MANAGEMENT—A QUANTITATIVE PERSPECTIVE

MARIO PANETTA TIS

N. PAUL LOOMBA

Professor and Chairman
Department of Management
Baruch College
City University of New York

Management–
A Quantitative
Perspective

Macmillan Publishing Co., Inc.
New York
Collier Macmillan Publishers
London

A portion of this material has been reprinted from *Linear
Programming: A Managerial Perspective*, copyright © 1964 by
McGraw-Hill, Inc., and copyright © 1976 by Narendra Paul Loomba.

Macmillan Publishing Co., Inc.
866 Third Avenue, New York, New York 10022

Collier Macmillan Canada, Ltd.

Library of Congress Cataloging in Publication Data

Loomba, Narendra Paul, (date)

  Management, a quantitative perspective.

  Includes bibliographies and index.
  1. Management—Mathematical models. 2. Operations
research. I. Title.
HD30.25.L66   658.4   77-1489
ISBN 0-02-371640-1

Printing: 1 2 3 4 5 6 7 8   Year: 8 9 0 1 2 3 4

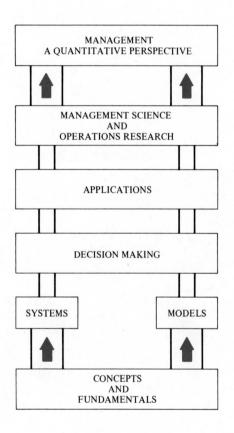

The main purpose of this book is to describe, explain, and illustrate how managers *can* and *should* make decisions for achieving personal as well as organizational goals and objectives. Hence, the book is directed toward two major audiences: (1) men and women who are currently enrolled in colleges and aspire to assume managerial positions in the world of business, politics, government, industry, health services, and social institutions, and (2) practicing managers who wish to keep informed regarding new tools, techniques, and methods of management analysis and decision making.

The book comprises sixteen chapters and five appendixes. A schematic representation of the organization of the book is shown in Exhibit A, which reflects a *conceptual* structure of the book in terms of six parts. The title of a specific part gives an indication of the common thread that runs through the chapters grouped under that part.

It is customary to include in the preface a description of the contents of various chapters. We shall deviate from this custom because we provide, on the page opposite each chapter opening, a list of major concepts and topics discussed in the chapter. However, it is desirable to describe the main purpose of each part.

PART I   Conceptual Foundations

The main purpose of Part I is to build a theoretical foundation for the topics, tools, techniques, methods, and models covered in the book. Part I provides a framework for managerial thinking. It describes and explains the quantitative approach to building and solving decision models—and designing managerial strategies.

PART II   Decision Theory

The purpose of Part II is to present an integrated view of managerial decision making. This part explains how rational choices can be identified under conditions of certainty, risk, uncertainty, and conflict. In addition, the reader is exposed to decision making under dynamic circumstances in which not one but a set of sequential decisions is required. The overall review of decision theory presented in this part sets the stage for the planning and control models presented in subsequent chapters.

PART III   Analysis and Planning

The main purpose of Part III is to describe and explain how managerial planning can be made more efficient and effective by utilizing management science models. Planning and control are related concepts, and in real life they cannot be separated. However, for purposes of classification we have

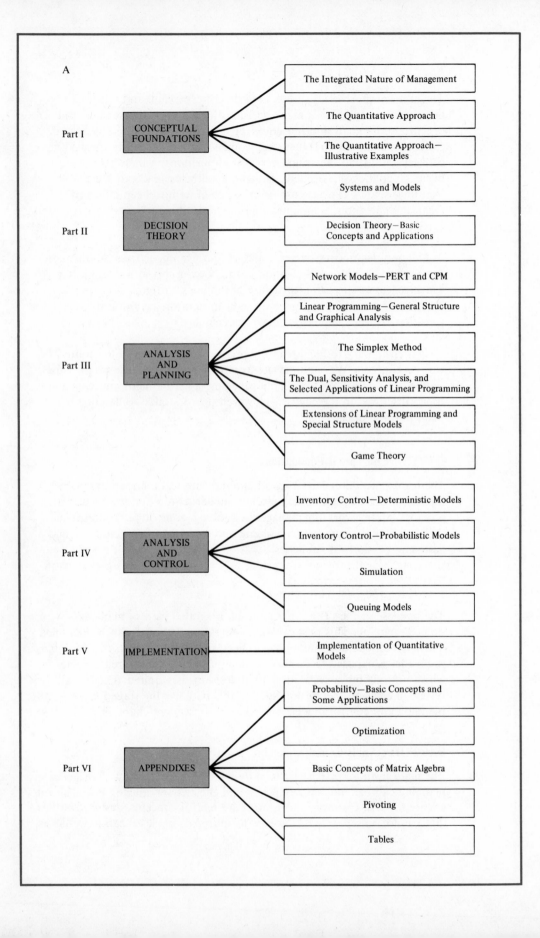

A

Part I — CONCEPTUAL FOUNDATIONS
- The Integrated Nature of Management
- The Quantitative Approach
- The Quantitative Approach—Illustrative Examples
- Systems and Models

Part II — DECISION THEORY
- Decision Theory—Basic Concepts and Applications

Part III — ANALYSIS AND PLANNING
- Network Models—PERT and CPM
- Linear Programming—General Structure and Graphical Analysis
- The Simplex Method
- The Dual, Sensitivity Analysis, and Selected Applications of Linear Programming
- Extensions of Linear Programming and Special Structure Models
- Game Theory

Part IV — ANALYSIS AND CONTROL
- Inventory Control—Deterministic Models
- Inventory Control—Probabilistic Models
- Simulation
- Queuing Models

Part V — IMPLEMENTATION
- Implementation of Quantitative Models

Part VI — APPENDIXES
- Probability—Basic Concepts and Some Applications
- Optimization
- Basic Concepts of Matrix Algebra
- Pivoting
- Tables

included *PERT, CPM, linear programming*, and *game theory* under the umbrella of analysis and planning.

PART IV   Analysis and Control

The major focus of this part is on the managerial function of control. Selected models of *inventory control* are described, developed, and illustrated with specific examples. The nature, structure, and potential of *simulation* as well as *queuing* models are examined and explained with reference to actual decision problems.

PART V   Implementation

The purpose of Part V is to present some of the important issues and aspects of implementation of quantitative models. The implementation of quantitative models is of the utmost importance because, without actual implementation, quantitative decision models will amount to no more than an interesting academic exercise. This part examines various relationships and interactions involved in the *process of implementation*.

PART VI   Appendixes

In Part VI we present a comprehensive coverage of the required probability, statistical, and mathematical concepts. This part also includes a set of tables needed to solve problems given at the end of various chapters.

With rare exceptions, most books dealing with quantitative approaches to management are narrow and mechanistic. Seldom do they provide a "macro" view of the topic under discussion. Nor do they integrate the *behavioral* and *practical* considerations of management with the quantitative decision models. This book seeks to attend to these and other deficiencies and provides the reader with a comprehensive and balanced treatment of management. In each chapter we provide the reader with a "macro" orientation before proceeding to "micro" interests. The perspective and focus are no doubt *quantitative*, but the reader is continuously made aware of the role and importance of *qualitative* and *behavioral* factors in the process of management.

We should mention four additional unique features of this book. First, mathematical content within the chapters is minimal. However, in the appendixes that appear at the end of the book we have provided a comprehensive coverage of the required probability, statistical, and mathematical concepts. Second, throughout the book we have listed, in footnotes, further references and comments to provide additional depth and comprehensiveness. Third, this book is not a collection of unrelated topics. It is, instead, a *unified entity* that integrates different chapters and sections of the book in a meaningful whole. Fourth, and most important, we have prepared a separate volume entitled *Study Guide and Cases* to reinforce and supplement this book. The major purpose of the *Study Guide and Cases* is to serve as a *linking mechanism* between the main text and the classroom. These features make it possible for the instructor to select the level of mathematical sophistication and the depth of analysis to suit the specific needs of his or her students. They also enable the instructor to present a broadened perspective of each chapter and to utilize the cases as illustrations of the practical applications of management science. It should be emphasized that most of the case studies represent real-life experiences.

This book is specifically written for courses usually taught under such headings as: *Quantitative Management, Quantitative Approaches to Management, Introduction to Management Science, Introduction to Operations Research, Introduction to Decision Sciences*. The book affords a vast degree of flexibility in terms of comprehensiveness and level of mathematical sophistication. It can, therefore, be adopted for undergraduate as well as graduate courses.

I am grateful to many of my students, friends, and colleagues for their advice and help. Professors A. O. Holsinger of Baruch College, Donald Moscato of Iona College, J. Donald Phillips of the University of Alabama, Gary Wicklund of the University of Iowa, and George Schneller of Rider College reviewed the entire manuscript and made valuable suggestions. Professors Lou Stern, Georghios Sphicas, John Humes, and Jack Shapiro, who are my colleagues in the Department of Management, Baruch College, gave me their professional as well as personal support in developing this book.

I owe a great deal to my graduate students and research assistants because they developed *all* of the examples and problems included in the book. In this regard I want to express my thanks to David Cadden, John Affisco, Daniel Shimshak, and Rakesh Gupta. I am particularly grateful to Rakesh Gupta because he read the entire manuscript several times and helped me improve the book.

I wish to acknowledge the patience and excellent typing of Julia Borick. I appreciate her understanding and cooperation. My thanks also go to Kay Martin and Vi McCormack of the Department of Management.

Last, and most important, I wish to acknowledge the continuing support, understanding, patience, and encouragement that I receive so generously from all the members of my family. My daughters, Sonya and Sheela, my son, Lalit, my friend and wife, Mary, and my faithful companion with the wagging tail, Raju—each provided the necessary inspiration to undertake and complete this project.

N. Paul Loomba
Scarsdale, New York

PART III
Analysis and Planning

CHAPTER 6 NETWORK MODELS—PERT AND CPM

CHAPTER 7 LINEAR PROGRAMMING—GENERAL STRUCTURE AND GRAPHICAL ANALYSIS

CHAPTER 11   GAME THEORY

PART IV
Analysis and Control

CHAPTER 12   INVENTORY CONTROL—DETERMINISTIC MODELS

CHAPTER 13   INVENTORY CONTROL—PROBABILISTIC MODELS

CHAPTER 14   SIMULATION

Appendixes

PART I

Conceptual Foundations

CHAPTER 1

The Integrated Nature of Management

MAJOR CONCEPTS AND TOPICS DISCUSSED IN THIS CHAPTER

Definition and Importance of Management

Various Perspectives on Management

Schools of Management Thought

Scientific management
Administrative management
Human relations
Behavioral science
Management science

Integrated Nature of Management

1.1
Introduction

The essence of management is to make decisions for the purpose of achieving individual, group, and organizational objectives. Management is a multidimensional and dynamic concept. It is multidimensional because management problems and their solutions have consequences in several dimensions, particularly the human, economic, social, and political. Management is a dynamic concept because the environment within which managerial decisions are made is always in a state of flux. Hence, managers are often required to regard not only economic considerations but other criteria as well (e.g., human, social, political) while making complex decisions in a changing environment. A formal model to faithfully depict complex reality can soon become too cumbersome—difficult to formulate, solve, and implement. The manager therefore must, and does, make certain simplifying assumptions in practice. The usual approach is to analyze the problem in economic terms and then implement the solution only if it does not do violence to human, social, and political constraints.

We recognize the existence and importance of multidimensional problems, and objectives, in organizations. We also recognize the managerial need for making certain simplifying assumptions in order to arrive at a "first-cut" solution, which can then be modified to meet the demands of reality. Yet there exists the need to *explicitly* state these assumptions and then, to the extent possible, capture the essence of problems by formulating them in quantitative terms. In this manner, a "quantitative approach"[1] can usefully be employed at any level of complexity ranging from simple deterministic[2] problems involving a *single* objective to complex, probabilistic problems with *multiple* objectives that have human, social, and political, as well as economic dimensions.

In real life, societies choose their goals and priorities through the political system—rather than through the mechanism of the free market, as was claimed by classical economists. Hence, the manager must make decisions based not only on economic criteria but also on political realities. However, in this book, we shall restrict our scope to the discussion of those problems that are *essentially* economic, and in which the decision to choose a course of action is often made solely on the basis of *economic* criteria.

The practice and theory of management have evolved, especially during the last 75 years, along different lines of inquiry and with focus on particular aspects of management. The advances in the field of management are described in the literature under the general heading "schools of management thought." As we discuss the main characteristics of these schools of management, it will become clear that: (1) the discipline of management has effectively integrated concepts, tools, techniques, and viewpoints of different academic fields; and (2) the

---

[1] Briefly, the quantitative approach requires the conscious use—in making decisions—of data, information, and decision criteria that can be objectively measured. We discuss and illustrate the quantitative approach in Chapter 2.

[2] Briefly, deterministic problems assume that available courses of action as well as their outcomes are known with certainty. Probabilistic problems assume that outcomes cannot be assumed to be certain; however, it is possible to attach a measure of probability to each outcome (i.e., we can specify the "odds"). For further discussion, see Chapter 5.

quantitative approach to management can be usefully employed in all aspects of management, and has either explicit or implicit relevance to all schools of management.

The purpose of this chapter is to provide a background of management against which the role, potential, and limitations of the quantitative approach can be appreciated. First, we provide the reader with a macro view of management. This is followed by an enumeration of the reasons that have made management such an important area in modern society. We then present and summarize the salient features of different schools of management.

1.2
What Is Management?[3]

The term "management" has many connotations, implications, and aspects. The scope of management is so wide and diverse that it is difficult to coin any single definition that can fully convey its importance to man and society. We shall therefore examine management from several points of view.

Management involves the sum total of all activities undertaken to achieve the goals and objectives of an individual or an organization. It is *simultaneously* the integration of effort, the design of organizational structure, the acquisition and judicious use of resources, motivating people, providing leadership, planning strategies, controlling, innovating, and otherwise creating an environment in which individual and group goals can be achieved.

Management is not a static concept. It is rather a *dynamic, complex,* and *social* phenomenon. It is dynamic because it is not independent of time, change, or value systems. It is complex and social because it involves people; the totality of their interpersonal relationships; aspects of leadership, motivation, productivity, and morale; and an innumerable combination of technical, economic, political, psychological, and social factors. Management is not single-dimensional; it is a *multidimensional* phenomenon because managers make decisions in an environment that has economic, physical, social, psychological, political, and technical components. Managers must deal with man–machine systems of various complexities. They must understand, and attempt to influence, human behavior in an organizational setting.

Management is *universal* in the sense that all organizations, regardless of their specific objectives, type of work, geographical or cultural environment, must be managed. Indeed, management is *the* central activity needed for human progress and survival. In the interdependent world of our times, organizations, particularly large and complex organizations, provide the framework for productive effort; and these organizations must be managed. The effective management of organizations is therefore one of the most important and central tasks of the society. Without proper management our social structure cannot survive the stresses and strains created by an amazingly fast rate of social and technological change.

Management transcends the traditional boundaries of narrowly defined disciplines and by its very nature is an *interdisciplinary* field. Neither the students nor the study of management can be confined within the narrow walls of a single

[3] Sections 1.2 to 1.9 are based on Chapter 11 of Levey and Loomba [1973].

The Integrated Nature of Management   Chapter 1

discipline. Substantial contributions to the field of management have been made from such diverse fields as philosophy, political science, economics, engineering, mathematics, statistics, sociology, psychology, anthropology, and social psychology.

In view of its extremely broad scope and complex nature, we can coin several useful definitions of the term "management." Each will have a special significance as it relates to a particular management situation or to a specific approach to solving management problems. For example, management has been viewed as a *function*, a *process*, a *profession*, and as an *elite* or a *class* of people. Management has also been described as an *art* and as a *science*. And, along with material, capital, and labor, management is considered a *resource*. It is perhaps the most valuable resource because it provides the primary force for converting other resources into products and services.

As a *function*, management refers to the kinds of tasks and activities that are performed by managers. The specific nature of the activities are determined by such managerial functions as planning, organizing, directing, leadership, and control. The functional view of management implies that managers of organizations, public or private, producing goods or services, must essentially perform the same basic tasks and functions. They must establish organizational goals and objectives; secure sufficient financial and human resources; assemble materials, tools, and machinery; organize capabilities in terms of authority, responsibility, and accountability relationships; provide direction and leadership; institute control mechanisms; and in general create and maintain a motivating and rewarding environment. It is clear from this partial list that managerial tasks are extremely varied and complex. The efficient and effective performance of these tasks and functions is the responsibility of the managers.

As a *process*, management refers to the series of systematic, sequential or overlapping, and interdependent steps by which goals and objectives are achieved. The process of management is the vehicle through which managerial functions are performed. The skills involved in the designing, instituting, and controlling of this process are teachable, learnable, and transferable—hence the evolution of the *discipline* of management. The process concept of management is useful for two reasons. First, it has a time orientation and so reflects the dynamic nature of management. Second, within the process framework, it is possible to concentrate on decision making (how choices are made among alternatives), which is the essence of management.

Management, like law and medicine, is a recognized *profession*. All major colleges and universities offer professional degrees in management. Several professional societies, such as The Academy of Management, AIDS (American Institute of Decision Sciences), TIMS (The Institute of Management Sciences), and ORSA (Operations Research Society of America), have been formed for the purpose of interchanging information and encouraging professional development in different branches of management.[4] Several professional journals are being published in which persons from educational, business, health, and governmental organizations publish articles relating to the practice, applications, and theory of management. Professional societies have also been organized, and management journals are being published in Europe, Asia, Africa, South America, and other

[4] Important branches of management are: management science, behavioral science, labor relations, personnel management, and general management (i.e., interaction between business and society). The quantitative approach to management can be applied in each of these branches.

parts of the globe. Private business firms and management consulting firms frequently offer training seminars in such specialized areas as management science, sensitivity training, and transactional analysis. Recruiting firms that cater only to persons with specialized backgrounds (management science, industrial relations, behavioral science, etc.) have been organized in the United States and abroad. Thus, not only does management meet all the tests of being a profession, it is already entering an advanced stage of specialization of its various components. This overspecialization has created the need for, and increased the value of, concepts or techniques that can serve as *integrative* devices. As we shall describe in Chapter 2, the *quantitative approach* to management meets this need.

Management also refers to an *elite* or *class of people*. In this sense, management is the group of people directing the affairs of a business firm, or for that matter, of any organization. The *management* is that group in an organization which has the legal authority to direct and control the organization. We refer sometimes to the dichotomy of "labor" and "management"; but as most of us know, such a dichotomy does not have any general validity, except perhaps during those times when labor unions are engaged in contract negotiations.

A very general definition of management views it as an *art* of getting things done with and through people. It is an art because individual variations in approaching, and successfully solving, the same type of managerial problems can be observed in actual business practice. It is an art because management problems are often amenable to individual styles that are based on creativity, judgment, intuition, and experience rather than on the systematic methods of science. As an art, the ingredients of management are intuition rather than logic, guesses rather than measurement, and group discussion that leads to consensus rather than experimental verification that is precise and admits no deviation.[5]

Management as a *science* adopts the view that a substantial portion of management consists of "phenomena that can be measured, relationships that can be represented quantitatively, causal chains whose internal consistency can be logically verified, and conclusions which can be tested experimentally."[6] In this manner, knowledge and experience can be accumulated systematically, and the tested procedures can be utilized without the level of risk faced by the original researchers. The objective of this approach is to bring as many management phenomena as is realistically possible under the domain of *programmed* decision making.[7] The higher the percentage of decisions that can be handled with the tools, techniques, and methods of management science, the greater is the freedom of the manager to devote his time to creative—as opposed to routine—activities. The phenomenal progress in the field of management in terms of more powerful tools and techniques of analysis, and better methodology for solving complex problems, has been made possible only because the art of management has increasingly been supplemented by the science of management. However, there are some inherent limitations in viewing management as a science because the preconditions of a truly scientific analysis are rather severe. A pragmatic synthesis of art and science appears to be the prescription for modern management.

---

[5] Feeney [1971, p. 2].

[6] Feeney [1971, p. 1].

[7] Decisions are *programmed* to the extent that they are routine, repetitive, and can be handled with definite procedures.

The above discussion of the various aspects of management has been presented to emphasize management's importance to society as well as its inherent complexity. We now provide a definition of management which is both descriptive and useful.

> Management is the process of integrating the efforts of a purposeful group, or organization, whose members have at least one common goal.

Our definition of management implies at least three things. First, management involves goal-oriented persons whose efforts must be integrated in the context of a group or an organization. These persons have biases, norms, cultural identifications, attitudes, individual aspirations, group goals, and organizational loyalties. What motivates people of diverse backgrounds in an organizational setting? How can we bring organizational members to their highest level of development, satisfaction, and fulfillment? What can we do to generate a constructive, purposeful environment that is conducive to productivity as well as quality of life?[8] Answers to such questions are being provided by behavioral scientists who have produced research, generalizations, and theories relating to human behavior in organizations. The focus of the behavioral science approach to the study of management is on individual, group, and organization behavior. Behavioral scientists attempt to understand those factors or variables (and their interrelationships) that can give us an insight into such phenomena as leadership, motivation, communication, and organizational performance. The academic disciplines useful in conducting this type of inquiry are psychology, sociology, and anthropology. The area of behavioral sciences is an important area of research and study, but we shall not delve into it in this text. However, our definition implies the significance of understanding human behavior in organizations. It can be stated in this context that one of the prime responsibilities of management is to bring out what is best in people.

The second implication of our definition of management is that the problem of defining goals and objectives is of the utmost importance. It is obvious that until and unless there is *at least* one common goal, the very foundation of the concept of management is shaken. This emphasizes the role of management as the *catalyst* for evolving a set of common goals. This is not an easy task. Human nature is such that there is an inherent conflict among various goals and objectives that an individual wishes to achieve at different points in time. This conflict occurs in a number of ways: (1) conflict between an individual's own objectives (e.g., more money or more leisure time); (2) conflict between *role-defined* goals (e.g., more time at work or with family); (3) conflict between individual and group goals (e.g., an individual's personal attitude toward war as opposed to the stand of the political party to which he belongs); (4) conflict between goals of different groups to which an individual belongs at the same time (e.g., a union member serving on a contract-negotiating team while holding a large amount of company stock); and (5) conflict between individual and organizational goals (e.g., employee's desire for identification with producing the *whole* product versus the company's need for improving productivity through the device of mass producing the parts and then assembling the product). Such examples of conflict among goals and objectives can be

---

[8] In an article published in *The New York Times* [June 18, 1974, p. 39] Tom Wicker describes how by adapting the work to the workers' needs, productivity was increased by 46 percent in 2 years at an IBM plant in Amsterdam. The increased productivity was accompanied by "sharply improved" quality, lower absenteeism, and lower staff turnover.

seen by all of us in everyday life. The responsibility of management in this context is to understand the nature of conflict and arrive at a set of *viable* and *achievable* goals and objectives for the organization (e.g., sales volume, return on investment, share of the market, customer service, diversification, and social responsibility).

Managers must also choose the *means* (or plans) to achieve these goals and objectives. In practice, managerial plans are based upon, and derived from, organizational objectives, and managers employ a set of tools, techniques, or other facilitative mechanisms to implement these plans. It should be stated here that in this text we do not address ourselves to the important question of how individual, group, and organizational goals are formulated.[9] Instead, we narrow our inquiry to those problems where the main goal can be stated in quantitative terms, and the problem can be solved by quantitative methods. Although the quantitative methods are of assistance in the rational choice of both goals and means, they are more relevant and practical in the selection and implementation of the means. Yet, we must not discount the "spirit" of the quantitative approach (i.e., a conscious and systematic analysis), which is at the heart of resolving policy issues and forming organizational goals.

The third implication of our definition resides in two words: "process" and "integration." As stated earlier, the process framework emphasizes the time orientation, the dynamic nature, and the decision-making aspects of management. And, if we admit the existence of conflicting goals and objectives in organizations, then the integration of efforts of organizational members becomes the basic ingredient of management. The integration of effort takes place at several levels and in different forms. Starting from the top level, strategic, and policy-type questions (e.g., which markets to enter, which products to produce) to the very basic operational questions (e.g., determination of product mix, level of inventories), the responsibility of management is to make resource-allocation decisions. Each decision, regardless of the level or part of the organization where it is made, must be integrated into a purposeful "whole." We emphasize this point here because we shall not have the opportunity to repeat this important assertion in individual chapters.

Actually, in most cases in this text we shall formulate and solve problems with the *implicit* assumption that these problems exist by themselves; that they are separate from other problems of the organization; and that they have no effect on other problems or parts of the organization. This is a *severe* assumption and it flies in the face of interdependence, which is the predominant reality of modern life. Then, why do we make such an assumption? The answer lies in the nature of management practice and the purpose of this book. In real life, managers break problems, especially complex problems, into simple components and solve the component problems one by one, as if each component existed by itself. The solutions to individual components are then integrated to yield a solution to the original problem.

The purpose of this book is to illustrate the quantitative approach to management. Although it is possible to apply the quantitative approach to simple as well as complex problems, we plan to restrict our scope to a set of very basic problems. The problems to which we address ourselves have two attributes. First, they are prototypes of problems that managers face with increasing frequency in

---

[9] How organizational goals are arrived at is an important area of study. See Simon [1964].

real life. Second, they are the type of problems that are ideally suited for the learning of how the quantitative approach to management works.

1.3
The Importance of Management

Management has become the most important resource because modern societies are characterized by certain unique phenomena. Perhaps the most significant of these phenomena that call for integration of effort and place a heavy premium on management are: (1) the emergence and importance of organizations, particularly large organizations; (2) the fact of interdependence among various sectors of the economy; and (3) an increasing rate of change not only in terms of new technology, inventions, and innovations, but also in *value systems* that ultimately affect every phase of our lives. We briefly discuss each of these three points.

An organization can be viewed as a system of cooperative effort, designed to achieve a set of goals that are, in several respects, common to organizational members. Organizations have emerged and survived because they provide the only efficient means through which basic resources are converted into products and services needed for human survival. Organizations are important because we spend a vast proportion of our lives as participants, clients, or customers of formal or informal organizations. They provide a setting in which individuals attempt to satisfy their needs to exercise authority, gain social status and prestige, mold the direction of future events, and have the power base from which to influence the behavior of other persons and organizations. Given the prevalence and importance of organizations, it is easy to appreciate why managers and students of management must gain an understanding of the environment, nature, structure, processes, and behavior of organizations. Each and every one of these aspects of organizations constitutes a major field of management study.[10]

In modern societies these large and complex organizations must operate under the most uncertain and dynamic environment. They must be managed and managed effectively—for the welfare of man and society. We see therefore that the emergence of organizations, particularly the large and complex organizations, has contributed significantly to the importance of management.

The fact of interdependence among various sectors of our economy, and even among various nations of the world, can perhaps best be illustrated by the economic consequences that followed the 1973 Arab oil embargo. In a chain reaction, prices of raw materials, food, products, and services increased at a very fast pace. The rates of inflation in most countries climbed to a two-digit level and the stability of the world monetary system was shaken. A similar type of interdependence, though of a less dramatic nature, exists among government, business, industry, and the individual. To understand the complexities of these relationships, to plan for contingencies, and to be able to survive is the job of management. This requirement, too, attests to the importance of management.

Management is also very important in our society because of an increasing rate of change, not only in terms of new technology, inventions, and innovations, but also in value systems that ultimately affect every phase of our lives. The pace of new

[10] See, for example, Huse and Bowditch [1973] or Filley and House [1975].

technological inventions; managerial innovations; and changing economic, political, and social patterns is such that obsolescence, technical as well as professional, is an ever-present threat. For example, it took only seven years before IBM's System/360 was superseded by the introduction of a vastly improved System/370 series. This had a profound effect on the entire computer industry. RCA was virtually forced to abandon the computer field, and in 1972 the company had to absorb a loss of some $220 million for making the original decision to enter the computer field. The computer leasing industry suffered a severe financial blow within the short span of only three or four years. Computer leasing companies (Rockwood Computer, Granite Management, DPF, to name only a few) that had become the favorites of Wall Street during the middle sixties, were pushed almost to the brink of financial collapse. This is but one example of the consequences of *change* that are inherent in developing and managing modern organizations.

Apart from technological changes, the managers of modern organizations must face the information explosion, ambiguity, uncertainty, and most importantly, the realities of rapidly changing value systems. Our attitudes toward such psycho-socio-economic factors as population growth, family, sex, size of cars, and pollution, are changing very rapidly. Management is important because managers must cope with rapid change and the consequences of rapid change. They must anticipate change, predict its impact, and plan its direction.

The central problem for the manager is not only to manage change, but to *create* change so that organizations can effectively serve society. A careful balance must be found between change and stability. The key to such a balance, and hence to order and survival, is *effective management*.

We end this section by asking this question: How do we judge the quality of management? A general answer is to say that the quality of management is related directly to the degree of success with which the managerial decisions have produced results in terms of stated goals and objectives.[11] And, it is to assist the manager in his process of making decisions that the quantitative approach has established its importance. The main purpose of the quantitative approach, then, is to improve, perhaps optimize,[12] the decisions that managers make in the process of management.

1.4
Schools of Management

It is in the nature of human beings to approach the same problem from different perspectives. Since management, by its very nature, is an extremely complex and multidimensional phenomenon, the study of management has historically proceeded along economic, physiological, social, and psychological, as well as interdisciplinary lines. Furthermore, as is the case in every discipline, particular kinds of developments, breakthroughs, and innovations in management have resulted in response to the needs and circumstances that existed during a given

[11] Here is a question that the reader may want to ponder. What is most often rewarded in real life? Good decisions or good outcomes (results)?

[12] To optimize is to arrive at the best possible solution. Another way to look at the concept of optimization is to say that every decision problem has a solution space, and to optimize is to find that point in the solution space that will yield the best value to the decision maker. See Appendix B.

period of time. For example, it was during the period of industrial revolution that the principles of division of labor and specialization were used to develop a factory system of production. The sole concern in that period was with higher productivity through an improved machine technology. Later, during the last part of the nineteenth and the early part of the twentieth century, management paid considerable attention to the physiological aspects of man. The contributions of Frederick Taylor (time study), Frank Gilbreth (motion study), and Henry Gantt (control charts for scheduling and controlling production) were a consequence of efforts directed at maximizing output from a man–machine system—rather than just the machines. Since that time, management theorists have attempted to describe and explain the social, technical, political, and psychological foundations as well as other relevant aspects of management. Such contributions to the description, analysis, theory, and practice of management have been grouped and discussed in the literature under the heading "schools of management" or "schools of management thought."

Management literature offers several different classifications of the schools of management. As in any system of classification, our aim is to increase order, decrease ambiguity, and establish a basis for communication. However, the process of classification is always subject to two opposing forces. One relates to creating too few groups, so that items in the same classification have overlapping characteristics. The opposing force is to create too many categories, so that items in different classes have the same characteristics. In such "soft" areas as social sciences,[13] we must always realize that attempts to classify do not always result in "neat" categories. Hence, what we call schools of management should not be viewed as hard and fast classifications of management thought, but only as a device to organize ideas for purposes of communication, learning, and teaching. In this chapter, we shall discuss five schools of management: (1) scientific management, (2) administrative management, (3) human relations, (4) behavioral science, and (5) management science (or operations research). Our order of listing corresponds more or less to the chronological sequence in which these schools have evolved. A list of major contributors to, as well as the main characteristics of, each school are summarized in Table 1.1.

It is not our intention to give a detailed history of the development of management thought.[14] We shall present instead only the salient features of various schools of management. This is important for at least two reasons. First, by gaining a familiarity with different schools of management, the reader will be able to realize the historical development of management theory and practice. Second, by understanding the salient features of the various schools, we shall be able to appreciate the role and potential of the quantitative approach.

[13] By "social sciences" we usually mean psychology, sociology, anthropology, economics, history, and political science. The term "behavioral sciences" usually refers to psychology, sociology, and anthropology.

[14] For a detailed history of management thought, see George [1972].

Table 1.1 *Schools of Management Thought*

School of Management Thought	*Major Contributors*	*Main Focus or Characteristics*
1. Scientific Management	Frederick Taylor Frank Gilbreth Henry Gantt	• Scientific method applied to production problems • Time study • Motion study • Functional organization
2. Administrative management	H. Fayol L. Urwick J. Mooney A. Riley	• Management "principles" • Macro orientation for administrative design • Reliance on experience and intuition rather than empirical data
3. Human relations	Mary Parker Follett Elton Mayo	• Importance of human motivation • Group approach to management • Beginning of scientific experimentation on human problems
4. Behavioral science	Chris Argyris Rensis Likert Herbert Simon James March	• Rigorous application of scientific method to individual, and organization behavior problems • Emphasis on psychology, sociology, and anthropology for research in organization theory
5. Management science	P. M. S. Blackett George Dantzig C. West Churchman Russell Ackoff Richard Bellman	• Mathematical models of management problems • Scientific method • Use of interdisciplinary teams • Systems approach

1.5
Scientific Management (1890–1916)

The *scientific management school* is associated with the contributions of Frederick W. Taylor, Frank Gilbreth, and Henry Gantt.[15] This school derives its name from the basic philosophy that all tasks, whether related to physical production or managerial functions, can and should be analyzed by the methods of science involving observation, data collection, hypothesis[16] formulation, testing, and actual implementation. In practice, however, the pioneers of scientific management concentrated their efforts mainly on physical production and production-type activities, although some attention was paid to managerial problems at the level of shop foremen.

The thrust of the scientific management school was to achieve specialization in terms of work, the worker, and the management by employing the scientific method[17] to study, analyze, and understand problems and phenomena. And the guiding force of the scientific management movement was the economic factor. The pioneers of the scientific management movement based their work on the fundamental assumption that economic forces are more or less the sole motivators for human performance.

The scientific management school is of interest to us for the following reasons. First and foremost, it marks the beginning of the first significant attempts to provide a scientific basis for improving the practice of management. Second, there began to emerge, for the first time, a body of knowledge that provided the nucleus and the impetus for various theories of management. For example, scientific management neglected, for the most part, the human aspects of organizational tasks, and concentrated primarily on the use of men as adjuncts to machines.[18] The next logical step in the development of management theory would be to examine the question of whether, in addition to its technical bases, productivity is also related to psychological and sociological factors. And it was precisely this concern that eventually led to the development of the human relations school.

Again, scientific management emphasized essentially the functional specialization of the separate parts rather than the management system as a whole. In other words, the orientation of scientific management was of the micro type, as opposed to a macro or systems approach to management. The need to remove this weakness, in conjunction with demands generated by important practical problems, provided the forces that shaped the management science (or operations research) school. As we shall observe in the following paragraphs, the behavioral science school combines the scientific approach of the scientific management school with the human concern of the human relations school.

---

[15] Frederick W. Taylor is known as the founder of the scientific management movement. His famous work, *Principles of Scientific Management*, was published in 1911. Gilbreth pioneered motion study and Gantt is known for developing control charts.

[16] A hypothesis is a statement of belief regarding a phenomenon, fact, or relationship among various variables. A hypothesis must always be tested against facts before it is *accepted* or *rejected*. See Section 2.6.

[17] We discuss some details of the scientific method in Section 2.6.

[18] March and Simon [1958, p. 13].

1.6
Administrative Management (1910–1930)

The *administrative management school* concentrated on the questions of departmentalization, coordination, and organization involved in the design and management of organizations. This school is associated with the work of such men as H. Fayol, L. H. Gulick, L. Urwick, J. D. Mooney, and A. C. Riley. The major contributions of this school, in contrast to scientific management, can be appreciated with two observations. First, while Taylor produced a set of operating procedures applicable to specific situations, administrative management advanced a set of management principles applicable in all types of management situations. Second, while Taylor's work was based on scientific investigation, the principles of management were evolved on the basis of common sense and experience rather than from empirical evidence.

The principles of management, advanced by the administrative management school, fall into two groups. The first relates to the process of *designing* an administrative organization on a rational basis, while the second focuses on those aspects that are important *after* the organization design has been completed. In the first group, the argument starts from the premise that any general-purpose organization has a set of basic tasks or functions that must be performed. Furthermore, these tasks can be subdivided into different types of activities, such as production, finance, marketing, service, supervisory, and coordinative activities. The main job of management is to combine these activities in a well-defined administrative structure, with the overall objective of achieving the minimum cost for performing these activities. In the organizing process, activities are combined into well-defined units of work, which, in turn, are combined into well-defined departments, divisions, and so on to the highest level of aggregation appropriate for a given organization. Finally, horizontal as well as vertical relationships, in terms of responsibility, authority, and accountability, are established. The administrative design could be based on such considerations as organization by *process, purpose, clientele, place,* or *time.*

The second group of principles was directed to management problems encountered in "running"—as opposed to designing—an organization. Principles such as *unity of command* (an employee should receive orders only from one boss) and *scalar chain* (one should normally not short-circuit one's immediate superior) are two of the several general principles of management advanced by the administrative management school.

Like the scientific management school, the administrative management school largely ignored the psychological and sociological factors associated with human behavior. The administrative management school is important for these two reasons. First, it advanced the scope of management concern beyond the production orientation that was characteristic of the scientific management school. Second, its failure to "confront theory with evidence" provided the impetus for the evolution of the behavioral science school.[19]

The scientific and the administrative management schools provided the spark for several new developments in terms of improved tools, techniques, and methods

[19] March and Simon [1958, p. 32].

for management practice. Considerable progress was made during the 1920s, 1930s, and 1940s in the actual application of improved management technology. However, as mentioned earlier, neither the scientific management nor the administrative management school paid sufficient attention to psychological and sociological factors associated with human behavior. It was to fill this gap that first the human relations and then the behavioral science school appeared on the scene.

1.7
Human Relations (1930–1950)

The *human relations school* is of importance because it represents the first systematic attempts to study and analyze the relationship of human factors to productivity. The contributions of Mary Parker Follett and Elton Mayo and his associates will be described briefly to bring out the flavor of this school.

The central question that Miss Follett attempted to answer was this: How can society go beyond the boundaries implied by its physical resources and individual capabilities? Her answer, in simple words, was to create cooperative working groups in organizations by recognizing the importance of motivational factors of the individual *and* the group. She recognized the importance of psychology (dealing with individual behavior) and sociology (dealing with group behavior) and advocated the use of the "group" approach to management in an environment based on good human relations. Miss Follett felt that coordination of group efforts to achieve the most efficient results was the central core of management. And, effective coordination could be achieved through proper education, improved harmony, group thinking, and by promoting a cooperative organization. It should be noted that Miss Follett's work was not "experimental" in nature.

Elton Mayo and his associates are known for their experimental studies that attempted to relate productivity to a set of physical and social factors. The experiments were conducted (between 1924 and 1932) at Western Electric's Hawthorne Works in Chicago. The purpose of the experiments was to relate certain physical variables to productivity by comparing the output of a "test" group (where these variables were changed) to that of a "control" group (where these variables were kept at a constant level). The variables that were investigated included the degree of illumination, number and duration of rest periods, changes in working hours, and shorter work weeks. The researchers found that physical factors are not the sole determinants of productivity. They proposed that man is not a simple econotechnical creature but that he has a very important socioemotional dimension and that social groups have a great impact on behavior and productivity.

Mayo's experiments established the importance of the sociological concept of group effort to the practice of management. Mayo observed that an organization is a social system consisting of cliques, informal groups, and status levels; and that this system was a mixture of factors that are logical and economic—as well as nonlogical, emotional, and human. This meant that, in addition to meeting the economic goals of the organization, management must satisfy the social and psychological needs of the workers.

The human relations schools has been criticized for two reasons. In practice, the proponents of this philosophy were perceived as "manipulators" who emphasized motivational factors only for superficial reasons. Second, it still lacked a genuinely scientific basis for inquiry into human behavior.

The contributions of the three schools described thus far (scientific management, administrative management, and human relations) pushed the frontiers of management to a critical mass. A tremendous interest was generated in integrating the most important elements of these schools and then applying them to the management problems of an increasingly complex world. These efforts resulted in the evolution of behavioral science and management science schools. All the schools of management, therefore, are related. This relationship and the integrated nature of management is shown in Figure 1.1. As shown in Figure 1.1, the behavioral science school built essentially on the foundations of the *scientific method* and the *concern for human behavior*. The foundations of the management science school include the *scientific method* and the *macro* or *systems orientation*. In the actual practice of management, managers do not depend upon a single school; they invariably draw on the concepts or combination of concepts developed by different schools of management. The integrated nature of management thought, as depicted in Figure 1.1, must be recognized and appreciated by students of management.

The drive to evolve integrated management concepts was based on the recognition, by both the practitioners and scholars of management, that two particular aspects of management had thus far not received sufficient attention. The first related to the application of the scientific method for understanding human behavior in organizations. The concern here was to investigate, on a

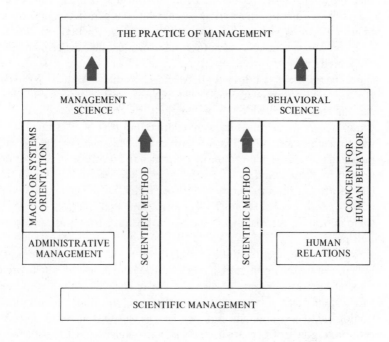

Figure 1.1. The Integrated Nature of Management Thought.

scientific basis, the psychological, sociological, and anthropological dimensions of management. As a result, several empirical studies were conducted to understand the behavior of individuals and groups within organizations—under various kinds of economic, social, political, and technological environments. These studies form the central core of the behavioral science school.

The second aspect of management that needed careful study was the idea of a "systems" as opposed to a "functional" approach to management. The philosophy of the systems effort was that the goals and objectives of the separate parts of an organization are often in conflict; that the reconciliation of these conflicting goals and objectives is *the* executive function; and that such executive-type problems must be solved in terms of effectiveness of the *entire* system rather than its separate parts. The scientific research conducted with the philosophy of the systems approach has resulted in the evolution of the management science school.

1.8
Behavioral Science (1950–   )

As indicated in Figure 1.1, the *behavioral science school* stands on two foundations, the scientific method and the concern for human behavior in organizations. It concentrates on that area of management which deals with individual behavior, group behavior, and behavior of organizations. The behavioral science approach is rooted in the belief that actual human behavior in organizations, at whatever level, can be understood only if it is observed, described, and then explained on a scientific (inductive) basis.[20] The attempt then is to describe, explain, understand, and predict organization behavior, based on scientific investigation and experimentation. Specific areas of investigation that have attracted the attention of behavioral scientists include such topics as employee morale, job satisfaction, motivation, and interpersonal relations. Behavioral research and studies have also been conducted on several aspects of social interactions, patterns of power and authority, communication, and leadership—as well as their relationships to organizational performance and success. Although it is difficult to draw hard and fast boundaries in management research, behavioral sciences refer usually to the disciplines of psychology (useful in the study of individual human behavior), sociology (useful in the study of human behavior in groups), and anthropology (useful in the study of human behavior derived from a cultural orientation).

Behavioral science is essentially *descriptive* in nature (it describes what *is*; how people *do* behave). As we shall discuss below, management science is essentially *prescriptive* or *normative* in nature (it prescribes what *ought* to be; it prescribes how people *should* behave).

Organizations are simultaneously economic, technical, psychological, and social systems. Behavioral scientists emphasize the psychosocial subsystems, while the management scientists emphasize the economic–technical subsystems. A truly effective systems approach would pay sufficient attention to all the subsystems of an organization.

---

[20] The inductive approach leads to general conclusions based on specific cases. It is experimental in nature. See Section 2.6.

1.9
Management Science (1950–   )

As indicated in Figure 1.1, the *management science school* is built on two foundations, the scientific method and the systems orientation. What is management science and what do management scientists do? We define management science as that branch of the field of management which employs a rational, logical, systematic, and scientific approach in analyzing the process of management and management problems. To the extent possible, problems are examined with a systems orientation. Also, in practice, management scientists develop scientific models that project the consequences of alternative courses of action, and that incorporate the elements of chance, risk, and uncertainty to help managers make rational choices and design optimal policies.

As mentioned earlier, the focus of management scientists has mainly been on the economic–technical subsystems of organizations. Management science is essentially normative in nature—that is, it prescribes a specific managerial course of action. It tells the manager how he should behave. It outlines specific solutions to specific problems, based on a set of assumptions that are often very bold.

The terms "management science," "operations research," "decision sciences," "systems sciences," and "systems analysis" are often used interchangeably in the literature. Management science, as we know it today, made its start in the United Kingdom during World War II, when a team of scientists was given the assignment of solving several complex military problems: selecting optimum gun sites, determination of optimum convoy size, optimum depth for detonating antisubmarine charges, optimum civil defense plans, and location of the most vulnerable spots in bombers. Management science pioneers used a research methodology combining the inductive approach with the use of "analogy." That is, wherever possible, an analogy with previously developed and tested logical structures was utilized in the process of model building. The knowledge gained from wartime experiences was refined to arrive at a number of well-defined models (i.e., their general structure was precisely identified), dealing with problems of resource allocation, inventory control, queuing, routing, replacement, and so on. The attempt was to develop a variety of models, with known properties and deductively derived solutions, that can be "matched" and applied on a routine basis to certain types of recurring problems. This was indeed done—with increasing frequency and success in the 1950s and 1960s. Important contributors to promoting the philosophy and application of management science include C. West Churchman, Russell Ackoff, George Dantzig, and Richard Bellman, among others.[21]

Management science is both a body of knowledge and an approach for analyzing and solving management problems. As a *body of knowledge*, management science consists of various management theories, methods, models, and specific tools and techniques that can be used to handle a wide range of management problems. Management theories range all the way from individual, group, and organization behavior to theories of planning, control, and theories

---

[21] See Dantzig [1963, Chap. 2].

dealing with inventory, maintenance, and production scheduling. Management science models have been used to analyze wide areas of strategic, administrative, and operational problems. Linear programming, dynamic programming, stochastic programming, Markov chains, and simulation models provide some examples of management science models. Program evaluation and review technique, critical path method, sensitivity analysis, different types of information models, and cost-effectiveness models are additional examples of topics that constitute the body of knowledge in management science.

As an *approach*, management science refers to the attitude with which management scientists view, analyze, and solve management problems. The approach is that of a man of science; grounded in the discipline of inductive as well as deductive inference, model building, and theory construction.[22] The essence of this approach is, first, that problems must be expressed quantitatively and, second, that symbolic (as opposed to verbal) modes of expression and reasoning are to be preferred.

Management science has been effective in two ways. First, the scientific approach has yielded dividends in improving the "art" of management. Second, several breakthroughs have been made in isolating, and solving, complex decision problems at the operational level. We refer here to such problems as: scheduling, inventory, facilities location, distribution, queuing, replacement, maintenance, design, and information systems. However, the record is not so bright when one considers the arena of administrative and strategic decision classes.[23] It appears that further advances in the applications of management science can only be made by redefining several basic ideological premises, by finding ways to handle policy-type questions, and by accommodating relevant behavioral aspects in the formal models.[24]

Management science is characterized by: (1) the systems approach, (2) interdisciplinary teamwork, (3) application of the scientific method, and (4) the use of models. We shall discuss these four concepts in Chapter 2. It should be noted here that, in the management literature, the terms "management science" and "the quantitative approach" are often used synonymously. However, in our view, the quantitative approach is appropriate, useful, and relevant in all schools of management, although it has been most conspicuous in the management science area.

1.10
Summary

In this chapter, we have introduced the reader to the nature, scope, role, and importance of management. We examined management from several perspectives, such as the function, profession, resource, process, discipline, science, and art concepts. We also emphasized that management is a multidimensional and dynamic reality, not a static concept. Our discussion of various aspects of

---

[22] See Section 2.6 for a description of the deductive approach.

[23] See, for example, Gruber and Niles [1971] or Ansoff [1965, Chap. 2].

[24] We refer the reader to two excellent articles on this topic: Wagner [1971] and Argyris [1971].

management suggested the following definition: *Management is the process of integrating the efforts of a purposeful group, or organization, whose members have at least one common goal.* The important implications of this definition were noted. The importance of management was traced to three important phenomena of our times: large organizations, interdependence, and an increasing rate of change. Each of these factors was briefly discussed with respect to actual business developments.

We have shown in this chapter that there are certain fundamental threads that run through and integrate various schools of management. A brief account of the evolution of management thought was presented by describing the salient features of scientific management, administrative management, human relations, behavioral science, and management science schools. The integrated nature of management was established by relating the foundations and characteristics of various schools of management. A claim was made that the quantitative approach to decision making is appropriate, useful, and relevant in all branches and schools of management. What is the quantitative approach? How can managers employ it to solve decision problems? These and related questions will be discussed in Chapter 2.

References

Ansoff, H. I. *Corporate Strategy.* New York: McGraw-Hill Book Company, 1965.

Argyris, C. "Management Information Systems: The Challenge to Rationality and Emotionality." *Management Science* (Feb. 1971), B275–B292.

Dantzig, G. B. *Linear Programming and Extensions.* Princeton, N.J.: Princeton University Press, 1963.

Donnelly, J. H., J. L. Gibson, and J. M. Ivancevich. *Fundamentals of Management*, rev. ed. Dallas, Tex.: Business Publications, Inc., 1975.

Feeney, G. J. "The Role of the Professional in Operation Research and Management Science." *TIMS Interfaces* (Aug. 1971), 1–12.

Filley, A. C., and R. J. House. *Managerial Process and Organizational Behavior*, 2nd ed. Glenview, Ill.: Scott, Foresman and Company, 1975.

George, C. S., Jr. *The History of Management Thought.* Englewood Cliffs, N.J.: Prentice-Hall, Inc., 1972.

Gruber, W. H., and J. S. Niles. "Problems in the Utilitization of Management Science/Operations Research." *TIMS Interfaces* (Nov. 1971), 12–19.

Huse, E. F., and J. L. Bowditch. *Behavior in Organizations: A Systems Approach to Managing.* Reading, Mass.: Addison-Wesley Publishing Company, Inc., 1973.

Koontz, H., and C. O'Donnell. *Management*, 6th ed. New York: McGraw-Hill Book Company, 1976.

Levey, S., and N. P. Loomba. *Health Care Administration: A Managerial Perspective.* Philadelphia: J. B. Lippincott Company, 1973.

March, J. G., and H. A. Simon. *Organizations.* New York: John Wiley & Sons, Inc., 1958.

Mintzberg, H. *The Nature of Managerial Work.* New York: Harper & Row, Publishers, 1973.

Simon, H. A. "On the Concept of Organization Goal." *Administrative Science Quarterly* (June 1964), 1–22.

Taylor, F. W. *Principles of Scientific Management.* New York: Harper & Row, Publishers, 1911.

Turban, E., and N. P. Loomba. *Readings in Management Science.* Dallas, Tex.: Business Publications, Inc., 1976.

Wagner, H. M. "The ABC's of OR." *Operations Research* (Oct. 1971), 1259–1281.

Weber, R. E. *Management.* Homewood, Ill.: Richard D. Irwin, Inc., 1975.

Review Questions and Problems

1.1. What is your concept of the term "management"? Describe the various perspectives on management discussed in this chapter.

1.2. Management functions within a dynamic environment. What are some of the factors that managers may consider as dynamic or changing?

1.3. Management has been viewed as an art as well as a science. Discuss the importance of each view and describe how the two can, and indeed should, be applied simultaneously in the actual practice of management.

1.4. What factors in modern society contribute to the increasing importance of management?

1.5. List and describe different schools of management. List the main characteristics of each school.

1.6. What are the four most important characteristics of management science? Explain their significance in your own words.

1.7. Read the preface to this book and discuss why the present chapter serves as the proper foundation for understanding the quantitative approach to management.

The Quantitative Approach

MAJOR CONCEPTS AND TOPICS
DISCUSSED IN THIS CHAPTER

Thrust, Requirements, Substance, Spirit, Potential, and Limitations of the Quantitative Approach

The Concept of Utility

The Idea and Implications of the Systems Approach

Interdisciplinary Teamwork

The Scientific Method

The inductive approach
The deductive approach

The Use of Models

Basic Structure of a Decision Model

Objectives and goals
Variables and parameters
General versus specific solution
Implementation and control

Payoff Matrix Formulation of a Decision Problem

Marginal Approach to Decision Problems

2.1
Introduction

The nature, role, and importance of management were examined in Chapter 1 from different perspectives. The main characteristics of different schools of management were described to provide a background against which the idea, thrust, potential, and limitations of the quantitative approach to management can be appreciated. The purpose of this chapter is to give an operational meaning to the quantitative approach. We first explain the requirements, substance, and the spirit of the quantitative approach. This is followed by a discussion of the four pillars of the quantitative approach: systems orientation, interdisciplinary teamwork, scientific method, and use of models. Finally, we show how *general* models can be used to solve *specific* problems. This is accomplished by expressing some typical business problems in quantitative terms and solving them by the application of quantitative models.

2.2
The Quantitative Approach

The *quantitative approach* to management requires that decision problems be defined, analyzed, and solved in a conscious, rational, logical, systematic, and scientific manner—based on data, facts, information, and logic—and not on mere whim or guess. A vital ingredient of the quantitative approach is that choices are made by the application of decision criteria that can be *objectively measured*. Within the boundaries imposed by these requirements, there are several levels and variants of the quantitative approach. Depending on the degree of mathematical sophistication employed, the range varies from calculating a simple breakeven point,[1] constructing a realistic balance sheet or income statement, and developing a behavioral model of job satisfaction, to the building and utilization of such modern models of management science as linear programming, queuing models, and simulation models.[2] One common thread in all variants of the quantitative approach is that numbers or symbols are employed to represent phenomena of interest or models of reality.

The scope of quantitative methods (the mechanisms through which the quantitative approach is implemented) is very broad.[3] They are applicable in defining and solving problems in all types of organizations: business, government, military, and private nonprofit organizations. The most familiar applications are

---

[1] Breakeven point (BEP) for a firm (or for a product) is the volume of sales at which *total* revenues equal the sum of *fixed* and *variable* costs.

[2] A classification of *prototype* problems (or models) is: (1) allocation, (2) inventory, (3) replacement, (4) queuing, (5) sequencing and coordination, (6) routing, (7) competitive, and (8) search. See Ackoff and Sasieni [1968, p. 11]. As used in this text, the term "model" means a mathematical or quantitative representation of some problem.

[3] In practice, the terms "tools," "techniques," and "methods" are often used interchangeably. For a distinction between the meaning of these terms, see Ackoff [1962, pp. 5–7].

found in business organizations: plant location, profit planning, inventory control, production scheduling, return on investment (ROI) analysis, portfolio selection, marketing research, and so on. Quantitative techniques such as PPB (planning, programming, and budgeting)[4] and PERT (program evaluation and review technique)[5] are being employed in making policy and operational decisions in government, military, and private nonprofit organizations.

The main purpose of this book is to present and illustrate the *quantitative approach* to management at an elementary level, concentrating essentially on those managerial problems that are most frequently encountered in business firms. We plan to accomplish this purpose by considering a selected set of managerial problems, formulating and stating them in such terms that they can be solved by *structured* and *well-defined* solution procedures, and finally arriving at specific and objectively measurable answers. How to determine the breakeven point for a firm? How to choose an optimum product mix? How to make an optimum allocation of resources? What is the best inventory policy? How can we use additional information to formulate a new product strategy? How many service outlets will lead to an optimum operation of a service facility, such as a bank or a grocery store? These are the types of problems that are best solved by the methods and models developed by the quantitative approach.

The availability of well-structured models and methods is only one, and perhaps less important, aspect of the quantitative approach. The second, and more important aspect, is the *attitude* of search, conducted on a *scientific* basis, for increased knowledge in the *management* of organizations. Actually, the emergence of well-structured, and useful, quantitative methods is the result of this attitude, namely, the conscious, rational, logical, systematic, and scientific approach to problem solving. The point we want to emphasize is that the attitude encompassed in the quantitative approach is perhaps more important than the specific methods or techniques. It is only by adopting this attitude that the boundaries and application of the quantitative approach can be advanced to include those areas where, at first glance, quantitative data and facts are hard to come by. It is therefore possible, and desirable, to apply the quantitative approach not only to the traditional business areas (e.g., production, finance, and marketing) but also to such questions as social responsibility, ecology,[6] public policy, international relations, interpersonal relations, individual and group behavior, and organizational structure and behavior. Since the focus of this book is on describing and explaining a selected set of methods (or models), it is all the more important that the reader keep in mind the true potential of the quantitative approach.

The quantitative approach is *not* a fixed formula to be uniformly applied to all types of problems. It is, on the other hand, a style of management. The quantitative approach does not preclude the qualitative or judgmental elements that almost always exert a substantial influence on managerial decision making. Quite the contrary! In actual practice, the quantitative approach must build upon, be modified by, and continually benefit from the experiences and creative insights of business managers. In our view, the quantitative approach imposes a special

---

[4] PPB (planning, programming, and budgeting) is a quantitative technique for making allocation decisions. See Levey and Loomba [1973, Chap. 7].

[5] PERT (program evaluation and review technique) is a planning and control technique based on network theory. See Levey and Loomba [1973, pp. 516–518]. We describe PERT in Chapter 6.

[6] One entire issue of *Management Science* (Vol. 9, No. 10, June 1973) is devoted to the application of management science to ecology and the quality of life.

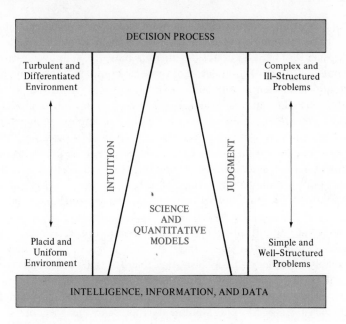

Figure 2.1. Symbiotic Relationship Between Qualitative Thinking and Quantitative Models.

responsibility on the manager. It attempts to cultivate a managerial style that demands a conscious, systematic, and scientific analysis—and resolution—of decision problems.

In the real world, there exists a symbiotic (i.e., mutually supportive) relationship among intuition, judgment, science, quantitative attitudes, practices, methods, and models. As shown in Figure 2.1, the decision process is always supported by a mixture of qualitative (intuition, judgment) and quantitative models.[7] The higher the degree of complexity and the degree of turbulence in the environment, the greater is the importance of the qualitative approach to management. Conversely, the lower the degree of complexity (i.e., simple and well-structured problems) and the degree of turbulence in the environment (i.e., uniform environment), the greater is the potential of quantitative models.

Progress in the domain of quantitative approaches to management has been recorded along two dimensions. First, research efforts have been and are being directed to discover and develop more efficient tools and techniques to solve decision problems of all types. Second, through a continuous process of testing new frontiers, attempts have been made to expand the boundaries and application potential of the available techniques. This, too, is an important aspect of the quantitative approach which the reader must keep in mind. New developments and innovations are taking place continually, and the bulk of the material in this book is of a very basic and elementary nature. Our purpose is to ignite a spark, and we hope that the reader will keep on asking critical questions as he enters the ranks of management and attempts to use the knowledge and attitude gained by reading this book.

[7] Figure 2.1 was suggested and developed by my colleague A. O. Holsinger of the Department of Management, Baruch College (CUNY).

The quantitative approach is assuming an increasing degree of importance in the theory and practice of management. What factors are responsible for this development? The answer resides in four main reasons. First of all, decision problems of modern management are so complex that only a conscious, systematic, and scientifically based analysis can yield realistic solutions. Second, we now have at our disposal a repertory of quantitative models that have demonstrated their potential in solving these complex managerial problems. Third, the availability of modern computers has made it possible, both in terms of time and cost, to actually apply these models to real-life problems in all types of organizations—business, industry, military, government, health, and so on. Last, and most important, if managers are to fully utilize the potentials of management science models and computers, then problems will have to be stated in quantitative terms.

The terms "quantitative approach," "operations research," "management science," "systems analysis," and "systems sciences" are often used interchangeably. However, it is also possible to find definitions that attempt differentiation between these terms. We shall consider the quantitative approach as having the greatest scope because even the most elementary attempt to quantify (e.g., in very basic accounting statements) represents an aspect of the quantitative approach. Higher-level and more sophisticated models of operations research and management science are obviously quantitative in nature.

A decision problem can be formulated, analyzed, and solved in a number of different ways, ranging from a solution based on intuition and applying simple logic to the idea of building an elaborate mathematical model. From a quantitative point of view we shall only discuss these four approaches: (1) an inductive approach based on observation, problem definition, hypothesis formulation, testing the hypothesis, rejecting or accepting the hypothesis, implementation, and control (Section 2.6); (2) a deductive approach in which a general model is used to solve a specific problem (Section 2.6); (3) formulating the specific problem in the form of a payoff matrix (payoff matrix-formulation approach) (Section 2.9), and identifying the optimal strategy by the application of a decision criterion; and (4) formulating the problem so that the idea of marginal approach can be applied either to develop a general model or to solve a specific problem (Section 2.10).

These approaches are related to each other, and managers can use them separately, sequentially, or on a combined basis. Knowing which approach to use in a given circumstance is one of the most important ingredients of success in management. The choice is usually made on the basis of reliability, validity, and economic consideration.

2.3
The Concept of Utility

The question of *measuring* the attainment of objectives is extremely important in the quantitative approach. Regardless of the type of decision model employed, we must be able to measure the extent to which our attempts at achieving a goal, or a set of goals, have been successful. In this connection, we must examine two issues. First, is the objective single-dimensional? That is, can it be measured with a single measure of performance, such as profit? Or, is the objective multidimensional?[8] That is, do we have conflicting goals (make more money, spend less time in commuting) that require two different measures of performance (dollars and time)? The second issue deals with the *type* of scale that is used for measurement. The scale of measurement can be objective[9] or subjective. For example, when stated in monetary units, the goal of profit maximization is assumed to be objectively measured. However, since the same amount of money might not provide equal satisfaction to different persons, a subjective scale of measurement may have to be employed. Then, how can we build a model that permits an objective and rational analysis and, at the same time, takes into account this element of subjectivity? The answer resides in the concept of utility.

By the term *utility* we mean the satisfaction or happiness that one derives from a specified amount of money, a commodity (e.g., food), or an activity (e.g., playing tennis). We shall restrict our discussion to utility of money. Utility can be positive (for profit), zero, or negative (for loss), and it is measured in units called *utils* (or utiles). We can think of total utility (corresponding to a specified amount of money), marginal utility (corresponding to marginal increment in utility as a result of marginal or additional increment of money), average utility, and expected utility (in the case of probabilistic situations—see Appendix A, Section A.4).

Table 2.1 explains the ideas of total and marginal utility. The *marginal* utility measures the impact of the *last* unit. As shown in Table 2.1, while the marginal utility of $1,000 is 0.6 when the profit increases from $5,000 to $6,000, it is only 0.3 when the profit increases from $9,000 to $10,000. Actually as shown in Table 2.1, we experience less and less satisfaction (as measured by marginal utility) for each additional $1,000 in profits. This is the case of the diminishing marginal utility of money.

The idea of utility is important because utility is highly *subjective* and the utility of the same amount of money or payoff is different for different individuals. For example, the utility of $50,000 is not the same for a rich man as it is for a poor man. Such individual differences in utility for money explain why different people exhibit different attitudes toward taking risks. We can identify three types of attitudes and

Table 2.1

Profit	Total Utility	Marginal Utility*
$5,000	4.1	—
$6,000	4.7	0.6
$7,000	5.2	0.5
$8,000	5.6	0.4
$9,000	6.0	0.4
$10,000	6.3	0.3

* Values in Table 2.1 are read from the risk-aversion case in Figure 2.2.

[8] A multidimensional problem involves conflict among goals. For a brief discussion of how to handle multidimensional problems, see Loomba [1976, p. 50].

[9] Objective scales of measurement have been classified into four categories: (1) nominal scale, (2) ordinal scale, (3) interval scale, and (4) ratio scale. See Starr [1971, pp. 50–53]. Also, see Green and Tull [1975, p. 50].

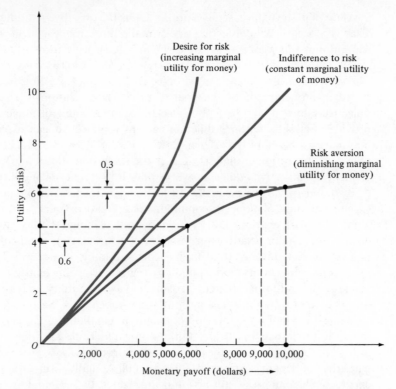

Figure 2.2. The Concept of Utility. (Adapted from Brigham and Pappas [1976, p. 69.]) From *Managerial Economics* Second Edition, by Eugene F. Brigham and James L. Pappas, Copyright © 1976 by The Dryden Press, A Division of Holt, Rinehart and Winston. Reprinted by permission of Holt, Rinehart and Winston.

behavior toward risk: (1) risk aversion, (2) indifference to risk, and (3) a desire for risk. These attitudes can be described in terms of marginal utility, as shown in Figure 2.2.

The assumption in risk-aversion behavior is that each additional unit of monetary payoff yields a decreased amount of satisfaction. That is, in risk aversion we assume a *diminishing marginal utility* of money. Most business managers exhibit risk-aversion behavior.

The assumption in the behavior that exhibits indifference to risk is that the manager has a *constant marginal utility* of money. When we use monetary payoffs as the decision criterion, we are essentially using the assumption of constant marginal utility.

The assumption in the behavior that exhibits a desire for risk is that the decision maker has an *increasing marginal utility* of money. In real life, gamblers tend to exhibit an increasing marginal utility of money.

In this text, we shall measure utility by simple monetary payoffs. This implies a constant marginal utility of money.[10]

---

[10] The actual measurement of utility poses a very difficult problem in real-life situations. See Swalm [1966], Hammond [1967], and Stimson [1969]. Also see Section 5.4.

The systems view of problems, an interdisciplinary teamwork, the philosophy of the scientific method, and the use of models are the four main pillars of the quantitative approach. We shall explain each one in turn in Sections 2.4 to 2.7.

2.4
The Systems Approach

The systems view of problems referred to usually as the *systems approach*, implies that each problem should be examined, to the extent possible and economically feasible, from the point of view of the overall system of which the problem is but one part. The systems approach means that the manager makes a *conscious* attempt to understand the relationships among various parts of the organization and their role in supporting the overall performance of the organization. Before solving a problem in any functional area, or at any organizational level, or in any specific sector of the organization, the manager must understand fully how the overall system will respond to changes in its component parts. For example, a cost-reduction program in the production division must also be examined at a higher level in terms of its possible consequences for other departments, and in such other dimensions as employee morale and job satisfaction. In short, the systems approach is based on the conviction that before implementing any functional solution, one must examine its ultimate effect on other functional areas and on the *entire* system. Furthermore, the process of problem formulation and definition at lower levels of the organization must, if at all possible, fit into the boundaries defined by higher-level objectives. This implies comprehensiveness, in terms of both objectives and problem formulation. However, practical considerations of time, information, cost, and feasibility often force the manager to solve parts of the problem individually and in sequence. This is in contradiction to the idea of overall optimization, which is the goal of management science. But, suboptimization[11] is a fact of life and the importance of management science lies in helping the manager understand when it is necessary and when it can be avoided.

2.5
Interdisciplinary Teamwork

The idea of *interdisciplinary teamwork* is necessary in solving complex management problems because of the advanced state of specialization in many disciplines. The body of specialized knowledge has grown to a point where it is impossible for one person to be a specialist in more than one branch of a scientific discipline. Yet the problems of modern-day life are multidimensional, not single-dimensional. Furthermore, the same problems can be viewed, with beneficial results, by persons from different disciplines. There are no such things as physical problems, biological problems, social problems, psychological problems,

---

[11] *Suboptimization* occurs when there are conflicting goals and objectives or imperfect information. We discuss *optimization* in Appendix B.

economic problems, and so on. There are only problems; the various disciplines of science only represent different ways of looking at them.[12] Large and complex problems need to be subjected to analysis by a team of specialists representing a wide range of skills. This multidisciplinary view produces cross-fertilization of ideas, takes advantage of accumulated knowledge, and makes certain that all ramifications of the problem have been considered. Many organizational problems, for example, have economic, social, political, engineering, physical, biological, and psychological aspects. Although it is impossible for one person to specialize in such a range of disciplines, it is conceivable that a team can be organized so that each aspect of the problem could be analyzed by a specialist in that field. By pooling their specialized talents, the team members can develop better and advanced solutions to old problems and new solutions to new and complex problems. The scientifically trained person from each discipline attempts to grasp the essence of a problem and relate it structurally to similar problems in his or her own field. If there is a structural similarity between the new problem and the one familiar to the scientist, there is a possibility that old and tested solution methods can be applied to the new problem. When the entire team is attempting to develop analogies in this manner, the possibility of finding a solution increases markedly.

2.6
The Scientific Method[13]

Perhaps the most important feature of the quantitative approach is the use of the *scientific method* and the building of decision models. The philosophy of the scientific method requires that the practice of management be based, to the greatest extent possible, on a systematic effort of observation, problem definition, hypothesis formulation, testing of the hypothesis, and implementation of the results obtained or knowledge gained with provisions for feedback. That is, the scientific method consists of observing, measuring, recording, and refining data; building a model that describes, explains, and predicts the behavior of the system under study; and testing and improving the model with the ultimate purpose of increasing managerial efficiency and effectiveness.

Before we describe and illustrate the scientific method, it will be useful to note two important aspects of science: (1) it comprises a body of systematic knowledge, consisting of concepts, laws, principles, and theories used in explaining a set of phenomena; and (2) it involves a process of inquiry or a procedure for answering questions, solving problems, and designing better procedures.

The body of systematic knowledge is accumulated through inductive and deductive research conducted for the purpose of explaining phenomena. We depict this process in Figure 2.3.

[12] Ackoff and Sasieni [1968, p. 7].

[13] For a comprehensive discussion of the ideas presented in this section, we recommend Rigby [1965].

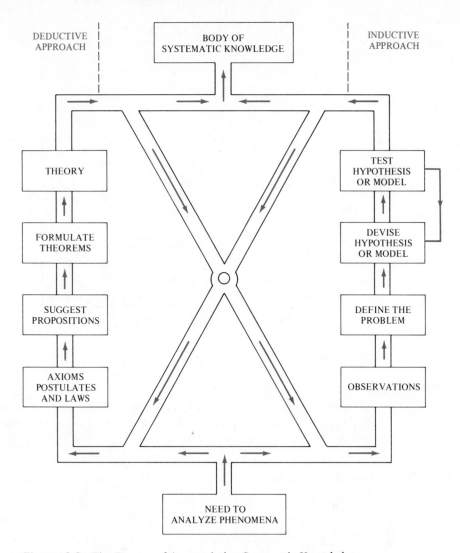

Figure 2.3. The Process of Accumulating Systematic Knowledge.

The Inductive Approach

The *inductive approach* for the purpose of reaching conclusions or making statements is based on empirical evidence. A schematic representation of the inductive approach is shown in Figure 2.4. The method of induction involves the collection of hard data in specific situations and then the making of a general statement to cover all similar situations. The direction of inference, therefore, is from "specific to general." For example, if the task is to evolve a general formula for calculating the circumference of a circle, we shall have to undertake *actual* measurements for several specific circles and then infer (inductively) that

$$\text{circumference of a circle} = 2\pi r$$

where

$$r = \text{radius}, \quad \pi = 3.1416$$

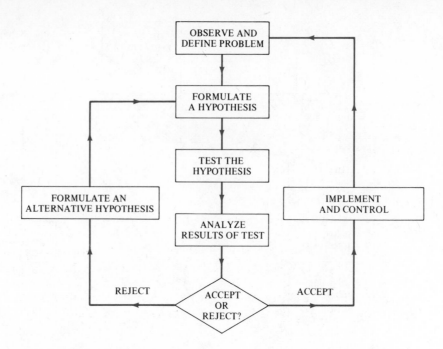

Figure 2.4. The Inductive Approach.

Similarly, if we were asked to identify the highest point on a curve, the inductive approach will require the *actual* measurement of *all* the points before we can identify the highest point on the curve.

The Deductive Approach

The *deductive approach* for the purpose of reaching conclusions or making statements depends on the techniques of mathematics—rather than on empirical evidence. For example, the general formula for calculating the circumference of a circle will be derived from other established "truths"; no actual empirical measurements of specific circles are needed. Similarly, if we are asked to identify the highest point on a curve, the deductive approach requires only that the first derivative of the mathematical expression (e.g., $Y = 2X^2 + 3$) be taken and equated to zero as the first step toward identifying the highest point on the curve.[14] We accept the truth of the general procedure for identifying maxima or minima and then employ the procedure to specific situations. Again, note two things. First, no actual measurements are required; the validity of our conclusion depends only on the validity of the mathematical procedure that is being employed. Second, the direction of the deductive approach is from "general to specific." A schematic representation of the deductive approach is shown in Figure 2.5.

We give one more example to illustrate the difference between the deductive and the inductive approach. Assume that John is taller than Rakesh; and Rakesh is taller than Carmine. Then, based on the deductive approach, we can say that John is taller than Carmine. However, if an inductive approach were to be used, we will

[14] See Appendix B.

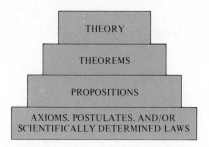

Figure 2.5. The Deductive Approach.

have to actually measure the heights before we can conclude that John is taller than Carmine.[15]

The second aspect of science relates to the procedures of inquiry involving *qualitative* research (e.g., asking the right questions to define the problem); *quantitative* research to discover, establish, and explain relationships (e.g., the behavior of different types of costs in inventory problems); and *analysis* and *interpretation* (to suggest optimal courses of managerial actions).[16] The focus of this book, as described in Section 2.2, is on the quantitative approach. We shall build quantitative models of decision problems, and obtain optimal courses of managerial actions based on the analysis, solution, and interpretation of these models.

Let us now return to the theme of scientific method. Based on the preceding discussion, we can say that the scientific method can be divided into four stages: (1) observation[17] and problem definition, (2) formulation of a hypothesis or a generalized model, (3) testing the hypothesis or some of the predictions (arrived at deductively) from the generalized model, and (4) implementing the solution or the model. We can illustrate these four stages by considering a very simple example.

2.6.1 ILLUSTRATION OF THE SCIENTIFIC METHOD

Example 2.1 | The Ace Cat Food company is a national producer of cat food and has always held a commanding share of the market. However, sales data indicate that in the past 6 months, sales declined sharply in the Middle Atlantic region. This led management to inquire into the possible causes of the sales downturn. An investigation revealed that a year ago the company's major competitor, Feline Cat Food Co., introduced a new form of package design in the Middle Atlantic region. The new package included a plastic lid that could be used to reseal the can once it was opened. This eliminated the problem of leaving an uncovered can of cat food in the refrigerator.

The Ace Company assumed that since its product, as well as its price, were almost identical to Feline, the decline in sales was caused by the impact of Feline's new package in this geographical area. The management of the Ace Company proposed that if it packaged its product in a manner similar to Feline,

---

[15] If $A > B$, and $B > C$, then, deductively, $A > C$.

[16] Rigby [1965, p. 5].

[17] As used in this text, the term "observation" includes the task of data collection.

it could regain its former share of the market. They decided to produce a small amount of the product in a new container and run a market test. The market test proved that their prediction was correct; sales did increase until the former share of the market was attained.

However, if the market test with the new container had not been successful, other causes for the decline in the sales would have to be hypothesized and tested. For example, if the hypothesis that the sales decline was a consequence of the competitor having introduced a new container had been rejected by the market test, it might mean that the assumption regarding the similarity of the products was not a correct assumption. A second hypothesis could then have been formulated: "Improvement in the product quality will help recapture the lost share of the market." Again, as the management of the Ace Company investigates various possible courses of action, their data, generated by carefully controlled experimentation, might show that the decline in Ace's sales was really a consequence of the competitor's expanded promotion, advertising, or any number of additional factors not originally considered. In other words, the idea behind the scientific method is to *empirically* test a course of action *before* it is adopted or rejected. We now illustrate the four stages of the scientific method with reference to our example.

Stage 1. *Observation and problem definition.*

A decline in sales of the Ace Cat Food Company in the Middle Atlantic region triggered management to think that the company had a problem with declining sales and that the causes of the problem should be located and corrective steps taken.

In this stage, observations might lead to a problem definition, or alternatively, the awareness and recognition, or *assumption*, of a problem will lead to observations and then to problem definition.[18] The major idea is to *systematically observe* the system whose behavior must be understood and explained. In the managerial context, this step is triggered with the purpose of solving a problem and gaining an increased degree of control over the environment. In actual practice, this step can take place in one of two ways, as shown in Figure 2.6.

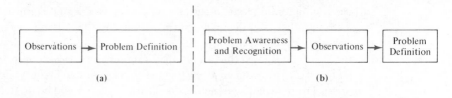

Figure 2.6. The Process of Problem Definition.

Stage 2. *Formulation of a hypothesis.*

The Ace Company, based on observation and certain assumptions, came to the belief that the decline in sales was caused by the competitor's introduction of a new container; hence the hypothesis: "If Ace introduced a new container, it would recapture the lost share of the market."

---

[18] A higher level of aspiration (e.g., double our profits in 5 years) on the part of the manager is an example of specifying goals, which, in turn, lead to problem definition.

The heart of this step is that, based on the observation(s), and with the eventual purpose of solving a problem, a course of action is suggested.[19] The *course of action* or *hypothesis* is a statement of belief (made with implicit predictive elements) which says that the problem will be solved if the suggested action is followed. A stringent requirement here is that the hypothesis should be so formulated that it can be "confronted" with data and then either accepted or rejected.

Depending upon the level of sophistication and the scope of the research, or the problem, the observations of stage 1 might be used to *infer* a *generalized* structure or model. The purpose in such cases is to predict consequences if one or more aspects of the system were changed. For example, if the observation process had been carefully designed and systematically carried out, we might have come up with a mathematical expression (model) that related sales with such other variables as price, promotion and advertising budget, and cat population. Then, from this mathematical model we could *deduce* changes in sales (the dependent variable) as a function of changes in one or more independent variables.[20] In such a case the model becomes the hypothesis to be tested against data.

Stage 3. *Testing the hypothesis.*

This step is the heart of the scientific method because it is here that the hypothesis (statement of belief that implies a managerial course of action) is "confronted" with empirical data. For example, the hypothesis "If Ace introduced a new container, it would recapture the lost share of the market" will be tested by actually producing and marketing a limited quantity of the product packaged in the new container. If the tests support the stated belief, the hypothesis is accepted; otherwise, it is rejected. If accepted, it becomes the basis of managerial actions. If rejected, alternative courses of action will have to be investigated. In this manner, each new alternative course of action will become the new hypothesis to be tested. It should be stated here that what we have described is the procedure for testing a single hypothesis. Many times, the experimentation involved in testing hypotheses is directed at comparing two or more courses of action. The tests can be conducted either simultaneously or successively.

Similarly, the actual system can be tested to ascertain whether some of the conclusions *deduced* in stage 2 will, in fact, be supported if actual changes are made in some part of the system.

Stage 4. *Implementation and control.*

The courses of action accepted through the experimentation of stage 3 are finally implemented as organizational actions. In our example, if the test run with the new container was successful, the Ace Company would set in motion all efforts that are necessary to package the cat food in new containers.

This step is the logical conclusion of the scientific approach to solving managerial problems. However, in actual practice, this is not the end of managerial actions. An effective system of control is needed to detect changes in the system and to take corrective actions if necessary. Thus, managers must institute a carefully designed system of control, based on provisions of feedback, whereby a sharp eye is

---

[19] The course of action is based on a series of assumptions that may or may not be explicitly stated.

[20] See Appendix 2A at the end of the chapter for a discussion of parameters, constants, and variables.

kept on the environment, changes in the parameters[21] of the system, assumptions of the plans, and so on.

What we have described above is the scientific method. The reader *must not* infer that actual business behavior is composed of such neat, convenient, and easily delineated phenomena. On the contrary, in the actual business world, pressures of time are immense, and the demands for managerial decisions come simultaneously from several directions. Managers therefore seldom have the time to conduct carefully designed experiments. Hence, in the real world, organizational arrangements are made so that specialized management science groups are established to experiment with models where time and cost considerations permit experimentation and development. However, more often than not, managerial problems require quick resolution. In such cases, the scientific method of management science boils down to a logical and rational approach to problem solving, with a clear recognition of the fact that *all* the data may either not be available or are impossible to get within the constraints of time and money. This is the approach of pragmatic managers. Sometimes labeled as the philosophy of satisficing,[22] rather than optimizing, such an approach recognizes the need for making timely decisions. We shall contend, however, that when managers behave in a satisficing fashion, they are—in effect—being rational and are, in a sense, optimizing. They are quick to realize the unacceptable costs that would result if there were a preoccupation with optimization under *all* circumstances. The interesting question therefore is: Does management science or the quantitative approach exclude such a pragmatic approach? Must management scientists doggedly, and blindly, carry out the mechanics of quantitative optimization, without proper regard to the behavioral aspects that reflect the realities of organizational life? Our answer is a most emphatic *no*. The boundaries of management science or the quantitative approach cannot be so narrowly drawn. If they are, the results will be counterproductive and there will never develop the kind of dialogue between the manager and the management scientist that is required for successful management practices.

2.7
The Use of Models

Managers deal with reality that is at once complex, dynamic, and multifaceted. It is neither possible, nor desirable, to consider each and every element of reality before deciding upon a course of action. Such an approach will be impractical because of the fact that time and financial resources are not unlimited. Nor can managers conduct actual experiments with reality, again because of different types of constraints (e.g., economic, legal, human, political). For example, the Pentagon cannot proceed to test the accuracy and effectiveness of the CRUISE missiles by actually firing these missiles on population or industrial targets. How, then, can managers gain insight into real-life problems and find solutions that must stand the

---

[21] See Appendix 2A.

[22] Satisficing is not a misspelled word. It can be thought of as a contraction of "sufficient to satisfy." In terms of managerial behavior, Russell Ackoff has suggested three categories of planning philosophies: (1) *optimizing*, (2) *satisficing*, and (3) *adaptivizing*. See Levey and Loomba [1973, p. 275].

test of the future? The answer resides in the concepts of systems and models.

A system defines a particular aspect or "cut" of reality that is important to the decision maker. For example, in a business firm, we have a production system, a marketing system, a financial system, and so on. A *model* is a relationship among specified variables and parameters of the system. A model is constructed to analyze and understand the system, so that better decisions can be made. For example, the financial system of a firm can be represented by such models as a balance sheet, an income statement, and a discounted cash flow statement.

A model, then, is a particular representation of a system, which, in turn, represents specified aspects of reality (see Figure 4.1 on p. 84). For example, a balance sheet that gives, at a given point in time, an instant picture of the assets, liabilities, and net worth of a corporation is a financial model. Similarly, an income statement that lists, for a given period of time such as 1 year, the revenues, expenditures, and net income of a corporation is also a financial model. A balance sheet and an annual income statement are thus examples of models that represent *some* aspects of the financial health of a corporation. Similarly, we can build quantitative or mathematical models of several types of managerial problems related to production, marketing, and other areas.

We emphasize the "particularity" of models because managers can perceive the same problem differently—depending upon their particular interests and attention focus. The management science or quantitative models, as opposed to verbal models, have the advantage that, given the same assumptions, different persons will arrive at the same conclusions. This assertion will become quite obvious from the quantitative model illustrated in Section 2.8.

The use of quantitative or mathematical models is the core of management science and the quantitative approach. As mentioned earlier, these models are either derived inductively or built on the basis of deductive reasoning. For example, if the sales of a product could be shown, on the basis of actual market research and empirical data, to be a particular function of price, advertising, income level of consumers, or some other factors, we would be building an inductive model. On the other hand, as shown in Section 2.8.1, the simple inventory model expressed by Equation (2.7) was built on a deductive basis.

Most of the models presented in this book are of the deductive variety, although simulation models (Chapter 14) are essentially inductive in nature. Further, as

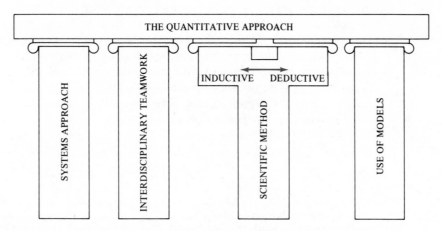

Figure 2.7. The Quantitative Approach.

shown in Figure 2.3, there are explicit as well as implicit interactions between the inductive and deductive approaches as models are built and applied. For example, the implementation and control phases of the solutions derived through deductive models are subject to empirical verification. And, as shown in Figure 2.5, certain foundations or stages of the deductive models could have been arrived at through scientific experimentation (i.e., inductively). We want to emphasize this relationship between the inductive and deductive approaches because in many texts dealing with quantitative management, this important idea is often either completely ignored or is not stated explicitly.

The conceptual relationship of the quantitative approach and its four main pillars is shown schematically in Figure 2.7.

2.8
Basic Structure of a Decision Model

Quantitative models[23] are developed, solved, and applied to specific problems to guide and assist the manager in making decisions. In each and every decision situation, regardless of its content or orientation, we propose a sequence of seven steps that must be executed—explicitly or implicitly. These steps constitute the basic structure of a decision model (enclosed within dashed lines in Figure 2.8).

Formulation of objectives and goals, the first step in our model, is usually preceded by a series of activities which are often referred to as *perception* and *intelligence*. The essential purpose of these activities is to *define the problem*. However, as mentioned earlier, the quantitative approach requires that the definition of the problem be subject to a conscious application of the scientific attitude and the systems orientation. This view is shown schematically in the top portion of Figure 2.8. We shall illustrate the quantitative modeling approach by applying the seven steps shown in Figure 2.8. to an inventory problem.

2.8.1 THE INVENTORY PROBLEM

In the case of many companies, particularly for large manufacturing concerns, inventories are of major significance. This is because millions of dollars can be tied up in inventories, which results in extremely high interest costs or opportunity costs.[24] Hence, if the inventories can be reduced by designing and implementing sound inventory control policies, the potential savings can be substantial. How to formulate and solve inventory control models with different assumptions is the subject matter of Chapters 12 and 13. Here we restrict our discussion to the basic *EOQ (economic order quantity) model*.

---

[23] The discussion here pertains to deductive models, although several of the same steps are also applicable to inductive models.

[24] The term "opportunity cost" refers to the cost involved in *not* following the best course of action with reference to specified conditions of a given decision problem. For example, if funds tied up in inventories could produce more profits in an alternative project, then the company is incurring certain opportunity costs.

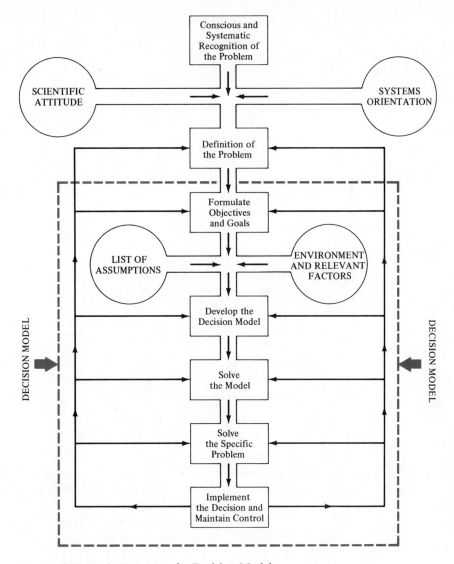

Figure 2.8. Basic Structure of a Decision Model.

The basic EOQ model reflects an inventory problem under deterministic conditions (i.e., no uncertainty exists; see Sections 5.3 to 5.5), no quantity discounts, and linear inventory usage (i.e., usage per day is constant). The behavior of costs in the basic EOQ model is shown in Figure 2.9 (see p. 42).

Let us illustrate the model by considering an inventory situation in which we purchase a single product and stock it to meet an annual demand that is known with certainty. We adopt the following notation:

D = demand per year (units/year)

N = number of orders per year

S = incremental cost of processing one order ($/order)

Q = quantity per order (units/order)

C = cost or purchase price per unit ($/unit)

H = holding or carrying costs expressed as a percentage of average dollar inventory (%age)

T = total inventory cost ($/year)

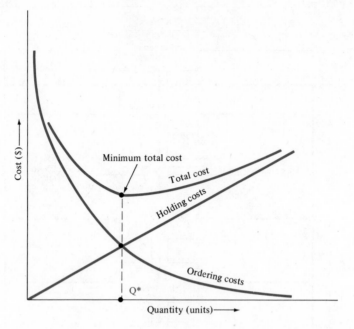

Figure 2.9. Basic EOQ Model (Q^* = optimum order quantity).

In illustrating each of the seven steps of Figure 2.8 we shall use a two-pronged attack. First, whenever appropriate, we shall discuss the philosophical aspects of the particular step. Second, we shall illustrate the step with reference to the inventory problem. In this manner, we can appreciate the broad perspective of the quantitative modeling approach and simultaneously grasp the details of a specific decision problem.

Step 1. *Formulate a set of objectives and goals.*

General Discussion. By the term "objective" we mean a qualitative statement of a desired occurrence or state of affairs. "The P/E ratio[25] of our stock should be improved" is an example of a statement of one objective. By the term "goal" we mean a time-oriented target. For example, "we should increase our share of the market by at least 10 percent within the next year" is a statement of a goal. It would be useful for us to think of objectives and goals as being organized in an hierarchical system. That is, each objective can be subdivided into a set of goals. For example, the objective of increasing the P/E ratio[25] can be pursued by attempting to achieve, say, these goals during the *next fiscal year:* (1) increase our share of the market in the food division by 10 percent; (2) increase sales volume for the company by 30 percent, either by expansion of the present markets or through acquisition; (3)

[25] *P/E ratio* refers to the ratio of stock price to earning per share of stock.

initiate a company-wide program to cut operating costs by 10 percent; and (4) develop and test market two new products.

A few comments are in order at this point. First, it is in the nature of things that objectives are usually multidimensional. Thus, the manager must decide which dimension is relevant, what is an appropriate goal (time-oriented target) along each dimension, and what relative weights in terms of importance are to be attached to these goals. Second, if it is decided by the manager that, for purposes of analysis and planning, the objective is single-dimensional, the distinction between objective and the goal is only of theoretical value. Third, the manager must apply the appropriate scale for measurement along each dimension. Thus, while profits and costs are measured in dollars, it stands to reason that such factors as morale and motivation would have to be measured in nonmonetary units.

In this book, most of the models that we consider have *single-dimensional objectives that can be stated and measured in monetary terms.*

For the Inventory Problem. The sole objective in the inventory problem is to minimize total inventory cost, T. A quantitative statement of the general model (in terms of the criterion variable, T) is developed in step 4 and is shown in Equation (2.6) (on p. 47).

Step 2. *List assumptions of the decision problem.*

General Discussion. In this step, the manager can make different simplifying assumptions regarding future environment, technology, market conditions, behavior of the variables, and the like. These assumptions have the impact of deciding what type of decision model will be employed. For example, the manager can assume conditions of either complete certainty, or risk, or uncertainty (see Sections 5.3 to 5.5). Further, he could assume, albeit on the basis of statistical forecasts, specific values for some of the important factors, such as prime rate, tax rate, and so on. Similarly, assumptions can be made whether the variables are *linear* or *nonlinear* (see Appendix B), whether certain variables are to be treated as *continuous* or *discrete* (see Appendix 2A), and whether the decision problem is to be treated as a *static* or a *dynamic* problem (see Section 5.7).

For the Inventory Problem. We make these assumptions: (1) leadtime[26] is known with certainty, (2) purchase cost per unit is constant (i.e., quantity discounts are not available), (3) inventory depletes at a linear rate (i.e., demand per day is constant), (4) cost of processing a purchase order is constant, and (5) cost of holding or carrying inventories (when expressed as a percentage of average dollar inventory) is constant.

Note that, because of these assumptions, total inventory cost is minimized at the point where ordering costs equal holding costs (see Figure 2.9 and Appendix 12A).

Step 3. *State the context and environment of the decision problem and identify the relevant factors.*

General Discussion. The purpose of this step is to "take stock" of the prevailing circumstances and identify the relevant factors. In particular, the manager lists his

---

[26] We define *leadtime* as the time required between ordering lot size and receiving it.

or her resources; the constraints that limit freedom of action; future anticipated economic, political, social, and government policy trends (e.g., fiscal and monetary policies); and possible actions of competitors. Then a list of all the relevant factors that have a bearing on the problem is compiled and divided into two sets: variables and parameters.[27] The variables can be classified as shown in Figure 2.10.

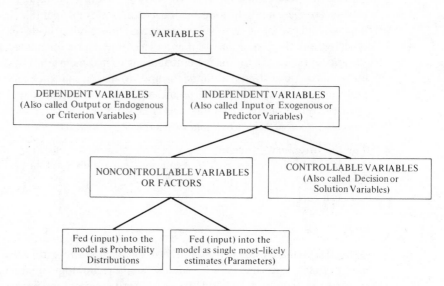

Figure 2.10. A Classification of Variables.

A *dependent* (*output, endogenous, criterion*) *variable* is that factor whose value is to be optimized (e.g., profit, cost, waiting time). The term "dependent" implies that the value of this variable is determined by (dependent upon) other variables or inputs to the system. For example, total inventory cost, T, is determined by such inputs to the system or model as the values of Q, D, S, and H. The term "output" implies that the value of the variable is the output generated by the interaction of the components of the system or model. For example, the components of the inventory system generate the output variable, T. The term "endogenous" implies that a variable, such as T, is internally generated by the system. The term "criterion" implies that we use the value of this variable as *the yardstick* for making a decision. For example: "Choose that value of the order quantity, Q, that will minimize total cost, T."

An *independent* (*input, exogenous, predictor*) *variable* is any factor that is an "input" to the system or model, and is often subject to an *independent* choice by the manager. The term "exogenous" implies that the input is externally generated (e.g., demand or prime rate). The term "predictor" implies that these values are being fed into the model for purposes of predicting the value of the dependent variable.

The input is either chosen by the manager (*controllable*) or dictated by the environment (*noncontrollable*). For example, the value of Q is chosen by the manager, and hence the variable Q is a controllable independent variable. A controllable variable is also referred to as a *decision variable* (manager decides its

[27] Any quantity that assumes various values is called a *variable*, while any quantity that remains fixed (in the context of a given problem or situation) is called a *parameter*. For further discussion, see Appendix 2A.

magnitude) or *solution variable* (the model solution identifies its value). The quantity to be ordered, number of machines to be purchased, number of shifts to be operated, number of part-time nurses to be hired, and number of units of specified products to be produced are examples of controllable (decision) variables. A particular combination of such controllable factors is termed a strategy. A strategy is a course of action that the manager might employ to achieve his objectives.

A *noncontrollable factor* is that over which the manager has little control. A noncontrollable factor, as an input to the system or model, can be a *fixed input* (i.e., a constant value, a single most-likely estimate) or a *variable input* (i.e., a probability distribution). For example, if we assume such factors as annual inventory demand, exchange rates among various currencies, prime interest rate, size of the federal budget, number of strikes, and number of new models that the competitors will introduce next year as constants during the planning horizon, we assume *single estimates* (values) for these factors. Then these factors represent fixed inputs to the model. On the other hand, if we assume a noncontrollable factor to be a variable, then it is entered into the model as a probability distribution (as opposed to a single estimate). For example, instead of being a constant demand, the annual inventory demand can be assumed to vary, and hence must be represented by a probability distribution.

Briefly, if noncontrollable factors are assumed as variables, they are fed into the model as probability distributions. If they are assumed as constants (e.g., price per unit of a product), with reference to a specific problem, they are considered parameters, and are fed into the model as single estimates. (See Figure 2.10.)

A specific combination of noncontrollable factors, emerging as a result of random and natural events, is called a state of nature. The term "state of nature" is employed to describe a particular configuration of the noncontrollable factors that the manager will face as the future unfolds. When a manager lists one or more future states of nature, he or she is, in effect, projecting a specific set of events that will affect the outcomes of the decision. Thus, a state of nature summarizes a configuration of noncontrollable factors emerging from several natural and random events, from actions of rational opponents, or both.

The purpose of the model is to relate the set of variables and parameters in order to faithfully reflect reality. The task of the manager is to choose those values of the decision variables that will result in the optimization of the dependent or criterion variable. The functional relationship of the criterion variable to the decision variables is called the objective function. The general model developed in Equation (2.6) on p. 47 can be viewed as an objective function.

It should be noted here that in real-life decision problems, the manager does not have complete freedom of choice even while selecting values for the controllable factors. The controllable factors can be manipulated only within certain ranges, and there are certain limits that cannot be violated. As we shall see in Chapter 7, which deals with linear programming, such limits are made explicit by introducing into the decision model a set of inequalities. As far as the noncontrollable variables are concerned, the manager attempts to study their behavior by building appropriate probability distributions. These distributions are then made the basis upon which forecasts regarding the behavior of the noncontrollable factors are made. For example, it is possible to record data and build appropriate daily probability distributions regarding the number of machine failures, number of manhours required to repair them, and so on. These distributions can then be used to project future machine breakdowns, number of repairmen needed, and so on.

For the Inventory Problem

- Because of the assumptions made in step 2, we see that D, S, C, and H can be treated as parameters.
- Q and N are *decision variables*. Since demand per year is fixed, we can say that

$$N = \frac{D}{Q} \quad \text{or} \quad Q = \frac{D}{N} \tag{2.1}$$

For example, if the demand is 3,000 units/year, and we place 10 orders, it is obvious that the order quantity must be 300 units.

- Our *criterion* (dependent) *variable* is T.

Step 4. *Develop the decision model.*

General Discussion. The purpose of this step is to state, in an explicit fashion, the specific relationship among different variables and parameters that are relevant to the problem. All the variables and parameters are denoted by symbols and the relationship is developed. What emerges is a decision model. The model could be a simple model that calls for straight (or unconstrained) optimization of a "reward," "payoff," or "utility" as a function of controllable and noncontrollable factors, as shown in Equation (2.2). Or it can be a more complex and sophisticated model as discussed in Appendix B at the end of the book. Equation (2.2) represents the general form of a decision model that relates the dependent (criterion) variable R to a set of decision variables X_i and noncontrollable factors Y_j.

$$R = F(X_i, Y_j) \tag{2.2}$$

where

R = result, reward, or payoff measured in dollars, utility, or some other unit

X_i = set of controllable (decision) variables[28]

Y_j = set of noncontrollable factors (variables and parameters) which is not under the direct control of the manager but which affects R

F = functional relationship between the dependent (criterion) variable R and the decision variables X_i and the noncontrollable factors Y_j

The decision models, developed in this step, can be classified in three categories. First, the model is of the type that has no constraints imposed on it, but it requires optimization. For example, the inventory model of Equation (2.6), $\left(T = \dfrac{DS}{Q} + \dfrac{Q}{2}CH\right)$, is of this type (i.e., unconstrained optimization). Second, the model can be of the variety in which the model consists of an objective function that is to be optimized subject to a set of constraints (i.e., constrained optimization). This, for example, is the model that we shall discuss in the product-mix example of Section 3.4. Third, the model is used not for optimization, but for obtaining information on some critical points. For example, the determination of the breakeven point (B.E.P.) in Section 3.2 is such a model.

---

[28] Subscripting is an economizing device for representing several variables by one symbol. For example, the variables X_1, X_2, and so on, are all represented by X_i.

For the Inventory Problem. We observe that in the type of inventory problem described above, all costs can be directed to one of four categories: (1) cost of inventory items, (2) costs involved in processing purchase orders, (3) holding or carrying costs, and (4) stockout costs (i.e., the costs that arise when the customer demand cannot be satisfied from the existing inventories). Under the deterministic assumptions of our problem (i.e., complete and deterministic information regarding demand and leadtime) we need concern ourselves with only two of the four categories. The first category is not relevant because no quantity discounts are available, and the fourth is not relevant because under the assumptions of certainty regarding demand and leadtime, we need not incur any stockout costs. Hence, for our problem, total inventory cost will equal the sum of ordering costs and the holding costs:

$$\text{total inventory cost} = \text{ordering costs} + \text{holding costs} \tag{2.3}$$

Our task is to find the optimal quantity that will minimize total inventory cost. That is, we want to build a general model and then solve that model for the optimal order quantity Q^*.

Ordering Costs

ordering costs = number of orders × cost of processing an order

$$= \quad N \quad \times \quad S$$

$$= \quad \frac{D}{Q} \quad \times \quad S$$

$$= \frac{D}{Q} S \tag{2.4}$$

Holding Costs

holding costs = average dollar inventory × percentage holding costs

$$= \frac{Q}{2} C \qquad\qquad \times H$$

$$= \frac{Q}{2} CH \tag{2.5}^{29}$$

If we substitute (2.4) and (2.5) in (2.3), we obtain our general model.

$$T = \frac{D}{Q} S + \frac{Q}{2} CH \tag{2.6}^{30}$$

We have now expressed, through the general model shown in Equation 2.6, a relationship among the criterion variable, T; the managerially controllable decision variable, Q; and the parameters $D, S, C,$ and H. This was done by building such *basic blocks* (i.e., submodels) as ordering cost $\left(\dfrac{D}{Q} S\right)$ and holding costs $\left(\dfrac{Q}{2} CH\right)$ and then aggregating them into a general model.

---

[29] Note that since inventory usage is linear, average inventory *in units* $= \dfrac{Q}{2}$, and *in dollars* $= \dfrac{Q}{2} C$.

[30] Note again the dimensional consistency of Equation (2.6). Each term of (2.6) has a dimension of $/year.

Step 5. *Solve the model.*

General Discussion. The purpose of this step is to derive a *general solution* or a *general methodology*.

The general solution is in terms of specified decision variable(s), or for some *critical* information. For example, in Equation (2.7) that follows $\left[Q^* = \sqrt{\dfrac{2DS}{CH}} \right]$, we have a general solution in terms of the decision variable Q. And, in Equation 3.8 of Chapter 3 $\left[Q = \dfrac{F}{P-C} \right]$ the general solution for *BEP* yields the critical information regarding breakeven quantity, Q.

An example of developing a *general methodology* is provided by the linear programming model. Although the actual derivation is beyond the scope of this book, a *general methodology* (the simplex method) for solving linear programming problems has been developed. We illustrate the application of the simplex method in Chapter 8.

The *general solution* is derived by the use of logic or mathematics, fulfilling some condition or test of optimality. For example, the optimal order quantity, Q^* (read Q star) can be either derived from Equation (2.6) by using mathematics[31] or by meeting the *condition of optimality* that requires equating ordering and holding costs.[32]

In Section 3.2 of Chapter 3 we derive a general solution for *BEP* by meeting the condition that, at the breakeven point, profit is zero (or total revenue equals total cost).

For the Inventory Problem. The model given in Equation (2.6) can now be solved for optimal order quantity. The mathematical derivation is shown in Section 12.11.1. Here we derive the answer by imposing the condition of optimality that ordering costs equal holding costs. Thus, equating Equation (2.4) and (2.5), we obtain

$$\frac{D}{Q}S = \frac{Q}{2}CH$$

or

$$Q^* = \sqrt{\frac{2DS}{CH}} \tag{2.7}$$

The symbol Q^* represents the optimal order quantity for this problem.

Step 6. *Apply the general model solution to solve the specific problem.*

General Discussion. The purpose of this step is to determine an *actual* strategy. That is, the general model is used to determine the optimal strategy. In this step, we distinguish two important categories: (1) direct procedure, and (2) iterative procedure.

In the *direct procedure*, the general model can directly (i.e., in a nonrepetitive or noniterative manner) identify the numerical value of the decision variable(s) for the

---

[31] This is done by taking the first derivative of the total cost, T, with respect to Q, equating the first derivative to zero, and then solving the resulting equation for the optimal value of Q. We discuss this approach in Chapter 12. Also see Appendix B.

[32] This point is fully explained in Section 12.11.1.

specific problem. As we shall show below, all we have to do is to substitute the numerical values of specified parameters in Equation (2.7) and *directly* obtain the numerical value of $Q*$ (i.e., the optimal strategy for the specific problem is identified in a nonrepetitive or noniterative manner). Similarly, we can directly determine the numerical value of the BEP quantity, Q, for the specific problem by using Equation (3.8),

$$\left(Q = \frac{F}{P - C} \right).$$

In the *iterative procedure* (exemplified by the simplex method to be described in Chapter 8), we *cannot* directly identify the optimal strategy for the specific problem. Instead, the procedure requires several iterations (each iteration identifies a better strategy) that lead us, in a finite number of trials, to the optimal solution. Here, the general model generates alternative strategies that must be tested for feasibility and optimality. The task of the manager here is to consider only those strategies that are feasible and viable in view of the available resources and specified constraints. Also, the test of optimality is the instrument by which the manager determines whether a given strategy is optimal (best).

For the Inventory Problem. Assume that in a specific problem, we have the following data:

$$D = 4{,}000 \text{ units/year}$$
$$S = \$20/\text{order}$$
$$H = 20 \text{ percent}$$
$$C = \$5/\text{unit}$$

Then we can immediately determine the optimal order quantity by utilizing Equation (2.7):

$$Q* = \sqrt{\frac{2(4{,}000)(20)}{(5)(0.20)}} = 400 \text{ units/order}$$

Step 7. *Implement the decision and maintain a system of control.*

General Discussion. This is the action step. Having identified the optimal strategy, the manager takes all the necessary steps to implement it. The question of follow-up and control, however, is of the utmost importance because the entire decision model is based on a set of assumptions, including the important assumption that the system is stable. If the optimal strategy is to remain optimal, a system of surveillance and control must be maintained to see whether any significant changes have taken place. If so, the circumstances would call for seeking a new optimal strategy. Depending upon the specific formulation of the decision problem, the decision environment, or the predilections of the manager, some of the seven steps of the decision model may be combined, or subsumed under different titles. But they must be considered and executed—explicitly or implicitly, consciously or unconsciously.

For the Inventory Problem. The purpose of this step is twofold. First, the decision on the lot size (derived in step 6) is to be integrated with, and implemented by, the organization's system of inventory control. Second, the behavior of the various parameters of the problem must be monitored continually to maintain control and make changes in the ordering policy when and if necessary.

2.9
Payoff Matrix Formulation of a Decision Problem

In the preceding section, we defined the terms "strategy" (a course of action that implies a particular combination of controllable factors) and "state of nature" (a particular combination of noncontrollable factors). A payoff represents a monetary reward or utility that is a consequence of a specific strategy *in conjunction* with a given state of nature. When payoffs are arranged in the form of a table (or matrix),[33] we obtain a payoff matrix, as shown in Table 2.2.

Conceptually speaking, the number of possible strategies in a decision problem can be infinite (e.g., in a linear programming problem) or finite. If the number of strategies is infinite, we need an efficient and powerful procedure for evaluating the strategies so that the optimal strategy can be quickly and economically identified. This is precisely what is accomplished by the simplex method (see Section 8.5). However, in many decision problems there are only a handful of viable strategies. That is, reality dictates that only a finite number of strategies can be considered. Such problems, with a finite set of strategies, a finite number of states of nature, and hence a finite number of payoffs, can be conveniently expressed in the form of a matrix. Table 2.2 represents a decision problem with two alternative strategies and three different states of nature.

Table 2.2

		State of Nature		
		N_1	N_2	N_3
		Utility or Payoff		
Strategy	S_1	10	15	3
	S_2	2	-6	20

The numerical value of a payoff is determined by the manager and is entered at the intersection of a specified strategy and a given state of nature. For example, in Table 2.2, the payoff associated with strategy S_1 is $10 *if* state of nature N_1 occurs; it is $15 *if* state of nature N_2 occurs. That is, a payoff associated with any strategy is *conditional* upon the occurrence of a specified state of nature. That is why such a payoff matrix (or payoff table) is often described as a conditional payoff matrix

Once the payoff matrix has been constructed, the next task is to choose the optimal strategy according to a specified criterion. The last step, of course, is to

---

[33] A *matrix* is an array of ordered numbers. See Appendix C.

implement the decision and maintain control. The matrix-formulation mode of solving a decision problem points up the importance of generating strategies, specifying states of nature, and estimating payoffs. It is discussed further in Chapter 5.

2.10
Marginal Approach to Decision Problems

Suppose that we are making a profit of $100 by selling two chairs, and a profit of $144 by selling three chairs. Then the *marginal* profit for the third chair is $44, while the average profit is $48 (as compared to $50 when only two chairs are being sold). Hence, the marginal approach requires that we determine the effect of selling the last unit (what happens *at the margin*). In general, the marginal approach measures the net effect on the dependent (criterion) variable as a result of unitary change in an independent (decision) variable

A simple application of the marginal approach is reflected in the decision rule: continue to increase the scale of production up to the point where marginal revenue is greater than or equal to marginal cost. The logic of this decision rule is obvious. The production of *one more* unit results in two monetary consequences: marginal cost (negative utility) and marginal revenue (positive utility). As long as marginal revenue is greater than marginal cost, the manager will want to consider producing *one more* unit. He or she will stop as soon as marginal revenue equals marginal cost. Any production beyond that point will contribute a loss, as it would be in a region where marginal costs exceeds marginal revenue. The marginal approach is useful in solving several decision problems and is a valuable tool in economic theory. It is particularly useful in situations where the number of finite strategies is so large that the payoff matrix formulation will lead to rather extensive calculations. We further illustrate the application of the marginal approach in Section 13.2.2.

2.11
Summary

An attempt was made in this chapter to give operational meaning to the quantitative approach to decision making and model building. The meaning, spirit, and main thrust of the quantitative approach were described. It was suggested that the quantitative approach is the *attitude* of analyzing and solving problems on a conscious, rational, logical, systematic, and scientific basis. From a quantitative point of view, four different but essentially related approaches to decision problems were listed: (1) the inductive approach, (2) the deductive approach, (3) the payoff matrix-formulation approach, and (4) the marginal approach.

The systems approach, interdisciplinary teamwork, the scientific method, and the use of models were listed as the four pillars of the quantitative approach. A very brief description, supported by simple examples, was provided for each. The meaning of the systems approach was explained. It was stated that the systems approach requires that the effect of any change or problem be analyzed, to the extent possible, from the point of view of the overall system. The thrust of the interdisciplinary-teamwork concept is to pool the advantages of specialized knowledge from various disciplines.

We discussed the scientific method in moderate detail. The difference between the inductive and deductive approaches for drawing inferences and building models was explained. How the scientific method works was explained with the aid of a business example. The four stages of the scientific method (inductive approach) were illustrated.

The basic structure of a deductive decision model was established. The decision process was divided into a sequence of seven steps: (1) formulate a set of objectives and goals, (2) list the assumptions of the decision problem, (3) state the context and environment of the decision problem and identify the relevant factors, (4) develop the decision model, (5) solve the model, (6) apply the general model solution to solve the specific problem, and (7) implement the decision and maintain a system of control. Each of these steps was described and explained.

We then presented the matrix-formulation approach to decision problems and, finally, the idea of the marginal approach to solving decision problems.

This chapter has laid the conceptual foundations of the quantitative approach. We shall provide these ideas with substance by presenting a selected set of illustrative examples in Chapter 3.

References

Ackoff, R. L. *Scientific Method: Optimizing Applied Research Decisions.* New York: John Wiley & Sons, Inc., 1962.

Ackoff, R. L., and M. W. Sasieni. *Fundamentals of Operations Research.* New York: John Wiley & Sons, Inc., 1968.

Brigham, E., and J. Pappas. *Managerial Economics,* 2nd ed. New York: The Dryden Press, 1976.

Churchman, C. W., L. Auerbach, and S. Sadan. *Thinking for Decisions: Deductive Quantitative Methods.* Chicago: Science Research Associates, Inc., 1975.

Green, P. E., and D. S. Tull. *Research for Marketing Decisions.* Englewood Cliffs, N.J.: Prentice-Hall, Inc., 1975.

Hammond, J. S., III. "Better Decisions with Preference Theory." *Harvard Business Review* (Nov.–Dec. 1967), 123–141.

Hayes, R. H. "Qualitative Insights from Quantitative Methods." *Harvard Business Review* (July–Aug. 1969), 108–117.

Hillier, F. S., and G. J. Lieberman. *Introduction to Operations Research,* 2nd ed. San Francisco: Holden-Day, Inc., 1974.

Levey, S., and N. P. Loomba. *Health Care Administration.* Philadelphia: J. B. Lippincott Company, 1973.

Levin, R. I., and C. A. Kirkpatrick. *Quantitative Approaches to Management,* 3rd ed. New York: McGraw-Hill Book Company, 1975.

Loomba, N. P. *Linear Programming: A Managerial Perspective,* 2nd ed. New York: Macmillan Publishing Co., Inc., 1976.

Loomba, N. P., and E. Turban. *Applied Programming for Management*. New York: Holt, Rinehart and Winston, 1974.

Morris, W. T. "On the Art of Modeling". *Management Science* (Aug. 1967), 707–717.

Rigby, P. *Conceptual Foundations of Business Research*. New York: John Wiley & Sons, Inc., 1965.

Starr, M. K. *Management: A Modern Approach*. New York: Harcourt Brace Jovanovich, 1971.

Stimson, D. H. "Utility Measurement in Public Health Decision Making." *Management Science*, Vol. 16, No. 2 (Oct. 1969), B17–B30.

Swalm, R. O. "Utility Theory—Insights into Risk Taking." *Harvard Business Review* (Nov.–Dec. 1966), 123–136.

Turban, E., and N. P. Loomba. *Readings in Management Science*. Dallas, Tex.: Business Publications, Inc., 1976.

Wagner, H. M. *Principles of Management Science*, 2nd ed. Englewood Cliffs, N.J.: Prentice-Hall, Inc., 1975.

Review Questions and Problems

2.1. Describe the basic philosophy of the quantitative approach to management.

2.2. Discuss the main structure of these four approaches to problem formulation and solution: inductive approach, deductive approach, payoff matrix-formulation approach, and the marginal approach.

2.3. Distinguish between the inductive and deductive approaches to model building. Give examples of each.

2.4. Define the term "utility." In general, what type of utility function is inferred from the decisions made by business managers? What is the underlying assumption if decisions are made solely on the basis of monetary payoffs?

2.5. What are the main pillars of the quantitative approach? Describe the nature and role of each.

2.6. Describe the basic structure of a decision model by listing the sequence of seven steps presented in this chapter. Formulate a business problem and analyze it by applying these steps.

2.7. What is the purpose of building models? What characteristics must a model possess to be useful?

2.8. Define the following terms.
(a) Variable.
(b) Parameter.
(c) Independent (or input) variable.
(d) Dependent (or criterion) variable.
(e) Decision (or solution) variable.
(f) Controllable factors.
(g) Noncontrollable factors.

2.9. Develop a simple problem and illustrate the following terms.
(a) Strategy.
(b) State of nature.
(c) Objective function.
(d) System.
(e) Model.

    (f) Unconstrained optimization.

    (g) Constrained optimization.

2.10. Distinguish between the *direct* and *iterative* procedures for obtaining solutions to specific problems.

Appendix 2A
Parameters, Constants, and Variables

In order to grasp the nature of quantitative models, one must be familiar with such terms as parameters, constants, and variables. An attempt will be made in the following paragraphs to give *tangible* meaning to these terms.

Suppose that an industrial worker has a wage rate of $2/hour. Then, if he works 40 hours in a particular week, his total earnings for that week are $80. During some other week he may have worked a total of only 30 hours, in which case he would have earned $60. In any case, his total earnings for a particular week, assuming no overtime, can always be calculated as follows:

$$\text{total earnings} = 2 \times \text{number of hours worked}$$

If we let

$$H = \text{number of hours worked}$$

$$T = \text{total earnings}$$

then

$$T = 2H \tag{2A.1}$$

is the relationship between this worker's total earnings and the number of hours worked.

Similarly, another worker might have a wage rate of $4/hour; the total earnings will then be given by the equation $T = 4H$. Briefly, if the number of hours worked were the only criterion for wage payment, we could say that $T = KH$, where K is a constant, for a particular worker or for a particular class of workers, to be determined or assigned in a specific situation. This type of constant, which is fixed for a specific situation, problem, or context (but can vary from one problem context to another), is called a *parameter*. This is in contrast to such *absolute constants* as pi (denoted by the symbol π, which has an approximate value of 3.1416), whose value remains the same in *all* problems, situations, and contexts.

In our simple illustration we note two kinds of mathematical quantities. One type (the quantity 2 in this example) remains fixed and, as mentioned earlier, is called a parameter. The other type, exemplified by T and H, is allowed to vary. Quantities such as H and T, since they can assume various values in a given problem, are called *variables*.

Variables can be classified in a number of ways. For example, a variable can be *discrete* (subject to counting, e.g., 2 cars, 3 houses) or *continuous* (subject to measurement, e.g., temperature, height).

A variable can relate to either a certain (deterministic) or an uncertain (probabilistic or stochastic) environment. In a deterministic environment, a variable will reflect the value of things that vary but whose magnitudes are known with certainty [e.g., variable T in Equation (2A.1)]. On the other hand, a variable is *random* (*probabilistic* or *stochastic*) if its value is determined by "chance" (e.g., the number of persons arriving at a subway station during a specified period of time). For further discussion regarding a random variable, see Appendix A at the end of the book.

Another classification of variables was presented in Figure 2.10 and discussed in Section 2.8. With respect to Figure 2.10, we make three additional comments at this stage. First, whether a variable is designated as exogenous (independent, input, predictor) or endogenous (dependent, output, criterion) depends upon the scope of the problem and the purpose of the model. As an example, for the manager of a firm, the demand for an inventory item is an exogenous variable. However, from the point of view of the entire industry, the demand forecast for that item is an endogenous variable. Second, whether a given quantity is viewed as a parameter or a noncontrollable independent variable depends upon the nature of the problem and the perspective of the manager. To the extent that the price of a product is influenced by market forces, it is a noncontrollable variable and could be entered as such in the formulation of a model. However, if the manager assumes that the price per unit will stay constant (in the context of a given problem), it then becomes a parameter of the problem. Third, in certain problems, in order to be more faithful to the factors that are not under the direct control of the manager, parameters are replaced by random variables that have specified probability distributions. In any case, parameters are constant values that help describe the behavior of one or more aspects of the problem or a component of the problem. For example, if a given component of a problem (e.g., demand for a product in the context of an inventory problem) could be specified as a normally distributed random variable, its *mean* (expected value) and *standard deviation* are its two parameters, and they describe the behavior of the problem component.

CHAPTER 3

The Quantitative Approach– Illustrative Examples

MAJOR CONCEPTS AND TOPICS
DISCUSSED IN THIS CHAPTER

Breakeven Analysis

Illustration of the Modeling Approach

Determination of the breakeven point
Determination of the optimal product mix
Determination of the minimum-cost transportation program

Sensitivity Analysis and Its Managerial Uses

3.1
Introduction

We have now established that the quantitative approach to model building and decision making can take several forms, depending upon the nature of the problem and the efficiency of the specific solution procedure. In particular, we explained four different but related approaches: (1) the inductive approach, (2) the deductive approach, (3) the payoff matrix-formulation approach, and (4) the marginal analysis approach. An example of the inductive approach (reliance on experimentation, specific to general) was described in Section 2.6. In this chapter, we show how some typical business problems can be solved by the use of deductive decision models (general to specific). The payoff matrix-formulation approach is illustrated in Chapter 5 and the marginal analysis approach in Section 13.2.2.

3.2
Breakeven Analysis

It is often useful for managers to have some insight into the behavior of costs, volume of output, revenues, and profits. Of particular interest is the point or volume of output at which the firm can *break even*. The analysis conducted to determine the breakeven point (BEP) is known as *breakeven analysis*.

The purpose of breakeven analysis (sometimes called cost–volume–profit analysis) is twofold: (1) to study the interrelationships among costs, volume of output, revenues and profits; and (2) to determine the breakeven point (BEP) for a firm that produces a single product or a set of products. The breakeven point is defined as the level of output (in terms of physical units, dollars, or percent plant capacity) at which total revenues equal total costs. It is obvious from the definition of BEP that: (1) at the breakeven point the level of profits is zero, (2) the firm will incur a loss if it operates below the breakeven point, and (3) profits begin to accrue only when the level of output exceeds the breakeven point.

Breakeven analysis consists essentially of two steps. The first step is to establish the nature and behavior of revenues and costs. That is, we must answer such questions as: Are revenues linear (price per unit remains constant, regardless of the number of units sold) or nonlinear? What are the relevant costs and how must they be classified? Do we expect some sudden shifts in price or costs at specified levels of output (e.g., price discounts)? The second step is to calculate the actual breakeven point.

We shall illustrate breakeven analysis with reference to a *single-product* case described in Example 3.1. We assume that price per unit remains constant, regardless of sales volume or production level. We consider only two categories of costs: fixed costs and variable costs. By *fixed costs* we mean those costs that remain constant regardless of sales volume or production level. Examples of fixed costs include executive salaries, rent, insurance premiums, and depreciation. *Variable costs* are those costs that vary directly with the level of production or sales volume. Examples of variable costs are direct labor costs, material costs, and sales commissions. We assume that no changes in fixed costs take place during the planning horizon and that variable cost *per unit* is constant. Our assumptions imply linear behavior of revenues and costs.

Example 3.1 | The management of a small company is thinking of introducing a new product in a stable market. The production manager and the marketing manager have agreed on the following "quantitative" information relating to the new product:

> fixed costs = $12,000/year
>
> variable costs = $3/unit
>
> sale price = $6/unit
>
> plant capacity = 5,000 units/year

The management wants to determine the breakeven point for this product as a *guide* to decision making. It should be noted here that this information will constitute only *one* of the decision inputs for deciding whether the new product should be introduced. (Why?)

As mentioned in Section 2.2, a managerial problem, or any other problem for that matter, can be solved in a number of ways, ranging from the use of intuition, or simple logic, to the idea of building a general model. One approach, for example, is to solve the specific problem by utilizing the given information *directly*. In our breakeven-point problem, for example, we note that every time a unit is sold, the sales price not only covers the variable cost of that unit but also generates $3 to recover fixed costs. Hence, our BEP problem boils down to this: If, for every unit sold, we generate $3 to recover fixed costs, how many units must be sold to recover the total fixed costs of $12,000? The answer is obviously 4,000 units. Similarly, we can obtain a solution to our problem by graphical means, as shown in Figure 3.1. Notice that our specific problem has been solved by utilizing the given information directly, without any recourse to a *general* model.

3.2.1 BREAKEVEN POINT IN UNITS

The second approach for solving a problem is to use, whenever appropriate and possible, a general model to solve a specific problem. The general model can be graphical or mathematical.[1] The development and utilization of general models is the essence of the quantitative approach.

In Figure 3.2, we present a graphical version of the *general linear breakeven-point model*.

Note the following:

- Fixed costs are plotted horizontally, as they do not change during the planning horizon. Line *AF* represents fixed costs.
- Variable costs are linear (i.e., variable cost per unit is constant). Variable cost is

---

[1] Chapter 4 is devoted to a discussion of models.

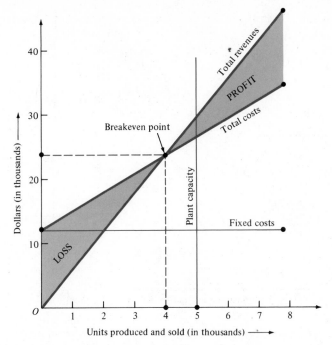

Figure 3.1.
fixed costs	= $12,000/year
variable costs	= $3/unit
price	= $6/unit
BEP (quantity)	= 4,000 units
BEP (dollars)	= $24,000
BEP (percent capacity)	= 80 percent

represented by the straight line *OV.* Note that line *OV* originates from the origin and has a slope that equals variable cost per unit.

- Total costs are determined by adding variable costs to the fixed costs. That is why line *AT,* which represents total costs, originates from point *A* in Figure 3.2 and is parallel to the variable cost line *OV.*
- Total revenues are also linear (i.e., price per unit is constant). Total revenue is represented by the straight line *OR.* Note that line *OR* originates from the origin and has a slope that equals price per unit.
- The breakeven point, *B,* is the point at which total revenues equal total costs. A vertical line drawn from this point will yield the breakeven point in physical units (point *Q*), while a horizontal line drawn from the same point will yield breakeven point in dollars (point *D*).
- The region of loss and the region of profit are shown in Figure 3.2.

We now derive a *general* mathematical model for the linear BEP case and then apply this model to solve our problem. The steps involved are those presented in Section 2.8.

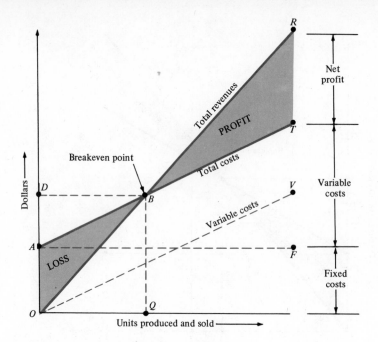

Figure 3.2. Linear Breakeven Chart
Q = breakeven-point quantity
D = breakeven-point dollars

Step 1. *Formulate a set of objectives and goals.*

In this simple model, the objective is to *develop information* regarding the breakeven point for the firm. This information is then used for making managerial decisions (e.g., of the various possibilities, the equipment to be purchased should have the lowest breakeven point).

Step 2. *State the relevant assumptions.*

We assume that: (1) fixed costs do not change during the planning horizon, (2) variable cost *per unit* remains constant, and (3) revenue *per unit* remains constant.

Step 3. *Identify the relevant factors of the decision problem.*

We make a list of all the *relevant* components or factors of the decision problem and then classify them in terms of variables and parameters. In our case, the only relevant factors are price per unit, variable cost per unit, fixed costs, breakeven quantity, and the planning horizon (given as 1 year). Further, the only variable is the breakeven quantity, as we are assuming that price per unit, variable cost per unit, and fixed costs remain constant (and hence are treated as parameters).

Step 4. *Develop the decision model.*

Next we develop a decision model that relates different variables and parameters. This requires that we represent different variables and parameters by specific symbols and then develop the model. We adopt the following symbolic notation:

Q = number of units produced and sold (units)

P = price per unit (\$/unit)

V = variable cost per unit (\$/unit)

R = total revenues per time period (\$/year)

T = total costs per time period (\$/year)

F = fixed costs per time period (\$/year)

π = total profit per time period (\$/year)

Recall that *the condition* for BEP is that profits be zero, or total revenues equal total costs. This condition, plus the assumptions regarding the behavior of revenues and costs, provide all the ingredients needed for developing this model. The general model emerges as we link total revenue and total cost to the concept of profit. Since, at BEP, total profit is zero, we can write

total profit = total revenue − total cost = 0

or

$$\pi = R - T = 0 \tag{3.1}$$

Now,

R = price per unit sold × number of units sold

$$= P(Q) \tag{3.2}$$

And

$$T = \text{fixed costs} + \text{variable costs} \tag{3.3}$$

Since variable costs = variable cost per unit × number of units produced,

$$\text{variable costs} = V(Q) \tag{3.4}$$

Hence, from (3.3),

$$T = F + V(Q) \tag{3.5}$$

Put (3.2) and (3.5) in Equation (3.1). Then

$$\pi = R - T = P(Q) - [F + V(Q)] = 0$$
$$= P(Q) - F - V(Q) = 0 \tag{3.6}$$

Equation (3.6) is our general decision model for the linear BEP case. We can also derive the general model by the condition that, at BEP, total revenues equal total costs ($R = T$).

From (3.2),

$$R = P(Q)$$

From (3.5),

$$T = F + V(Q)$$

Hence, the condition that $R = T$ becomes

$$P(Q) = F + V(Q) \tag{3.7}$$

Note that (3.7) can also be derived directly from (3.6) and that (3.6) and (3.7) represent the same general model.

Step 5. *Solve the model.*

The next step is to solve the model. That is, the model is used to solve for the relevant variable in a *general* form. Here, we want to solve for the breakeven quantity, Q, as illustrated below. We solve (3.7) for Q:

$$P(Q) = F + V(Q)$$

or

$$P(Q) - V(Q) = F$$

or

$$Q(P - V) = F$$

or

$$Q = \frac{F}{P - V} \tag{3.8}$$

The quantity Q, given by (3.8), is the breakeven quantity (BEP). Our general model for the linear BEP case, therefore, is

$$\text{BEP (in units)} = \frac{F}{P - V} \tag{3.9}$$

Step 6. *Solve the specific problem.*

We are now in a position to utilize the general model to solve our specific problem. If we substitute in (3.9) the values of F (fixed costs), P (price per unit), and V (variable cost per unit) as given in Example 3.1, we find that BEP is 4,000 units.

From (3.9),

$$\text{BEP (in units)} = \frac{F}{P - V} = \frac{12,000}{6 - 3} = 4,000 \text{ units}$$

The answer is exactly the same as obtained earlier by direct reasoning or by the graphical approach.

Step 7. *Implement the decision and maintain a system of control.*

In the simple BEP model, the idea of this step is to use the BEP information in making managerial decisions of the type involved in the purchase of machinery or equipment. Further, the *actual* (versus *assumed*) behavior of costs and revenue must be continually monitored to maintain control.

3.2.2 BREAKEVEN POINT IN DOLLARS

In the quantitative approach we continue to build upon available facts and results. For this purpose the concept of dimensional analysis is very useful. Stated briefly, *dimensional analysis* refers to the consistency of dimensions in each term of an equation. Let us illustrate by saying that the management of our company wants the BEP expressed in dollars rather than physical units. We note first that Equation (3.9) has the dimension of "units." Since we wish to derive an expression for sales volume in dollars, we multiply the right-hand side of (3.9) by P and obtain:[2]

$$\text{BEP (in \$)} = P\left(\frac{F}{P - V}\right) \tag{3.10}$$

We can also express (3.10) as

$$\text{BEP (in \$)} = \frac{F}{1 - (V/P)} \tag{3.11}$$

Thus, (3.11) is another formulation of a general model of the linear BEP case. Now, we can use either (3.10) or (3.11) to solve our problem. From (3.10),

$$\text{BEP} = 6 \cdot \left(\frac{12{,}000}{6 - 3}\right) = \$24{,}000$$

From (3.11),

$$\text{BEP} = \frac{12{,}000}{1 - \frac{3}{6}} = \$24{,}000$$

Again, the answer is the same as was obtained by applying the graphical approach in Figure 3.1.

3.2.3 BREAKEVEN POINT IN PERCENT CAPACITY

We now derive the BEP formula in terms of percent capacity. This, too, is accomplished by the use of dimensional analysis. It stands to reason that "percent capacity" dimension can be realized if we divide BEP units by total capacity (also stated in units) and multiply the resulting ratio by 100. Accordingly, we divide the right-hand side of (3.9) by "total capacity in units" and then multiply it by 100. Thus,

$$\frac{\text{BEP (in units)}}{\text{total capacity (in units)}} \times 100 = \frac{\dfrac{F}{(P - V)}}{\text{total capacity (in units)}} \times 100$$

Hence,

$$\text{BEP (in \% capacity)} = \frac{F}{P - V} \times \frac{100}{\text{total capacity (in units)}} \tag{3.12}$$

For our problem,

$$\text{BEP (in \% capacity)} = \frac{12{,}000}{6 - 3} \times \frac{100}{5{,}000} = 80 \text{ percent}$$

---

[2] Note that the dimension of P is \$/unit. Since the dimension of (3.9) was units, its product with \$/unit yields: units × \$/unit = \$.

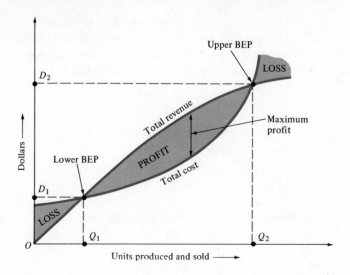

Figure 3.3

Although it provides a useful insight into making financial decisions, we note certain limitations of breakdown analysis. First, it is a static model, covering a fixed period of time. It cannot easily handle situations in which the firm is subject to a series of sudden changes in prices, costs, technology, and so on. Second, it is useful only in short-term planning. It is not helpful in problems that involve long-term and large-scale financial investment. In such cases, managers depend upon simulation models, discounted cash-flow analysis, and other advanced methods of financial analysis.[3] Third, the scope of the linear BEP model is limited because, in real-life problems, costs and revenue are often nonlinear. In such cases, a nonlinear breakeven chart, such as shown in Figure 3.3, can be constructed. Note that, in the nonlinear case, we have two breakeven points, and the goal of the manager here is to determine the point of maximum profit.

Despite its limitations, breakeven analysis is a valuable *guide* for decision making. Here, we have used the linear BEP case to illustrate how a general quantitative model can be developed and used to solve specific problems.

3.3
Sensitivity Analysis

Managerial decisions are often made with specific assumptions regarding the values and behavior of selected factors. For example, an investment decision is usually based on estimated cash flows, future interest rates, market competition, price levels, and so on. Similarly, as we saw in Section 3.2, the BEP of a product is determined on the basis of estimated and assumed behavior of fixed costs, variable costs, and total revenues. It is important, therefore, to know how

---

[3] Simulation models are discussed in Chapter 14. The basic discounted cash-flow model discounts future income streams in order to evaluate the desirability of an investment.

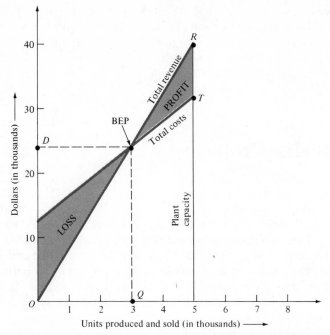

Figure 3.4. fixed costs   = $12,000/year
variable costs   = $4/unit
price   = $8/unit
BEP (quantity)   = 3,000 units
BEP (dollars)   = $24,000
BEP (percent capacity) = 60 percent

"sensitive" is our solution to changes in the values of certain factors. The term "sensitive" refers to the magnitude of change that takes place in the "solution" as a result of changes in one or more factors. For example, it is useful to know the percentage change in BEP as a result of certain changes in fixed costs, variable cost per unit, or price per unit. The investigation of such changes is referred to in the literature as *sensitivity analysis.* Practicing managers engage in sensitivity analysis when they ask "what if" types of questions. *What* will happen to BEP *if* the price per unit changes by 5 percent? *What if* the variable cost increases by 10 percent?

There are two ways to conduct sensitivity analysis. First, the problem can be "re-solved" after taking the assumed changes into account. Thus, as shown in Figure 3.4, a new BEP is determined after the data of Example 3.1 have been changed to reflect a price increase of $2/unit, and an increase of $1/unit in the variable cost.

The second approach for conducting a sensitivity analysis is to establish ranges between which certain factors can change but still have no effect on the optimal solution. This type of investigation is useful in such linear programming problems as the product-mix problem and the transportation problem (e.g., see Section 9.6).

A great managerial advantage of sensitivity analysis is that it yields information regarding the types of controls that are needed in specific situations. For example, if a "solution" is highly sensitive to specified factors or parameters, it would call for a very tight system of monitoring and control. It would also imply that extreme care should be taken in statistical estimation procedures that are used to determine the values of such factors or parameters. We shall discuss sensitivity analysis further in Chapter 9.

3.4
The Product-Mix Problem

Typically, the product-mix problem lists the technological requirements of, and the resources for, producing two or more products. Also given are the profit contribution[4] per unit of each product and the available capacities of the resources. The problem requires the design of an *optimal product mix* (or program of production) so that the total profit contribution is maximized. In such problems we assume limited resources, a given planning horizon (i.e., the production program is designed for a specified period of time), a fixed state of technology, and linear behavior in all relationships.

Example 3.2 The Morgan Production Company produces wooden dowels, which they sell primarily to furniture manufacturers. The market conditions are such that the company can sell its entire production at constant prices. Morgan produces two types of dowels, A and B. Profit per unit from types A and B is $7 and $6, respectively. During the production process the dowels must go through two processes: cutting and finishing. The capacities of the cutting and finishing departments are 300 and 270 hours/month, respectively. Each unit of type *A* dowel requires 2 hours to cut and 1 hour to finish. Each unit of type *B* dowel requires 1 hour to cut and 3 hours to finish. The relevant data for our problem are summarized in Table 3.1. Our objective is to design an optimal program that will maximize total profits.

Table 3.1 *Process Time Data per Unit of Product*

Process	Product A	Product B	Capacity per Month (hours)
Cutting	2	1	300
Finishing	1	3	270
Profit per Unit	$7	$6	

---

[4] *Profit contribution* is defined as the difference between the price per unit and the average variable cost per unit. Thus, as different sales levels are considered, profit contribution is available to cover fixed costs and provide profits. The concept of profit contribution is useful in making pricing and product-mix decisions, especially in the short run.

As before, the quantitative approach requires that we state our problem in the form of a mathematical model. The steps involved are those listed in Section 2.8.

Step 1. *Formulate a set of objectives and goals.*

The sole objective here is to maximize profits. Denote the amount of profit by Z (the criterion variable). Let X (decision variable) represent the amount of product A to be produced and Y (decision variable) represent the amount of product B to be produced.

Since our objective is to maximize profits by designing an optimal mix of products A and B, we can develop an objective function that relates the dependent (criterion) variable to the independent (decision) variables. Note that 1 unit of product A generates \$7 and 1 unit of product B generates \$6. Hence, we can say that $Z = 7X + 6Y$ and that we want to choose those values of X and Y that will maximize Z. Hence, the objective function is

Maximize

$$Z = 7X + 6Y \tag{3.13}$$

However, we see that taken by itself a linear function,[5] such as $7X + 6Y$, can be made infinitely large. This obviously does not make any sense in a business context. What, then, is the solution to this dilemma? The answer lies in the fact that the resources are limited. That is, we must maximize, but subject to certain specified constraints. That is why the problems in which we are required to either maximize or minimize an objective function, subject to specified constraints, fall in the category called constrained optimization (see Appendix B).

It should be noted that some problems call for unconstrained optimization,[6] as in the case of the basic inventory model shown in Figure 2.9 on p. 42. That is, no constraints were explicitly specified or entered into the model. Again, in some problems we require some *critical* information, but the constraints need not be used in the determination of such information. For example, in the linear BEP chart shown in Figure 3.2, the BEP in units was determined without any reference to plant capacity. However, here too, the manager cannot ignore the practical importance of plant capacity.

Step 2. *State the relevant assumptions.*

We assume complete certainty, linearity, fixed technology, constant profit per unit, divisibility, and a static decision model.[7]

Step 3. *Identify the relevant factors of the decision problem.*

- There are two resources here (the capacities of the cutting and finishing departments). These capacities are assumed to be constant

---

[5] In a linear function each term has only one variable and the exponent of each variable is 1.

[6] In optimization problems (constrained or unconstrained), the optimum solution is always obtained by applying a specified *condition of optimality*. For example, in Figure B.10, *minimum* total cost is obtained by applying the condition that the slope of the total-cost curve must be zero at its minimum point (i.e., we take the first derivative of total cost with respect to Q and equate it to zero).

[7] These assumptions are explained in Section 7.2.1. We list them here only to keep alive the "rhythm" of the quantitative modeling approach described in Section 2.8.

during the planning horizon. Thus, resource capacities are treated as parameters.

- Technology is fixed. That is, the amounts of resources required to produce each unit of product A and product B remain constant, regardless of the volume of production. These amounts, known as input–output coefficients, are also treated as parameters.
- Profit per unit of production for each product remains constant for the planning horizon. Although influenced by market forces, the two profit coefficients are also treated as parameters because of the constancy assumption.
- We have two decision variables, the amount of product A to be produced (denote by variable X) and the amount of product B to be produced (denote by variable Y).
- The dependent or the criterion variable is the amount of profit (denote by variable Z) that is generated by various combinations of products A and B (i.e., different values of X and Y).

Step 4. *Develop the decision model.*

- The linear objective function from step 1 is

Maximize

$$Z = 7X + 6Y \tag{3.13}$$

- The capacity constraints here are of the "less than or equal to" type. The reason is obvious. The optimal program of production can use the entire available capacity or perhaps less, but the capacity constraint cannot be violated. The two capacity constraints can be stated as:

$$
\begin{aligned}
2X + 1Y &\leqslant 300 \qquad \text{cutting department} \\
1X + 3Y &\leqslant 270 \qquad \text{finishing department}
\end{aligned}
\tag{3.14}
$$

- Another obvious constraint is that the level of production can be zero or positive, but it cannot be negative. This means that

$$X \geqslant 0 \qquad \text{and} \qquad Y \geqslant 0 \tag{3.15}$$

Now, if we combine the submodels described in (3.13) to (3.15), we obtain the following mathematical model for the problem shown in Table 3.1.

Maximize

$$\boxed{Z = 7X + 6Y} \qquad \text{objective function}$$

subject to constraints

$$
\boxed{
\begin{aligned}
2X + \ Y &\leqslant 300 \\
X + 3Y &\leqslant 270 \\
X, \quad Y &\geqslant \ 0
\end{aligned}
}
\qquad \text{constraints}
\tag{3.16}
$$

Our *specific* product-mix problem has now been stated mathematically.

It should be noted that, in the usual case, the result of step 4 is in terms of a *general* relationship. This could have been the case if we had specified the product-mix problem of Table 3.1 in general terms. However, to project the "image" of a business context, we provided specific numbers in Table 3.1. That is why the decision model (3.16) represents a specific decision problem.

Step 5. *Solve the model.*

The result of this step is usually a *general model* in terms of specified decision variables [e.g., the derivation of Q^* shown in Equation (2.7) on p. 48.] or a *general methodology*. For example, as we shall illustrate in Chapter 8, a general methodology (the simplex method) for solving such problems has been developed. By applying this general methodology, we can solve *any* product-mix problem that conforms to the structure and assumptions of the general model.

Step 6. *Solve the specific problem.*

How the general methodology of the simplex method is applied to solve product-mix problems of the type stated in (3.16) is illustrated in Chapter 8. It can be verified that the optimal solution to our problem is

$X = 126$ that is, produce 126 units of product A

$Y = 48$ that is, produce 48 units of product B

maximum profit = $1,170

Step 7. *Implement the decision and maintain a system of control.*

The purpose of this step is twofold. First, the production plan designed in step 6 is to be implemented through proper organizational channels. Second, the behavior of the various parameters of the problem (i.e., *actual* versus *assumed* values of resources, input–output coefficients, profit per unit, etc.) must be continually monitored in order to maintain control (i.e., keep on checking the validity of the current optimal plan of production).

3.4.1 CONCLUDING REMARKS ON THE PRODUCT-MIX PROBLEM

Both the breakeven problem and the product-mix problem are examples of quantitative formulations of specific situations that require managerial decisions. It should be obvious, however, that the product-mix problem was expressed at a higher level of sophistication. For one thing, in the product-mix problem we *explicitly* stated a goal, the maximization of profits. Second, the linear inequalities given in (3.16) express, in a "quantitative" fashion, the fact of *interdependence* implied by the production technology. The point that we wish to emphasize is that although we can employ the quantitative attitude in almost any managerial problem, the specific model that we use, and the level of sophistication that is appropriate, depend to a large degree on the particular demands of the decision situation and the nature of the problem.

3.5
The Transportation Problem

For several manufacturing and distribution companies, especially the large firms, the problem of transporting or shipping goods from plants to warehouses is of special significance. This is because a large percentage of the annual expenses of such companies is consumed by transportation and transportation-related activities. The potential for cost savings by designing and implementing an optimal transportation program is, in many cases, substantial. A very simple transportation problem involving two plants (or origins) and two warehouses (or destinations) is shown in Table 3.2.

Table 3.2

Origins	Destination		Monthly Supply (units)
	D_1	D_2	
O_1	2 X_{11}	3 X_{12}	80
O_2	4 X_{21}	2 X_{22}	120
Monthly Demand (units)	75	125	

As shown in Table 3.2, the supply capacities of the two plants or "Origins" are 80 and 120 units/month, respectively. The demands of the two warehouses or "Destinations" are, respectively, 75 and 125 units/month. The cost to ship 1 unit of commodity from each plant to each warehouse is shown in the upper right-hand corner of the appropriate cell.

As before, the quantitative approach requires that we state the problem in the form of a mathematical model. The steps involved are those listed in Section 2.8.

Step 1. *Formulate a set of objectives and goals.*

The sole objective here is to minimize total transportation costs. Denote total costs by T (the criterion variable). Let X_{11}, X_{12}, X_{21}, and X_{22} (decision variables) denote the amount of goods to be shipped through the four routes, as shown in Table 3.2.[8] Since our objective is to minimize total transportation cost,

---

[8] The first subscript in the decision variable X_{ij} refers to the plant, and the second subscript refers to the warehouse. Thus, X_{12} is the amount of goods to be shipped from plant (origin) 1 to warehouse (destination) 2.

we can develop an *objective function* that relates the criterion (dependent) variable to the decision (independent) variables.

As can be verified from Table 3.2, the objective function is

Minimize

$$T = 2X_{11} + 3X_{12} + 4X_{21} + 2X_{22} \tag{3.17}$$

That is, choose values for the four decision variables such that total cost, T, is minimized. But, (3.17) is a linear function, and its minimization makes sense *only* if we impose some constraints.[9] These constraints are developed in step 4.

Step 2. *State the relevant assumptions.*

We assume complete certainty, linearity, and a static model. We also assume that: (1) transportation cost per unit of goods shipped between each plant and warehouse is known and remains constant, (2) supply capacities of all the plants and demand requirements of all the warehouses are known, and (3) we are dealing with a homogeneous commodity. These assumptions and their consequences are explained in Chapter 10.

Step 3. *Identify the relevant factors of the decision problem.*

- Because of the assumptions made, unit transportation costs, supply capacities, and demand requirements are fixed and hence can be treated as parameters.
- As explained earlier, the four *decision variables* are X_{11}, X_{12}, X_{21}, and X_{22}.
- The dependent or the *criterion variable* (denote by T) is the amount of total cost incurred as specific values are assigned to the four decision variables.

Step 4. *Develop the decision model.*

- The linear objective function from step 1 is

  Minimize

  $$T = 2X_{11} + 3X_{12} + 4X_{21} + 2X_{22} \tag{3.17}$$

- There are four constraints here: two relating to the plant capacities, and two relating to the warehouse demands.

  For Plant Capacities

  $$\begin{array}{ll} X_{11} + X_{12} = 80 & \text{for plant } O_1 \\ X_{21} + X_{22} = 120 & \text{for plant } O_2 \end{array} \tag{3.18}$$

  For Warehouse Demands

  $$\begin{array}{ll} X_{11} + X_{21} = 75 & \text{for warehouse } D_1 \\ X_{12} + X_{22} = 125 & \text{for warehouse } D_2 \end{array} \tag{3.19}$$

[9] Otherwise, a linear function such as (3.17) can be made negative infinity. And that does not make any sense in the business context.

- Another obvious constraint is that there can be no negative shipments. This means that

$$X_{11}, X_{12}, X_{21}, X_{22} \geqslant 0 \qquad (3.20)$$

Now, if we combine the submodels described in (3.17) to (3.20), we obtain the following mathematical model for the problem shown in Table 3.2:

Minimize

$$T = 2X_{11} + 3X_{12} + 4X_{21} + 2X_{22}$$

subject to the constraints

$$
\left.
\begin{aligned}
X_{11} + X_{12} \quad\quad\quad\quad &= 80 \\
X_{21} + X_{22} &= 120 \\
X_{11} \quad\quad + X_{21} \quad\quad &= 75 \\
X_{12} \quad\quad + X_{22} &= 125
\end{aligned}
\right\} \qquad (3.21)
$$

and

$$X_{11}, \quad X_{12}, \quad X_{21}, \quad X_{22} \geqslant 0$$

Our specific problem has now been stated mathematically.

It should be noted again that, in the usual case, the result of step 4 is in terms of a *general* relationship. This could have been the case if we had specified the transportation problem of Table 3.2 in general terms. However, to project the "image" of a business context, we provided specific numbers in Table 3.2. That is why the decision model (3.21) represents a specific decision problem.

Step 5. *Solve the model.*

As before, the result of this step is a general model or methodology. As we shall illustrate in Chapter 10, a general methodology (*transportation algorithm*) for solving transportation problems has been developed.[10] By applying this general methodology we can solve any specific transportation problem.

Step 6. *Solve the specific problem.*

How to solve transportation problems of the type stated in (3.21) is illustrated in Chapter 10. It can be verified that the optimal solution to our problem is

$$X_{11} = 75 \text{ units} \qquad X_{12} = 5 \text{ units}$$
$$X_{21} = 0 \text{ units} \qquad X_{22} = 120 \text{ units}$$

total transportation cost = $405

Step 7. *Implement the decision and maintain a system of control.*

As before, the intent of this step is to implement the transportation plan of step 6 and to monitor the behavior of various parameters to maintain control.

---

[10] An *algorithm* is a systematic step-by-step procedure to solve a problem.

3.6
Summary

In this chapter, we applied the quantitative approach for building and solving decision models of some typical business problems. Linear breakeven point (BEP) models were derived and then applied to a simple problem. We explained how a product-mix problem can be formulated as a quantitative (linear programming) model. Next, we illustrated the quantitative formulation of the transportation problem. In each case, we illustrated the seven steps of the modeling approach as depicted in Figure 2.8 on p. 41.

The concepts of systems and models are of the utmost importance to managers, and will be discussed in detail in Chapter 4.

References

See the References at the end of Chapter 2.

Review Questions and Problems

3.1. Describe the purpose of breakeven analysis. What are the limitations of breakeven analysis?

3.2. What purpose is served by dimensional analysis of the various terms of an equation? How do we use the concept of dimensional analysis in deriving BEP formulas in dollars and in percent capacity?

3.3. The Phytrum Funnel Firm produces funnels that sell for $1.75 each. It costs the firm (in unit variable cost) $0.75 to produce one funnel. The fixed costs are calculated to be $3,000/month. How many units would have to be produced each year to break even? If the total annual capacity of the plant is 72,000 units, what is the breakeven point in terms of percent capacity? In dollars?

3.4. The Slumber Lumber Company currently operates under the following conditions. A cord of wood sells for $10 and costs $6 to cut; the fixed costs are $30,000/year. The firm has an option to purchase a new piece of equipment from the Texas Chain Saw Corporation. The new equipment would increase fixed costs by $3,000/year but reduce variable costs to $4.50/cord. How would the new equipment affect the breakeven point?

3.5. The EER Wax Company wants to determine the optimal product mix of their general-use wax and heavy-duty wax. They have a limited supply of the chemicals that are used in the manufacture of the two waxes: 200 gallons of chemical A and 360 gallons of chemical B. One unit of general-use wax uses 2 gallons of A and 6 gallons of B and generates a profit of $3. One unit of heavy-duty wax uses 5 gallons of A and 3 gallons of B and gives a profit of $2.

(a) What is the criterion variable? Decision variables? Parameters?
(b) Build the objective function.
(c) State the problem in the form of a mathematical model.

3.6. Shaky Rent-a-Car has opened two new locations in addition to the two previous ones. They want to move 75 cars into the new locations at minimum total cost. The data are summarized in Table 3.3.

Table 3.3

Old Location	New Location		Supply
	C	D	
A	3	4	30
B	2	6	45
Demand	25	50	

(a) What is the criterion variable? Decision variables? Parameters?
(b) Build the objective function.
(c) State the problem in the form of a mathematical model.

3.7. Convert the model shown in Equation (2.6) on p. 47, such that N becomes the decision variable. Then solve for N by applying the condition of optimality that ordering costs equal holding costs.

3.8. An electrical company requires 20,000 units of switches per year to meet production demand. The cost per switch, C, is \$2.50 and the incremental cost of processing one order, S, is \$10/order. Assume that the holding cost, H, is 25 percent of average dollar inventory. Determine the optimum number of orders per year. What is the optimal order quantity?

3.9. A research clinic uses 100,000 test tubes per year at a cost of \$0.02/tube. The incremental cost of processing each order is \$12, and the holding cost is 5 percent of average dollar inventory. What is the optimal order quantity?

Systems and Models

MAJOR CONCEPTS AND TOPICS
DISCUSSED IN THIS CHAPTER

The Concept of a System

Systems analysis and systems design

Basic Considerations for a System

The total system's objectives and their performance measures
The system environment or fixed constraints
Resources of the system
Components and parts of the system, their goals, and measures of performance
Management of the system

The Concept of a Model

The Purpose of Models

Relationship Among Reality, System, and Model

Classification of Models

Physical, graphic, schematic, analog, and mathematical models
Static versus dynamic models
Linear versus nonlinear models
Deterministic versus probabilistic models
Allocation, inventory, queuing, replacement, and competitive models
Analytical versus simulation models

4.1
Introduction

The integrated nature of management thought was discussed in Chapter 1. The underlying concept that makes this integration meaningful is the concept of a *system*. We briefly described the idea of the systems approach in Section 2.4. Systems and models are related concepts, and both of them are extremely fundamental to the study and practice of management. In this chapter, we briefly describe the concept of a system and illustrate systems thinking with a business example. We then discuss models, and describe the purpose and thrust of models. Finally, we present several different classifications of models and briefly discuss some of the models included in these classifications.[1]

4.2
The Concept of a System

Managers make decisions in the real world. Their energies are devoted to influencing and affecting events in such a manner that they can achieve a desired state of affairs such as increased profit margin, better productivity, job satisfaction, and a larger share of the market. In order to gain influence, and control, over the environment, managers must understand "reality" and experiment with reality so that causal relationships can be discovered. One way to understand reality would be to observe it, conduct direct experimentation, and interact with it in real time. However, reality is so rich, complex, and dynamic that direct experimentation on or with reality is often too expensive, or sometimes even impossible because of time, legal, or other constraints. What, then, is the solution to this important problem? The answer lies in the concepts of systems and models that serve as aids to analysis, understanding, and managerial decision making.

In order to "get a handle" on his problems, a manager abstracts certain important parts from reality, makes certain assumptions, and delineates the boundaries of his interest. This, in effect, is the process of defining a system. The relevant system thus is that part of reality which is of major consequence to the decision maker. For example, for the inventory control manager of a business firm, the "system" consists of inventory items, their prices, and their demand rates; behavior of such costs as ordering costs, holding costs, and stockout costs; manufacturing or purchase leadtimes; and the like. The inventory manager is not directly involved with, say, promotion and advertising strategies. Similarly, the "system" that is relevant to the financial vice-president of a large business firm is not like the systems that are of direct interest to the marketing, production, or legal vice-presidents. There are of course many elements that will be common among these "subsystems," because they are all parts of a larger system—the entire business organization. What we want to emphasize is that the boundaries of the system and what is included in the system are determined by the decision

---

[1] The discussion in this chapter is adapted from Levey and Loomba [1973, Chap. 2].

maker. How a system is defined, determined, viewed, analyzed, or designed is a function of the interest and purpose of the manager. What the manager *perceives* to be important will be included in the system, while those elements and relationships that are not relevant to his purpose will be ignored.

The concept of a system presupposes interdependence, relationships, and a purpose. Hence, a system can be defined as a set of interrelated and interdependent parts designed to achieve a set of goals and objectives. This definition of the term implies that almost anything that is the focus of our attention can be viewed as a system. This is because most entities, be they abstract or concrete, consist of two or more parts, and they owe their existence to the fact that they serve a purpose.

Depending upon the purpose of our conceptualization, we can think in terms of business systems, political systems, social systems, health care systems, financial systems, production systems, marketing systems, and so on. Furthermore, the same entity can be viewed in terms of different types of systems. For example, a business firm and its behavior can be analyzed in terms of economic systems, social systems, and so on. Each of these perspectives is useful to the manager. However, in this text, we view, formulate, and solve problems as if they are parts of a system that is purely *economic* in nature.

Systems exist in *hierarchies*, and managers can *create* their own systems and system hierarchies for purposes of planning and control. For example, if we consider a manufacturing firm as a system, then we have a production subsystem, a financial subsystem, a marketing subsystem, and so on. Similarly, we can *create* a special R&D (research and development) system that combines elements from each of the subsystems of the firm. What this implies is that if a system can be divided into a subsystem, then for certain purposes, the subsystem can be viewed as a complete system. Alternatively, depending upon the level from where the problem should be studied, we can always take certain systems and combine them into a *special* system or a larger system. Again, the point to emphasize is that the scope, level, boundaries, components, and the links of a system are determined by several considerations—they are *not* chosen arbitrarily.

Let us summarize two important aspects of the systems concept. First, there is the *systems approach* to the solution of managerial problems, which we described briefly in Section 2.4. The systems approach embodies a philosophy of management; it is a *way of thinking* that is global rather than local, and macro rather than micro. It is a "systemic" view of things. The idea behind this view is that goals of the lower-level subsystems are usually in conflict, and that for the overall benefit of the entire system, resolution of such conflicts can take place only when the problems are analyzed at the highest level possible.

The second aspect relates to the analysis and design of systems. Here, subsequent to the perspective and information obtained from a macro point of view, managers have to engage in some micro types of activities. The essential requirement at the micro level is to view the system as a *means* for accomplishing the goals established by the manager. The purpose is to choose the hardware and the software so as to efficiently run the system on a day-to-day basis. These are the practical, as opposed to the conceptual, aspects of the systems concept, and the related activities are referred to as systems analysis and systems design.

Systems analysis is the process of describing the system and then discovering the relevant relationships among various parts of the system. *Systems design* builds upon the results and information obtained from systems analysis. It is the process of designing the *operating structure* of the system. For example, in the inventory control problem, once the objective of minimizing total cost has been stated, the function of systems analysis is to identify such points of the system as the demand rates, safety stock requirements, service levels, ordering costs, holding costs, and so on. Then the behavior of these costs is specified and their relationships to the overall performance of the system (i.e., total cost) are determined. Part of the purpose of the systems design in the inventory control problem is to specify whether the *fixed-order* or the *fixed-period* system will be used.[2]

Systems design concentrates on the configuration of the system (i.e., *how* the different parts of the system are connected). The purpose of systems design is to consider alternative arrangements, evaluate each in terms of its impact on the system's measure of performance, and then choose the optimal arrangement. For example, different order sizes and reorder points will result in different total costs of an inventory system. The idea of the optimal system design is to weigh the effect of alternative arrangements and then choose that configuration which minimizes total inventory costs. The idea of systems design is particularly important in computer-based management information systems (commonly known as MIS).

It should be obvious from this discussion that a system connotes order as opposed to chaos; implies a logical as opposed to a haphazard attack on problems; and a global rather than a local point of view. The essence of a system is that its parts are *supposed* to work for the overall objective of the whole.

4.3
Basic Considerations for a System

In order to analyze, understand, and manage a system, managers must consider the following five items:[3] (1) the total system's objectives and their performance measures; (2) the system environment or the fixed constraints; (3) the resources of the system; (4) the components or parts of the system, their goals, and measures of performance; and (5) the management of the system. Let us illustrate these considerations with respect to a business firm. Consider, for example, LILCO, a privately owned utility company. One possible analysis of such a system in terms of the five elements described above is as follows.

The Total System's Objectives and Their Performance Measures

Since LILCO is a privately owned utility, one of its primary objectives is to make a profit, or a fair rate of return on investment. The performance measure for this could be the magnitude of return on investment, earnings per share, or the like. If additional objectives were to be named, they would fall under the umbrella of public needs. Included in this category are customer satisfaction with the present

---

[2] We discuss inventory control in Chapters 12 and 13. Briefly, *fixed order* means that order size is fixed, but the time of ordering fluctuates. In the *fixed-period* system, the time of ordering is fixed while the order size is varied.

[3] Churchman [1968, p. 29].

service, and growth to meet future demand. Specific measures of performance for these additional objectives will have to be designated.

It should be noted here that in the business world, managers often break down the overall system into subsystems. They then define the subsystem of interest in such a manner that it has a single objective whose achievement can be measured with a single measure of performance. For example, in the product-mix example of Section 3.4, *the* objective of the subsystem was to maximize profits from the sale of two products. Similarly, in the transportation problem presented in Section 3.5, *the* objective of the subsystem was to minimize total costs of transportation.

The System Environment or the Fixed Constraints

Foremost of the fixed constraints on LILCO are those imposed by law. These include the area to be serviced and rulings of the State Public Service Commission. The Commission has regulatory power over rates charged to customers and must give its approval to transactions involving capitalization (stock and bond issues, etc.). Consumer demand, a constraint faced by all business organizations, is also very much in evidence at LILCO. During the winter months, when the demand is low, the plants are working below their capacity, but operational arrangements have to be worked out to satisfy the high demand during the summer months.

Let us again consider the product-mix example of Section 3.4. The constraints that we assume to be fixed in that example are the cutting and finishing capacities and the state of technology.[4] Similarly, in the transportation problem of Section 3.5, the constraints that we assume to be fixed are the supply capacities of the plants and the demand requirements of the warehouses.

Resources of the System

The resources of LILCO are similar to those available to most business firms: human resources, plant, property, equipment, technology, capital, and management talent. However, LILCO has an additional resource that is unique to many utilities. This resource is the virtual monopoly, created by law, which LILCO enjoys in its designated areas of service.

It should be noted here that the same things can be visualized as either a constraint or a resource. For example, in the product-mix example of Section 3.4, the cutting and finishing capacities can be considered either as constraints within which the manufacturer must run his operations—or they can be considered as resources[5] needed to produce the products. What constitutes a constraint or a resource is determined by the particular perspective with which the problem is formulated and analyzed. Furthermore, the manager may or may not have to make an explicit statement of the resources of the system. For example, in the transportation problem of Section 3.5, company trucks may be needed to transport the goods. Yet, the problem or the "system" was so stated that there was no need to make an explicit statement regarding this resource.

---

[4] By *state of technology* we mean the input-output coefficients. In our example, these coefficients represent the number of cutting and finishing hours required to produce 1 unit of product *A* or product *B*.

[5] Obviously, these resources have a value. In Section 9.3 we illustrate how this value can be determined.

Components and Parts of the System, Their Goals, and Measures of Performance

As LILCO is a large utility, we can identify several components within its system structure. We shall however, list only two: the Research and Development (R&D) Department, and the Finance Department.

The goals of the components of a system and their respective measures of performance are usually set, coordinated, and measured by top management. For example, the management of LILCO can set this goal for its R&D department: Design a nuclear generating facility within, say, a period of one year, and with a budget of $2.5 million. The measure of performance of the R&D department can be in terms of number of new designs, new patents, or as a ratio of completed to assigned projects. Similarly, a goal for the Finance Department could be to obtain capitalization, by some specified date, for the construction of the plant. A measure of performance of the Finance Department can be in terms of percentage completion of its targeted capitalization drive. The activities of the two departments are coordinated by top management.

The rationale for explicitly considering the components of the system, their goals, and their respective measures of performance is to resolve any serious conflicts that might exist among different parts of the system. In many cases, as in our product-mix and transportation problems, the systems are simple and the managers do not have to worry about the separate components of the system. In such cases we can think of the system as being fully integrated so that the goals of its components are in full harmony with the overall objective of the system.

Management of the System

Management of the system is performed by a hierarchy of executives who coordinate the efforts of the different components in order to achieve a set of system goals and objectives. As in every organization, communication and decision making are the key factors at LILCO. Management information systems must be used to keep management in touch with what is being done within each component and in the field. The management, in turn, must communicate goals and decisions to each of the system's components.

In the product-mix and transportation problems, the management of the system is assumed to be the development of "programs" that will maximize profits and minimize costs. All systems, needless to say, must be managed effectively in order to achieve the objectives of the system.

4.4
What Is a Model?

Just as a system represents a specific part of the reality that is of interest to the manager, a model is a *particular* account of a system. We can therefore define the term "model" as follows: A *model* is a particular account of a system which, in turn, represents a specific part of reality, an object of interest, or a subject of inquiry in real life. This relationship is depicted in Figure 4.1.

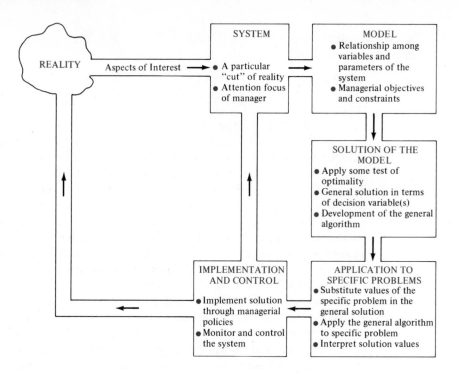

Figure 4.1. Relationship Among Reality, System, and Model.

After a system has been defined or a problem has been conceptualized, it must somehow be represented. The representation is through the device of models that embody our attempt to *abstract the essence* of reality. The means of representation may be physical, graphic, schematic, analog, mathematical, symbolic, or a combination of these.

Forrester describes models as follows:[6]

> Models have become widely accepted as a means for studying complex phenomena. A model is a substitute for some real equipment or system. The value of a model arises from its improving our understanding of obscure behavior characteristics more effectively than could be done by observing the real system. A model, compared to the real system it represents, can yield information at lower cost. Knowledge can be obtained more quickly and for conditions not observable in real life.

Considerable progress has been made in the use of models to solve certain types of *repetitive* business problems. For example, models have been developed to handle not just individual problems, but an entire *class* of problems, such as inventory problems. Allocation, queuing, and competitive problems are additional examples of *classes* of problems whose structure can be mathematically described.[7]

---

[6] Forrester [1961, p. 49].

[7] Inventory models are presented in Chapters 12 and 13. Linear programming, a prime example of an allocation model, is described in Chapter 7. See Section 5.6 and Chapter 11 for a discussion of some competitive models. Chapter 15 covers queuing models.

As mentioned in Chapter 2, the use of models is the heart of the quantitative approach. How to build, analyze, solve, and apply models to obtain optimal strategies for specific problems was illustrated in Chapter 3.

4.5
The Purpose of Models

The ultimate purpose of a model is to give the manager an improved degree of control over his operations and environment. The degree of control is related directly to the accuracy of prediction regarding the future behavior of the system. Hence, it can be stated that the "quality" of a model is measured by its capability to accurately predict the future.

Before a model acquires predictive powers, the analyst must go through the preliminary steps of describing and explaining the system. We can therefore say that models are built to *describe, explain,* and *predict* the behavior of a system. If a model proves to be a reliable predictor of system behavior, it can also be used to *prescribe* preferred courses of action. Thus, depending upon the immediate purpose of the manager, or stage of model development or sophistication, models can be descriptive (describe what *is*), explanatory (explain behavior by establishing relationships between model components), predictive (predict behavior under a variety of assumed conditions), prescriptive or normative (provide guidelines for what ought to be), or consist of a combination of characteristics that are drawn from each of these categories.[8]

When, for example, we study for a stated period of time the behavior of demand for an inventory item and list various demand levels and their respective frequencies, we are in the process of building a *descriptive* model. Here, usually the model *describes* the behavior of demand by a probability distribution.

When, for example, we conduct a correlation analysis that attempts to *explain* variations of a variable such as stock prices by "associating" them, say, with earnings per share or dividends, we are building an *explanatory model*. Similarly, models can be built to explain variations in productivity by virtue of such factors as wages, promotion policy, and education levels.

When, by the aid of data, we can establish a specific relationship between, say, stock prices (within an industry group) and earnings per share, we are building a *predictive* model. Once the model is complete, it gives us the means with which to predict the price of a stock in the specific industry, *given* any level of earnings per share. The analysis with which a predictive model of this type is built is known as *regression analysis.*[9]

When, for example, we use linear programming to solve our product-mix problem given in Section 3.4, the model *prescribes* the optimal solution (the most

---

[8] See, for example, Horowitz [1970, Chap. 1] and Simon [1959].

[9] Regression analysis deals with the estimation, based on actual data, of some mathematical relationship (linear or nonlinear) between the dependent variable and a set of independent variables. See Boot and Cox [1974].

preferred course of action). We discuss linear programming in Chapters 7, 8, and 9. Also, in Chapter 5, we present several prescriptive decision models.

To build models that faithfully represent the real world is not an easy task. The reality is so complex that it is often very difficult to visualize and understand it completely. Furthermore, even when we have a sufficient understanding of reality, our attempt at representing it by models may succeed only partially. First, the state of the art of model building may not measure up to the task (as is the case when we attempt to build models of human behavior). Second, even when a model does succeed in capturing reality in all of its complex aspects, it is usually mathematically intractable. We are therefore forced in many cases to "simplify" reality in order to build useful models of it. This, for example, was the case when we derived the EOQ inventory model of Equation (2.7) on p. 48, based on the assumptions of certainty, linearity, and so on. The assumptions may not necessarily represent the real world. However, they provide a useful point from which to start. Later, unrealistic assumptions can be dropped, perhaps one at a time, so that, slowly but surely, our model moves closer to reality.

Thus, there are necessarily some inherent weaknesses when models are employed to represent reality. But this does not mean that we should reject the approach of building and using models to solve real-life problems. On the contrary, the modeling approach is not only sound but is the best available approach in analyzing and solving complex decision problems. It is much easier, more feasible, less costly, and less time-consuming to obtain relevant information (regarding the behavior of the system under various conditions) from models rather than from experimentation with the reality that the model represents. A model is useful when it is simple to understand, has explanatory and predictive power, and permits us to draw valid inferences regarding the behavior of the system.

The real issue in building a model is its utility in explaining and predicting the behavior of the system that it represents. The model should be able to explain relationships between various components of the system, between each component and the overall system, and the response of the system to changes in its components. After the model has been constructed it should be tested and, if possible, elaborated upon and enriched.[10]

4.6
Classification of Models

We can establish several classifications of models, depending upon the purpose or criterion of classification. We have already discussed a classification *by purpose* that consisted of four categories: descriptive, explanatory, predictive, and prescriptive models. In this section, we present a number of additional classification systems, based on different criteria.

---

[10] The process of alternate testing and elaboration has been described by Morris [1967].

4.6.1 CLASSIFICATION ACCORDING TO DEGREE OF ABSTRACTION

Figure 4.2 shows a second classification of models according to the *degree of abstraction*. Any three-dimensional model that looks like the real thing but is either reduced in size (e.g., toy airplane) or scaled up (e.g., plastic model of the human heart) is a physical (iconic) model. Physical models are easy to observe, build, and describe, but they are difficult to manipulate and not very useful for prediction. Three-dimensional models of plant layouts, housing developments, and city planning proposals are often employed for improving the detail and quality of plans.

An organization chart is a graphic[11] (block-type) model depicting the intended system of organizational authority–responsibility relationships. The flow process chart showing what happens (operation, storage, delay, inspection, etc.) at different stages during the complete processing of a product is a schematic model. Schematic models are extremely useful in giving a visual picture of the system under study ("A picture," as they say, "is worth a thousand words"). The main features of a computer program are often represented by a schematic description of steps that connect the start to the end of the computer program. Any PERT/CPM-type model is a schematic representation of a complete project showing a network of "events" and "activities." We present PERT (program evaluation and review technique) and CPM (critical path method) in Chapter 6.

Analog models represent a system (or object of inquiry) by utilizing a set of properties different from that which the original system possesses. For example, an analog computer is the physical (mechanical or electrical) representation of the variables in a problem. Different colors on a map may represent water, desert, continents, and so on; or they may represent military alliances between nations. Similarly, a map is an analog model showing roads, highways, towns, and their interrelationships. Graphic, schematic, and analog models are easier to manipulate and more general than physical models.

Mathematical or symbolic models represent systems (or reality) by employing mathematical symbols and relationships. Mathematical models are precise, most

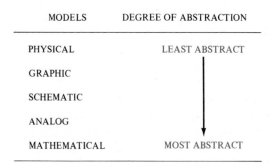

Figure 4.2. Classification According to Degree of Abstraction.

[11] The graphic, schematic, and analog model are of the same species—the difference is one of degree rather than kind.

abstract, general rather than specific, and can be manipulated easily by utilizing the laws of mathematics. The mathematical model for *any* straight line, for example, is $Y = a + bX$, where *a* and *b* are, respectively, the intercept and slope of the line. A specific straight line can be represented by assigning numerical values to the parameters *a* and *b*.

4.6.2 CLASSIFICATION ACCORDING TO BEHAVIOR CHARACTERISTICS

A third classification of models, developed by J. W. Forrester,[12] is shown in Figure 4.3. Forrester's classification, based on specified *behavior characteristics*, is useful in understanding the nature and role of models in representing management and economic behavior of organizations. Of particular interest in this classification are the categories of static versus dynamic models, and linear versus nonlinear models. Essentially, static models do not consider the impact of changes that take place during the planning horizon. That is, they are independent of time. Also, in static models, only one decision is needed for the duration of a given time period. We present a number of static decision models in Chapter 5. It should also be noted here that linear programming is a static decision model.

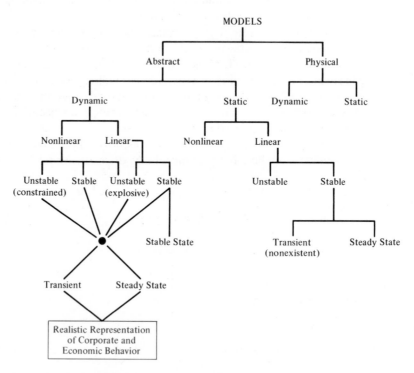

Figure 4.3. Classification According to Behavior Characteristics. (From Forrester [1961, p. 49].)

[12] Forrester [1961, p. 49].

Dynamic models are characterized by the fact that, in a given situation, not one but a series (sequence) of interdependent decisions must be made by the manager. In general, dynamic models consider time as one of the variables and admit the impact of changes generated by time. At the heart of dynamic models is the concept of "stages." A stage (i.e., decision point) can correspond to the variable time (e.g., monthly production schedules) or to well-specified milestones (e.g., decisions on design, test-market, full-scale production, etc., associated with the managerial problem of product development). We shall present a simple dynamic model in Section 5.7.

Linear models are characterized by the fact, or assumption, that each and every component of the model exhibits a linear[13] behavior. The linear programming model is obviously a linear model, as is the submodel that represents ordering costs in the inventory model discussed in Section 2.8. A nonlinear model is characterized by the fact, or assumption, that one or more components of the model exhibit nonlinear behavior. We can, for example, assume that the linear objective function in Equation (3.16), $[Z = 7X + 6Y]$, can become nonlinear $(Z = 7X^2 + 6XY + Y^2)$, even though all the constraints remain linear. In this manner, we shall have formulated a nonlinear programming problem.[14] Similarly, as shown in Figure 3.3 on p. 66, managers are often confronted with nonlinear breakeven problems.

4.6.3 CLASSIFICATION ACCORDING TO DEGREE OF CERTAINTY

Models can also be classified according to the *degree of assumed certainty*. Under this classification we can divide models into deterministic versus probabilistic models.[15] Deterministic models assume conditions of complete certainty and perfect knowledge. This implies that each decision or strategy results in a *unique* and *known* payoff or consequence. It should be noted that linear programming, transportation, and the assignment models are examples of deterministic models. A basic deterministic decision model is presented in Section 5.3.

Probabilistic models handle those situations in which the consequences or payoffs of managerial actions cannot be predicted with certainty. This implies that each decision or strategy can result in more than one payoff. The concept of probability, which we discuss in Appendix A, is employed in solving probabilistic models. A basic probabilistic decision model is presented in Section 5.4. It should be noted that simulation models deal essentially with probabilistic systems, as we shall see in Chapter 14.

4.6.4 CLASSIFICATION ACCORDING TO FORM (STRUCTURE)

As discussed briefly in Section 4.4, we can also classify models according to their *form* (i.e., structure) and *content* (i.e., functional area). The form refers to the *structure* of the problem—the way in which different components of the problem

---

[13] Linearity implies *proportionality* and *additivity*. See Section 7.2.1.

[14] For an elementary treatment of nonlinear programming, see Loomba and Turban [1974].

[15] Another possible classification (based on the criterion of degree of certainty) will be discussed in Chapter 5 under the headings: (1) complete certainty (i.e., deterministic), (2) risk (i.e., probabilistic), and (3) complete uncertainty.

are related to each other. The content refers to the situation which the problem is designed to represent. For example, the linear programming (form) can be applied to solve problems in such diverse areas (content) as production, finance, or marketing. While the manager concerns himself with the content, the form of the problem is the concern of the scientist, who arrives at it by testing the pattern, relevance, and coherence behind the manager's behavior.[16] Once the general form (structure) of an often-repeated (and repeatable) process can be expressed in mathematical terms, we have a model.

As explained earlier, the structure of the model can be derived by the use of inductive approach, deductive approach, or both. But once the model successfully captures the properties of a specific process, it can be applied in different situational contexts. The manager's task is to provide the "content" of his strategy in relation to a chosen "form." For example, inventory models deal with a process in which "something is stored to meet future demand," and this class of problems is fairly general (e.g., inventory problem exists in homes, grocery stores, hospitals, business firms, factories, warehouses, banks). A general inventory model, once it is tested and proved, can be used to solve a whole class of similar problems regardless of the situational context. The manager's job is to examine whether the problem at hand meets the requirement of having similar properties and structure as that of one of the tested models. If so, the general model can be used to solve the problem. If not, a specific model to solve the problem at hand must be built from scratch.

Described below are some models classified according to form.

Allocation models deal with the problem of allocating scarce resources among competing activities. The allocation is made according to a decision criterion, such as maximization of profits or minimization of costs. The general linear programming model and the special structure transportation model and the assignment model (Chapter 10) are examples of allocation models.

Inventory models deal with that class of problems when "something is stored to meet a future need." Typically, an inventory model is built by stating total inventory cost in terms of various cost categories, such as ordering costs, holding costs, and then solving for an optimum *order quantity*, or optimum *number of orders*, according to a decision criterion—such as minimization of total costs. We present a selected set of inventory models in Chapters 12 and 13.

Queuing models are designed to solve a class of problems in which a set of customers arrive for service at a set of service facilities. In such situations, because of probabilistic arrival patterns of customers, three things can happen. First, there is a *perfect match* between the requirements of the customers and the capacities of the service facilities. In such a case, we do not have a problem. Second, the demand for services exceeds the supply of services, and therefore the customers have to "wait" for service. Third, the supply of services exceeds the demand for services, and hence the service facilities have to "wait" or remain idle. Obviously, specific costs are associated with the waiting of customers and the idle service facilities. Further, these two categories of costs move in opposite directions. For example, by adding more facilities we decrease the cost of customer waiting but increase the cost of idle facilities. The purpose of queuing models is to help design a system that will minimize a stated measure of performance, such as the sum of

---

[16] Beer [1966, p. 73].

the costs of customer waiting and idle facilities. We discuss some elementary queuing models in Chapter 15.

Replacement models serve to solve a class of problems in which equipment or parts must be replaced because of deterioration or complete failure. Customarily, replacement problems are considered in two categories. The first deals with equipment that deteriorates with time. For example, equipment may lose efficiency as a result of either use or the appearance of better equipment on the market. Lathes, drilling machines, planers, and electronic devices are representative of the type of equipment that deteriorates as a result of use or obsolescence. The second category deals with items that have a more or less constant efficiency with time. When they fail, they do so suddenly and completely. A typical example of a problem in the second category is the decision regarding a replacement policy for light bulbs.

Methods of analysis for formulating replacement policies with regard to these two categories are dissimilar because of the different nature and cost behavior of the equipment involved in each category. For equipment that deteriorates with time, for example, the analyst must consider, among other costs, the operating and maintenance costs that increase with time. It is necessary, when considering problems in this category, to decide upon an optimum interval of time after which the present equipment should be replaced with another candidate.

The category dealing with items that fail suddenly and completely calls for an analysis in which some sort of mortality distribution is predicted for the items in question. Based on this distribution, the replacement policy has the objective of minimizing costs by determining a certain interval after which all items are replaced (within this interval individual items that fail are replaced immediately). Although this category of problems deals with decreasing, constant, and increasing probabilities of failure with time, a commonly used illustration is that of group replacement of light bulbs having an increasing probability of failure. In particular, the problem is to determine some interval of time such that the combined cost of replacing individual items within this interval and replacing all items at the end of the interval is minimized. We present a simple replacement problem in Appendix A (Section A.8).

Competitive models help analyze those situations in which two or more *rational* opponents are involved in choosing strategies in order to optimize a measure of effectiveness. In the management literature, these models are included in the category of *game theory*. We present a very elementary model in Section 5.6, and then discuss some aspects of game theory in Chapter 11.

4.6.5 CLASSIFICATION ACCORDING TO PROCEDURE OF SOLUTION

In general, solutions to mathematical models can be derived by using two types of procedures: (1) analytical and (2) simulation. In the analytical procedure, two categories can be identified. In the first category, we have a *general solution* in an abstract form (i.e., the solution is specified by symbols), and it can be used *directly* to solve a specific problem (i.e., we can obtain the optimal strategy in a noniterative manner). This, for example, is the case in the inventory model presented in Section 2.8.

In the second category, we have a *general methodology*[17] that is applied (inductively) to solve a specific problem. This category of the analytical procedure is *iterative* (numerical) in nature. In the iterative case, the specific problem is *not* solved directly. Instead, the general methodology (algorithm) is applied to produce a specific numerical solution, and then, on successive trials (iterations), "better" solutions are produced until the optimal solution is identified. This, for example, is the case when we apply the simplex method to solve a linear programming problem (Chapter 8).

In the simulation procedure, the solution is *not* derived deductively. Instead, the model is *experimented* upon by inserting into the model specific values of controllable variables, under assumed conditions, and then observing their effect on the criterion variable. For example, we can *test* the effect of different numbers of checkout counters (controllable variable), under assumed conditions of customer arrivals, on total cost of operation (criterion variable) of a grocery store. As we shall explain in Chapter 14, simulation procedures use the concept of random sampling. They describe "what is happening" to the system, for a selected period of time, under a variety of assumed conditions.

Thus, depending upon the procedure of solution employed, we can classify models into the categories of analytical and simulation models.

Analytical models have a specified mathematical structure and they can be "solved" by known analytical or mathematical techniques. For example, the inventory control model illustrated in Section 2.8 is an analytical model. The nonlinear profit-maximization model depicted in Figure 3.3 is also an analytical model. Various decision models presented in Chapter 5 are additional examples of analytical models. Briefly, any optimization model (that calls for maximizing or minimizing a criterion variable) is an analytical model.

In general, two difficulties arise in the formulation and solution of analytical models. First, the "reality" in certain cases may be so complex that we cannot build adequate analytical models. Second, even if we succeed in building a reasonably adequate model of certain complex problems, we might not be able to "solve" these models—either because it may be beyond the current state of the art

Table 4.1 *Classification of Models*

Criterion of Classification	Categories of Models
• Purpose	• Descriptive, explanatory, predictive, prescriptive
• Degree of abstraction	• Physical, graphic, schematic, analog, mathematical
• Specified behavior characteristics	• Static, dynamic
	• Linear, nonlinear
• Degree of certainty	• Deterministic, probabilistic
	• Certainty, risk, uncertainty
• Form or structure	• Allocation, inventory, queuing, replacement, competitive
• Procedure or method of solution	• Analytical, simulation

[17] Also called an *algorithm* (a systematic step-by-step procedure to solve a problem).

or perhaps it might be too costly. In such cases the alternative is to analyze and solve the problem by means of simulation.

A simulation model is experimentation (computer-assisted or manual) on a mathematical structure of a real-life system in order to describe and evaluate the system behavior through real time under a variety of assumptions. A simulation model also consists of a mathematical structure, but it is *not* solved mathematically to yield a general solution. Instead, it is experimented upon to yield a series of outputs. We shall discuss simulation models in Chapter 14.

Table 4.1 summarizes our discussion on classification of models.

4.7
Summary

In this chapter, we discussed the concepts of systems and models. A system was viewed as a specific part of reality—that part which is of interest to the manager. A system was defined as a set of interrelated and interdependent parts, designed to achieve a set of goals and objectives. We then described two important aspects of the systems concept: (1) the systems approach, and (2) the analysis and design of systems. This discussion was followed by a list of five basic considerations that must be examined with respect to *any* system. These basic considerations were illustrated with the aid of an actual example in which a utility company was considered as a system.

A model was defined as a *particular* account of a system. This was followed by a discussion regarding the ultimate purpose of models—an improved degree of control over the environment. This is accomplished by models that are descriptive, explanatory, predictive, or prescriptive. The meaning and focus of these models were briefly described.

Finally, we gave six different classifications of models, based on these criteria: (1) purpose, (2) degree of abstraction, (3) specified behavior characteristics, (4) degree of certainty, (5) form (structure), and (6) procedure of solution. A brief discussion of each type of model was presented to build a proper background for the rest of the book.

The first four chapters have been devoted to the achievement of these main goals: (1) to discuss the nature and importance of management; (2) to explain the quantitative approach and its four pillars: the systems approach, interdisciplinary teamwork, the scientific method, and the use of models; (3) to establish interrelationships among reality, systems, and models; and (4) to describe the purpose of models and become familiar with different types of models. We are now ready to examine the applications of some of these models to decision problems faced by individuals and organizations. We turn our attention to this task in Chapter 5.

References

Ackoff, R. L. "Towards a System of Systems Concepts." *Management Science*, Vol. 17, No. 11 (July 1971), 661–671.

Beer, S. *Decision and Control.* New York: John Wiley & Sons, Inc., 1966.

Boot, J. G. C., and E. B. Cox. *Statistical Analysis for Managerial Decisions*, 2nd ed. New York: McGraw-Hill Book Company, 1974.

Churchman, C. W. *The Systems Approach*. New York: Delacorte Press, 1968.

Davis, G. B. *Management Information Systems*. New York: McGraw-Hill Book Company, 1974.

Eilon, S. "Mathematical Modeling for Management." *Interfaces*, Vol. 4, No. 2 (Feb. 1974), 32–38.

Forrester, J. W. *Industrial Dynamics*. Cambridge, Mass.: The MIT Press, and New York: John Wiley & Sons, Inc., 1961.

Hayes, R. H., and R. L. Nolan. "What Kind of Corporate Modeling Functions Best." *Harvard Business Review*, Vol. 52, No. 3 (May–June 1974), 102–112.

Horowitz, I. *Decision Making: The Theory of the Firm*. New York: Holt, Rinehart and Winston, 1970.

Johnson, R. A., F. E. Kast, and J. E. Rosenzweig. *The Theory and Management of Systems*, 3rd ed. New York: McGraw-Hill Book Company, 1973.

Levey, S., and N. P. Loomba. *Health Care Administration*. Philadelphia: J. B. Lippincott Company, 1973.

Lilier, G. L. "Model Relativism: A Situational Approach to Model Building." *Interfaces*, Vol. 5, No. 3 (May 1975), 11–18.

Loomba, N. P., and E. Turban. *Applied Programming for Management*. New York: Holt, Rinehart and Winston, 1974.

Mantell, L. H. "The Systems Approach and Good Management." *Business Horizons*, Vol. 15, No. 5 (Oct. 1972), 43–51.

Morris, W. T. "On the Art of Modeling." *Management Science*, Vol. 13 (Aug. 1967), 707–717.

Simon, H. A. "Theories of Decision Making in Economics and Behavioral Science." *American Economic Review* (June 1959), 253–281.

Urban, G. L. "Building Models for Decision Makers." *Interfaces*, Vol. 4, No. 3 (May 1974), 1–11.

Von Bertalanffy, L. *General Systems Theory*. New York: George Braziller, Inc., 1969.

Review Questions and Problems

4.1. Define and relate the terms "reality," "system," and "model."

4.2. List the differences between systems analysis and systems design. Give an example of each.

4.3. What are the five basic considerations of a system? Select a system of interest (from your work, home, or college) and establish these considerations.

4.4. Explain the nature and purpose of models.

4.5. What is the purpose of a mathematical model? How does a model achieve this purpose? Consider in your answer the concept that a model is an abstraction of reality.

4.6. Distinguish between descriptive and prescriptive models. State whether the following models are descriptive or prescriptive: linear programming, balance sheet, tax return, annual budget, and opinion poll.

4.7. List five different criteria of classification of models. Classify a set of models within each criterion.

4.8. Describe the main characteristics of the selected categories of models shown in Table 4.1.

4.9. What is the difference between static and dynamic models? Give an example of each.

4.10. What are the main differences between analytical models and simulation models? Under what conditions might one be preferable to the other for predictive purposes?

4.11. What types of systems can best be studied through the use of simulation models?

PART II

Decision Theory

Decision Theory— Basic Concepts and Applications

5.1
Introduction

As described in Chapter 4, if we classify decision models according to the *degree of certainty*, we identify two types of models: deterministic models (the manager *assumes* complete certainty and each strategy results in a *unique* payoff) and probabilistic models (each strategy leads to more than one payoff and the manager attaches a probability measure to these payoffs). Theoretically, the scale of assumed certainty can range from complete certainty to complete uncertainty. Hence, we can think of *decision making under certainty* (DMUC) and *decision making under uncertainty* (DMUU) as the two extreme points on a scale. The region that falls between these extreme points corresponds to the concept of probabilistic models, and we refer to it as *decision making under risk* (DMUR) Figure 5.1 illustrates this classification of decision models.

We want to emphasize two things at this time. First, as implied in Figure 5.1, most of the decision problems fall in the category of decision making under risk. Second, the assumed degree of certainty is only one aspect of a decision problem. Other specifications, such as linear or nonlinear behavior, static or dynamic conditions, single or multiple objectives, must also be made before designing a model to solve the problem.

Decision theory deals with decision making under conditions of risk and uncertainty. For our purposes, we shall consider all types of decision models, including deterministic models, to be under the domain of decision theory.

Several quantitative decision models that help managers identify optimal or best courses of action have been developed and are available in the management

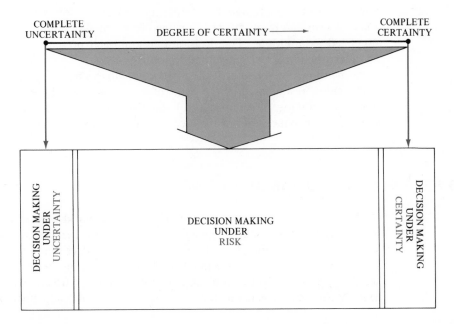

Figure 5.1. Decision Classification Based upon Degree of Certainty.

literature. Before we present a selected set of these decision models, we want to expose the reader to some of the basic concepts of decision making. Accordingly, we first discuss these issues: What is a decision? Why must decisions be made? What is involved in the process of decision making? What are some of the ways of classifying decisions? Answers to these questions will provide us with the background against which the potential as well as limitations of the decision models discussed in this chapter can be better appreciated. Then, we discuss and illustrate a selected set of decision models. In all the models we shall assume a finite set of strategies, and each decision problem will be formulated as a payoff matrix. Also, we shall illustrate each model with respect to a business problem.

5.2
Some Aspects of Decisions and Decision Making[1]

5.2.1 WHAT IS A DECISION?

A *decision* is the conclusion of a process designed to weigh the relative utilities of a set of available alternatives so that the most preferred course of action can be selected for implementation. *Decision making* involves all the thinking and activities that are required to identify the most preferred choice. In particular, the making of a decision requires a set of goals and objectives, a system of priorities, an enumeration of alternative courses of feasible and viable actions, the projection of consequences associated with different alternatives, and a system of choice criteria by which the most preferred course is identified. Although it is possible to analyze the making of a specific decision as an isolated phenomenon, decisions are essentially *sequential* in nature. The sequential nature of decisions is obvious from the fact that in the interdependent world of today each decision has consequences and implications far beyond its original boundaries drawn under simplified assumptions. The decision-tree approach presented in Section 5.7 considers the impact of sequential decisions.

As mentioned in Chapter 1, the essence of management is to make decisions that commit resources in the pursuit of organizational objectives. Planning, organizing, staffing, direction, control, leadership, communication, and all other functions of management are executed through the making and implementation of decisions.

5.2.2 WHY MUST DECISIONS BE MADE?

Decisions must be made because we are living in a world whose resources are scarce, and because all human beings are motivated by a set of wants and needs. These needs can be biological, physical, financial, social, ego, or higher-level self-actualization needs. Each individual, in playing the various roles that he or she accepts in life, is motivated to act and make decisions to satisfy a set of wants and needs. We can say, in general, that people would act in such a manner as to create

---

[1] This section is adapted from Levey and Loomba [1973, Chap. 4].

a "state of affairs" most conducive to satisfy their aspirations. These aspirations can be stated in terms of objectives and time-oriented goals. Decisions are made to achieve these goals and objectives.

5.2.3 DECISIONS AND CONFLICT

One very obvious problem in decision making is to recognize the inherent conflict that exists among various goals relevant to any decision situation. For example, at the *individual* level, there is always the conflict between the desire to make more money and to have more leisure time. Similarly, in the organizational context, there is always present the conflict of interest among various departments, divisions, and managers. The traditional conflict of interest among marketing, production, and financial departments can be described in terms of diversity of product lines, standardization, and requirements of working capital. For example, the marketing people would like to offer to their customers as much variety and range of products as is required to capture the largest share of the market. This, however, would mean smaller production runs, frequent change-overs, and difficult production scheduling. Also, the level of the capital tied up in inventories will have to be increased, a requirement that might not be within the reach of the finance division. The implicit conflicts among the three divisions of the firm are obvious. The job of the top management is to make decisions in such a manner as to resolve such conflicts while pursuing overall goals such as return on investment, market share, and so on.

5.2.4 TWO PHASES OF THE PROCESS OF DECISION MAKING

Decision theory, the body of knowledge that deals with the analysis and making of decisions, is an important area of study. This is evident from the significant contributions of such diverse disciplines as philosophy, economics, psychology, sociology, statistics, political science, and operations research to the area of decision theory. Regardless of the perspective, the process of decision making consists of two phases. One relates to the preliminary questions of how to formulate goals and objectives, enumerate environmental constraints, identify alternative strategies, and project relevant payoffs. The second concentrates on the question of how to choose the optimal strategy when we are given a set of objectives, strategies, and payoffs. Our emphasis in this chapter is on the second phase, namely, how to choose the optimal strategy under a specified set of assumptions, including all available strategies and their associated payoffs.

5.2.5 CLASSIFICATIONS OF DECISIONS

Decisions can be classified in a number of ways, depending upon the criterion or purpose of classification. For example, decisions can be *strategic* (relating to a firm's outside environment, such as product-market mix), *administrative* (dealing with the acquisition and structuring of resources, such as organization design), or *operational* (dealing with repetitive, day-to-day problems such as inventory control).

Depending upon the nature of the problems, decisions can be classified as programmed or nonprogrammed decisions.[2] Programmed decisions are those that are meant to solve repetitive and well-structured problems. For example, decisions on inventory control, production scheduling, and product-mix design, are programmed decisions. Decisions are programmed to the extent that they are routine, repetitive, have a definite structure, and can be handled with well-defined procedures. Such decisions, once the organization has developed specific processes for handling them, can be processed by computers. Hence, once the system is in a steady state, programmed decisions do not demand a large proportion of the manager's time. The significance of this statement lies in the corollary that, to the extent possible, managers must find ways to bring as many organizational decisions as possible under the umbrella of the "programmed" category. In this manner, they can devote their energies to performing more creative activities.

Nonprogrammed decisions are those that handle nonroutine, novel, ill-structured, and policy-type problems. Decisions on mergers and acquisitions, product-market mix, plant location, and so on, are typical examples of nonprogrammed decisions. In general, decisions are nonprogrammed to the extent that they are novel and unstructured and the organization has not developed well-established procedures for handling them.

Depending upon the scope, complexity, and the number of people affected, decisions can be *individual* or *managerial*. In the modern world of specialization and interdependence, most of the decisions have managerial characteristics and consequences.

Decisions can also be classified in terms of the *sphere of interest*. For example, we can think in terms of economic, political, or social decisions. This classification points up a very important aspect of decisions: Decisions usually involve multiple, rather than single, dimensions along which time-oriented goals are established.

Finally, decision problems can be *static* (requiring *one* decision for the entire planning horizon) or *dynamic* (requiring a series of decisions that are sequential in nature and that affect each other).

As established in Chapter 4, decision models can be descriptive or prescriptive. The focus of *descriptive decision models* is to study how people *actually* make decisions, not how they *ought* to make decisions. The purpose of descriptive models is to discover the factors that lead to success, and bring the findings to the attention of the practicing manager. The focus of *prescriptive* (or *normative*) *decision models* is on how decisions *should* be made. The normative models prescribe for the manager the most preferred courses of action. The normative models (or prescriptive models) are so constructed that the decision criterion is part and parcel of the total model [e.g., the linear programming model shown in Equation (3.16) on p. 70 includes the decision criterion of maximizing profits]. All normative models are based on the assumption of rationality, which requires: (1) the ability to state objectives clearly and to rank them in some order of preference according to a set of decision criteria, and (2) the employment of proper means to optimize the achievement of objectives. Rationality also demands that when the time comes to choose a course of action, the manager makes the choice according to the *agreed upon* criterion or criteria.

---

[2] Simon [1960, p. 5].

While the normative decision models assume complete rationality and think of the manager as an economic man endowed with infinite wisdom, the descriptive decision models view the manager as an administrative man with limited knowledge and ability. The administrative man theory is based on the assumption that in real life, managers do not really optimize and they do not possess infinite rationality. Instead, the actual behavior of managers can be described more in terms of "satisficing" and "bounded rationality".[3]

It should now be observed that most of the decision models presented in this book are normative and they deal with administrative and operational, programmed, single-dimensional, and static decisions. In addition, we often assume linear behavior. Hence, before developing or using a decision model, it is extremely necessary that we establish and understand basic facts or assumptions on these various aspects of the decision problem.

5.3
Decision Making Under Certainty (Deterministic Outcomes)

Decision making under certainty (DMUC) implies that all the relevant information required to make the decision is known with complete certainty. DMUC is a deterministic model that assumes complete knowledge, stability, and nonambiguity. With reference to the decision matrix, we assume that the manager can enumerate all possible strategies, knows fully the requirements to carry them out, and can project, for each strategy, *exactly one* payoff. That is, each strategy results in a *unique* payoff. This means that DMUC assumes the existence of only one state of nature.

We present two models representing DMUC, one with a single objective and the other with multiple objectives. In the case where we assume a single objective,

Table 5.1

Strategy	State of Nature N
	Utility or Payoff
S_1	u_1
S_2	u_2
S_3	u_3
.	.
.	.
.	.
S_n	u_n

---

[3] Simon [1957, p. 198]. "Satisficing" implies that in real life most managers accept "good enough" (as opposed to "best") solutions. The idea of "bounded rationality" is that human beings have limits to rationality. We also discussed the idea of satisficing (as opposed to optimizing) in the last paragraph of Section 2.6.

we can measure the attainment of the objective with a single measure of performance, such as profit or cost. The theoretical model in this case can be represented by a unicolumn payoff matrix, as shown in Table 5.1.

Shown in Table 5.1 are various possible strategies and their respective utilities u_1, $u_2, \ldots, u_n$. We emphasize again that in DMUC there is only one state of nature, N, and a single measure of performance. In the single objective case, the task is to compare all strategies, in terms of their payoffs or utilities, and then choose the strategy that yields the highest payoff or utility. Such a strategy is called the *optimal strategy*.

Example 5.1: DMUC with a Single Objective

Hermes, Inc., will launch one of its heaviest campaigns to promote a special product. The promotion budget is not yet finalized, but they know that some $5,000,000 will be available for advertising and promotion.

Management wants to determine how much they should spend for television spots, which is the most appropriate medium for their product. They have created five "TV campaign strategies" with their projected outcomes in terms of increase in sales. The decision criterion to be used in identifying the optimal strategy is that of maximum utility. That is, the strategy that yields the maximum utility is the optimal strategy. Utility, for the purposes of this problem, was defined as the ratio of outcome (i.e., increase in sales) to cost. Shown in Table 5.2 are the strategies and their respective payoffs.

Clearly, the optimal strategy in this case is S_3, as it yields the maximum utility.

Table 5.2

Strategy	Cost (millions of dollars)	Increase in Sales (millions of dollars)	Utility or Payoff	
S_1	1.80	1.78	0.988	
S_2	2.00	2.02	1.010	
S_3	2.25	2.42	1.075	← Maximum utility
S_4	2.75	2.68	0.974	
S_5	3.20	3.24	1.012	

Example 5.2: DMUC with Multiple Objectives[4]

Let us consider the case of Atlas Products, Inc., a manufacturing company that is developing its annual plans in terms of three objectives: (1) increased profits, (2) increased market share, and (3) increased sales. Note that the *profit* objective could be stated in, and measured by, absolute dollar volume, or percentage increase, or return on investment (ROI). The *market share* is to be measured in terms of percentage of the total market, while *sales growth* could be measured either in dollars or in percentage terms.

---

[4] This example can be omitted without loss of continuity.

Let us assume that Atlas management has formulated three different strategies for achieving the stated objectives. Now, in order to formulate the payoff matrix for this problem, we need two things. First, we must assign *relative weights* to each of the three objectives. Second, for each strategy we will have to project a "score" in each of the three dimensions (one dimension for each objective) and express these scores in terms of utilities. The relative weights of the three objectives, and the projected utilities of each strategy (with respect to each objective), are shown in Table 5.3. The optimal strategy is the one that yields the maximum weighted or composite utility.

The *weighted* or *composite utility* for a given strategy is calculated by multiplying the utilities under each objective by their respective weights and then summing the products. For strategy S_1, for example, we derive the composite utility, CU, as follows:

$$7(0.2) + 4(0.5) + 9(0.3) = 6.1$$

The composite utility for the other two strategies can be calculated similarly.

As shown in Table 5.3, S_3 is the optimal strategy, as it yields the maximum composite utility.

Table 5.3

Measures of Performance (of Three Objectives)	ROI (Profit)	% increase (Market Share)	% increase (Sales Growth)	Weighted or Composite Utility
Weights	0.2	0.5	0.3	(CU)
Strategy S_1	7	4	9	6.1
S_2	3	6	7	5.7
S_3	5	5	10	6.5 ← Maximum utility

In addition to the procedure illustrated above, here are some additional ways of handling multiple objective decisions. First, multidimensional objectives (with various measures of performance) can be assigned different weights so that the problem can be solved by dimensional analysis.[5] The multidimensionality can also be handled by: (1) arriving at a single measure of performance (e.g., utility) by means of somehow transforming[6] multidimensional objectives to a single measure of performance; and (2) optimizing with respect to one objective and satisficing with respect to the others (this is accomplished by structuring the problem into a programming format in which the most important objective is optimized subject to constraints that contain "acceptable" values of the other objectives).[7]

[5] Starr [1971, pp. 278–284].

[6] This can be done mathematically or by constructing tradeoff functions. Tradeoff functions may be either objective or subjective in nature. See Ackoff and Sasieni [1968, p. 35, 46–49]. The "indifference curve" of the economist is also an example of the tradeoff function.

[7] For a discussion of the concept of satisficing (as opposed to optimizing), see Simon [1957, pp. 204–205].

5.4
Decision Making Under Risk
(Probabilistic Outcomes)

Decision making under risk (DMUR) describes a situation in which each strategy results in more than one outcome or payoff—and the manager attaches a probability measure to these payoffs. That is, this model covers the case when the manager projects two or more outcomes for each strategy *and* he or she knows, or is willing to assume, the relevant probability distributions of the outcomes. In particular, we assume the following: (1) the availability of more than one strategy, (2) the existence of more than one state of nature, (3) the relevant outcomes, and (4) a probability distribution of the outcomes associated with *each* strategy.

The optimal strategy in DMUR is identified by the strategy that has the *highest expected utility*. In other words, we apply the expected-value criterion[8] in DMUR models. If the model has a profit-type objective, the optimal strategy is the one with the highest expected value. If, on the other hand, it is a cost-type objective, the optimal strategy is the one with the lowest expected value.

Example 5.3

Assume that you are invited to play this game. A coin will be tossed and you will receive $4 each time a head appears; however, you will pay $5 each time a tail appears. Will you agree to play the game?

The answer is intuitively no. Let us, however, apply the expected value criterion before a decision is made. Here, the two *monetary* outcomes are $+4$ and -5, and their probabilities are $\frac{1}{2}$ and $\frac{1}{2}$. Hence,

$$\text{expected monetary value (EMV)} = u_1 p_1 + u_2 p_2$$
$$= (+4)\tfrac{1}{2} + (-5)\tfrac{1}{2} = -0.50$$

That is, on the average, you can expect to lose $0.50 per game played. Hence, *if* you apply the expected value criterion, you will not agree to play this game. Note that the expected loss of $0.50 cannot itself occur in *any one* play of the game. Expected value is thus a long-range prediction of average loss (or gain).

Several comments regarding decision making under risk are in order at this time.
• Decision problems with finite strategies require the comparison of expected values of different strategies. Hence, in DMUR, we must build *conditional payoff* tables, as illustrated in Examples 5.4 and 5.5.

---

[8] In decision making under risk we deal with probabilistic situations that are described by random variables (i.e., the outcome of the strategy is a variable, not a fixed quantity). We assume that it is possible to attach a measure of probability to *each* value assumed by the random variable. Then the concept of expected value determines what happens (or what we can expect) *on the average*. It is calculated as:

$$\text{expected value} = u_1 p_1 + u_2 p_2 + u_3 p_3 + \cdots + u_n p_n$$

where u's represent the monetary or utility values of various *discrete* outcomes, and p's represent their respective probabilities. Note that an expected value is nothing more than the *weighted average* of payoffs. For further discussion, see Appendix A.

- Note that we assume a *repetitive* experiment. This may or may not be a valid assumption in some business problems.
- The decision in the above example was made purely on monetary grounds. Now, suppose that you are an extremely rich person and the playing of this game provides you with the opportunity of spending an evening with a very attractive person (and you have other than monetary outcomes in mind). Then the *utility* of each monetary outcome of this game (i.e., $+4$ or -5) is positive. Consequently, the expected utility is positive and, under this criterion, your decision will be to play the game. The idea is that, in the final analysis, it is the utility, rather than the monetary value, that is weighed by the decision maker.
- The *expected value criterion* does not take into account the "quality of risk" (i.e., the *range* or *standard deviation* of the outcomes is not considered—see Section 14.8 and Appendix A).
- How do managers adjust or make allowances for risk while making decisions? The answer is that each manager utilizes, consciously or unconsciously, a trade-off function between risk and return. In general, the higher the perceived risk, the higher is the required return.
- The adjustment for risk in real life can be made by following several approaches. We mention two here: (1) adjustment is made by multiplying the projected payoff by a "certainty equivalent[9] adjustment factor," and (2) adjustment is made by increasing the required rate of return to include a "risk premium."

Example 5.4 Think of the marketing manager of an insurance company who has kept complete records of the sales effort of the sales personnel. These records contain data regarding the number of insurance policies sold and net revenues received by the company as a function of four different sales strategies. The manager has constructed the conditional payoff matrix given in Table 5.4, based on his records. Note that the states of nature refer to the number of policies sold. The numbers within the table represent utilities.

Table 5.4

State of Nature	N_1	N_2	N_3	Expected Utility or
Probability	0.2	0.5	0.3	Payoff (EU)

Strategy	Utility or Payoff			
S_1 (1 call, 0 follow-up)	4	6	10	6.8
S_2 (1 call, 1 follow-up)	6	5	9	6.4
S_3 (1 call, 2 follow-up)	2	10	8	7.8 ← Maximum utility
S_4 (1 call, 3 follow-up)	10	3	7	5.6

[9] Here is the idea of certainty equivalent. Suppose that you have a choice between receiving a deterministic payoff of $1,000 and a gambling experiment (i.e., probabilistic payoff) in which you can win either $10,000 with a probability of 0.50 or lose $2,000 with a probability of 0.50 (i.e., expected value = $4,000). Now let us assume that your utility function is such that you are indifferent between the two alternatives. Then, in this situation, $1,000 is the "certainty equivalent" of an expected return of $4,000; and the certainty equivalent adjustment factor is $\frac{1,000}{4,000} = 0.25$.

Now, suppose that you are a new salesperson and that you have access to the original records as well as the payoff matrix. Which strategy would you follow?

Since this is a decision problem involving risk, we apply the expected-value criterion. Further, since the payoffs are stated in terms of utility, we calculate, for each strategy, its expected utility, EU. For strategy S_3,

$$EU = 2(0.2) + 10(0.5) + 8(0.3)$$
$$= 7.8$$

Expected utilities for other strategies are calculated in a similar fashion.

As shown in Table 5.4, strategy S_3 (1 call, 2 follow-up) yields the maximum EU and hence is the optimal strategy. Perhaps more than a certain number of follow-ups irritate the potential clients and hence are counterproductive.

Example 5.5 | A company is planning for its sales targets and the strategies to achieve these targets. The data in terms of three sales targets, their respective utilities, various strategies (e.g., different combinations of price, advertising, sales force, new store outlets), and appropriate probability distributions are given in Table 5.5. What is the optimal strategy?

The expected monetary value of each strategy is calculated, as before, by multiplying different monetary outcomes by their respective probabilities and summing the products. For strategy S_2, we have

$$EMV \text{ (for } S_2) = 50(0.2) + 75(0.5) + 100(0.3)$$
$$= 77.5$$

The expected utility for S_2 is calculated as follows:

$$EU \text{ (for } S_2) = 4(0.2) + 7(0.5) + 9(0.3)$$
$$= 7.0$$

The EMV (expected monetary value) and EU (expected utility) for strategies S_1 and S_3 are calculated in a similar fashion and are shown in Table 5.5.

Clearly, as shown in Table 5.5, the optimal strategy (both in terms of EMV and EU) is S_2.

Table 5.5

Sales Target (in millions of dollars)	50	75	100	Expected Monetary Value (EMV)	Expected Utility (EU)
Utility	4	7	9		
	Probabilities				
Strategy S_1	0.6	0.3	0.1	62.5	5.4
Strategy S_2	0.2	0.5	0.3	77.5	7.0 ← Optimal
Strategy S_3	0.5	0.3	0.2	67.5	5.9

It should be noted that Table 5.5 represents an alternative formulation (as compared to Table 5.4) of a DMUR problem with a single objective.[10] In Table 5.4, utilities are entered within the body of the conditional payoff matrix, and a *single* probability distribution is associated with specified states of nature. In Table 5.5, sales targets are selected and, for *each* strategy, a probability distribution is specified in terms of achieving the sales targets. These probabilities are entered *within the body* of the conditional payoff matrix.

Each strategy, designed to generate sales, also results in costs to the company. For example, strategy S_1 might involve certain advertising, promotional, and other related expenditures. The utility measures reflect the differences between appropriate sales revenues and the costs associated with the strategies mounted to obtain these sales. These utilities are shown under appropriate sales targets. In practice, the approach of Table 5.5 is often a more realistic representation of the way managers think.

Two things should be noted in connection with the application of the expected-value criterion in DMUR. First, the optimal strategy is chosen strictly on the basis of a *weighted* outcome, and no account is being taken of the "quality" of risk. That is, the *range* of the outcomes is not being considered.[11] Second, the probability distributions are assumed to stay constant and hence they reflect a *stable* system. This may or may not be the case in actual practice.

5.4.1 CALCULATION OF INDIFFERENCE PROBABILITIES AND THE VALUE OF PERFECT INFORMATION

As we have seen in Examples 5.4 and 5.5, the DMUR problem requires the construction of a conditional payoff matrix. This means that the manager has to enumerate strategies, list possible states of nature (i.e., future conditions), attach the probability measure to each state of nature, and estimate various payoffs. Then he can identify his optimal strategy by using the criterion of expected value. Now, we ask two questions: First, how much error can he make in his probability estimates without having to change his optimal strategy? The answer to this question is provided by the concept of "indifference" probabilities. Second, since probabilities, in a sense, represent the manager's degree of belief regarding the occurrence of a specified state of nature, what price is he willing to pay for additional information? The answer to this question is provided by the concept of "value of perfect information."

Example 5.6 | Think of a typical marketing decision problem in which a company has to decide whether or not to introduce a new product. Let us assume that a major competitor of this company is about to introduce a competitive product. Now, although 100 percent reliable information regarding the competitor's plans is not always available, the marketing manager can make certain probabilistic

---

[10] Matrix formulation can also be used to solve a DMUR problem with multiple objectives. See Eilon [1969].

[11] This problem can be surmounted by considering each strategy in terms of two dimensions, the *expected value* and the *variance*. See Appendix A.

statements based on experience, research surveys, "informed" friend, or "spy network." Let us adopt the following notation:

$$C_1 = \text{competitor introduces new product}$$

$$p(C_1) = p_1 = \text{probability that the competitor introduces a new product}$$

$$C_2 = \text{competitor does not introduce a new product}$$

$$p(C_2) = p_2 = \text{probability that the competitor does not introduce a new product}$$

$$S_1 = \text{company decides to introduce new product}$$

$$S_2 = \text{company decides not to introduce new product}$$

We assume the conditional payoff matrix given in Table 5.6 for our problem. Table 5.6 represents a typical conditional payoff table. For example, if our manager introduces the new product *and* then if the competitor does not introduce a new product, the payoff to our manager is $10 million. Similarly, we can interpret other conditional payoffs shown within the body of the payoff matrix.

Table 5.6

		Competitor's Strategy		Expected Monetary Value (EMV)
		C_1	C_2	
Probability		0.6	0.4	
Strategy	S_1	6	10	7.6
	S_2	4	15	8.4 ← Optimal

Calculation of Expected Value. We treat this problem as a static DMUR problem with a single objective. Hence, the optimal strategy can be identified by applying the expected-value criterion.

$$\text{EMV of } S_1 = E(S_1) = 0.6(6) + 0.4(10) = 7.6$$

$$\text{EMV of } S_2 = E(S_2) = 0.6(4) + 0.4(15) = 8.4 \leftarrow \text{optimal strategy}$$

Since EMV of S_2 is higher than the EMV of S_1, the optimal strategy is S_2.

Calculation of Indifference Probabilities. Our manager can now proceed to calculate the "indifference" probabilities. That is, he can determine the limits for $p(C_1)$ and $p(C_2)$ at which he will be indifferent with respect to the two strategies because both of them will have the same expected values. That is, indifference probabilities can be calculated by letting EMV of $S_1 = $ EMV of S_2. Now, if we let p_1 be the probability of C_1, then the probability of $C_2 = 1 - p_1$ (since C_1 and C_2 are the only two strategies of our competitor and these probabilities must add up to 1). Therefore,

$$\text{EMV of } S_1 = 6(p_1) + 10(1 - p_1)$$
$$= 10 - 4p_1 \tag{5.1}$$

$$\text{EMV of } S_2 = 4(p_1) + 15(1 - p_1)$$
$$= 15 - 11p_1 \tag{5.2}$$

At the point of indifference, we have the condition that EMV of strategy S_1 equals EMV of strategy S_2. Hence, equating (5.1) with (5.2), we get

$$10 - 4p_1 = 15 - 11p_1$$

or

$$p_1 = \tfrac{5}{7}$$

and

$$p_2 = 1 - \tfrac{5}{7} = \tfrac{2}{7}$$

Hence, the two indifference probabilities are $p(C_1) = \tfrac{5}{7}$; and $p(C_2) = \tfrac{2}{7}$. In a way, this calculation indicates the sensitivity to the probability estimation made by the manager with respect to the two strategies. Note that $p(C_2)$ could be as low as $\tfrac{2}{7}$, as compared to the current value of 0.4, and still the optimal strategy will be S_2.

Value of Perfect Information. From the payoff matrix given in Table 5.6, it is possible to place a tentative value on what can be called *perfect information*. Let us argue that we know of an extremely reliable consulting agency (Scarsdale Consulting Group) that can be retained to provide additional information with respect to our competitor's plan. Our next question is, obviously, how much we should pay the consulting agency for this assignment. An upper limit to what we should pay can be established if we assume a situation in which we would get *completely* reliable or *perfect* information. *Before* we decide to retain the agency, we can reason that if we knew for certain that the competitor will choose C_1, then we shall choose S_1 and gain a payoff of 6. Similarly, if we knew for certain that the competitor will choose C_2, we shall select S_2 and gain a payoff of 15. However, since this is a probabilistic problem assuming a stable system, the competitor will choose C_1 during 60 percent of the time, and choose C_2 during 40 percent of the time. Thus, the *expected value under perfect information* (EVPI) is

$$\text{EVPI} = 0.6(6) + 0.4(15) = 9.6$$

Hence, the *upper limit* or "worth" of perfect information is the difference between the value of the "expected value under perfect information" (EVPI) and the expected monetary value (EMV) of the optimal strategy calculated under straightforward conditions of risk. In our case, then, the

$$\text{\textit{value of perfect information}} = \text{EVPI} - \text{EMV of } S_2$$
$$= 9.6 - 8.4 = 1.2 \tag{5.3}$$

That is, we should not retain the consulting agency if it asks for a fee that exceeds $1.2 million.

5.4.2 THE CONCEPT OF OPPORTUNITY LOSS

Any payoff matrix can be converted into an *opportunity-loss* matrix. The rationale behind the concept of opportunity loss (or opportunity cost) is this: What is the cost in lost opportunity if we did not choose the best strategy for a specified state of nature or competitor's strategy? We illustrate the concept with respect to Table 5.6, where the payoffs represent profits (utility). For example, if C_1 is to be the future, then the best strategy for the manager in Table 5.6 is S_1 (payoff of 6), and hence the opportunity loss would be zero. However, if the manager chose S_2, then the payoff (with C_1 occurring) would be 4 (rather than 6), and hence there would be an opportunity loss of 2. That is, in order to calculate opportunity losses for a column of a conditional *profit payoff matrix*, we follow this rule: *Subtract each number in the column from the largest number in that column.*[12] Accordingly, the opportunity-loss matrix for the payoff matrix in Table 5.6 is as shown in Table 5.7.

Table 5.7

		Competitor's Strategy		Expected Opportunity Loss (EOL)
		C_1	C_2	
Probability		0.6	0.4	
Strategy	S_1	0	5	2
	S_2	2	0	1.2 ← Minimum

Now, if we calculate the expected opportunity loss (EOL) for each strategy, then the opportunity-loss matrix can be used for two purposes. First, the strategy with the *minimum* opportunity loss is the optimal strategy. Thus, as can be seen in Table 5.7, S_2 is the optimal strategy. Second, the value of the minimum EOL equals the value of perfect information. This can be verified by checking the minimum EOL value with the value obtained in (5.3).

It stands to reason that any additional information has "value" to the extent that it decreases the level of uncertainty. Hence, the acquisition of perfect information *should* completely remove uncertainty surrounding a decision problem. This observation provides yet another perspective on the idea of the value of perfect information. That is,

cost of uncertainty = value of perfect information = minimum EOL.

We can state, therefore, that the opportunity-loss matrix is equivalent to the original payoff matrix. It provides us with another perspective on the decision problem.

5.5
Decision Making Under Uncertainty

Conceptually, a decision problem under the assumption of complete uncertainty (DMUU) can be formulated in exactly the same manner as the DMUR model, except that no probabilities are attached to the various states of nature. Table 5.8 compares the certainty, risk, and the uncertainty models.

[12] The rule for a *cost payoff matrix* is: Subtract the lowest number from each number in that column.

Table 5.8

Decision Making Under Certainty		Decision Making Under Risk				Decision Making Under Uncertainty			
	State of Nature		State of Nature				State of Nature		
	N		N_1	N_2	N_3		N_1	N_2	N_3
		Probability	p_1	p_2	p_3				
	Utility or Payoff		Utility or Payoff				Utility or Payoff		
Strategy		Strategy				Strategy			
S_1	u_1	S_1	u_{11}	u_{12}	u_{13}	S_1	u_{11}	u_{12}	u_{13}
S_2	u_2	S_2	u_{21}	u_{22}	u_{23}	S_2	u_{21}	u_{22}	u_{23}
S_3	u_3	S_3	u_{31}	u_{32}	u_{33}	S_3	u_{31}	u_{32}	u_{33}

Decision Making Under Certainty	Decision Making Under Risk	Decision Making Under Uncertainty
• *One* state of nature • Single-column matrix • Deterministic outcomes • Optimal strategy is the one with the highest utility	• More than one state of nature • Multiple-column matrix • Probabilistic outcomes (i.e., probabilities are attached to various states of nature) • Optimal strategy is identified by the use of the expected value criterion	• More than one state of nature • Multiple-column matrix • Uncertain outcomes (i.e., probabilities are *not* attached to various states of nature) • Optimal strategy is identified by using a number of different criteria

While discussing DMUU, we shall assume that we are dealing with a single objective that has just one measure of performance, such as dollars.

Let us illustrate DMUU and various approaches for solving problems with the help of an example.

Example 5.7: Decision Making Under Uncertainty

The management of Hermes, Inc., is considering the use of a newly discovered chemical which, when added to detergents, will make the washing soft, thus eliminating the necessity of adding softeners. The management is considering, at the present time, these three alternative strategies:

S_1: add the new chemical to the currently marketed detergent Propo and sell it under the label "New Improved Propo"

S_2: Introduce a brand new detergent under the name "Soft Giant"

S_3: develop a new product and enter the softener market under the name "Body Comfort"

The management has decided for the time being that only one of the three strategies is economically feasible.[13] The marketing research department is requested to develop a conditional payoff matrix for this problem. After

---

[13] Given sufficient resources and profitable markets, the company could obviously select all three strategies simultaneously.

Table 5.9

		State of Nature		
		N_1	N_2	N_3
		Utility or Payoff		
Strategy	S_1	15	12	18
	S_2	9	14	10
	S_3	13	4	26

conducting sufficient research, based on personal interviews and anticipating the possible reactions of the competitors, the marketing research department submits a payoff matrix shown in Table 5.9.

We emphasize again that in DMUU no probability distribution is attached to the set of the states of nature. Note also that in Table 5.9 the numbers within the payoff matrix are all positive, indicating that no matter what strategy is chosen, the company stands to make money. In some cases, the payoff matrix can include negative entries, representing estimates of potential loss.

Let us now examine the conditional payoff matrix given in Table 5.9 and consider the various ways in which the optimal strategy can be identified. It should be obvious that, given the same payoff matrix and complete uncertainty (DMUU), different individuals might choose different strategies, depending upon their subjective values, experiences, propensity for risk, and personal habits. For example, an *optimistic* person would choose S_3, even though this strategy also includes the lowest payoff of 4. Conversely, a person who wishes to avoid risks will choose strategy S_1.

It is because of the possibility of applying different choice criteria that the models used to solve DMUU problems are sometimes referred to as choice criteria models. We illustrate below the applications of some widely known choice criteria.

5.5.1 CRITERION OF PESSIMISM

When we apply the criterion of pessimism to solve a problem under uncertainty, we first determine the *worst* possible outcome in each strategy, and then identify "the *best* of the *worst*" outcome in order to select the optimal strategy. With

Table 5.10

		State of Nature			Worst, or Minimum, Outcome
		N_1	N_2	N_3	
		Utility or Payoff			
Strategy	S_1	15	12	18	12 ← Maximin
	S_2	9	14	10	9
	S_3	13	4	26	4

respect to our problem stated in Table 5.9, we obtain the analysis as shown in Table 5.10.

Clearly, as shown in Table 5.10, according to the criterion of pessimism, the optimal strategy is S_1. Since, while applying the criterion of pessimism, the idea is to choose the "maximum" of the "minimum" values, the choice process is also called *maximin*.

5.5.2 CRITERION OF OPTIMISM

Here, we first determine the *best* possible outcome in each strategy and then identify "the *best* of the *best*" outcome in order to select the optimal strategy. With respect to our example, the analysis is shown in Table 5.11. As shown in Table 5.11, according to the criterion of optimism, the optimal strategy is S_3. Since, while applying the criterion of optimism, the idea is to choose the "maximum" of the "maximum" values, the choice process is also called *maximax*.

Table 5.11

		State of Nature			Best, or Maximum, Outcome
		N_1	N_2	N_3	
		Utility or Payoff			
	S_1	15	12	18	18
Strategy	S_2	9	14	10	14
	S_3	13	4	26	26 ← Maximax

The *maximin* case assumes complete pessimism, while the *maximax* case assumes complete optimism. It stands to reason that we could also develop a choice criterion that would consider the *degree* of optimism or pessimism. In such a case the decision maker would attach some weights to the "best" and the "worst" outcomes in order to reflect his degree of optimism or pessimism. We illustrate this weighting procedure by assuming a *coefficient of optimism* of 0.6. The results are shown in Table 5.12. Note that numbers in the maximum payoff column come from Table 5.11, while the numbers in the minimum payoff column are from Table 5.10. As shown in Table 5.12, with a coefficient of optimism of 0.6, strategy S_3 is the optimal strategy. The reader can verify that, for a coefficient of optimism of 0.4, the optimal strategy in our example will be S_1.

Table 5.12

		Best, or Maximum, Payoff	Worst, or Minimum, Payoff	Weighted Payoff
Weight		0.6	0.4	
	S_1	18	12	$0.6(18) + 0.4(12) = 15.6$
Strategy	S_2	14	9	$0.6(14) + 0.4(9) = 12.0$
	S_3	26	4	$0.6(26) + 0.4(4) = 17.2$ ← Maximum

5.5.3 CRITERION OF REGRET

Here, we first determine the *regret (or opportunity-loss) matrix* in the following manner. Take the first column and identify the highest value in the column. Then subtract all the individual values of the first column, cell by cell, from the highest value of the first column. What we obtain is the first column of the regret matrix. Repeat the same procedure for *all* the columns of the original payoff matrix in order to obtain the regret matrix. The regret matrix for the payoff matrix given in Table 5.9 is shown in Table 5.13.

Table 5.13

		State of Nature		
		N_1	N_2	N_3
		Regret or Opportunity Loss		
	S_1	0	2	8
Strategy	S_2	6	0	16
	S_3	2	10	0

The rationale of the criterion of regret can be explained as follows: If the payoff matrix is known, then for a *given* state of nature, it is easy to identify the best strategy. And, therefore, by matching a given state of nature, with its best strategy we shall experience no regret— that is, a regret of zero. However, other than the best strategy would result in some amount or degree of regret, because the best strategy was not followed.

Let us illustrate the preceding argument with respect to the first column of the original payoff matrix given in Table 5.9. It is clear that if we assume that N_1 is going to happen, then the best strategy is S_1 and it will bring no regret to the decision maker. However if S_2 were to be chosen, and if N_1 did indeed occur, the amount or degree of regret *could* be expressed by the number $15 - 9 = 6$. Similarly, the degree of regret for S_3, in the context of N_1, *could* be expressed by the number $15 - 13 = 2$. Similar arguments were applied in determining the second and the third columns of the regret matrix shown in Table 5.13.

We state now the general rule to derive the regret matrix, provided the payoffs represent profits or positive utilities:[14] *In each column, identify the highest number and then subtract all the individual numbers of that column, cell by cell, from the highest number to obtain the corresponding column of the regret matrix.*

Let us now look at the regret matrix of Table 5.13 and see how the criterion of regret is used to select the optimal strategy. We first determine the *maximum* regret that the decision maker can experience for *each* strategy (see Table 5.14) and then identify the "*minimum* of the *maximum*" regret values in order to select the optimal strategy.

[14] If the payoffs are costs, we identify the lowest number and then subtract that number from all the numbers in a given column.

Decision Theory—Basic Concepts and Applications   Chapter 5

Table 5.14

		State of Nature			Maximum Regret
		N_1	N_2	N_3	
		Regret or Opportunity Loss			
	S_1	0	2	8	8
Strategy	S_2	6	0	16	16
	S_3	2	10	0	8

We see in Table 5.14 that, according to the criterion of regret, there are two strategies (S_1 and S_3) that are optimal. This would mean that some additional elements, including personal biases, would influence the actual choice of the decision maker. It should be noted that since the application of the criterion of regret requires the choice of "minimum of the maximum" regret values, this choice process can be called *minimax regret*.

5.5.4 EQUAL-PROBABILITY CRITERION

The idea here is that since we do not have any *objective* evidence of a probability distribution for the states of nature, we can use a *subjective* criterion. Furthermore, lacking any objective evidence, it is reasonable to assign equal probabilities to each state of nature. This subjective assumption of equal probabilities is sometimes referred to as the *Laplace* criterion, or *criterion of insufficient reason*, in the management literature.

Once equal probabilities are attached to each state of nature, we revert to decision making under risk and hence can use the expected-value criterion (see Table 5.15). The application of the equal probability assumption, as shown in Table 5.15, yields S_1 as the optimal strategy.

Table 5.15

		State of Nature			Expected Monetary Value (EMV)
		N_1	N_2	N_3	
Probability		$\frac{1}{3}$	$\frac{1}{3}$	$\frac{1}{3}$	
		Utility or Payoff			
	S_1	15	12	18	15 ← Maximum
Strategy	S_2	9	14	10	11
	S_3	13	4	26	$14\frac{1}{3}$

5.6
Decision Making Under Conflict or Competition

In all the decision models illustrated thus far, we simplified reality by assuming that the manager has a finite set of strategies and that he is required to identify the optimal strategy in circumstances that range from complete certainty to complete uncertainty. In each model we made two further assumptions: (1) various possible future environments that the decision maker will face can be enumerated by a finite set of states of nature, and (2) the complete payoff matrix is known. Our concept of state of nature included all actions by competitors, government, nature, and random chance events. We can now consider another simplified model of reality—the situation in which two *rational* opponents are required to select optimal strategies, given a series of assumptions, including: (1) the strategies of each party are known to both opponents, (2) the payoff matrix is known to each opponent, (3) both opponents choose their strategies *simultaneously*, (4) the loss of one party equals *exactly* the gain of the other party, (5) decision conditions remain the same, and (6) it is a *repetitive* decision-making problem.

A typical payoff matrix for the decision model described above is shown in Table 5.16. We refer to the two opponents as *players*, and we adopt the convention that a positive payoff will mean a gain to the *row player A* (or the *maximizing player*) and a loss to the *column player B* (or the *minimizing player*). As we shall explain in Chapter 11, this represents a 2-person, zero-sum game (exactly 2 players are involved and the sum of gains and losses equals zero).

For the decision problem given in Table 5.16, the optimal strategy for player *A* is identified by the *maximin* outcome, while the optimal strategy for player *B* is identified by the *minimax* outcome. Why? Because each player has to adopt a strategy that cannot be upset by his competitor. Note that by choosing A_2, player *A* has placed himself in the most preferred position in the sense that his payoff of 9 cannot be upset by player *B*. Similarly, by choosing B_1, player *B* can also assure for himself an outcome that cannot be upset by his competitor. For example, note that if player *A* plays A_2, any strategy other than B_1 will leave player *B* worse off. Similarly, if player *B* plays B_1, any strategy other than A_2 will leave player *A*

Table 5.16

		Player B				Minimum of Row Values
		B_1	B_2	B_3	B_4	
Player A	A_1	8	12	7	3	3
	A_2	⑨	14	10	16	9 ← Maximin
	A_3	7	4	26	5	4
Maximum of Column Values		9 ↑ Minimax	14	26	16	

Decision Theory—Basic Concepts and Applications   Chapter 5

worse off. By choosing A_2 and B_1, the two players have put themselves in the most preferred position in the sense that no competitive action will leave them any worse off. Each player, it should be noted, has applied the criterion of pessimism in choosing his optimal strategy.

Decision making under conditions of conflict or competition is the domain of what is called *game theory*. In Table 5.16, we have given a 2-person zero-sum game which can be solved by employing a *pure* strategy approach. That is, each player selects a *single* strategy and that is the *only* strategy the player will use in *each* play of the game. However, there exist examples of 2-person zero-sum games that cannot be solved by the pure strategy approach. In such cases, the optimal strategy for each person is not a single strategy, but a combination or mix of two or more strategies. Referred to as the *mixed-strategy* approach, we shall describe it, and other elements of game theory, in Chapter 11.

5.7
Decision Trees

Decision-making models described in Sections 5.3 to 5.6 are referred to as *single-stage* decision problems. This is because in each of these models, we assumed that the available data regarding payoffs, strategies, states of nature, competitor's actions, and probability distributions is not subject to revision, and that the entire decision horizon is considered as a single stage. And only *one* decision is made. These single-stage models are static decision models—because the available data are not revised under the assumption that time does not change any basic facts, and that no new information is sought. There are, however, business situations where the manager needs to make not one, but a *sequence* of decisions. The problem then becomes a *multistage* problem because the outcome of one decision affects subsequent decisions. In situations that require a sequence of decisions, the manager can utilize a simple but very useful schematic device known as *decision trees*. A decision tree is a schematic representation of a decision problem. For example, the decision problem of Table 5.6 can be represented by the decision tree shown in Figure 5.2.

A decision tree consists of *nodes, branches, probability estimates*, and *payoffs*. There are two types of nodes: decision nodes and chance nodes. A *decision node*, usually designated by a square, □, requires that a conscious decision be made to choose one of the branches that emanate from that node (i.e., one of the available strategies must be chosen). For example, DN #1 in Figure 5.2 is a decision node at which the manager must decide to choose one of the two available strategies. A *chance node*, usually designated by a circle, ○, shows different possible events (states of nature, competitor's actions, or some other conditions) that can confront a chosen strategy. For example, there are two chance nodes in Figure 5.2 (CN #1 and CN #2), and there are two different possible events (competitor introduces or competitor does not introduce) at each of the chance nodes.

The *branches* emanate from and connect various nodes. We shall identify two types of branches: decision branches and chance branches. A *decision branch* (denote by two parallel lines, =) represents a strategy or course of action. Note that two decision branches emanate from decision node DN #1 in Figure 5.2. A

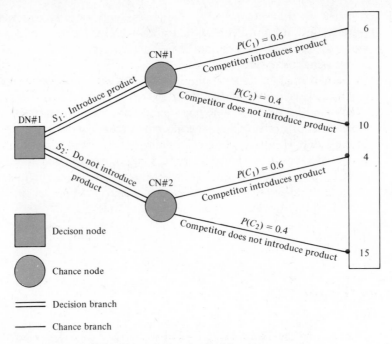

Figure 5.2. Single-Stage Stochastic Decision Tree

chance branch (denote by a single line, —) represents a chance determined event. Indicated alongside the chance branches are their respective probabilities. Note that two chance branches emanate from each of the two chance nodes in Figure 5.2. Any branch that marks the end of a decision tree (i.e., it is not followed by either a decision or a chance node) will be called a *terminal branch*. A terminal branch can represent a decision alternative or chance outcome.

The payoffs can be positive (e.g., profit or sales) or negative (e.g., expenditure or cost) and they can be associated with a decision branch or a chance branch. We shall place payoffs alongside appropriate branches except that the payoffs associated with the *terminal* branches of the decision tree will be shown at the end of these branches.

A decision tree can be *deterministic* or *probabilistic* (*stochastic*), and it can represent a single-stage (one decision) or multistage (a sequence of decisions) problem. This classification is shown in Figure 5.3.

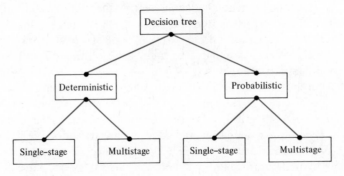

Figure 5.3. A Classification of Decision Trees

5.7.1 DETERMINISTIC DECISION TREES

A deterministic decision tree represents a problem in which *each* possible alternative and its outcome is known with certainty. That is, a deterministic tree does not contain *any* chance node.

A single-stage deterministic decision tree is one that contains no chance nodes and involves the making of only one decision. Any *single-column* payoff matrix (e.g., Table 5.1) can be translated as a single-stage deterministic decision tree. Although it can provide visual clarity, a single-stage deterministic decision tree does not command any major advantages over the payoff matrix formulation of the deterministic decision problem.

Table 5.17

	Profit or Payoff (dollars)		
Strategy	First Year	Second Year	Total
S_1: replace now	4,000	6,000	10,000
S_2: replace after 1 year	5,000	4,000	9,000
S_3: do not replace	5,000	3,000	8,000

A multistage deterministic decision tree is one that contains no chance nodes and involves the making of a *sequence* of decisions. We show a simple multistage deterministic decision tree in Figure 5.4. The decision tree represented in Figure

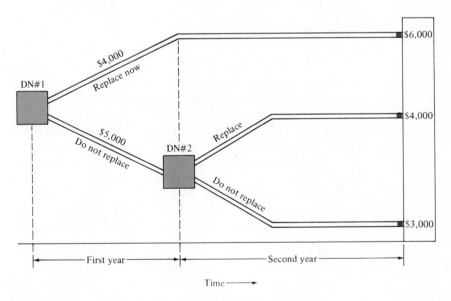

Figure 5.4. A Multistage Deterministic Decision Tree.

5.4 reflects three different strategies in a machine-replacement problem. These strategies and their respective payoffs are summarized in Table 5.17. It is obvious that the optimal strategy in our simple example is S_1 (replace now) as it yields the highest payoff. Further, note that we have solved the problem by simple enumeration.[15]

5.7.2 STOCHASTIC DECISION TREES

Stochastic decision trees are characterized by the presence of chance nodes. A single-stage stochastic decision tree is one that contains at least one chance node and involves the making of only one decision. Conceptually, any conditional payoff matrix can be represented as a single-stage stochastic decision tree, and vice versa. However, such problems (involving one decision) are best formulated and solved by the payoff matrix approach. An example of a single-stage (one decision) stochastic decision tree was shown in Figure 5.2.

A multistage stochastic decision tree is one that contains at least one chance node and involves the making of a sequence of decisions. The decision-tree approach is most useful in analyzing and solving multistage stochastic decision problems. Next, we illustrate a multistage stochastic decision tree with the aid of an example. As mentioned earlier, the decision-tree approach is most useful in analyzing and solving multistage decision problems.

Example 5.8

Based on the recommendation of their strategic planning group, Lehigh manufacturing company has decided to enter the market with a new consumer product. The company has just established a corporate management science group with members drawn from research and development, manufacturing, finance, and marketing departments. The group was asked to prepare and present an investment analysis that will consider expenditures for building a plant, sales forecasts for the new product, and net cash flows covering the expected life of the plant. After having considered several alternatives, the following strategies were presented to top management.

Strategy A. *Build a large plant with an estimated cost of $2 million.*

This alternative can face two states of nature or market conditions: high demand with a probability of 0.70, or low demand with a probability of 0.30. If the demand is high, the company can expect to receive an annual cash flow of $500,000 for 7 years. If the demand is low, the annual cash flow would be only $100,000 because of large fixed costs and inefficiencies caused by small volume.

As shown in Figure 5.5, strategy A ultimately (depending upon whether the demand is high or low) branches into two possibilities, identified in the decision tree by terminal points A_1 and A_2.

Strategy B. *Build a small plant with an estimated cost of $1 million.*

This alternative also faces two states of nature: high demand with a probability of 0.70, or low demand with a probability of 0.30. If the demand is low and remains

---

[15] Large deterministic decision trees give rise to thousands of strategies. In such cases, *dynamic programming* is a very useful technique. See Loomba and Turban [1974, p. 383].

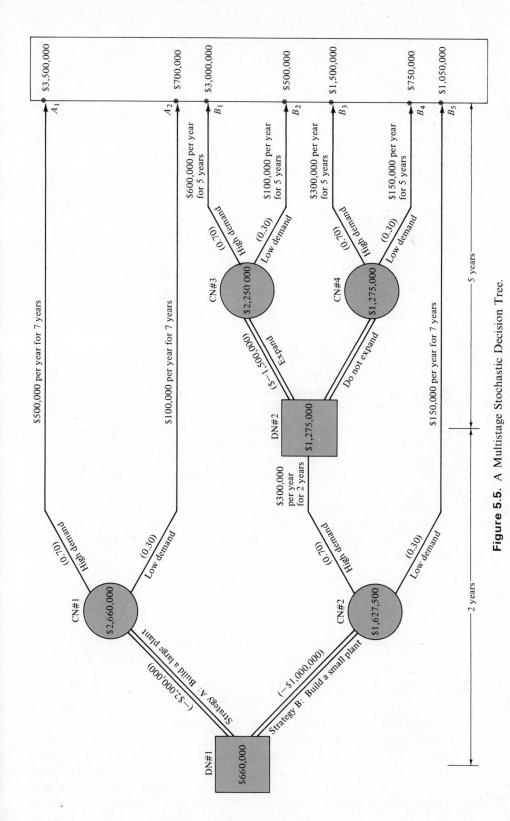

Figure 5.5. A Multistage Stochastic Decision Tree.

low for 2 years, the plant is not expanded. However, if initial demand is high and remains high for 2 years, we face *another decision* of whether or not to expand the plant. It is assumed that the cost of expanding the plant at that time is $1.5 million. Further, it is assumed that after this second decision, the probabilities of high and low demand remain the same.

As shown in Figure 5.5, strategy *B* eventually branches into five possibilities, identified in the decision tree by terminal points B_1, B_2, B_3, B_4, and B_5.

Estimates of annual cash flows and probabilities of high demand and low demand are shown in Figure 5.5. Which strategy should be selected?

As indicated in Figure 5.5, a decision tree is portrayed in such a manner that the starting point is a decision node and the progression is from left to right. Various paths through the tree are indicated by the number of branches, and the manner, in which various decision and chance nodes are connected by means of branches. Along the branches emanating from decision nodes, we write down the decision alternatives and/or their monetary payoffs or costs. Along the branches emanating from chance nodes, we write down the outcomes, their associated probabilities, and monetary payoffs. Finally, at the extreme right-hand side of the decision tree (at the end of terminal branches after which no decision or chance node is encountered, and which represents the end of the planning horizon) we place the relevant *payoffs*. That is, at the end of each terminal branch, we place the payoff associated with that branch.

Once the relevant information regarding decision nodes, chance nodes, decision and chance branches, rewards or costs of decision branches, probabilities, and payoffs associated with chance branches are known, we can proceed with the actual analysis.

Analysis. The analysis of a decision tree consists of calculating the *position* value of each node through the process of *rollback*. The concept of rollback implies that we start from the end of the tree (where the payoffs associated with the terminal branches are indicated) and go back toward the first decision node (DN #1). That is, we proceed from right to left.

As we roll back, we can face either a chance node or a decision node. The position value of a *chance node* is simply the *expected value* of the payoffs represented by various branches that emanate from the node. For example, the position value of chance node 1 (CN#1) is

$$0.7(7 \times 500,000) + 0.3(7 \times 100,000) = \$2,660,000$$

Similarly, position values of chance nodes 3 and 4 (CN#3 and CN#4) are calculated as follows:

position value for CN#3: $0.7(5 \times 600,000) + 0.3(5 \times 100,000)$
$$= \$2,250,000$$
position value for CN#4: $0.7(5 \times 300,000) + 0.3(5 \times 150,000)$
$$= \$1,275,000$$

The position value of a *decision node* is the highest (assuming positive payoffs) of the position values of nodes, or the node, to which it is connected, *less* the cost involved in the specific branch leading to that node. For example, as we roll back to decision node 2 (DN#2), we note that $1.5 million (cost of expansion) must be subtracted from the CN#3 position value of $2.25 million. That is, this branch yields a position value of $2.25 - 1.50 = \$750,000$. And this must be compared with the CN#4 position value of $1,275,000. The higher of the two values (i.e., $1.275 million) is the position value of DN#2. The position value of a node will be placed inside the symbol for the node (see Figure 5.5).

Next, we roll back to CN#2. As in CN#3 and CN#4, the position value of CN#2 is also calculated by the *expected value concept*. However, in the case of CN#2, one of the branches emanating from it leads, with a probability of 0.7, to a decision node (the payoff for this branch is a total cash flow of $600,000 plus the position value of DN#2), while the other is a terminal branch, having a probability of 0.3, with its own payoff of $1,050,000. Hence, the position value of CN#2 is

$$0.7(\$600,000 + 1,275,000) + 0.3(7 \times 150,000) = \$1,627,500$$

We are now ready to roll back to DN#1. As shown in Figure 5.5, the position values of CN#1 and CN#2 that are connected to decision node 1 are already calculated. From the position value of CN#1, we subtract $2 million (cost of building the large plant) and obtain: 2,660,000 − 2,000,000 = $660,000. From the position value of CN#2, we subtract $1 million (cost of building the small plant) and obtain: 1,627,500 − 1,000,000 = $627,500. Thus, when we compare the two decision branches emanating from DN#1, we find that strategy A (build large plant) yields the higher payoff. Hence, the position value of DN#1 is $660,000. That is, strategy A is our optimal strategy, and its expected value is $660,000.

We can now summarize the elements and concepts needed to construct a decision tree:

- All decision and chance nodes.
- Branches that connect various decision and chance nodes.
- Payoff (rewards or costs)—if any—associated with branches emanating from decision nodes.
- Probability values associated with branches emanating from chance nodes.
- Payoffs associated with each chance branch.
- Payoffs associated with each terminal branch at the conclusion of each path that can be traced through various combinations that form the tree.
- Position values of chance and decision nodes.
- The process of rollback.

Our decision-tree problem described in Example 5.8 involved a sequence of only two decisions, and each chance node had only two branches. This is obviously a simplified example, designed only to show the concept, structure, and mechanics of the decision-tree approach. The following are only some of the refinements that can be introduced in order to more faithfully reflect reality.

1. The sequence of decisions can involve a larger number of decisions.
2. At each decision node, we can consider a larger number of strategies.
3. At each chance node, we can consider a larger number of chance branches. Actually, we can even assume continuous probability distributions at each chance node.
4. We can introduce more sophisticated and more detailed projections of cash flows.

5. We can use the concept of *discounted* dollars that would take into account the fact that present dollars are worth more than future dollars.
6. We can also obtain an idea of the *quality of risk* associated with relevant decision-tree paths. That is, in addition to calculating the *expected value*, we can calculate such parameters as *range* and *standard deviation* of the payoff distribution associated with each relevant path. See Appendix A.
7. We can conduct Bayesian analysis that permits introduction of new information and revision of probabilities.[16]

The decision-tree approach traces explicitly all possible *paths* that one *could* follow in a multistage decision problem. It provides a deep insight into the various ramifications of sequential decisions as they affect each other, and the final payoffs associated with each possible path. The decision-tree approach can be implemented manually or with the aid of computers.

5.8
Summary

This chapter was devoted to a discussion of the basic elements of decision theory. We examined several aspects of decisions and decision making. Different classifications of decisions were presented.

We then discussed and illustrated a selected set of decision models, such as decision making under conditions of certainty, risk, uncertainty, and conflict. The concepts of indifference probabilities and the value of perfect information were explained. It was emphasized that most of the decision models discussed in this book are normative, and they deal with administrative and operational, programmed, single-dimensional, and static decisions. Finally, we briefly described the basic elements, structure, and mechanics of the decision-tree approach to solving decision problems. The decision-tree approach was illustrated with the aid of a simple investment example. Admittedly, neither the problems nor the decisions are that simple in the real world. However, the attempts to analyze decision problems in a quantitative fashion yield not only some "ball park" figures, but also valuable qualitative insights into the entire decision environment.

Decision trees are very useful for representing *combinatorial problems* (i.e., large combinations of choices emerge as a result of sequential and interdependent decisions); and that is very similar to the structure of such planning models as PERT and CPM, which will be presented in Chapter 6.

References

Ackoff, R. L., and M. W. Sasieni. *Fundamentals of Operations Research.* New York: John Wiley & Sons, Inc., 1968.
Ansoff, H. I. *Corporate Strategy.* New York: McGraw-Hill Book Company, 1965.

[16] See Green and Tull [1975]. Also see Section A.3.8.

Bross, I. D. J. *Design for Decision.* New York: Macmillan Publishing Co., Inc., 1953.

Canada, J. R. "Decision Flow Networks." *Industrial Engineering,* Vol. 6, No. 6 (June 1974), 30–37.

Conrath, D. W. "From Statistical Decision Theory to Practice: Some Problems with the Transition." *Management Science,* Vol. 19, No. 8 (Apr. 1973), 873–883.

Duncan, J. W. *Decision Making and Social Issues.* Hinsdale, Ill.: The Dryden Press, 1973.

Dunford, R. R. "Decisions, Decisions." *Industrial Research,* Vol. 16, No. 7 (July 1974), 27–30.

Eilon, S. "What Is a Decision?" *Management Science,* Vol. 16, No. 4 (Dec. 1969), B172–B189.

Flinn, R. A., and E. Turban "Decision Tree Analysis for Industrial Research." *Research Management,* Vol. 13, No. 1 (Jan. 1970), 27–34.

Green, P. E., and D. S. Tull. *Research for Marketing Decisions.* Englewood Cliffs, N.J.: Prentice-Hall, Inc., 1975.

Hammond, J. S., III. "Better Decision with Preference Theory." *Harvard Business Review* (Nov.–Dec. 1967), 123–141,

Ives, D. "Decision Theory and the Practicing Manager." *Business Horizons,* Vol. 16, No. 3 (June 1973), 38–40.

Levey, S., and N. P. Loomba. *Health Care Administration.* Philadelphia: J. B. Lippincott Company, 1973.

Lindgren, B. W. *Elements of Decision Theory.* New York: Macmillan Publishing Co., Inc., 1971.

Lindley, D. V. *Making Decisions.* London: John Wiley & Sons, Inc., 1971.

Longbottom, D. A. "The Application of Decision Analysis to a New Product Planning Decision." *Management Decision,* Vol. 24, No. 1 (Mar. 1973), 9–17.

Loomba, N. P., and E. Turban. *Applied Programming for Management.* New York: Holt, Rinehart and Winston, 1974.

Luce, R. D., and H. Raiffa. *Games and Decisions.* New York: John Wiley & Sons, Inc., 1958.

Mack, R. P. *Planning on Uncertainty.* New York: John Wiley & Sons, Inc., 1971.

Meador, C. L., and D. N. Ness. "Decision Support Systems: An Application to Corporate Planning." *Sloan Management Review,* Vol. 15, No. 2 (Winter 1974), 51–68.

Miller, D. W., and M. K. Starr. *Executive Decisions and Operations Research,* 2nd ed. Englewood Cliffs, N.J.: Prentice-Hall, Inc., 1969.

Miller, D. W., and M. K. Starr. *The Structure of Human Decisions.* Englewood Cliffs, N.J.: Prentice-Hall, Inc., 1967.

Morton, S. M. S. *Management Decision Systems.* Boston: Harvard University Press, 1971.

Newman, J. W. *Management Applications of Decision Theory.* New York: Harper & Row, Publishers, 1971.

Radford, K. J. *Managerial Decision Making.* Reston, Va: Reston Publishing Company, Inc., 1975.

Simon, H. A. *Models of Man.* New York: John Wiley & Sons, Inc., 1957.

Simon, H. A. *The New Science of Management Decisions.* New York: Harper & Row, Publishers, 1960.

Starr, M. K. *Management: A Modern Approach.* New York: Harcourt Brace Jovanovich, 1971.

Sullivan, W. G., and W. W. Claycombe. "The Use of Decision Trees in Planning Plant Expansion." *Advanced Management Journal,* Vol 40, No. 1 (Winter 1975), 29–39.

Swalm, R. O. "Utility Theory—Insights into Risk Taking." *Harvard Business Review* (Nov.–Dec. 1966), 123–136.

Terry, H. "Comparative Evaluation Performance Using Multiple Criteria," *Management Science,* Vol. 9 (1963), 431–442.

Thomas, H. *Decision Theory and the Manager.* London: Sir Isaac Pitman & Sons Ltd., 1972.

Torgerson, W. S. *Theory and Methods of Scaling.* New York: John Wiley & Sons, Inc., 1958.

Turban, E., and N. P. Loomba. *Readings in Management Science.* Dallas, Tex.: Business Publications, Inc., 1976.

Von Neumann, J., and O. Morgenstern. *Theory of Games and Economic Behavior.* Princeton. N.J.: Princeton University Press. 1947.

Review Questions and Problems

5.1. What is a decision? Differentiate between programmed and nonprogrammed decisions.

5.2. Define the term "decision theory." Describe decision models based on the criterion of degree of certainty.

5.3. Explain the concept of "expected value." Give the general formula for calculating the expected value when we have a finite number of outcomes.

5.4. Does the expected-value criterion ignore the "quality" of risk? If so, how can you remove this deficiency?

5.5. Briefly describe the nature of descriptive and prescriptive decision models.

5.6. Table 5.18 shows a decision problem involving three strategies and three states of nature. Payoffs represent profits.

Table 5.18

		State of Nature		
		N_1	N_2	N_3
Strategy	S_1	47	49	33
	S_2	32	25	41
	S_3	51	30	14

(a) What is the optimal strategy if we apply the criterion of pessimism? Equal probability criterion?

(b) Develop a regret matrix and apply the minimax regret criterion to identify the optimal strategy.

5.7. An automobile manufacturer has developed a new type of engine which is far less polluting than other types. Management wants to increase sales using one of the following three strategies:

S_1: offer the new engine as an option in luxury models

S_2: offer it as an option in the economy models

S_3: design a new car for the new engine

The marketing department feels that sales will be affected by falling gas prices (N_1), rising gas prices (N_2), and a possible gas shortage (N_3). Table 5.19 shows the payoffs in millions of dollars.

(a) What would be the optimal strategy if we use: (1) the criterion of pessimism, (2) the criterion of optimism, and (3) the coefficient of optimism = 0.25?

(b) Find the optimal strategy if the equal-probability criterion is used.

Table 5.19

		State of Nature		
		N_1	N_2	N_3
Strategy	S_1	35	21	13
	S_2	24	30	17
	S_3	28	26	15

5.8. H. Kondriak decided to see a doctor after his "cold" had persisted for 2 days. He was faced with three choices; see a private doctor (S_1), go to a clinic by appointment (S_2), or go to the free clinic (S_3) where no appointment was necessary. He had conflicting objectives; low cost (weight of 0.50), familiarity with the doctor (0.35) and short wait (0.15). What should Mr. Kondriak do, given the utilities in Table 5.20? Which type of decision model is represented by Table 5.20?

Table 5.20

Objective		Low Cost	Familiar Doctor	Short Wait
Weight		0.50	0.35	0.15
Strategy	S_1	1	5	4
	S_2	4	3	3
	S_3	5	1	1

5.9. The Nevor-Cey-Dye Hospital (NCD) is trying to obtain funds for a drug rehabilitation program from three sources: federal (N_1), state (N_2), or city (N_3) governments. The Board of NCD has estimated a probability distribution of funding based on past aid to similar projects. The strategies, states of nature and their respective probabilities, and utilities of the outcomes are given in Table 5.21.

Table 5.21

	State of Nature		
	N_1	N_2	N_3
Probability	0.3	0.5	0.2
Strategy			
S_1: psychiatric counseling	2	4	9
S_2: vocational counseling	3	5	7
S_3: medical treatment	5	6	4
S_4: combination of S_1, S_2, and S_3	4	8	3

(a) What is the optimal strategy?

(b) What is the value of perfect information in this decision model?

5.10. Sporting Girl, a manufacturer of women's sportswear, is considering three different media-mix strategies for their advertising campaign. The probabilities shown in Table 5.22 were determined by an economic consulting firm. What type of decision model is this? What is the optimal strategy?

Table 5.22

Sales Target (in thousands)		60	100	120
Utility		4	8	10
			Probabilities	
Strategy	S_1	0.5	0.3	0.2
	S_2	0.2	0.6	0.2
	S_3	0.2	0.5	0.3

5.11. Pride and Prejudice Supermarket has three weighted objectives which can be achieved by using three different strategies. However, the strategies have different utilities, because of personnel and cost requirements. Use the data in Table 5.23 to determine the strategy that would maximize P&P's utility.

Table 5.23

Objective		Greater Exposure	Larger Market Share	Quicker Service
Weight		0.3	0.2	0.5
	S_1	8	4	10
Strategy	S_2	7	6	7
	S_3	9	7	2

5.12 John Schuss wants to go skiing. However, if the weather should turn warm, the slopes will become unusable and he would waste a trip. The weather forecast, given by the National Weather Service, and his utilities are given in Table 5.24.

Table 5.24

Weather Condition	Warm	Cold
Probability	0.4	0.6
S_1: go skiing	−4	8
S_2: don't go	5	1

(a) What should John Schuss's rational decision be?
(b) If he does not believe the NWS prediction, determine the range of probabilities within which he will make the same decision as in part (a).
(c) What is the value of perfect information?

5.13. Dr. F. Stein, Administrator of the NCD Hospital, has been under pressure by the community to expand the outpatient department. In addition, the need to expand the inpatient facilities by 10 beds is pressing. The cost of expanding the outpatient facility is $50,000. A community survey suggests that there is a 50 percent chance that outpatient visits will increase by 25 percent over last year's 5000 visits, a 40 percent chance that visits will increase by 10 percent, and a 10 percent chance that no increase will take place. Each visit nets $15 for the hospital. The inpatient occupancy rate is projected (with certainty) to be 90 percent. A filled bed nets the hospital $16,000/year. The cost of expanding inpatient facilities is $100,000.

The budget does not permit the expansion of both departments. What should Dr. Stein's decision be? Construct a decision tree.

5.14. Senator Philip Buster has to vote on a bill for the production of the Boomerang missile. Since this is an election year, his performance is being scrutinized by the citizens of his state, who are very conscientious and public-spirited. Senator Buster can take only pro or con positions. However, after taking an initial position he has to decide between taking active part in the debate or simply casting his vote. Either decision would mean a change in the number of votes for Senator Buster in the upcoming elections. A con position will cost him 5 percent of the labor vote (i.e., workers in the state's defense industry) and a further decrease of 2 percent if he argues the con position. If he just casts his vote, no more votes would be lost. A pro position on the production of the missile will mean a loss of 7 percent; arguing the position a further 2 percent loss of the liberal vote (assume that the number of potential labor votes equals the number of potential liberal votes). Casting a pro vote would mean an additional 1 percent loss of liberal votes. Build a decision tree and determine the strategy that minimizes the number of lost votes. Is this a multistage deterministic decision tree?

5.15 Richard Heir received a house worth $1 million and $1 million in cash from his eccentric grandfather's estate with the proviso that after 2 years he give $1 million to the Save the Lemming Foundation. If, at the end of 2 years, Rich had less than $1 million in cash, the house would have to be sold to meet the donation to the foundation. Rich can invest the cash in the stock market or put it in the bank at 6 percent interest. Each investment would be for 2 years. The payoffs in terms of annual rate of return and the probabilities are given in Table 5.25.

Table 5.25

Annual Rate of Return (percent)	Probability
20	0.20
5	0.50
−25	0.30

If the money is put in the bank, then at the end of 1 year he can either invest the interest in the stock market with the same annual rate of return distribution as shown in Table 5.25 or he can leave the interest in the bank. Use a decision tree to determine the strategy that will maximize Rich Heir's monetary holdings at the end of 2 years. Assume that during the second year the value of rate of return is the same as during the first year.

PART III

Analysis and Planning

CHAPTER 6

Network Models— PERT and CPM

MAJOR CONCEPTS AND TOPICS
DISCUSSED IN THIS CHAPTER

Philosophical Foundations of PERT and CPM

General Framework of PERT and CPM

Activities, events, and critical path(s)

Basic Concepts, Elements, Purpose, Focus, and Evolution of PERT and CPM Models

Probabilistic Analysis in PERT

Analysis versus simulation

The Mechanics of PERT

PERT/COST Networks

CPM Networks and Project Crashing

The Mechanics of CPM

6.1
Introduction

A *network* is a graphical representation of a project, depicting the flow as well as the sequence of well-defined activities (an *activity* defines the actual work to be performed) and events (an *event* marks the beginning or end of an activity). Developed during the 1950s, both PERT (program evaluation and review technique) and CPM (critical path method) are network models.

The purpose of this chapter is to present PERT and CPM models, describe basic concepts used in the construction and analysis of these models, and illustrate the mechanics of the models with the aid of specific examples.

6.2
Philosophical Foundations of PERT and CPM

Planning and control are two of the most important functions of management. *Planning* involves the formulation of objectives and goals that are subsequently translated into specific plans and projects. The function of *control* is to institute a mechanism that can trigger a warning signal if *actual* performance is deviating (in terms of time, cost, or some other measure of effectiveness) from the plan. If such a deviation is unacceptable to the manager, he will take corrective action to bring performance in conformity with the plans. In other cases, the manager may have to develop more realistic plans so that a viable correspondence between plans and performance can be maintained. This brief description of planning and control leads to two observations. First, successful planning requires an appropriate and effective system of control. Second, an economical and effective system of control is based on the principle of management by exception. That is, the need for corrective action should arise only in exceptional situations, and that in most cases performance should be in conformity with the plans. These two concepts (an integrated planning and control system, and management by exception) provide the philosophical foundations of PERT and CPM models.

6.3
The General Framework of PERT and CPM

The PERT and CPM models are extremely useful for the purpose of planning, analyzing, scheduling, and controlling the progress and completion of large and complex projects. In both PERT and CPM the working procedure consists of five steps: (1) analyze and break down the project in terms of specific activities and/or events; (2) determine the interdependence and sequence of activities and produce a network; (3) assign estimates of time, cost, or both to all the activities of the network; (4) identify the longest or critical path through the network; and (5) monitor, evaluate, and control the progress of the project by replanning, rescheduling, and reassignment of resources.

The central task in the control aspect of these models is to identify the *longest* path through the network. The longest path is the critical path because it equals the minimum time required to complete the project. If, for any reason, the project must be completed in less time than the critical path time, additional resources must be devoted (e.g., overtime work) to expedite one or more activities comprising the critical path. Paths other than the critical path (i.e., *noncritical* or *slack* paths) offer flexibility in scheduling and transferring resources, because they take less time to complete than the critical path.

The PERT and CPM models are similar in terms of their basic structure, rationale, and mode of analysis. However, in general, two distinctions are made between PERT and CPM. The first relates to the way in which activity times are estimated, and the second concerns the cost estimates for completing various activities. The PERT activity-time estimates are probabilistic (three *different* time estimates, based on the concept of probability of completing the activity, are made for *each* activity), while in CPM the assumption is made that activity times are deterministic (i.e., under specified conditions, a *single* time estimate is made for *each* activity). The second usual distinction is that while in PERT the activity costs are not explicitly provided, the CPM model does give explicit estimates of activity costs.[1] Furthermore, in CPM, two sets of estimates are provided. One set gives *normal time* and *normal cost* required to complete each activity under normal conditions. The second set gives *crash time* and *crash cost* required to complete each activity under conditions that gain reduction in project completion time by expending more money. The purpose of this dual estimate is to enable the management to obtain a clear picture of the costs associated with deliberate acceleration of the project completion.

6.4
The Purpose and Focus of PERT and CPM Models

The purpose of PERT and CPM is to enable the manager to plan, schedule, monitor, evaluate, and control all the work activities involved in the completion of a project. Although the concept, as well as the mechanics, of PERT and CPM can be used in any type of work, the focus of these models is on *one-time* projects. That is, these models are particularly suited for the coordination and control of one-time projects. Let us explain the meaning of such projects.

For purposes of implementation, business or organizational plans are subdivided into specific projects, jobs, and tasks to be performed. A specific project, job, or task can be further subdivided into well-defined work activities that have identifiable start and completion points. Depending upon the type and nature of the business, work activities can be either *one-time* or *repetitive*. For example, the *design* of a new car is a one-time project, consisting of one-time activities. However, the mass production of a car involves repetitive activities.

---

[1] Our discussion assumes that the only measure of effectiveness in PERT is time. Recent versions, known as PERT/COST, do consider costs explicitly. See Section 6.9.

Here is another example of a one-time project. The mayor of a large urban city has established the goal of reducing next year's expense budget by a specified amount. This goal is translated into specific budget cuts in various administrative units and agencies of the city. The managers of these agencies are asked to develop and submit detailed information on such questions as: What must be done (i.e., concrete action steps or activities)? What is the *order* or *sequence* of these activities (i.e., *precedence* relationships)? Who will perform these activities and what is needed to complete the activities (i.e., specification of personnel and other resources)? When will these activities be performed (i.e., specification of the time estimates including the beginning and completion dates)? Note that this is a special project consisting of one-time activities, and that the information needed to complete the project must of necessity come from different points in the city system. The main task, therefore, is to *coordinate* the performance of the different units involved in the project. This requires that activities of the various units be scheduled, monitored, and evaluated for purposes of control. As we shall see in Section 6.8, this is accomplished by building a project network and by identifying the longest path through the network.

A network model can be analyzed manually, translated into a mathematical model,[2] or programmed into a computer. Here, we shall concentrate on the manual version, since our purpose is to explain the basic procedure for building and solving PERT and CPM models. This should suffice to familiarize the reader with the basic concepts, structure, and mechanics of PERT and CPM. Large-scale and complex problems must of necessity be handled by appropriate computer programs.

6.5
Evolution of PERT and CPM

PERT and CPM models are based upon, and have evolved from, Gantt-type bar charts and milestone charts, as shown in Figure 6.1. Note that the simple bar chart shows *only* the start and finish times of the tasks involved in completing the overall project. It does not show any significant milestones or events (that could be used for exercising on-going control) within a task. The milestone chart is an improvement on the bar chart because it identifies significant milestones or events and shows dependencies (i.e., precedence relationships) *within* tasks. However, the milestone chart does not show interrelationships and interdependencies of events *among* tasks. This deficiency is eliminated by the PERT network, as shown in Figure 6.1. The name "program evaluation and review technique" suggests and implies this: Monitor and evaluate the progress of the scheduled program activities; review and implement necessary changes to achieve program objectives. And this is exactly what is accomplished by PERT.

Program evaluation and review technique was developed in 1958 by the Special Projects Office of the U.S. Navy. The development was a result of the research conducted for the purpose of coordinating and expediting the work of several thousand contractors involved in the Polaris missile program. It is

---

[2] For a linear programming formulation of the PERT–CPM model, see Moder and Phillips [1964] and Lee and Moore [1975, p. 402].

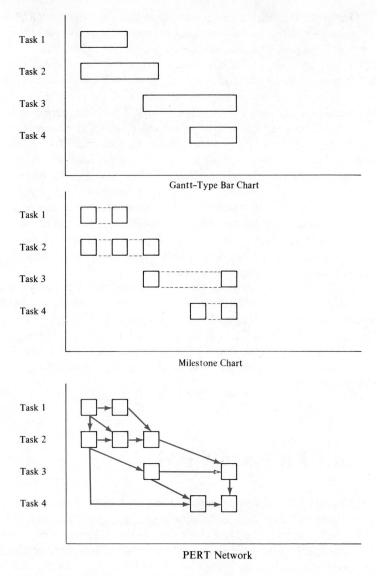

Task 1

Task 2

Task 3

Task 4

Gantt–Type Bar Chart

Task 1

Task 2

Task 3

Task 4

Milestone Chart

Task 1

Task 2

Task 3

Task 4

PERT Network

Figure 6.1. Evolution of PERT and CPM.

claimed that, with the aid of PERT, the completion of the Polaris missile program was expedited by almost 2 years.

As mentioned earlier, PERT is a probabilistic model. Realizing the uncertainties involved in the time required to complete different work activities, the originators of PERT decided that three different time estimates (most optimistic, most realistic, and most pessimistic) for completing each activity should be obtained. The three time estimates are denoted as follows:

a = most optimistic time (this is the shortest time, assuming most favorable conditions)

m = most likely time (this refers to the *mode* of the distribution. In practice, this implies the most realistic time required to complete an activity)

b = most pessimistic time (this is the longest time, assuming most unfavorable conditions)

Further, it was assumed that activity time estimates are distributed according to a *unimodal beta distribution*. The beta distribution was assumed by the developers of PERT because it provides flexibility whereby, depending upon the relative values of a, m, and b, the distribution can be skewed to the right or left. A beta distribution that is skewed to the right is shown in Figure 6.2. (*Note:* In Figure 6.2 and in other figures that represent continuous probability distributions in this book, we have often labeled the vertical axis as "probability.")

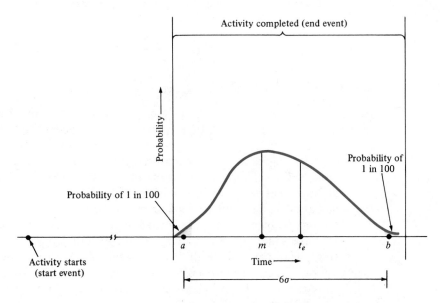

Figure 6.2. Discussion of the Beta Distribution for Activity Completion Time.

a = most optimistic time estimate. Assume that $a = 10$ weeks. Then the probability of completing the activity within "10 or less" weeks is $\dfrac{1}{100}$.

m = most likely time. This is the *mode* of the distribution. Assume that $m = 16$ weeks. This means that most of the time this activity will take 16 weeks to complete.

b = most pessimistic time estimate. Assume that $b = 40$ weeks. Then the probability that the activity will take more than 40 weeks is $\dfrac{1}{100}$.

t_e = *expected* time for completing the activity. It is a weighted average of a, m, and b and is calculated as follows:

$$t = \frac{a + 4m + b}{6} = \frac{10 + 4(16) + 40}{6} = 19 \text{ weeks}$$

The meaning of $t_e = 19$ is that there is a 50:50 chance that the actual completion of the activity can be earlier or later than 19 weeks.

σ = standard deviation of the distribution of time estimates for completing the activity. It measures the *spread* or *dispersion* of the distribution, and is calculated as follows:

$$\sigma = \frac{b - a}{6} = \frac{40 - 10}{6} = 5 \text{ weeks.}$$

Strictly speaking, in continuous distributions the probability is *not* measured by the vertical height but by the area under the curve *between* two specified values of the random variable. For further discussion, see the note on p. 501.)

It should now be emphasized that in PERT we are assuming that the estimated time to complete each activity is a probability distribution, such as shown in Figure 6.2. Out of the entire distribution we choose only three points (time estimates). Now, for this probability distribution we can calculate two parameters: *expected time* for completing the activity, t_e, and the *standard deviation, σ* (read "sigma"). The two parameters are calculated (they only provide approximations for the beta distribution) as follows:

$$t_e = \frac{a + 4m + b}{6} \tag{6.1}$$

$$\sigma = \frac{b - a}{6} \tag{6.2}$$

The branches of the PERT network can show either t_e or the three different time estimates. Once the three time estimates for each activity are obtained, we need precedence relationships (i.e., proper sequencing to reflect interrelationships and interdependencies among activities) in order to develop a PERT network. A very simple PERT network consisting of two activities (activity 1–2 and activity 2–3) and three events (events 1, 2, and 3) is shown in Figure 6.3. Note that there is only one path (1–2–3) in the network shown in Figure 6.3.

In real-life problems, a PERT network consists of several paths, and the control on the time required to complete the overall project is exercised by identifying the longest (critical) path through the network. Actually, the identification of the critical path is one of the central tasks in analyzing a PERT network. In Section 6.8, we shall present a step-by-step procedure for building, analyzing, and using a PERT model.

The critical path method (CPM) was developed in 1957 by the Du Pont Company in connection with the building and maintenance of chemical plants. The name "critical path method" suggests and implies this: Identify the critical (longest) path through the network and use it to exercise control on the progress of the project. As described earlier, CPM is very similar to PERT. Both models portray the interrelationships and interdependencies of activities and events that comprise a work project. However, as mentioned earlier. CPM is deterministic rather than probabilistic. That is, for each activity, *under specified conditions*, there is a *single* time estimate.[3] Also, for each activity, a deterministic estimate of *normal cost* and *crash cost* is provided. A very simple CPM network consisting of two activities and three events is shown in Figure 6.4. In the CPM network shown

Figure 6.3

[3] Actually, two time estimates, each of which is deterministic, are obtained. One, called *normal time*, is the time estimate under normal conditions. The other, called *crash time*, is the time estimate that would result by incurring more than normal costs.

Figure 6.4

in Figure 6.4, the numbers without the parentheses show the normal time and normal cost data, and the numbers within the parentheses show the crash time and crash cost data. Note that in CPM we consider an *explicit tradeoff* between time and cost. As can be ascertained from Figure 6.4, if we want to gain time by expediting activity 1–2, the cost is $250/week, while the cost of expediting activity 2–3 is $400/week. It stands to reason, therefore, that activity 1–2 should be *crashed* before activity 2–3, assuming that we want to finish the project in less than the indicated normal time of 14 weeks.

In Section 6.10, we shall present a step-by-step procedure for building, analyzing, and using a CPM model.

6.6
Basic Concepts of PERT and CPM

In this section, we describe some basic concepts that are common to both PERT and CPM. In order to fix ideas, we shall employ the PERT network shown in Figure 6.5. The network shown in the figure represents a project for constructing a new yacht. The project consists of eight activities and seven events. In Table 6.1 we describe these activities and provide three different time estimates for completing each activity. These time estimates are used to calculate the *expected time* of completion, t_e, and *standard deviation*, σ, for each activity. These t_e and σ are listed in the last two columns of Table 6.1 and are placed alongside the branches of Figure 6.5.

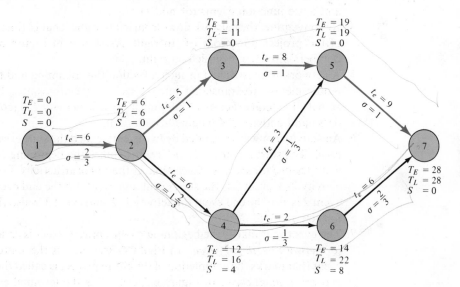

Figure 6.5

Table 6.1

Activity	Description	Time Estimate (weeks)			Expected Time (weeks) $t_e = \dfrac{a + 4m + b}{6}$	Standard Deviation (weeks) $\sigma = \dfrac{b - a}{6}$
		(a)	(m)	(b)		
1–2	Construction of hull	4	6	8	6	$\frac{2}{3}$
2–3	Construction of deck	2	5	8	5	1
2–4	Engine installation	3	5	13	6	$1\frac{2}{3}$
3–5	Construction of superstructure	5	8	11	8	1
4–5	Plumbing and wiring	2	3	4	3	$\frac{1}{3}$
4–6	Radar installation	1	2	3	2	$\frac{1}{3}$
5–7	Interior finishing	6	9	12	9	1
6–7	Painting	4	6	8	6	$\frac{2}{3}$

We can now make the following observations:

1. A *network*, whether it is PERT or CPM, consists of interrelated and interdependent activities and events.

2. An *activity* refers to the actual process of doing work. It involves the expenditure of effort, time, money, and other resources. An activity is denoted by an arrow, →. As shown in Figure 6.5, the *arcs* or *branches* of the network represent activities.

3. An *event* refers to a specific and identifiable milestone, or accomplishment of work, at a specified point in time. Events only signify the start or end of activities and therefore do *not* require the expenditure of effort, time, money, or other resources. An event is denoted by a circle, ◯. As shown in Figure 6.5, the *nodes* of a network represent events. If an event signifies the start or completion of more than one activity, it is called a *junction event*. Events 2, 4 and 5 are junction events (or nodes).

4. By convention, the network flows from left to right. That is, time and progress of the project flow from left to right. As shown in Figure 6.5, the event numbers also flow from left to right.

5. A network is constructed in such a fashion that planning and technological requirements are translated into precedence relationships. For example, activity 1–2 (construction of hull) must precede activity 2–3 (construction of deck) and activity 2–4 (engine installation).

6. An activity is always bounded by two events, called the *start event* and the *end event*. The start (or *predecessor event*) signifies the beginning of an activity, while the end (or *successor event*) marks the end of an activity. For example, in activity 2–3, event 2 is the start event and event 3 is the end event. Note that event 2 is also the end event for activity 1–2, and event 3 is also the start event for activity 3–5.

7. The event that marks the beginning of the entire project is called the *source* (or *network beginning*) *event*. In Figure 6.5, event 1 is the source event. The event that marks the completion of the entire project is called the *terminal* (or *network ending*) *event*. In Figure 6.5, event 7 is the terminal event.

8. No activity can start until its start event is complete. For example, activity

5–7 (interior finishing) cannot start until event 5 is complete (i.e., superstructure has been constructed and plumbing and wiring are in place).

9. No event is complete until *all* activities leading to that event are complete. For example, event 5 in Figure 6.5 is not complete until activities 3–5 and 4–5 are complete.

10. A corollary of observations 8 and 9 is that *loops* or *cycles* are not permitted in networks. Why a loop is not permitted in a network becomes clear if we examine the loop shown in Figure 6.6. Note that event 1 is not complete until activity 3–1 is complete. However, activity 3–1 is not complete until event 3 is realized. But event 3 cannot be realized until activity 2–3 is complete. However, activity 2–3 is not complete until event 2 is realized, and this requires the completion of activity 1–2. But activity 1–2 is not complete until event 1 is complete. Thus, we have completed a full cycle, and find that we cannot progress out of this loop. That is why loops or cycles are not permitted in networks. A managerial rationale behind the requirement of not permitting loops is that, by definition, planning time does not repeat itself.[4]

11. In order to incorporate technological or managerial requirements, it is sometimes necessary to insert a *dummy* activity into the network model. Denoted by a dashed arrow,-----→, a dummy activity does *not* require any time, effort, or resources for its completion. Let us illustrate. In Figure 6.5, activity 2–4 precedes activity 4–6. Now, assume that we impose the additional requirement that activity 2–3 also precedes activity 4–6. This means that activity 4–6 can start only upon the completion of both activities 2–4 *and* 2–3. In order to incorporate this new planning requirement, we add the dummy activity 3–4, as shown in Figure 6.7.

12. A network *path* consists of a set of activities that connect the network beginning event to the network ending event. A network consists of several paths. The longest path (in terms of time) is called the the *critical path*. Paths other than the critical path are called *noncritical* or *slack paths*. There are three different paths in the network shown in Figure 6.5. They are listed and properly labeled in Table 6.2.

Table 6.2

Path	Length of Path
1–2–3–5–7	$6 + 5 + 8 + 9 = 28$ weeks ← critical path
1–2–4–6–7	$6 + 6 + 2 + 6 = 20$ weeks ← slack path
1–2–4–5–7	$6 + 6 + 3 + 9 = 24$ weeks ← slack path

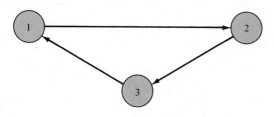

Figure 6.6

[4] See Starr [1971, p. 326].

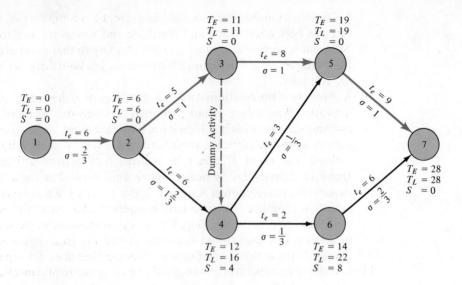

Figure 6.7

13. Each event of the PERT network can be assigned two specific time dimensions. One is the earliest expected event time, T_E, and the other is the latest allowable event time, T_L. Each time dimension relates to the time elapsed from the point of starting the project. As such, T_E or T_L can easily be converted to calendar dates.

Calculation of Earliest Expected Event Time, T_E

Note that event 5 is realized only when activity 3–5 is complete *and* activity 4–5 is complete. Now if we reach event 5 via 1–2–4–5, it takes 15 weeks. However, if we reach event 5 via 1–2–3–5, it takes 19 weeks. Hence, it stands to reason that the earliest expected time, T_E, for event 5 is 19 weeks.[5]

We now provide a generalized procedure for calculating T_E for an event.

Step 1. *For each event, identify the various paths that connect the network beginning event to that event.*

Step 2. *Proceeding forward (left to right), add t_e of the activities along each such path.*

Step 3. *The longest chain or path determines its T_E.*

That is, the *highest* value obtained in step 2 is T_E of the event. It is obvious that T_E of the network beginning event is zero. In Table 6.3 we provide the T_E for all the events shown in Figure 6.5.

Another rule for calculating the T_E of an event is as follows: *For each event, identify its predecessor events and their respective T_E. To each predecessor T_E add the respective t_e of the activity that leads to the event under consideration. Then the highest of such values is the T_E of that event.*

---

[5] Note that this is a direct consequence of observation 9: "No event is complete until all activities leading to that event are complete."

Table 6.3

Event	T_E (weeks)
1	0
2	6
3	11
4	12
5	19
6	14
7	28

Consider, again, event 5. It has two *predecessor events*, 3 and 4. Now the above rule is applied, as shown in Table 6.4.

Table 6.4

Event	Predecessor Event	T_E of Predecessor Event(s)	t_e of Activity Leading to Event	T_E of Event
1	(Network beginning event)			0
2	1	0	6	6
3	2	6	5	11
4	2	6	6	12
5	3	11	$+$ $8 = 19\sqrt{}$	19
	and			
	4	12	$+$ $3 = 15$	
6	4	12	2	14
7	5	19	$+$ $9 = 28\sqrt{}$	28
	and			
	6	14	$+$ $6 = 20$	

Calculation of Latest Allowable Event Time, T_L

If we want to finish the project on time, it is obvious that T_L of the network beginning event must equal its T_E. Hence, by definition, T_L of the network beginning event is zero. Similarly, the T_L of the network ending event must equal its T_E. Thus, for event 7, $T_L = 28$ weeks.

Now consider event 4. Starting backward from the terminal event 7, we trace two paths to event 4. One path (7–6–4) is 8 weeks, and the second path (7–5–4) is 12 weeks. This means that the latest allowable time for completing event 4 is 20 $(28 - 8 = 20)$, in view of path (7–6–4). However, the latest allowable time for event 4 is 16 $(28 - 12 = 16)$, in view of path (7–5–4). It stands to reason that event 4 must be realized by 16 weeks, and not by 20 weeks, if the terminal event 7 is to be realized by 28 weeks.

We now provide a generalized procedure for calculating T_L of an event.

Step 1. *For each event, identify various paths that connect the network ending event to that event.*

Step 2. *Proceeding backward (right to left) subtract t_e of the activities along each such path.*

Step 3. *The longest chain or path determines its T_L.*

That is, the *lowest* value obtained in step 2 is the T_L of the event. In Table 6.5, we provide the T_L for all the events shown in Figure 6.5.

Table 6.5

Event	T_L (weeks)
7	28
6	22
5	19
4	16
3	11
2	6
1	0

Another rule for calculating the T_L of an event is as follows: *For each event, identify its successor events and their respective T_L. From each successor T_L, subtract the respective t_e of the activity that originates from the event under consideration. Then, the lowest of such values is the T_L of that event.*

Consider, again, event 4. It has two successor events, 5 and 6. Now, the above rule is applied as shown in Table 6.6.

Table 6.6

Event	Successor Event	T_L of Successor Event	t_e of Activity Originating from Event	T_L of Event
7	(Network ending event)			28
6	7	28	6	22
5	7	28	9	19
4	5	19	$-\ 3 = 16\surd$	16
	and			
	6	22	$-\ 2 = 20$	
3	5	19	8	11
2	3	11	$-\ 5 = 6\surd$	6
	and			
	4	16	$-\ 6 = 10$	

Network Models—PERT and CPM   Chapter 6

14. Associated with each event is a measure called *slack*. The slack of an event represents the time by which we can delay the realization of that event *without* jeopardizing the timely realization of successor events. The slack of an event is denoted by S, and is calculated as follows:

$$S = T_L - T_E \qquad\qquad (6.3)$$

In Table 6.7, we calculate the slacks of all the events shown in Figure 6.5.

Table 6.7

Event	T_L	T_E	Slack
1	0	0	0
2	6	6	0
3	11	11	0
4	16	12	4
5	19	19	0
6	22	14	8
7	28	28	0

Note that slack is *usually* zero or positive. However, if for some business reason the project must be expedited (say the project were one fourth complete and then management announces a bonus for completing the project earlier than the T_E of the terminal event), then a negative slack *could* exist along the critical path. A negative slack implies that the project is behind schedule.

We noted earlier that path 1–2–3–5–7 is the critical path in Figure 6.5. Observe from Table 6.7 that the slack of each of the events on the critical path is zero. Hence, we can say that the critical path is the path with zero slack. However, considering the possibility of negative slack, the following definition of critical path is more appropriate. The critical path is the path with the least algebraic value of slack. The concept of slack is important because it indicates a measure of flexibility for the manager in terms of scheduling activities, allocating resources, and achieving a balanced rate of production.

The Concept of Activity Slack

Another means of utilizing the concept of slack for planning and controlling the network is to calculate the *slack associated with each activity*. If we examine Figure 6.5, we note that there are two *noncritical paths* through the network: path 1–2–4–6–7 and path 1–2–4–5–7. On any noncritical path, we can identify activities in terms of *critical* activities and *noncritical* activities. For example, on path 1–2–4–6–7, activity 1–2 is the only critical activity, while activities 2–4, 4–6, and 6–7 are noncritical activities. Similarly, on path 1–2–4–5–7, activities 1–2 and 5–7 are critical while activities 2–4 and 4–5 are noncritical.

It is obvious that each noncritical path contains some slack and that one or more noncritical activities along each noncritical path can be delayed in terms of starting or completing dates without delaying the overall project completion time. The availability of slack along noncritical paths offers the manager a great deal of flexibility—because the slack of a noncritical path can be distributed over the noncritical activities of that path to suit the specific needs of the project.

We can calculate total slack associated with a noncritical path (also called *floating slack* of a noncritical path) as follows:

total slack on a noncritical path

$$= \text{(sum of } t_e \text{ of critical path)} - \text{(sum of } t_e \text{ of noncritical path)}$$

For example, total slack on the noncritical path 1–2–4–6–7 is

$$(6 + 5 + 8 + 9) - (6 + 6 + 2 + 6) = 8 \text{ weeks}$$

This slack can be distributed over the three noncritical activities 2–4, 4–6, and 6–7 in a number of ways. However, two things should be noted. First, it is possible to calculate the *maximum possible slack* that can theoretically be used in a noncritical activity *A–B* as follows:

maximum possible slack that can be used in a noncritical activity *A–B*

$$= (T_L \text{ of event } B - T_E \text{ of event } A) - t_e \text{ of activity } A\text{–}B$$

For example, maximum possible slack that can be used in each of the activities above is:

for activity 2–4: $(16 - 6) - 6 = 4$ weeks

for activity 4–6: $(22 - 12) - 2 = 8$ weeks

for activity 6–7: $(28 - 14) - 6 = 8$ weeks

Second, these slacks are not independent of each other and, in the final analysis, after we have allocated slacks to different noncritical activities on a *given* noncritical path, the sum of these allocations cannot exceed the total possible slack for that path.

Now, *one* obvious way of distributing this slack of 8 weeks is to allocate a slack of 4 weeks to activity 2–4 and a slack of 4 weeks to activity 4–6.

Information regarding activity slack is extremely useful. In complex projects, this information can be transmitted to different work centers and to specialized craft work (e.g., electrical, plumbing, etc.). In this manner, various subsystems of the network can plan and control their work more effectively.

6.7
Probabilistic Analysis in PERT

As described earlier, we assume that time estimates to complete each and every activity in a PERT network have a probabilistic distribution. Thus, for each activity on the critical path we have a separate distribution of time estimates. Since the critical path 1–2–3–5–7 in Figure 6.5 consists of four activities (activities 1–2, 2–3, 3–5, and 5–7), this gives rise to four separate probability distributions, each of which resembles the distribution shown in Figure 6.2. Having recognized this, the next logical question is: How can we combine these individual distributions to obtain a single distribution that shows the time estimates for completing the critical path and hence the entire project?[6] The task is accomplished by making these two assumptions: (1) the activities are independent in

---

[6] Note that, by definition, the project is complete only when the critical path is complete.

terms of their variance (i.e., the completion times of the activities are assumed to be independent), and (2) the completion time for the critical path is normally distributed. Based on these assumptions, we calculate the expected time and standard deviation of the critical path 1–2–3–5–7 (see Figure 6.8) as follows. The expected time of the critical path is calculated by simply adding together the t_e of the individual activities on the critical path. Thus, expected time, t_e, for the critical path = project t_e = sum of t_e of activities on the critical path. In our case,

t_e of the critical path (1–2–3–5–7) = $6 + 5 + 8 + 9 = 28$ weeks

The standard deviation of the critical path is calculated as follows:[7]

$$\sigma_{\text{critical path}} = \sigma_{\text{project}} = \sqrt{\sigma_{1-2}^2 + \sigma_{2-3}^2 + \sigma_{3-5}^2 + \sigma_{5-7}^2}$$

$$\sigma_{\text{project}} = \sqrt{\tfrac{4}{9} + 1 + 1 + 1} = 1.86 \text{ weeks}$$

We have now calculated the expected completion time, t_e, and the standard deviation, σ, of the project, under the assumption that the time estimates of the critical path (and hence the project) are normally distributed. We are, therefore, in a position to answer such questions as: What is the probability of completing the project by a certain date? What is the date by which management can be 90 or 95 percent confident of completing the project? Let us illustrate these concepts with reference to our example.

The completion time distribution of our project is shown in Figure 6.9. Now, let us pose this question: What is the probability of completing this project as late as 30 weeks from the beginning date? The question asks for the shaded area as shown in Figure 6.10. We calculate the area by using Table I in Appendix E.[8]

$$Z = \frac{\text{absolute difference from the mean}}{\text{standard deviation}} = \frac{30 - 28}{1.86}$$

$$= 1.08 \text{ standard deviations}$$

Hence, we look under column 2 in Table I (next to the value of 1.08 under column 1) and find that the shaded area between t_e and 30 is approximately 0.36. The area to the left of 30 is obviously $0.50 + 0.36 = 0.86$. That is, the probability of completing the project by 30 weeks is 86 percent. Or, we can say that the probability of being late (i.e., completing the project *after* 30 weeks) is 14 percent.

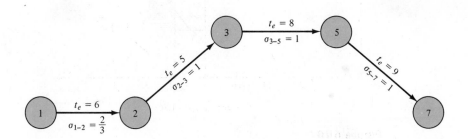

Figure 6.8

---

[7] The formula is based on this fact: The variance of the sum equals the sum of the variance (for independent activities).

[8] See Section A.6.1, which explains the procedure for finding areas between specified points under a normal curve.

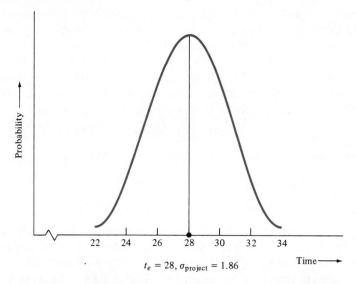

$t_e = 28, \sigma_{\text{project}} = 1.86$

Time ———→

Figure 6.9. Completion Time Probability Distribution of the Entire Project.
- Combines the activities on the critical path 1–2–3–5–7 in Figure 6.5.
- Assumes independence among the probability distributions of completion times for activities on the critical path.
- Assumes that the completion time of the entire project is normally distributed.

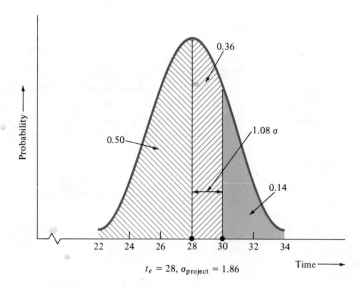

$t_e = 28, \sigma_{\text{project}} = 1.86$

Time ———→

Figure 6.10

What is the time by which management can be 95 percent confident of completing the project? The question asks for point C in Figure 6.11. As shown in Figure 6.11, if management wants to be 95 percent confident of completing the project by a point in time labeled C, then the area under the curve from t_e to C is

Network Models—PERT and CPM   Chapter 6

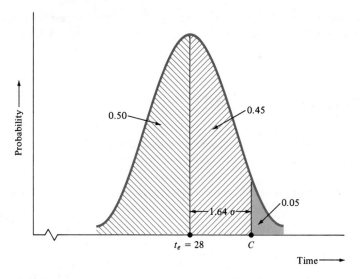

Figure 6.11

45 percent (i.e., 95 percent area is to the left of point C). Now, we find from Table I in Appendix E that this corresponds to a distance of 1.64σ. Hence,

$$C = t_e + 1.64\sigma_{\text{project}}$$
$$= 28 + 1.64(1.86)$$
$$= 28 + 3.05$$
$$= 31.05 \text{ weeks}$$

Hence, management can be 95 percent confident that the project will be complete by 31.05 weeks after its start date.

Our analysis of the network shown in Figure 6.5 is now complete. The insight gained from this analysis provides the foundation for the step-by-step procedure for planning, scheduling, and analyzing a PERT network.

6.7.1 ANALYSIS VERSUS SIMULATION

Behind the probabilistic analysis in PERT are two assumptions: (1) estimates of t_e are unbiased (i.e., if these estimates are used repeatedly, we would be *on the average* correct), and (2) the activity times are independent of one another. However, in real life, both of these assumptions may be open to question. The actual behavior of PERT networks depends upon the *interaction* of each activity with all other activities. This means that, as opposed to what the formal analysis of the PERT network tells us, in actual performance, one of the near-critical paths (rather than the critical path identified by the analysis) *may* turn out to be the critical path. Consider, for example, a near-critical path whose length is close to the critical path but whose variance is much larger. This near-critical path *could* turn out to be the actual critical path, and our normal probability analysis would then lead to wrong conclusions. The next question is: How can we overcome this deficiency of normal probability analysis? The answer resides in the concept of simulation.[9] In Section 14.10, we shall simulate a simple PERT network.

6.8
The Mechanics of PERT

The construction, analysis, and management of a PERT network consists of the following 12 steps.

Step 1. *Define the overall project, including the project objective and target completion date.*

Step 2. *Break down the project into well-defined activities.*

Identify the source event (i.e., network beginning event) and the terminal event (i.e., network completion event). For *each* activity, identify its start event and end event.

Step 3. *Give serial numbers to each event and arrange them in the proper sequence as required by planning and technological requirements.*

This establishes precedence relationships.

Step 4. *Construct the actual PERT network, interconnecting all the activities and events as required by the precedence relationships.*

Step 5. *For each activity, calculate its expected completion time, t_e, and standard deviation.*

- Obtain the most optimistic time estimate: *a.*
- Obtain the most likely time estimate: *m.*
- Obtain the most pessimistic time estimate: *b.*

Then

$$t_e = \frac{a + 4m + b}{6}$$

$$\sigma = \frac{b - a}{6}$$

Step 6. *Determine the critical path.*

- Identify all paths through the network.
- Determine the length of each path by adding the expected times, t_e, of the activities on the path.
- The path with the *longest* expected time is the critical path.

Step 7. *Calculate the earliest expected time, T_E, for each event.*

T_E for the network beginning event is zero. For other events, we employ the following rule: For each event, identify its predecessor events and their respective

---

[9] We shall discuss simulation in Chapter 14.

T_E. To each predecessor T_E, add the respective t_e of the activity that leads to the event under consideration. Then the *highest* of such values is the T_E of that event.

Step 8. *Calculate the latest allowable time, T_L, for each event.*

T_L for the network completion event equals its T_E (calculated in step 7). For other events, we employ the following rule: For each event, identify its successor events and their respective T_L. From each successor T_L, subtract the respective t_e of the activity that originates from the event under consideration. Then the *lowest* of such values is the T_L of that event.

Step 9. *Calculate slack, S, for each event.*

$$S = T_L - T_E$$

Step 10. *Conduct the necessary probability analysis on the PERT network to generate management information regarding project completion.*

Step 11. *Distribute the PERT network to those who are going to work on the project.*

Step 12. *Monitor the progress of the project and make changes when and if necessary.*

6.9
PERT/COST Networks

A PERT network is labeled PERT/TIME when we assume that the *only* measure of effectiveness is time. This assumption implies that an acceptable level of cost control can be achieved by merely keeping strict control on the time spent for completing various activities of the network. However, such an assumption suffers from two major deficiencies. First, it does not permit a *direct* focus on the dimension of cost—a dimension that is an important part of performance evaluation of managers and organizations. Second, it does not integrate the network planning and control activities into the overall financial and budgetary plans of the organization. To correct these deficiencies, the concept of PERT/TIME has been expanded to include the dimension of cost. The resulting network is called PERT/COST.

A PERT/COST network is built in essentially the same manner as, and is an expansion of, the PERT/TIME network. A project is broken down into small, well-defined, units or activities for which accurate estimates regarding time, cost, manpower, material, overhead, equipment, and machines can be obtained. The cost estimates for each unit can be single estimates, three different estimates, or several estimates reflected in a time–cost curve (that provide time–cost options for purposes of control). Then, depending upon the technology and construction requirements, *work packages* and *cost centers* are defined and assigned to front-line supervisors. The concept of PERT/TIME is used as an integrating device for the work packages.

Once the PERT/COST network is complete, it permits the accumulation of actual costs as the project is being completed. Thus, an on-going mechanism for cost control is available that permits comparison of *actual* versus *budgeted* costs on the basis of work packages or cost centers. Any cost *overruns* can be quickly detected and corrective action initiated to exercise managerial control. It is clear that the major purpose of PERT/COST is to help the manager obtain an optimum mix of time and cost in completing specified projects.[10]

6.10
CPM Networks and Project Crashing

As mentioned earlier, a CPM network is deterministic. The CPM approach is useful when we can assume that both time and cost of completing various project activities are known with certainty. Two sets of time and cost figures are obtained for each activity: (1) *normal* time and *normal* cost, and (2) *crash* time and *crash* cost. What we have, therefore, is a time–cost tradeoff function for *each* activity. Further, it is usually assumed that the relationship between time and cost is linear, as shown in Figure 6.12.

As shown in Figure 6.12, point K represents the crash cost (maximum cost) and crash time (minimum time) for the activity, and point L represents the normal cost (minimum cost) and normal time (maximum time). We can calculate the slope of the cost–time line (for each activity) to measure the cost–time tradeoff. That is, how much additional cost will be incurred by saving one unit of time (say, 1 week) in completing an activity?

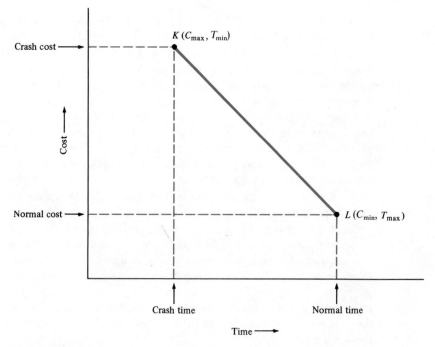

Figure 6.12

[10] For a brief description of PERT/COST, see Vollmann [1973, pp. 199–207].

$$\text{slope of the cost–time line} = \frac{\Delta \text{ cost}}{\Delta \text{ time}} = \frac{\text{crash cost} - \text{normal cost}}{\text{crash time} - \text{normal time}}$$

(The symbol Δ measures change and is read "delta.")

The idea of project crashing is that, under certain circumstances, it is necessary and desirable to expedite project completion even though it will result in higher costs. Since, in CPM, we know both the minimum project completion time and the cost–time relationships of all activities, our objective is to design a program that will yield *minimum project completion time with the least increase in costs over the normal costs.*

Let us illustrate these concepts with the aid of the network shown in Figure 6.13. The normal, as well as crash time and cost data for the network of Figure 6.13 are given in Table 6.8. In the last column of Table 6.8, we list, for each activity, $\Delta\text{cost}/\Delta\text{time}$ (i.e., change in cost per week). Note that $\Delta\text{cost}/\Delta\text{time}$ will always yield a negative slope (see Figure 6.12).

Table 6.8

	Time (weeks)		Cost (dollars)		$\dfrac{\Delta\text{cost}}{\Delta\text{time}}$ (Change in Cost per Week) (dollars)
Activity	Normal	Crash	Normal	Crash	
1–2	10	7	1,000	1,600	200
1–3	15	10	2,000	3,000	200
2–4	8	6	1,800	2,600	400
2–5	20	16	4,500	5,300	200
3–6	30	20	7,200	9,600	240
4–5	14	12	5,000	6,000	500
5–6	12	9	3,300	4,500	400
Total			24,800	32,600	

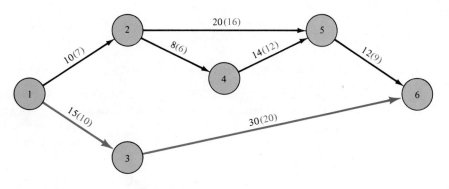

Figure 6.13

On each branch of the network in Figure 6.13 we show the normal as well as the crash time. The normal time is shown without the parentheses, while the crash time is within the parentheses. Thus, 10(7) shown on branch 1–2 indicates that the normal completion time for activity 1–2 is 10 weeks and its crash time is 7 weeks.

We shall use the convention that the number without the parentheses represents the normal time, while the number within the parentheses represents the crash time.

6.10.1 THE MECHANICS OF CPM

The construction of the CPM network requires the general steps of project definition, breakdown of project into activities, identification and numbering of events, and structuring the network to reflect required precedence relationships. These are the same steps that were followed in building a PERT network in Section 6.8 (steps 1 to 4), and therefore we need not repeat them. The analysis phase of the CPM requires three steps, and we discuss them below in connection with the network of Figure 6.13.

Step 1. *Identify the normal critical path and the crash critical path.*

It can be ascertained from Figure 6.13 that the network has three different paths, as enumerated in Table 6.9. It is clear from Table 6.9 that the normal critical path is 1–3–6 (45 weeks) and that, under normal conditions, the cost of the entire project is $24,800 (see Table 6.8). Also, our crash critical path is 1–2–4–5–6 (34 weeks) and that, under crash conditions, the cost of the entire project is $32,600 (see Table 6.8). Our task, then, is to design a program that will complete the project within 34 weeks with the least increase in cost above $24,800. It is logical to assume that we shall start by crashing the *least expensive* activity on the normal critical path. The procedure is described and illustrated next.

Table 6.9

Path	Length of Path (weeks)	
	Normal	Crash
1–3–6	45	30
1–2–5–6	42	32
1–2–4–5–6	44	34

Step 2. *On the normal critical path, identify the least expensive activity to crash.*

Crash this activity and note whether the critical path has changed. If not, crash the next least expensive activity on this critical path and so on, until a new critical path emerges, with its own least expensive activity to crash. Continue this process until an *irreducible critical path* on which all activities are on their crash times has been obtained.

We describe in Table 6.10 how step 2 works. Remember, we start our analysis with the *normal critical path*.

Table 6.10. *Network Crashing*

Step 1	Step 2							Step 3
1–3–6 (normal critical path)	(45) →crash 1→ →40 (1–3)	40	(40) →crash 4→ →30 (3–6)	30	30	30	30	→uncrash 3–6 by 4 weeks→ (34)
1–2–5–6	42	42	39	36	36	36 →crash 6→ →32 (2–5)	32	→uncrash 2–5 by 2 weeks→ (34)
1–2–4–5–6	44	(44) →crash 2→ (41) →crash 3→ →38 (1–2) (5–6)	38	(38) →crash 5→ →36 (2–4)	36	(36) →crash 7→ (34) (4–5)	34	- - - - - - → (34)

- Circled numbers show the length of the *critical path* (in weeks).

- $\xrightarrow{\text{crash}}$ indicates the sequential number of the crash (on top of the arrow) and the particular activity that is to be crashed (underneath the arrow) on a specified path.

First Crash. There are only two uncrashed activities on the normal critical path (1–3 and 3–6). Of these, activity 1–3 is the least expensive activity ($200/week), and hence we crash it by 5 weeks. As shown in Table 6.10, this reduces path 1–3–6 to 40 weeks and changes the critical path to 1–2–4–5–6 (44 weeks).

Second Crash. There are four uncrashed activities on the new critical path (1–2, 2–4, 4–5, and 5–6). Of these, activity 1–2 is the least expensive activity ($200/week), and hence we crash it by 3 weeks. As shown in Table 6.10, the critical path is still 1–2–4–5–6; but it has decreased to 41 weeks.

Third Crash. There are three uncrashed activities on the current critical path (2–4, 4–5, and 5–6). Of these, activities 2–4 and 5–6 are least expensive ($400/week). We can crash any of them; however, we crash activity 5–6, as it yields a larger reduction in completion time (3 weeks). As shown in Table 6.10, this changes the critical path to 1–3–6 (40 weeks).

Fourth Crash. There is only one uncrashed activity (i.e., 3–6) on the current critical path. We crash it by 10 weeks and, as shown in Table 6.10, the critical path is again 1–2–4–5–6 (38 weeks).

Fifth Crash. Now there are only two uncrashed activities on the critical path (2–4 and 4–5). Of these, activity 2–4 is least expensive ($400/week) and hence we crash it by 2 weeks. As shown in Table 6.10, this means that we now have two critical paths (1–2–5–6 and 1–2–4–5–6) of 36 weeks each.

Sixth Crash. If we compare the two critical paths (1–2–5–6 and 1–2–4–5–6), we find that only two uncrashed activities remain (2–5 and 4–5). Since activity 2–5 is least expensive ($200/week), we crash it by 4 weeks. As shown in Table 6.10, this results in making path 1–2–4–5–6 the critical path.

Seventh Crash. There now remains only one uncrashed activity on the current critical path (activity 4–5). We crash it, and note that the critical path is still 1–2–4–5–6, but it is irreducible (i.e., all activities on this path are at their crash times). Therefore, we have completed step 2.

Step 3. *Examine the noncritical paths and uncrash activities on such paths (beginning with the most expensive activity) to the point after which further uncrashing will create a longer critical path.*

In Table 6.10 we show how step 3 works. We also note that: (1) the minimum completion time of 34 weeks has been achieved, (2) the noncritical path 1–3–6 is 30 weeks long and hence can be uncrashed by no more than 4 weeks, and (3) noncritical path 1–2–5–6 is 32 weeks long and hence can be uncrashed by no more than 2 weeks.

Of the two activities on the noncritical path 1–3–6, activity 3–6 is most expensive ($240/week), and hence we uncrash it by 4 weeks.

Of the three activities on the noncritical path 1–2–5–6, activities 1–2 and 5–6 cannot be uncrashed, as they are included in the crash critical path 1–2–4–5–6. However, we can uncrash activity 2–5 ($200/week), and hence we uncrash it by 2 weeks.

We have now executed step 3, and our analysis of the CPM network of Figure 6.13 is complete. We have obtained minimum completion time with the least increase in costs above the normal project cost. The final time status of the activities and their cost consequences are summarized in Table 6.11. It should be noted that the minimum project completion time of 34 weeks has been obtained at a cost of $31,240, as compared to the crash project cost of $32,600.

Table 6.11

	Final Time and Cost of Activities		
	Time (weeks)		
Activity	Normal	Crash	Cost (dollars)
1–2		7	1,600
1–3		10	3,000
2–4		6	2,600
2–5	18 weeks total		4,900
3–6	24 weeks total		8,640
4–5		12	6,000
5–6		9	4,500
			31,240

It should be emphasized that the CPM model is well suited to accommodate the reality of budgetary constraints. For example, we can answer this question: What is the minimum project-completion time if our budget for the network in Figure 6.13 is $27,000? To answer this question we start at the end of step 3 and, of the crashed activities at that stage, we uncrash the most expensive activity first. Then, keeping an eye on the critical path, we keep on uncrashing activities until the project cost is reduced to the level of the budget constraint. The reader is encouraged to find the new minimum project completion time, assuming a budget of $27,000.

Also, it should be noted that by following the steps illustrated in Table 6.10, we can easily derive a series of points that relate project cost to specified times of completion. For example, we can answer this question: What is the minimum cost to complete the project in 39 days? (See Problem 6.16.)

6.11
Computer Programs for Network Models

A wide range of computer programs for building, analyzing, and operating network models are available in the market. They differ in terms of their capacity (i.e., the ability to handle the number of activities and events), form of input (card, tape, etc.), form of output, and generation of different types of management reports. In Table 6.12, we list a selected set of computer programs and provide the name of the company that can supply detailed information regarding these programs. It should be mentioned that some of these programs were developed by organizations other than the ones that we have listed as source references.

Table 6.12 *Computer Programs for PERT and CPM*

Name of Company or Source	*Computer Program or Routine*
Burroughs Corporation	• Project Audit Report (PAR) • TIME-PERT
Control Data Corporation	• PERT I and PERT II
General Electric Company	• Automatic Scheduling with Time Integrated Resource Allocation (ASTRA) • Critical Path Method Program • Project Monitor and Control Method (PROMOCOM)
Grumman Data Systems	• CPM***
International Business Machines Corporation	• A Gantt Reporter for Master Planning • CPM–PERT Time • Critical Path and Manpower Leveling System • Critical Path Schedule Bar Graph Generator Program • ICES/360 Project I • Least Cost Estimating and Scheduling (LESS) • Management Planning and Control System (MPACS) • NASA PERT and Companion Cost • PERT II, PERT III, and PERT IV • PERT COST • Resource Allocation and Multi-project Scheduling (RAMPS)
Philco Corporation	• WCC PERT
Radio Corporation of America	• APEX • PERT/TIME
Scientific Time Sharing Corporation	• L-834 (PERT*PLUS) • L-835 (MINIPERT)
Service Bureau Corporation	• General Resource Allocation and Scheduling Procedure (GRASP)

As an actual case study of the application of computers in implementing PERT/CPM systems, we cite the construction of the World Trade Center in New York City. The Port Authority of New York and New Jersey developed a system for the World Trade Center project that incorporated some of the most desirable features of both CPM and PERT. The system was developed to use the Authority's computers (IBM 360/40 installation).

Using the critical path technique, planning and scheduling functions were performed separately. Planning consisted of determining all items of work or activities necessary for completion of a contract, their interrelationships, and order of performance. Scheduling involved translation of the plan into a timetable by assignment of time estimates or durations for the accomplishment of each activity. The incorporation of costs converted the network into a total system.

As each contract was awarded, the Authority received a CPM plan from the contractor including time and cost. Activity durations represented the best time estimates based on experience and past performance. All the CPMs submitted by contractors were integrated into an overall network that contained every item of work in the most efficient sequence.

The CPM network approach then facilitated control of a contract by providing a means for updating the plan and determining the effect of a change in plan on the schedule. The schedule printouts that were used by the contractor to control his work, were also used by the Port Authority's engineers to measure the contractor's performance. They also provided the basis for computing monthly payments to the contractor. The plan and schedule were continually revised to reflect the work as it was performed.

The result was a master construction plan that was flexible enough to adjust to construction contract changes, redesign, accidents, late deliveries, transportation failures, bad weather, labor shortages, and strikes without losing time. When something went wrong, crashing the job with men and overtime would maintain the time schedule.

The CPM model scheduled thousands of elements of World Trade Center construction, construction materials, and up to $10 million each month in contractor payments. It brought together the right men, materials, and tools at the right place for the right work at the right time over a multiyear program.

6.12
Summary

In this chapter, we described the philosophical foundations and general framework of PERT and CPM models. PERT is a probabilistic model, while CPM is a deterministic model. Both models are extremely useful for planning and controlling projects that involve interrelated and interdependent activities.

Such basic concepts of network models as events, activities, expected activity time (t_e), variance of activity time (σ^2), earliest expected event time (T_E), latest allowable event time (T_L), event slack (S), and critical path were explained. These concepts were then utilized in the analysis of a PERT network. We then briefly described the nature and objective of PERT/COST networks. This was followed by a description of CPM networks. The major objective of the CPM model is to gain an insight into the time–cost tradeoffs for the project. This concept was illustrated by analyzing a CPM network. Finally, we provided a reference table containing a number of computer programs for implementing network models.

References

Battersby, A. *Network Analysis for Planning and Scheduling*, 3rd ed. New York: John Wiley & Sons, Inc., 1970.

Cleland, D. I., and W. R. King. *Systems Analysis and Project Management*, 2nd ed. New York: McGraw-Hill Book Company, 1975.

Crowston, W. B. "Models for Project Management." *Sloan Management Review*, Vol. 12, No. 3 (Spring 1971), 25–42.

Kaimann, R. A., and F. R. Probst. "PERT–Review Possibilities." *Journal of Systems Management*, Vol. 23, No. 6 (June 1972), 39–41.

Lee, S. M., and L. J. Moore. *Introduction to Decision Science.* New York: Petrocelli/Charter, Inc., 1975.

McMillan, C., and R. F. Gonzalez. *Systems Analysis: A Computer Approach to Decision Models.* Homewood, Ill.: Richard D. Irwin, Inc., 1973.

Moder, J. J., and C. R. Phillips. *Project Management with CPM and PERT.* New York: Van Nostrand Reinhold Company, 1964.

Sauls, E. "The Use of GERT." *Journal of Systems Management*, Vol. 23, No. 6 (June 1972), 14–17.

Schorberger, R. J. "Custom Tailored PERT/CPM Systems." *Business Horizons*, Vol. 15, No. 6 (Dec. 1972), 64–66.

Siemens, N. "A Simple CPM Time–Cost Tradeoff Algorithm." *Management Science*, Vol. 17, No. 6 (Feb. 1971), B354–B363.

Starr, M. K. *Management: A Modern Approach.* New York: Harcourt Brace Jovanovich, 1971.

Vollmann, T. E. *Operations Management.* Reading, Mass.: Addison-Wesley Publishing Company, Inc., 1973.

Whitehouse, G. E. "Project Management Techniques." *Industrial Engineering*, Vol. 5, No. 3 (Mar. 1973), 24–29.

Whitehouse, G. E. *Systems Analysis and Design Using Network Techniques.* Englewood Cliffs, N.J.: Prentice-Hall, Inc., 1973.

Wiest, J., and F. Levy. *Management Guide to PERT–CPM.* Englewood Cliffs, N.J.: Prentice-Hall, Inc., 1972.

Review Questions and Problems

6.1. Define and illustrate the following terms: (a) network, (b) activity, (c) event, and (d) critical path.

6.2. What are the philosophical foundations of PERT and CPM? Describe how a PERT network is related to a Gantt-type bar chart and milestone chart.

6.3. Describe the basic procedure (five steps) that is common in building a PERT and a CPM network. What are the two characteristics that distinguish PERT and CPM?

6.4. List the various steps in building and analyzing a PERT network and illustrate them with respect to the network shown in Figure 6.14.

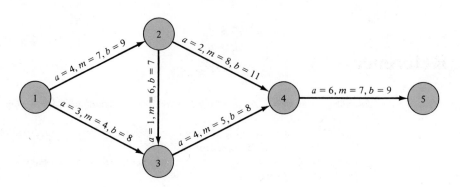

Figure 6.14

6.5. List the various steps in building and analyzing a CPM network and illustrate them with respect to the network shown in Figure 6.15.

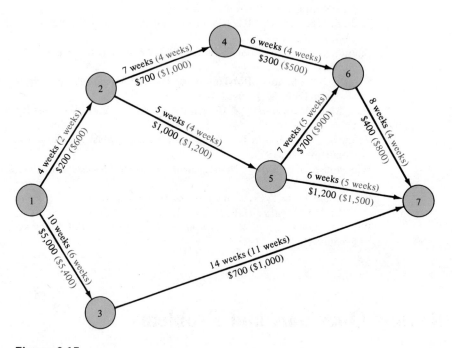

Figure 6.15

6.6. State the rules for calculating T_E and T_L of a PERT network. Explain, in your own words, the rationale for the rules.

6.7. For the network shown in Figure 6.16, calculate the following: T_E, T_L, event slack, and critical path.

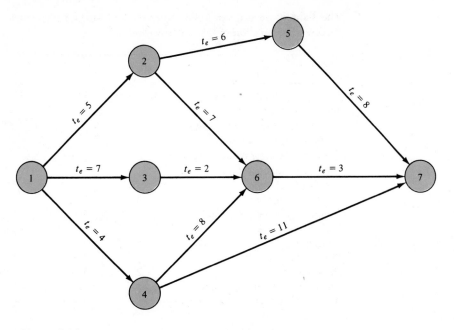

Figure 6.16

6.8. Beth Israel Medical Center is considering the installation of a radiation-therapy unit for serious internal malignancies. This would involve the following activities:

Activity	Description	t_e (weeks)
1–2	Prototype testing	3
2–3	Feasibility study	3
3–4	Board approval	1
4–6	City license	1
2–7	Signing of contractor	1
4–5	State license	1
5–10	Electrical work	3
6–8	Hiring of personnel	2
7–8	Purchasing of equipment	4
8–9	Installation of apparatus	3
5–8	Safety licensing	1
9–10	Testing equipment	1
7–10	Training operators	2

Draw the appropriate PERT network. Determine T_E, T_L, and S for each event. Identify the critical path.

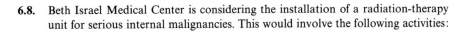

6.9. The Remington Hospital has decided to build a new intensive-care unit on its first floor. This will entail 5,000 square feet, which presently is composed of patients' rooms on an ambulatory-care floor and extra floor space in the central supply wing.

The planning department has designed the following timetable of activities for the successful completion of the intensive-care unit.

Description	t_e (weeks)	Activity
Overall plan and objective	2	1–2
Blueprints and diagrams	3	1–3
Competitive bids placed, sorted, and contract awarded	6	1–4
Ordering fixtures, plumbing and electrical dismantling, removal of walls	5	2–3
Installing supports	3	2–5
Plumbing and heating installation, electrical work	2	3–5
Ceiling and wall preparation	4	4–7
Supply partitioning	6	4–8
Painting and decorating	2	5–6
Floor preparation and tiling	2	6–7
Arrival of and assembling of beds and equipment	5	6–8
Installation of central nurses' facility, telephone and intercom system in patient rooms	3	7–9
Bed-monitoring system, oxygen setups in patient rooms, computer hookup at nurses station	7	8–10
Intensive-care-unit analysis, testing, and inspection	4	9–10

Draw the PERT network, Determine the T_E, T_L, and S for each event. Identify the critical path.

6.10. Jackson Community Hospital has a small automated hematology lab. The following procedure is used in the laboratory operation.

Description	Activity	t_e (minutes)
Blood sample taken	1–2	4
Lab collects sample	2–3	2
Emergency samples given priority	2–4	1
Initial reports on samples	3–4	5
Inadequate samples rejected	3–6	6
Secondary report on samples	4–5	15
Reports on emergency samples sent down	5–6	5
All other reports issued	6–7	9

Design the appropriate PERT network. Calculate T_E, T_L, and S (slack) for each event.

6.11. Senator Papoon's campaign coordinators believe that winning the New York primary is extremely crucial. Hence, they have hired Dewey, Cheatum, and Howe Consulting Company to develop their preliminary plans. The consultants have set up a PERT network for the activities involved in the campaign as follows:

Description	Activity	t_e (weeks)
Signature campaign to get on ballot	1–2	10
Initial district canvassing	2–3	7
Development of marketing approaches	2–4	12
Contact county chairmen	3–4	3
Initiate phase 1 of campaign	3–5	4
Total district canvassing	4–6	9
Secure delegates	5–7	2
Initiate phase 2 of campaign	6–8	15
Preliminary TV, radio advertising program	7–8	7
Senator Papoon starts final phase of campaign	8–9	8

Identify the critical path for the network and the T_E, T_L, and S for each event.

6.12. The Townhouse Construction Company attempts to build houses according to a PERT methodology. The construction activities include:

Description	Activity
Laying foundation	1–2
Digging basement	1–3
Install plumbing and wiring	2–4
Constructing frame	3–5
Insulating	4–5
Finishing	5–6

Management has interviewed its foreman, and has arrived at the following time estimates for the activities:

Activity	a	b	m
1–2	3	9	6
1–3	6	12	9
2–4	4	8	6
3–5	1	4	3
4–5	5	9	7
5–6	5	15	10

Calculate: (a) the expected time, t_e, for individual activities; (b) the completion time of the project; (c) the standard deviation of project completion time; and (d) the time in which management can be 95 percent confident of completing the project.

6.13. The PERT and CPM models are usually associated with large-scale projects. However, the U.S. Air Force Systems decided that it was an appropriate technique for studying the launch procedures for the SRAM (short-range attack missile). Times associated with the launch activities have a beta distribution and are measured in minutes.

Description	Activity	a	m	b
Update navigational data	1–2	1	4	7
Activate on-board computer	1–3	2	4	5
Preliminary systems check	2–4	1	2	4
Tie in radar ranging data	2–5	3	5	12
Input initial firing command	3–4	1	2	4
Input ECM requirements	3–6	2	4	5
Update navigational data	4–7	1	4	7
Final systems check	5–7	2	4	6
Arming procedures activated	6–7	1	2	4

Determine the expected time (t_e) and standard deviation (σ) for each activity. Determine the critical path. What is the time by which the Air Force can be 99 percent confident of launching the missile? What is the probability that all procedures will be completed in 15 minutes? In 13 minutes?

6.14. A marketing firm is studying the possibility of introducing a new product. In order to facilitate the product's development, the firm wants to build a PERT chart based on the following activities:

Description	Activity	Time (weeks)		
		a	m	b
Market survey	1–2	2	3.5	5
Product test 1	1–3	3.5	5	6.5
Market analysis	2–4	4	4.5	7
Product test 2	3–5	3	5	6.5
Small market test	4–5	2.5	4	5.5
Promotion campaign	4–6	4.5	5	5.5
FDA approval	5–6	1	3	4
Product test 3	6–7	2	3	4
Citywide distribution	4–7	6	7.5	10
Test final analysis	7–8	3	4	4.5
General distribution	8–9	8	11	16

Determine the critical path. What is the probability that the entire project would be completed by the end of 30 weeks?

6.15. A prerequisite for the funding of a government research project is the construction of a CPM network. The data on time and cost of various activities are as follows:

	Time (weeks)		Cost (dollars)		_SLOPE_	_CRASH SAVES_	_COST/DAY._
Activity	Normal	Crash	Normal	Crash			
1–2	16	14	1,500	2,000	500	2	250
1–3	25	20	2,000	2,500	500	5	100
2–4	10	7	2,500	4,000	1500	3	500
3–4	32	26	1,000	1,600	600	6	100 / 100
3–5	40	35	1,750	2,250	500	5	550
4–5	16	12	4,000	6,000	2000	4	360
4–6	12	8	3,000	4,200	1200	4	
5–6	9	6	1,500	3,000	1500	3	550

Determine: (a) the normal critical path, (b) the crash critical path, and (c) the minimum project completion time with the least increase in the costs over normal costs.

6.16. The Otto D. Struct Demolition Company has given a bid to level a building complex that has been condemned by the city. The firm, prior to bidding has examined the project and has determined the activities required for the job and their associated times and costs. The relevant information is as follows:

		Time (weeks)		Cost (dollars)	
Activity	Description	Normal	Crash	Normal	Crash
1–2	Surveying	3	2	1,000	1,500
2–3	Internal demolition	4	2	2,000	4,000
2–4	Debris removal	4	3	2,500	3,500
3–5	Raising protective barrier around buildings	3	1	1,500	2,500
4–5	Setting of explosive charges	4	2	6,000	12,000
5–6	Final debris removal	6	3	2,000	5,000

Determine: (a) the normal critical path, (b) the crash critical path, (c) the first and last activities to be crashed, and (d) the minimum project completion time with the least increase in the costs over normal costs.

Find the minimum completion time, assuming a budget of $24,000. What is the minimum cost to complete the project in 12 weeks?

CHAPTER 7

Linear Programming– General Structure and Graphical Analysis

**MAJOR CONCEPTS AND TOPICS
DISCUSSED IN THIS CHAPTER**

Basic Assumptions of Linear Programming

Deterministic conditions, linearity, fixed technology, constant prices and costs, continuous variables, static conditions

Basic Terminology of Linear Programming and Linear Programming Solutions

General Structure of a Linear Programming Problem

Linear objective function
Linear structural constraints
Nonnegativity constraints

The Graphical Approach for Analyzing and Solving a Linear Programming Problem

Special Cases

Multiple optimal solutions
The degenerate basic feasible solution
The unbounded problem
No feasible solution

The Significance of Extreme-Point Solutions

7.1
Introduction

Linear programming is a general model for optimum allocation of scarce or limited resources to competing products (or *activities*) under such assumptions as certainty, linearity, fixed technology, and constant profit per unit. A glimpse of a typical linear programming problem was provided in Section 3.4, where we developed a quantitative formulation of the product-mix problem. Recall that the essence of the product-mix problem is to make an optimum allocation of scarce resources to competing activities.

Linear programming is one of the most versatile, powerful, and useful techniques for making managerial decisions. It has been employed in solving a broad range of problems in business, government, industry, hospitals, libraries, and education. As a technique of decision making, it has demonstrated its value in such diverse areas as production, finance, marketing, research and development, and personnel. Determination of optimal product-mix, transportation schedule, plant location, assignment of personnel and machines, media selection, and investment-portfolio selection are but a few examples of the type of problems that can be solved by linear programming.

The purpose of this chapter is to explain the basic elements and structure of linear programming problems and their solutions. We shall employ the graphical method of solving a linear programming problem to achieve this purpose.

7.2
Basic Assumptions, Terminology, and General Structure

Let us consider a product-mix problem in which two sizes of paper towels (products *A* and *B*) are to be produced by utilizing three different processes (cutting, folding, and packaging). The paper toweling is received from another manufacturing firm in the form of large rolls. These rolls are cut, folded, and packaged in two sizes. The technical specifications of the problem and the production processes are summarized in Table 7.1.

Table 7.1 *Process Time Data per Unit of Product*

	Product		Capacity Constraint
Process	*A*	*B*	*per Time Period*
Cutting	10	6	2,500
Folding	5	10	2,000
Packaging	1	2	500
Profit per Unit	$23	$32	

The data in the table represent the technical specifications of the two products. The production of 1 unit of product *A*, for example, requires 10 units of processing time (say minutes) in the cutting department, 5 units in the folding department, and 1 unit in the packaging department. When sold, product *A* yields a profit contribution of $23/unit. The total available capacity in the cutting department is 2,500 units. Similar information is available in Table 7.1 for producing 1 unit of product *B*. Note that each product must be processed through all three departments.

Our objective is to design or identify a production program that will maximize profit and yet not demand resources in excess of those that are assumed as given in the problem. In other words, our task is to design or identify the optimal program.

7.2.1 BASIC ASSUMPTIONS

We now state some important assumptions with respect to the information contained in Table 7.1. These assumptions also hold in the general linear programming model.

1. We assume that the manager here is *completely certain* (i.e., deterministic conditions) regarding technology, resources, strategies (different production programs), and their respective consequences (profits). That is, each strategy results in a unique payoff.
2. We assume that all relationships in the problem exhibit *linearity*.[1] The assumption of linearity is quite useful, and often approximates reality in such problems as blending of gasoline, determination of optimal diets, and production planning and scheduling.[2]
3. We assume a *fixed technology*. That is, we consider production requirements to be fixed during the planning horizon.[3]
4. We assume that *profit per unit* of each product remains *constant*, regardless of the level of production.
5. We assume that all decision variables are *continuous*. That is, we can produce products in fractional units. This is often referred to as the assumption of *divisibility*.
6. Only *one* decision is required for the planning horizon. This means that linear programming is a *static* model. This implies a *single-stage* decision problem (as opposed to a multistage, dynamic decision problem).
7. All variables must assume *nonnegative* values.

---

[1] The term "linear" implies proportionality and additivity. *Proportionality* refers to the fact that doubling (or tripling) the production of a product will exactly double (or triple) the profit and the required resources. *Additivity* means that the effect of two different programs of production is the same as that of a joint program involving the same activity (production) levels.

[2] Whenever the assumption of linearity is not warranted, the problem might be expressed as a nonlinear programming problem. Nonlinear programming deals with those problems in which the objective function and/or constraints are nonlinear. For a simple presentation of some nonlinear programming methods, see Chapter 7 of Loomba and Turban [1974].

[3] By *planning horizon* we refer to that time period for which the manager is designing the production program.

7.2.2 BASIC TERMINOLOGY

Linear programming is a method of determining an optimal program of interdependent activities in view of limited resources that are available to the manager during a specified period of time. As explained earlier, the term "linear" implies proportionality and additivity. The term *program* refers to a course of action covering a specified period of time. A specific production schedule, product mix, stock portfolio, advertising media mix, are examples of programs. Since it is always possible to design a number of different programs, managers attempt to identify those programs that are best or optimal in terms of some measure of effectiveness. A program is *optimal* if it *maximizes* or *minimizes* some measure or criterion of effectiveness, such as profit, cost, or sales.

The term *programming* refers to a systematic procedure by which a particular program or plan of action is designed. Programming consists of a series of instructions and computational rules for solving a problem that can be executed manually or can be fed into the computer. In Chapter 8 we describe in detail the simplex method, one of several available methods that can systematically solve linear programming problems. The simplex method was developed by the American mathematician George B. Dantzig in 1947.

The term *activity* refers to any candidate (product, service, project, etc.) that is competing with other candidates (or activities) for limited resources. Thus, in Table 7.1, we have two competing activities (products *A* and *B*). A specific amount of production of a product measures its *activity level*.

Note that the three manufacturing departments represent the *resources*, and these resources are *limited* in terms of available capacities during the planning horizon. In addition to the terminology described above, we shall define and explain several other terms and concepts relating to linear programming problems, and their solutions, in this and the next three chapters.

7.2.3 GENERAL STRUCTURE OF A LINEAR PROGRAMMING PROBLEM

For the problem of Table 7.1, the optimal program is the program that will yield maximum profit. If the problem had been of the type in which the manager was mainly interested in costs, the objective would have been the minimization of costs, and the optimal program will result in minimum costs. The idea is that in any linear programming problem, the manager must identify a measurable objective or criterion of effectiveness. This type of objective can usually be quantified and becomes the objective function of the problem. Assumption of linearity implies that it is a linear objective function. If we denote the profit by the variable Z, and the number of units of A and B to be produced by the variables X and Y, respectively, then, for our problem, the linear objective function is given by[4]

$$Z = 23X + 32Y \tag{7.1}$$

---

[4] In large linear programming problems, different variables are usually denoted by $X_1, X_2, X_3, \ldots$. This procedure has the advantage of accommodating as many variables as needed, since the entire real-number system is available for specific identification. At the elementary levels of exposition, it is convenient to use a system that does not involve subscripts.

The objective function, it should be noted, is nothing more than a mathematical expression that describes the manner in which profit accumulates as a function of the number of different products produced. Note also that the objective function relates the criterion variable Z (profit) to decision variables X and Y (number of units of A and B).

A quick examination of any linear function indicates that its maximization, or minimization, does not make sense without imposing some sort of additional constraints. For example, the maximization of the linear objective function given by (7.1) will result in a value of positive infinity. However, when such a function is subject to certain constraints (e.g., those representing the limited resources), only those values of X and Y can be considered that will not violate the constraints implied by the problem specifications.

Referring again to Table 7.1, we note that the current capacity of each manufacturing department is fixed for the planning horizon, and hence we have limited resources. The technical specifications of the problem and how they relate to the fixed resource capacities are expressed by a set of structural constraints. The assumption of linearity implies that such a set is linear. Since any production program (i.e., values of X and Y) must be such that it cannot demand resources in excess of the given capacities, the linear structural constraints for our problem must be expressed as inequalities of the "less than or equal to" type. For our problem, there are three structural constraints:

$$\left. \begin{array}{r} 10X + 6Y \leqslant 2{,}500 \\ 5X + 10Y \leqslant 2{,}000 \\ 1X + 2Y \leqslant 500 \end{array} \right\} \tag{7.2}$$

Although all inequalities in (7.2) are of the "less than or equal to" type, it should be noted here that the linear structural constraints can be of three types:

Type	Mathematical Symbol
Less than or equal to	$\leqslant$
Greater than or equal to	$\geqslant$
Equality	$=$

A production program, by definition, must be such that a particular activity or candidate is either included in, or excluded from, the production program. This means that negative production, which has no physical counterpart, is not permitted in the solution of a linear programming problem. This obvious fact is made an integral part of the linear programming problem by stating a set of nonnegativity constraints. For our problem, the nonnegativity constraints are

$$X \geqslant 0, \qquad Y \geqslant 0 \tag{7.3}$$

We can now summarize the three components of any linear programming problem. These components describe the general structure of the linear programming model.[5]

1. A linear objective function.
2. A set of linear structural constraints.
3. A set of nonnegativity constraints.

The linear programming problem considered in this section can be stated mathematically as:

Maximize

$$Z = 23X + 32Y$$ linear objective function

subject to the constraints

$$10X + 6Y \leqslant 2,500$$
$$5X + 10Y \leqslant 2,000$$ linear structural constraints   (7.4)
$$1X + 2Y \leqslant 500$$

and

$$X \geqslant 0, \quad Y \geqslant 0$$ nonnegativity constraints

Our problem is to design an optimal program. What this means mathematically is that we must choose those values of X and Y that will maximize (7.1) and not violate the constraints given by (7.2) and (7.3). Note that the complete problem stated by (7.4) is nothing more than a mathematical statement of the situation confronted by the manager.

We now make some additional remarks regarding terminology.

1. The variables included in the linear objective function (e.g., X and Y), which we have termed activities or candidates, are also called the *decision variables*. The manager's task here is twofold: which variables to include in the objective function; and what values to assign to these variables to optimize the objective function. The question of what the activities or the decision variables are is purely a matter of managerial judgment based on experience and market conditions. However, once the choice has been made as to what the decision variables in a given situation are, the problem of assigning values to these variables (i.e., how much to produce) is solved by the linear programming model.

2. The coefficients of the decision variables in the objective function are termed *profit* (for the maximization case) or *cost* (for the minimization case) *coefficients* (or simply *objective function coefficients*). For example, the numbers 23 and 32 are

---

[5] Linear programming is one branch of mathematical programming. Any mathematical programming problem also consists essentially of three components: (1) an objective function that can be linear or nonlinear; (2) a set of structural constraints that can be linear or nonlinear; and (3) a set of constraints on the variables that can be nonnegativity constraints, constraints that specify ranges, or constraints which specify that variables can assume only discrete or integer values. See Loomba and Turban [1974, p. 4]. For a brief discussion of integer programming, see Loomba [1976, Chap. 11].

the two profit coefficients in (7.1). The information regarding these coefficients is obtained from the sales department. Profit or cost coefficients are denoted by C_j.

3. The coefficients of the decision variables in the structural constraints are known as *input–output coefficients*. The prefix "input–output" is appropriate because the value of the coefficients here indicates the magnitude of specific input resource required to achieve an output level of 1 unit. Thus, as seen in the first constraint of (7.2), 10 units of the cutting resource is needed to produce 1 unit of A. Similarly, the other input–output coefficients in (7.2) express the state of production technology of the problem. The information regarding input–output coefficients comes from such departments of the firm as the production department and research and development. The pertinent questions for the manager here relate to the reliability of information and possible future changes resulting from changes in technology. The input–output coefficients are denoted by a_{ij}.

4. The numbers on the right-hand side of the structural constraints express the maximum availability of resources ($\leqslant$), minimum requirements of certain characteristics or variation thereof ($\geqslant$), or exact requirements ($=$). As seen from (7.2), all the constraints of our problem are of the "less than or equal to" type. The information regarding the magnitude of the capacity or requirement levels comes from a number of sources, such as the finance department, production department, and the quality-control department. Whether or not to acquire additional capacities of specified resources is an important managerial decision. As we shall see in Chapter 9, linear programming provides valuable assistance in making such decisions. The numbers on the right-hand side are denoted by b_i.

Finally, we observe, without proof, that if a linear programming problem can be solved, it can yield an infinite number of solutions.[6] This property will become evident when we present a graphical approach for analyzing and solving linear programming problems. This property also means that if linear programming problems are to be solved in a finite number of steps, some efficient method of search must be available for identifying the optimal program. The simplex method, to be described in Chapter 8, is one of the efficient methods that have been developed for solving linear programming problems.

7.3
Linear Programming—A Graphical Approach

When stated mathematically, the technical specifications of any linear programming problem are translated as a certain number of rows and a certain number of columns. The number of rows (constraints) is determined by the number of resources, or characteristics, specified by the technology of the problem. For example, in the product-mix problem of Section 7.2, we have three rows (constraints). The number of columns (variables) is determined by the number of activities or candidates. For example, in the example of Section 7.2, we have two columns (variables). We shall always denote the number of rows by the letter m and the number of columns by the letter n. The number of rows and the number of columns of the structural constraints determine the *dimensions* of a

---

[6] For an explanation, see Sections 7.3.3 and 7.8.

linear programming problem. In general, we can think of a linear programming problem as an $m \times n$ (read m by n) problem.

How can we proceed to graph such problems of $m \times n$ dimensions? One obvious restriction is that to graph a set of structural constraints, we are limited to those cases in which either the number of rows, or the number of columns, is 2 or less.[7] If the number of columns (i.e., activities or variables) is 2, we can consider any $m \times 2$ problem and graph the constraints in the two-dimensional activity space. For example, we have graphed in Figure 7.6 the problem that is shown in Table 7.1 and stated mathematically by (7.4). If the number of rows (i.e., resources or constraints) is two, we can consider any $2 \times n$ problem and graph the constraints in the two-dimensional *resource space*.[8] We shall restrict our discussion of the graphical method to *activity space*

The preceding remarks were made to indicate that, theoretically, the graphical approach can be employed to solve any $m \times 2$ or $2 \times n$ linear programming problem. That is, we are, for all practical purposes, restricted to a two-dimensional space. The graphical method is, therefore, not an efficient method of solving large real-life linear programming problems. The value of the graphical approach lies in its ability to show, without the benefit of a rigorous mathematical proof, several different characteristics of linear programming problems and their solutions.

The graphical method consists of graphing the structural constraints and thereby determining the region of feasible solutions, graphing the objective function, and identifying the optimal solution. We shall illustrate the graphical method by solving the problem given in Table 7.1 and stated mathematically in (7.4).

7.3.1 GRAPHING THE STRUCTURAL CONSTRAINTS

As mentioned earlier, the structural constraints can be of three types: (1) less than or equal to ($\leqslant$), (2) greater than or equal to ($\geqslant$), or (3) equality ($=$). Next, we provide an example of each type:

Constraint	Graphical Representation
$2X + 4Y \leqslant 20$	Figure 7.1a
$2X + 4Y \geqslant 20$	Figure 7.1b
$2X + 4Y = 20$	Figure 7.1c

Note that in Figure 7.1a, the "less than or equal to" type of constraint is represented by the entire shaded area below the line $2X + 4Y = 20$. Similarly, in Figure 7.1b the "greater than or equal to" type of constraint is represented by the entire shaded area above the line $2X + 4Y = 20$. In Figure 7.1c, the equality

---

[7] It is possible to graph in a three-dimensional space; however, we ignore that option because it is neither efficient nor does it have any significant pedagogical value.

[8] See Loomba [1976, p. 74].

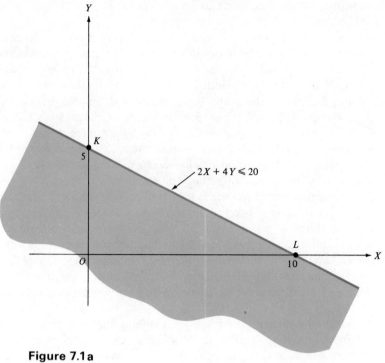

Figure 7.1a

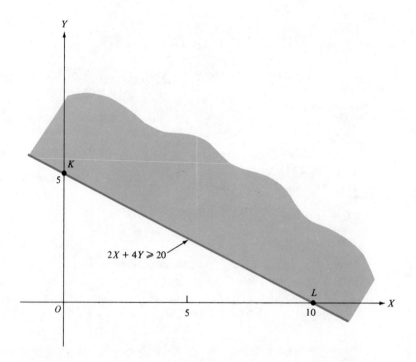

Figure 7.1b

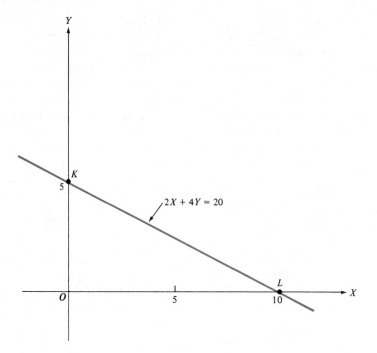

Figure 7.1c

constraint is represented by a line alone; no shaded area is involved.[9] It should be noted here that if we plot the constraints $X \geqslant 0$ and $Y \geqslant 0$ in each of Figures 7.1a to 7.1c, the result will be to restrict everything to the first quadrant.

Let us now return to our problem of Table 7.1. For each of the three constraints embodied in Table 7.1 we can write an inequality of the "less than or equal to" type. It is desirable that the reader gain familiarity with these inequalities and their physical interpretation. Let us consider the inequality that represents the cutting department capacity. If we let variables X and Y denote, respectively, the units of products A and B to be produced, the inequality for the cutting department is

$$10X + 6Y \leqslant 2{,}500$$

This inequality is simply an algebraic way of expressing the information given in Table 7.1 in connection with the cutting process. It gives algebraic expression to one of the three structural constraints in our problem. A descriptive translation of this inequality is: Each unit of product A requires 10 units of the cutting capacity, and each unit of product B requires 6 units of the cutting capacity; the amount of A (i.e., a specific value of X) and the amount of B (i.e., a specific value of Y) to be produced should be such that the total demand on the capacity of the cutting department does not exceed 2,500 units. Thus, any specific combination of values of X and Y that does not violate this and the other given constraints is a *feasible solution*.

[9] When graphed, a linear equation with two variables generates a straight line in a two-dimensional space. A linear equation with three variables generates a *plane* in a three-dimensional space. A linear equation with four or more variables generates a *hyperplane* in a space of appropriate dimensions.

Let us assume that we wish to produce just 2 units of product A and 2 units of product B. This program ($X = 2$, $Y = 2$) can give us two types of information in connection with each resource: (1) the total capacity used by this program, and (2) whether or not the capacity constraint has been violated. For this program the total cutting capacity used is $10(2) + 6(2) = 32$ units, and the remaining cutting capacity, therefore, is $2,500 - 32 = 2,468$ units. The constraint on the capacity of the cutting department obviously has not been violated. For each program, a similar check must be made of all resources.

As can easily be ascertained, $X = 2$, and $Y = 10$ is also a possible solution for this problem. Furthermore, this program results in a higher level of profit than our first program of $X = 2$ and $Y = 2$. However, there may be other programs that will yield even larger profits than the second program ($X = 2$, $Y = 10$). If so, we must discover them. This suggests that the search for a better program must continue until an optimal solution is determined. The optimal solution for our problem is the specific program that will yield the highest level of profit without violating any of the structural constraints. We shall identify the optimal solution by employing the graphical approach.

The first task in the graphical approach is to write all the constraints for the problem and then graph them in the activity space.[10] In our problem, for cutting capacity,

$$10X + 6Y \leqslant 2,500 \tag{7.5}$$

for folding capacity,

$$5X + 10Y \leqslant 2,000 \tag{7.6}$$

and for packaging capacity,

$$1X + 2Y \leqslant 500 \tag{7.7}$$

This set of inequalities can be graphed easily. Inequality (7.5), for example, is graphed in Figure 7.2.

To obtain the X and Y intercepts for inequality (7.5), we proceed as follows. Let $X = 0$; then

$$Y = \frac{2,500}{6} = 416\frac{2}{3} \quad \text{(point K)}$$

Let $Y = 0$; then

$$X = \frac{2,500}{10} = 250 \quad \text{(point L)}$$

Joining points K and L gives us a line whose equation is

$$10X + 6Y = 2,500$$

However, since we do not wish to plot this equation, but rather the inequality $10X + 6Y \leqslant 2,500$, the region of interest is represented by the shaded area in Figure 7.2. Clearly, the shaded area also includes negative values of X and Y

---

[10] We speak of *activity space* because here the two-dimensional space in which we graph the inequalities will have as its coordinates the activities X and Y. If we graph the problem so that "resources" are the coordinates, we have a *resource space*. In the resource space, activities are plotted as rays. For a simple discussion, see Loomba [1976, pp. 74–78].

Linear Programming—General Structure and Graphical Analysis   Chapter 7

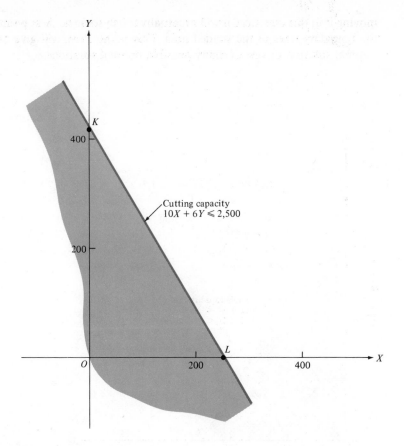

Figure 7.2

which imply negative production and have no real physical counterpart. In order to exclude any possibility of negative production, a set of nonnegativity constraints is introduced. In our example, the nonnegativity constraints are $X \geqslant 0$, $Y \geqslant 0$; and they imply that we are restricted to producing zero or more units of products A and B.

The addition of nonnegativity constraints restricts the area of possible solutions to the first quadrant of the XY plane, as shown in Figure 7.3. Similarly, Figures 7.4 and 7.5 show the areas of possible nonnegative solutions for the folding and packaging capacities, respectively. If we combine Figures 7.3, 7.4, and 7.5, we obtain Figure 7.6, the shaded area of which represents the region of all feasible solutions for our problem.

Any point in the shaded area and/or on the boundary of the shaded area of Figure 7.6 is a possible solution. In other words, *there is an infinite number of solutions for this problem if we assume divisibility of the production units.* Our objective is to pick at least one point (X, Y) from the shaded (feasible) area of Figure 7.6 that will maximize profit or yield the highest value for the linear objective function: $Z = 23X + 32Y$.

How can we proceed to accomplish this? It is at this point that we are guided by the objective function. If, somehow, we can graph the objective function in Figure 7.6, determine its direction of maximum increase, and start and keep on moving it in this direction, it will eventually touch some farthest point on one of the boundary lines of the shaded area. This point, then, will give us a unique optimal solution or one of many possible optimal solutions.

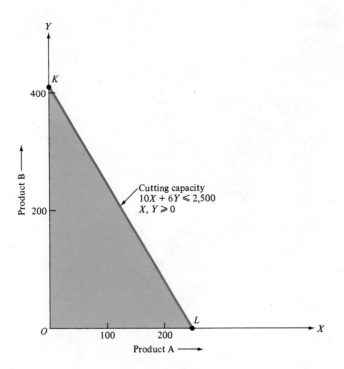

Figure 7.3

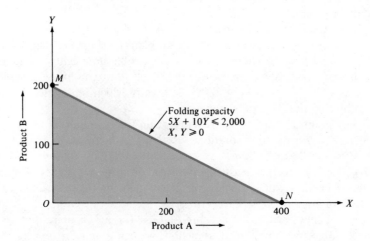

Figure 7.4

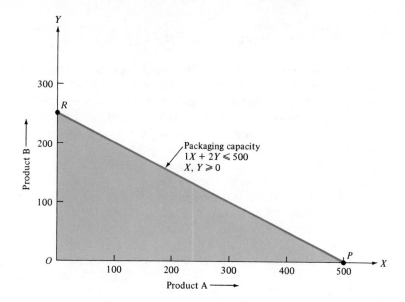

Figure 7.5

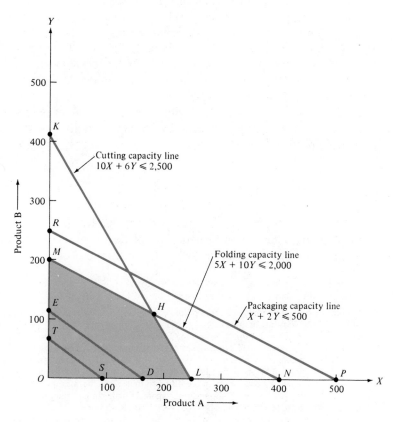

Figure 7.6

7.3.2 GRAPHING THE OBJECTIVE FUNCTION

The objective function can be of the minimizing or the maximizing type. For our problem we are to maximize the linear profit function: $Z = 23X + 32Y$. This function can be graphed for different values of total profit, such as $736 or $1,472. The graph of the linear profit function for a specific amount of profit results in a straight line and is known as an *isoprofit line*. Each point on a specific isoprofit line corresponds to a program; and each point yields the same profit as any other point on that line. How do we graph an isoprofit line? By choosing a specific profit level, finding those values of X and Y that yield this profit level, and then joining these two values with a straight line. For example, how many units of product A alone, and how many units of product B alone, are required to produce a profit of, say $736?[11] Since profit per unit of product A is $23, the answer is obviously $X = 32$. Similarly, since profit per unit of product B is $32, it will require a value of $Y = 23$ to produce a profit of $736. Thus, one set of two isoprofit points is $X = 32$, $Y = 0$; and $X = 0$, $Y = 23$. Another set of isoprofit points in Figure 7.6 is $X = 96$, $Y = 0$ (point S), and $X = 0$, $Y = 69$ (point T). When we join these two points (S and T), we obtain the $2,208 isoprofit line ST, as shown in Figure 7.6. All points on this line are within the region of feasible solutions; hence, all represent feasible programs, each yielding a profit of $2,208. Thus, an isoprofit line is the locus of all points (i.e., all possible combinations of X and Y) that yield the same profit. In a similar fashion we could have drawn other isoprofit lines, yielding different levels of profit contribution. For example, line DE in Figure 7.6 represents the $3,680 isoprofit line. A comparison of lines DE and ST shows that the $3,680 isoprofit line ($DE$) is parallel to the $2,208 isoprofit lines ($ST$) (i.e., they have the same slopes) and is located farther away from the origin. This was to be expected, since per unit profit of each product is fixed, and larger total profit will be obtained as we move away from the origin. Note also that, in the two-dimensional activity space, the slope of any isoprofit line is determined by the profit coefficients in the linear objective function. (Why?). For example, in our problem the slope of any profit line is given by $-\frac{23}{32}$.

7.3.3 FINDING THE OPTIMAL SOLUTION

Let us examine the convex[12] polygon *OMHL* shown in Figure 7.6. We assert, without giving a formal mathematical proof, that an optimal solution to a linear programming problem can always be found at one of the corner (or extreme)

---

[11] Any arbitrary profit figure will work. However, it is always convenient to pick a profit number that gives an integer as an answer and places the isoprofit line within the region of feasible solutions.

[12] A convex polygon consists of a set of points having the property that the segment joining any two points in the set is entirely in the convex set. There is a mathematical theorem which states: The points that are simultaneous solutions of a system of linear inequalities of the "less than or equal to" type form a polygonal convex set. For purposes of visualization, refer to Figures 7.7 and 7.8; the former represents a polygonal convex set, whereas the latter does not. Note that if points C and D in Figure 7.8 are joined, the definition of a convex polygon is seen to be violated.

Although Figures 7.7 and 7.8 are in two-dimensional space, the concept of a convex set is general and can be extended to any n-dimensional space. Furthermore, since all linear programming problems contain structural constraints that are of the "less than or equal to" type or, if not, can be converted to the "less than or equal to" type, the solutions to linear programming problems form a convex set

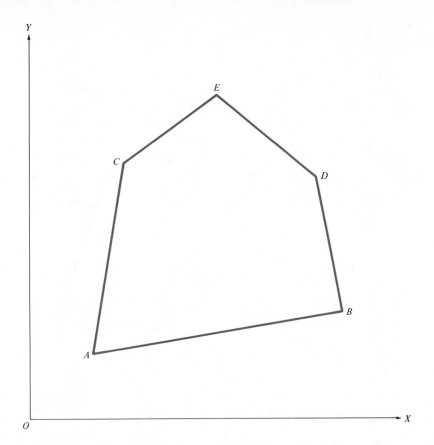

Figure 7.7. Convex Set.

points of the region of feasible solutions. This can be seen by examining three possible situations regarding the relationships between the linear objective function of a problem involving just two activities and the corner points of the convex set. Let us examine the feasible region $OMHL$ in Figure 7.6, which reflects our two-activity problem. First, if per unit profit of A is overwhelmingly large as compared to per unit profit of B, we must produce A alone, and hence the optimal solution must be at the corner point L. Second, if the per unit profit of B is overwhelmingly large as compared to per unit profit of A, we must produce B alone and the optimal solution must be at the corner point M. Third, if the relationship of per unit profits for products A and B is such that the optimal solution cannot include just one product, but must include both products, the optimal solution can always be located at a corner point, such as H in Figure 7.6. The truth of the third case can easily be substantiated if we consider the slope of an isoprofit line with respect to the slopes of lines MH and HL in Figure 7.6.[13]

The above remarks were made with reference to Figure 7.6, but they are meant to assert the following general statement: If there exists a solution to a linear

[13] If the isoprofit line is parallel to MH, each point on MH (including point H) is an optimal solution. Similarly, if the isoprofit line is parallel to HL, each point on HL (including point H) is an optimal solution. If the isoprofit line is not parallel to any boundary line (such as MH and HL), it pays to move it as far away from the origin as possible, and we shall eventually stop at point H.

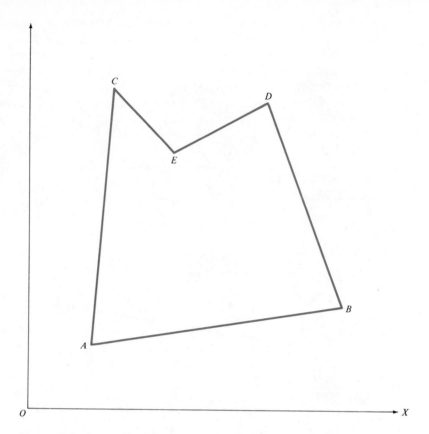

Figure 7.8. Nonconvex Set.

programming problem, an optimal solution can always be found at an extreme (or corner) point of the convex set of feasible solutions.

Let us hark back to our problem and the consideration of the isoprofit lines in Figure 7.6. Since the objective is to maximize profit, we should keep on drawing such isoprofit lines for higher profits as long as any part of the highest isoprofit line remains within the feasible (shaded) region. Obviously, we shall have to stop only when we have hit either a corner point of the convex polygon $OMHL$ or one of its boundary lines. In either case we would have found our optimal solution(s).

In a profit-maximization problem involving only two activities the isoprofit line farthest from the origin but still within the feasible-solution area is used to determine the optimal solution. Two cases can arise. First, this farthest feasible isoprofit line may be coincident with one of the boundary lines of the convex polygon. If this is the case, all points on the boundary line that is coincident with the isoprofit line are feasible, as well as optimal, solutions.[14] Second, the farthest feasible isoprofit line may not coincide with any of the boundary lines of the convex polygon. If this is the case, one of the corner points of the convex polygon provides the optimal and unique solution.

[14] In a two-activity case, if the slope of any of the boundary lines is the same as that of any isoprofit line, we can conclude that the linear programming problem has many alternative optimal solutions. In such a case any isoprofit line will be either parallel to or coincident with one of the boundary lines of the convex polygon.

In our case, we observe that the isoprofit line farthest from the origin and still within the region of feasible solutions passes through the point H. Hence, point H represents the optimal solution from among an infinite number of solutions represented by the shaded area of Figure 7.6.

The coordinates of the point H can be determined either directly from the graph or by a simultaneous solution of the two lines intersecting at point H. The equations of these lines, representing the cutting and folding capacities, are already known to us. The determination of the coordinates of point H is illustrated next. For the cutting department,

$$10X + 6Y = 2,500$$

or

$$Y = \frac{1,250}{3} - \frac{5}{3}X \tag{7.8}$$

For the folding department,

$$5X + 10Y = 2,000$$

or

$$Y = 200 - \frac{1}{2}X \tag{7.9}$$

Equating Equations (7.8) and (7.9), we obtain

$$\frac{1,250}{3} - \frac{5}{3}X = 200 - \frac{1}{2}X$$

or

$$X = \frac{1,300}{7} = 185\frac{5}{7} \text{ units} \tag{7.10}$$

Substituting (7.10) in (7.9), we find that

$$Y = 200 - \frac{1}{2}\left(\frac{1,300}{7}\right)$$

$$= \frac{750}{7} = 107\frac{1}{7} \text{ units}$$

Hence, the optimal solution is to produce $\frac{1,300}{7}$ units of X (product A) and $\frac{750}{7}$ units of Y (product B). The profit for this program is

$$23\left(\frac{1,300}{7}\right) + 32\left(\frac{750}{7}\right) = \$7,700$$

When we substitute $X = \frac{1,300}{7}$ and $Y = \frac{750}{7}$ in the inequalities (7.5) to (7.7), we note that this program fully utilizes the capacities of the cutting and folding departments but leaves 100 units of the packaging department capacity unused.

This can also be observed by examining Figure 7.6, in which the packaging-capacity line is far above the shaded area.

Referring again to Figure 7.6, we make the following comments:

1. Any solution that does not violate the structural and the nonnegativity constraints is a *feasible solution*.

2. Because of the assumption that all variables are continuous, a linear programming problem has an *infinite number of solutions*. Each and every point in the set *OMHL* represents a possible or feasible solution. The set of such solutions is a convex set, regardless of the number of activities or constraints involved. For the two-dimensional case, the convex set is represented as a shaded area such as that shown in Figure 7.6.

3. The structural constraints can be of two types: redundant or *nonbinding*, and active or *binding*. As can be seen in Figure 7.6, the packaging-capacity constraint is nonbinding. That is why the line representing the packaging capacity does not determine any of the boundary lines of the convex set *OMHL*. Also, because the packaging capacity is nonbinding, it is not fully utilized. Note that our optimal solution leaves 100 units of the packaging capacity unused.

4. Of the infinite number of solutions defined by the convex set, the optimal solution can always be found at one of its extreme points. Hence, an efficient search technique is to test only the extreme point (or corner) solutions for optimality. Any extreme point solution is called a basic feasible solution.[15] The solutions at points *O*, *M*, *H*, and *L* are basic feasible solutions.

7.4
The Minimization Problem

In this section, we shall apply the graphical method to solve a minimization problem. The structural constraints of the problem will be graphed in the activity space.

Let us consider a minimization problem in which we are to determine the least-cost diet. The problem calls for meeting minimum weekly requirements of two nutrients by purchasing a mix of two foods. The specifications for the problem are shown in Table 7.2.

---

[15] Actually, there are two types of basic feasible solutions: *nondegenerate basic feasible* and *degenerate basic feasible*. The distinction is in terms of number of positive variables in a solution and the number of structural constraints, m. If the number of positive variables in the solution equals m, we have a nondegenerate basic feasible solution. If it is less than m, we have a degenerate basic feasible solution. In this book, we shall use the term "basic feasible solution" or just "basic" solution to denote nondegenerate basic feasible solutions. A degenerate basic feasible solution is shown by point A in Figure 7.11. Also, see Figure 7.14.

Table 7.2

Nutrient	Food A	Food B	Weekly Requirement (milligrams)
I	2	3	3,500
II	6	2	7,000
Cost per Unit of Food (cents)	10.0	4.5	

The problem can be stated mathematically as

Minimize

$$Z = 10X + 4.5Y$$

subject to the constraints

$$2X + 3Y \geqslant 3,500$$
$$6X + 2Y \geqslant 7,000$$

and

$$X, \quad Y \geqslant \quad 0$$

(7.11)

We have graphed this problem in Figure 7.9.

The graphical procedure for solving a two-activity minimization case is exactly the same as the one described for the maximization case. The only difference is that the linear objective function is graphed in the form of isocost lines, as opposed to the isoprofit lines of the maximization case. After the structural constraints of the problem have been graphed to define the region of feasible solutions, we can draw isocost lines of successively lower values. The isocost line that is closest to the origin and yet lies within the convex set will help identify the optimal solution. The optimal solution, as the reader can verify from Figure 7.9, is found at the corner point C.[16]

7.5
Special Cases

In most cases, linear programming problems yield unique optimal solutions. However, the following special cases should be noted: (1) multiple optimal solutions, (2) degenerate basic feasible solution, (3) unbounded solution, and (4) no feasible solution.

[16] The optimal solution: food A = 1,000 units, food B = 500 units, and total cost = $122.50.

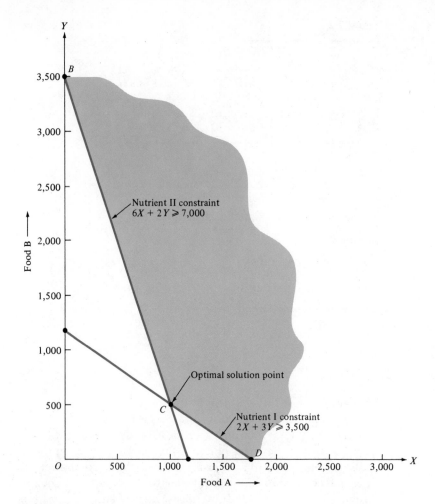

Figure 7.9

7.5.1 MULTIPLE OPTIMAL SOLUTIONS

A linear programming problem yields multiple optimal solutions whenever its objective function is parallel to any one of the boundary lines (i.e., constraints) that define the set of feasible solutions. Let us illustrate by considering the following problem.

Maximize

$$Z = 10X + 20Y$$

subject to the constraints

$$10X + 6Y \leqslant 2{,}500$$
$$5X + 10Y \leqslant 2{,}000$$
$$1X + 2Y \leqslant 500$$

and

$$X, \quad Y \geqslant 0$$

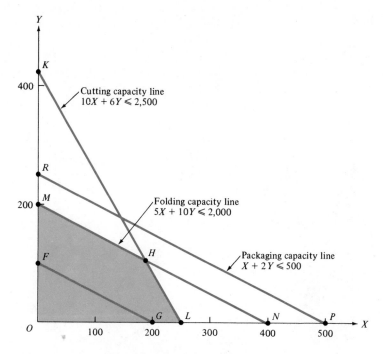

Figure 7.10. Multiple Optimal Solutions.

We have graphed this problem in Figure 7.10. Note that the $2,000 isoprofit line FG is parallel to the boundary line MH. If we draw successively higher isoprofit lines away from the origin, we can observe that the highest isoprofit line is the one that will be coincident with the line MH. This means that the two corner points M and H, as well as any other point on the line MH, represent optimal solutions. Hence, we have a special case in which we have multiple optimal solutions rather than a unique optimal solution.[17] The existence of multiple optimal solutions gives the manager some degree of flexibility in terms of determining the exact product mix.

7.5.2 THE DEGENERATE BASIC FEASIBLE SOLUTION

A degenerate basic feasible solution, like the nondegenerate basic feasible solution, is also a corner-point solution. However, the degenerate basic feasible solution has the property that the number of positive variables that comprise the solution is less than the number of structural constraints m. A graphical illustration of a degenerate basic feasible solution (at point A) is provided in Figure 7.11.

---

[17] In linear programming problems, if we can identify two optimal corner points (such as M and H), then any *linear combination* of these points is also an optimal solution. See Section C.6.3 in Appendix C for the definition of a linear combination.

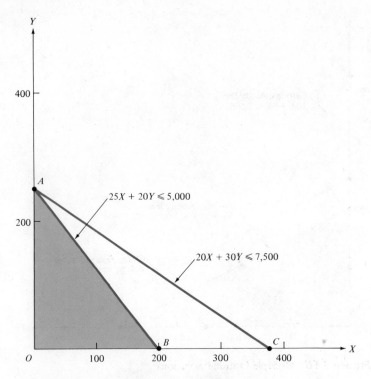

Figure 7.11. Degenerate Basic Feasible Solution (at Point A).

Let us consider the following problem.

Maximize

$$Z = 40X + 50Y$$

subject to the constraints

$$25X + 20Y \leqslant 5,000$$
$$20X + 30Y \leqslant 7,500$$

and

$$X, \quad Y \geqslant \quad 0$$

(7.12)

The constraint set (7.12) has been graphed in Figure 7.11.

The optimal solution, as the reader can verify, is at point A, which means that $X = 0, Y = 250$. That is, the number of *positive* variables in the optimal solution is 1, while the number of structural constraints, m, is 2. Hence, it is a degenerate basic feasible solution. Note also that the second constraint is active just at one point in Figure 7.11. The problem of degeneracy is discussed further in Chapter 8.

7.5.3 THE UNBOUNDED PROBLEM

The constraint set of a linear programming problem can be either bounded or unbounded. Figure 7.6 is an example of a bounded problem because the convex set $OMHL$ is closed from all sides. In such problems, there is always an upper (or lower) bound on the objective function. For example, the upper bound on the profit in our problem was $7,700. Most real-life linear programming problems are bounded problems. However, we can construct linear programming problems in which objective functions are not bounded.

A problem is unbounded if its constraints are such that they result in a convex set that is open. Figure 7.12 shows an unbounded problem. The unbounded problem is of no practical significance. An unbounded linear programming problem can result from an improper formulation of the real-life problem.

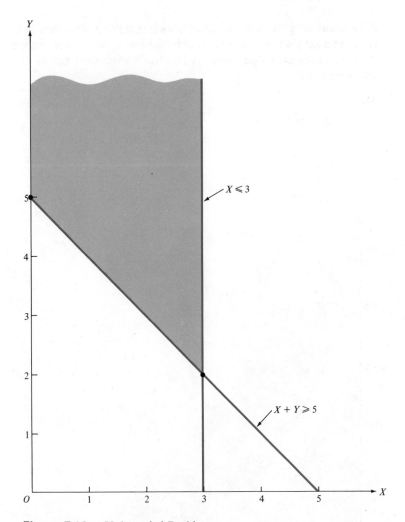

Figure 7.12. Unbounded Problem.

The unbounded problem graphed in Figure 7.12 is mathematically stated as follows:

Maximize

$$Z = 3X + 2Y$$

subject to the constraints

$$X \quad \leqslant 3$$
$$X + Y \geqslant 5$$

and

$$X, \quad Y \geqslant 0$$

7.5.4 NO FEASIBLE SOLUTION

If the linear programming problem is such that the intersection of its constraints yields an empty set, we have a case of no feasible solution. This happens whenever the constraints are inconsistent (i.e., mutually exclusive). Let us illustrate by the following problem.

Maximize

$$Z = 10X + 20Y$$

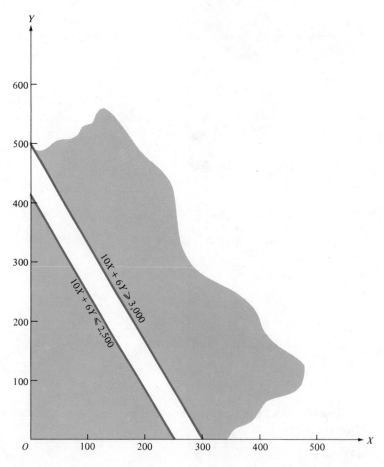

Figure 7.13.   No-Feasible-Solution Case.

subject to the constraints

$$10X + 6Y \leqslant 2,500$$
$$10X + 6Y \geqslant 3,000$$

and

$$X, \quad Y \geqslant \quad 0$$

The constraints of the preceding problem are graphed in Figure 7.13. It is clear that no point in Figure 7.13 can simultaneously satisfy all the inequalities. Hence, we have a special case in which no feasible solution can be found. The no-feasible-solution case can reflect a managerial situation in which the demands on the system cannot simultaneously be satisfied. This type of situation calls for managerial ability to resolve the impossible conflicting demands to a level that will permit organizational decisions to be made.

7.6
The Significance of Extreme-Point Solutions

If we examine Figure 7.6 (maximization case) or Figure 7.9 (minimization case), we find that in each case the optimal solution lies at one of the extreme points of the convex set of feasible solutions.[18] This is not an accident. It is instead a direct consequence of this important assertion made in Section 7.3.3: An optimal solution to a linear programming problem can always be found at one of the corner (or extreme) points of the region of feasible solutions. The importance of this assertion lies in the fact that, in order to identify the optimal solution, we have to search only a finite number of extreme-point solutions, rather than an infinite number of solutions that comprise the convex set of feasible solutions. For example, to identify the optimal solution in Figure 7.6, we have to search and compare only the four extreme-point solutions (points O, M, H and L). Similarly, to identify the optimal solution in Figure 7.9, we have to search and compare only three extreme-point solutions (points B, C, and D).

The fact that we have to search and compare only the extreme-point (or corner-point) solutions implies this: The optimal solution must lie at one of the intersections of the structural constraints *taken as equalities*. For example, we note the following in Figure 7.6.

> point O lies at the intersection of line $X = 0$, and line $Y = 0$
>
> point M lies at the intersection of line $X = 0$,
> and line $5X + 10Y = 2,000$
>
> point H lies at the intersection of line $5X + 10Y = 2,000$,
> and line $10X + 6Y = 2,500$
>
> point L lies at the intersection of line $Y = 0$,
> and line $10X + 6Y = 2,500$

---

[18] Note that in a two-dimensional space, an extreme point is generated by the intersection of two lines. It can be visualized that in a three-dimensional space, an extreme point is generated by the intersection of three *planes*. We can say that, in any n-dimensional space, we need the intersection of n *hyperplanes* to generate an extreme point.

The idea that extreme-point solutions, from which the optimal solution is identified, are generated by the intersection of constraints as equalities leads us to the next question: How can inequalities be converted into equalities? We discuss this issue in the next section.

7.7
Transformation of Inequalities into Equalities

There are essentially two types of inequalities: (1) less than or equal to ($\leqslant$), and (2) greater than or equal to ($\geqslant$). The "less than or equal to" inequality is used to indicate the upper limit of a resource. For example, the resource limitation for the cutting department can be expressed as

$$10X + 6Y \leqslant 2,500 \tag{7.13}$$

It is obvious that the values of X and Y must be so chosen that when inserted in (7.13), the left-hand side of the inequality must be *less than or equal to* the right-hand side. If a set of values (say $X = 100$, $Y = 100$) is such that the left-hand side is indeed less than the right-hand side, we observe that the cutting resource is not fully utilized and that some *slack* is left. For example, for $X = 100$, $Y = 100$, the slack (or the idle capacity) is 900 units. In other words, *slack* is the number of units of a resource not used. The magnitude of the slack is a variable because its value is determined by what values are assigned to X and Y. For example, if $X = 100$, $Y = 50$, the slack is 1,200 units. Note that the slack cannot be negative.

For any set of values X and Y, the addition of the slack variable to the left-hand side will make the left-hand side equal to the right-hand side.[19] Hence the rule:

> An inequality of the "less than or equal to" type is transformed into an equality by the addition of a nonnegative slack variable.

We shall denote slack variables with the letters S_1, S_2, S_3,... . The slack variables can be thought of as imaginary products, each requiring for its production 1 unit of capacity from *only one* of the resources and 0 units of capacity from the others, and each yielding a profit of zero. The production of 1 unit of S_1, for example, requires 1 unit of cutting capacity but 0 units of folding capacity and 0 units of packaging capacity.

Thus, with the addition of slack variables (one for each constraint), the resource inequalities stated in (7.4) become

$$\left. \begin{array}{rcrcrcl} 10X + & 6Y + & 1S_1 & & & = & 2,500 \\ 5X + & 10Y & & + 1S_2 & & = & 2,000 \\ 1X + & 2Y & & & + 1S_3 & = & 500 \end{array} \right\} \tag{7.14}$$

Note that the value of S_1 represents idle cutting department capacity. Similarly, values of S_2 and S_3 represent idle capacities of the folding and packaging departments, respectively. This fact becomes clear if in (7.14) we let $X = 0$ and $Y = 0$.

[19] If $X = 100$ and $Y = 100$, then the slack is 900. Hence, according to Equation (7.13), 10(100) + 6(100) + 900 = 2,500.

Let us now consider the nutrient I constraint from (7.11):

$$2X + 3Y \geqslant 3,500 \tag{7.15}$$

Again, it is obvious that the values of X and Y must be so chosen that when inserted in (7.15) the left-hand side of the inequality must be greater than or equal to the right-hand side. If the X and Y values are such that they make the left-hand side greater than the right-hand side, the equality can be restored by *subtracting* a nonnegative *surplus* variable. A specific value of the surplus variable represents the excess of nutrient I over the required level of 3,500. This argument leads us to the following rule:

> An inequality of the "greater than or equal to" type is transformed into an equality by the subtraction of a nonnegative surplus variable.

We shall denote surplus variables by the letters $R_1, R_2, R_3, \ldots$. Thus, with the subtraction of surplus variables (one for each constraint), the two inequalities stated in (7.11) become

$$\begin{aligned} 2X + 3Y - 1R_1 \qquad\; &= 3,500 \\ 6X + 2Y \qquad - 1R_2 &= 7,000 \end{aligned} \tag{7.16}$$

Note that R_1 and R_2 represent the surplus amount of nutrients I and II, respectively. For example, if we designed a program with $X = 1,000$ and $Y = 1,000$, it is clear from (7.16) that this *particular* program contains 1,500 surplus units of nutrient I (i.e., $R_1 = 1,500$), and 1,000 surplus units of nutrient II (i.e., $R_2 = 1,000$).

7.8
The Number of Extreme Points and Terminology of Linear Programming Solutions

Note that the 3×2 inequality constraint set stated in (7.4) became a 3×5 equality constraint set in (7.14). That is, in (7.14) we have five variables, as opposed to two variables in (7.4). Of these, two are real variables (X and Y) and three are slack variables (S_1, S_2, and S_3). This argument can be extended to cover the general $m \times n$ linear programming problem.

Let us think of a linear programming problem with m structural constraints and n activities (real variables). If the m constraints are stated as inequalities, we can convert them into equalities by the addition or subtraction of a total of m slack or surplus variables. Then we have a system of m equations with $m + n$ variables.[20] Since the number of equations is less than the number of variables (m is less than $m + n$), we have an infinite[21] number of solutions. This property, that a linear programming problem has an infinite number of solutions, was also demonstrated in the graphical method (see Section 7.3.3). Furthermore, it was

[20] The $m + n$ variables consist of n real variables and m slack or surplus variables.

[21] For example, consider the single equation system $X + Y = 10$. In this system, the number of equations (one) is less than the number of variables (two); and hence we have an infinite number of solutions. The reader can check that for every arbitrary value of X, there is a value of Y so that $X + Y = 10$.

stated in Section 7.3.3 that in order to locate the optimal solution, we have to search only the extreme (or corner) points of the convex set. This property of only searching the corner points reduces the search process to a finite effort, but even then there is a very large number of such corner points.[22] These corner points are systematically identified. That is, values of real, slack, and surplus variables associated with these corner points are calculated. Then, the corner-point solution with the highest profit (or lowest cost) is the optimal solution.

In summary, obtaining a solution to linear programming problems involves assigning specific values to the real variables and the slack or surplus variables without violating the given structural constraints and the nonnegativity constraints. The following terminology, depending upon whether or not the solution is an extreme-point solution and depending upon the number of positive components in the solution, is used to identify different types of solutions:

1. Non-extreme-point solution: any solution that does not lie at one of the corner points of the convex set and contains more than m positive components.
2. Extreme-point solution: any solution that lies at a corner point of the convex set. There are two types of extreme-point solutions: (a) basic feasible, and (b) degenerate basic feasible.
   (a) Basic feasible solution: any solution that contains exactly m positive components.
   (b) Degenerate basic feasible solution: any solution that contains less than m positive components.
3. Optimal solution: any basic feasible or degenerate basic feasible solution that either maximizes or minimizes the objective function.

A schematic representation of the above classification is shown in Figure 7.14.

In light of the above discussion we summarize in Table 7.3 the nature of extreme-point solutions of Figure 7.6.

Table 7.3

Solution Point (Basic Feasible Solution)	Variables in Solution (Basic Variables)	Variables Not in Solution (Non-basic Variables)	Total Profit (dollars)
O	S_1, S_2, S_3	X, Y	0
M	S_1, Y, S_3	X, S_2	6,400
H	X, Y, S_3	S_1, S_2	7,700
L	X, S_2, S_3	S_1, Y	5,750

[22] For example, the number of possible corner points in an $m \times (m + n)$ system is given by the combination of "$(m + n)$ things taken m at a time." This is calculated as

$$\binom{m + n}{m} = \frac{(m + n)!}{(m)!(m + n - m)!}$$

If $m = 3$ and $n = 2$, then

$$\binom{3 + 2}{3} = \frac{5!}{3!\,2!} = \frac{5 \times 4 \times 3 \times 2 \times 1}{(3 \times 2 \times 1)(2 \times 1)} = 10$$

It should be noted that the number of possible corner points increases very rapidly as $(m + n)$ increases.

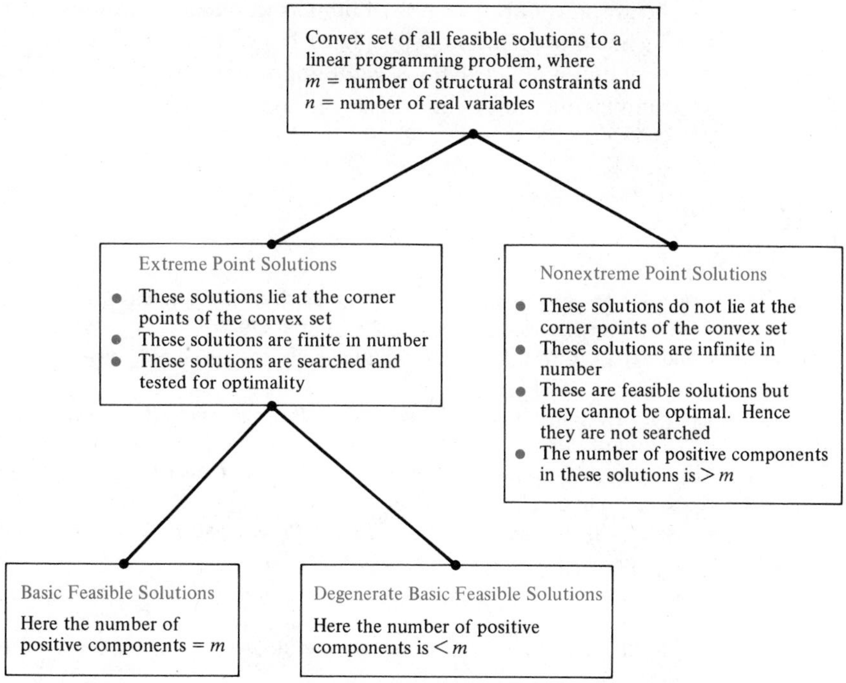

Convex set of all feasible solutions to a linear programming problem, where m = number of structural constraints and n = number of real variables
Extreme Point Solutions
• These solutions lie at the corner points of the convex set
• These solutions are finite in number
• These solutions are searched and tested for optimality
Nonextreme Point Solutions
• These solutions do not lie at the corner points of the convex set
• These solutions are infinite in number
• These are feasible solutions but they cannot be optimal. Hence they are not searched
• The number of positive components in these solutions is $> m$
Basic Feasible Solutions
Here the number of positive components $= m$
Degenerate Basic Feasible Solutions
Here the number of positive components is $< m$

Figure 7.14

7.9 Summary

In this chapter, we described the basic assumptions, terminology, and general structure of linear programming problems and their solutions. We employed the graphical method to establish several important ideas that are relevant to describing and understanding the nature and behavior of the linear programming model.

A simple linear programming problem was graphed in the activity space. The activity-space representation permitted us to define different types of solutions, such as feasible, basic feasible, and degenerate basic feasible solutions. The set of solutions was found to be convex, and it was indicated that the number of solutions is infinite.

It was established that the optimal solution to a linear programming problem can always be found at one of the extreme points of the convex solution set. Since the number of these extreme points is finite, the search for the optimal solution can be completed in a finite number of steps.

The usual case in linear programming problems is that the optimal solution can be found and is unique. There are, however, certain special cases, such as: (1) multiple optimal solutions, (2) the degenerate basic feasible solution, (3) the unbounded solution, and (4) no feasible solution. Each of these special cases was illustrated graphically.

The graphical approach is of limited value and is not an efficient method of solving linear programming problems. However, as we discovered in this chapter, it is very useful in clarifying several important concepts in linear programming. The simplex method is more general and is discussed in Chapter 8.

References

Beale, E. M. L. *Applications of Mathematical Programming Techniques*. New York: American Elsevier Publishing Co., Inc., 1970.

Childress, R. L. *Sets, Matrices, and Linear Programming*. Englewood Cliffs, N.J.: Prentice-Hall, Inc., 1974.

Cooper, L., and D. Steinberg. *Linear Programming*. Philadelphia: W. B. Saunders Company, 1974.

Daellenbach, H. G., and E. G. Bell. *User's Guide to Linear Programming*. Englewood Cliffs, N.J.: Prentice-Hall, Inc., 1970.

Gass, S. I. *An Illustrated Guide to Linear Programming*. New York: McGraw-Hill Book Company, 1970.

Gass, S. I. *Linear Programming*, 4th ed. New York: McGraw-Hill Book Company, 1975.

Kaplan, E. L. *Linear Programming*. Philadelphia: W. B. Saunders Company, 1972.

Lee, S. M. *Goal Programming for Decision Analysis*. Philadelphia: Auerbach Publishers, Inc., 1974.

Lee, S. M. *Linear Optimization for Management*. New York: Mason/Charter Publishers, Inc., 1976.

Loomba, N. P. *Linear Programming*. New York: McGraw-Hill Book Company, 1964.

Loomba, N. P. *Linear Programming: A Managerial Perspective*, 2nd ed. New York: Macmillan Publishing Co., Inc., 1976.

Loomba, N. P., and E. Turban. *Applied Programming for Management*. New York: Holt, Rinehart and Winston, 1974.

McMillan, C. *Mathematical Programming*. New York: John Wiley & Sons, Inc., 1974.

Markowitz, H. "Portfolio Selection." *Journal of Finance*, Vol. 7, No. 1 (Mar. 1952), 77–91.

Sposito, V. A. *Linear and Nonlinear Programming*. Ames, Iowa: Iowa State University Press, 1975.

Strum, J. E. *Introduction to Linear Programming*. San Francisco: Holden-Day, Inc., 1972.

Wagner, H. M. *Principles of Management Science with Applications to Executive Decisions*. Englewood Cliffs, N.J.: Prentice-Hall, Inc., 1975.

Review Questions and Problems

7.1. State the basic assumptions of the linear programming model.

7.2. Define and illustrate the following terms: linearity, program, programming, activity, activity level, optimal program.

7.3. What components describe the general structure of a linear programming model?

7.4. Define and illustrate the following terms: decision variables, cost or profit coefficients, input–output coefficients, capacity limits.

7.5. Define and illustrate the following terms: convex set, feasible solution, extreme-point solution, basic feasible solution, degenerate basic feasible solution, isoprofit line, binding constraint, nonbinding constraint, basic variables, nonbasic variables.

7.6 Explain the statement that there is an infinite number of solutions to a linear programming problem (provided a solution exists). Illustrate this concept graphically.

7.7. Explain the statement that an optimal solution to a linear programming, problem can always be found at one of the extreme points of the convex solution set. Illustrate this concept graphically.

7.8. Illustrate, graphically, the following special cases of the linear programming problem:
(a) Multiple optimal solutions
(b) Degenerate basic feasible solution
(c) The unbounded problem
(d) No feasible solution

7.9. Explain the significance of and attach a physical interpretation to:
(a) Slack variables
(b) Surplus variables

7.10. Use the graphical method to solve the following linear programming problem:

Maximize

$$Z = 3X + 2Y$$

subject to the constraints

$$4X + 5Y \leqslant 60$$
$$2X + 2Y \leqslant 30$$
$$X, \quad Y \geqslant 0$$

(a) What is the significance of the optimal solution?
(b) What happens to the optimal solution if the objective function is changed to $Z = 8X + 10Y$?
(c) If we add the new constraint: $2X + 2Y \geqslant 40$?

7.11. Use the graphical method to optimize the following problem.

Minimize

$$Z = 6X + 7.5Y$$

subject to the constraints

$$7X + \quad 3Y \geqslant 210$$
$$6X + 12Y \geqslant 180$$
$$4Y \geqslant \quad 20$$

and

$$X, \quad Y \geqslant 0$$

7.12. The E.E.R. Wax Company wants to determine the optimal product mix of their general-use wax and heavy-duty wax. They have a limited supply of the chemicals used in the manufacture of the two waxes. The pertinent data are summarized in Table 7.4. Formulate and solve the problem.

Table 7.4

| Chemical | Product | | Gallons Available |
	General-Use Wax	Heavy-Duty Wax	
A	2	5	200
B	6	3	360
Profit per Gallon	$3	$2	

7.13. Twenty-First-Century Hyena is planning next year's shooting schedule. They intend to use linear programming techniques as a possible guide. They make films for television and theater release. On the average a television film costs $750,000 and is sold for $1.25 million. A theater release film costs approximately $2 million and returns $3 million. It takes 12 weeks to shoot a television film; a theater film takes 30 weeks. Management knows that for the next year they have the facilities for the equivalent of 600 weeks of shooting time. It is also known that at least seven films must be made for television. Use the graphical method to determine the number and type of films that will maximize profits. How is the optimal solution changed if, in addition, the shooting budget is limited to $25 million?

7.14. A municipality is opening a new airport. The city government is concerned with providing adequate transportation to the facility. It can purchase buses and/or use a remodeled section of railroad track. Each bus costs $30,000 and carries 40 passengers. Each railroad car costs $45,000 and carries 100 passengers. The daily demand fluctuates between 15,000 and 60,000 people. The budget for the project is $2,700,000.
(a) If a bus can make 10 trips/day and a railway car can make 17 trips/day, what is the optimal number of people transported?
(b) What is the optimal number if the budget is reduced by $500,000?
(c) If there were a choice of remodeling the track at a cost of $500,000, would you remodel the track or just rely upon buses? Assume you have the same budget as in part (b).

7.15. The Food and Agricultural Organization's research department has developed two high nutrient foods, one using soybean derivatives and the other fish meal. Each unit of soybean food has 20 units of nutrient I and 60 units of nutrient II. Each unit of fish meal food has 30 units of nutrient I and 20 units of nutrient II. The FAO has determined the per capita daily minimum requirements of nutrients I and II to be 350 and 700 units, respectively. The cost of producing the soybean food is 20 cents/unit and 9 cents/unit for fish meal food. The FAO wants to send food packets (separate for each individual) to famine-ridden areas. Determine the units of soybean food and fish meal food that should be in each packet in order to minimize costs.

7.16. The Slumber Lumber Company produces two products: bed frames and bed canopies. The profit margin, per dozen, is $60 for bed frames and $50 for canopies. Both products go through cutting and sanding processes, which have a capacity of 40 and 50 hours/week, respectively. Each dozen bed frames consume 2 hours of cutting and 1 hour of sanding capacity. Every dozen units of canopies use up 1.25 hours of cutting and 1 hour of sanding capacity. How can the company maximize its profits? Do we have a nonbinding constraint? If so, what is the amount of unused sanding capacity?

CHAPTER 8

The Simplex Method

MAJOR CONCEPTS AND TOPICS
DISCUSSED IN THIS CHAPTER

The Rationale and Mechanics of the Simplex Method

Slack, surplus, and artificial slack variables
Initial basic feasible solution
Test for optimality
Rules of transformation for the key and nonkey rows of a simplex tableau

Economic Interpretation of the $C_j - Z_j$ Numbers in the Optimal Program

Special Cases of Linear Programming in the Context of the Simplex Terminology and Format

Multiple optimal solutions
No feasible solution
Unbounded solution
Degenerate basic feasible solutions

Degeneracy

8.1
Introduction

Among the various methods of solving linear programming problems, the simplex method is one of the most general and powerful. The graphical method was presented primarily to give readers a feel for linear programming problems and to acquaint them with some of the technical terminology so essential in understanding the rationale and mechanics of the simplex method. In practice, linear programming problems of any significance are usually solved by application of the simplex method or a variant of the simplex method.[1] In this chapter, we illustrate the simplex method by applying it to the maximization problem of Table 8.1.

8.2
Rationale for the Simplex Method

The simplex method rests on two concepts: feasibility and optimality. The search for the optimal solution starts from a basic feasible solution or program.[2] The solution is tested for optimality, and if it is optimal, the search is stopped. If the test of optimality shows that the current solution is not optimal, a new and better basic feasible solution is designed. The feasibility of the new solution is guaranteed by the mechanics of the simplex method, as is the fact that each successive solution is designed only if it is better than each of the previous solutions. This *iterative process* is continued until an optimal solution has been obtained.

The simplex method is based on the property that the optimal solution to a linear programming problem, if it exists, can always be found in one of the basic feasible solutions. Thus, in the simplex method, the first step is always to obtain a basic feasible solution. This solution is then tested for optimality by examining the net effect on the linear objective function of introducing one of the nonbasic variables to replace at least one of the current basic variables. If any improvement potential is noted, the replacement is made, always by introducing only one nonbasic variable at a time. The replacement process is such that the new solution is always feasible.

The simplex method is quite simple and mechanical in nature. The iterative steps of the simplex method are repeated until a finite optimal solution, if it exists, is determined. Otherwise, the method indicates either that the given linear programming problem has no solution or that no finite solution exists.

---

[1] Revised simplex and dual simplex are two such variants. See Loomba and Turban [1974].

[2] As in the graphical method, we search only the extreme-point solutions.

8.3
The Simplex Method—An Illustrative Example

To fix ideas and to facilitate comparison with the graphical method, we solve the same problem that was solved graphically in Section 7.3. For quick reference, the data of Table 7.1 are reproduced as Table 8.1.

Table 8.1 *Process Time Data per Unit of Product*

Department	Product A	Product B	Capacity
Cutting	10	6	2,500
Folding	5	10	2,000
Packaging	1	2	500
Profit per Unit	$23	$32	

Our first step is to translate the technical data into inequalities; convert these inequalities into equations by the addition of slack[3] variables; express the nonnegativity constraints and state the corresponding linear objective function. The slack variable may be given the familiar physical interpretation that the capacities of cutting, folding, and packaging departments not utilized in producing products A and B are, respectively, used to produce imaginary products S_1, S_2, and S_3, each giving a per unit profit contribution of zero.

Our problem, then, can be stated as follows:

Maximize

$$Z = 23X + 32Y + 0S_1 + 0S_2 + 0S_3$$

subject to the constraints

$$\begin{aligned} 10X + 6Y + 1S_1 + 0S_2 + 0S_3 &= 2{,}500 \\ 5X + 10Y + 0S_1 + 1S_2 + 0S_3 &= 2{,}000 \\ 1X + 2Y + 0S_1 + 0S_2 + 1S_3 &= 500 \end{aligned}$$ (8.1)

and

$$X, \quad Y, \quad S_1, \quad S_2, \quad S_3 \geqslant 0$$

In the simplex method each program is given in the form of a matrix or tableau. Although there are various forms for a simplex tableau, we shall follow the one given in Figure 8.1, which contains an initial program for the problem given in Table 8.1. The nomenclature of the simplex tableau, as identified in

---

[3] If the inequalities are of the "greater than or equal to" type, the surplus variables are subtracted from the left sides of the inequalities. A strict equality requires the addition of an artificial variable whose objective function coefficient represents a huge penalty. See Section 8.5.4.

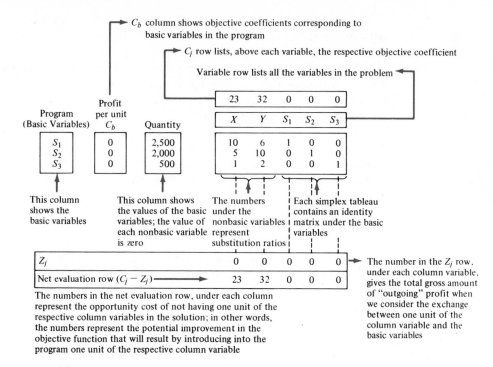

Figure 8.1

Figure 8.1, will be followed whenever we are dealing with subject matter related to linear programming.

8.3.1 DESIGN AN INITIAL PROGRAM

The first program in the simplex method is that which involves only the slack variables. This program is summarized in the first simplex tableau (Table 8.2). The interpretation of the data in Table 8.2 must be fully grasped in order that the simplex method can be understood. Let us, therefore, discuss the contents of the simplex tableau shown in Table 8.2. Other simplex tableaus will have similar interpretations.

Table 8.2 *First Program*

Program (Basic Variables)	Profit per Unit, C_b	Quantity	$C_j \rightarrow 23$ X	32 Y	0 S_1	0 S_2	0 S_3
S_1	0	2,500	10	6	1	0	0
S_2	0	2,000	5	10	0	1	0
S_3	0	500	1	2	0	0	1
Z_j			0	0	0	0	0
$C_j - Z_j$			23	32	0	0	0

1. In the column labeled "Program" are listed the variables that are included in the solution (products being produced). These are the basic variables.[4] Thus, in our first program, we are producing only S_1, S_2, and S_3.

2. In the column labeled "Profit per Unit" are listed the profit coefficients of the basic variables that are included in the specific program. Thus, the profit coefficients of S_1, S_2, and S_3 are all zero. The column title C_b stands for "profit or cost coefficients of the basic variables."

3. In the column labeled "Quantity" are listed the values of the basic variables included in the solution (quantities of the products being produced in the program). Since our initial program consists of producing 2,500 units of S_1, 2,000 units of S_2, and 500 units of S_3, these values are listed in the "Quantity" column. Any variables that are not listed under the "Program" column are the nonbasic variables. Their values are, by definition, zero. Hence, in view of the initial program of Table 8.2, X and Y are the nonbasic variables, and each has a value of zero.

4. The total profit contribution resulting from a specific program can be calculated by multiplying corresponding entries in the "Profit per Unit" column and the "Quantity" column and adding the products. Thus, total profit contribution in our first program is zero.

$$2,500(0) + 2,000(0) + 500(0) = 0$$

5. Numbers in the main body (entries in columns X and Y) can be interpreted to mean *physical ratios of substitution* if the program consists only of the slack variables. These physical ratios of substitution[5] in Table 8.2 correspond exactly to the given technical specifications. For example, the number 10 gives the ratio of substitution between X and S_1.[6] In other words, if we wish to produce 1 unit of X, 10 units of S_1 must be sacrificed. That is, available cutting capacity will be reduced by 10 units. The numbers 5 and 1 have similar interpretations. By the same token, to produce 1 unit of Y we must "sacrifice" 6 units of S_1, 10 units of S_2, and 2 units of S_3.

6. Like the numbers in the main body, the entries in the "identity" columns, S_1, S_2, and S_3 in Table 8.2 can be interpreted as ratios of exchange. Thus, the numbers in column S_1 represent, respectively, the ratios of exchange between S_1 and the basic variables S_1, S_2, and S_3. Note that the numbers under the basic variable columns (in Table 8.2 the basic variables are S_1, S_2 and S_3) always consist of unit vectors. (See Appendix C for a discussion of matrices and vectors.) Further, the unit vector is so constructed that the number 1 is at the intersection of the row and column of the same basic variable, while zeros appear at the intersection of different basic variables. This assertion can be checked in any simplex tableau.

7. The C_j numbers at the top of the columns of all the variables represent the coefficients of the respective variables in the objective function.

8. The numbers in the Z_j row, under each variable, give the total *gross amount* of outgoing profit when we consider the exchange between one unit of column variable and the basic variables.

---

[4] Associated with each basic variable is a vector that can be termed basic vector. A set of basic vectors comprises a basis. Thus, associated with each simplex tableau is a basis. When we proceed from one tableau to another, we change from one basis to another. The nature and role of a basis is discussed in Appendix C.

[5] In subsequent tableaus, these numbers are *algebraic ratios of exchange*.

[6] Note that 10 lies at the intersection of column X and row S_1.

9. The numbers in the net evaluation row, $C_j - Z_j$,[7] give the *net effect* of exchange between *one unit* of each variable and basic variables. They are always zero under the basic variables. Thus, they are zero under S_1, S_2, and S_3 in Table 8.2. Under the nonbasic variables, they can be positive, negative, or zero.

8.3.2 TEST FOR OPTIMALITY

In so far as the total profit contribution resulting from our initial program is zero, it can obviously be improved and hence is not the optimal program. However, the test of optimality can be formalized in terms of the signs of the entries $(C_j - Z_j)$ in the net evaluation row. In maximization problems, the program is optimal if each $C_j - Z_j$ is either zero or negative. In minimization problems, the program is optimal if each $C_j - Z_j$ is zero or positive. Let us explain.

Assume that we wish to change the program in Table 8.2 by introducing (producing) 1 unit of Y. This would, as explained previously, involve sacrificing 6 units of S_1, 10 units of S_2, and 2 units of S_3. The net effect of this exchange on the profit function would be

$$\boxed{+1(32)} \quad - \quad \boxed{6(0) + 10(0) + 2(0)} \quad = 32 = \quad \boxed{C_j - Z_j}$$

$$C_j = \text{incoming unit} \qquad Z_j = \text{outgoing total} \qquad \text{net effect}$$
$$\text{profit} \qquad\qquad\qquad \text{profit}$$

In other words, the introduction of 1 unit of Y at this stage of the solution will increase the value of the profit function by $32. Thus, the opportunity cost of not having this unit of Y in our initial program is $32. It is this number, $C_j - Z_j$, that is entered in the net evaluation row under column Y. Similarly, as can easily be ascertained, the opportunity cost of not having product X in our solution, at this stage, is $23/unit. This, then, is the significance of the $C_j - Z_j$ numbers in the net evaluation row. The mechanics of calculating the $C_j - Z_j$ in any tableau is as follows.

To get a number $C_j - Z_j$, under any column j, first multiply the exchange (or substitution) ratios in that column by the corresponding profit coefficients of the basic variables that appear under the C_b column; add the products (to yield Z_j) and then subtract this sum from the corresponding number listed in the C_j row.[9]

The numbers $C_j - Z_j$ in the net evaluation now represent the potential improvement in the objective function that will result from the introduction into the program of 1 unit of each of the respective variables. Thus, by definition, these numbers represent the opportunity costs of *not* having 1 unit of each variable in the solution. Since we are dealing with a linear programming model that assumes

---

[7] C_j is the profit coefficient of any variable j; Z_j is the sum of the products of the exchange ratios under the jth variable and the corresponding profit coefficients of the basic variables.

Opportunity cost is the cost involved in *not* following the best course of action.

[9] Mathematically,

$$C_j - Z_j = C_j - \sum_{i=1}^{m} a_{ij}C_i, \qquad j = 1, 2, \ldots, n \tag{8.2}$$

where a_{ij} is the *substitution ratio* at the intersection of the ith row and jth column.

certainty, the presence of any positive opportunity cost (or positive $C_j - Z_j$ in maximization problems) in the net evaluation row of a given simplex tableau indicates that an optimal solution has not been obtained, and therefore a better program can be designed. This is the test that will be used in this book for obtaining an optimal solution of a maximization problem.

By use of a similar argument it can be shown that the test of optimality for minimization problems requires that each $C_j - Z_j$ be either positive or zero. We summarize next the criteria for tests of optimality.

For maximization problems: If one or more $C_j - Z_j$ are positive, the solution is *not* optimal. If each $C_j - Z_j$ is either negative or zero, the solution is optimal.

For minimization problems: If one or more $C_j - Z_j$ are negative, the solution is *not* optimal. If each $C_j - Z_j$ is either positive or zero, the solution is optimal.

The $C_j - Z_j$ for Table 8.2 are calculated and listed in the net evaluation row. An examination of these numbers shows that they are either positive or zero. Hence, our first program is not optimal and must be revised.

8.3.3   REVISE THE CURRENT PROGRAM

Once a program is found to be nonoptimal, we must design a new and better program. How the simplex method accomplishes this task is explained below.

1. *Identify, from the set of nonbasic variables, the incoming variable (or the key column).* Note that, in Table 8.3, variables X and Y are the nonbasic variables. Further, the two positive $C_j - Z_j$ (23, 32) in the net evaluation row of Table 8.3 indicate, respectively, the magnitudes of the opportunity costs of not including 1 unit of variables (products) X and Y, at this solution stage. Since the highest opportunity cost falls under column Y, the variable (product) Y should be brought into the new program first. Hence, Y is the incoming variable, and column Y is called the key column.[10] The rule for determining the key column is: *The key column is the column under which the largest positive $C_j - Z_j$ appears.*

2. *Identify the outgoing variable (or the key row[11]).* After we have decided to bring in variable (product) Y to replace at least one of the basic variables (products) $(S_1, S_2, \text{ or } S_3)$ in the current program, the question becomes: How many units of Y can be brought in without exceeding the existing capacity of any one of the resources? In linear programming terms, this means that we must calculate the maximum allowable number of units of Y that can be brought into the program without violating the nonnegativity constraints. If we examine Table 8.3, we note that to bring in 1 unit of Y, we must sacrifice 6 units of S_1, 10 units of S_2, and 2 units of S_3. Insofar as we are currently producing only 2,500 units of S_1, it is clear that no more than $416\frac{2}{3}$ units $\left(\dfrac{2{,}500}{6} = 416\frac{2}{3}\right)$ of Y can be brought in without violating the capacity constraint of the cutting department. Similarly, at this stage of the solution, the production of Y is limited to 200 units $\left(\dfrac{2{,}000}{10} = 200\right)$ and 250 units $\left(\dfrac{500}{2} = 250\right)$ by the available capacities of the folding department and packaging department, respectively. The limiting case,

---

[10] Also referred to in the literature as the *pivot column*. See Appendix D.

[11] Also referred to in the literature as the *pivot row*. See Appendix D.

Table 8.3 *First Program*

Program (Basic Variables)	Profit per Unit, C_b	Quantity	$C_j \rightarrow$ 23 X	32 Y	0 S_1	0 S_2	0 S_3	Replacement Quantity
S_1	0	2,500	10	6	1	0	0	$416\frac{2}{3}$
S_2	0	2,000	5	10	0	1	0	200 → outgoing variable
S_3	0	500	1	2	0	0	1	250
Z_j			0	0	0	0	0	
$C_j - Z_j$			23	32	0	0	0	

incoming variable

therefore, arises from row S_2 in Table 8.3. This, then, is our key row (the outgoing variable), and 200 units is the maximum quantity of the product Y that can be produced, at this stage of the solution, without violating the nonnegativity constraints. The mechanics for identifying the key row will now be discussed.

Divide the entries under the "Quantity" column by the corresponding *positive*[12] entries of the key column, and compare these ratios. *The row in which the smallest ratio falls is the key row.* These ratios are, in effect, maximum possible replacement quantities that indicate the limiting values of the incoming variable as a replacement for each of the basic variables. Hence, from now on we shall refer to them as, and list them under, a column named "Replacement Quantity."

The calculations that help identify the outgoing variable or the key row are as follows. For the cutting department (row S_1),

$$\frac{2,500}{6} = 416\tfrac{2}{3} \text{ units}$$

For the folding department (row S_2),

$$\frac{2,000}{10} = 200 \text{ units} \rightarrow \text{key row}$$

For the packaging department (row S_3),

$$\frac{500}{2} = 250 \text{ units}$$

While going through the simplex algorithm, it is convenient to place these replacement-quantity calculations on the extreme right-hand side of a given tableau. The limiting replacement quantity of the incoming variable (product) is then identified by the *lowest nonnegative value.*[13] The outgoing variable or the key row is indicated by an arrow of the form $\rightarrow$, as shown in Table 8.3.

3. *Identify the key number (or the pivot*[14] *element).* Once the key row and the key column have been determined, the identification of the key number is a simple matter. *The number that lies at the intersection of the key row and the key column of a given tableau is the key number.* Thus, the key number in Table 8.3 is 10. The identification of the key column and the key row has shown us that the variable (product) Y will replace variable (product) S_2 and that no more than 200 units of Y can be produced under the current capacity restrictions. Our next task is to determine the exact composition of the remainder of the revised program. In other words, we must find the reductions in S_1 and S_3 due to the fact that 200 units of Y are to be included in the revised program. Furthermore, we must build an entire new simplex tableau for the revised program.

Since it takes 10 units of folding department capacity to produce 1 unit of Y, it is evident that all 2,000 units (200 × 10) of the folding capacity are exhausted. However, as we noted earlier, the production of 1 unit of Y also requires 6 units of

---

[12] A negative entry in the key column, when interpreted as a ratio of exchange, would mean that the introduction of the incoming variable increases rather than decreases the magnitude of the outgoing variable in which this negative entry exists. The current magnitude of this outgoing variable, therefore, would provide no limit to the introduction of the incoming variable. Similarly, an exchange ratio of zero would provide no limit. Hence, in identifying the key row, only the positive ratios of substitution need be examined.

[13] Note that a replacement quantity of "zero" would always constitute the lowest nonnegative value.

[14] See Appendix D.

Table 8.4 *Second Program*

Program (Basic Variables)	Profit per Unit, C_b	Quantity	$C_j \to$ 23 X	32 Y	0 S_1	0 S_2	0 S_3	Replacement Quantity
S_1	0	1,300	7	0	1	$-\frac{3}{5}$	0	$\frac{1300}{7} \to$ outgoing variable
Y	32	200	$\frac{1}{2}$	1	0	$\frac{1}{10}$	0	400
S_3	0	100	0	0	0	$-\frac{1}{5}$	1	
Z_j			16	32	0	$\frac{16}{5}$	0	
$C_j - Z_j$			7	0	0	$-\frac{16}{5}$	0	

incoming variable

cutting department capacity and 2 units of packaging department capacity. Thus, the remaining capacity of the cutting department is $2,500 - (200 \times 6) = 1,300$, and the remaining capacity of the packaging department is $500 - (200 \times 2) = 100$ units.

Another way to say the same thing is that our second program calls for producing $S_1 = 1,300$, $Y = 200$, $S_3 = 100$; and $X = 0$, $S_2 = 0$. The three products (S_1, Y, and S_3) included in the second program are listed in the "Program" column in Table 8.4. This second program here corresponds to point M in Figure 7.6 on p. 183.

Table 8.4, which contains our second program, is derived from Table 8.3, which represented our initial program. The simplex tableaus are so constructed that the number of rows in each tableau is the same, even though in some cases the values of one or more basic variables appear as zero under the "Quantity" column. Further, any given tableau, during solution stages, has two types of rows: (1) the key row, and (2) the nonkey rows. Thus, to derive a new tableau from an old tableau, all we have to do is to establish rules of transformation for these two types of rows. These rules of transformation form the mechanical foundations of the simplex method. The rules are to be applied to the entire set of entries of each row, starting with, and to the right of, the "Quantity" column.

Transformation of the Key Row

The rule for transforming the key row is: *Divide all the numbers in the key row by the key number. The resulting numbers form the corresponding row in the next tableau* (to be placed in exactly the same position).

Thus, the second row in Table 8.4 (row Y) is derived from the second row in Table 8.3 (row S_2) by simply dividing all the numbers in row S_2 by 10 (the key number). The new row Y (Table 8.4) is

$$200 \quad \frac{1}{2} \quad 1 \quad 0 \quad \frac{1}{10} \quad 0$$

Transformation of the Nonkey Rows

The rule for transforming a nonkey row is: *Subtract from the old row number (in each column) the product of the corresponding key-row number and the corresponding fixed ratio* (formed by dividing the old row number in the key column by the key number). *The result will give the corresponding new row number* (to be placed in exactly the same position).

This rule can be placed in the following equation form:

new row number = old row number

  − (corresponding number in key row × corresponding fixed ratio)

where

$$\text{fixed ratio} = \frac{\text{old row number in key column}}{\text{key number}}$$

Thus, the new row S_1 for Table 8.4 is derived as follows (corresponding fixed ratio $= \frac{6}{10} = 0.6$):

old row number	−	corresponding number in old key row	×	corresponding fixed ratio	=	new row number
2,500	−	2,000	×	0.6	=	1,300
10	−	5	×	0.6	=	7
6	−	10	×	0.6	=	0
1	−	0	×	0.6	=	1
0	−	1	×	0.6	=	$-0.6 = -\frac{3}{5}$
0	−	0	×	0.6	=	0

Similarly, the new S_3 row in Table 8.4 is derived as follows (corresponding fixed ratio $= \frac{2}{10} = 0.2$):

old row number	−	corresponding number in old key row	×	corresponding fixed ratio	=	new row number
500	−	2,000	×	0.2	=	100
1	−	5	×	0.2	=	0
2	−	10	×	0.2	=	0
0	−	0	×	0.2	=	0
0	−	1	×	0.2	=	$-0.2 = -\frac{1}{5}$
1	−	0	×	0.2	=	1

The results are entered in the second simplex tableau, shown in Table 8.4. As indicated in the table, our second program calls for the production of $S_1 = 1,300$, $Y = 200$, and $S_3 = 100$ units. The variables X and S_2 are not in the solution (program) and therefore assume values of zero. The total profit contribution resulting from this program is $0(1,300) + 32(200) + 0(100) = \$6,400$.

The $C_j - Z_j$ numbers of the net evaluation row are calculated as before, according to Equation (8.2), and are shown in Table 8.4.[15]

8.3.4 DESIGN ANOTHER IMPROVED PROGRAM

As the net evaluation row of Table 8.4 shows, we still have one positive $C_j - Z_j$ under the X column. Its value of $+7$ indicates a positive opportunity cost of not having 1 unit of X in the program. Hence, program 2 shown in Table 8.4 is not an optimal program. This calls for designing a new program and therefore deriving a new simplex tableau. The procedure for deriving this third simplex tableau (Table 8.5) is exactly the same as was followed in deriving the second simplex tableau.

Derivation of Table 8.5

Were there more than one positive $C_j - Z_j$ number in the net evaluation row of a simplex tableau, we would select the largest one to identify the key column (the incoming variable). Since in Table 8.4 there is only one positive $C_j - Z_j$, we choose X (the column under which the positive $C_j - Z_j$ appears) to be the incoming product. Thus, the column labeled X is the key column. As before, we

---

[15] The $C_j - Z_j$ row can also be treated as a nonkey row and can, therefore, be transformed from one tableau to the next by following the rules of transformation for the nonkey row. Readers can verify this statement by directly calculating the net evaluation row of Table 8.4 from that of Table 8.3. Also, see Appendix D in which we use pivoting to design new and improved programs.

must now determine the limit on the quantity of X that can be introduced into the program and thus identify the key row. The maximum replacement quantities of variables S_1 and Y are shown on the right side of Table 8.4 under the "Replacement Quantity" column.[16] They indicate that row S_1 is the key row, and hence 7 is the key number.

Now, we must derive Table 8.5. Since the first row S_1 in Table 8.4 is the key row, we divide all the numbers in this row by 7 (the key number) to obtain the first row X in Table 8.5.

$$\frac{1,300}{7} \quad 1 \quad 0 \quad \frac{1}{7} \quad \frac{-3}{35} \quad 0$$

The nonkey row Y in Table 8.4 is transformed to row Y in Table 8.5 as follows (note that the corresponding fixed ratio $= \frac{1}{14}$):

old row number	$-$	$\left(\begin{array}{c}\text{corresponding number} \\ \text{in old key row}\end{array}\right.$	$\times$	$\left.\begin{array}{c}\text{corresponding} \\ \text{fixed ratio}\end{array}\right)$	$=$	new row number
200	$-$	1,300	$\times$	$\dfrac{1}{14}$	$=$	$\dfrac{750}{7}$
$\dfrac{1}{2}$	$-$	7	$\times$	$\dfrac{1}{14}$	$=$	0
1	$-$	0	$\times$	$\dfrac{1}{14}$	$=$	1
0	$-$	1	$\times$	$\dfrac{1}{14}$	$=$	$-\dfrac{1}{14}$
$\dfrac{1}{10}$	$-$	$-\dfrac{3}{5}$	$\times$	$\dfrac{1}{14}$	$=$	$\dfrac{1}{7}$
0	$-$	0	$\times$	$\dfrac{1}{14}$	$=$	0

Since the fixed ratio for the nonkey row S_3 (Table 8.4) is zero, the corresponding row in the next program (Table 8.5) is exactly the same. (Why?) As can be ascertained, all the $C_j - Z_j$ numbers in the net evaluation row of Table 8.5 are now either negative or zero, indicating the optimality of program 3. This program yields a profit of $7,700.

Table 8.5 *Optimal Program*

Program (Basic Variables)	Profit per Unit, C_b	Quantity	$C_j \rightarrow 23$ X	32 Y	0 S_1	0 S_2	0 S_3
X	23	$\frac{1300}{7}$	1	0	$\frac{1}{7}$	$-\frac{3}{35}$	0
Y	32	$\frac{750}{7}$	0	1	$-\frac{1}{14}$	$\frac{1}{7}$	0
S_3	0	100	0	0	0	$-\frac{1}{5}$	1
Z_j			23	32	1	$\frac{13}{5}$	0
$C_j - Z_j$			0	0	-1	$-\frac{13}{5}$	0

[16] We need not check row S_3 because its ratio of substitution (under the key column) is zero. Remember that replacement quantities need to be calculated only for positive ratios of exchange (substitution).

8.4
Economic Interpretation of the $C_j - Z_j$ Numbers in the Optimal Program

The economic interpretation of the $C_j - Z_j$ numbers in the net evaluation row of the optimal program is helpful for managerial decisions. Since the net evaluation of S_1 at this stage is -1.0, the introduction of 1 unit of S_1 (letting 1 unit of the cutting department capacity stay idle) will decrease the objective function by $1. By the same reasoning, if we had 1 more unit of the cutting capacity, the objective function could be increased by $1. In other words, $1 is the marginal worth, artificial accounting price, or shadow price of 1 unit of cutting capacity. Information regarding the marginal worths of various resources can help the manager decide whether additional resources should be purchased and at what prices.

The term marginal worth conveys the idea of the economists' concept of the worth of a marginal unit of a given resource. Here, as can be seen from the $C_j - Z_j$ row (under column S_2) of Table 8.5, the marginal worth of the folding capacity is $2.60. The marginal worth of the packaging capacity, however, is zero (see the $C_j - Z_j$ value under S_3 in Table 8.5). This makes economic sense because the optimal tableau indicates that we still have a spare capacity of 100 units in the packaging department ($S_3 = 100$). Hence, its marginal worth must be zero. The value of all the available resources can be calculated by multiplying the given capacity levels of the different resources by their respective marginal worths and adding the products. In our case, this value is equal to $7,700 = 2,500(1) + 2,000(2.60) + 500(0)$. Comparing this *imputed* value of the available resources with the value of the objective function in the optimal program (Table 8.5), we find that their magnitudes are exactly the same $\left[23\left(\frac{1300}{7}\right) + 32\left(\frac{750}{7}\right) = \$7,700 \right]$.

The fact that the value of the objective function in the optimal program equals the *imputed* value of the available resources is one component of a linear programming problem called the dual problem (Chapter 9).

8.5
The Simplex Method (Minimization Case)

8.5.1 PRELIMINARIES

One way to solve a minimization problem is to convert it to a maximization problem and then solve it by the simplex algorithm illustrated in Section 8.4. The conversion from minimization to maximization (or vice versa) can be made by just changing the signs of the cost (or profit) coefficients in the objective function. The constraints are left untouched. The solution to the converted problem is the same as that to the original problem, except that the sign of the optimal value of the objective function of the converted problem is changed to obtain the optimal value of the objective function of the original problem.[17]

The assertion of the above paragraph can be verified by taking the minimization problem of Table 8.6, converting it to a maximization problem (change the signs of the objective function coefficients), solving it by the simplex method, and then comparing the results with the solution to the original minimization problem, shown in Table 8.9. Figure 8.2 shows the optimal corner point C, which corresponds to $X = 15$ and $Y = 2.5$.

Our purpose in this section is to illustrate the straightforward application of the simplex method to minimization problems. The simplex algorithm that we illustrated in the maximization case in Section 8.4 is also applicable to minimization problems. There is, however, one specific difference. It relates to the test of optimality and hence to the choice of the incoming variable. As described earlier, in the maximization case the optimality is established when all $C_j - Z_j$ are either negative or zero (and hence the variable with the largest positive $C_j - Z_j$ is chosen as the incoming variable). Conversely, in the minimization case, the optimality is established when all $C_j - Z_j$ are either positive or zero (and hence the variable with the largest negative $C_j - Z_j$ is chosen as the incoming variable).

8.5.2 THE PROBLEM

The technical specifications of a diet-type problem are given in Table 8.6. The data indicate that 1 unit of F_1 (say, 1 ounce) contains 2 units of vitamin A and 3 units of vitamin B. Similarly, 1 unit of F_2 contains 4 units of vitamin A and 2 units

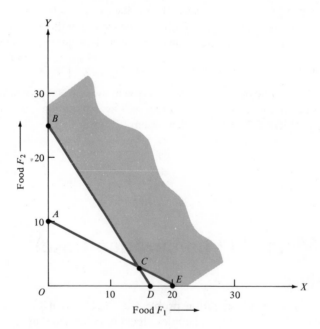

Figure 8.2

[17] Using the matrix notation, $\min \mathbf{CX} = -\max (-\mathbf{C})\mathbf{X}$. Also, $\max \mathbf{CX} = -\min (-\mathbf{C})\mathbf{X}$. See Appendix C.

of vitamin B. The daily requirement for vitamin A is at least 40 units, and for vitamin B at least 50 units.[18] Our objective is to determine optimal quantities of foods F_1 and F_2 to be purchased so that the daily vitamin requirements are met and, simultaneously, the cost of purchasing the foods is minimized. Assuming that X represents the quantity of food F_1 and Y the quantity of food F_2 to be purchased, and Z the total cost, we may state the problem in algebraic terms as follows:

Table 8.6

| | Food | | Daily |
Vitamin	F_1	F_2	Requirement
A	2	4	40
B	3	2	50
Cost per Unit (cents)	3	2.5	

Minimize

$$Z = 3X + 2.5Y$$

subject to the constraints

$$2X + 4Y \geqslant 40$$
$$3X + 2Y \geqslant 50$$

and

$$X, \quad Y \geqslant 0$$

8.5.3 TRANSFORMING THE INEQUALITIES INTO EQUALITIES

As opposed to those in the problem discussed in Section 8.3, the structural constraints here are of the "greater than or equal to" type. Hence, converting the inequalities into equalities requires the subtraction of surplus rather than the addition of slack variables. Let variables R_1 and R_2 represent, respectively, the quantity of vitamin A in excess of 40 units and the quantity of vitamin B in excess of 50 units. The introduction of these surplus variables converts the above inequalities into the following equations:

$$2X + 4Y - R_1 \qquad = 40 \tag{8.3}$$
$$3X + 2Y \qquad - R_2 = 50 \tag{8.4}$$

Variables R_1 and R_2 have the property that 1 unit of R_1 contains 1 unit of vitamin A and 1 unit of R_2 contains 1 unit of vitamin B. Variable R_1 appears only when we buy foods F_1 and F_2 with the purpose of satisfying the requirement for vitamin A, and R_2 appears only when we buy foods F_1 and F_2 to satisfy the requirement for vitamin B. Thus, if a specific program of purchasing foods F_1 and

---

[18] Any intake of vitamins in excess of daily requirements is assumed not to be harmful.

F_2 is such that the presence of R_1 and R_2 is required to satisfy Equations (8.3) and (8.4), the magnitudes of R_1 and R_2 will represent, respectively, the quantity of vitamin A in excess of 40 units and the quantity of vitamin B in excess of 50 units.

With the above interpretation, it is easy to see that variables R_1 and R_2 are restricted to nonnegative values, and each has a cost coefficient of zero. A complete statement of the problem, therefore, is:

Minimize

$$Z = 3X + 2.5Y + OR_1 + OR_2$$

subject to the constraints

$$2X + 4Y - 1R_1 + 0R_2 = 40 \qquad (8.5)$$
$$3X + 2Y + 0R_1 - 1R_2 = 50 \qquad (8.6)$$

and

$$X, \quad Y, \quad R_1, \quad R_2 \geqslant 0$$

8.5.4 ARTIFICIAL SLACK VARIABLES

Let us examine Equation (8.5). If we let real variables X and Y equal zero, we obtain a value of -40 for the surplus variable R_1. Any such negative value is unacceptable because it violates the nonnegativity constraint for R_1 and does not make any sense in terms of physical interpretation. We face a similar difficulty in connection with Equation (8.6). Hence, the initial program cannot be designed by letting X and Y equal zero. Some further modification of the structural constraints must be made. We propose, therefore, at this stage, to modify the statement of our problem in such a way that we can make X and Y equal to zero in the above equations and still have positive-valued variables that satisfy these equations. This is accomplished by introducing into the original inequalities, in addition to the surplus variables, the artificial variables. The artificial variables will be represented by the capital letter A with the proper subscript. Thus we can modify Equations (8.5) and (8.6) with the addition of artificial variables A_1 and A_2, respectively:

$$2X + 4Y - 1R_1 + 0R_2 + A_1 = 40 \qquad (8.7)$$
$$3X + 2Y + 0R_1 - 1R_2 + A_2 = 50 \qquad (8.8)$$

In this problem the artificial variables A_1 and A_2 can be thought of as imaginary foods, each unit containing 1 unit of the pertinent vitamin. For example, we can assume here that 1 unit of A_1 contains 1 unit of vitamin A, whereas 1 unit of A_2 contains 1 unit of vitamin B. In this sense A_1 is similar to R_1, and A_2 is similar to R_2. Also, both A_1 and A_2 are restricted to nonnegative values, for obvious reasons. However, the correspondence between the surplus and artificial variables does not hold in the matter of cost coefficients. Whereas surplus variables have zeros as their cost coefficients, each artificial slack variable is assigned an infinitely large cost coefficient (usually denoted by $+M$). (*Note:* If, for any reason, an artificial variable is utilized in a maximization problem, its eventual exit from the simplex tableau, or program, is assumed by assigning to it an objective coefficient of $-M$.)

Thus, the addition of the surplus and artificial variables converts the original problem to the following:

Minimize

$$Z = 3X + 2.5Y + 0R_1 + 0R_2 + MA_1 + MA_2$$

subject to the constraints

$$2X + 4Y - 1R_1 + 0R_2 + 1A_1 + 0A_2 = 40 \qquad (8.9)$$
$$3X + 2Y + 0R_1 - 1R_2 + 0A_1 + 1A_2 = 50 \qquad (8.10)$$

and

$$X, \quad Y, \quad R_1, \quad R_2, \quad A_1, \quad A_2 \geqslant 0$$

If in Equations (8.9) and (8.10) we let variables $X, Y, R_1,$ and R_2 assume values of zero, the artificial variables A_1 and A_2 will have positive values. We can see, therefore, that the inclusion of artificial variables will permit us to design an initial program in which no units of foods F_1 and F_2 are purchased and yet the nonnegativity constraints are not violated.[19]

In other words, these artificial variables enable us to make a convenient and correct start in obtaining an optimal solution by the simplex method. Further, having attached to each artificial variable an extremely large cost coefficient M, we can be certain that these variables can never enter into the optimal solution.[20] The inclusion of even 1 unit of an artificial slack variable in any program would result in a prohibitive cost. The deck is stacked, so to speak, and we would *intuitively* expect a quick exit of the artificial variables from any basic feasible solution. The solution to our modified problem (modified by the inclusion of A_1 and A_2, etc.) will, therefore, give us the solution to the original problem.

It should be stated here that if the original specifications of a problem are such that a given constraint is a strict equality (as opposed to an inequality), we also modify the problem by adding an artificial slack variable whose objective function coefficient imposes a huge, and hence unacceptable, penalty. As already discussed, such a modification permits us to obtain a basic feasible program with which to start the simplex search. The artificial variable with the unacceptably high penalty will never enter the optimal program, and hence the optimal solution to the modified problem is the optimal solution to the original problem.

8.5.5 DESIGN AN INITIAL PROGRAM

The first program is obtained by letting each of the variables $X, Y, R_1,$ and R_2 assume a value of zero. This means, as can be seen in Equations (8.9) and (8.10), that the initial program calls for purchasing 40 units of A_1 and 50 units of A_2. This program is given in Table 8.7.

[19] The reader will recall that such an initial program, when applied to Equations (8.5) and (8.6), violated the nonnegativity constraints for variables R_1 and R_2.

[20] If, in any linear programming problem involving artificial slack variables, the application of the simplex method fails to remove all artificial slack variables from the solution basis, the original problem has no solution.

Table 8.7 *First Tableau*

Program (Basic Variables)	Cost per Unit, C_b	Quantity	$C_j \rightarrow$ 3 X	2.5 Y	0 R_1	0 R_2	M A_1	M A_2	Replacement Quantity
A_1	M	40	2	4	-1	0	1	0	$10 \rightarrow$ outgoing variable
A_2	M	50	3	2	0	-1	0	1	25
Z_j			$5M$	$6M$	$-M$	$-M$	M	M	
$C_j - Z_j$			$3 - 5M$	$\frac{5}{2} - 6M$	M	M	0	0	

incoming variable

222

8.5.6 TEST FOR OPTIMALITY

The $C_j - Z_j$ numbers in the net evaluation row are calculated, as before, according to Equation (8.2). Since $C_j - Z_j$ are negative under both X and Y, our initial program is not optimal. The negatives of the entries in the net evaluation row represent the opportunity costs of not having 1 unit of each of the variables in the program. For example, the opportunity cost of not having 1 unit of Y in the solution is $-(2.5 - 6M) = 6M - 2.5$ cents, a positive opportunity cost that must be eliminated. Since a positive opportunity cost corresponds to a negative entry in the net evaluation row in the case of a minimization problem, we can state the following decision rule for testing the optimality of a given program in a minimization problem: As long as there exists even a single negative $(C_j - Z_j)$ number in the net evaluation row of a minimization problem, the optimal solution has not been obtained.

8.5.7 REVISE THE INITIAL PROGRAM

As in the simplex method for solving a maximization problem, revision of the current program in the case of a minimization problem requires: (1) identification of the key column, (2) identification of the key row and the key number, and (3) transformation of the key row and the nonkey rows into the new tableau that contains the revised program. The mechanics of these steps are exactly the same as in the maximization problem. However, as mentioned earlier, in the minimization case it is the largest negative entry in the net evaluation row (as opposed to the largest positive entry in the maximization case) which identifies the key column. The reason for this is obvious. In the minimization case, if the net evaluation entry under a particular column variable is negative, it is indicative of the fact that the inclusion of this variable in the new basis (by replacement of one of the current basic variables) will decrease the value of the objective function.

Since $C_j - Z_j$ for column Y is the largest negative number, we select Y as the incoming variable (key column).[21]

Next we must determine how many units of Y can be brought in without making either A_1 or A_2 negative. From row A_1, the maximum amount of Y that can be brought into the solution is $\frac{40}{4} = 10$ units. From row A_2, the maximum amount of Y that can be brought into the solution is $\frac{50}{2} = 25$ units. We see, therefore, that row A_1 provides the limiting case. This is, in other words, our outgoing variable (key row), and the key number is 4.

The rest of the procedure for revising the program is exactly the same as that followed in the simplex method for a maximization problem. The key row (row A_1 in this case) is transformed by dividing all its entries by the key number; the nonkey row (row A_2 in this case) is transformed according to the transformation rule for the nonkey row. Accordingly, a new program is designed. Table 8.8 lists the second program along with other pertinent information. Since there are negative $C_j - Z_j$ in Table 8.8, the second program is not the optimal program.

[21] Insofar as M represents a very large cost, the comparative magnitudes of the net-evaluation-row entries can be ascertained simply by comparing the number of M's. Thus, in Table 8.7, the net evaluation entry $\frac{5}{2} - 6M$ is, in absolute terms, larger than $3 - 5M$. This means that, for reducing the cost function, 1 unit of Y is preferable, at this stage to 1 unit of X.

Table 8.8 *Second Tableau*

Program (Basic Variables)	Cost per Unit, C_b	Quantity	$C_j \to$ 3 X	2.5 Y	0 R_1	0 R_2	M A_1	M A_2	Replacement Quantity
Y	2.5	10	$\frac{1}{2}$	1	$-\frac{1}{4}$	0	$\frac{1}{4}$	0	20
A_2	M	30	2	0	$\frac{1}{2}$	-1	$-\frac{1}{2}$	1	$15 \to$ outgoing variable
Z_j			$\frac{5}{4} + 2M$	2.5	$\frac{1}{2}M - \frac{5}{8}$	$-M$	$\frac{5}{8} - \frac{1}{2}M$	M	
$C_j - Z_j$			$\frac{7}{4} - 2M$	0	$\frac{5}{8} - \frac{1}{2}M$	M	$\frac{3}{2}M - \frac{5}{8}$	0	

incoming variable

8.5.8 REVISE THE SECOND PROGRAM

The net evaluation row of Table 8.8 has negative entries under columns X and R_1. Since the $C_j - Z_j$ under column X has a larger negative value than that under column R_1, the variable X should be brought into the solution next. That is, variable X is the incoming variable. Further, we see that A_2 is the outgoing variable. The new program will, therefore, consist of Y and X. Our revised program, given in Table 8.9, is derived in precisely the same manner as before, by following the rules of transformation.

Table 8.9 *Third and Optimal Tableau*

Program (Basic Variables)	Cost per Unit, C_b	Quantity	$C_j \to 3$ X	2.5 Y	0 R_1	0 R_2	M A_1	M A_2
Y	2.5	$\frac{5}{2}$	0	1	$-\frac{3}{8}$	$\frac{1}{4}$	$\frac{3}{8}$	$-\frac{1}{4}$
X	3	15	1	0	$\frac{1}{4}$	$-\frac{1}{2}$	$-\frac{1}{4}$	$\frac{1}{2}$
Z_j			3	$\frac{5}{2}$	$-\frac{3}{16}$	$-\frac{7}{8}$	$\frac{3}{16}$	$\frac{7}{8}$
$C_j - Z_j$			0	0	$\frac{3}{16}$	$\frac{7}{8}$	$M-\frac{3}{16}$	$M-\frac{7}{8}$

Since all the $C_j - Z_j$ in the net evaluation row of Table 8.9 are zero or positive, the optimal solution to our problem has been obtained. This optimal program assigns a value of 15 to variable X and $\frac{5}{2}$ to variable Y. In other words, this optimal program calls for purchasing 15 units of food F_1 and $\frac{5}{2}$ units of food F_2 daily, with an attendant cost of 51.25 cents. As a quick check will show, this program meets the daily requirements of vitamins A and B.

An economic interpretation of the $C_j - Z_j$ numbers, under the slack variables in the optimal tableau of a maximization problem was presented in Section 8.4. It will be recalled that, in the maximization case, the $C_j - Z_j$ number (in the optimal tableau) associated with a slack variable represented the marginal worth or imputed price per unit of a given resource. Further, we showed in Section 8.4 that the sum total of the imputed values of all the resources was exactly equal to the value of the objective function in the optimal program. A similar situation obtains for the $C_j - Z_j$ numbers in the optimal tableau of a minimization problem. In the minimization case, the $C_j - Z_j$ number (in the optimal tableau) associated with a surplus variable represents the marginal worth or imputed value that is assigned to one unit of the required item or characteristic. For example, the $C_j - Z_j$ number under R_1 in the optimal program shown in Table 8.9 is $\frac{3}{16}$. This means that we have assigned an imputed value of $\frac{3}{16}$ cent to 1 unit of vitamin A. Similarly, as can be seen from Table 8.9 (examine the $C_j - Z_j$ number under R_2), the imputed value of 1 unit of vitamin B is $\frac{7}{8}$ cent. Further, note that the sum total of the imputed values of the two stated requirements of vitamins $[\frac{3}{16}(40) + \frac{7}{8}(50)$ $= 51.25$ cents] exactly equals the total cost of the optimal program shown in Table 8.9.

One final note on the mechanics of the simplex method in minimization problems. Once an artificial slack variable leaves the basis, its exit is final—because its prohibitively high cost coefficient will never permit it to reenter the basis. Hence, we can reduce the size of the tableau and thus the number of calculations if, as soon as an artificial slack variable leaves the basis, we cross out the corresponding column headed by that artificial slack variable.

8.6
Special Cases

The usual case in linear programming problems is that we have a unique optimal solution. However, the following special cases should be noted: (1) multiple optimal solutions, (2) no feasible solution, (3) unbounded solution, and (4) degenerate basic feasible solution (degeneracy). All four special cases were stated and briefly explained in Chapter 7. Here, we describe these cases with reference to the simplex terminology and format.

Multiple Optimal Solutions

If any of the $C_j - Z_j$ numbers of the nonbasic variables, in the optimal simplex tableau, are zero, we have multiple optimal solutions.

No Feasible Solution

The case of "no feasible solution" represents a problem where the set of constraints is inconsistent (i.e., mutually exclusive). In the simplex algorithm, this case will occur if the solution is optimal (i.e., the test of optimality is satisfied), but some artificial variable remains in the optimal solution with a nonzero value.

Unbounded Solution

Think of a simplex tableau with *only one* unfavorable $C_j - Z_j$. This identifies the only incoming candidate. Assume now that all ratios of substitution under this key column are either zero or negative. This means that no change in the basis can be made, and no current basic variable can be reduced to zero. Actually, as the incoming variable is introduced, we continue to increase, without bounds, those basic variables whose ratios of substitution are negative. This illustrates an unbounded solution.

8.7
Degeneracy

It will be recalled that the simplex method is based on a set of rules whereby we proceed from one basic feasible solution to the next until an optimal solution, if it exists, is obtained. To proceed from one solution to the next by the simplex method, as the reader will recall, requires the identification of the key column and the key row.

Selection of the key column is a simple task, for it simply involves the identification of the column that contains the largest positive entry (maximization case) or the largest negative entry (minimization case) in the net evaluation row of a simplex tableau. However, in selecting the key row for purposes of replacing one of the basic variables, we can face two difficulties.

1. The initial simplex tableau may be such that one or more variables currently in the basis have a value of zero (one or more entries in the "Quantity" column are zero). If this happens, the minimum replacement quantity will be zero. It will then appear that the replacement process cannot be continued because the variable to be replaced is already zero.
2. The minimum replacement quantities for two or more variables currently in the basis may be the same. If this happens, there is a tie in terms of selection of the key row. In this case, removal of one of the tied variables will also reduce the other tied variable(s) to zero. In the next simplex tableau of this case, therefore, one or more of the basic variables will have a value of zero.

Both the above conditions give rise to a phenomenon known as *degeneracy*. Attempts to solve a degenerate linear programming problem will show that either: (1) after a finite number of iterations the optimum solution can be obtained, or (2) the problem begins to cycle,[22] thereby preventing the attainment of the optimal solution.

Let us illustrate the same example that was used to illustrate a degenerate basic feasible solution in Section 7.5.2 (see Figure 7.11 on p. 192).

Maximize

$$Z = 40X + 50Y$$

subject to the constraints

$$25X + 20Y \leqslant 5{,}000$$
$$20X + 30Y \leqslant 7{,}500$$

and

$$X, \quad Y \geqslant \quad 0$$

8.7.1 DESIGN AN INITIAL PROGRAM

Shown in Table 8.10 is the first program in which both the basic variables are the slack variables S_1 and S_2. Calculation of the net evaluation row in Table 8.10 shows that column Y is the key column. As previously, our next task is to choose a key row by identifying that basic variable which is to be replaced by the incoming variable (in this case the incoming variable is Y). But there is no unique key row in Table 8.10, since both row S_1 and row S_2 provide the limiting case. In other words, we have a tie between row S_1 and S_2.

---

[22] That is, during the solution stages, we keep returning to the same basis.

Table 8.10 *First Tableau*

Program (Basic Variables)	Profit per Unit, C_b	Quantity	$C_j \to$ 40 X	50 Y	0 S_1	0 S_2	Replacement Quantity
S_1	0	5,000	25	20	1	0	250 → outgoing variable
S_2	0	7,500	20	30	0	1	250
Z_j			0	0	0	0	
$C_j - Z_j$			40	50	0	0	

└── incoming variable

The introduction of 250 units of Y at this stage will require removing all units of S_1 and S_2 from the solution. This means that our next program will consist of only 250 units of Y. It appears, therefore, that our next tableau would have only one row instead of the two rows contained in Table 8.10. However, in the simplex algorithm, all tableaus, during all the solution stages, have the same number of rows. How, then, do we proceed in the case in which a tie appears? The answer is that, insofar as the simplex tableau format requires the replacement of only one basic variable at a time, we should somehow break the tie between row S_1 and row S_2 by designating one of them as the key row. Then, only that variable which falls in the key row should be shown as removed from the basis. The other will remain a basic variable, but its value will be zero. The mechanics for accomplishing this will be discussed in the following paragraphs.

8.7.2 SOLVING A DEGENERATE PROBLEM

In Table 8.10, we have encountered a degenerate situation. How do we resolve the degeneracy? Some rule is obviously needed to break the tie between the two basic variables S_1 and S_2. Several arbitrary rules have been suggested for making this decision. One such rule is that the variable whose subscript is smallest[23] should be removed first. Another rule calls for removing that variable whose subscript is found first in a table of random numbers. Another alternative, of course, is to remove one of the tied variables at will. All these alternatives are arbitrary, but they do permit the continuation of the solution by the simplex method.

We arbitrarily designate S_1 as the key row. The key number, then, is 20. Following the rules of transformation, we change the basic variables from S_1, S_2 (in Table 8.10) to Y, S_2 (in Table 8.11). The second program is shown in Table 8.11. Since all the $C_j - Z_j$ in Table 8.11 are either negative or zero, we have arrived at the optimal solution. However, the optimal solution is a *degenerate basic feasible solution* (the number of positive basic variables is *less than m*).

In Figure 7.11, we presented a graphical representation of our degenerate problem. The optimal solution of Table 8.11 corresponds to point A in Figure

Table 8.11 *Second and Optimal Tableau*

Program (Basic Variables)	Profit per Unit, C_b	Quantity	$C_j \rightarrow 40$ X	50 Y	0 S_1	0 S_2
Y	50	250	1.25	1	0.05	0
S_2	0	0	-17.5	0	-1.5	1
Z_j			62.5	50	2.5	0
$C_j - Z_j$			-22.5	0	-2.5	0

[23] If we had denoted X, Y, S_1, S_2 by X_1, X_2, X_3, X_4, then, from Table 8.10, X_3 would be removed first, since it would have the smaller subscript of the tied variables. That is, S_1 would be removed.

7.11. It should be noted that in this problem the resolution of degeneracy was a simple matter. No matter which of the tied variables was removed first, we would have obtained the same solution, although the *number of iterations* would have been greater had we removed S_2 first. Two remarks must be made at this time. First, an arbitrary removal of one of the tied variables may mean that a much larger number of iterations will be necessary to arrive at the optimal solution than would be the case if some other tied variable were removed from the basis. Second, a more serious situation may arise if an arbitrary selection of the tied variable leads us to what we earlier called *cycling*. In cycling, we start from a given set of basic variables and, after a few iterations, return to the same set so that an optimal solution may never be reached.

Although cycling is a theoretical possibility, it seldom occurs in practical problems. However, general methods of resolving degeneracy have been devised which, if followed, will ensure against falling into the cycle process.[24]

8.8
Summary

In this chapter, we presented both the rationale and the mechanics of the simplex method. In terms of the rationale, the simplex method rests on two concepts: feasibility and optimality. The search for the optimal solution consists of an iterative process that starts from a basic feasible solution, applies a test of optimality, obtains if necessary a better basic feasible solution, and stops only when an optimal solution has been identified.

In terms of mechanics, the first step is to state the problem mathematically. Then the inequality constraints are converted into equality constraints (by the inclusion of slack, surplus, or artificial variables) and the objective function is properly modified (profit or cost coefficient of zero for slack or surplus variables; profit coefficient of $-M$ and cost coefficient of $+M$ for artificial slack variables). The next step is to design an initial program (and display it as a simplex tableau) that usually includes only the slack, surplus, or artificial variables. Then a test of optimality is applied by noting the signs of the $C_j - Z_j$ (net evaluation numbers). If a given program is not optimal, it is revised according to definite rules of transformation for the key row and nonkey rows of the simplex tableau that contains the program. This procedure is repeated until an optimal solution (if it exists) is obtained. A schematic diagram of this iterative procedure is given in Figure 8.3.

The $C_j - Z_j$ numbers in the net evaluation row of the optimal simplex tableau have an economic interpretation. They yield the marginal worth of a given resource, or the imputed value of one unit of the required item or characteristic (e.g., the imputed value of a unit of a vitamin).

We also illustrated how, in the context of the simplex terminology and format, we can identify the special cases of multiple optimal solutions, no feasible solution, unbounded solution, and degenerate basic feasible solution.

[24] See Charnes et al. [1953]. For an illustration, see Loomba [1964, p. 158].

Finally, we used the simplex method to illustrate a minimization problem and the case of degeneracy in linear programming.

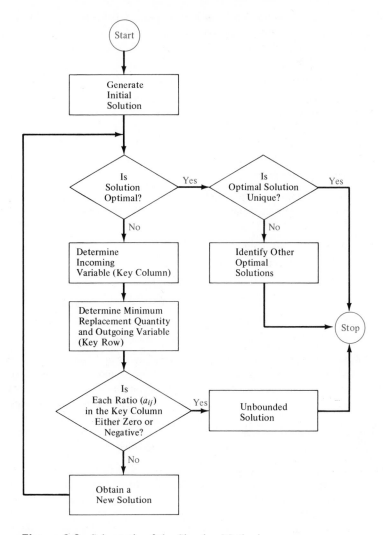

Figure 8.3. Schematic of the Simplex Method.

References

See the References at the end of Chapter 7.

Review Questions and Problems

8.1. Describe the rationale of the simplex method.

8.2. What is meant by the term "opportunity cost"? How is the concept of opportunity cost employed in designing a test for optimality?

8.3. What is the significance of $C_j - Z_j$ numbers in a simplex tableau? Describe the rule for calculating $C_j - Z_j$ numbers. Interpret the economic significance of $C_j - Z_j$ numbers in terms of marginal worth. In terms of imputed value.

8.4. Illustrate the following terms with respect to Table 8.3.
  (a) Key column (the "incoming" variable that is currently nonbasic)
  (b) Key row (the "outgoing" variable that is currently basic)
  (c) Key number
  (d) Minimum replacement quantity

8.5. State the transformation rules for: (a) the key row, and (b) the nonkey rows. Explain the rationale for these rules by the argument established in Appendix D.

8.6. What role do the artificial variables play in the simplex method?

8.7. What are the decision rules of testing optimality for maximization problems? For minimization problems?

8.8. What conditions must exist in a simplex tableau to establish the existence of multiple optimal solutions? No feasible solutions? Unbounded solution? Degeneracy?

8.9. Which variable would you enter into the second simplex tableau for each of the following objective functions:
  (a) Maximize $10X_1 + 3X_2 + 4X_3 + 11X_4$
  (b) Maximize $-3X_1 - 2X_2 - 7X_3 - 6X_4$
  (c) Minimize $10X_1 + 3X_2 + 4X_3 + 11X_4$
  (d) Minimize $3X_1 + 2X_2 - 7X_3 + 6X_4$

8.10. Speedy Pharmaceutical has developed a new drug designed to ward off drowsiness. There are three ingredients, two compounds and an inert filler. In order to be effective the drug must contain 250 mg of compound A and 300 mg of compound B. Each pill weighs 10 grams. The FDA, after conducting tests, has suggested that no more than 450 mg of compound A and 600 mg of compound B be in each pill. Compound A costs \$0.02/gram, compound B costs \$0.15/gram, and the filler costs \$0.07/gram. Formulate the problem and solve for the optimal mix.

8.11. The Pisa Tower Construction Company is in need of a particular mixture of cement. Limestone and clay, the two ingredients, cost \$6 and \$10 per ton, respectively. The company needs 300 tons of the mixture for a project. To assure that the mixture will have the proper hardening qualities, the company knows that it must use at least 140 tons of clay and no more than 180 tons of limestone. Use the simplex method to determine the mixture of clay and limestone that will minimize cost.

8.12. The Tastee Ice Cream Corporation must use a mixture of cream and milk in preparing its products. For the coming month the company expects to produce 250 dozen gallons of ice cream and wants to minimize cost. Management feels that the proper mixture of cream and milk would require at least 130 dozen gallons of cream and no more than 150 dozen gallons of milk. Cream costs \$12/dozen gallons and milk costs \$8/dozen gallons. Using the simplex method, determine the optimal mixture for cost minimization.

8.13. The Lite Company produces two types of lamps, contemporary and colonial. The company earns net profit of \$9 for each contemporary lamp sold and \$6 for each colonial. Each unit of both lamp types must pass through two processing areas: assembly and wiring. Assembly has 72 hours and wiring has 60 hours available per week. Each contemporary lamp requires 6 hours in assembly and 4 hours in wiring.

The Simplex Method   Chapter 8

Each colonial lamp requires 4 hours in assembly and 2 hours in wiring. Use the simplex method to determine the product mix that will maximize profit for the Lite Company. What does the solution suggest for the Lite Company in the way of future production?

8.14. The Nut'n'Bolt Company manufactures two types of screws, wooden and metal. Each screw has to go through two machines, slotting and threading. Each machine can be run a maximum of 40 hours/week. One hundred wooden screws need 1 minute on the threading machine and 2 minutes on the slotting machine. One hundred metal screws need 12 minutes and 1 minute on the threading and slotting machines, respectively. If the profit is 5 cents/hundred for wooden screws and 11 cents/hundred for metal screws, what is the optimal product mix?

8.15. EMU Airlines flies three types of airplanes: short range, medium range, and long range. The company leases the planes from a manufacturer. The profit contribution (in millions of dollars) of the planes is: long range, 5; medium range, 4; and short range, 2. The airline employs 10 mechanics, 25 pilots, and 75 stewardesses. The long-range plane needs 1 mechanic, 4 pilots, and 3 stewardesses. The medium-range plane requires 4 mechanics, 2 pilots, and 3 stewardesses. Each short-range plane requires 2 mechanics, 1 pilot, and 3 stewardesses. How many planes of each type should the airline lease in order to maximize profits? (Ignore the fact that the number of planes is indivisible.)

CHAPTER 9

The Dual, Sensitivity Analysis, and Selected Applications of Linear Programming

MAJOR CONCEPTS AND TOPICS DISCUSSED IN THIS CHAPTER

The Concepts of the Primal and Dual Problems

Seller's maximization problem
Buyer's minimization problem
The dual variables
Artificial accounting prices, shadow prices, implicit prices, and marginal worths

Comparison of the Optimal Tableaus of the Primal and Its Dual

Sensitivity Analysis

Changes in the objective function coefficients (C_j)
Changes in the input–output coefficients (a_{ij})
Changes in resource or requirement level (b_i)

The Process of Building a Linear Programming Model

Problem formulation
Building the objective function
Building the constraints
Preparation for solution by computer

Selected Applications of Linear Programming

Computer Programs for Linear Programming

9.1
Introduction

In this chapter, we turn our attention to accomplishing these five tasks:

1. Describe and illustrate the concept of the dual problem.
2. Describe and illustrate the idea of sensitivity analysis.
3. Emphasize the *process* of building a linear programming model.
4. Indicate the application potential of linear programming by considering some practical problems in selected areas.
5. Provide a selected set of computer programs for linear programming.

9.2
The Concept of the Dual

Linear programming problems exist in pairs. Thus, in linear programming, associated with every maximization problem is a minimization problem. Conversely, associated with every minimization problem is a maximization problem. As we shall see in this chapter, it is possible to state an original linear programming problem (maximization or minimization) and derive its dual problem according to well-known relationships of duality.[1] The original linear programming problem is called the *primal problem*, and the derived problem is called the *dual problem*.

The concept of the dual problem is important for several reasons.[2] We mention two here. First, the variables of the dual problem can convey important information to managers in terms of formulating their future plans. Second, in some cases the dual problem can be instrumental in arriving at the optimal solution to the original problem in many fewer iterations (thereby reducing the cost and time of computation). For example, it takes much less computational effort to solve by the simplex method the dual of a linear programming problem whose original dimension[3] is, say, $5,000 \times 2$.

The format of the simplex method is such that when the primal problem is solved, the dual is automatically being solved. Thus, the optimal solution to the dual can be read from the optimal tableau of the primal problem (see Figure 9.1).

The concept of the dual will be explained in this chapter by means of an example.

[1] See Section 3.4 of Loomba and Turban [1974].

[2] See Loomba and Turban [1974, p. 91].

[3] The dual of this problem will have a dimension of $2 \times 5,000$. That is, an $m \times n$ primal problem reflects itself as an $n \times m$ dual problem.

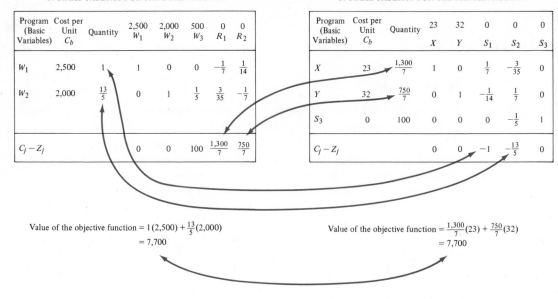

Value of the objective function $= 1(2{,}500) + \frac{13}{5}(2{,}000)$

$= 7{,}700$

Value of the objective function $= \frac{1{,}300}{7}(23) + \frac{750}{7}(32)$

$= 7{,}700$

Figure 9.1. Comparison of the Primal and Dual Optimal Tableaus.

9.3
The Dual to a Maximization Problem

Let us consider the maximization problem of Table 9.1. As previously mentioned, the mathematical statement of the problem is

Maximize

$$Z = 23X + 32Y$$

subject to the constraints

$$10X + 6Y \leqslant 2{,}500 \text{ (machine-hours)}$$
$$5X + 10Y \leqslant 2{,}000 \text{ (machine-hours)}$$
$$1X + 2Y \leqslant 500 \text{ (man-hours)}$$
$$X, \quad Y \geqslant 0$$

Table 9.1 *Process Time Data per Unit of Product*

Department	Product		Resource Capacity per Time Period
	A	*B*	
Cutting	10	6	2,500
Folding	5	10	2,000
Packaging	1	2	500
Profit per Unit	$23	$32	

The maximization problem stated above is our primal problem. Associated with it is a linear programming minimization problem that is dual to the given problem. We propose to formulate the dual by means of an intuitive argument.

Think of the primal problem here as the *seller's maximization problem* because the seller wishes to maximize his profits. Also, it should be noted that: (1) technology is fixed, and (2) profits are generated because the seller has certain resources. Therefore, it is obvious that it will be useful, for purposes of managerial planning, to know what profits are generated by the respective resources. We answer this question by formulating a hypothetical buyer's problem.

Associated with the seller's maximization problem is a *buyer's minimization problem*. Let us explain the rationale. The buyer, it is assumed, will consider the purchase of the resources in full knowledge of the technical specifications given in Table 9.1.[4] If the buyer wishes to get an idea of his total outlay, he will have to determine how much he must pay to buy all the resources. Assume that he designates variables W_1, W_2, and W_3, to represent the per unit price or value that he will assign to cutting, folding, and packaging capacities, respectively, while making his purchase plans. The total outlay, which the buyer wishes to minimize, will be determined by the function $2,500W_1 + 2,000W_2 + 500W_3$. The objective function of the buyer, therefore, is

Minimize

$$Z = 2,500W_1 + 2,000W_2 + 500W_3 \tag{9.1}$$

The linear function of (9.1) must be minimized in view of the knowledge that the current technology yields a profit of \$23 by spending 10 machine-hours of the cutting department, 5 machine-hours of the folding department, and 1 man-hour of the packaging department. Hence, the specific values for the variables W_1, W_2, and W_3 must be assigned in such a manner that $10W_1 + 5W_2 + 1W_3$ generates *at least* \$23. By the same reasoning, and *simultaneously*, these assigned values must be such that $6W_1 + 10W_2 + 2W_3$ generates *at least* \$32. Hence, in the buyer's problem, the two structural constraints are

$$10W_1 + 5W_2 + 1W_3 \geqslant 23$$
$$6W_1 + 10W_2 + 2W_3 \geqslant 32$$

In addition, the assigned values to the resources in our problem must be nonnegative. That is, W_1, W_2, and W_3 must each be greater than or equal to zero.

We can now state the dual to the given primal problem.

Minimize

$$Z = 2,500W_1 + 2,000W_2 + 500W_3$$

subject to the constraints

$$10W_1 + 5W_2 + 1W_3 \geqslant 23$$
$$6W_1 + 10W_2 + 2W_3 \geqslant 32$$
$$W_1, \quad W_2, \quad W_3 \geqslant 0$$

Let us make some observations regarding the dual problem stated above.

1. The variables W_1, W_2, W_3, ..., are called the *dual variables*. The values

---

[4] This is because linear programming is a deterministic model that assumes static conditions and full knowledge of all actions as well as their consequences. See Section 7.2.1.

assigned to the dual variables in the optimal tableau of the dual problem represent artificial accounting prices, or implicit prices, or shadow prices, or marginal worths of the various resources. As mentioned in Section 9.4, the values of the dual variables can also be read from the net evaluation row of the optimal tableau of the primal problem. That is, the $C_j - Z_j$ of the optimal simplex tableau of the primal automatically yield the optimal solution to the dual (see Figure 9.1).

The dimension of any dual variable is determined by the units of the constraint to which the dual variable corresponds. Thus, note that the dimension of W_1 as well as W_2 is dollars/machine-hour, while the dimension of W_3 is dollars/man-hour. Similarly, if a constraint had been specified in, say, pounds, the dimension of its dual variable would have been dollars/pound. Furthermore, if one more (marginal) unit of a specified resource is made available, the value of the objective function will increase by an amount equal to the value of the dual variable associated with that resource.

2. Since, by definition, the entire profit in the maximization must be traced to the given resources, the buyer's total outlay, at the equilibrium point, must equal the total profit. That is, the optimal value of the objective function of the primal equals the optimal value of the objective function of the dual.

3. The example that we have provided is that of a symmetrical dual. Here all structural constraints are inequalities, and all variables are restricted to non-negative values.[5] The "symmetry" in our example can be observed if we place the primal and the dual next to each other, as shown in Table 9.2.

Note that:

- If in the primal, the objective function is to be maximized, then in the dual it is to be minimized. Conversely, if in the primal the objective function is to be minimized, then in the dual it is to be maximized.
- Objective function coefficients of the primal appear as right-hand-side numbers in the dual, and vice versa.
- The right-hand-side numbers of the primal appear as objective function coefficients in the dual, and vice versa.
- The input–output coefficient matrix of the dual is the transpose of the input–output coefficient matrix of the primal, and vice versa.[6]
- If the inequalities in the primal are of the "less than or equal to" type, then in the dual they are of the "greater than or equal to" type. Conversely, if the

Table 9.2

Primal	Dual
Maximize $23X + 32Y$ subject to the constraints	Minimize $2{,}500W_1 + 2{,}000W_2 + 500W_3$ subject to the constraints
$10X + 6Y \leqslant 2{,}500$	$10W_1 + 5W_2 + 1W_3 \geqslant 23$
$5X + 10Y \leqslant 2{,}000$	$6W_1 + 10W_2 + 2W_3 \geqslant 32$
$1X + 2Y \leqslant 500$	$W_1, \quad W_2, \quad W_3 \geqslant 0$
$X, \quad Y \geqslant 0$	

[5] For a discussion of unsymmetrical dual, see Loomba and Turban [1974, p. 92].

[6] For a definition of the terms *matrix* and *transpose*, see Appendix C.

inequalities in the primal are of the "greater than or equal to" type; then in the dual they are of the "less than or equal to" type.

These comments and some additional items of correspondence are now summarized in Table 9.3.

Table 9.3

Primal	Dual
Maximize	Minimize
Objective function	Right-hand side
Right-hand side	Objective function
ith row of input–output coefficients	ith column of input–output coefficients
jth column of input–output coefficients	jth row of input–output coefficients
ith relation an inequality $(\leqslant)$	ith variable nonnegative
ith relation an equality $(=)$	ith variable unrestricted in sign
jth variable nonnegative	jth relation an inequality $(\geqslant)$
jth variable unrestricted in sign	jth relation an equality $(=)$

9.4
Solving the Dual Problem

The simplex algorithm can now be applied to the following dual problem:

Minimize

$$Z = 2{,}500W_1 + 2{,}000W_2 + 500W_3 - 0R_1 - 0R_2 + MA_1 + MA_2$$

subject to the constraints

$$10W_1 + 5W_2 + 1W_3 - 1R_1 + 0R_2 + 1A_1 + 0A_2 = 23$$
$$6W_1 + 10W_2 + 2W_3 + 0R_1 - 1R_2 + 0A_1 + 1A_2 = 32$$

and

$$W_1, \quad W_2, \quad W_3, \quad R_1, \quad R_2, \quad A_1, \quad A_2 \geqslant 0$$

The various solution stages are summarized in Tables 9.4 to 9.6. Because all the $C_j - Z_j$ are positive or zero in Table 9.6, the third tableau represents the optimal program. The optimal program is

$$W_1 = 1, W_2 = 2.6 \quad \text{and} \quad W_3 = 0, R_1 = 0, R_2 = 0$$

The meaning of this program is as follows:

W_1 = marginal worth of 1 unit of the cutting department resource
  = \$1.00/machine-hour

W_2 = marginal worth of 1 unit of the folding department resource
  = \$2.60/machine-hour

W_3 = marginal worth of 1 unit of the packaging department resource
  = \$0.00/man-hour

Table 9.4 *First Tableau*

Program (Basic Variables)	Cost per Unit, C_b	Quantity	$C_j \rightarrow$ 2,500 W_1	2,000 W_2	500 W_3	0 R_1	0 R_2	M A_1	M A_2	Replacement Quantity
A_1	M	23	10	5	1	-1	0	1	0	$2\frac{3}{10} \rightarrow$ outgoing variable
A_2	M	32	6	10	2	0	-1	0	1	$5\frac{1}{3}$
Z_j			16M	15M	3M	-M	-M	M	M	
$C_j - Z_j$			2,500 - 16M	2,000 - 15M	500 - 3M	M	M	0	0	

incoming variable

Table 9.5 *Second Tableau*

Program (Basic Variables)	Cost per Unit, C_b	Quantity	$C_j \rightarrow$ 2,500 W_1	2,000 W_2	500 W_3	0 R_1	0 R_2	M A_1	M A_2	Replacement Quantity
W_1	2,500	2.3	1	0.5	0.1	-0.1	0	0.1	0	4.6
A_2	M	18.2	0	7	1.4	0.6	-1	-0.6	1	$2.6 \rightarrow$ outgoing variable
Z_j			2,500	$1,250+7M$	$250+\frac{14}{10}M$	$-250+\frac{6}{10}M$	$-M$	$250-\frac{6}{10}M$	M	
$C_j - Z_j$			0	$750-7M$	$250-1.4M$	$250-0.6M$	M	$-250+1.6M$	0	

— incoming variable

Table 9.6 *Third and Optimal Tableau*

Program (Basic Variables)	Cost per Unit, C_b	Quantity	$C_j \rightarrow$ 2,500 W_1	2,000 W_2	500 W_3	0 R_1	0 R_2	M A_1	M A_2
W_1	2,500	1	1	0	0	$-\frac{1}{7}$	$\frac{1}{14}$	$\frac{1}{7}$	$-\frac{1}{14}$
W_2	2,000	2.6	0	1	0.2	$\frac{3}{35}$	$-\frac{1}{7}$	$-\frac{3}{35}$	$\frac{1}{7}$
Z_j			2,500	2,000	400	$-\frac{1300}{7}$	$-\frac{750}{7}$	$\frac{1300}{7}$	$\frac{750}{7}$
$C_j - Z_j$			0	0	100	$\frac{1300}{7}$	$\frac{750}{7}$	$M-\frac{1300}{7}$	$M-\frac{750}{7}$

When we examine the $C_j - Z_j$ numbers in the net evaluation row of Table 8.5, on p. 216, (also see optimal tableau for the primal shown in Figure 9.1), we note that the *absolute values* of the $C_j - Z_j$ under the slack variables S_1, S_2, and S_3 are precisely 1, 2.6, and 0. The fact that the marginal value of the packaging department resource is zero is supported by the fact that in the optimal program in Table 8.5, p. 216, $S_3 = 100$ (i.e., the optimal program leaves 100 units of the packaging capacity unused). Also, see Figure 9.1.

In Figure 9.1, we compare the optimal tableaus of the primal and the dual and indicate their relationships to each other. Note that the A_1 and A_2 columns of Table 9.6 (optimal tableau) have been omitted in Figure 9.1. This is perfectly all right because, as the reader will recall, the artificial variables have no physical interpretation. They are a device to obtain, in an easy manner, the first basic feasible solution, when the constraints are either equalities or inequalities of the "greater than or equal to" type.

9.5
Comparison of the Optimal Tableaus of the Primal and Its Dual

We place in Figure 9.1 the optimal tableau of the primal (Table 8.5) next to the optimal tableau of its dual (Table 9.6) and make some important observations.

- The objective functions of the two optimal tableaus assume identical values.
- The $C_j - Z_j$ entries (with signs changed) in the net evaluation row under columns S_1 and S_2 of the optimal tableau of the primal are the same as entries under the "Quantity" column in the optimal tableau of the dual problem. That is, the optimal solution to the dual can be retrieved from appropriate $C_j - Z_j$ of the optimal simplex tableau of the primal.
- Since S_3 is a basic variable in the optimal tableau of the primal, it indicates unused packaging capacity. Hence, $W_3 = 0$, as can be inferred from the optimal tableau of the dual.
- The magnitudes of the variables X and Y in the primal optimal tableau are exactly the same as the entries in the net evaluation row under columns R_1 and R_2 of the optimal tableau of the dual problem. This type of correspondence between the optimal tableaus of the primal and its dual always exists. Thus, the solution to a primal problem in linear programming can always provide a solution to its dual.

The relationships just described should be carefully checked and grasped by the reader.

9.6
Sensitivity Analysis

Optimal solutions to linear programming problems are obtained under a set of assumptions such as fixed technology, fixed prices, and fixed levels of resources or requirements. These assumptions, implying certainty, complete knowledge, and static conditions, permit us to design an optimal program. The conditions in the real world, however, might be different from those that are assumed by the model. It is, therefore, desirable to determine *how sensitive* the optimal solution is to different types of changes in the problem data and parameters. The changes whose effect on the optimal solution needs to be analyzed include: (1) changes in such parameters as objective function coefficients (C_j), input–output coefficients (a_{ij}), resource or requirement levels (b_i); and (2) possible addition or deletion of products or methods of production. *Sensitivity analysis, postoptimality analysis,* and *parametric programming* are various names for investigating the relationships between optimal solutions and possible changes in various components of the problem.

Managers conduct sensitivity analysis when, in their planning processes, they ask what are called the "what-if" questions. The what-if questions are like a double-edged sword. They are designed to project the consequences of possible changes in the future, as well as the impact of the possible errors of estimation of the past. Thus, the need for sensitivity analysis (or *what-if* analysis) arises from two sources. First, we want to know the effect of, and hence be prepared for, possible future changes in various parameters and components of the problem. Second, we want to know the degree of error, in estimating certain parameters, that could be absorbed by the current optimal solution. In other words, sensitivity analysis answers questions regarding what errors of estimation could have been committed, or what possible future changes can occur, without disturbing the optimality of the current optimal solution

The results of sensitivity analysis establish *ranges* (upper limits and lower limits) for various parameters $(C_j, a_{ij}, b_i,$ etc.) within which the current optimal program will remain optimal. In this sense, sensitivity analysis is a major guide to managerial planning and control. Further, it should be noted that sensitivity analysis avoids the need for *reworking the entire problem* from the very beginning each time a change is investigated or incorporated. Rather, the current optimal solution can be used to study the effect of changes with minimal computational effort. It is possible to illustrate sensitivity analysis with respect to changes in C_j, a_{ij}, and b_i; adding or deleting a new column (i.e., a new product); and adding or deleting a new row (i.e., a new process).[7] This, however, requires a level of mathematics beyond the scope of this book. For this reason, we shall limit our discussion of sensitivity analysis to a two-dimensional linear programming problem that is amenable to graphical representation.

We shall present a brief descriptive analysis of changes in the objective function coefficients (C_j), changes in the input–output coefficients (a_{ij}), and changes in resource or requirement levels (b_i). Since it is possible to handle sensitivity analysis of C_j within the framework of the simplex method, we present a more detailed analysis for C_j.

9.6.1   CHANGES IN THE OBJECTIVE FUNCTION COEFFICIENTS (C_j)

Consider the maximization problem of Table 7.1 from p. 171. This problem was graphed in Figure 7.6 on p. 183. The sensitivity analysis of C_j in this problem requires the determination of a *range* for each profit coefficient. Changing the

---

[7] For illustrative examples, see Loomba [1976]. Also, see Loomba and Turban [1974, pp. 137–147].

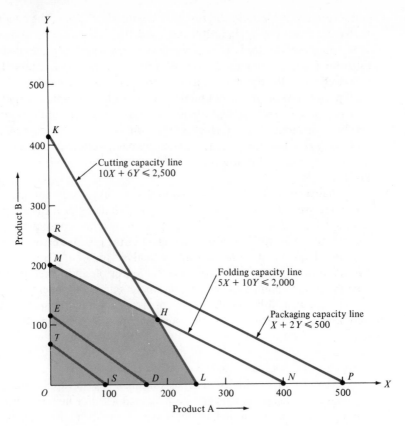

Figure 9.2

profit coefficients boils down to changing the slope of the isoprofit line. Thus, the question is: What values of the slope of the isoprofit line will shift the optimal solution from the current extreme point to another adjacent extreme point of the convex set?

To answer this question, we refer to Figure 7.6 (reproduced as Figure 9.2). We note the following in Figure 9.2.

- Slope of the isoprofit line $= \dfrac{-C_1}{C_2} = \dfrac{-23}{32}$

- Current optimal extreme point is H.

- Two adjacent extreme points are point M and L.

- Slope of line $MH = \dfrac{-5}{10} = \dfrac{-1}{2}$

- Slope of line $HL = \dfrac{-10}{6}$

Since the slope of any isoprofit line (e.g., line ED in Figure 9.2) is given by $\dfrac{-C_1}{C_2}$, the question here is twofold. First, if we let C_2 remain at \$32, what value must C_1 take before the slope of the isoprofit line will change to make point M the optimal point? This will happen when $-C_1/C_2$ is "less than or equal to" $-1/2$. Second, with $C_2 = \$32$, what value must C_1 take before the slope of the isoprofit line will change to make point L the optimal point? This will happen when $-C_1/C_2$ is "greater than or equal to" $-10/6$. We can ask similar questions regarding C_2, assuming that C_1 is held at \$23. It is clear, therefore, that the range of C_1 or C_2 can be investigated as follows:

$$\frac{-10}{6} \leqslant \frac{-C_1}{C_2} \leqslant \frac{-1}{2} \tag{9.2}$$

To investigate the range of C_1, we let C_2 assume its current value of \$32. Thus,

$$\frac{-10}{6} \leqslant \frac{-C_1}{32} \leqslant \frac{-1}{2}$$

The *minimum* profit coefficient C_1 (for which the current solution remains optimal) is given by

$$\frac{-C_1}{32} \leqslant \frac{-1}{2}$$

or

$$C_1 \geqslant 16$$

That is, the *lower limit* for C_1 is \$16. It is clear from (9.2) that the *maximum* profit coefficient C_1 (for which the current solution remains optimal) is given by

$$\frac{-10}{6} \leqslant \frac{-C_1}{32}$$

or

$$C_1 \leqslant 53\tfrac{1}{3}$$

That is, the *upper limit* for C_1 is $53\tfrac{1}{3}$. Hence, the range of C_1 for which the current solution remains optimal is

$$\$16 \leqslant C_1 \leqslant \$53\tfrac{1}{3}$$

The range for C_2 for this problem can also be established. We leave this task to the reader ($13.80 \leqslant C_2 \leqslant 46.00$). Next we present a more detailed analysis of changes in C_j.

The sensitivity of the optimal solution to changes in the objective function coefficients (C_j) is investigated by checking the sign, in the optimal tableau, of the new net-evaluation numbers, $(C_j + G) - Z_j$. The variable G reflects the amount of change in C_j, and it can be positive or negative. For maximization problems, the current basis remains optimal as long as each $(C_j + G) - Z_j$ remains nonpositive. Conversely, for minimization problems, the current basis remains optimal as long as each $(C_j + G) - Z_j$ remains nonnegative.

Let us advance some intuitive arguments to establish the required actions in carrying out the analysis for changes in C_j. Consider first the idea of a *nonbasic variable* in maximization problems. It is clear that a nonbasic variable can enter the solution only if its profit coefficient is increased beyond a certain limit. Hence, in maximization problems, we must determine the *upper limit* of the profit coefficient of each nonbasic variable. Beyond that limit the optimality of the current solution is destroyed. Conversely, in minimization problems, sensitivity analysis requires the determination of the *lower limit* of C_j for a nonbasic variable. Hence, for nonbasic variables we have to determine either the upper limit (in maximization problems) or the lower limit (in minimization problems).

However, when it comes to conducting sensitivity analysis on the objective function coefficients of the *basic variables*, we must investigate the *range* (i.e., both the upper and lower limits). The determination of the range is necessary because an increase in the objective function coefficient of a basic variable would mean that, at some point, resources from other products should be diverted to this more profitable product. Similarly, a decrease in the objective function coefficient of the same basic variable would mean that, at some point, resources should be diverted away from this less-profitable product. We summarize the implications of our intuitive arguments in Table 9.7.

Table 9.7 *Sensitivity Analysis for* C_j

Type of Variable	Maximization Case	Minimization Case
Nonbasic	Determine the *upper* limit	Determine the *lower* limit
Basic	Determine the *range*	Determine the *range*

While determining the range (i.e., both the upper and lower limits) for C_j of a basic variable, it can happen that only one of the limits is meaningful. If such is indeed the case in a specific situation, it will be identified by the mechanics of the analysis, as we shall illustrate in the following example.

Example 9.1 | Let us illustrate sensitivity analysis for C_j with respect to the maximization problem whose technical specifications appear in Table 9.8. The optimal simplex tableau for the problem is given in Table 9.9. In the optimal solution we observe that X, S_2, and S_3 are basic variables, and Y and S_1 are nonbasic variables.

Table 9.8

Department	Product A	B	Capacity
Cutting	10	6	2,500
Folding	5	10	2,000
Packaging	1	2	500
Profit per Unit	$50	$25	

Table 9.9 *Optimal Solution*

Program (Basic Variables)	Profit per Unit, C_b	Quantity	$C_j \rightarrow$ 50 X	25 Y	0 S_1	0 S_2	0 S_3
X	50	250	1	$\frac{3}{5}$	$\frac{1}{10}$	0	0
S_2	0	750	0	7	$-\frac{1}{2}$	1	0
S_3	0	250	0	0	$\frac{7}{5}$	0	1
Z_j			50	30	5	0	0
$C_j - Z_j$			0	-5	-5	0	0

Analysis for C_j of Nonbasic Variables

Let us first consider the case of a *nonbasic* variable. In the optimal tableau of a maximization problem, a nonbasic variable (the product is not being produced) has a negative $C_j - Z_j$.[8] The negative sign indicates that the production of the product would, at that solution stage, decrease the profit. The question that we want to answer is this: By what amount will the profit coefficient of the nonbasic variable have to be increased to destroy the optimality of the current program? Let this amount be G_2 for the nonbasic variable Y, and let the corresponding profit coefficient be $C'_2 = C_2 + G_2$. The optimality of the solution shown in Table 9.9 is destroyed as soon as

$$C'_2 - Z_2 > 0 \quad \text{or} \quad (C_2 + G_2) - Z_2 > 0 \tag{9.3}$$

We see from column Y of Table 9.9 that $C_2 = 25$ and $Z_2 = 30$. Substituting these values in (9.3), we obtain $(25 + G_2) - 30 > 0$, or $G_2 > 5$. That is, the *change* in profit coefficient of the nonbasic variable Y will have to be more than 5 in order to destroy the optimality of the current optimal solution. Hence, the upper limit for C_2 is $25 + 5 = 30$. That is, as soon as the profit coefficient of Y is higher than 30, we must make Y a basic variable.

In our example, the only other nonbasic variable is S_1. Since S_1 is a slack variable, we shall not bother to conduct sensitivity analysis on its profit coefficient.

We repeat that in maximization problems we are interested in determining the upper limit beyond which the profit coefficient of a nonbasic variable will *destroy optimality* of the current solution. This upper limit for the profit coefficients of the nonbasic variables in maximization problems is determined from the criterion

$$(C_j + G) - Z_j > 0 \tag{9.4}$$

[*Note:* Alternatively, we can say that the current solution will *remain optimal* only if each $(C_j + G) - Z_j \leqslant 0$.]

In minimization problems, we are interested in determining the lower limit below which the cost coefficient of a nonbasic variable will *destroy optimality* of the current solution. This lower limit for the cost coefficients of the nonbasic variables in minimization problems is determined from the criterion

---

[8] In the case of multiple optimal solution, the $C_j - Z_j$ could be zero.

$$(C_j + G) - Z_j < 0 \qquad (9.5)$$

[*Note:* Alternatively we can say that the current solution will *remain optimal* only if each $(C_j + G) - Z_j \geqslant 0$.]

Analysis for C_j of Basic Variables

Let us now investigate the effect of the changes in a *basic* variable. In Table 9.9, we see that variables X, S_2, and S_3 are the basic variables. Let us consider variable X whose current profit coefficient is 50. Let us change this coefficient to $50 + G_1$ and then proceed with our analysis. The change in the profit coefficient of X is reflected in Table 9.10. Note that Table 9.10 is the same as Table 9.9 except that the profit coefficient of X has been changed from 50 to $50 + G_1$ (as a result, rows Z_j and $C_j - Z_j$ of Table 9.10 have also been changed).

Since this is a maximization problem, the solution shown in Table 9.10 will remain optimal only if each $C_j - Z_j \leqslant 0$. Hence, to determine the value of G_1, we must solve the following set of linear inequalities:

$$-5 - \frac{3}{5}G_1 \leqslant 0 \qquad (9.6)$$

$$-5 - \frac{1}{10}G_1 \leqslant 0 \qquad (9.7)$$

From the first inequality, $G_1 \geqslant -\frac{25}{3}$; from the second equality, $G_1 \geqslant -50$. That is, the binding constraint is $G_1 \geqslant -\frac{25}{3}$. Hence, we conclude that the profit coefficient of X must decrease by more than $8\frac{1}{3}$ in order to destroy the current optimal solution.

Note that we have established the lower limit[9] for the profit coefficient of X. The nature of the two inequalities (9.6) and (9.7) was such that only one side of the range was determined. If both sides of the range (i.e., the lower as well as the upper limit) were meaningful, the inequalities, such as (9.6) and (9.7), will generate both limits.

Table 9.10

Program (Basic Variables)	Profit per Unit, C_b	Quantity	$C_j \rightarrow$ $50 + G_1$ X	25 Y	0 S_1	0 S_2	0 S_3
X	$50 + G_1$	250	1	$\frac{3}{5}$	$\frac{1}{10}$	0	0
S_2	0	750	0	7	$-\frac{1}{2}$	1	0
S_3	0	250	0	0	$\frac{7}{5}$	0	1
Z_j			$50 + G_1$	$30 + \frac{3}{5}G_1$	$5 + \frac{1}{10}G_1$	0	0
$C_j - Z_j$			0	$-5 - \frac{3}{5}G_1$	$-5 - \frac{1}{10}G_1$	0	0

[9] The lower limit for C_1, the profit coefficient of X, is $50 - \frac{25}{3} = 41\frac{2}{3}$. While conducting sensitivity analysis on a basic variable, it should be noted that, in the established range, the basic variables remain the same. But the values of the basic variables and objective function change.

An examination of Table 9.10 indicates why an upper limit for the profit coefficient of X (i.e., C_1) is not meaningful in terms of sensitivity analysis. No matter how much C_1 is increased, it will never affect the optimality of the solution shown in Table 9.10. The product X is the only *real* variable in the current optimal solution.

Whenever a range exists for C_j of basic variables, it will automatically be established by the simultaneous solution of the linear inequalities shown in (9.8) and (9.9).

For maximization problems:

$$(C_j + G) - Z_j \leqslant 0 \qquad j = 1, 2, \ldots \qquad (9.8)$$

For minimization problems:

$$(C_j + G) - Z_j \geqslant 0 \qquad j = 1, 2, \ldots \qquad (9.9)$$

It should be noted that if sensitivity analysis were performed on the C_j's of the problem stated in Table 9.1 (the same problem as shown in Table 9.8 except that $C_1 = \$23$ and $C_2 = \$32$), then the two ranges for the profit coefficients are as shown below:

	Lower Limit	Upper Limit
For C_1	$(23 - 7) = 16.00$	$(23 + \frac{91}{3}) = 53\frac{1}{3}$
For C_2	$(32 - \frac{91}{5}) = 13.80$	$(32 + 14) = 46.00$

The range for C_1 was established earlier by graphical analysis. The reader should verify these results by conducting sensitivity analysis on C_1 and C_2 of Table 9.1 by the more comprehensive simplex format presented in this section. [*Hint:* Use Table 8.5 for determining the inequalities shown in (9.8)].

9.6.2 CHANGES IN THE INPUT–OUTPUT COEFFICIENTS (a_{ij})

Changes in the input–output coefficients reflect potential changes in the state of technology. An improvement in technology means that less resources will be required to produce a product and hence the values of a_{ij} will be reduced. Thus, if for a nonbasic variable, the value of a_{ij} is reduced, it will affect the $C_j - Z_j$ of that nonbasic variable. Hence, the question for the nonbasic variable is: To what value can the a_{ij} of a nonbasic variable be reduced before it will destroy the optimality of the current solution? The analysis of a_{ij} for a basic variable is a bit more complicated.[10]

In graphical terms, changes in a_{ij} mean that the convex solution set will change. Note that changes in a_{ij} do not affect the slope of the isoprofit line. Therefore, in Figure 9.2, we could conduct sensitivity analysis of a_{ij} by establishing the new area of feasible solutions (i.e., new convex solution set) and then testing whether the current optimal solution at point H remains optimal.

[10] See Loomba and Turban [1974, p. 145].

9.6.3 CHANGES IN RESOURCE OR REQUIREMENT LEVELS (b_i)

Knowledge of how sensitive the optimal solution is to changes in resources or requirements (b_i) is often important to managers because of changing conditions in the marketplace. It is extremely useful for planning purposes to know the ranges within which each available resource, or stated requirement, can vary without affecting the *feasibility* of the current basic variables. It is interesting to note that changes in b_i affect the magnitudes of the basic variables as well as the value of the objective function. However, the $C_j - Z_j$ (the net evaluation row numbers) are not affected. Hence, the current solution remains optimal until one of the basic variables becomes infeasible. It is this fact that is used for conducting sensitivity analysis for changes in each b_i.[11]

In terms of graphical discussion, changes in b_i mean that the convex solution set will change. For example, if we increase b_1 from 2,500 to 4,000 in Table 9.1, the area of feasible solutions will change from OMHL (in Figure 9.2) to a larger area. If we decrease b_1 from 2,500 to 1,200, the area of feasible solutions will become smaller. Thus, the question is: What is the upper limit and the lower limit on b_1 before the optimal solution will shift from the current extreme-point solution?

Note that changes in b_i do not affect the slope of the isoprofit line. It should also be stated that we establish *ranges* for b_i.

9.7
The Process of Building a Linear Programming Model[12]

In Section 2.8, we explained in detail the basic structure of a decision model with reference to *any* decision problem. Here we concentrate on the *formulation* of a linear programming model. In Section 9.8, we shall provide some illustrative examples.

9.7.1 PROBLEM FORMULATION

The need for the decision arises because a problem is perceived or triggered by an information or control system. For example, an aggressive company president driven by ambition can arbitrarily set the goal of doubling his annual sales over a 5-year period. Starting with this goal, he will set in motion a series of actions (e.g., acquisition of other companies, introduction of new products, penetration of new markets) that lead to the need and desirability of defining or formulating problems at various levels of the organization. Similarly, a poor income statement can trigger the need to search for underlying causes that must then be formulated as problems. It is quite obvious that organizational problems are seldom isolated problems; they affect, and are in turn affected by, other problems in the organization. For example, the determination of optimal inventory levels

---

[11] For a simple example, see Loomba [1976, p. 202].

[12] This section is adapted from Loomba and Turban [1974, pp. 58–59].

cannot be divorced from the consideration of available storage space or the constraints of working capital. However, in the real world, each problem is, to some extent, isolated and then solved. Its solution is then tested against the realities and power structure of organizational life. To a large extent, we proceed in exactly the same way when we formulate a linear programming problem. The problem is defined in terms of optimizing an objective function. Various solutions to the problem are then tested against the realities of available resources. The optimal solution is that which gives the best value of the objective function and does not violate any constraints. The search for the optimal solution can be conducted either manually or by using a computer. Thus, while formulating a linear programming problem, we must keep in mind these three aspects: (1) building the objective function, (2) building the constraints, and (3) preparation for solving the problem by computer.

9.7.2 BUILDING THE OBJECTIVE FUNCTION

The initial and probably the most difficult aspect of formulating a linear programming problem is the construction of its objective function. The function relates the objective or goal (dependent or criterion variable) to a set of independent (decision) variables and parameters. One of the first tasks is to identify both the independent (decision) variables and their structural relationship to the dependent (criterion) variable. When such problems are formulated, our focus is usually on a single dependent (criterion) variable, such as total profit, total cost, or percentage share of the market. Unfortunately, in many practical problems objectives are not single-dimensional; hence, it is necessary to convert a multiple-objective problem to a single-objective problem. We now describe three approaches for handling multiple-dimensional problems.

Expressing All Objectives But One in the Form of Constraints

Suppose that a company has three objectives: maximizing profit, maximizing the share of the market, and maximizing the growth rate. It could then specify two of these objectives in the form of constraints, thus leaving a single objective function to be maximized. For example, the company can state its objective as the maximization of its share of the market, subject to the constraints that it achieve at least $1.50 profit per share and at least a 10 percent annual rate of growth. An important consideration in this approach is how to choose those objectives that should be expressed as constraints and then determine their minimum acceptable levels.[13]

Expressing All Objectives as a Single Objective

Theoretically, it is possible to express any number of objectives as a single objective if we can find a common denominator, such as money or utility, that will express the tradeoff relationships among the various objectives. The major problem in such an approach is how to build the tradeoff relationships among the various objectives.

[13] The concept of *satisficing*, discussed in Section 5.2, is highly relevant here.

In many practical cases one finds that when multiple objectives are expressed as a single objective function, the resultant objective function is often nonlinear. However, nonlinear models are usually more difficult to solve than linear programming problems. The reason for considering the question of multiple objectives rather than a single objective is to bring the model as close to reality as possible. However, the attempt to reflect reality can often lead to difficulty, both in terms of formulating the problem and building its mathematical model. The result is that in several cases the models are so complicated that it is impossible (or too expensive) to find optimal solutions for them. The only recourse in such cases is either to sacrifice part of the reality and arrive at a simpler formulation, or to seek "approximate" or "good enough" (rather than optimal) solutions for the more realistic but more complicated problem. Finding the proper balance between the reality and the amount of complexity is a major problem for the model builder.

Goal Programming[14]

Goal programming is another method of handling multidimensional problems. The procedure entails listing various goals, ranking them in terms of priority, and specifying quantitative targets for each goal. These targets are incorporated as constraints, and the objective function is made up of deviations (overachievement as well as underachievement) from specified targets. The objective in goal programming is the minimization of these deviations. It should be noted that the assumed behavior in goal programming is that of a *satisficer* rather than of an *optimizer*.

9.7.3 BUILDING THE CONSTRAINTS

The specification of the constraints is derived from the existing state of technology; available levels of physical, economic, and other resources; and stated requirements relating to important factors. Each constraint is built after estimating the respective input–output coefficients that tie a resource, or a requirement, to specified decision variables (activities). Wherever possible, only the significant factors should be expressed as constraints, since the computational work in linear programming is proportional approximately to the cube of the number of constraints involved, and since an excessive number of constraints might outstrip the capabilities of the computer.

9.7.4 PREPARATION FOR SOLUTION BY COMPUTERS

Most real-life problems are too large and complex to be solved manually, so the availability of a computer is a necessity. In formulating and solving a linear programming problem, we should bear in mind that the problem should be so structured that it will be possible to solve it by computer.

A large number of computer packages (programs) are available that can be used to solve many problems if the problems are structured to conform to the

---

[14] For a very lucid explanation of goal programming, see Lee [1974].

package design. In some cases, all we have to do is to provide the computer with the coefficients of the objective function, the input–output coefficients of the constraints, resource capacities or requirements and the number of variables; the output is the solution to that problem. However, if the problem cannot be simplified to fit one of the packages, a program has to be devised to meet its particular requirements. This can be a costly and time-consuming process.

Computers are very important but are not the only aspect of linear programming applications and implementation. We shall discuss this matter further in Chapter 16. A selected set of computer programs for linear programming is shown in Table 9.15.

9.8
Selected Applications of Linear Programming[15]

Having grasped the basic ideas of linear programming, the process of building a linear programming model, relationships between the primal and the dual, and sensitivity analysis, we can extend our horizon to the practical world of linear programming. Linear programming is an extremely versatile tool for structuring decision problems faced by managers in different fields of endeavor. In this section we present a few examples that are considered classical in the practical applications of linear programming.

It should be emphasized at this point that duality is a *mathematical property* of linear programming. The meaning of the dual variable associated with a specified constraint is this: The value of a specified dual variable measures the change in the objective function in response to a 1-unit change in the corresponding constraint. This interpretation of the dual variable can in many (*but not all*) cases be translated into managerial guidance for policy formulation. In the examples that follow, we shall, whenever desirable, give a managerial interpretation to the dual variables.

9.8.1 THE PRODUCT-MIX PROBLEM

An example of the product-mix problem was presented in Sections 3.4 and 7.2. A product-mix problem exists whenever the manager is to determine an optimal production program or product mix (which products to produce and in what quantities). Such a problem can be solved by linear programming if the objective is to maximize a linear objective function, subject to a set of linear and nonnegativity constraints. Typically, in a product-mix problem, the inequality constraints are of the "less than or equal to" type.[16]

The product-mix problem is a problem that arises in all types of business situations. Portfolio-selection and media-selection problems (Sections 9.8.5 and 9.8.6) are, in effect, examples of the product-mix problem in the areas of finance and marketing.

---

[15] This section may be omitted without loss of continuity.

[16] This is because we have to maximize a linear objective function. What, for example, would be the practical consequence of a linear programming problem in which the linear function is to be maximized and *all* constraints are of the "greater than or equal to" type?

As explained in Section 9.3, the values of the dual variables associated with a primal product-mix problem represent the marginal worths of the resources. This information is of the utmost importance to managers in terms of planning for expansion of operations.

9.8.2 THE DIET PROBLEM

The diet (or feed-mix) problem arises whenever the manager is to determine the *optimal* combination of diet, or feed mix, that will satisfy specified nutritional requirements and minimize the total cost of purchasing the diet. An example of the diet problem was presented in Section 7.4.

In the diet problem, the objective is to minimize a linear objective function, subject to a set of linear and nonnegativity constraints. Typically, in the diet problem, the constraints are of the "greater than or equal to" type, because some minimum quantities of specified nutrients must be supplied by the diet.[17] The dual of the diet problem of Section 7.4 (see Table 7.2 on p. 189) can be stated as

Maximize

$$3,500W_1 + 7,000W_2$$

subject to the constraints

$$2W_1 + 6W_2 \leqslant 10$$
$$3W_1 + 2W_2 \leqslant 4.5$$

and

$$W_1, \quad W_2 \geqslant 0$$

(9.10)

The meaning of the dual variables in this case becomes clear if we reason as follows. The two foods in Table 7.2 have value because they contain nutrients I and II. The dual, therefore, can be viewed as the seller's problem, in which a value must be placed (in terms of cents per unit of nutrient) in such a way that the quantities of nutrients sold generate maximum revenue and, *at the same time*, meet the constraint of the competitive market prices of the two foods. Note that the dimensions of the two variables are:

$$W_1 = \text{cents/unit of nutrient I}$$
$$W_2 = \text{cents/unit of nutrient II}$$

If we solve the dual problem stated in (9.10), we find that $W_1 = 0.5$ cents, and $W_2 = 1.5$ cents. The managerial utility of this information is that we can shift to other types of food if a better "buy" is available. The knowledge of the values of W_1 and W_2 permits us to evaluate and compare different foods in terms of their nutritional contents and costs.

---

[17] The "greater than or equal to" types of inequalities are a natural consequence of the situation in which a linear function is to be minimized. What, for example, would be the practical consequence of a linear programming problem in which the linear function is to be minimized and *all* constraints are of the "less than or equal to" type?

9.8.3 THE TRANSPORTATION PROBLEM

The transportation problem was discussed in Section 3.5. The transportation problem is a special case of the general linear programming model. It deals with designing an optimal transportation program when a homogeneous commodity is to be shipped from a set of origins (e.g., plants) to a set of destinations (e.g., warehouses). We discuss the transportation problem further in Chapter 10.

We shall see in Section 10.10 that the concept of the dual is used in testing the optimality of transportation programs.

9.8.4 THE ASSIGNMENT PROBLEM

The assignment problem is also a special case of the general linear programming model. It deals with designing an optimal assignment in which *exactly one* origin (e.g., a machine) is matched with *exactly one* destination (e.g., a job). We discuss the assignment problem in Chapter 10. It should be noted that the assignment method (see Section 10.20) is also based on the concept of the dual variables.

9.8.5 THE PORTFOLIO-SELECTION PROBLEM

A *portfolio-selection problem* arises whenever a given amount of money is to be allocated among several investment opportunities. The portfolio-selection problem is quite general in the sense that it can exist for individuals, trust-fund managers, or corporations. The components of the portfolio can be stocks, bonds, savings certificates, projects, companies to be acquired, or plants to be opened. The portfolio-selection problem, like other allocation problems, can be formulated at different levels of mathematical sophistication and solved by applying different methods of solution. For example, the objective function to be maximized can be nonlinear rather than linear.[18] As another example, a single-period allocation problem in which a specified amount of money is to be allocated to different plants can be formulated as a multistage problem and solved by dynamic programming.[19] In this section we present a simplified portfolio-selection problem.

Assume that the management of Atlas Corporation wants to invest, for a specified period, a sum of $1,000,000. The finance department of the company is asked to provide data regarding expected yields from good-quality common and preferred stocks, corporate bonds, government bonds, and saving certificates. The relevant information regarding expected annual yields of different categories of investment is shown in Table 9.11.

---

[18] See Markowitz [1952].

[19] For a simple illustration, see Loomba and Turban [1974, p. 369].

Table 9.11

Category of Investment	Expected Annual Yield (percent)
Common stocks	5
Preferred stocks	7
Corporate bonds	10
Government bonds	8
Saving certificates	6

Assume that these returns are stable and that, for the planning horizon, they will remain constant.[20] Assume further that the diversification goals of the management are specified by these statements (or constraints):

1. Investment in common and preferred stocks should not be more than 30 percent of the total investment.
2. Investment in government bonds should not be less than the investment in savings certificates.
3. The investment in corporate and government bonds should not be more than 50 percent of the total investment.

Our problem, then, is to select the investment portfolio that will maximize expected annual return, R, and simultaneously meet the diversification and other constraints.

In formulating this problem, we introduce a slight variation in defining the activities. That is, here we define activities, or the decision variables, as percentages rather than as quantity levels. Thus, we define $x_1, x_2, x_3, x_4,$ and x_5 as percentages of the total portfolio (or investment) to be allocated, respectively, to common stocks, preferred stocks, corporate bonds, government bonds, and saving certificates. The problem can now be stated mathematically as follows[21]:

Maximize

$$R = 0.05x_1 + 0.07x_2 + 0.10x_3 + 0.08x_4 + 0.06x_5$$

subject to the constraints

$$
\left.
\begin{aligned}
x_1 + x_2 &\leqslant 0.30 \\
x_4 - x_5 &\geqslant 0.0 \\
x_3 + x_4 &\leqslant 0.50 \\
x_1 + x_2 + x_3 + x_4 + x_5 &= 1.00
\end{aligned}
\right\} \quad (9.11)
$$

and

$$x_1, \quad x_2, \quad x_3, \quad x_4, \quad x_5 \geqslant 0$$

[20] This is a bold assumption. In practice, the manager must attach some sort of risk factor to each category of investment. A linear programming formulation that takes this modification into account is easily obtainable. See Problem 9.13 at the end of the chapter.

[21] The second statement can be expressed as $x_4 \geqslant x_5$ or $x_4 - x_5 \geqslant 0.0$.

The equality constraint in (9.11) represents the fact that our total investment must equal 100 percent.

9.8.6 THE MEDIA-SELECTION PROBLEM

The DISCO Manufacturing Company has decided to spend $200,000, during the next fiscal year, to advertise its electrical ovens. The management of DISCO is in the process of designing an advertising program that will use one or more of these four media: television, radio, newspapers, and magazines. Their marketing research department recommends that the allocation of advertising budget be made in such a way that the exposure, E, of the company's product is maximized. Past experience and records indicate the data in terms of exposure per dollar spent in advertising (Table 9.12). Also, as shown in the table, the management has specified certain maximum expenditures in each media. Assume further that the combined expenditures for newspapers and magazines should not be less than the allocation for radio. Let x_1, x_2, x_3, and x_4 represent the *dollar amounts* to be expended on television, radio, newspapers, and magazines, respectively. Then our media-selection problem can be mathematically stated as follows:[22]

Table 9.12

Media	Exposure per Dollar Spent in Advertising	Maximum Expenditures
Television	7	100,000
Radio	4	20,000
Newspapers	5	50,000
Magazines	3	30,000

Maximize

$$E = 7x_1 + 4x_2 + 5x_3 + 3x_4$$

subject to the constraints

$$
\left.
\begin{aligned}
x_1 &\leqslant 100,000 \\
x_2 &\leqslant 20,000 \\
x_3 &\leqslant 50,000 \\
x_4 &\leqslant 30,000 \\
-x_2 + x_3 + x_4 &\geqslant 0
\end{aligned}
\right\} \qquad (9.12)
$$

and

$$x_1, \quad x_2, \quad x_3, \quad x_4 \geqslant 0$$

[22] The requirement that the combined expenditures for newspapers and magazines should not be less than the allocation for radio can be expressed as $x_3 + x_4 \geqslant x_2$ or $-x_2 + x_3 + x_4 \geqslant 0$.

9.8.7 THE BLENDING PROBLEM

The *blending problem* is very much like the diet problem. Typically, the idea is to produce a blend out of specified commodities or constituents whose characteristics and costs are given. Minimum acceptable characteristics are given and are specified in terms of percentages rather than in absolute amounts. The objective function to be minimized is formulated not in total cost, but in terms of such measures as cost per gallon or cost per pound of alloy. In an alloy-blending problem, we may be required to have specified percentages of certain metals, such as copper, tin, or zinc, to produce an alloy. The information regarding the metal contents and unit costs of certain alloys available in the market is given. The problem, then, is to design a blend that minimizes cost per pound and also satisfies the stated requirements. Table 9.13 specifies such a problem.

Let x_1, x_2, and x_3 represent, respectively, the *percentages* of alloys A, B, and C in 1 pound of the blended alloy. It is then clear that one of the constraints must be $x_1 + x_2 + x_3 = 1$. The remaining information is quite clear from Table 9.13. Mathematically, the problem can be stated as follows:

Minimize

$$13x_1 + 11x_2 + 9x_3$$

subject to the constraints

$$
\left.
\begin{aligned}
0.3x_1 + 0.1x_2 + 0.7x_3 &= 0.20 \\
0.5x_1 + 0.6x_2 + 0.1x_3 &= 0.53 \\
0.2x_1 + 0.3x_2 + 0.2x_3 &= 0.27 \\
x_1 + x_2 + x_3 &= 1
\end{aligned}
\right.
\qquad (9.13)
$$

and

$$x_1, \quad x_2, \quad x_3 \geqslant 0$$

A second variation of the blending problem results if we are to design an optimal mix of production runs that consume *inputs per run* (as opposed to input

Table 9.13

Metal Content	Alloy Available in the Market			Required Blend
	A	B	C	
Copper	0.3	0.1	0.7	0.20
Tin	0.5	0.6	0.1	0.53
Zinc	0.2	0.3	0.2	0.27
Cost per Pound	$13	$11	$9	

per unit of output) and produce specified outputs of *joint products per run.*[23] Consider, for example, the problem of designing an optimal mix (in terms of runs) of two production processes in an oil refinery. The refinery uses two production processes (I and II) to produce two types of gasoline (regular and premium). Each run of process I requires 3 units of crude A and 8 units of crude B to produce 6 units of regular gasoline and 4 units of premium gasoline. Each run of process II requires 6 units of crude A and 4 units of crude B to produce 5 units of regular gasoline and 7 units of premium gasoline. The availability of supply of crudes A and B is 300 and 400 units, respectively. The refinery must produce 200 units of regular gasoline and 150 units of premium gasoline. The problem data are organized in Table 9.14. Assume that the profits per production run from process I and II are $10 and $15, respectively. Let x_1 and x_2 be the *number of production runs* of processes I and II, respectively. Our problem can then be mathematically stated as follows:

Maximize

$$10x_1 + 15x_2$$

subject to the constraints

$$\left.\begin{array}{r}3x_1 + 6x_2 \leqslant 300 \\ 8x_1 + 4x_2 \leqslant 400\end{array}\right\} \text{ supply constraints}$$

$$\left.\begin{array}{r}6x_1 + 5x_2 \geqslant 200 \\ 4x_1 + 7x_2 \geqslant 150\end{array}\right\} \text{ output constraints}$$

$$x_1, \quad x_2 \geqslant 0$$

Table 9.14

Production Process	Input per Production Run (units)		Output per Production Run (units)	
	Crude A	Crude B	Regular Gasoline	Premium Gasoline
I	3	8	6	4
II	6	4	5	7
	300	400	200	150
	Input supply		Output requirement	

[23] Several other variations of the blending problem exist. For another variation, see Problem 9.14. Yet another variation is presented in Problem 9.15, which is a prototype of a simple production planning problem.

9.9
Computer Programs for Linear Programming

In real life, linear programming problems are solved not manually, but with the aid of a computer. The selection of the computer and the specific program (code) is not an easy task. Questions relating to *speed, precision, storage size, turnaround*

Table 9.15 *Computer Programs or Routines for Linear Programming*

Name of Company or Source	Computer Programs for Linear Programming
Bendix Corporation	• G20 Linear Programming Code One
CEIR	• LP90 (available through SHARE as IK LP90)
Control Data Corporation	• 3600 Ophelie Linear Programming System
	• 6400 Optima Program
General Electric Company	• 225 Linear Programming System
	• LPINST***
	• LINPRO***
Grumman Data Systems	• ASSIGNMT***
	• INTPRO***
	• LINPROG***
	• RESIMPX***
	• SIMPLEX***
	• TRANSPT***
Honeywell Corporation	• 800/1800 Advanced Linear Programming System (ALPS)
International Business Machine Corporation	• 1410 Basic Linear Programming System
	• Branch and Bound Mixed Integer Program (BBMIP)
	• Direct Search Zero–One Integer Program
	• IPLP 6
	• IPM 1
	• IPM 3
	• Large-Scale Transportation Problem
	• 1620–1311 Linear Programming System
	• 7040/44 Linear Programming System II
	• 1130 Linear Programming—Mathematical Optimization Subroutine System
	• System/360 Mathematical Programming System (MPSX) with MIP Option
	• Transportation Problem Code
	• Transportation Problem System
	• Zero–One Integer Program with Heuristics
Philco Corporation	• LP2000 Linear Programming
Rand Corporation	• MFOR Program
Scientific Time Sharing Corporation	• Remote MPSX Linear Programming System
Univac Corporation	• 1107 Linear Programming

time, *cost*, and *specific needs* of the user must be considered. More than 100 linear programming codes for a vast variety of computers are available on the market. In Table 9.15, we provide a selected set of these codes, along with the name of the company or source that can be contacted for detailed information.

9.10
Summary

In this chapter, we have presented the important concept of the dual problem in linear programming. Linear programming problems exist in pairs, the primal and its dual. Relationships between the primal and the dual were discussed and their correspondence was established. The derivation of the dual problem, by utilizing the primal, was illustrated. We then presented the idea of sensitivity analysis and discussed how managers can use sensitivity analysis for purposes of planning and control. How to conduct sensitivity analysis on objective function coefficients (C_j) was illustrated with specific examples. A very brief and descriptive presentation was made with respect to sensitivity analysis of input–output coefficients (a_{ij}), and resource or requirement levels (b_i). Then the process of building a linear programming model was described.

Linear programming is an extremely versatile tool for structuring decision problems faced by managers in different fields of endeavor. For this reason, we presented a set of classical applications of linear programming. Wherever appropriate, the meaning or role of the dual variables in these applications was stated. In addition, we provided a selected set of linear programming codes, along with the name of the company or source that may be contacted for detailed information.

The concept of the dual variable is important for several reasons. For example, it is helpful in assigning marginal worth to a given resource so that rational decisions can be made in terms of acquiring additional resources from the marketplace. The concept of the dual variable has also been used in designing a method for testing the optimality of transportation programs. It is also related to the mechanics of the assignment model. In Chapter 10, we present both the transportation and the assignment models.

References

See the References at the end of Chapter 7.

Review Questions and Problems

9.1. Explain the concept of duality. What is the economic interpretation of the dual variables if the primal is a maximization problem? What is the significance of the dual variables if the primal is a minimization problem?

9.2. Examine Figure 9.1 and restate the rules of correspondence between the primal and the dual (see Section 9.3).

9.3. What managerial insights or benefits can be gained by conducting sensitivity analysis in linear programming? Is sensitivity analysis limited to linear programming?

9.4. Explain in graphical terms (with reference to a two-dimensional linear programming problem), the implication of changes in: objective function coefficients (C_j), input–output coefficients (a_{ij}), and resource or requirement levels (b_i).

9.5. What is the mathematical significance of duality? Give a general interpretation of the value of a specified dual variable.

9.6. Describe in your own words the various steps in the process of building a linear programming model.

9.7. The Ellis-Dee Pharmaceutical Company is about to introduce a new drug, Utopin. Present plans call for the production of Utopin in a capsule and injection form, each of which goes through distilling and packaging. The production and profit data are given in Table 9.16.

Table 9.16

Process	Capsule	Injection	Capacity (hours)
Distilling	5	12	150
Packaging	10	5	100
Profit per Unit	$2	$3	

(a) Formulate the maximization problem (primal).
(b) Formulate and solve the dual using the simplex algorithm.

9.8. Maximize

$$23X + 32Y + 18Z$$

subject to the constraints

$$10X + 6Y + 2Z \leqslant 2,500$$
$$5X + 10Y + 5Z \leqslant 2,000$$
$$X + 2Y + 2Z \leqslant 500$$

and

$$X, \quad Y, \quad Z \geqslant 0$$

(a) Write and solve the dual of this problem.
(b) Will the dual optimal solution remain optimal if the profit coefficient of X is reduced from 23 to 15?
(c) Will the dual optimal solution change if the resource capacity of the first constraint in the primal problem is increased to 3,000?

9.9. A small winery manufactures two types of wine, Burbo's Better and Burbo's Best. Burbo's Better sells for $20/quart, and Burbo's Best sells for $30/quart. Two men mix the two wines. It takes a man 2 hours to mix a quart of Burbo's Better and 6 hours to mix a quart of Burbo's Best. Each man works an 8-hour day, with 30 minutes for lunch. The quantity of alcohol that the plant can use is limited to 18 ounces daily. Six ounces are used in each quart of Burbo's Better and 3 ounces in each quart of Burbo's Best. How many quarts of each should the winery make? Solve this problem via its dual.

9.10. Wung Lee's Chinese Restaurant serves two types of chow mein, chicken and shrimp. There is a $2 profit on each pound of shrimp chow mein, and a $1 profit on chicken chow mein. From past experience Wung Lee knows that he should not make more than 10 pounds of chicken chow mein and 8 pounds of shrimp chow mein each day. The two cooks work an 8-hour day, with 30 minutes for lunch. A pound of chicken chow mein takes 2 hours to cook, whereas a pound of shrimp chow mein takes 1 hour. How many pounds of each type of chow mein should Wung Lee make? Utilize the dual approach in solving this problem.

9.11. The alloying metals of iron, nickel, and chrome are to be mixed to form an alloy to be used in the manufacture of valve seats. The proportion of iron has to be limited to 4 times the proportion of nickel. The sum of proportions of nickel and chrome has to be at least 4 percent of the proportion of iron. The alloying metals have an impurity content of 0.1 percent, 0.03 percent, and 0.2 percent, respectively. It is known from the laboratory tests that the percentage of sulfur impurity in the alloy should not exceed 0.075 percent. If the metals cost $1, $5, and $7/kilogram, respectively:
(a) Find the optimal proportions of the alloying metals.
(b) What is the dual of this problem? How will you interpret the dual variables?
(c) Will the optimal solution change if the cost of nickel increases by 20 percent?

9.12. The Ketcham Every Time Company manufactures two types of baseball gloves. The profit from the high-quality glove is $4, and the profit from the low-quality glove is $2. Machine A is the only machine on which these gloves can be made. It takes 30 minutes to manufacture a low-quality glove, whereas 2 hours are needed to make a high-quality glove. The plant works two 8-hour shifts. There is enough material to make 24 low-quality gloves per day. It takes twice as much material to manufacture a high-quality glove. How many of each type of glove should the company make? Form the dual and obtain the values of the dual variables from a regular simplex solution of this problem.

9.13. Assume that the management of Scarsdale Mutual, Inc., wants to invest a sum of $1,000,000. The finance department has provided the following data regarding the yields and the risk factor (beta factor) for the securities:

Category of Investment	Expected Annual Yield	Risk or Beta Factor
Common stocks type A (utilities)	5	1
Common stocks type B (blue chip)	8	1.6
Corporate bonds	10	0.5
Government bonds	8	0
Saving certificates	6	0

Assume that the yields and risk factors remain constant for the planning horizon. Cast the problem in the linear programming format. Do not solve. The constraints are as follows:

(a) The investment in government bonds and saving certificates should not be more than 50 percent of the total investment.
(b) Common stocks should not constitute more than 40 percent of the portfolio.
(c) The beta factor of the portfolio should be less than or equal to 1.

9.14. The Wild Horses Oil Company makes three brands of gasoline: Man o' War, Trigger, and Swayback. Wild Horses makes its products by blending two grades of gasoline, each with a different octane rating. Each brand of gas must have an octane rating greater than a predetermined minimum. In gasoline blending, final octane rating is linearly proportional to component octanes (i.e., a blend of 50 percent 100-octane and 50 percent 200-octane gasoline is 150 octane). The other relevant data are given in Tables 9.17 and 9.18. There is no limit to the amount of each gasoline that may be sold. Formulate as a linear programming problem.

Table 9.17

Blending Component	Octane	Cost per Gallon (cents)	Supply per Week (gallons)
A	200	10	20,000
B	130	8	10,000

Table 9.18

Brand	Minimum Octane	Sale Price per Gallon (cents)
Man o' War	180	24
Trigger	160	21
Swayback	140	12

9.15. Let us consider a production planning problem in which the finished products consist of two components A and B. One unit of the finished product consists of 2 units of component A and 3 units of component B. These components are produced by two departments, which use the same raw materials but different methods of production. The components require two different raw materials that are available in limited quantities. The available supplies for the planning horizon are 300 units of raw material 1 and 400 units of raw material 2. The data for the problem are shown in Table 9.19. Formulate as a linear programming problem to maximize the output of the finished products.

Table 9.19

Department	Input per Production Run (units)		Output per Production Run (units)	
	Raw Material 1	Raw Material 2	Component A	Component B
I	3	8	6	4
II	6	4	5	6

Optional Problem

9.16. Formulate and solve the dual to Problems 7.12, 7.15, 8.10, and 8.15. Compare the answers with the solutions of the primal problems and try to give an economic interpretation of the dual variables.

CHAPTER 10

Extensions of Linear Programming and Special Structure Models

MAJOR CONCEPTS AND TOPICS DISCUSSED IN THIS CHAPTER

Extensions of Linear Programming

The Transportation Model

Structure, approach, and mechanics
Stepping-stone method
Modified distribution method (MODI)
Multiple optimal solutions and degeneracy in transportation problems

The Assignment Model

Structure, approach, and mechanics

Integer Programming

10.1
Introduction

Linear programming is only one component of the broad field known as mathematical programming. Nonlinear programming, stochastic programming, integer programming, and dynamic programming are some examples of programming methods other than linear programming. Each programming method, or model, represents an efficient optimization technique to solve a problem with a specific structure. And the specific structure in each category is determined by a set of assumptions. For example, as outlined in Chapter 7, the structure of the general linear programming model is based essentially on the following important assumptions:

1. *Certainty* (we assume complete knowledge regarding technology, resources, strategies, and their respective payoffs—and each strategy results in a unique payoff).
2. *Linearity* (the objective function as well as all the constraints are assumed to be linear).
3. *Divisibility* (all variables are assumed to be continuous, and hence they can assume integer as well as fractional values).
4. *Single-stage* (the problem assumes a fixed planning horizon and requires only *one* decision—i.e., it is a *static* model).
5. *Nonnegativity* (all variables must assume nonnegative values—i.e., an absolute lower bound, but no upper bound, is specified for all variables).
6. *Fixed technology* (we assume production requirements to be fixed during the planning horizon).
7. *Constant profit or cost per unit* (we assume that regardless of the level of production, profit or cost per unit remains constant).

What will happen if we make the general linear programming model more or less restrictive? That is, what kind of a modified model will evolve, and how shall we solve the modified model when we make some additional demands on, or assumptions in, the general linear programming model to more accurately reflect real-life problems? What, for example, will emerge if we impose on the general linear programming model the restriction that some or all variables can only assume nonnegative integer values?[1] The additional constraint that requires some or all variables to assume only nonnegative integer values gives rise to the integer (linear) programming problem.

The purpose of this chapter is threefold. First, we shall examine some of the assumptions of linear programming and describe how, by modifying these assumptions, we enter the domain of some important mathematical programming methods. Second, we shall describe in detail two *special-structure* linear programming models: the *transportation model* and the *assignment model*. Finally, we briefly explain the idea of integer programming.

---

[1] An integer is a whole number as distinguished from a fraction. The numbers 0, 1, and 2 are nonnegative integers. For a brief description of integer programming, see Loomba [1976, Chap. 11].

10.2
Extensions of Linear Programming

By extensions of linear programming we shall mean any model that emerges when one (or more) of the assumptions of the general linear programming model is modified to make the model either more or less restrictive. Let us examine a few modifications in the assumptions of the general linear programming model that lead to some of the most important mathematical programming models.

If the assumption of *certainty* is modified by assuming that some or all parameters of the problem are described by random variables (i.e., they are probabilistic rather than deterministic), we are in the domain of *stochastic programming*. The idea of stochastic programming is to convert the probabilistic problem into an equivalent deterministic problem, and then solve the problem.[2]

If the assumption of *linearity* were to be modified by assuming the existence of a nonlinear objective function or nonlinear constraints, we enter the domain of *nonlinear programming*. A nonlinear programming problem arises whenever we have either a nonlinear objective function, or a set of nonlinear constraints, or both.[3]

If the assumption of *divisibility* is modified by restricting some or all variables to integer values, we are in the domain of *integer programming*. The idea of integer programming is explained in Section 10.24.

If we go beyond the *single-stage* assumption of linear programming and consider those problems which require not one but a sequence of decisions, we are in the domain of *dynamic programming*. In dynamic programming the planning horizon is divided into more than one stage (multistage as opposed to single-stage), and the outcome of a decision at one stage affects the subsequent decision for the next stage, and so on. There are a host of business and economic problems that are multistage (or multiperiod), and they can be solved by dynamic programming.[4] Multistage decision-tree approach is an example of dynamic programming (see Section 5.7).

The simple nonnegativity assumption imposes no upper bound on the values of the variables. However, in many real-life problems it may be necessary to specify the upper bounds for some or all variables. When this happens, the linear programming problem is transformed into what is known as the *bounded-variable problem*. An efficient algorithm, which is based on the simplex method, has been developed to solve the bounded-variable problem.[5] It should also be observed that the general linear programming model can handle *unrestricted* variables X_j (i.e., the variable can assume positive as well as negative values) by a simple transformation,

$$X_j = Y_j - W_j, \quad \text{with } Y_j, W_j \geqslant 0$$

---

[2] For a brief and simple illustration, see Wagner [1975, pp. 382–391], and Taha [1971, pp. 649–53].

[3] For a brief discussion of nonlinear programming, see Chapter 7 of Loomba and Turban [1974].

[4] See Chapter 8 of Loomba and Turban [1974]. The chapter (89 pp. long) illustrates dynamic programming by employing a variety of illustrative examples.

[5] For a simple illustration, see Chapter 10 of Chung [1963].

Finally, we can obtain two special-structure models (*transportation* and *assignment* models) by making certain modifications in the general linear programming model. These models are discussed in subsequent sections.

10.3
The Transportation Model

The transportation model deals with a special class of linear programming problems in which the objective is to "transport" a homogeneous commodity from various "origins" to different "destinations" at a minimum total cost.[6] The supply available at each origin and the quantity demanded by each destination are given in the statement of the problem. Also given is the cost of shipping a unit of goods from a known origin to a known destination.

Given the information regarding the total capacities of the origins, the total requirements of the destinations, and the shipping cost per unit of goods for available shipping routes, the transportation model is used to determine the optimal shipping program(s) that results in minimum total shipping costs. The transportation model can be extended to solve problems related to topics such as production planning, machine assignment, and plant location.

Insofar as the transportation problem is a special case of the general linear programming problem, it can always be solved by the simplex method. However, the transportation algorithm, which we shall develop in later sections of this chapter, provides a much more efficient method of handling such a problem.

At this time we make two remarks in reference to the general linear programming problem. First, the input–output coefficients a_{ij} are not restricted to any particular value or values. For example, a particular a_{ij} may be specified to have a value of 10, -20, 1, or 0. Second, no restrictions are imposed regarding the homogeneity of units among the various inequalities or equations that represent the structural constraints. Of the given constraints, some may refer to available capacities of machines that perform different kinds of operations, while others may specify different types of, say, chemical characteristics. In other words, the units of any one constraint may not be the same as those of the other constraints and hence may not be interchangeable with the units of any other constraint. We can illustrate this by referring back to the vitamin problem of Section 7.4, in which the structural constraints were concerned with two types of vitamins that were not interchangeable.

The transportation problem, in comparison with the general linear programming problem, restricts the values that can be assigned to the input–output coefficients to 0 or 1. And it limits the "dimension" of the constraints to only one type of unit, so that they are homogeneous and hence interchangeable. Hence, the general linear programming problem can be reduced to what is called a transportation problem if: (1) the input–output coefficients a_{ij}'s (coefficients of the real variables in the constraints) are restricted to the values 0 or 1, and (2) there exists a homogeneity of units among the constraints. Hence, the transportation problem is a special case of the linear programming problem.

---

[6] Of course, if the payoff measure is of the profit variety, the objective will be to maximize total payoff.

10.4
An Illustrative Example

A manufacturing concern has three plants located in three different cities, all producing the same product. The total supply potential of the firm is absorbed by four large customers. Let us identify the three plants as O_1, O_2, and O_3, and the customers as D_1, D_2, D_3, and D_4. The relevant data on plant capacities, destination requirements, and shipping costs for individual shipping routes are recorded, in general terms, in Table 10.1.[7]

Table 10.1

Origin	Destination				Origin Capacity per Time Period
	D_1	D_2	D_3	D_4	
O_1	c_{11} x_{11}	c_{12} x_{12}	c_{13} x_{13}	c_{14} x_{14}	b_1
O_2	c_{21} x_{21}	c_{22} x_{22}	c_{23} x_{23}	c_{24} x_{24}	b_2
O_3	c_{31} x_{31}	c_{32} x_{32}	c_{33} x_{33}	c_{34} x_{34}	b_3
Destination Requirement per Time Period	d_1	d_2	d_3	d_4	

- c_{ij} = cost of shipping 1 unit of goods from ith origin to jth destination.
- x_{ij} = number of units to be shipped from ith origin to jth destination.
- $\sum b_i = \sum d_j$. That is, total origin capacities equal total destination requirements.

Note that the first subscript in each symbol used in Table 10.1 refers to the specific origin and the second subscript to the particular destination. For example, c_{12} is the cost of shipping 1 unit of goods from origin O_1 to destination D_2, and the variable x_{34} is the quantity to be shipped from origin O_3 to destination D_4. Origin capacities and destination requirements are given along the outside rims of Table 10.1 and are usually referred to as rim requirements. Our problem is to choose the strategy (a particular program of shipping) that will satisfy the *rim requirements* at a minimum total cost.

---

[7] The matrix of the transportation problem in Table 10.1 has three rows and four columns and hence is not a square matrix. This is to emphasize the point that a transportation problem is not restricted to a square matrix. As we shall see, the "assignment model" is restricted to a square matrix in the sense that one origin cannot simultaneously be associated with more than one destination. In the transportation problem, one origin can simultaneously supply goods to many destinations.

The transportation problem described above, like the general linear programming problem, consists of three components. First, we can formulate a linear objective function that is to be minimized. This function will represent the total shipping cost of all the goods to be sent from the three origins to the four destinations. Second, we can write a set of linear structural constraints. There are seven structural constraints for this problem: three reflecting the row or origin capacities and four reflecting the column or destination requirements. Three constraints (one for each row) relate the origin capacities and the goods to be received by different destinations. These are called *row* or *capacity constraints*. The other four constraints (one for each column) show the relationships between destination requirements and the goods to be shipped from different origins. These are called *column* or *requirement constraints*. Third, we can specify a set of nonnegativity constraints for the variables x_{ij}. They will state that no negative shipment is permitted. The general correspondence between a typical linear programming problem and the transportation problem is thus complete.

It should be noted that if the sum of origin capacities ($\sum b_i$) equals the sum of destination requirements ($\sum d_j$), the problem is called the *balanced* transportation problem. If the sum of origin capacities is not equal to the sum of destination requirements, the problem is *unbalanced*.

The unbalanced problem can be converted to a balanced problem by the simple device of adding a *dummy origin* (to supply the excess requirement) or a *dummy destination* (to absorb the excess capacity). In the row (representing dummy origin) or the column (representing dummy destination), all transportation costs are assumed to be zero. We illustrate the conversion of the unbalanced problem to a balanced problem in Section 10.12.

A little reflection will show that for the transportation problem of Table 10.1, only six rather than seven structural constraints need be specified. In view of the fact that the sum of the origin capacities equals the sum of the destination requirements ($\sum b_i = \sum d_j$), any solution satisfying six of the seven constraints will automatically satisfy the remaining constraint. In general, therefore, if m represents the number of rows and n represents the number of columns in a given transportation problem, we can state the problem completely with $m + n - 1$ equations. This means that a *basic feasible solution* of a transportation problem has exactly $m + n - 1$ positive components (as compared to $m + n$ positive components required for a basic feasible solution for the general linear programming problem having $m + n$ structural constraints).

Second, if origin capacities equal destination requirements, it is always possible to design an initial basic feasible solution in such a manner that the rim requirements are satisfied. This can be accomplished in one of the ways described in Section 10.6.

10.5
Approach of the Transportation Method

The transportation method consists of three basic steps. The first step involves making the initial shipping assignment in such a manner that a basic feasible solution is obtained. This means that $m + n - 1$ cells (routes) of the transportation matrix are used for shipping purposes. The cells having the shipping assignment will be called *occupied cells*, while the remaining cells of the transportation matrix will be referred to as *empty cells*.

The purpose of the second step is to test the optimality of the solution. This is done by determining the opportunity costs associated with the empty cells. The opportunity costs of the empty cells can be calculated individually for each cell or simultaneously for the whole matrix. If the opportunity costs of all the empty cells are nonpositive, we can be confident that an optimal solution has been obtained.[8] On the other hand, if even a single empty cell has a positive opportunity cost, we proceed to step 3.

The third step involves determining a new and better basic feasible solution. This involves using a heretofore empty cell so that the highest rate of improvement in the objective function is obtained. Once this new basic feasible solution has been obtained, we repeat steps 2 and 3 until an optimal solution has been designed.

10.6
Methods of Making the Initial Assignment (First Step)

The first step in the transportation method, as stated above, consists in making an initial assignment in such a manner that a basic feasible solution (number of occupied cells equals $m + n - 1$) is obtained. Of the various methods of making such an assignment, we shall illustrate (1) the northwest-corner rule, and (2) the least-cost method.[9]

10.6.1 THE NORTHWEST-CORNER RULE

According to this rule, the first allocation is made to the cell occupying the upper left-hand (northwest) corner of the matrix. Further, this allocation is of such a magnitude that either the origin capacity of the first row is exhausted, or the destination requirement of the first column is satisfied, or both. If the origin capacity of row 1 is exhausted first, we move down the first column and make another allocation which either exhausts the origin capacity of row 2 or satisfies the remaining destination requirement of column 1. On the other hand, if the first allocation completely satisfies the destination requirement of column 1, we move to the right in row 1 and make a second allocation which either exhaust the remaining capacity of row 1 or satisfies the destination requirement of column 2, and so on. In this manner, starting from the upper left-hand corner (i.e., northwest corner) of the given transportation matrix, satisfying the individual destination

---

[8] The transportation problem falls under the category of decision making under certainty (models that deal with decision making under certainty are referred to as *deterministic models*; see Section 5.3). Hence, the optimal solution must not contain any positive opportunity costs (opportunity cost is the cost involved in *not* following the best course of action). It will be recalled that the test for optimality in the simplex method was also based on the concept of opportunity cost.

[9] Another method is Vogel's approximation method (VAM). See Loomba [1976, pp. 216–222].

requirements, and exhausting the origin capacities one at a time, we move toward the lower right-hand corner until all the rim requirements are satisfied. It should be noted that when we follow the northwest-corner rule, we pay no attention to the relative costs of the different routes while making the first assignment.

Table 10.2

Origin	Destination				Origin Capacity per Time Period
	D_1	D_2	D_3	D_4	
O_1	12	4	9	5	55
O_2	8	1	6	6	45
O_3	1	12	4	7	30
Destination Requirement per Time Period	40	20	50	20	130

We now apply the northwest-corner rule to the transportation problem shown in Table 10.2. For this problem, application of the northwest-corner rule dictates that we first "load" or "fill" cell O_1D_1, which lies in the upper left-hand (northwest) corner. The product requirement of D_1 is 40 units, and the capacity of O_1 is 55 units; the lower of these two numbers (i.e., 40) is placed in cell O_1D_1. This means that the requirement of D_1 is fully satisfied, but we still have 15 units (55 − 40) of unused capacity at O_1. Thus, we move to the right of cell O_1D_1 in the first row. At this stage we note that the destination requirement of column D_2 is 20 units. Knowing that 15 units of capacity O_1 are still unused, we route all 15 units to destination D_2 (place 15 in cell O_1D_2). This completely exhausts the capacity O_1, but column D_2 still needs 5 units (20 − 15) to satisfy its requirement. Thus, we move down column D_2 and supply these 5 units from capacity O_2 (place 5 in cell O_2D_2). This leaves 40 units of unused capacity at O_2; these are routed to D_3 (place 40 in cell O_2D_3). The remaining requirement of 10 units (50 − 40) for D_3 is supplied from O_3 (place 10 in cell O_3D_3). This leaves 20 units of unused capacity at O_3; these are routed to D_4 (place 20 in cell O_3D_4). The entire table has now been loaded, resulting in the initial program given in Table 10.3. The circled numbers in the table give the number of units shipped from a particular origin to a specific destination. The cells in which these circled numbers are entered are the occupied cells. The rest of the cells are the empty cells. The occupied cells correspond to the basic variables; the empty cells correspond to the nonbasic variables of the simplex method.

Table 10.3 *Initial Assignment by the Northwest-Corner Rule*

Origin	Destination				Total
	D_1	D_2	D_3	D_4	
O_1	12 (40)	4 (15)	9	5	55
O_2	8	1 (5)	6 (40)	6	45
O_3	1	12	4 (10)	7 (20)	30
Total	40	20	50	20	130

It is to be observed that the number of occupied cells is

$$m + n - 1 = 3 + 4 - 1 = 6$$
$$= (\text{number of rows} + \text{number of columns} - 1)$$

Therefore, the solution, at this stage, is not degenerate.[10]

The total cost of this assignment is

$$(40 \times 12) + (15 \times 4) + (5 \times 1) + (40 \times 6) + (10 \times 4) + (20 \times 7) = \$965.$$

It should be noted that the last allocation (cell $O_3 D_4$) simultaneously satisfied the requirement of column D_4 and exhausted the capacity of O_3. This is the normal situation in the last allocation made by the northwest-corner rule; and if this occurs only in the last allocation, we can be certain of having a basic feasible solution. However, if any allocation previous to the last allocation happens to be such that it simultaneously satisfies the requirement of some destination and exhausts the capacity of some origin, then the number of occupied cells will be less than $m + n - 1$. This will mean that we have a degenerate basic feasible solution.[11]

10.6.2 THE LEAST-COST METHOD

The least-cost method starts by making the first allocation to that cell whose shipping cost per unit is lowest. This lowest-cost cell is loaded or filled as much as possible in view of the origin capacity of its row and the destination requirement

---

[10] A basic feasible solution for a transportation problem requires exactly $m + n - 1$ positive components. Thus, whenever a transportation program has $m + n - 1$ occupied cells, the solution is not degenerate.

[11] In most cases, the initial assignment made by following the northwest-corner rule will be such that the number of occupied or filled cells equals $m + n - 1$, where m is the number of rows and n is the number of columns. When this happens, we have a basic feasible solution. If the number of occupied cells in the initial assignment is less than $m + n - 1$, the problem is said to be degenerate at the very beginning. This type of degeneracy, occurring during the solution stages, can easily be resolved by judicious placement of a small number, ε (epsilon), in the empty cell(s). The epsilon is to be placed in that cell (or cells) which will help complete the different loops for all the empty cells. See Section 10.14.

of its column. Then we move to the next lowest-cost cell and make an allocation in view of the remaining capacity and requirement of its row and column, and so on. Should there be a tie for lowest-cost cell during any allocation, we can exercise "judgment" in breaking the tie or we can arbitrarily choose a cell for allocation.

Let us illustrate the least-cost method for the transportation problem of Table 10.2. The illustration is summarized in Table 10.4. We note that cells O_2D_2 and O_3D_1 each have a shipping cost of \$1/unit. Thus, there is a tie for the first allocation. We arbitrarily choose cell O_3D_1 for the first allocation and route 30 units from O_3 to D_1. This means that the capacity of O_3 is fully utilized (cross off row O_3 with a light pencil). The second allocation is made to cell O_2D_2, and we ship 20 units through this route (place 20 in cell O_2D_2 and cross off column D_2). Of those remaining, cell O_1D_4 has the lowest cost, and we route 20 units through O_1D_4 (place 20 in cell O_1D_4 and cross off column D_4). Of those remaining, cell O_2D_3 has the lowest cost, and we route 25 units (the remaining capacity of row O_2) through cell O_2D_3 (place 25 in cell O_2D_3 and cross off row O_2). We are now left with 35 units at O_1, while D_1 and D_3 still require 10 and 25 units, respectively. Hence, we route 10 units through O_1D_1 and 25 units through O_1D_3. All the rim requirements have now been satisfied, and we have the initial assignment in Table 10.4. The dotted lines crossing the cost squares (c_{ij}'s) have been numbered to show the order in which different rows and columns were crossed off, as an aid to making the initial assignment by the least-cost method.

Table 10.4 *Initial Assignment by the Least-Cost Method*

Origin	D_1	D_2	D_3	D_4	Total	
			Destination			
O_1	12 (10)	4	9 (25)	5 (20)	~~55~~ ~~35~~ ~~10~~ 0	
O_2	8	1 (20)	6 (25)	6	~~45~~ ~~25~~ 0	4th
O_3	1 (30)	12	4	7	~~30~~ 0	1st
Total	~~40~~ ~~10~~ 0	~~20~~ 0	~~50~~ ~~25~~ 0	~~20~~ 0		
	6th	2nd	5th	3rd		

It is to be observed that the number of occupied cells is six (i.e., $m + n - 1$), and thus we have a basic feasible solution. The total cost of this assignment is \$645. It is \$320 less than the cost of the initial solution obtained by the northwest-corner rule.

10.7
Test for Optimality (Second Step)

Once the initial basic feasible solution has been obtained, our next step is to test its optimality. There are two methods for testing optimality in transportation problems. In one method, test of optimality is conducted by directly calculating the opportunity cost of each empty cell. This is the *stepping-stone method*. In the stepping-stone method, each empty cell (associated with a nonbasic variable) is evaluated by transferring into it one unit from an occupied cell (associated with a basic variable). The effect on the objective function of such an exchange is then measured in terms of opportunity cost. Similarly, opportunity costs for all empty cells are calculated, one at a time. Even if a single opportunity cost (or cell evaluator) is positive, our program is not optimal. A new and better program is then designed. We illustrate the stepping-stone method in Section 10.9.

The second method of testing optimality is called the modified distribution method (MODI). This method is based on the concept of dual variables, which are used for evaluating the empty cells of a given program. As we shall see in Section 10.10, there is a simple way of assigning values to the dual variables associated with a given solution. Once this is done, the opportunity costs of all the empty cells of a program can easily be calculated. As compared to the stepping-stone method, the MODI method of testing optimality is simpler and more efficient.

In both the stepping-stone method and the MODI method, after the nonoptimality of a program has been established, the most favorable empty cell is identified. Then a new program is designed so that this most favorable empty cell becomes one of the occupied cells.

10.8
Design a New and Better Program (Third Step)

If the second step of the transportation method (i.e., test for optimality) indicates an optimal solution, the problem has been solved. Otherwise, a new and better basic feasible solution must be designed. The procedure for designing the new and better program is based on the overall constraint that all the rim requirements are fully met. As in the simplex method, all we do is exchange a nonbasic variable (most favorable empty cell) for at least one basic variable (one of the occupied cell). While making the transfer of goods to accomplish this, we must make certain that row as well as column requirements remain satisfied.

We continue to design new and better programs until an optimal program has been obtained. That is, we repeat steps 2 and 3 until an optimal solution has been designed.

Extensions of Linear Programming and Special Structure Models   Chapter 10

10.9
The Stepping-Stone Method
(for Testing Optimality)

As indicated in Section 10.7, the stepping-stone method tests the optimality of a solution by determining the opportunity cost of each empty cell in that solution. How do we determine the opportunity cost associated with an empty cell? Let us answer this question with respect to empty cell O_2D_1 in Table 10.3.

Assume that we shift 1 unit of goods to cell O_2D_1. Now, in order to satisfy the rim requirements, this will necessitate changes as shown in Table 10.5. The changes are guided by a closed path. The *closed path* is indicated by arrows, and identified by plus $(+)$ and minus $(-)$ signs in appropriate cells. *In the stepping-stone method, a separate closed path is needed to evaluate each empty cell.*

Table 10.5

	D_1	D_2
O_1	[12] (40) $-1 \longrightarrow$	[4] (15) $+1$
O_2	[ ] $\square$ $+1 \longleftarrow$	[8] [1] (5) -1

Unit Changes Along the Closed Path	Cost Consequence
Add 1 unit to O_2D_1: $+1$	$+\$8$
Take 1 unit out of O_1D_1: -1	$-\$12$
Add 1 unit to O_1D_2: $+1$	$+\$4$
Take 1 unit out of O_2D_2: -1	$-\$1$
	$-\$1$

Note that the shifting of one unit to O_2D_1 yields a negative cost change. This means that, in view of the current program shown in Table 10.3, we can save $1 if we effect the shifting of 1 unit as shown in Table 10.5. This also implies: (1) the opportunity cost of *not* utilizing cell O_2D_1 is $1 (i.e., opportunity cost is negative of the net cost consequence), and (2) we should shift as many units into cell O_2D_1 as possible.

As shown in Table 10.5, the maximum number that we can shift is given by the *minimum* of the circled numbers in the minus signed cells (here cells O_1D_1 and O_2D_2). Why?

If such a shift were to be made, we shall obtain a new program whose optimality must be tested by evaluating each empty cell in the program.

We can now recapitulate the transportation method in which optimality is tested by the stepping-stone procedure:

Step 1. *Design a basic feasible solution by making an initial assignment.*

For example, in Table 10.4 we designed a basic feasible solution by using the least-cost method. This first program is reproduced in Table 10.7.

Check on step 1: Since the number of occupied cells in this program equals $m + n - 1$, that is, $3 + 4 - 1 = 6$, this is indeed a basic feasible solution, and not a degenerate solution.

Step 2. *Test for optimality (determine the opportunity costs of the empty cells).*

We repeat: In the stepping-stone method, a separate closed path with proper plus and minus signs must be completed for each of the empty cells before the respective opportunity costs can be calculated.[12] Since our first program has a total of six empty cells, six different closed loops must be drawn. The opportunity cost associated with each empty cell is calculated in Table 10.6. An examination of these opportunity costs shows that cell O_2D_1 is the only cell with a positive opportunity cost. Hence, cell O_2D_1 must be included in our next program.

A comment about the opportunity cost of zero (for empty cell O_1D_2) is in order. An opportunity cost of zero associated with a particular empty cell at any stage of the problem solution indicates that if this cell is included in the next program, the total cost of the new program will be the same as that of the current program. Thus, we list "indifferent" in the "Action" column of Table 10.6.[13]

Step 3. *Design a new and better program.*

Having ascertained that a given program is not optimal (one or more empty cells have positive opportunity cost), we next revise the program to obtain a new basic feasible solution. The revised program must include that empty cell of the current program whose opportunity cost is highest. No choice is available here, since cell O_2D_1 is the only empty cell that has a positive opportunity cost (see Table 10.6).

The revision of the first program is guided by the closed loop of the empty cell to be included (in this case cell O_2D_1) and is as shown in Table 10.7. Since 10 is the smallest circled number of the negative cells in the closed loop, it is added to the cells that contain plus signs and subtracted from the cells that contain minus signs.

The next question is: Does the revised program represent an optimal solution? To answer this question, we have to repeat step 2, as discussed previously (i.e., calculate the opportunity cost of each empty cell). Should the result of step 2 indicate a nonoptimal solution, we would repeat step 3 and obtain another basic feasible solution.

Determination of the opportunity costs of all the empty cells of the second program (Table 10.7) will reveal that an optimal solution has indeed been derived. The reader is encouraged to verify this by the application of step 2 to Table 10.7.

---

[12] While tracing this *closed path*, one should start with the empty cell being evaluated and draw an arrow from that empty cell to an occupied cell in the same row or column. Then a plus sign is placed in the empty cell and a negative sign in the occupied cell to which the arrow was drawn. Next, one moves horizontally or vertically (never diagonally) to another occupied cell, and so on, until one is back to the original empty cell. At each turn of the path, plus and minus signs are placed alternately. Further, there is the important restriction that there is exactly one positive terminal and exactly one negative terminal in any row or column through which the path happens to pass. Obviously, this restriction is imposed to ensure that the rim requirement will not be violated when the units are shifted (to obtain a new program) along this closed loop. Mechanically, this implies that during the tracing of the closed loop, right-angle turns must be made only at the occupied cells. The starting point of a closed path is identified by the symbol □.

[13] If this happens in the optimal solution, it implies the existence of multiple optimal solutions.

Table 10.6

Empty Cell	Closed Path	Net Cost Change	Opportunity Cost	Action
O_1D_2	$+O_1D_2 - O_1D_3 + O_2D_3 - O_2D_2$	$+4 - 9 + 6 - 1 = 0$	0	Indifferent
O_2D_1	$+O_2D_1 - O_1D_1 + O_1D_3 - O_2D_3$	$+8 - 12 + 9 - 6 = -1$	$+1$	Candidate for inclusion in next program
O_2D_4	$+O_2D_4 - O_1D_4 + O_1D_3 - O_2D_3$	$+6 - 5 + 9 - 6 = 4$	-4	Do not include in next program
O_3D_2	$+O_3D_2 - O_3D_1 + O_1D_1 - O_1D_3 + O_2D_3 - O_2D_2$	$+12 - 1 + 12 - 9 + 6 - 1 = +19$	-19	Do not include in next program
O_3D_3	$+O_3D_3 - O_1D_3 + O_1D_1 - O_3D_1$	$+4 - 9 + 12 - 1 = +6$	-6	Do not include in next program
O_3D_4	$+O_3D_4 - O_1D_4 + O_1D_1 - O_3D_1$	$+7 - 5 + 12 - 1 = +13$	-13	Do not include in next program

Table 10.7

First Program

	D_1	D_2	D_3	D_4
	12	4	9	5
O_1	⑩		㉕	⑳
	8	1	6	6
O_2		⑳	㉕	
	1	12	4	7
O_3	㉚			

Second and Optimal Program

	D_1	D_2	D_3	D_4
	12	4	9	5
O_1			㉟	⑳
	8	1	6	6
O_2	⑩	⑳	⑮	
	1	12	4	7
O_3	㉚			

10.10
The Modified Distribution Method
(for Testing Optimality)

For testing optimality of a transportation program (i.e., how the opportunity costs of the empty cells are calculated), the stepping-stone method and the modified distribution method (MODI) differ as follows. In the stepping-stone method, we first draw closed paths for each of the empty cells, and then use these paths to calculate the opportunity costs (see Table 10.6). Then, having identified the most favorable empty cell (i.e., cell with the highest opportunity cost), we use its closed path to effect the transfer of goods and obtain a new basic feasible solution.

In the modified distribution method, as we shall illustrate below, test of optimality is conducted (i.e., opportunity costs of the empty cells are calculated) by the utilization of dual variables, without first having to draw closed paths for each empty cell. As a matter of fact, the MODI method easily permits us to identify the most favorable empty cell as soon as a set of values for the dual variables has been chosen. Then a closed path through the most favorable empty cell is drawn so that a new basic feasible solution can be obtained under the guidance of the closed path. Note that in the modified distribution method, we need draw only one closed path *after* the highest-opportunity-cost cell has been identified. Thus, the procedure for calculating the opportunity costs of the empty cells in MODI is independent of the tracing of the closed path.

We shall illustrate the mechanics and rationale of the modified-distribution method by solving the transportation problem for which a basic feasible solution (step 1) is shown in Table 10.8.

Table 10.8 *Initial Assignment by Least-Cost Method*

Origin	Destination				Total
	D_1	D_2	D_3	D_4	
O_1	12 ◯	4	9 ◯	5 ◯	55
O_2	8	1 ◯	6 ◯	6	45
O_3	1 ◯	12	4	7	30
Total	40	20	50	20	

Step 2. *Test for optimality (determine the opportunity cost of the empty cells).*

In the program shown in Table 10.8, we have six occupied cells. In linear programming terms, this means that six variables (i.e., $x_{11}, x_{13}, x_{14}, x_{22}, x_{23}$, and x_{31}) are basic variables. It will be recalled from the simplex method that the opportunity cost (represented by the $C_j - Z_j$ numbers in the net evaluation row) of any basic variable is zero. Similarly, it can be shown in the case of the transportation problem that the opportunity cost of each of the occupied cells (cells containing the basic variables) is zero. Now, if we assign a complete set of row numbers, u_i (to be placed at the extreme right-hand side of the table containing a given program) and a complete set of column numbers, v_j (to be placed at the bottom of the table) in such a way that the shipping cost per unit of each of the occupied cells equals the sum of its row and column numbers, we shall satisfy the condition that the opportunity cost of each occupied cell be zero.[14] Further, since the sum of the row and column numbers of any occupied cell equals the cost of that cell (a basic variable), the sum of the row and column numbers corresponding to each empty cell (nonbasic routes) gives the implied cost of that empty cell. The implied cost of any empty cell, therefore, is given by:

$$\text{implied cost} = \text{row number} + \text{column number} = u_i + v_j$$

and

$$\text{opportunity cost} = \text{implied cost} - \text{actual cost}$$
$$= (u_i + v_j) - c_{ij}$$

Thus, by the assignment of row and column numbers, we can calculate the implied cost as well as the opportunity cost of each empty cell without drawing a closed path. We must now tackle the problem of assigning these row and column numbers.

For each occupied cell, we have to choose u_i (row number) and v_j (column number) such that c_{ij} (the actual shipping cost per unit in the occupied cell) equals the sum of u_i and v_j. For the occupied cell falling in row 1 and column 1, for example, u_1 and v_1 are chosen such that $c_{11} = u_1 + v_1$. Similarly, for cell O_1D_2, we must choose u_1 and v_2 such that $c_{12} = u_1 + v_2$. This process must be carried out for all the occupied cells. But it should be realized that although a basic feasible solution for a transportation problem consists of $m + n - 1$ variables (in other words, there are $m + n - 1$ occupied cells), we must assign $m + n$ values to obtain a complete set of row and column numbers. Hence, to determine all the

---

[14] The transportation problem, when represented in the simplex tableau format, consists of column vectors representing structural and other variables. Then, in each column vector, the entries are either 1 or 0. It is this special property of the transportation problem which makes it quite easy to test optimality by the MODI method. If the dual of the transportation problem is formed, the coefficients of all the dual variables will also be 1 or zero. Now, consider a 2×2 transportation problem. It is clear that its basic feasible solution has exactly three positive components in the primal. This means that in the dual only three relationships need to be satisfied as equations. In the dual, while searching for the values of the dual variables, we assign values such that three constraints are satisfied as exact equalities, and these values must simultaneously satisfy the fourth "less than or equal to" constraint. These remarks can be extended to any $(m \times n)$ minimization problem. Their practical significance is this: A set of row numbers u_i and a set of column numbers v_j are chosen so that the opportunity cost of each cell is given by $u_i + v_i - c_{ij}$, where c_{ij} is the actual shipping cost per unit of the cell falling in ith row and jth column. Thus, if we choose u_i and v_j such that for all the occupied cells (basic routes) $c_{ij} = u_i + v_j$, we satisfy the requirement that the opportunity cost of each occupied cell is zero. For the empty cells (nonbasic routes), opportunity cost is given by $u_i + v_j - c_{ij}$.

row and column numbers, one arbitrary number, serving as either a row or a column number, must be chosen. Once one row number or column number has been chosen arbitrarily, the rest of the row and column numbers can be determined by the relationship $c_{ij} = u_i + v_j$. This relationship, as stated earlier, must hold for all the occupied cells. Insofar as any arbitrary number can be chosen to represent one of the u_i's or v_j's, we shall follow the practice of making u_1 take the value zero. This completes the description of the procedure for determining the row and column numbers.

The row and column numbers to check the optimality of Table 10.8 are shown in Table 10.9.

Table 10.9

Origin	Destination				Row Number
	D_1	D_2	D_3	D_4	
O_1	12 (10)	4 4	9 (25)	5 (20)	0
O_2	8 9	1 (20)	6 (25)	6 2	-3
O_3	1 (30)	12 -7	4 -2	7 -6	-11
Column Number	12	4	9	5	

If we arbitrarily choose a value of zero for u_1 and consider the occupied cell $O_1 D_1$, our question is: What value must be given to v_1 so that $c_{11} = u_1 + v_1$, or $12 = 0 + v_1$? Obviously, v_1 must take a value of 12.

Considering the occupied cell $O_3 D_1$, our question is: What value must be given to u_3 so that $c_{31} = u_3 + v_1$, or $1 = u_3 + 12$? Obviously, $u_3 = -11$. Similarly, we calculate other u_i and v_j numbers and enter them in Table 10.9.

Once all the row and column numbers have been calculated, our next task is to calculate the implied costs $(u_i + v_j)$ and the opportunity costs $(u_i + v_j - c_{ij})$ of the empty cells. The *uncircled numbers* in the matrix represent the implied costs of the empty cells. Comparison of the implied and actual costs of each empty cell shows that only cell $O_2 D_1$ has a positive opportunity cost of $+\$1$. For cell $O_2 D_1$, opportunity cost = implied cost − actual cost = $9 - 8 = +1$. A similar calculation for cell $O_1 D_2$ shows that its opportunity cost is zero. The opportunity costs for the rest of the empty cells are negative.

Having identified the presence of positive opportunity cost, we know that this program is not an optimal program. Hence, it must be revised to include that empty cell which has the highest opportunity cost (in this case, cell $O_2 D_1$).

Before we revise the preceding program, let us summarize the role of the row and column numbers. Insofar as the row and column numbers are assigned in such a manner that the actual cost of every occupied cell equals the sum of its row and column numbers, the sum of the row and column numbers of each empty cell gives the implied cost of that empty cell (unused route). If the implied cost of the empty cell is less than its actual cost, this route should be left out of our shipping program. If, on the other hand, the implied cost $(u_i + v_j)$ of an empty cell is more than its actual cost (c_{ij}), this route would be a candidate for inclusion in our next program. In summary, to evaluate and improve a given program in which the objective is to minimize a given function, the rules given in Table 10.10 apply.

Table 10.10

Implied Cost	Actual Cost	Action
$u_i + v_j$ > c_{ij}		A better program can be designed by including this cell in the solution
$u_i + v_j$ = c_{ij}		Indifferent; however, an alternative program with the same total cost and including this cell can be designed.
$u_i + v_j$ < c_{ij}		Do not include this cell in the program.

For a transportation problem in which the objective is to maximize a given function, the signs of the inequalities given in Table 10.10 must be reversed to establish the guidelines for action.

It should be noted that $(u_i + v_j)$ is mathematically and conceptually the same as Z_j in the simplex method.

Let us now return to our problem.

Step 3. *Design a new and better program.*

The revision of any program is guided by a closed path drawn for the most favorable empty cell that is to be included in the next program. Here the closed path for cell O_2D_1 is drawn (see Table 10.9) and the program is revised in exactly the same manner as shown in Table 10.7. The revised program is then tested for optimality (by assigning values to row numbers, u_i, and column numbers, v_j) as shown in Table 10.11. A comparison of the uncircled numbers (representing the implied costs) in the empty cells and the respective actual costs shows that no empty cell has a positive opportunity cost.[15] Hence, this is an optimal solution.[16]

---

[15] The fact that empty cell O_1D_2 has an opportunity cost of zero means that an alternative program which will include cell O_1D_2 and have the same total shipping cost as this program can be designed.

[16] The implied cost of any empty cell gives an indication of the cost sensitivity of that unused route. The cells O_3D_2, O_3D_3, and O_3D_4 in Table 10.11 are insensitive to transportation costs, whereas O_1D_1, O_1D_2, and O_2D_4 are not. For example, the transportation cost of cell O_3D_2 can be decreased by as much as $11 without affecting the optimality of the current solution. However, if the transportation cost of cell O_1D_2 is decreased by even $1, the current optimality is destroyed.

Table 10.11

Origin	D$_1$	D$_2$	D$_3$	D$_4$	Row Number
	Destination				
O$_1$	[12] 11	[4] 4	[9] (35)	[5] (20)	0
O$_2$	[8] (10)	[1] (20)	[6] (15)	[6] 2	−3
O$_3$	[1] (30)	[12] −6	[4] −1	[7] −5	−10
Column Number	11	4	9	5	

10.11
The Transportation Problem (Maximization Case)

Except for one transformation, a transportation problem in which the objective is to maximize a given function can also be solved by the MODI algorithm. The transformation is made by subtracting all the c_{ij}'s from the highest c_{ij} (profit) of the given transportation matrix. The transformed c_{ij}'s give us the relative costs, and the problem then becomes a minimization problem. Once an optimal solution to this transformed minimization problem has been found, the value of the objective function can be calculated by inserting the original values of the c_{ij}'s for those routes which form the basis (occupied cells) in the optimal solution.

10.12
Balancing the Transportation Problem

To solve a given transportation problem by the methods discussed in this chapter, we must establish equality between the total capacities of the origins and the total requirements of the destinations. Three cases can occur.

Case 1. *Supply equals demand* ($\Sigma b_i = \Sigma d_j$).

In this case, the total capacity of the origins equals the total requirement of the destinations. The problem can be arranged in the form of a matrix, along with the relevant cost data, and the transportation algorithm may be applied directly to obtain a solution.

Case 2. *Supply exceeds demand* ($\Sigma b_i > \Sigma d_j$).

In this case, the total capacity of the origins exceeds the total requirement of the destinations. A "dummy" destination can be added to the matrix to absorb the excess capacity. The cost of shipping from each origin to this dummy destination is assumed to be zero. The addition of a dummy destination establishes equality between the total origin capacities and total destination requirements. The problem is then amenable to solution by the transportation algorithm.

Example 10.1 | Table 10.12 gives both the unbalanced and balanced forms of a transportation problem in which the total given capacity of the origins exceeds the total given requirement of the destinations ($\Sigma b_i > \Sigma d_j$). The balanced problem can be solved by the transportation method, and the optimal solution will identify the particular origin at which the excess capacity should be left idle.

Case 3. *Demand exceeds supply* ($\Sigma b_i < \Sigma d_j$).

In this case, the total capacity of the origins is less than the total requirement of the destinations. A dummy origin can be added to the transportation matrix to meet the excess demand. The cost of shipping from the dummy origin to each destination is assumed to be zero. The addition of a dummy origin in this case establishes equality between the total capacity of the origins and the total requirement of the destinations.[17]

Example 10.2 | Table 10.13 gives both the unbalanced and balanced forms of a transportation problem in which the total given capacity of the origins is less than the total requirement of the destinations ($\Sigma b_i < \Sigma d_j$). The balanced problem can be solved by the transportation method, and the optimal solution will identify the particular destination whose requirement cannot be fully satisfied.

In the initial assignment for a transportation problem that has been balanced by the addition of a dummy origin or a dummy destination, only the last necessary allocations should be made to the dummy cells. This procedure, in general, will result in fewer iterations.

---

[17] The reader will observe that in a transportation problem, the role of the dummy column or dummy row that contains dummy variables is parallel to the role of the slack variables in the general linear programming problems illustrated previously.

Extensions of Linear Programming and Special Structure Models   Chapter 10

Table 10.12
Unbalanced Form

	D_1	D_2	D_3	Origin Capacity
O_1	5	3	2	200
O_2	6	4	1	400
Destination Requirement	200	200	150	

Balanced Form

	D_1	D_2	D_3	Dummy	Origin Capacity
O_1	5	3	2	0	200
O_2	6	4	1	0	400
Destination Requirement	200	200	150	50	

Table 10.13

Unbalanced Form

	D_1	D_2	D_3	Origin Capacity
O_1	5	3	2	200
O_2	6	4	1	400
Destination Requirement	300	200	150	

Balanced Form

	D_1	D_2	D_3	Origin Capacity
O_1	5	3	2	200
O_2	6	4	1	400
Dummy	0	0	0	50
Destination Requirement	300	200	150	

10.13
Comparison of the Transportation and the Simplex Methods

Some important observations can be made regarding parallels in the general transportation model and the simplex method. First, the role of the dummy variables in the transportation problem is similar to the role of the slack variables in the general linear programming problem. Second, the occupied cells and empty cells of the transportation program correspond, respectively, to the basic variables and nonbasic variables of the simplex tableau.

Third, the revision of a given transportation program is parallel to the process of obtaining a new basis in the simplex method. Let us explain this point further. A given transportation program, it will be recalled, is improved by filling one empty cell (the one that has the highest opportunity cost) at a time. In this process, all the units from at least one currently occupied cell are removed. Thus, a new cell is filled and becomes an occupied cell, and *at least* one of the previously occupied cells joins the category of empty cells. The total number of occupied cells, therefore, can either remain constant (only one previously occupied cell becomes an empty cell) or decrease (more than one of the previously occupied cells become empty cells) from one program to the next.

If the number of occupied cells remains the same from one program to the next, the process is similar to a simplex iteration in which one nonbasic variable is introduced into the solution to remove one of the basic variables currently in the solution. Of course, in this case we obtain a new basic feasible solution. If, on the other hand, the process of filling one empty cell results in the simultaneous vacating of two or more of the currently occupied cells, the transportation problem becomes degenerate. The latter situation, as the reader will observe, is parallel to the simplex iteration in which the introduction of one new (nonbasic) variable removes, simultaneously, two or more of the current basic variables.

10.14
Degeneracy in Transportation Problems

It was established earlier that a basic feasible solution for a transportation problem consists of $m + n - 1$ basic variables. This means that the number of occupied cells in a given transportation program is 1 less than the number of rows and columns in the transportation matrix. Whenever the number of occupied cells is less than $m + n - 1$, the transportation problem is said to be degenerate.

Degeneracy in transportation problems can develop in two ways. First, the problem may become degenerate when the initial program is designed via one of the initial-assignment methods discussed earlier. Second, the transportation problem may become degenerate during the solution stages. This happens when the inclusion of the most favorable empty cell (the cell having the highest opportunity cost) results in the simultaneous vacating of two or more of the currently occupied cells. To resolve degeneracy in both cases, we can allocate an extremely small amount of goods (close to zero) to one or more of the empty cells,[18] so the number of occupied cells becomes $m + n - 1$. The cell containing this extremely small allocation is, of course, considered to be an occupied cell.

In linear programming literature, this extremely small amount is usually denoted by the Greek letter ε (epsilon). The amount ε is assumed to be so small that its addition to or subtraction from a given number does not change that number. For example, $50 + \varepsilon = 50$, and $200 - \varepsilon = 200$. Of course, if ε is subtracted from itself, the result is assumed to be zero; that is, $\varepsilon - \varepsilon = 0$.

Once the number of occupied cells is $m + n - 1$, the transportation method can be applied in a straightforward manner. If, in the optimal solution, an occupied cell has ε units, it implies that no units are shipped through that route.

10.15
Multiple Optimal Solutions

An optimal solution to a given transportation problem is not always a unique solution. The existence of more than one optimal solution for a transportation problem can be determined by examining the opportunity costs of the empty cells in the optimal program designed by following the transportation algorithm. If any empty cell has an opportunity cost of zero in the optimal program, another optimal program with the same total shipping cost as the first can always be designed. The second optimal program is obtained by revising the first program so as to include the zero-opportunity-cost cell.

In terms of practical significance, the possibility of designing alternative solutions gives valuable flexibility to the manager. It should also be realized that an examination of the opportunity costs of the empty cells (in the optimal program) enables us to identify solutions in descending order of preference in terms of total shipping cost.

10.16
The Assignment Model

The assignment model deals with a special class of linear programming problems in which the objective is to assign a number of "origins" to the same number of "destinations" at a minimum total cost.[19] The assignment is to be made on a one-to-one basis. That is, *each origin can associate with one and only one destination* (and vice versa). This feature implies the existence of two specific characteristics in a linear programming problem, which, when present, give rise to an assignment

---

[18] This extremely small amount may be allocated to any empty cell subject to the condition that this will make possible the determination of a unique set of row and column numbers.

[19] Of course, if the payoff is of the profit variety, the objective is to maximize total payoff.

problem. First, the payoff matrix for the given problem is a square matrix.[20] Second, the optimal solution (or any solution within the given constraints) for the problem is such that there can be one and only one assignment in a given row or column of the payoff matrix.

Payoffs for each assignment are assumed to be known and independent of each other. With information about the number of origins and destinations and the payoffs associated with each available assignment, the assignment model is used to choose the strategy that maximizes or minimizes the total payoff, depending upon whether the particular payoff represents a gain or a loss to the decision maker.

10.17
A Simple Assignment Problem

We illustrate in Table 10.14a the payoff matrix for a 3×3 assignment problem. The cost coefficients c_{ij} give the cost of matching the ith job to jth machine. Our task is to assign to each x_{ij} one of two values (1 or 0) in such a manner that the total assignment cost is minimized. Once the assignment has been made, we have two types of cells: *assignment cells* and *nonassignment cells*. The value of x_{ij} for assignment cells is 1; it is 0 for all nonassignment cells. This is an important property of the assignment model (i.e., $x_{ij} = 1$ or 0).

In Table 10.14b, we enter specific cost data for a very simple assignment problem. The format of Table 10.14b is the same as that of a transportation problem, except that for each row the total capacity is 1, and for each column the total requirement is also 1.

It is easy to conclude that the minimum-cost assignment for the problem shown in Table 10.14b is: Assign O_1 to D_1; O_2 to D_2; and O_3 to D_3. This fact is shown by placing 1's in the assignment cells and 0's in the nonassignment cells. The total cost of this optimal assignment is $33.

Note that in the optimal assignment matrix (Table 10.14b), *each row* and *each column* contains *exactly one* assignment cell. This reflects another important property of the assignment model: The sum of x_{ij} for each row, and for each column, in the optimal assignment matrix must be 1.

In Table 10.14c, we represent the cost data for our assignment problem in a format that is different from the transportation-type format. It is customary to employ the format of Table 10.14c to state assignment problems, and we shall use this format to describe the mechanics of the assignment model.

---

[20] Insofar as any assignment problem must have a square payoff matrix (say $n \times n$), a basic feasible solution should have $n + n - 1$ occupied cells. But, owing to the structural constraints of the assignment problem, any solution of such a problem cannot have more than n assignments (i.e., n occupied cells). Hence, the assignment problem is inherently degenerate. If the given payoff matrix is not a square matrix, we can convert it to a square matrix by adding a dummy row or dummy column. The costs in the dummy row or dummy column are zero.

Table 10.14a

Job	Machine		
	D_1	D_2	D_3
O_1	c_{11} x_{11}	c_{12} x_{12}	c_{13} x_{13}
O_2	c_{21} x_{21}	c_{22} x_{22}	c_{23} x_{23}
O_3	c_{31} x_{31}	c_{32} x_{32}	c_{33} x_{33}

Table 10.14b

Job	Machine			Total
	D_1	D_2	D_3	
O_1	[10] 1	[15] 0	[20] 0	1
O_2	[19] 0	[12] 1	[16] 0	1
O_3	[12] 0	[14] 0	[11] 1	1
Total	1	1	1	

Table 10.14c

Job	Machine		
	D_1	D_2	D_3
O_1	10	15	20
O_2	19	12	16
O_3	12	14	11

10.18
Methods of Solving an Assignment Problem

Let us consider the 3×3 assignment problem whose cost data are shown in Table 10.14c. The problem can be solved by: (1) the simplex method,[21] (2) the transportation algorithm,[22] (3) enumeration, and (4) the assignment method.

We need not repeat the simplex method or the transportation algorithm, as they have already been described. The method of enumeration requires enumerating all *possible* assignments and then choosing the least-cost assignment. For example, there are $3! = 3 \times 2 \times 1 = 6$ possible assignments for the problem of Table 10.14c. For an $n \times n$ assignment problem, the number of possible assignments equals $n!$. One has only to think of a 10×10 assignment problem (3,628,800 possible assignments), not to speak of larger dimensions, to realize that it is impractical to solve such combinatorial problems by enumeration.

Next we describe the *assignment model* or the *assignment method* of solving assignment problems in which the payoffs represent costs (rather than profits) and the payoff matrices are square matrices.

10.19
Approach of the Assignment Model (Minimization Case)

The assignment method consists of three basic steps. The first step involves the derivation of a *total-opportunity-cost matrix* from the given payoff matrix of the problem. This is done, as we shall illustrate in Section 10.20, by: (1) subtracting the lowest number of each column of the given payoff matrix from all the other numbers in its column, and (2) subtracting the lowest number of each row of the matrix obtained in (1) from all the other numbers in its row. The total-opportunity-cost matrix thus derived will have at least one zero in each row and column. Any cell that has an entry of zero in the total-opportunity-cost matrix is considered to be a candidate for assignment. The significance of the total-opportunity-cost matrix is that it presents some possible assignment alternatives in which the opportunity costs of some or all assignments may be zero.

The purpose of the second step is to determine whether an optimal assignment, guided by the total-opportunity-cost matrix derived in step 1, can be made. This is accomplished, as we shall see in the next section, by a simple test. If the test shows that an optimal assignment (with a total opportunity cost of zero) can be made, the problem is solved.[23] On the other hand, if an optimal assignment cannot be made, we proceed to step 3.

---

[21] Added constraints are: $x_{ij} = 1$ or 0, and $\sum x_{ij} = 1$ for each row and column.

[22] Added constraints are: each $b_i = 1$, each $d_j = 1$ (see Table 10.14b).

[23] Insofar as the assignment problem involves decision making under certainty, the total opportunity cost of the optimal solution must be zero.

The purpose of the third step is to revise the current total-opportunity-cost matrix to derive better assignments. **The procedure by which this is accomplished either redistributes the zeros of the current total-opportunity-cost matrix or creates one or more new zero cells. The result is another total-opportunity-cost matrix which enables us to find a less costly assignment. In other words, the result of step 3 brings us back to the beginning of step 2, and we again search for an optimal solution. Thus steps 2 and 3 are repeated as many times as are necessary to find an optimal solution that has a total opportunity cost of zero.**

10.20
Illustration of the Assignment Method

Let us consider the assignment problem whose cost data are shown in Table 10.15.

Table 10.15

Job	D_1	D_2	D_3
		Machine	
O_1	20	27	30
O_2	10	18	16
O_3	14	16	12

Step 1. *Determine the total-opportunity-cost matrix.*

Opportunity cost is the cost involved in not following the best course of action. With respect to a matrix, we can consider two types of opportunity costs:

1. The column opportunity cost, which reflects the relative efficiency of a given column with respect to rows.
2. The row opportunity cost, which reflects the relative efficiency of a given row with respect to columns.

If we examine column D_1, we observe that machine D_1 is most efficient with respect to job O_2; hence, the opportunity cost of matching D_1 with O_2 is zero ($10 - 10 = 0$). On the other hand, if we were to match D_1 with O_1, it will involve an opportunity cost of \$10 (i.e., $20 - 10 = 10$). Similarly, the opportunity cost of assigning O_3 to D_1 is \$4 (i.e., $14 - 10 = 4$). By similar argument, it is possible to determine the column opportunity costs for columns D_2 and D_3. It should be clear by now that the column opportunity cost of a matrix can be determined by subtracting the lowest number, in each column, from all the numbers in that column. For the assignment problem of Table 10.15, the column-opportunity-cost matrix is shown in Table 10.16.

Table 10.16 *Column-Opportunity-Cost Matrix*

	D_1	D_2	D_3
O_1	10	11	18
O_2	0	2	4
O_3	4	0	0

The column-opportunity-cost matrix was derived by determining the relative efficiency of a given column (machine) with respect to all the rows (jobs). It should now be observed that we can also analyze alternatives by examining the relative efficiency of a given row (job) with respect to all the columns (machines). For example, consider job O_1 with respect to the three machines. It is obvious that the row opportunity cost of assigning O_1 to D_1 is zero ($20 - 20 = 0$). However, the row opportunity cost of assigning O_1 to D_2 is $7 (i.e., $27 - 20 = 7$); and the row opportunity cost of assigning O_1 to D_3 is $10 (i.e., $30 - 20 = 10$). By similar argument, it is possible to determine the row opportunity costs of rows O_2 and O_3. It is clear that the row opportunity cost of a matrix can be determined by subtracting the lowest number in each row from all the numbers in that row. For the assignment problem of Table 10.15, the row-opportunity-cost matrix is shown in Table 10.17. Thus, in an assignment problem, any match between an origin and a destination gives rise to two types of opportunity costs. One is the opportunity cost with respect to the lowest payoff in the column to which the assignment cell belongs (we have called it column opportunity cost). The other is the opportunity cost with respect to the lowest payoff in the row to which the assignment cell belongs (we have called it row opportunity cost).

Table 10.17 *Row-Opportunity-Cost Matrix*

	D_1	D_2	D_3
O_1	0	7	10
O_2	0	8	6
O_3	2	4	0

It should be emphasized that *total opportunity cost* is a relative concept. It measures relative efficiencies for the entire payoff matrix rather than relative efficiencies with respect only to columns or rows. It is possible to determine the total-opportunity-cost matrix directly from the original payoff matrix by performing two operations in sequence. First, subtract the lowest number, in each column, from all the numbers in the relevant column; then take the resultant matrix and subtract, in each row, the lowest number from all the numbers in that row. What we obtain is the total-opportunity-cost matrix, as shown in Table 10.18.

Table 10.18 *Derivation of the Total-Opportunity-Cost Matrix*

	Original Cost Matrix				*Column-Opportunity- Cost Matrix*				*Total-Opportunity- Cost Matrix*		
	D_1	D_2	D_3		D_1	D_2	D_3		D_1	D_2	D_3
O_1	20	27	30	O_1	10	11	18	O_1	0	1	8
O_2	10	18	16	O_2	0	2	4	O_2	0	2	4
O_3	14	16	12	O_3	4	0	0	O_3	4	0	0

Let us summarize the two operations required in calculating the total-opportunity-cost matrix for any assignment problem:

1. Subtract the lowest entry in each column of the given payoff matrix from all the entries in its column.
2. Subtract the lowest entry in each row of the matrix obtained in (1) from all the numbers in its row.

Step 2. *Test for optimality (determine whether an optimal assignment can be made).*

An optimal assignment in this problem can always be made if we can locate three zero cells[24] in the total-opportunity-cost matrix (see Table 10.18) such that a complete assignment to these cells can be made with a total opportunity cost of zero. This can happen only when no two such zero cells are in the same row or column, regardless of the number of zero cells in the total-opportunity-cost matrix. Thus, of the four zero cells in the total-opportunity-cost matrix of Table 10.18, only two zero cells are useful for the purpose of obtaining an optimal assignment. On the other hand, if we had an additional zero, say in cell $O_1 D_2$, we *could* locate a set of three zero cells such that an optimal assignment (with a total opportunity cost of zero) could be made.

Based on the above discussion, a simple test has been devised to determine whether an optimal assignment can be made. It consists in drawing and counting the *minimum* number of horizontal and vertical (*not* diagonal) lines necessary to cover all the *zero cells* in the total-opportunity-cost matrix. If the number of lines equals the number of rows (or the number of columns) of the given payoff matrix, an optimal assignment can be made, and the problem is solved. On the other hand, if the minimum number of lines needed to cover all the zero cells is less than the number of rows, or columns, an optimal assignment cannot be made, and it is necessary to construct a revised total-opportunity-cost matrix.

An application of this test to the total-opportunity-cost matrix of Table 10.18 shows that an optimal assignment cannot be made at this stage. It takes only two lines (row O_3 and column D_1) to cover all the zero cells in the total-opportunity-cost matrix (see Table 10.19a), whereas the number of rows is 3. Hence, a revised total-opportunity-cost matrix, which will lead us toward an optimal assignment, must be obtained.

---

[24] For an $n \times n$ assignment problem, we must locate n such zero cells. Such zeros, no two (or more) of which lie in the same row or column, are said to form a set of *independent* zeros.

Step 3. *Revise the current total-opportunity-cost matrix.*

After the application of the test of step 2, the cells of the total-opportunity-cost matrix can be classified into two categories:

1. The *covered cells*, which have been covered by the lines.
2. The *uncovered cells*, which have not been covered by the lines.

The fact that an optimal assignment cannot be made may be interpreted to mean that the relative opportunity costs of some of the cells are wrong.[25] To correct this situation we must obtain a set of three independent zero cells by revising the current total-opportunity-cost matrix. The result of the revision, therefore, must be such that either one of the zeros of the current total-opportunity-cost matrix (Table 10.19a) is transferred to one of the uncovered nonzero cells or a new zero appears in one of the uncovered nonzero cells. We would, intuitively, want this cell to emerge as a new independent zero cell. The procedure for accomplishing this consists in: (1) subtracting the lowest entry in the uncovered cells of the total-opportunity-cost matrix from all the uncovered cells, and (2) adding the same lowest entry to *only* those cells in which the covering lines of step 2 cross. See Section 10.11 of Loomba [1976].

In our example, the lowest entry in the uncovered cells of the total-opportunity-cost matrix (Table 10.19a) is 1 (cell O_1D_2). Subtracting this from all the uncovered cells and adding it to only those cells (in this case, cell O_3D_1) in which the covering lines of step 2 cross, we obtain a revised total-opportunity-cost matrix (see Table 10.19b). An application of the test of step 2 to the revised total-opportunity-cost matrix shows that the minimum number of lines needed to cover all the zeros is 3.[26] Since the number of rows of this matrix is also 3, an optimal assignment can be made.

Table 10.19a

	D_1	D_2	D_3	
O_1	0	1	8	
O_2	0	2	4	
O_3	4	0	0	→ covering line 1

covering line 2

Table 10.19b

	D_1	D_2	D_3
O_1	0	0	7
O_2	0	1	3
O_3	5	0	0

Once it is established that an optimal assignment can be made, we search for a row or column in which there is only one zero cell. The first assignment is made to that zero cell, and the row and column in which this cell lies are crossed out. The remaining rows and columns of the matrix are examined, to find that row or column in which there remains only one zero cell. Another assignment is made, and the respective row and column are crossed out. The procedure is repeated until a complete assignment has been made. The optimal-assignment sequence

[25] We know that the assignment problem involves decision making under certainty, and hence there must be at least one strategy (assignment) that involves a total opportunity cost of zero.

[26] Each line must be drawn in such a manner that it covers the *largest* number of zeros in the matrix.

for our problem is shown in Table 10.20. Since cell O_3D_3 is the only zero cell in column D_3, we make the first assignment to cell O_3D_3 and cross out row O_3 and column D_3.[27] In the reduced matrix, we note that cell O_1D_2 is the only zero cell in column D_2. Hence, we make the second assignment to cell O_1D_2 and cross out row O_1 and column D_2. This leaves only one zero cell open (cell O_2D_1), and therefore the third assignment is made to that cell. Thus, we have the following optimal assignment:

Table 10.20a				Table 10.20b				Table 10.20c		
	D_1	D_2	D_3		D_1	D_2	D_3		D_1	D_2	D_3
O_1	0	0	7	O_1	0	0	7	O_1	0	0	7
O_2	0	1	3	O_2	0	1	3	O_2	×0	1	3
O_3	5	0	×0	O_3	5	0	0	O_3	5	0	0

Assign job O_1 to machine D_2.
Assign job O_2 to machine D_1.
Assign job O_3 to machine D_3.

The total opportunity cost associated with this optimal assignment is, of course, zero. The total cost of this assignment, as can be easily verified from the original cost matrix, is $49.

10.21
The Assignment Method (Maximization Case)

Except for one transformation, an assignment problem in which the objective is to maximize the total payoff can be solved by the assignment algorithm presented in Section 10.20. The transformation involves subtracting all the entries of the original payoff matrix from the highest entry of the original payoff matrix. The transformed entries give us the "relative costs," and the problem then becomes a minimization problem. Once the optimal assignment for this transformed minimization problem has been identified, the total value of the optimal assignment can be found by adding the original payoffs of those cells to which the assignments have been made.

10.22
Multiple Optimal Solutions

After having established the fact that an optimal solution for an assignment problem exists, we may find that the number and positions of the zero cells in the final total-opportunity-cost matrix are such that more than one optimal

[27] The making of an assignment is shown by placing the symbol × in the appropriate cell.

assignment can be made. The presence of multiple optimal solutions for an assignment problem can be identified by the fact that, while assignments are being made via the final[28] total-opportunity-cost matrix, a row or column that contains *only one* zero cell cannot be located.

10.23
Integer Programming

The general linear programming model assumes divisibility. That is, all the variables are assumed to be continuous, and hence they can be assigned any nonnegative integer as well as fractional value. However, in many problems, the assumption of divisibility does not reflect the realities of life. For example, we cannot build 2.2 plants or 2.25 machines. Nor does an optimal solution that asks for the scheduling of 3.5 flights have any operational meaning. We must schedule either 3 or 4 flights. Similarly, we can cite several other problems or examples in which the decision variables must assume only integer values. Thus, there is the need at some times to impose, on the general linear programming model, an additional constraint that some or all of the variables can assume only integer values. When this is done, the resulting model is termed the *integer* (*linear*) *programming* model. It consists of four components: (1) a linear objective function, (2) a set of linear constraints, (3) a set of nonnegativity constraints, and (4) integer-value constraints for some or all variables. When all variables are restricted to integer values, we have an *all-integer* problem. If only some of the variables are restricted to integer values, we have a *mixed-integer* problem.

Various methods have been developed to solve integer programming problems.[29] As compared to the simplex algorithm, the computational effort required for solving integer programming problems is rather extensive. For this reason, we do not illustrate any integer programming methods.[30] However, to provide an intuitive understanding of integer programming we describe the idea of rounding off a noninteger solution and present a graphical analysis of a simple integer programming problem.

10.23.1 ROUNDING OFF THE NONINTEGER SOLUTION

One obvious approach for obtaining an integer solution is to first arrive at the optimal noninteger solution and then round off the values of the noninteger basic variables to their nearest value. The major advantage of this approach is the economy of time and cost, since the alternative of solving the problem by a regular integer programming algorithm will often require additional computations. The major disadvantages of this approach are: (1) the rounded

---

[28] Such as the revised total-opportunity-cost matrix of Table 10.19b. It is final in the sense that we know that this matrix can guide us in making an optimal assignment, and thus it need not be revised.

[29] These seven are discussed in Loomba and Turban [1974]: (1) rounding off a noninteger solution, (2) complete enumeration, (3) graphical approach, (4) Gomory's method, (5) Land and Doig's method, (6) branch-and-bound method, and (7) heuristic programming.

[30] See Loomba [1976, Chap. 11].

solution might not be the real optimal integer solution, and (2) the rounded solution might be an infeasible solution. Hence, when using the rounding-off approach, each rounded solution must be carefully tested for feasibility.

Let us consider the optimal noninteger solution to our familiar product-mix problem [shown in Table 7.1 and stated in (7.4)]: $X = 185\frac{5}{7}$; $Y = 107\frac{1}{7}$; profit = \$7,700. We shall now examine four rounding alternatives, carefully testing each for feasibility (see Table 10.21). Note that the \$7,688 profit associated with the optimal integer solution is less than the \$7,700 profit associated with the optimal noninteger solution. The difference (in this case, \$12) between the objective function of the optimal noninteger solution and the optimal integer solution represents the *cost of indivisibility*

Table 10.21

Rounding Alternative	Is the Rounded Solution Feasible?	Profit	
Case I: $X = 186$ $Y = 107$	No		
Case II: $X = 185$ $Y = 108$	No		
Case III: $X = 185$ $Y = 107$	Yes	\$7,679	
Case IV: $X = 184$ $Y = 108$	Yes	\$7,688	← optimal integer solution

10.23.2 GRAPHICAL ANALYSIS

Let us analyze the following integer programming problem by utilizing its graphical representation.

Maximize

$$Z = 6X + 4Y$$

subject to the constraints

$$\left.\begin{array}{rl} 1.2X + 2Y &\leqslant 14.4 \\ X &\leqslant 8 \\ Y &\leqslant 4 \end{array}\right\} \quad (10.1)$$

and

$$X, \quad Y \geqslant 0, \quad \text{and integer}$$

The integer programming problem given by (10.1) represents a managerial decision in which an optimal integer mix of two types of equipment is to be determined, assuming that the payoffs (objective function coefficients) associated with each unit of the two types of equipment are known.

Let us start by finding the optimal solution to the problem stated in (10.1) by the graphical method presented in Chapter 7. Shown in Figure 10.1 are the relevant constraints, the feasible convex set *OABCD*, and the optimal solution point *C*. The optimal *noninteger* solution is $X = 8$, $Y = 2.4$, and profit = \$57.60. The optimal *integer* solution to this problem, as the reader can verify, is $X = 8$, $Y = 2$ (point *E*), and profit = \$56. Let us examine Figure 10.1 in order to get a "feel" of the integer programming problem and see how some of the integer programming algorithms operate.

First, it should be noted that while any point in the convex set *OABCD* can be a feasible linear programming solution, only the points shown by the *lattice points* can be feasible integer solutions.[31] Second, if the simplex algorithm is to be used in integer programming, the convex set *OABCD* should, somehow, be reduced in such a manner that the extreme (or corner) points of the reduced convex set become all-integer points. This reduction, for example, can be accomplished by constructing one or more "cutting planes." We have drawn a cutting plane *GEF*

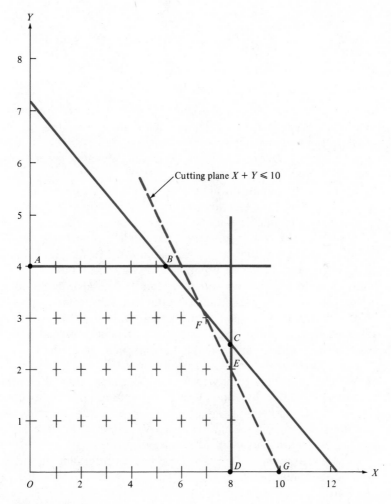

Figure 10.1

---

[31] *Lattice points*, marked by the sign + in Figure 10.1, are those whose coordinates are integer numbers. Whole numbers on either of the axes are obviously integer.

in Figure 10.1 that represents the constraint $X + Y \leqslant 10$.[32] These cutting planes are generated by an integer programming algorithm known as *Gomory's method*. The heart of Gomory's method is to construct a convex set (with a minimum area) that covers all the integer values (lattice points) of the original noninteger convex set. This is accomplished by constructing the cutting planes that are imposed, one at a time, on the original convex set. The cutting planes reflect the additional linear constraints (called *Gomorian constraints*) that are added to the problem in order to converge on the integer solution.

The graphical analysis points up the important fact that the set of feasible integer solutions is always less than or equal to the set of feasible solutions without the integer constraints. This means that the optimal value of an integer solution will always be less than or equal to the optimal value of a noninteger solution to the same problem (maximization case). Hence, the manager must pay a price for imposing the indivisibility requirement.

10.24
Summary

In this chapter, we examined some extensions of linear programming. These extensions emerged as we made the general linear programming model less or more restrictive. In particular we described, very briefly, stochastic programming, nonlinear programming, integer programming, dynamic programming, and the bounded-variable problem.

Two special-structure linear programming models (the transportation and the assignment models) are of special importance because of their simplicity and application potential. These models were discussed in detail.

The approach of the transportation model (or method) consists of three iterative steps: (1) making the initial assignment, (2) testing for optimality, and (3) designing a new and better program, if necessary. Methods of executing these steps were illustrated with specific examples. We also discussed the cases of degeneracy and multiple optimal solutions in transportation problems.

The structure of the assignment model was described and illustrated. Four different methods of solving an assignment problem were listed. Of these, the assignment model (or algorithm) is the most efficient method.

The approach of the assignment model consists of three iterative steps: (1) deriving the total-opportunity-cost matrix (this represents an initial assignment), (2) testing for optimality, and (3) revising the total-opportunity-cost matrix (to obtain a new and better assignment), if necessary. The execution of these steps was illustrated with a specific example. We also discussed the case of multiple optimal solutions in assignment problems.

Finally, we presented the basic idea of integer programming and illustrated its structure graphically.

---

[32] This constraint ($X + Y \leqslant 10$), which represents the cutting plane, was derived by using Gomory's method. In the simple problem shown in Figure 10.1, it is not difficult to argue that a cutting plane drawn through the lattice points E and F would yield the minimum convex set that covers all the integer solutions. Gomory's method is illustrated in Section 6.5 of Loomba and Turban [1974].

References

See the References at the end of Chapter 7.

Review Questions and Problems

10.1. Give a brief description of the structure of these models: stochastic programming, nonlinear programming, integer programming, dynamic programming, bounded-variable problem.

10.2. What are the additional constraints that reduce the general linear programming problem to the transportation problem? To the assignment problem?

10.3. (a) Explain why a basic feasible solution to a transportation problem has exactly $m + n - 1$ components.

(b) What happens if the initial assignment in a transportation problem gives less than $m + n - 1$ occupied cells, where m is the number of origins and n is the number of destinations? How can such a problem be solved?

10.4. What is a balanced transportation problem? Describe the approach of the transportation algorithm.

10.5. Explain the rationale of the MODI method of testing optimality. How does MODI method differ from the stepping-stone method?

10.6. What are the rim requirements? What role do they play in revising a given transportation program?

10.7. What are the row and column numbers? Relate the concept of dual variables to the row and column numbers.

10.8. Distinguish between the terms "opportunity cost" and "implied cost" of an empty cell.

10.9. The assignment problem is inherently degenerate. Explain.

10.10. Describe the approach of the assignment model.

10.11. Under what conditions can the assignment problem have multiple optimal solutions?

10.12. Why must the solution set for an integer programming problem be less than or equal to the solution set for the same problem without the integer constraint?

10.13. Formulate the transportation problem of Table 10.22 as a linear programming problem.

Table 10.22

Origin	Destination D₁	D₂	D₃	Capacity
O_1	4	5	7	40
O_2	6	3	8	50
O_3	5	2	3	60
Demand	50	45	55	

10.14. The Holee Bagel Corporation has three flour mills and four distributorships. Determine the best transportation schedule for the data given in Table 10.23. Use the northwest-corner rule and the MODI method.

Table 10.23

	Queens	Yonkers	Newark	Scranton	Mill Capacity
Hartford Mill	5	3	6	7	35
Hoboken Mill	2	8	1	9	60
Philadelphia Mill	10	4	8	3	25
Distributor Demand	30	45	25	20	

10.15. The Corner Job Shop has three employees who have varying proficiencies in three skills. Table 10.24 shows the manager's assessment of the wage cost for each employee for three jobs. Determine the optimal assignment.

Table 10.24

Job	Employee E_1	E_2	E_3
J_1	100	124	140
J_2	60	80	96
J_3	88	76	68

10.16. The Slumber Lumber Company has received a contract to supply lumber for three construction projects. It plans to send 1,000-kilogram truckloads from three lumberyards. The transportation cost/kilogram and other data are given in Table 10.25. What is the minimum total transportation cost? Use the MODI method.

Table 10.25

| | Project | | | Capacity |
Lumberyard	P_1	P_2	P_3	(truckloads)
L_1	⌐0.20	⌐0.60	⌐0.30	8
L_2	⌐0.40	⌐0.20	⌐0.70	11
L_3	⌐0.50	⌐0.80	⌐0.30	12
Project Requirement (truckloads)	10	12	9	

10.17. Three employees of a company are to be assigned to three jobs which can be done by any of them. Because of the different number of years with the firm, John, Jim, and Sally get different wages per hour, $6, $8, and $10, respectively. The amount of time in hours taken by each employee to do a job is given in Table 10.26. Determine the cost of the best assignment.

Table 10.26

Job	John	Jim	Sally
A	5	3	6
B	4	5	8
C	6	7	1

10.18. Within the First Army area, the Army Quartermaster Corps maintains four depots from which they ship goods to five bases. Table 10.27 gives the cost, capacity, and demand data. Determine the least-cost shipping schedule.

Table 10.27

Depot	Base					Capacity
	B_1	B_2	B_3	B_4	B_5	
D_1	8	5	6	8	9	1,500
D_2	12	7	9	10	10	2,100
D_3	6	6	8	9	8	1,400
D_4	10	8	6	9	8	1,800
Demand	2,000	750	950	1,500	1,600	

10.19. Five salesmen are to be assigned to five territories. Based on past performance, Table 10.28 shows the profit that can be generated by each salesman in each territory. Find the optimal assignment.

Table 10.28

Salesmen	Territory				
	T_1	T_2	T_3	T_4	T_5
S_1	26	14	10	12	9
S_2	31	27	30	14	16
S_3	15	18	16	25	30
S_4	17	12	21	30	25
S_5	20	19	25	16	10

CHAPTER 11

Game Theory

MAJOR CONCEPTS AND TOPICS
DISCUSSED IN THIS CHAPTER

Basic Elements of Game Theory

Strategy, maximizing player, minimizing player
Rule of dominance
Value of the game

The 2-Person Zero-Sum Game

Pure strategy
Mixed strategy

Game Theory and Linear Programming

11.1
Introduction

Game theory is a body of knowledge that deals with making decisions when two or more intelligent and rational opponents are involved under conditions of conflict or competition. Managers competing for share of the market, army generals engaged in the planning or execution of war, union leaders and management involved in collective bargaining, and chess players are all competitors involved in winning *the game*. The competitors in the game are called *players*. It is assumed that each player (an individual or a group) is capable of making independent and rational decisions.

Game-theory models differ from decision making under certainty and decision making under risk models in two respects. First, the opponent of the decision maker in a game-theory model is an active and rational opponent (in DMUC and DMUR models the opponent is the passive state of nature). Second, the decision criterion in a game model is the *maximin* or the *minimax* criterion[1] (in DMUC and DMUR models the criterion is the maximization or minimization of some measure of effectiveness such as profit or cost).

Game-theory models can be classified in a number of ways, depending on such factors as the *number of players, sum of gains and losses,* and the *number of strategies* employed in the game. For example, if the number of players is two, we refer to the game as a *2-person game*. Similarly, if the number of players is N (with $N \geqslant 3$), the game is called an *N-person game*.

If the sum of gains and losses of the game is zero, it is called a *zero-sum* (or *constant-sum*) game. Conversely, if the sum of gains and losses does not equal zero, the game is a *nonzero-sum* game.

A game of chess in which two players agree that the loser will pay \$5 to the winner is an example of the *2-person, zero-sum* game. A situation in which two major companies are competing for share of the market *can* be structured as a *2-person, zero-sum* game

A typical example of an *N*-person, nonzero-sum game is the situation when several companies are engaged in an intensive advertising campaign to capture a larger share of the market. It is nonzero-sum because the *total size* of the market usually increases owing to intensive advertising—with the result that the sum of gains and losses is positive.

The purpose of this chapter is to discuss 2-person, zero-sum games, and explain the relationship between linear programming and game theory.

11.2
Basic Elements of Game Theory

Let us consider a 2-person zero-sum game whose payoff matrix appears in Table 11.1.

----

[1] This was illustrated in Section 5.6.

Table 11.1

		Player B		
		B_1	B_2	B_3
Player A	A_1	6	9	2
	A_2	8	5	4

We make the following remarks:

1. The numbers within the payoff matrix represent the *outcomes* or *payoffs* of the different *plays* (strategies) of the game. The payoffs are stated in terms of a measure of effectiveness such as money, percent of market share, or utility.

By convention, in a 2-person, zero-sum game, the positive numbers denote a gain to the *row* or *maximizing* player, and loss to the *column* or *minimizing* player For example, if player A employs strategy A_1 and player B chooses strategy B_2, this results in a gain of 9 to A and loss of 9 to B.[2]

It is assumed that the payoff matrix is known to both players.

2. A *strategy* is a course of action or a complete plan. It is assumed that a strategy cannot be upset by competitors or nature (chance). In Table 11.1, player A has two strategies (A_1 and A_2) while player B has three strategies (B_1, B_2, and B_3).

3. *Rules* of the game describe the framework within which players choose their strategies. For example, we assume that players must choose their strategies *simultaneously* and that the game is *repetitive*

4. A strategy is termed *dominant* if each payoff in the strategy is superior to *each corresponding* payoff in an alternative strategy. For example, for player B, both strategies B_1 and B_2 are dominated by strategy B_3. Hence, for the purpose of solving this game, columns B_1 and B_2 could be removed from the payoff matrix. Then the game is solved. Player B chooses B_3 and player A chooses A_2. The value of this game is 4.

The *rule of dominance* can be used to reduce the size of the payoff matrix and the computational effort.

5. The *value* of the game refers to the *expected outcome per play* when both players follow their best or optimal strategies.

A game is termed *fair* if its value is zero, and *unfair* if its value is nonzero. Note that the value of the game in Table 11.1 is 4; hence, it is an unfair game.

6. An *optimal* strategy refers to the course of action, or complete plan, that leaves a player in the *most preferred position* regardless of the actions of his competitors. The meaning of the most preferred position is that any deviation from the optimal strategy, or plan, would result in decreased payoff.

7. The *purpose* of the game model is to identify the optimal strategy or plan for each player. Note that the optimal strategy for A is A_2, while B_3 is the optimal strategy for B.

Because of the severe assumptions implied or stated in items 1 to 3 above, the practical value of game theory is rather limited. However, the idea of decision

[2] This implies the assumption that the utility functions of the players are identical.

making under conditions of conflict (or cooperation) is at the core of managerial decisions. Hence, the concepts involved in game theory are very important for the following reasons:[3]

- It develops a framework for analyzing decision making in competitive (and sometimes in cooperative) situations. Such a framework is *not* available through any other analytical technique.
- It describes a systematic quantitative method (in 2-person zero-sum games) that enables the competitors to select rational strategies for the attainment of their goals.
- It describes and explains various phenomena in conflicting situations, such as bargaining and the formation of coalitions.

11.3
The 2-Person, Zero-Sum Game

There are two types of 2-person, zero-sum games. In one the most preferred position for each player is achieved by adopting a *single* strategy, and therefore the game is known as the *pure-strategy* game The second type requires the adoption by both players of a *mixture* of different strategies (as opposed to a single strategy) in order to achieve the most preferred position and is therefore referred to as the *mixed-strategy* game

11.3.1 PURE-STRATEGY GAME—AN ILLUSTRATIVE EXAMPLE

As described earlier, in a pure-strategy game, the optimal plan for each player is to employ a *single* strategy. In the pure-strategy game, the maximizing player identifies his optimal strategy by the application of the *maximin* criterion, while the minimizing player uses the *minimax* criterion to identify his optimal strategy. If the maximin value equals the minimax value, the game is solved. (The test here is that this value must simultaneously be the maximum of its column and minimum of its row. See the circled value of 4 in Table 11.2.) In such a case, a *point of equilibrium* has been reached, and this point is known as the *saddle point*.[4]

If the maximin value does not equal the minimax value, the point of equilibrium cannot be reached. This means that a saddle point does not exist, and the game cannot be solved by employing pure strategies. Consequently, as illustrated in Section 11.3.2, a game with no saddle points is solved by employing mixed strategies.

Consider a situation in which two major companies are in the process of devising their advertising strategies. Assume that company *A* has two strategies and company *B* has three strategies. These strategies and their respective payoffs

---

[3] Loomba and Turban [1974, p. 231].

[4] Visualize a saddle. Then, in the context of the saddle point, we can "think" of two surfaces; one slopes downward (along the sides of a horse), the other slopes upward (along the length of a horse). The saddle point is *simultaneously* the maximum of the downward-sloping surface and minimum of the upward-sloping surface. In the game-theory context, this means that the saddle point is the value that is *simultaneously* the maximum of its column and minimum of its row.

are structured in the form of a 2-person, zero-sum game. This structure is shown in Table 11.2.

Table 11.2

| | | Company B | | | |
		B_1	B_2	B_3	Row Minimum
Company A	A_1	1	9	2	1
	A_2	8	5	④	4 ← maximin
Column Maximum		8	5	4	
				↑ minimax	

Examine the payoff matrix of Table 11.2 from the point of view of the maximizing player, company A.[5] If strategy A_1 is chosen, it is obvious that company B will choose B_1 and the payoff to company A is 1. Now, if strategy A_2 is chosen, company B will choose B_3, and the payoff to company A is 4. Hence, it is obvious that company A will be in the most preferred position if it employs a *single* strategy (strategy A_2).

Let us now examine Table 11.2 from the point of view of the minimizing player, company B. First, note that strategy B_3 dominates strategy B_2; hence, company B will never choose B_2. Hence, column B_2 could be eliminated from the payoff matrix without affecting the outcome of the game.[6] Now, if strategy B_1 is chosen, it is obvious that company A will choose A_2, and B will lose 8 units. If strategy B_3 is chosen, company A will still choose A_2; however, the loss to B will be only 4 units. Hence, company B will be in its most preferred position if it employs a *single* strategy (strategy B_3).

We have shown, therefore, that the 2-person, zero-sum game shown in Table 11.2 is a pure strategy game. It has a saddle point, and its value is 4. The optimal strategy for company A is A_2, and the optimal strategy for company B is B_3.

Now, instead of going through an extensive argument, we can arrive at the same conclusion and solve this pure-strategy game by applying the *maximin* criterion (for the maximizing player) and the *minimax* criterion (for the minimizing player).

[5] The discussion here is for illustration only. Otherwise, as stated in Section 11.2, players choose their strategies simultaneously.

[6] The use of the dominance rule reduces the size of the problem but does not affect the solution of the game. For example, if we eliminate column B_2 from Table 11.2, the size of the game is reduced from 2 × 3 to 2 × 2, but the optimal strategies remain as A_2 and B_3. To the extent that the application of dominance requires extensive comparison of numbers, it is often recommended that the first step in solving a 2-person, zero-sum game should be the attempt to identify a saddle point. If the saddle point exists, the game is solved. Otherwise, use the rule of dominance and reduce the size of the matrix as much as possible. The repeated use of the rule of dominance might lead us to the identification of the optimal strategies. Otherwise, we employ the mixed-strategy technique or linear programming to solve the game. For a schematic representation of this procedure, see Figure 11.1.

Maximin Criterion (for the maximizing player)

Find the minimum of each row. The maximum of these minimum values is the maximin value. Then, for the pure-strategy game, the optimal strategy is the row in which the maximin value lies.

Note that for the game of Table 11.2, the two row-minimum values are 1 and 4. The maximum of these minimum values is 4. Hence, the *maximin* value of 4 is shown in Table 11.2.

Minimax Criterion (for the minimizing player)

Find the maximum of each column. The minimum of these maximum values is the minimax value. Then, for the pure strategy game, the optimal strategy is the column in which the minimax value lies.

Note that there are three columns, and the three column-maximum values are 8, 5, and 4. The minimum of these maximum values is 4. Hence, the *minimax* value of 4 is shown in Table 11.2.

Since maximin value equals minimax value, our next question is: Do we have a saddle point? The answer here is yes, because the value 4 is *simultaneously* the maximum of its column and the minimum of its row.

After we have satisfied ourselves that a saddle point exists, we can say that the optimal strategy for A is A_2, and the optimal strategy for B is B_3.

11.3.2 MIXED-STRATEGY GAME—AN ILLUSTRATIVE EXAMPLE

Consider a situation in which two major companies are in the process of devising a plan to compete for securing a very lucrative business contract. Let us assume that each company has three strategies (low bid, medium bid, and high bid). These strategies and their respective payoffs can be reflected in the form of a 2-person, zero-sum game, as shown in Table 11.3. Our problem is to identify the optimal strategy, or plan, for each of the two companies.

Table 11.3

| | | Company B | | | |
		B_2	B_2	B_3	Row Minimum
Company A	A_1	2	5	7	2 ← maximin
	A_2	−1	2	4	−1
	A_3	6	1	9	1
Column Maximum		6	5	9	
			↑ minimax		

As shown in Table 11.3, the maximin value does *not* equal the minimax value. Hence, we cannot identify a saddle point at this time. The game, therefore, is not a pure strategy game.

Next, we apply the rule of dominance and see whether this will lead us to a solution of the game. Note that in Table 11.3 strategy B_3 is dominated by strategy B_2; hence, we can drop column B_3. This is shown by enclosing column B_3 in Table 11.3.

After column B_3 is eliminated, we note that strategy A_2 is dominated by strategy A_1. Hence, strategy A_2 is eliminated from Table 11.3 (we show this by enclosing the two remaining outcomes in A_2).

Table 11.4

		Company B		
		B_1	B_2	Row Minimum
Company A	A_1	2	5	2 ← maximin
	A_3	6	1	1
Column Maximum		6	5	
			↑ minimax	

Our reduced payoff matrix, therefore, is as shown in Table 11.4. As shown in the table, the maximin value does not equal the minimax value. Hence, there is no saddle point and we cannot reach a point of equilibrium in this game.[7]

When there is no saddle point, we can solve the game by applying the concept of mixed strategies. A mixed-strategy game can be solved by: (1) the graphical method, (2) the analytical method, and (3) linear programming.

The Graphical Method for Solving Mixed-Strategy Games

All $2 \times n$ games (i.e., row player has two strategies and column player has n strategies) and $m \times 2$ games (i.e., row player has m strategies and column player has 2 strategies) can be solved graphically. That is, in order to solve the mixed strategy game graphically, one dimension of the payoff matrix must be 2. We shall not illustrate the graphical method for two reasons: (1) unlike the graphical method in linear programming, it does not provide any deep insights into game theory, and (2) its scope is very limited.[8]

---

[7] The extensive argument goes like this: If A_1, then B takes B_1. But if B_1, then A takes A_3. But if A_3, then B takes B_2. But if B_2, A takes A_1. Thus, we have completed a full circle without finding a point of equilibrium.

[8] The interested reader is referred to Lee and Moore [1975]. Also see Problem 11.14.

The Analytical Method for Solving Mixed-Strategy Games

We shall illustrate the analytical method by solving the game shown in Table 11.4. The basic idea behind the mixed-strategy approach is that a *pattern* of mixed strategies should be developed so that the *expected* gain (or loss) should be the *same*, regardless of the plan of the opponent. Furthermore, the pattern should be implemented in such a way that the opponent cannot discover it.

As we shall see below, the pattern is developed by assigning a probability distribution to different strategies. Also, the secret of the pattern is protected by selecting the strategies *at random* (but conforming in the long run to the probability distribution determined on the basis of equal expected gain, or expected loss).

For Company A. Let us assume that we employ strategy A_1 with a probability of p. Then, it is obvious that we employ strategy A_3 with a probability of $1 - p$.

Assume that company B employs strategy B_1. Then the expected gain to A is

$$2p + 6(1 - p) = 6 - 4p \tag{11.1}$$

Now, assume that company B employs B_2. Then the expected gain to A is

$$5p + 1(1 - p) = 1 + 4p \tag{11.2}$$

The optimal plan for company A requires that its expected gain be the same regardless of what company B does. Hence, equating (11.1) and (11.2), we get

$$6 - 4p = 1 + 4p$$

or

$$p = \tfrac{5}{8} = 0.625$$

That is, company A should employ strategy A_1 62.5 percent of the time, and employ strategy A_3 37.5 percent of the time. However, selection of the strategies is at random (in order to protect the secret of the pattern).

$$
\begin{aligned}
\text{expected gain to company } A &= 0.625(2) + 0.375(6) \\
&= 0.625(5) + 0.375(1) \\
&= 3.5
\end{aligned}
$$

For Company B. Assume that we employ strategy B_1 with a probability of q. Then it is obvious that we employ strategy B_2 with a probability of $1 - q$.

Assume that company A employs A_1. Then the expected loss to B is

$$2q + 5(1 - q) = 5 - 3q \tag{11.3}$$

Now, assume that company A employs A_3. Then the expected loss to B is

$$6q + 1(1 - q) = 1 + 5q \tag{11.4}$$

The optimal plan for company B requires that its expected gain be the same, regardless of what company A does. Hence, equating (11.3) and (11.4), we get

$$5 - 3q = 1 + 5q$$

or

$$q = \tfrac{4}{8} = \tfrac{1}{2} = 0.50$$

That is, company B should employ strategy B_1 50 percent of the time, and employ strategy B_2 50 percent of the time. Again, selection of strategies is to be random.

$$\text{expected loss to company } B = 0.50(2) + 0.50(5)$$
$$= 0.50(6) + 0.50(1)$$
$$= 3.5$$

We can now make two observations. First, note that by using mixed strategies, we have achieved a point of equilibrium in the sense that expected gain (*per play*) of the maximizing player equals expected loss (*per play*) of the minimizing player. Second, by using mixed strategies both players have improved their positions as compared to the maximin and minimax values shown in Table 11.4. Player A has increased his expected gain from 2 to 3.5, and player B has reduced his expected loss from 5 to 3.5.

11.4
Game Theory and Linear Programming

Graphical methods as well as the analytical method (illustrated in Section 11.3) are rather limited in scope. To solve mixed-strategy games of 3×3 or larger dimensions, we can employ linear programming.

Since our purpose here is to explain the procedure, we shall employ linear programming to solve the game shown in Table 11.4. We do this to save computational effort; otherwise, linear programming can be employed to 2-person, zero-sum games of any size.

Let us adopt the following notation:

$$V = \text{value of the game}$$

$\bar{x}_1$ and $\bar{x}_2$ = probabilities of selecting strategies A_1 and A_3, respectively

$\bar{y}_1$ and $\bar{y}_2$ = probabilities of selecting strategies B_1 and B_2, respectively

Since A is the maximizing player, we can write expected gain for A in terms of $\geqslant$ inequalities. That is, A might gain more than V if B employs a poor strategy. Hence, the expected value of gain for player A is given as follows:

$$2\bar{x}_1 + 6\bar{x}_2 \geqslant V \qquad \text{(when player } B \text{ employs strategy } B_1 \text{ all the time)}$$

$$5\bar{x}_1 + 1\bar{x}_2 \geqslant V \qquad \text{(when player } B \text{ employs strategy } B_2 \text{ all the time)}$$

We know that

$$\bar{x}_1 + \bar{x}_2 = 1$$

and

$$\bar{x}_1, \quad \bar{x}_2 \geqslant 0$$

(11.5)

Since B is the minimizing player, we can write expected loss for B in terms of $\leqslant$ inequalities. That is, B might lose less than V if A employs a poor strategy. Hence, the expected value of loss for player B is given as follows:

$$2\bar{y}_1 + 5\bar{y}_2 \leqslant V \qquad \text{(when player } A \text{ employs strategy } A_1 \text{ all the time)}$$

$$6\bar{y}_1 + 1\bar{y}_2 \leqslant V \qquad \text{(when player } A \text{ employs strategy } A_3 \text{ all the time)}$$

Also, we know that

$$\bar{y}_1 + \bar{y}_2 = 1$$

and

$$\bar{y}_1, \quad \bar{y}_2 \geqslant 0$$

$$\left.\begin{array}{c} \\ \\ \\ \\ \\ \\ \\ \end{array}\right\} \qquad (11.6)$$

By dividing each inequality and equation in (11.5) and (11.6) by V, we get

For Company A

$$\frac{2\bar{x}_1}{V} + \frac{6\bar{x}_2}{V} \geqslant 1$$

$$\frac{5\bar{x}_1}{V} + \frac{1\bar{x}_2}{V} \geqslant 1$$

$$\frac{\bar{x}_1}{V} + \frac{\bar{x}_2}{V} = \frac{1}{V}$$

For Company B

$$\frac{2\bar{y}_1}{V} + \frac{5\bar{y}_2}{V} \leqslant 1$$

$$\frac{6\bar{y}_1}{V} + \frac{1\bar{y}_2}{V} \leqslant 1$$

$$\frac{\bar{y}_1}{V} + \frac{\bar{y}_2}{V} = \frac{1}{V}$$

Now, let us define new variables:

$$\frac{\bar{x}_1}{V} = x_1, \qquad \frac{\bar{x}_2}{V} = x_2 \qquad (11.7)$$

$$\frac{\bar{y}_1}{V} = y_1, \qquad \frac{\bar{y}_2}{V} = y_2 \qquad (11.8)$$

Hence, we get the following:

For Company A

$$2x_1 + 6x_2 \geqslant 1$$
$$5x_1 + 1x_2 \geqslant 1$$
$$x_1 + x_2 = \frac{1}{V}$$

For Company B

$$2y_1 + 5y_2 \leqslant 1$$
$$6y_1 + 1y_2 \leqslant 1$$
$$y_1 + y_2 = \frac{1}{V}$$

Recall that company A is the maximizing player. Hence, its objective is to maximize V, which is equivalent to minimizing $\frac{1}{V}$. Since $x_1 + x_2 = \frac{1}{V}$, we can write for company A the following equivalent linear programming problem:

Minimize

$$x_1 + x_2$$

subject to the constraints

$$2x_1 + 6x_2 \geqslant 1$$
$$5x_1 + 1x_2 \geqslant 1$$
$$x_1, \quad x_2 \geqslant 0$$

(11.9)

Since company B is the minimizing player, its objective is to minimize V. This means that B must maximize $\dfrac{1}{V}$. Since $y_1 + y_2 = \dfrac{1}{V}$, we can write for company B the following equivalent linear programming problem:

Maximize

$$y_1 + y_2$$

subject to the constraints

$$2y_1 + 5y_2 \leqslant 1$$
$$6y_1 + 1y_2 \leqslant 1$$
$$y_1, \quad y_2 \geqslant 0$$

(11.10)

It should be noted that (11.9) is the dual to (11.10). Hence, it is necessary to solve only one problem. The solution to the dual can be retrieved from the optimal tableau of the primal.

We solve the primal linear programming problem of (11.10) by the simplex method. The optimal tableau is shown in Table 11.5.

The optimal solution is

$$y_1 = \tfrac{1}{7} \qquad y_2 = \tfrac{1}{7}$$

The optimal solution to the dual problem can be retrieved from the $(C_j - Z_j)$ row of Table 11.5.[9]

$$x_1 = \tfrac{5}{28}, \qquad x_2 = \tfrac{3}{28}$$

Table 11.5 *Optimal Tableau*

Program (Basic Variables)	*Profit per Unit* C_b	*Quantity*	$C_j \rightarrow 1$ y_1	1 y_2	0 S_1	0 S_2
y_2	1	$\tfrac{1}{7}$	1	0	$\tfrac{3}{14}$	$-\tfrac{1}{14}$
y_1	1	$\tfrac{1}{7}$	0	1	$-\tfrac{1}{28}$	$\tfrac{5}{28}$
Z_j			1	1	$\tfrac{5}{28}$	$\tfrac{3}{28}$
$C_j - Z_j$			0	0	$-\tfrac{5}{28}$	$-\tfrac{3}{28}$

[9] This argument was discussed in Chapter 9. See Figure 9.1.

Remember that our objective is to determine the optimal probability distributions for A and B. This is how we proceed.

The value of the game, V, as stated earlier, is found by

$$\frac{1}{V} = x_1 + x_2 = \frac{5}{28} + \frac{3}{28} = \frac{2}{7}$$

Hence,

$$V = \frac{7}{2} = 3.5$$

Note that this is the same value as was obtained by using the analytical method in Section 11.3.2.

Now, from (11.7),

$$\bar{x}_1 = V \cdot x_1 = \frac{7}{2} \cdot \frac{5}{28} = \frac{5}{8} = 0.625$$
$$\bar{x}_2 = V \cdot x_2 = \frac{7}{2} \cdot \frac{3}{28} = \frac{3}{8} = 0.375$$

This means that company A should employ strategy A_1 62.5 percent of the time, and strategy A_3 37.5 percent of the time. Note that this is the same probability distribution (mixture, pattern) that was obtained in Section 11.3.2.

From (11.8),

$$\bar{y}_1 = V \cdot y_1 = \frac{7}{2} \cdot \frac{1}{7} = \frac{1}{2} = 0.50$$
$$\bar{y}_2 = V \cdot y_2 = \frac{7}{2} \cdot \frac{1}{7} = \frac{1}{2} = 0.50$$

This means that company B should employ strategy B_1 50 percent of the time and strategy B_2 50 percent of the time. Note that this is the same probability distribution (mixture, pattern) that was obtained in Section 11.3.2.

11.5
Summary

Game theory is a body of knowledge that deals with making decisions when two or more intelligent and rational opponents are involved under conditions of conflict or competition. The rational thinking implied in game-theory models has been useful in testing strategies and policies involved in union bargaining, political negotiations, devising military options, making advertising and promotional decisions, and so on.

Game-theory models can be classified according to a number of criteria such as the number of players, sum of gains or losses, and the number of strategies employed. In this chapter we discussed only the 2-person, zero-sum game model. Basic elements of game theory were defined and illustrated with respect to a 2-person, zero-sum game, and the importance of game theory was described.

The 2-person, zero-sum game model can fall under one of two categories: (1) pure-strategy game, or (2) mixed-strategy game. Each of the two categories was illustrated with specific examples.

In conclusion, we established the relationship between game theory and linear programming. This provided another instance of the versatile power of the linear programming model. How a 2-person, zero-sum game can be solved as a linear programming model was illustrated with a specific example. In Figure 11.1, we summarize the procedure for solving 2-person, zero-sum games.

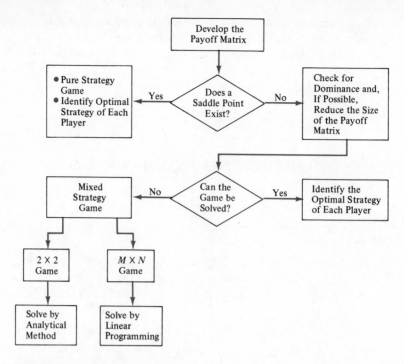

Figure 11.1. Schematic Representation of the Procedure for Solving 2-Person, Zero-Sum Games.

References

Davis, M. D. *Game Theory: A Nontechnical Introduction.* New York: Basic Books, Inc., 1970.

Lee, S. M., and L. J. Moore. *Introduction to Decision Science.* New York: Petrocelli/Charter, Inc., 1975.

Levin, R. L., and R. B. Desjardins. *Theory of Games and Strategies.* Scranton, Pa.: International Textbook Company, 1970.

Loomba, N. P., and E. Turban. *Applied Programming for Management.* New York: Holt, Rinehart and Winston, 1974.

Lucas, W. F. "An Overview of the Mathematical Theory of Games." *Management Science,* Vol. 18, No. 5, Part II (Jan. 1972), P3–P19.

Luce, R. D., and H. Raiffa. *Games and Decisions.* New York: John Wiley & Sons, Inc., 1957.

Shubik, M. *Games for Society, Business and War.* New York: North-Holland/American Elsevier, 1975.

Shubik, M. "On Gaming and Game Theory." *Management Science,* Vol. 18, No. 5, Part II (Jan. 1972), P37–P53.

Shubik, M. "On the Scope of Gaming." *Management Science,* Vol. 18, No. 5, Part II (Jan. 1972), P20–P36.

Shubik, M. *The Uses and Methods of Gaming.* New York: North-Holland/American Elsevier, 1975.

Singleton, R. R., and W. F. Tyndall. *Games and Programs.* San Francisco: W. H. Freeman and Company, 1974.

Von Neumann, J., and O. Morgenstern. *Theory of Games and Economic Behavior*. Princeton, N.J.: Princeton University Press, 1944.

Williams, J. D. *The Compleat Strategyst*, rev. ed. New York: McGraw-Hill Book Company, 1966.

Review Questions and Problems

11.1. What is the domain of game theory?

11.2. In what respects do the game-theory models differ from decision making under certainty (DMUC) and decision making under risk (DMUR) models?

11.3. What different criteria can be applied to classify game-theory models?

11.4. Describe and illustrate, with respect to Table 11.1, the basic elements of game theory.

11.5. What is a pure-strategy game? A mixed-strategy game?

11.6. What is a saddle point? Relate the concept of the saddle point to a pure-strategy game.

11.7. What is the significance of dominance in game theory? Can the idea of dominance be used in DMUR models?

11.8. Describe the maximin criterion. The minimax criterion.

11.9. How can we convert game models into linear programming problems?

11.10. For the payoff matrix, shown in Table 11.6, utilize the maximin (minimax) principle to determine the optimal strategy for each participant. What is the value of the game?

Table 11.6

		Player B		
		B_1	B_2	B_3
Player A	A_1	50	80	70
	A_2	70	90	80

11.11. The North American Air Defense Command (NORAD) and the Strategic Air Command (SAC) are participating in a large war-game exercise. Each will consider the other an opponent. The designated aggressor SAC has developed four strategies for "penetrating" the air defense network. NORAD has developed four "counterstrategies." Table 11.7 shows a payoff matrix which represents the number of targets "destroyed" by SAC. Determine the pure strategies for each player. Can one apply the rule of dominance?

Table 11.7

		NORAD			
		N_1	N_2	N_3	N_4
SAC	S_1	65	100	65	60
	S_2	68	27	29	27
	S_3	75	80	60	41
	S_4	102	40	77	60

11.12. Use the analytical method to solve the mixed-strategy game shown in Table 11.8.

Table 11.8

		Player B		
		B_1	B_2	B_3
Player A	A_1	45	50	25
	A_2	80	55	35
	A_3	70	40	60

11.13. Governor Peanut realizes that if he is to win his party's nomination, he must have some means to formulate, analyze, and choose a strategy that his opponent, Senator Papoon, cannot upset. His aides suggest that he utilize game theory for this purpose. Governor Peanut accepts this suggestion and his research staff provides the payoff matrix, shown in Table 11.9. Design the optimal strategy for Governor Peanut.

Table 11.9

		Senator Papoon		
		P_1	P_2	P_3
Governor Peanut	G_1	60	45	50
	G_2	80	35	40
	G_3	90	65	42

11.14. Examine the payoff matrix shown in Table 11.10. Assume that the probabilities of strategies A_1 and A_2 are p_1 and p_2, respectively. Assume, further, that the probabilities of B_1 and B_2 are q_1 and q_2, respectively.
(a) Determine the optimal strategy for player A. For player B.
(b) Plot the payoffs to A and graphically show the maximum point. (Assume linear relationships. Payoff to A is $15q_1 + 6q_2$ if A_1 is chosen. Payoff to A is $10q_1 + 15q_2$ if A_2 is chosen. Let q_1 vary from 0 to 1 as q_2 varies from 1 to 0.)

(c) Plot the payoffs to B and graphically show the minimum. (Assume that the payoff to B is $15p_1 + 10p_2$ if B_1 is chosen. The payoff to B is $6p_1 + 15p_2$ if B_2 is chosen.)

Table 11.10

		Minimizing Player B	
		B_1	B_2
Maximizing	A_1	15	6
Player A	A_2	10	15

11.15. The defense lawyer and district attorney in a criminal case could conceivably use a game-theory approach (see Table 11.11). Solve this game using the analytical approach.

Table 11.11

		Lawyer			
		L_1	L_2	L_3	L_4
	D_1	70	45	75	80
District Attorney	D_2	75	55	83	95
	D_3	85	60	70	25

11.16. A large multinational firm, Pay-Ore-Dye, Inc., is examining possible strategies to deal with an emerging nation in negotiating a mining rights contract. The firm visualizes the payoff matrix, shown in Table 11.12.

Table 11.12

		Firm			
		F_1	F_2	F_3	F_4
	N_1	-10	35	40	25
Nation	N_2	1	50	65	35
	N_3	40	25	15	20

Formulate this as a linear programming problem.

11.17. Two dog food manufacturers, Great Dane Ptomaine and Guts-for-Mutts are competing for an increased market share. The payoff matrix, shown in Table 11.13, shows the increase in market share for Great Dane Ptomaine and the decrease in market share for Guts-for-Mutts.

Table 11.13

		Guts-for-Mutts			
		Give Coupons	Decrease Price	Maintain Present Strategy	Increase Advertising
	Give Coupons	2	−2	4	1
	Decrease Price	6	1	12	3
Great Dane	Maintain Present Strategy	−3	2	0	6
Ptomaine	Increase Advertising	2	−3	7	1

Simplify the problem by the rule of dominance. Then, formulate the game as a linear programming problem and solve it.

PART IV

Analysis and Control

CHAPTER 12

Inventory Control— Deterministic Models

MAJOR CONCEPTS AND TOPICS
DISCUSSED IN THIS CHAPTER

Essential Aspects, Scope, and Importance of the Inventory Problem

Basic Blocks of Inventory Control

Systems of Inventory Control

Fixed-order system
Fixed-period system

Classifications of Physical Inventories

The ABC Classification

A Classification of Inventory Problems (Models)

Methods of Solving Inventory Models

Numerical approach
Analytical approach
Simulation approach

Deterministic Models of Inventory Control

Static Case
Dynamic Case

Inventory Model with Quantity Discounts

12.1
Introduction

The inventory problem arises whenever something is stored to meet a future demand. An *inventory*, therefore, is *any resource* (physical, financial, or human) that has value because it can satisfy a future need. The management of inventories involves two closely related functions: (1) *planning* for inventories, and (2) *control* of inventories. The planning aspect is concerned with such decisions as *what* to store or produce; *where* are the best sources for procurement of goods; *what* are the most economical arrangements for transportation, storage, inspection; and so on. The control aspect is concerned with decisions such as *when* to order or produce; *how much* to order or produce; and *what* type of inventory control system should be instituted in order to minimize total inventory costs (or maximize profits).

The heart of any inventory control system is an appropriate inventory model that expresses relationships between a criterion variable (total cost or profit) and a set of decision variables (e.g., order quantity Q). We shall restrict our attention to models that have "total inventory cost" (T) as the criterion variable and either the order quantity (Q), or the number of orders (N), or the level of safety stock (SS) as the decision variable. Thus, as illustrated in Section 12.11, an inventory model is a mathematical relationship that expresses "total inventory cost" as a function of decision variables such as the "order quantity" and the "number of orders." Inventory models provide the means for designing an optimal inventory policy in terms of *when* and *how much* to order (or produce).

In this chapter, we first discuss the scope and importance of the inventory problem. We then present a classification of inventories and inventory models. Finally, we illustrate a series of deterministic inventory models. Probabilistic inventory models are discussed in Chapter 13.

12.2
The Scope and Importance of the Inventory Problem

The very definition of the term *inventory* (something of value stored to meet a future demand) establishes both the very wide scope and the importance of the inventory problem. In terms of scope, we note that almost all aspects of organized human effort can in some ways be formulated as inventory problems. The inventory problem is indeed present in *any* purposeful organization: business firms, banks, hospitals, military, government, schools, or even an ordinary household. Here are some examples. A manufacturing firm must keep adequate physical inventories of raw materials, work-in-process, and finished goods in order to meet the demands at various stages of the production process and distribution. A retailer must keep inventories of hundreds of standard, fashion, and promotional items (physical resources) in order to meet regular as well as seasonal demands of his customers. Banks must maintain an inventory of cash (financial resource) in order to meet their loan commitments as well as daily withdrawals by individual depositers. An airline must schedule its flights so that an optimal level of inventory of seats (space resource) is available in order to accommodate the flow of customers. Training programs, such as airline hostess training programs, must determine the size of their classes (human resource) so that the demand for hostesses is adequately met.

The inventory problem is a typical example of the "executive-type" problems that are common to complex and large organizations. The nature of the inventory problem is such that it presents inherent conflicts among the goals of marketing (customer satisfaction by offering a broad range of products), production (cost minimization by producing a small range of standard items), and finance (minimization of working capital tied up in inventories). Furthermore, inventories play a significant role in the two most important financial documents of a firm, the *income statement* and the *balance sheet*. The inventory problem therefore has implications and dimensions that reach into all major branches of the business firm.

The importance of the inventory problem is based on the following reasons or purposes:

1. The inventory problem is all pervasive. The idea of "meeting a future need" is the very essence of management.
2. Inventories tie up a significant portion of an organization's working capital. For large manufacturing firms, inventory investment can amount to millions of dollars.[1] Even a small percentage reduction in manufacturing inventories can therefore result in substantial savings.
3. Inventories serve to "decouple" the procurement, production, and distribution functions of a firm. Thus, they permit the management of each function a greater degree of independence, flexibility, and efficiency.
4. Inventories make it possible to smoothen production even though the demand fluctuates due to economic and seasonal factors.
5. Inventories make it possible to meet production or customer demand, even though the supply may be irregular due to economic or seasonal factors.
6. Inventories permit managers to take advantage of quantity discounts.
7. Inventories reduce the impact of stockouts that result in loss of sales and customer goodwill.

12.3
Essential Aspects of the Inventory Problem

It was stated in Section 12.1 that the management of inventories involves two closely related functions of *planning* (*what* to store; *where* are the best sources for procurement) and *control* (*when* to order; *how much* to order). The inventory models presented in this and the next chapter answer the questions of *when* and *how much*. The questions of *what* and *from where* are also extremely important, but are beyond the scope of this book.

---

[1] For example, the value of inventories at F. W. Woolworth Company was close to $950 million at the end of 1976.

1. *What is to be stored?* The answer to this question is provided by the nature, purpose, and scope of the organization. The range of inventory items can vary from one to hundreds, or even to thousands. "*What* to store" is obviously a direct consequence of the basic mission of the firm, its customers, and the markets that it serves.

An important consequence of "what to store" is the type of inventory model that would be utilized in controlling inventories. For example, an inventory model can be single-product or multiproduct; single-location or multilocation; single-level or multilevel; single-period or multiperiod. In this as well as in the next chapter, we address ourselves only to single-product, single-location, and single-period models.

2. *Where are the best sources for procurement?* This question relates to the choice of a vendor and considers such factors as reliability of supply, quantity or price discounts, and quality. In Section 12.13 we shall discuss a deterministic model that considers quantity discounts.

3. *When to order or produce?* This question can be answered in two forms. The first relates to some *level* of inventory which triggers the ordering activity. For example, as soon as the level of inventory of an item drops to 50, we issue a procurement order. The second operational form of "when to order" relates directly to the dimension of *time*. For example, an inventory policy can state that a procurement order must be placed every 2 months.

4. *How much to order or produce?* This question relates to the *quantity* to be ordered or produced at one time. And, it is this question that is the major focus of the inventory models discussed in this and the next chapter.

The essential aspects of the inventory problem are integrated in Figure 12.1.

Figure 12.1. Essential Aspects of the Inventory Problem.

12.4
Basic Blocks of Inventory Control

Before presenting some models of inventory control, we give a brief discussion of: (1) the nature of inventory demand and supply, (2) categories of inventory costs, (3) systems of inventory control, and (4) methods of information feedback. These areas form the *basic blocks* from which an "integrated" inventory policy must be determined.

12.4.1 THE NATURE OF INVENTORY DEMAND AND SUPPLY

The question of inventory demand and supply has three distinct but related dimensions. First, since inventories are kept to meet future demand, we must predict the *nature of demand*. Is it the type of demand that can be reasonably assumed to occur with *certainty*? Such, for example, would be the case while production plans are being made to fulfill contractual obligations. If we say that the annual demand for an item is 5,000 units, we are assuming a single demand level and hence a *certain* or *deterministic demand*.

If the demand is of the type that different demand levels, along with their respective probabilities, must be specified, then we have a probabilistic demand. Table 12.1 illustrates an example of a *probabilistic demand*.

Demand predictions should also take note of such factors as seasonality, trends, introduction of new competitive items, and the like. In short, we must consider *all* relevant factors before assuming a particular demand situation.

The second dimension relates to the questions of supply and leadtime that determine the timing of receiving the materials. *Leadtime* is the time elapsed between the acts of ordering and actually receiving the materials. In manufacturing operations, leadtime refers to the time interval between setup of and actual output from the machines. As in the case of predicting the nature of demand, we must state the nature of leadtime. Can the leadtime be predicted with *certainty* (i.e., is it *deterministic*?). Or, is the leadtime of a varying nature so that it can only be specified by a *probabilistic distribution*?

When both the demand and the leadtime are assumed to be *certain*, we are in the domain of *deterministic models*. In Sections 12.11 and 12.12 we illustrate two different deterministic models.

Table 12.1 *Probabilistic Demand*

Annual Demand (units)	Probability
2,000	0.20
4,000	0.50
6,000	0.30

When either the demand, or the leadtime, or both are specified by probability distributions, we are in the domain of *probabilistic models*. In chapter 13, we shall illustrate probabilistic inventory models.

The third dimension relating to demand is the behavior of "units demanded during leadtime." Once the demand and leadtime characteristics of an inventory item have been specified, the nature of *units demanded during the leadtime period* can be predicted. Units demanded during the leadtime period may be *constant* or *varying*, depending upon the nature of the demand or *usage rate* during leadtime and the behavior of the leadtime. For example, assume that demand or usage per day, during leadtime, is known with certainty to be 10 units, and there is also a deterministic leadtime of 2 days. Then the number of units demanded during the leadtime is also known with certainty, and in this case is 20 units. However, if either the demand or leadtime or both have probabilistic distributions, units demanded during the leadtime will also have a probabilistic distribution.[2]

12.4.2 CATEGORIES OF INVENTORY COSTS

Regardless of the nature of demand, leadtime, and units demanded during the leadtime, four categories of inventory costs are associated with keeping inventories of an item. These costs are: (1) purchase costs of the inventory items, (2) ordering or setup costs, (3) holding costs, and (4) stockout costs. The optimal inventory strategy is usually based on, and determined from, these four categories of costs and their relationship to different inventory levels. Therefore, for any inventory situation, total inventory cost per year can be determined from the following cost equation:

$$
\left. \begin{aligned}
\text{Total inventory cost} = {} &\text{Purchase costs of inventory items} \\
&+ \text{Ordering costs} + \text{Holding costs} \\
&+ \text{Stockout costs}
\end{aligned} \right\} \quad (12.1)
$$

Purchase Costs of the Inventory Items

An inventory item can exhibit two types of purchase-cost behavior. First, we have the case when the purchase price is fixed and hence the *cost per unit, C,* is *constant* regardless of the quantity purchased. The second case arises when quantity discounts are available and hence the *cost per unit* is a *variable* (determined by the size of the purchase).

Ordering (or Setup) Costs

A company can meet its needs for materials and goods by either purchasing from outside suppliers or by setting up its own production facilities (buy or make). In either case there are some well-defined costs, called *procurement costs*, that must be incurred by the company. When the goods are purchased from the outside, these procurement costs are usually referred to as *ordering costs*, and they consist of all of the costs that are incurred in sending inquiries, writing purchase orders,

---

[2] The distribution of units demanded during leadtime can be obtained from either company records or by employing analytical or simulation methods.

receiving and inspecting goods, paying the bills, and performing related paperwork to keep the supplies flowing. A major portion of this category of costs consists of personnel salaries. Other components are expenses for telephones, paper forms, and supplies. If the company is engaged in supplying its own requirements (e.g., batch production of different items), the procurement costs are referred to as *setup costs*. The setup costs include all the costs required to setup the necessary production process to produce a "batch" of goods.

What is of interest in making inventory control decisions is the *incremental* cost of processing an order (or *incremental* cost of preparing for a production lot). Depending upon the level of activities, the incremental cost per order, S, is determined by the number of orders written and the total procurement costs per year.

Holding (or Carrying) Costs

Holding costs consist of all costs related to carrying inventories in stock. Examples of holding costs are: cost of money tied up in the inventory, storage cost, depreciation, insurance, taxes, deterioration, and obsolescence. Holding costs can be expressed in one of two ways. First, holding costs (H) can be expressed as a fixed percentage of *average dollar* inventory value. For example, accounting records of a company may show that the value of H is 20 percent. This means that if the *average dollar* inventory of this company is $20,000, the holding cost is $0.20(20,000) = \$4,000$/year. Second, holding cost (h) can be expressed as the cost of holding an inventory item for a time period such as 1 year. For example, the cost of holding 1 unit of an inventory item for 1 year can be $5 or $10, depending upon purchase price, cost of capital, and so on.

Stockout Costs

Stockout costs are incurred when a customer's demand cannot be fulfilled because the inventory is completely depleted. If the customer is willing to wait, the stockout cost consists of the cost of expediting the order and processing it under "RUSH" conditions. Sometimes the customer is not willing to wait and therefore "back-ordering" is not possible. In such cases, the stockout cost consists of loss of goodwill and loss of profit from that sale.

The four categories of costs just mentioned can essentially be grouped into two different sets. As the level of average inventory over a particular time period increases, one set of costs increases while the second decreases. For example, assuming a deterministic demand rate and no discounts for quantity purchases, the determination of economic order quantity (EOQ) requires balancing ordering costs (which decrease as average inventory levels increase) against holding costs (which increase as average inventory levels increase). For purposes of analysis and eventual development of an inventory model, therefore, one must identify all such costs; determine their relationship to various inventory levels; and measure them in relation to different strategies. Once the model has been developed, it can be solved by employing *numerical*, *analytical*, or *simulation* methods. This solution, in effect, yields a particular strategy which will result in an optimal value of the selected measure of effectiveness. In inventory models, the measure of effectiveness is usually the "total inventory cost" per year.

12.4.3 SYSTEMS OF INVENTORY CONTROL

By a system of inventory control we shall mean a framework for integrating the necessary information and data for the purpose of minimizing total inventory cost. In this chapter we shall present two major systems: (1) the fixed-order system, and (2) the fixed-period system.

Fixed-Order System

In the *fixed-order system* a purchase order is issued as soon as the supply on hand falls to a predetermined level called the *reorder point*. Further, the size of the purchase order, as determined by the model, is fixed. That is, the quantity ordered is always the same. In its simplest form, the order quantity in this system is constant, while the time between reordering fluctuates depending upon the rate of depletion. In other words, the "when" fluctuates with the rate of usage, but the "how much" remains constant.

A major advantage of the fixed-order system is its ease of operation. On the other side of the balance sheet, many operational complications can arise. For example, if a firm is purchasing different products from the same source, a rigid adherence to the system may result in loss of opportunities for price and freight discounts. Then, too, if the inventory must be stored at different locations in the plant, much of the automaticity of the fixed-order system is lost. The determination of optimum order quantity and the decision on the reorder point are, of course, the analytical aspects of this system.

Fixed-Period System

In the fixed-period system (sometimes called the *periodic-reordering or reordering-cycle system*) the *time* between reordering remains constant (e.g., review period of 4 months), while the *quantity* ordered is allowed to fluctuate, depending on the expected demand during the next review period. In other words, the "how much" fluctuates, but the "when" remains constant. At the end of each *review period*, the items are reviewed and an order is placed to bring the stocks up to a specific supply control level. The amount ordered is usually that which is sufficient to cover the demand for the purchasing leadtime plus one reorder cycle.

The most important advantage of this type of inventory control system lies in its adaptability for exercising tighter control on high-value items. This system is desirable where the firm faces fixed transportation schedules from the suppliers or where branch warehouses order hundreds of different items in each period from a central source of supply. The main disadvantage results from the necessity of determining different reorder cycles, order quantities, and safety stocks in a multi-item organization having different demand distributions, different carrying charges, and so on, for various inventory items.

A number of combinations or variations of the two basic systems (fixed order and fixed period) are possible. In practice, while designing a particular system of inventory control, the planner can take elements from different types of systems, depending upon the nature of the operations, demand for the different items, and other related factors pertinent to economical inventory control.

Any system of inventory control needs an information feedback mechanism in order to operate successfully. This is accomplished either by taking physical inventory at the end of a specific time interval, or by instituting perpetual inventory procedures. The perpetual inventory procedure keeps a running record of material received, material on order, material issued, and balance on hand. In most large organizations, perpetual inventory records are maintained. This is especially feasible where the volume of business is large enough to justify the installation of a computer.

12.5
Classification of Physical Inventories

Inventories can be classified in a number of ways, depending upon the criterion of classification. In case of physical inventories, the *stage of completion* in the production process can be used as the criterion. The result is three categories: raw materials, work-in-process, and finished goods.

A more general classification emerges if we use the *purpose* of inventories as the criterion of classification:

1. *Inventories in transit*

Transit or *movement* inventories exist because goods must be moved from one location to another. For example, inventories moved by trucks, freight trains, and ships are transit inventories. The optimal size of transit inventories is determined by such factors as the transit time, demand rate, and transportation costs.

2. *Cycle or lot-size inventories*

Cycle or *lot-size* inventories exist because stocks are purchased (or produced) to obtain quantity discounts (or to reduce per unit setup costs) and to reduce ordering, transportation, and handling costs. The optimal lot size is based on such factors as quantity discounts, ordering costs, and holding costs.

3. *Safety or uncertainty inventories*

Safety (buffer) stock or *uncertainty* (fluctuation) inventories are held to provide a cushion (or buffer) against unpredictable fluctuations in supply and demand. Obviously, when both demand and supply are known with certainty, there is no need for safety or buffer stock. The optimal size of the safety stock is determined by such factors as holding costs and stockout costs.

4. *Anticipation or seasonal inventories*

Anticipation or *seasonal* inventories build up when the purchasing or production rate is higher than the current demand. Some of the uses of anticipation inventories are: to accommodate seasonal peak sales (e.g., Christmas sales), take advantage of anticipated future price rises, and smoothen production and employment rates by building inventories during low demand periods and by depleting them during high demand periods. The optimal size of anticipation inventories is influenced by such factors as projected prices, stockout costs, and holding costs.

12.6
The ABC Classification

Even before a decision on the choice of a specific inventory control system is made, inventories can be classified according to their relative importance in terms of *annual dollar volume*. This importance is established by evolving a relationship so that each inventory item can be placed in one of three classes (A, B or C) that relate percentages in terms of number of items and annual dollar volume. Known in the literature as the ABC system, it classifies all inventory items in three classes. The A class consists of those items which constitute only 5 to 25 percent of all items but account for 65 to 85 percent of a company's total dollar volume. The B class items constitute another 10 to 25 percent of all items and account for 15 to 20 percent of dollar volume. The C class consists of 50 to 80 percent of items but accounts for 5 to 15 percent of dollar volume. Since it costs money to develop and operate an inventory control system, the ABC system is an effective way to isolate those costly items on which control efforts must be focused. It is a very effective device for exercising *selective* control.

In Table 12.2, we present a typical ABC classification.

12.7
A Classification of Inventory Problems (or Models)

Inventory problems (or models) can be classified in a variety of ways, depending upon the assumptions made with respect to such factors as the criterion of effectiveness (e.g., cost-minimization and profit-maximization models); static versus dynamic behavior (this relates to the number of ordering decisions made

Table 12.2 *The ABC Classification*

Percentage in Terms of Number of Items	Class	Percentage in Terms of Annual Dollar Volume
5	A	
15		80
	B	
80	C	15
		5

	Deterministic (assumption of certainty)	Probabilistic (assumption of probabilistic behavior)
Static (single order)	• Trivial Inventory Problems	• Christmas Tree Problem • Newsboy Problem
Dynamic (multiple orders)	• Simple EOQ Models • Dynamic Programming Models	• Majority of Inventory Problems

Figure 12.2. Matrix of Inventory Models.

during the planning horizon time period—i.e., single or multiple orders); length of the planning horizon (finite or infinite); specific behavior of prices (e.g., constant or variable price schedule); specific nature and behavior of demand and leadtime (e.g., deterministic or probabilistic); and so on. The number of factors that can enter an inventory problem is so large that there is literally no end to the different types of inventory models that can be built. The published literature on the subject is enormous, and inventory theory is probably the most developed aspect of operations research.[3] Since the subject matter is so broad, we draw some arbitrary boundaries and discuss only a selected set of inventory models. However, the models that we discuss comprise the most widely used models in actual practice.

Shown in Figure 12.2 is a matrix of inventory models that emerges when we simultaneously apply the assumptions of: (1) deterministic versus probabilistic behavior, and (2) static versus dynamic behavior. Based on the matrix shown in Figure 12.2, we can build a classification scheme (see Figure 12.3) from which the models discussed in this and the next chapter are selected.

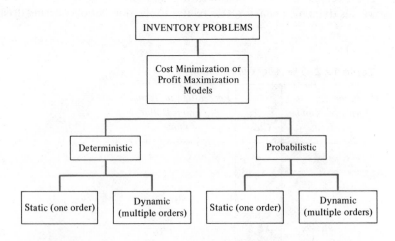

Figure 12.3. A Classification of Inventory Problems (Models).

[3] For an excellent summary of mathematical inventory theory, see Veinott [1966].

12.8
Methods of Solution

Inventory models can be solved by different methods. Of special importance are these three approaches: (1) numerical approach, (2) analytical approach, and (3) simulation approach.

12.8.1 THE NUMERICAL APPROACH

The numerical approach is essentially a trial-and-error method of determining the optimal inventory policy. The basic steps of the numerical approach are:

Step 1. *Identify the relevant cost components from a total inventory cost equation, such as Equation (12.1).*

In a *deterministic* problem with no quantity discounts, for example, the only relevant components of (12.1) are *ordering costs* and *holding costs*.

Step 2. *Identify the decision variable, such as the number of orders per year (N) or the order quantity (Q).*

Step 3. *For different selected values of the decision variable, calculate the total inventory cost.*

Step 4. *Identify the optimal value of the decision variable* (e.g., optimal number of orders).

The value of the decision variable that results in minimum total inventory cost yields the optimal inventory policy.

Example 12.1 | We illustrate the numerical approach by considering a manufacturer whose annual requirement, D, is 1,200 units, and purchase cost, C, is $1/unit. The average monthly demand (usage) is $100. Assume that the *incremental* ordering cost, S, is $12, and the holding cost, H, is 20 percent of the average dollar inventory. We assume *constant* usage and *deterministic* conditions.

Table 12.3

(1)	(2)	(3)	(4)	(5)	(6)
		Average*	*Ordering*	*Holding*	*Sum of*
Frequency of	*Number of*	*Inventory*	*Costs*	*Costs*	*Columns*
Orders	*Orders*	*(dollars)*	*(dollars)*	*(dollars)*	*4 and 5*
Annual	1	600	12	120	$132
Semiannual	2	300	24	60	84
Quarterly	4	150	48	30	78 ← Minimum
Monthly	12	50	144	10	154

* Based on the assumption of linear usage and an inventory of zero at the end of each order cycle, average inventory is one-half of the order quantity.

Hence, from the four cost categories of Equation (12.1), the two relevant categories are the *ordering costs* and *holding costs*.

The numerical approach to the above problem is illustrated in Table 12.3. As shown in Table 12.3, the minimum total inventory cost results when the number of orders, N, is 4. Hence, we are led to the conclusion that the best (optimal) inventory policy in this case is to place 4 orders per year. That is, an order of 300 units (order quantity) should be placed on a quarterly basis.

A note of caution with respect to the numerical approach is in order. The numerical approach yields the minimum cost *only* for the alternatives tried. It *might* miss the true optimum, as indeed is the case in our example. The real optimal solution for this problem yields a value of 3.16 orders, as can be shown by using the model derived in Section 12.11.2.[4]

12.8.2 THE ANALYTICAL APPROACH

The analytical approach (deductive variety) for solving an inventory model was discussed in Section 2.8.1. It consists of building a mathematical model to represent the inventory problem and then solving the model to arrive at the optimal value of a specified decision variable. We illustrate the analytical approach in Sections 12.11 and 12.12.

12.8.3 THE SIMULATION APPROACH

The simulation approach for solving inventory problems is useful for probabilistic models. The idea and mechanics of the simulation approach are presented in Chapter 14.

12.9
Selected Models of Inventory Control

As mentioned earlier, a very large number of different inventory models can be formulated if each possible combination of such factors as nature of demand, nature of leadtime, service levels, number of products, number of locations, number of inventory levels, and availability of discounts is considered.

In this book we shall limit our discussion to models based on the classification scheme shown in Figure 12.3. In particular we shall discuss the following models in this chapter: deterministic model (static case), deterministic model (dynamic

---

[4]

$$N = \sqrt{\frac{DCH}{2S}} = \sqrt{\frac{1,200(1)(0.20)}{2(12)}} = 3.16 \text{ orders}$$

This translates into an order quantity of approximately 379 units (as opposed to 300 units when $N = 4$).

case; instantaneous buildup), deterministic model (dynamic case; gradual buildup), and deterministic model (with quantity discounts). We shall present probabilistic inventory models in Chapter 13.

12.10
Deterministic Model (Static Case)

Since this is a static case, we are dealing with a *single*-order situation. The assumption of *certainty* makes this problem a trivial case, as we do not require a mathematical model to solve a static problem under conditions of certainty.

Chartering a bus for a class trip, ordering cinema tickets for a party of friends, ordering meals at a restaurant are all examples of a static model under deterministic conditions.

12.11
Deterministic Model (Dynamic Case: Instantaneous Buildup of Inventory)

Since this is a dynamic case, we are dealing with an inventory problem that permits *multiple* orders during a planning horizon. The deterministic assumption means that both demand and leadtime are known with *certainty*. We illustrate this model after making the following additional assumptions.

1. Quantity discounts are not available. Hence, purchase cost per unit, C, is constant.
2. Demand rate is linear. That is, usage per day is constant.
3. Leadtime is constant.
4. Inventory builds up instantaneously.

Assume further that we are operating a fixed-order system. Then the dynamic deterministic model can be represented graphically as shown in Figure 12.4. In the inventory literature, this model is known as the basic EOQ (economic order quantity) model.

Figure 12.4 shows the behavior of inventory at hand with respect to time. It also shows the time of ordering, leadtime, linear usage, instantaneous buildup of inventory, quantity ordered, and the time at which the material is received. Note that an order is placed as soon as the level of inventory drops to the *reorder point*, R.

(*Note:* Our assumption of constant demand per day will lead to demand behavior that should be graphed as a stairway. However, in Figure 12.4, and also in other relevant figures, we approximate such demand by a straight line).

In Figure 12A.1 on p. 356, we represent the behavior of relevant costs of this model. Also, as explained in Appendix 12A, because of the *assumptions of this model*, the optimal order quantity, Q^*, can be calculated by equating ordering costs to holding costs.

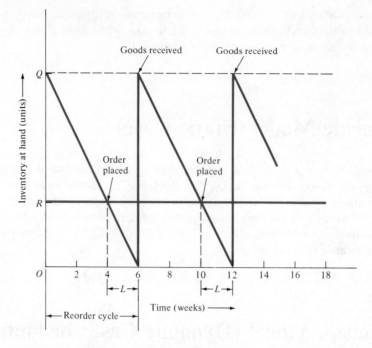

Figure 12.4. Basic EOQ Model. (Behavior of Inventories) (fixed-order system with no safety stock; deterministic model having constant demand and constant leadtime; instantaneous buildup of inventory)

R = reorder point	demand forecast = 100 units/week
Q = order quantity	reorder point = $2 \times 100 = 200$ units
L = leadtime	order quantity = 600 units
	leadtime = 2 weeks

We can now proceed to illustrate the analytical approach. Let us adopt the following notation:

T = total inventory cost ($/year)

D = demand per year (units/year)

C = cost or purchase price per unit ($/unit)

Q = quantity per order (units/order)

H = holding or carrying costs, expressed as a percentage of average dollar inventory (%)

N = number of orders per year

S = incremental cost of processing an order ($/order)

R = reorder point (units)

L = leadtime (some time period such as weeks or months)

Y = reorder cycle (the elapsed time between successive orders), stated in time units such as days, weeks, or months, or fraction of a year. Note that $Y = \dfrac{1}{N}$ and $N = \dfrac{D}{Q}$

12.11.1 DETERMINATION OF OPTIMAL LOT SIZE, Q*

The *analytical approach* for solving an inventory model consists essentially of four steps. We shall illustrate these steps symbolically as well as with the aid of an example. The objective is to determine Q^*.

Step 1. *Identify the relevant cost components from the total inventory cost equation, such as Equation (12.1).*

Recall that Equation (12.1) has four cost components: purchase costs of inventory items, ordering costs, holding costs, and stockout costs.

Since quantity discounts are not available, and annual demand is known with certainty, annual purchase costs of inventory items (DC) are constant, regardless of number of orders (N) or size of order (Q). Hence, they need not be included in the model.

Since both demand and leadtime are known with certainty, there is no need for a safety stock. Nor can there be any stockouts. Hence, stockout costs need not be included in the model.

Therefore, for the basic EOQ model the only relevant cost components are ordering costs and holding costs. Hence, the inventory model can be described by the following equation:

$$\text{total inventory cost} = \text{ordering costs} + \text{holding costs} \tag{12.2}$$

Step 2. *Identify the decision variable, such as the number of orders per year (N) or the order quantity (Q).*

Let us assume that the decision variable is Q.

Step 3. *Build a mathematical relationship that expresses total inventory cost in terms of its different cost components* (these cost components are to be stated in terms of the specified decision variable).

The two relevant cost components here are ordering costs and holding costs.

Ordering Costs

$$\begin{aligned}
\text{ordering costs} &= \text{number of orders} \times \text{incremental cost of processing an order} \\
&= N \quad\quad\quad\quad\quad\quad \times S \\
&= \frac{D}{Q} \quad\quad\quad\quad\quad\quad \times S \\
&= \frac{D}{Q} S
\end{aligned} \tag{12.3}$$

Illustrative Comments. For example, if $D = 6{,}000$ units/year and $Q = 500$ units/order, then number of orders per year $= N = \dfrac{6{,}000}{500} = 12$. Thus,

$$N = \frac{D}{Q} \quad \text{or} \quad Q = \frac{D}{N} \tag{12.4}$$

Also, reorder cycle

$$Y = \frac{1}{N} = \frac{Q}{D} = \frac{500 \text{ units/order}}{6,000 \text{ units/year}} = \frac{1}{12} \text{ year/order}$$

Thus, time required to exhaust one order is $\frac{1}{12}$ year or 1 month. Alternatively stated, the time between successive orders is 1 month. That is, the *reorder cycle* is 1 month. Note that $N = \frac{1}{Y} = 12$ orders/year.

Assume that $S = \$25$/order. Then

ordering costs $= NS = 12(25) = \$300$/year $\leftarrow$

Holding Costs

holding costs = average dollar inventory × percentage holding costs

$$= \frac{Q}{2} C \qquad \times H$$

$$= \frac{Q}{2} CH \qquad (12.5)$$

Illustrative Comments

- Average physical inventory $= \frac{Q}{2}$. This is because of the linear behavior of inventory as shown in Figure 12.4. Note that the reorder cycle begins with Q units and ends with zero units (and there is no safety stock). Thus, since the usage is linear,

$$\text{average inventory} = \frac{Q + 0}{2} = \frac{Q}{2}$$

Assume that $Q = 500$ units/order. Then

$$\text{average physical inventory} = \frac{500}{2} = 250 \text{ units}$$

- Average dollar inventory $= \frac{Q}{2} C$

Assume that $C = \$20$/unit. Then

$$\text{average dollar inventory} = \frac{500}{2} \text{units} \times \frac{\$20}{\text{unit}} = \$5,000$$

- Holding costs = average dollar inventory × percentage holding costs

$$= \frac{Q}{2} C \qquad \times H$$

Assume that $H = 0.06$. Then

$$\text{holding costs} = \frac{500}{2} (20)(0.06)$$

$$= \$300/\text{year} \leftarrow$$

Now, we are in a position to state Equation (12.2) mathematically. Put (12.3) and (12.5) in (12.2). Then

$$T = \frac{D}{Q}S + \frac{Q}{2}CH \tag{12.6}$$

Step 4. *By applying an appropriate mathematical technique, find the optimal value of the decision variable.*

For example, if we equate the first derivative[5] of T (with respect to Q) to zero, we obtain the optimal value for the decision variable Q. Thus, from (12.6),

$$\frac{dT}{dQ} = \frac{-DS}{Q^2} + \frac{CH}{2} = 0 \qquad\qquad Q^2 = \frac{2DS}{CH}$$

Hence, the optimal order quantity

$$Q^* = \sqrt{\frac{2DS}{CH}} \tag{12.7}$$

Illustrative Comment. We can now calculate Q^* directly by substituting the values of D, S, C, and H in (12.7). Assume that $D = 6,000$, $S = 25$, $C = 20$, and $H = 0.06$. Then

$$Q^* = \sqrt{\frac{2(6,000)(25)}{(20)(0.06)}} = 500 \text{ units/order}$$

Note that for this inventory problem, the ordering costs happen to equal holding costs. However, for the basic EOQ model shown in Figure 12.4, the *minimum* inventory cost results *when* ordering costs equal holding costs.[6]

Hence, there are two ways of solving the basic EOQ model shown in Figure 12.4. First, the model can be solved (i.e., we can obtain the general formula for optimal order quantity, Q^*) by using calculus. Second, the model can be solved by equating ordering costs to holding costs. **Both approaches are illustrated below:**

Derivation of Q^* by equating ordering cost to holding costs	*Derivation of Q^* by using differential calculus*

Ordering costs = holding costs. Hence, equating Equations (12.3) and (12.5),

From Equation (12.6),

$$\frac{D}{Q}S = \frac{Q}{2}CH$$

$$T = \frac{D}{Q}S + \frac{Q}{2}CH$$

$$\frac{dT}{dQ} = \frac{-DS}{Q^2} + \frac{CH}{2} = 0$$

$$Q^2 = \frac{2DS}{CH}$$

$$Q^2 = \frac{2DS}{CH}$$

$$Q^* = \sqrt{\frac{2DS}{CH}}$$

$$Q^* = \sqrt{\frac{2DS}{CH}} \tag{12.7}$$

[5] The concept of a derivative is explained in Appendix B.
[6] The condition that *minimum* inventory cost results when ordering costs equal holding costs is derived in Appendix 12A.

Example 12.2 The purchasing agent at Cadden Corporation forecasts a demand of 12,000 lamp shades of a certain size for the next year. The purchase cost of each lamp shade is $6. The accounting department has estimated that the incremental cost to process a purchase order is $18 and that the holding costs are 20 percent of average dollar inventory. Assume linear usage and deterministic conditions. What is the optimum order quantity?

The problem description indicates that it is a deterministic (dynamic) problem, requiring the calculation of Q^*. Hence, we can use (12.7) to calculate the optimum order quantity, Q^*. Here $D = 12,000$, $S = 18$, $C = 6$ and $H = 0.20$. Then

$$Q^* = \sqrt{\frac{2DS}{CH}} = \sqrt{\frac{2(12,000)(18)}{6(0.20)}}$$

$$= \sqrt{360,000} = 600 \text{ units/order}$$

12.11.2 DETERMINATION OF OPTIMAL NUMBER OF ORDERS, N*

Assume now that we want to specify N as the decision variable. This means that both ordering costs and holding costs in Equation (12.2) must be specified in terms of N.

$$\text{ordering costs} = NS \tag{12.8}$$

From (12.5),

$$\text{holding costs} = \frac{Q}{2}CH$$

We know from (12.4) that $Q = D/N$. Hence,

$$\text{holding costs} = \frac{D}{2N}CH \tag{12.9}$$

Put (12.8) and (12.9) in (12.2). Then

$$T = NS + \frac{D}{2N}CH \tag{12.10}$$

As in the case of Q^*, we can also solve the basic inventory models in terms of N^* in the following two ways:

Derivation of N* by equating ordering costs to holding costs	*Derivation of N* by using differential calculus*
Ordering costs = holding costs. Hence, equating Equations (12.8) and (12.9),	From Equation (12.10),
$$NS = \frac{D}{2N}CH$$	$$T = NS + \frac{D}{2N}CH$$
	$$\frac{dT}{dN} = S - \frac{DCH}{2N^2} = 0$$

or

$$N^2 = \frac{DCH}{2S}$$

or

$$N^* = \sqrt{\frac{DCH}{2S}}$$

or

$$N^2 = \frac{DCH}{2S}$$

or

$$N^* = \sqrt{\frac{DCH}{2S}} \qquad (12.11)$$

12.11.3 DETERMINATION OF OPTIMAL REVIEW TIME, Y*

Determination of N^* and Y^* is equivalent to thinking in terms of the fixed-period system, as follows. The dimension of N is

$$\frac{\text{number of orders}}{\text{year}}$$

Hence, the dimension of $1/N$ is

$$\frac{\text{year}}{\text{number of orders}}$$

That is, $\frac{1}{N}$ gives us *reorder cycle time* in fractions of a year. Thus, we can say that the *optimum review time*, Y^*, in the deterministic case can be calculated as

$$Y^* = \frac{1}{N^*} \qquad (12.12)$$

Note that $\frac{365}{N}$ gives the *reorder cycle time* in days (i.e., it equals the number of days for which the order quantity is sufficient).

Example 12.3
The Tough Hammer Company sells a standard hammer at a constant rate. The sales forecast for the coming year is 12,000 units. The incremental cost to process each order is $25, and the purchase price is $5/unit. If the holding costs are 12 percent of average dollar inventory, what is the optimal number of orders? Assume deterministic conditions.

The problem description indicates that it is a deterministic (dynamic) problem, requiring the calculation of N^*. Hence, we can use (12.11) to calculate the optimum number of orders, N^*. Here $D = 12,000$, $C = 5$, $H = 0.12$, and $S = 25$. Then

$$N^* = \sqrt{\frac{DCH}{2S}}$$

$$= \sqrt{\frac{(12,000)(5)(0.12)}{2(25)}} = 12 \text{ orders/year}$$

Since D is 12,000 units/year, this means that the company should place an order of 1,000 units every month.[7]

[7] The optimal order quantity can also be calculated directly by using (12.7).

The optimum review time,

$$Y^* = \frac{1}{N^*} = \tfrac{1}{12} \text{ year}$$

This means that the company should review inventory status every month. In the deterministic model, this means that we place an order at the end of each month.

12.12
Deterministic Model (Dynamic Case: Gradual Buildup of Inventory)

This model is applicable in those situations where batch production is involved. The assumption is that a production process is set up to produce a batch of Q units. The rate of production, P, is greater than D (the rate of demand or usage), so that by the time the production is halted the inventory builds up to a certain level. The demand is continuous and is met (with certainty) both during and after the production period. As soon as the inventory drops to a predetermined reorder point, R, the production setup for the next batch is started. The leadtime for completing the production setup is known with certainty, and, therefore, no stockouts are possible. Our objective is to determine the general formula for optimal production lot size, Q^*.

The behavior of the "gradual buildup" model is shown in Figure 12.5. Let us adopt the following notation and values:

P = production rate (units/year) = 100,000 units/year

D = demand rate (units/year) = 50,000 units/year

L = leadtime

Q = quantity to be produced per setup (units/setup)

S = incremental setup cost ($/setup) = $20

C = production cost per unit of the item being produced ($/unit)
= $40

N = number of setups (or orders) per year

H = holding cost expressed as a percentage of average dollar inventory (%) = 40 percent = 0.40

t = time duration of the production run (fraction of a year)

$P - D$ = rate of inventory buildup (units/year) = 100,000 − 50,000
= 50,000 units/year

R = re-setup point

Let us examine the triangle KBM in Figure 12.5 and make some observations.

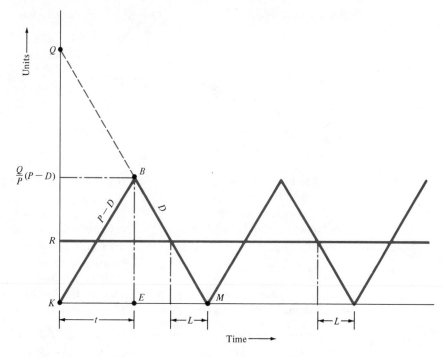

Figure 12.5. Deterministic Model—Gradual Buildup of Inventory.

P = production rate (units/year) = 100,000
D = demand rate (units/year) = 50,000
Q = quantity to be produced per setup (units/setup)
S = incremental setup cost ($/setup) = $20
C = production cost per unit of the item being produced ($/unit)
    = $40
N = number of setups (or orders) per year
H = holding cost expressed as a percentage of average dollar
    inventory = 40 percent = 0.40
t = time duration of the production run
$P - D$ = rate of inventory buildup (units/year) = 50,000 units/year
L = leadtime
R = re-setup point

Solution of the Model	*Illustrative Comments*
• The triangle KBM represents one inventory cycle.	
• Production starts at point K and stops at point E.	
• The rate at which the inventory builds up is the difference between the production and the demand (usage) rate (i.e., $P - D$).	• The buildup rate here is $100{,}000 - 50{,}000 = 50{,}000$ units per year = 1,000 units/week (assuming 50 working weeks) = 200 units/day (assuming 250 working days)

$P - D$	= 50,000 units/year

Solution of the Model	Illustrative Comments

- Production run time, $t = \dfrac{Q}{P}$

  - If $Q = 500$ units and
    $P = 100{,}000$ units/year

    Then $t = \dfrac{500}{100{,}000} = 0.005$ year

$$t = \frac{Q}{P}$$

$= 0.005$ year

- Since the buildup rate is $P - D$; and the production run is for a period of time t, total inventory at the end of time t, is

  $$t(P - D) = \frac{Q}{P}(P - D)$$

  That is, the height of point B (*maximum inventory*) is

  - If $t = 0.005$ year and $P - D = 50{,}000$ units/year, total inventory at the end of 0.005 year is $(0.005)(50{,}000) = 250$ units. This means that maximum inventory at hand in each inventory cycle is 250 units. That is, the height of point B (*maximum inventory*) is

$$\frac{Q}{P}(P - D)$$

$= 250$ units

- Since both the buildup rate $(P - D)$ and the usage rate (D) are constant (with zero inventory at the end of each cycle), the average inventory is one-half the maximum inventory. Hence, *average inventory in units* is

  $$= \frac{1}{2}\frac{Q}{P}(P - D)$$

  - This is obvious when we consider that one inventory cycle KBM consists of two triangles (KBE and BEM). For each triangle, the average inventory is one-half the maximum height B. Hence, the *average inventory in units* for each inventory cycle is

    $\frac{1}{2}$(height of point B)

$$\frac{1}{2}\frac{Q}{P}(P - D)$$

$= \dfrac{1}{2}(250) = 125$ units

- Average inventory (dollars)

$$= \frac{1}{2}\left[\frac{Q}{P}(P - D)\right]C$$

$= (125 \text{ units})\dfrac{\$40}{\text{unit}} = \$5{,}000/\text{year}$

- Holding costs

$$= \frac{1}{2}\left[\frac{Q}{P}(P - D)C\right]H$$

$= \$5{,}000 \times 0.40 = \$2{,}000/\text{year}$

- The number of setups is

$$N = \frac{D}{Q}$$

$$N = \frac{50,000}{500} = 100 \text{ setups/year}$$

- Ordering (setup) costs   • Setup costs

$$= \frac{D}{Q}S$$

$$= \frac{50,000}{500}(20) = \$2,000/\text{year}$$

Since this is a deterministic model and no quantity discounts are assumed, the total inventory cost equation (12.1) consists of only two components, as shown in (12.13).

$$T = \text{setup costs} + \text{holding costs}$$
$$= \frac{D}{Q}S \qquad + \frac{1}{2}\frac{Q}{P}(P - D)CH \tag{12.13}$$

We can now differentiate T with respect to Q and equate the first derivative to zero in order to obtain Q^*. However, Q^* can also be determined by equating setup costs to holding costs.

$$\text{setup costs} = \text{holding costs}$$

$$\frac{D}{Q}S = \frac{1}{2}\frac{Q}{P}(P - D)CH$$

$$Q^2 = \frac{2DS}{CH}\frac{P}{P - D}$$

$$Q^* = \sqrt{\frac{2DS}{CH}\left(\frac{P}{P - D}\right)} \tag{12.14}$$

Alternatively,[8]

$$Q^* = \sqrt{\frac{2DS}{CH}\left(\frac{1}{1 - \dfrac{D}{P}}\right)} \tag{12.15}$$

---

[8] Note that the only difference between (12.7), the EOQ formula for the instantaneous buildup case, and (12.15), the EOQ formula for the gradual buildup case, is the modifying factor $\dfrac{1}{1 - \dfrac{D}{P}}$, *which is always a number greater than 1. This is because the denominator* $1 - \dfrac{D}{P}$ *is always less than 1. When the value of the modifying factor* $\dfrac{1}{1 - \dfrac{D}{P}}$ *equals 1, (12.15) becomes (12.7). Note also that in the modifying factor* $\dfrac{1}{1 - \dfrac{D}{P}}$ *we can also use daily, weekly,* or *monthly demand and production rates. Why?*

Sec. 12.12   Deterministic Model (Dynamic Case: Gradual Buildup of Inventory)   **351**

Since we are dealing with a deterministic model, we can derive N^* and Y^* as follows:

$$N^* = \frac{D}{Q^*}, \qquad Y^* = \frac{1}{N^*}$$

Example 12.4

The Gupta Flange Company forecasts a demand of 36,000 flanges for the coming year. The production capacity of the company is 126,000 units/year. Production cost per unit is $12.60, and the holding costs are estimated to be 20 percent of average dollar inventory. The incremental setup cost is $225 per production run. What is the optimal quantity, Q^*, per setup, and N^*, the optimal number of setups? Assume deterministic conditions and constant buildup as well as usage rates. Here $D = 36,000$, $P = 126,000$, $S = 225$, $C = 12.60$, and $H = 0.20$. From (12.14),

$$Q^* = \sqrt{\frac{2DS}{CH} \frac{P}{P - D}}$$

$$= \sqrt{\frac{2(36,000)(225)}{(12.6)(0.20)} \frac{126,000}{126,000-36,000}}$$

$$= \sqrt{9,000,000} = 3,000 \text{ units/setup}$$

$$N^* = \frac{D}{Q^*} = \frac{36,000}{3,000} = 12 \text{ setups/year}$$

12.13
Deterministic Model (with Quantity Discounts)

In this model, we assume a dynamic (multiple-order) problem and instantaneous buildup of inventory. This is, therefore, the same model as shown in Figure 12.4, except that the purchase cost per unit, C, is not constant. The vendor offers a quantity discount according to a price–quantity schedule. For example, the vendor may offer a discount of 10 percent on all purchases made in lots of 100 units or more (single-price-break case). A more common practice is to offer multiple price breaks (or discounts) according to a schedule that shows a set of quantity ranges and a price per unit for *each* quantity range.

A major advantage of quantity discounts is to reduce the purchase costs and the ordering costs. A major disadvantage is to increase the holding costs, as the average inventory increases with large orders.

In Table 12.4, we present a multiple-price-break schedule. Also shown is the optimal order quantity Q^* for each price per unit.[9] Let us examine Table 12.4 and ask: Why not calculate Q^* for the lowest price per unit and then order in lots equal to Q^*? The answer resides in the concept of what we shall call *feasible* order quantity. Not always is it feasible to use Q^* for the lowest price per unit. A Q^* is feasible *only* if it falls within the quantity range corresponding to a specified price. Otherwise, it is a nonfeasible Q^*.

[9] Assume that $D = 3,000$, $S = 15$, and $H = 0.20$.

Table 12.4

(1)	(2)	(3)	(4)	
Quantity Range	Price per Unit, C	Price-break Number	$Q^* = \sqrt{\dfrac{2DS}{CH}}$	
1–49	$10	0	212	nonfeasible
50–99	9	1	223	nonfeasible
100–299	8	2	237 ←	feasible
300 and above	7	3	254	nonfeasible

For example, the optimal order quantity for $C = \$10$ is 212 units. However, this is not a feasible Q^* because at $C = \$10$, the quantity range is only $1 - 49$ units. Similarly, as shown in Table 12.4, $Q^* = 223$ units, and $Q^* = 254$ units are also not feasible. The only feasible Q^* in Table 12.4 is the one that corresponds to a price per unit of $8.

The objective in the quantity discount (or price-break) model is to minimize total inventory cost. It should be noted that in the deterministic case, only the first three components of Equation (12.1) are relevant: purchase costs of inventory items, ordering costs, and holding costs.

Let us illustrate the price-break model with the aid of an example.

Example 12.5 | Assume the following information with respect to a deterministic inventory problem with constant usage and instantaneous buildup of inventory:

$$D = 3{,}000 \text{ units/year}$$

$$S = \$15/\text{order}$$

$$H = 20 \text{ percent of average dollar inventory}$$

The quantity discount schedule is that shown in Table 12.4. The essence of the procedure for determining the optimal order quantity in the price-break model is to compare the total inventory cost for *each* feasible Q^* and *each* price-break quantity. The minimum total cost alternative identifies the optimal order quantity. We can employ the following five steps.

12.13.1 PROCEDURE FOR SOLVING THE DETERMINISTIC INVENTORY PROBLEM WITH QUANTITY DISCOUNTS

Step 1. *Calculate the optimal order quantity for the lowest price (highest discount).*

If the calculated Q^* is feasible, it will result in minimum total cost. Otherwise, proceed to step 2.

For our problem,

$$Q_3^* = \sqrt{\frac{2DS}{CH}} = \sqrt{\frac{2(3{,}000)15}{7(0.20)}} = 254$$

As can be ascertained from Table 12.4, $Q_3^* = 254$ is nonfeasible, since the $7 price per unit is available only for the quantity range of 300 units and above. Since Q^* for the lowest price is nonfeasible, we proceed to step 2.

Step 2. *Calculate Q^* for each different price per unit (C).*

For our problem, four different "prices per unit" are available, as shown in Table 12.4. For each C, we calculate Q^*. The results are shown in column 4 of Table 12.4.

Step 3. *Calculate total inventory cost, T, for each feasible Q^* calculated in step 2.*

As shown in column 4 of Table 12.4, the only feasible $Q^* = 237$ units, corresponding to $C = \$8$. Now, total cost T for this model consists of the first three components of Equation (12.1).[10] That is, in this model

total inventory cost = purchase costs + ordering costs + holding costs

$$T = DC \qquad + \frac{D}{Q}S \qquad + \frac{Q}{2}CH \qquad (12.16)$$

We calculate T for $Q^* = 237$, as shown in column (2), Table 12.5.

Step 4. *Calculate total inventory cost, T, for each price-break quantity.*

As shown in Table 12.4, we have three price breaks (at quantities 50, 100, and 300). That is, we have to calculate T for $C = \$9$, $C = \$8$, and $C = \$7$, according to Equation (12.16). The results are shown in Table 12.5.

Step 5. *The optimal Q^* is that which corresponds to the minimum T from steps 3 and 4.*

As shown in Table 12.5, the minimum T is $21,360, and hence the optimal order quantity is the price-break quantity of 300 units.

Table 12.5

	(1) $Q_3^* = 254$ for C = \$7	(2) $Q_2^* = 237$ for C = \$8	(3) Price Break at Quantity 300	(4) Price Break at Quantity 100	(5) Price Break at Quantity 50
Purchase costs (DC)		24,000	21,000	24,000	27,000
Ordering costs $\left(\frac{D}{Q}S\right)$	Nonfeasible Q^*	190	150	450	900
Holding costs $\left(\frac{Q}{2}CH\right)$		190	210	80	45
Total cost		24,380	21,360	24,530	27,945

↑
minimum
total
cost

[10] There are no stockout costs, as this is a deterministic model.

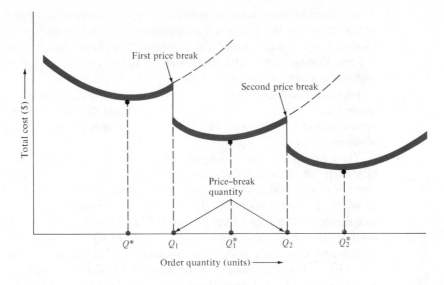

Figure 12.6. Quantity Discount Model.

In Figure 12.6 we show the general behavior of total inventory cost, T, with quantity discounts. Note that in Table 12.5, the minimum total cost occurs at a price-break quantity (as opposed to a Q^* quantity shown in Figure 12.6). We show Q^* with no discounts, and Q_1 and Q_2, which are two price-break quantities (i.e., minimum quantities required to qualify for specified discount prices). We also show Q_1^* optimal order quantity for the first discount price and Q_2^* optimal order quantity for the second discount price. The logic of the five-step procedure for solving the inventory model with quantity discounts can be seen from the structure of Figure 12.6. First, note that only the solid portion of the different curves are relevant. Second, the minimum total cost must take place either at *feasible* EOQ points such as Q^*, Q_1^* or Q_2^* (identified by step 3) or at price-break quantities such as Q_1 or Q_2 (identified by step 4). Finally, step 5 compares the results of steps 3 and 4 and locates the optimal order quantity that yields minimum total cost.

12.14
Summary

In this chapter, we defined the inventory problem, established its scope and importance, and presented its essential aspects. The basic blocks of inventory control were discussed. They are: (1) the nature of inventory demand and supply, (2) categories of inventory costs, (3) systems of inventory control, and (4) methods of information feedback.

Two systems of inventory control (fixed order and fixed period) were described. In the fixed-order system, the order quantity is constant, while the time between reordering fluctuates. In the fixed-period system, the time between reordering remains constant, while the quantity ordered is allowed to fluctuate.

Inventories can be classified in a number of ways, depending upon the criterion of classification. We presented classifications of inventories by stage of completion, purpose, and annual dollar volume. The classification by annual dollar volume, known as the ABC classification, is an excellent device for exercising selective control on high-value items.

Inventory problems (models) were classified by simultaneously applying the assumptions of (1) deterministic versus probabilistic behavior, and (2) static versus dynamic behavior. The focus of this chapter was on deterministic (dynamic) models.

Three approaches for solving inventory models were listed: (1) the numerical approach, (2) the analytical approach, and (3) the simulation approach. The numerical and analytical approaches were illustrated with specific examples.

We built and illustrated the use of deterministic inventory models in calculating Q^* (optimal order quantity), N^* (optimal number of orders), and Y^* (optimal time between reordering). The basic EOQ (economic order quantity) model was illustrated under the assumption of *instantaneous buildup* of inventories and *gradual buildup* of inventories. Finally, we developed a five-step procedure to solve a deterministic model with quantity discounts.

Although we did not address ourselves to the handling of inventory problems by linear programming, we make two observations. First, it is possible to formulate the inventory problem as a linear programming problem. Second, the transportation format can be used to set up and solve a production and inventory problem.

Appendix 12A

For the model stated in Equation (12.10), the behavior of ordering, holding, and total costs is shown in Figure 12A.1.

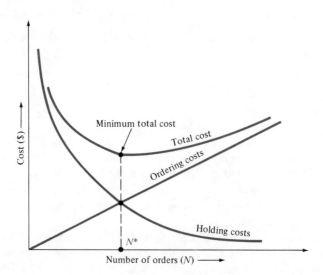

Figure 12A.1. Basic EOQ Model. (Behavior of Costs).

$$\text{ordering costs} = NS \qquad\qquad\qquad (12\text{A}.1)$$

$$\text{holding costs} = \frac{1}{2}\frac{D}{N}CH$$

Since D, C, and H are parameters, we can say that $K = \frac{1}{2}(DCH)$, where K is a constant. Hence,

$$\text{holding costs} = \frac{K}{N} \qquad\qquad\qquad (12\text{A}.2)$$

Total cost, T, is the sum of ordering costs and holding costs. Hence, adding (12A.1) and (12A.2),

$$T = NS + \frac{K}{N} \qquad\qquad\qquad (12\text{A}.3)$$

We identify the optimum number of orders, N^* (yielding *minimum* total cost), by taking the first derivative of T with respect to N and equating it to zero. Hence, from (12A.3),

$$\frac{dT}{dN} = S - \frac{K}{N^2} = 0$$

or

$$N^2 = \frac{K}{S}$$

Hence,

$$N^* = \sqrt{\frac{K}{S}} \qquad\qquad\qquad (12\text{A}.4)$$

Put (12A.4) in (12A.1):

$$\text{ordering costs} = \sqrt{\frac{K}{S}}(S) = \sqrt{KS} \qquad\qquad\qquad (12\text{A}.5)$$

Put (12A.4) in (12A.2):

$$\text{holding costs} = \frac{K}{\sqrt{K/S}} = \sqrt{KS} \qquad\qquad\qquad (12\text{A}.6)$$

Note that (12A.5) is equal to (12A.6) when the *optimum* value of N is used in determining ordering cost and holding cost. Hence, the minimum total cost, T, results when

$$\text{ordering costs} = \text{holding costs}$$

References

Buffa, E. S., and W. H. Taubert. *Production-Inventory Systems: Planning and Control*, rev. ed. Homewood, Ill.: Richard D. Irwin, Inc., 1972.

Edwards, J. D., and R. A. Roemmich. "Scientific Inventory Management." *MSU Business Topics*, Vol. 23, No. 4 (Autumn 1975), 42–46.

Gibson, D. W., and J. E. Butler. "Evaluation of Inventory Management." *Business Horizons*, Vol. 16, No. 3 (June 1973), 51–60.

Green, J. M. *Production and Inventory Control Handbook*. New York: McGraw-Hill Book Company, 1970.

Griffin, W. C. *Introduction to Operations Engineering*. Homewood, Ill.: Richard D. Irwin, Inc., 1971.

Heffernan, J. J. "Interaction in Production-Distribution Systems." *Sloan Management Review*, Vol. 12, No. 3 (Spring 1971), 63–76.

Jordan, H. H. "Relating Customer Service to Inventory Control." *Advanced Management Journal*, Vol. 39, No. 4 (Oct. 1974), 53–56.

Lewis, C. D. *Scientific Inventory Control*. New York: American Elsevier Publishing Co., Inc., 1970.

Magee, J. F., and D. M. Boodman. *Production Planning and Inventory Control*, 2nd ed. New York: McGraw-Hill Book Company, 1967.

Mayer, R. R. "The Interrelationship Between Lot Sizes and Safety Stocks in Inventory Control." *Journal of Industrial Engineering* (July–Aug. 1965), 268–274.

Naddor, E. *Inventory Systems*. New York: John Wiley & Sons, Inc., 1966.

Starr, M. K., and D. W. Miller. *Inventory Control: Theory and Practice*. Englewood Cliffs, N.J.: Prentice-Hall, Inc., 1962.

Thomas, A. B. *Inventory Control in Production and Management*. Boston: Cahners Publishing Co., Inc., 1970.

Veinott, A. F., Jr. "The Status of Mathematical Inventory Theory." *Management Science*, Vol. 12, No. 11 (1966), 754–777.

Wagner, H. "A Manager's Survey of Inventory and Production Control Systems." *Interfaces*, Vol. 2, No. 4 (Aug. 1972), 31–39.

Review Questions and Problems

12.1. Define the term "inventory." What are the essential aspects of the inventory problem?

12.2. Explain the statement: "The inventory problem is a typical example of the executive-type problems that are common to complex and large organizations."

12.3. What factors contribute to the importance of the inventory problem?

12.4. List and describe the basic blocks of inventory control.

12.5. List and describe the nature of various categories of inventory costs.

12.6. Describe the structure of the fixed-order system and the fixed-period system of inventory control.

12.7. Classify inventories by using "purpose" as the criterion of classification.

12.8. Give the rationale for the ABC system of classifying inventories.

12.9. What are the various criteria for classifying inventory problems (or models)? Develop a matrix of inventory models by applying these two criteria: (a) single versus multiple orders, and (b) deterministic versus probabilistic behavior.

12.10. Explain the nature of the following methods of solving inventory problems: (a) the numerical approach, (b) the analytical approach, and (c) the simulation approach.

12.11. The basic EOQ model discussed in Section 12.11 can be solved by equating ordering costs to holding costs. Describe the assumptions that make this approach possible.

12.12. In Section 12.13 we developed a basic deterministic model with quantity discounts. Discuss the rationale behind the five-step process for solving this model.

12.13. What is the optimal order quantity and the total cost for a firm if demand is 300 units/month, holding costs are $0.25/unit/day, and the incremental cost of processing an order is $5/order?

12.14. How many orders should be placed to minimize costs if demand is 20,000 units/year, cost per unit is $40, incremental cost of processing an order is $25/order, and holding costs are 10 percent of average dollar inventory?

12.15. A machine shop stocks three items in its inventory of raw materials. Item I costs $20/unit, item II costs $6/unit, and item III costs $1/unit. Annual demand for items I, II, and III is 200, 150, and 650 units, respectively. Use the ABC classification to determine which item should be controlled closely and rigorously.

12.16. Rapid Construction Company maintains inventories of a variety of raw materials. Cement is stored in bags in a warehouse. The Company typically uses 100,000 bags annually. The cost of cement is $10/bag. The incremental cost of processing an order is $50/order and holding costs are 25 percent of average dollar inventory. In addition, the supplier of cement has offered a 5 percent discount if lots of 5,000 bags are purchased. Should the company accept the quantity discount terms?

12.17. The Slumber Lumber Company uses varnish on its products. The company expects to use $10,000 worth of varnish in the coming year. The incremental cost of processing an order is $60/order and holding costs are 10 percent of average dollar inventory. How many orders should be placed in the coming year?

12.18. Determine the optimal order quantity and the reorder point for a fixed-order system if: demand = 180,000 units/year or 600 units/day, price = $1/unit, incremental cost of processing an order = $150/order, holding cost = 6 percent of average dollar inventory, and leadtime = 8 days.

12.19. The Pic-Mount Company has recently hired a new inventory control manager. The present policy of the Company has been to order 20,000 reams of paper five times a year. The new manager feels that a fixed-order system would be cheaper. The paper costs $30/ream, incremental cost of processing an order is $65/order, and holding costs are 15 percent of average dollar inventory. Determine the optimal order quantity. What are the cost savings over the fixed-period system? If the leadtime is 2 days, what is the reorder point? (Assume 250 working days.)

12.20. The Nevor-Cey-Dye Hospital uses 4,800 cartons of intravenous solution every year. The cost per carton is $20. The hospital has been ordering on a quarterly basis, incremental cost of processing an order is $10/order, and holding costs amount to 12 percent of average dollar inventory. What ordering policy will minimize costs? What are the savings with the new policy?

CHAPTER 13

Inventory Control–Probabilistic Models

MAJOR CONCEPTS AND TOPICS
DISCUSSED IN THIS CHAPTER

Nature, Behavior, and Structure of Probabilistic Inventory Models

Role of stockouts and safety (buffer) stocks

Probabilistic Model (Static Case)

The idea of cumulative probability distribution
The payoff matrix approach
The marginal analysis approach

Probabilistic Model (Dynamic Case)

Fixed-order system
Fixed-period system

The Concept of Service Level

Selected Measures of Managerial Efficiency in Inventory Control

Sensitivity Analysis in Inventory Control

Computerized Inventory Control Systems

13.1
Introduction

In Chapter 12, we presented a selected set of deterministic inventory models. The deterministic models *assume* that *all* aspects of the inventory problem are known with *complete certainty*, and that each strategy results in a *unique* payoff. However, as discussed in Section 12.4.1, if either the demand or the leadtime or both cannot be assumed to be known with certainty, their behavior must be described with probability distributions (discrete or continuous). The inventory problem (model) is of the *probabilistic* variety whenever one or more components of the problem must be described with probability distributions.

An important consideration in any probabilistic model is the possibility of *stockouts*. The stockouts can occur because of unexpected high demand during the leadtime (or between review periods) or unexpected delays in receiving goods (i.e., longer than expected leadtime).

The stockouts inflict certain costs such as lost sales or loss of customer goodwill and, therefore, necessary steps should be taken to reduce or avoid stockouts. The danger of stockouts is met by maintaining what is known as *safety* or *buffer stocks*. However, the maintenance of safety stocks imposes its own costs (e.g., holding costs of the safety stock).

In the matter of safety stocks we are clearly dealing with two categories of costs that move in opposite directions. As the level of the safety stock is increased, costs in one category (e.g., holding costs of safety stock) increase, while the costs in the second category (e.g., stockout costs consisting of lost profit and loss of customer goodwill) decrease. The optimal level of safety stock is that which leads to the minimization of the sum of holding costs of safety stock and stockout costs. This means that estimates on the costs of being out of stock must be made and fed into the probabilistic inventory model. For example, the manager may decide that the annual penalty for being 1 unit short is $10. There are various ways of formulating and solving probabilistic inventory models. In this chapter, we shall present the following models: probabilistic model (static case), and probabilistic model (dynamic case).

13.2
Probabilistic Model (Static Case)

The static case permits the possibility of only a single order and it is assumed that inventories *cannot* be carried over to the next period. This, for example, is the situation facing a newspaper distributor or the seller of Christmas trees. Appropriately, the probabilistic problem (static case) is known in the inventory literature as the "newsboy" problem, or "Christmas tree" problem, or the "single-episode" problem. The leadtime in such problems is often assumed to be certain (i.e., deterministic), while the demand is represented by a discrete probability distribution. Also, the stockout cost is assumed to be known. We shall illustrate two approaches for solving the probabilistic (static case) model. First, we shall represent the problem in the form of a payoff matrix and identify the optimal ordering policy by using the *expected value* criterion. In the second approach we shall use the concept of *marginal analysis*, and identify the optimal ordering policy by equating the marginal profit of the last unit *if* it is sold to the marginal loss of the last unit *if* it is *not* sold.

13.2.1 THE PAYOFF MATRIX APPROACH

The first step in the payoff matrix aproach is to formulate a conditional payoff matrix for the inventory problem. This requires that we consider a set of strategies and represent the cost or profit consequences of these strategies in the form of a conditional payoff matrix. The optimal strategy is then identified by the application of some decision criterion. For example, we shall apply the expected value criterion in solving the problems described in Example 13.1 and 13.2.

Example 13.1 | Let us consider an inventory problem with a deterministic leadtime but a probabilistic demand. The inventory item purchased every morning is a perishable commodity (i.e., its salvage value, W, at the end of the day is zero). Purchase cost per unit, C, is \$10; and its selling price per unit, SP, is \$15. The seller estimates the stockout (or shortage) penalty, K, to be \$2/unit. Shown in Table 13.1 is the daily demand distribution. What is the optimal order quantity?

Before solving the problem, we make the following observations:

1. It is the normal convention that cumulative probability of a random variable is specified on a "less than or equal to" basis. Now, assume a *continuous* variable, X, that represents, say, time for completing an activity. Then the cumulative probability would be denoted as $P(\text{time} \leqslant X)$. And if we want to know the cumulative probability of X on a "greater than or equal to" basis—$P(\text{time} \geqslant X)$—then we can calculate it *indirectly* by utilizing $P(\text{time} \leqslant X)$. That is,

$$P(\text{time} \geqslant X) = 1 - P(\text{time} \leqslant X)$$

However, for pedagogical reasons, we can build the cumulative probability on a "greater than or equal to" basis—$P(\text{time} \geqslant X)$—*directly* from the given probability distribution. This unconventional procedure is particularly useful when we are dealing with a discrete variable (e.g., daily demand, D). Therefore, in Table 13.1, we show cumulative probability as $P(\text{demand} \geqslant D)$. Note that

Table 13.1

Daily Demand, D	Probability, p(D)	Cumulative Probability, P (Demand ⩾ D)
20	0.10	1.00
21	0.50	0.90
22	0.30	0.40
23	0.10	0.10

for a discrete distribution (e.g., demand) we have the following relationship:

$$P(\text{demand} \geqslant D) = 1 - P(\text{demand} < D)$$

We shall follow the practice of giving cumulative probability on a "greater than or equal to" basis throughout this chapter. For further discussion, see Section A.7 in Appendix A.

2. Note that in Table 13.1 the probability of selling *exactly* 20 units is 0.10, but the cumulative probability of selling 20 or more ($\geqslant 20$) is 1.00. Similarly, the probability of selling exactly 21 units is 0.50; but the cumulative probability of selling 21 or more ($\geqslant 21$) is 0.90.

3. There is only *one* order; hence, the ordering costs are fixed. They can be assumed to be part of purchase cost, C.

4. Holding costs are a function of the order size and could be considered separately. However, in this simple model we shall assume them to be fixed and therefore not include them in the model.

5. The profit on a given day is a result of two events: how much is ordered on a given day, and the actual demand during that day. For example, if 20 units are ordered and the actual demand is also 20, the profit is $20(5) = \$100$. However, if the demand on that day were 21 units, the profit would be reduced by the penalty of being out of stock by 1 unit. That is, the profit or payoff would be $20(5) - 1(2) = \$98$.

6. It should be noted that the profit resulting from any ordering policy is dependent upon, or is a *condition* of, the actual demand. That is why the payoffs calculated in such problems are called *conditional payoffs*, and the resultant payoff matrices are called *conditional payoff matrices*.

7. This is a profit-maximization (as opposed to cost-minimization) model.

8. In this example, we can calculate any conditional profit or payoff as follows:

$$\text{profit} = D(SP - C) - K(X) - Y(C - W) \tag{13.1}$$

where

$$D = \text{units sold per day}$$
$$SP = \text{selling price per unit}$$
$$C = \text{purchase cost per unit}$$
$$X = \text{number of stockout units}$$
$$K = \text{stockout penalty per unit}$$
$$Y = \text{units not sold at the end of the day}$$
$$W = \text{salvage value (\$/unit)}$$

We are now in a position to build a payoff (profit) matrix for this problem.

Solution. It is obvious that in this case we have only four possible strategies (ordering alternatives): 20, 21, 22, or 23 units. For each of the ordering alternatives, there are four possible levels of demand, or states of nature (20, 21, 22, or 23 units), with a discrete probability distribution as shown in Table 13.1. Each strategy has a profit consequence that can be calculated by using Equation (13.1). Thus, we can construct the conditional payoff matrix shown in Table 13.2.

Table 13.2

Ordering Alternative		Daily Demand				Expected Value of Profit (dollars)
	Level:	20	21	22	23	
	Probability:	0.10	0.50	0.30	0.10	
20		100	98	96	94	97.20
21		90	105	103	101	102.50 ← maximum
22		80	95	110	108	99.30
23		70	85	100	115	91.00

Note that there are four payoff rows in Table 13.2, corresponding to the four ordering alternatives. The expected value of profit, corresponding to an ordering alternative, is determined by calculating the weighted sum (using probability weights) of the payoffs associated with that alternative. The calculations for the first two strategies are shown below.[1]

$$\text{expected value (order 20 units)} = 100(0.10) + 98(0.50) + 96(0.30)$$
$$+ 94(0.10) = \$97.20$$

$$\text{expected value (order 21 units)} = 90(0.10) + 105(0.50) + 103(0.30)$$
$$+ 101(0.10) = \$102.50$$

The optimal strategy (ordering alternative) is that which yields the *maximum expected profit*. As can be ascertained from the last column in Table 13.2, the maximum expected profit is $102.50, and hence the optimal inventory policy is to place daily an order of 21 units.[2]

Example 13.2

Consider the same inventory problem as that described in Example 13.1 except that the inventory item has a salvage value of $5.

Solution. Our task, as before, is to construct a payoff matrix for all possible strategies (order 20, 21, 22, or 23 units). The payoffs are to be calculated with the realization that the inventory item has a salvage value of $5/unit. We can calculate each payoff by using Equation (13.1). The resulting payoff matrix is shown in Table 13.3. The expected value of each ordering strategy is

---

[1] The reader will recall that the "expected value" is calculated as

$$EV = O_1 p_1 + O_2 p_2 + \cdots + O_n p_n$$

where

O_i = *i*th outcome or payoff

p_i = probability of the *i*th outcome or payoff

[2] The reader should revisit Section 2.9 and Sections 5.4 to 5.6 in order to appreciate the application of the payoff-matrix-formulation approach to decision problems.

calculated, as before, by summing the products of relevant payoffs and the probabilities of those payoffs. As can be seen in the last column of Table 13.3, the maximum expected profit is $103.00. This corresponds to the ordering alternative of 21 units. Hence, again, the optimal inventory policy is to place a daily order of 21 units.

Table 13.3

Ordering Alternative	Daily Demand					Expected Value of Profit (dollars)
	Level:	20	21	22	23	
	Probability:	0.10	0.50	0.30	0.10	
20		100	98	96	94	97.20
21		95	105	103	101	103.00 ← maximum
22		90	100	110	108	102.80
23		85	95	105	115	99.00

13.2.2 THE MARGINAL ANALYSIS APPROACH

The concept of marginal analysis is based on the idea of considering the *net* consequences of taking an action. The term "marginal" refers to the situation of considering the *last* (*additional; on the margin*) action in a series of repetitive actions. Assume that we are currently following a policy of $Q^* = 20$. Then, the determination of the *net* consequence of adding the 21st unit (i.e., make $Q = 21$) is an example of *marginal analysis*. Marginal analysis is straightforward if we assume conditions of certainty. For example, suppose that we are considering the problem of adding the 100th unit to an inventory and we know with certainty that its cost is $95 and that we can sell it for $100. The *net* consequence of adding this unit to the inventory therefore, is $5 and our decision, based on marginal analysis, will be to add the 100th unit. Thus, we can establish a decision rule for inventory decisions under certainty: *Keep on adding to the inventory up to the point when the net gain from the last unit ceases to be positive.*

The marginal analysis concept can also be applied to probabilistic situations. As in the certainty case, we determine the *net* consequence of taking the *last* action. However, the presence of probabilities requires that the consequences of the last action be weighted by appropriate probabilities. This is done by calculating and comparing the *expected values* of losses and gains that emerge from the marginal action. That is, in probabilistic problems, marginal analysis requires the calculation of *expected net gain*. Thus, we should compare the *expected marginal gain* (if the last unit is sold) with the *expected marginal loss* (if the last unit is *not* sold). Accordingly, we can establish the following decision rule for probabilistic inventory problems: *Increase the order quantity to that point at which the expected marginal gain from the last unit is greater than or equal to the expected marginal loss.* That is,

expected marginal gain ⩾ expected marginal loss

or

$$P(MG) \geqslant (1 - P)(ML) \tag{13.2}$$

where

P = probability of selling the last unit = cumulative probability, $P(\text{demand} \geqslant D)$

$1 - P$ = probability of *not* selling the last unit = $1 - P(\text{demand} \geqslant D)$

MG = marginal gain if the last unit is sold

ML = marginal loss if the last unit is *not* sold

From (13.2),

$$P(MG + ML) \geqslant ML$$

or

$$P^* \geqslant \frac{ML}{MG + ML} \tag{13.3}$$

Note that P^* is the optimal cumulative probability of selling the *last* unit.[3] The optimal Q^* is identified with the help of P^*, as can be seen in Table 13.4.

Discrete Probability Distribution of Demand

We shall illustrate next the marginal analysis approach as applied to an inventory problem in which the probabilistic demand is given by a discrete distribution.

Example 13.3 | Consider a probabilistic (static) inventory problem with

$$C = \$12/\text{unit}$$
$$SP = \$20/\text{unit}$$

The probability distribution for daily demand is shown in Table 13.4.

Table 13.4

Daily Demand, D	Probability of Demand, $p(D)$	Cumulative Probability of Demand, $P(\text{demand} \geqslant D)$
15	0.10	1.00
16	0.15	0.90
17	0.50	0.75 ← optimal
18	0.25	0.25

Assume the salvage value as well as stockout cost to be zero. What is the optimal order quantity?

---

[3] The ratio $\dfrac{ML}{MG + ML}$ is sometimes called the *critical ratio*. It is equivalent to $\dfrac{C_o}{C_u + C_o}$, where C_o = cost of overstocking and C_u = cost of understocking.

Solution

$$\text{marginal gain} = MG = \text{selling price} - \text{cost} = 20 - 12 = \$8$$

marginal loss = ML = $12 (the same as the purchase cost, since salvage value is zero)

From (13.3), the optimal cumulative probability

$$P* = \frac{ML}{MG + ML} = \frac{12}{8 + 12} = 0.60$$

The value of $P*$ (optimal cumulative probability) of 0.60 says that if the cumulative probability of selling the last unit is 0.60 *or more* we add that unit to our inventory. Now, in the cumulative probability column— $P(\text{demand} \geqslant D)$ —we move from bottom to top. Hence, in the third column of Table 13.4 we find that the *first* cumulative probability P that fulfills this condition (i.e., the condition that the cumulative probability of selling the last unit is 0.60 *or more*) is 0.75. Hence, the optimal order quantity is 17 units. Also, this policy will yield the maximum expected profit.

We can now calculate the expected marginal gain and expected marginal loss from the 17th unit:

$$\text{expected marginal gain} = P(MG) \qquad = (0.75)(8) \qquad = \$6$$
$$\text{expected marginal loss} = (1 - P)(ML) = (1 - 0.75)(12) = \$3$$

Hence, the expected benefit from stocking the 17th unit is

$$\text{expected marginal gain} - \text{expected marginal loss} = 6 - 3 = \$3$$

Note that if we add the 18th unit to our inventory (i.e., make $Q = 18$), the expected marginal loss (for the 18th unit) will exceed the expected marginal profit (from the 18th unit). The reader should verify this assertion.

Continuous Probability Distribution of Demand

The marginal analysis approach can also be used when the demand is represented by a *continuous* (rather than a discrete) probability distribution. We illustrate with the aid of an example.

Example 13.4 Let us assume a probabilistic (static) inventory problem in which we have to decide on the optimum size of the one-shot order. Assume, further, the following data: cost $(C) = \$10.00/\text{unit}$, selling price $(SP) = \$19.50/\text{unit}$, and salvage value $(W) = \$5.00/\text{unit}$.

Daily demand can be approximated by a normal distribution with mean $(\bar{D}) = 20$ units and standard deviation $(\sigma) = 5$ units.

Solution. Our inventory problem can be solved with reference to Figures 13.1 and 13.2. Figure 13.1 represents a normal probability distribution of daily demand. Point $\bar{D}$ represents average daily sales (i.e., mean = 20 units). Since the distribution is normal, we can make the following statements.[4]

---

[4] See Table I in Appendix E.

1. Mean ± 1 standard deviation = 20 ± 5; hence, the probability that daily sales will range between 15 and 25 units is 0.6826. This corresponds to an area of 68.26 percent under the curve in Figure 13.1.
2. Mean ± 2 standard deviations = 20 ± 10; hence, the probability that daily sales will range between 10 and 30 units is 0.9544. This corresponds to an area of 95.44 percent under the curve in Figure 13.1.
3. Mean ± 3 standard deviations = 20 ± 15; hence, the probability that daily sales will range between 5 and 35 units is 0.9974. This corresponds to an area of 99.74 percent under the curve in Figure 13.1.
4. The area under the curve between any two points on the horizontal axis (in Figure 13.1) represents the probability that daily sales will be between the range marked by the two points.
5. The area under the curve to the right of any point (sales level) represents the probability of selling that many *or more* units.
6. The area under the curve to the left of any point (sales level) represents the probability of selling that many *or less* units. In Figure 13.2, we have shown a cumulative probability of selling a given quantity *or more*. For example, the probability of selling $Q = 22$ units *or more* is 0.344.

We are now in a position to solve our problem. Here

$$MG = SP - C = 19.50 - 10.00 = \$9.50$$
$$ML = C - W = 10.00 - 5.00 = \$5.00$$

From (13.3),

$$P^* = \frac{ML}{MG + ML} = \frac{5.00}{9.50 + 5.00} = 0.344$$

Since the optimal cumulative probability P^* is 0.344, we are saying that the optimal order quantity Q^* is such that the cumulative probability of selling the Qth unit is 0.344. This is shown as 34.4 percent of the area in Figure 13.1 and is also shown as point A on the vertical axis in Figure 13.2.

Let point Q in Figure 13.1 represent the optimal order quantity. The shaded area to the right of point Q in Figure 13.1 is 34.4 percent and the area under the curve to the right of $\bar{D}$ is 50 percent. Hence, the area under the curve between points $\bar{D}$ and Q is $50 - 34.4 = 15.6$ percent. As can be seen from Table I of Appendix E, this implies that point Q is 0.40 standard deviations to the right of point $\bar{D}$. Thus,

$$Q^* = \bar{D} + 0.40(\sigma)$$
$$= 20 + 0.40(5)$$
$$= 22 \text{ units}$$

Hence, the optimal order quantity Q^* is 22 units.

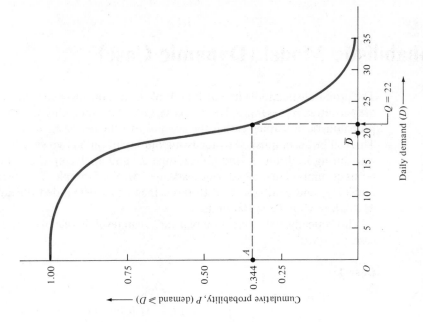

Figure 13.2. Cumulative Probability Distribution of Daily Demand, $P(\text{demand} \geq D)$.

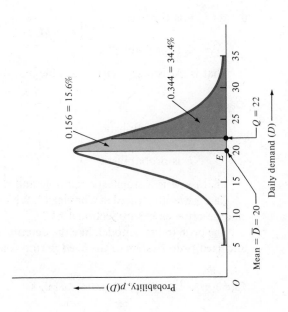

Figure 13.1. Normal Probability Distribution of Daily Demand.

13.3
Probabilistic Model (Dynamic Case)

The probabilistic model in which multiple orders during a specified time period are permitted represents a dynamic case. One of the most important issues in the probabilistic (dynamic) case is the *analysis of inventory behavior during leadtime* This can be accomplished by focussing our attention on two variables: (1) usage *rate* during leadtime, u, and (2) leadtime, L; and analyzing their interaction in terms of "units demanded during leadtime," M. For example, if usage rate, $u = 10$ units/day, and leadtime, $L = 10$ days, then units demanded during leadtime, $M = uL = 10 \times 10 = 100$ units.

Theoretically, the interaction of u and L can result in one of the following four cases:

Case 1

$$\left. \begin{array}{l} u \text{ is constant} \\[1em] L \text{ is constant} \end{array} \right\} \Rightarrow uL = M \text{ is constant}$$

This is obviously a deterministic situation.

Case 2

$$\left. \begin{array}{l} u \text{ is probabilistic} \\[1em] L \text{ is constant} \end{array} \right\} \Rightarrow uL = M \text{ is probabilistic}$$

That is, M is a stochastic variable and we have a probabilistic model.

Case 3

$$\left. \begin{array}{l} u \text{ is constant} \\[1em] L \text{ is probabilistic} \end{array} \right\} \Rightarrow uL = M \text{ is probabilistic}$$

That is, M is a stochastic variable and we have a probabilistic model.

Case 4

$$\left. \begin{array}{l} u \text{ is probabilistic} \\[1em] L \text{ is probabilistic} \end{array} \right\} \Rightarrow uL = M \text{ is probabilistic}$$

That is, M is a stochastic variable and we have a probabilistic model.

Case 1 was illustrated in Chapter 12. We shall illustrate case 2 in Example 13.5 and describe case 3 in Section 13.3.2.[5]

The probabilistic model, like the deterministic model, can be operated under the fixed-order system or the fixed-period system. The behavior of a probabilistic

[5] See Buffa and Taubert [1972, p. 106] for case 4.

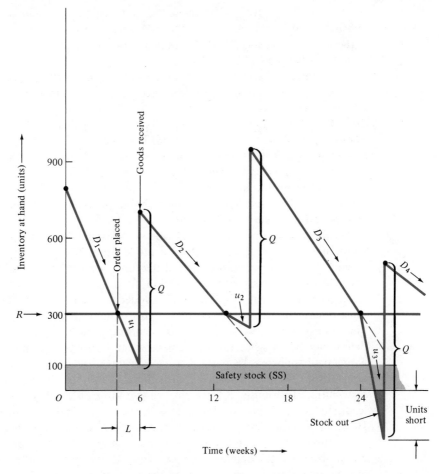

Figure 13.3. Probabilistic Model (fixed-order system with safety stock; constant leadtime but probabilistic demand; instantaneous buildup of inventory)

Q = order quantity = 800-SS = 700 units
R = reorder point (with safety stock) = 300 units
SS = safety stock = 100 units
L = leadtime = 2 weeks

model under the fixed-order system is shown in Figure 13.3 (assumptions: constant leadtime, probabilistic demand, instantaneous buildup of inventory).

13.3.1 FIXED-ORDER SYSTEM

It should be noted that in the fixed-order system, stockouts can occur *only* during the leadtime period. This is evident from the way the fixed-order system is operated. In the fixed-order system, stockouts cannot occur *before* the reorder point R, regardless of any changes in the demand rate. This is because R represents a positive inventory level, and hence stockouts cannot occur. As soon as the inventory dips to R, an order is placed. After the reorder point R (i.e., during the leadtime), however, if the demand is unusually high, or if the leadtime is unusually long, the stockouts can occur. Hence, in the fixed-order system, the size of the safety stocks should be determined to provide protection for *one* leadtime period.

[*Note*: By comparison, the size of the safety stock in the *fixed-period* system must be larger (assuming the same service policy). As an extremely conservative service policy (to accommodate fluctuations of *both* demand rate and leadtime), the safety stock in the fixed-period system must provide protection for one leadtime period *plus* one review period. This conclusion can be drawn from the following argument. Assume that at a specific review time, the manager decides not to reorder. Hence, one review period must pass before the next order is placed and the goods from *that* order will arrive after one leadtime period. Hence, the safety stock in the fixed-period system should provide protection for one lead-time period *plus* one review period.]

The determination of the optimal safety stock is dependent upon three things: (1) the nature of "units demanded during leadtime," M, as determined by the interaction of u (usage *rate* during leadtime) and L (leadtime); (2) penalty for being out of stock (i.e., stockout costs); and (3) holding costs of the safety stock.[6]

Regarding the behavior of "units demanded during leadtime," M, the manager must obtain the necessary information from the past records of the company. Since in Figure 13.3 we have assumed a constant leadtime, the behavior of M is determined by the behavior of u (remember, $M = uL$). Now, since we are dealing with a probabilistic sales pattern, usage *rate* during leadtime can be represented either by a discrete probability distribution or by a continuous probability distribution. In Figure 13.3, we have shown three different "usage *rates* during leadtime," u_1, u_2, and u_3. Note that u_1 is the same as the regular demand rate. However, u_2 represents a decreased rate, while u_3 represents an accelerated rate (as compared to demand rates before the reorder points). [*Note*: It should be emphasized that the demand rate (i.e., demand before the reorder point, R) and "usage rate during leadtime" (i.e., demand after R) are both probabilistic variables. However, we have shown them in Figure 13.3 as "weighted averages" calculated from their respective probability distributions, and represented them by straight lines. This simplification makes it easier to "see" what goes on in a probabilistic inventory system.]

The second factor in the determination of safety stock is the magnitude of stockout cost, K. Stockout costs are essentially a matter of managerial judgment, although the amount of lost profit does provide an insight. Stockout costs are usually expressed as a penalty for being 1 unit short per ordering cycle (the terms "reorder cycle," "reordering cycle," "ordering cycle," and "order cycles" are used interchangeably in this book).

The third factor, holding costs of safety stock, is comprised of such costs as the cost of capital, insurance, taxes, and obsolescence. They can be expressed as a *percentage* of average dollar inventory (denoted by capital letter H), or as an absolute number showing the cost of holding 1 unit per year (denoted by lower-case letter h).

---

[6] Another factor is the relationship (interaction) between the size of order, Q, and the size of safety stock, SS. As a general rule, the larger the Q, the lower is the level of SS. However, we shall ignore this factor in our model.

Discrete Probability Distribution of Demand

We now proceed to illustrate a probabilistic (dynamic) inventory problem (fixed-order system) with the aid of an example. We shall assume that the probability distribution of demand is discrete. Further, realizing that stockouts can occur *only* during leadtime, we want to focus on that pattern of demand which is realized during the leadtime. That is why we concern ourselves with the behavior of "usage rate during leadtime," u, "leadtime," L, and "units demanded during leadtime," M.

Example 13.5

The ABC Company has found that its average daily demand for an inventory item is 10 units (or $D = 3,000$ units, assuming 300 working days in a year). The company has kept good records on the behavior of M—"units demanded during leadtime." That is, the probability distribution of M is known. Shown in columns 1 and 2 of Table 13.5 is the probability distribution of M.

Information regarding purchase costs, holding costs, ordering costs, and stockout costs follows:

$$C = \$300/\text{unit}$$

$$h = \$30/\text{unit/year}^7$$

$$S = \$450/\text{order}$$

$$K = \text{penalty for being 1 unit short } per\ order\ cycle = \$20/\text{unit/order cycle}$$

$$L = \text{normal leadtime} = 2 \text{ working days}$$

If we recognize that the demand is probabilistic and leadtime deterministic, what is the optimal safety stock?

Solution. Before solving for the optimal safety stock and the optimal order quantity, we make the following comments with reference to Table 13.5.

Columns 1 and 2: The data in columns 1 and 2 are based on the company records. The information from column 1 regarding units demanded during leadtime, M, and from column 2 regarding the probability of units demanded during leadtime, $p(M)$, can be used to calculate the *expected value* of units

---

[7] Note that the holding cost here has been specified on the basis of "holding 1 unit per year," and the lower-case letter h is used to denote the holding cost. Previously, we used the capital letter H to represent the holding cost as a percentage of average dollar inventory. If we use H, then $Q^* = \sqrt{\dfrac{2DS}{CH}}$.

If we use h, then $Q^* = \sqrt{\dfrac{2DS}{h}}$, as can be quickly ascertained by letting

$$\text{ordering costs} = \text{holding costs}$$

$$\frac{D}{Q}S = \frac{Q}{2}h$$

Hence,

$$Q^* = \sqrt{\frac{2DS}{h}} \tag{13.4}$$

Table 13.5

(1) Units Demanded During Leadtime, (M)	(2) Probability of Units Demanded During Leadtime, p(M)	(3) Cumulative Probability of Units Demanded During Leadtime, P (units demanded ≥ M)	(4) Probability of Being Safe if R = M	(5) Probability of Being Short if R = M	(6) Level of Safety Stock, SS if R = M
10	0.05	1.00	0.05	0.95	
15	0.20	0.95	0.25	0.75	0
20	0.50	0.75	0.75	0.25	5
25	0.20	0.25	0.95	0.05	10
30	0.05	0.05	1.00	0.00	

demanded during leadtime (denote by $\overline{M}$). Thus,

$$\overline{M} = p_1 M_1 + p_2 M_2 + p_3 M_3 + p_4 M_4 + p_5 M_5$$
$$= 0.05(10) + 0.20(15) + 0.50(20) + 0.20(25) + 0.05(30)$$
$$= 20 \text{ units}$$

Column 3: Cumulative Probability of Units Demanded During the Leadtime, P **(units demanded** $\geqslant M$**).** The cumulative probability that units demanded during leadtime will be 10 *or more* is obviously 1.00.

The cumulative probability that units demanded will be 15 *or more* is $0.20 + 0.50 + 0.20 + 0.05 = 0.95$.

The cumulative probability of units demanded being 20 or more, 25 or more, or 30 or more is similarly derived.

Column 4: Probability of Being Safe if $R = M$**.** If $R = 10$, we are safe only if $M = 10$, and hence the probability of being safe $= 0.05$.

If $R = 15$, we are safe if $M = 10$ or $M = 15$. Hence, the probability of being safe $= 0.05 + 0.20 = 0.25$.

If $R = 20$, we are safe if $M = 10$, $M = 15$, or $M = 20$. Hence, the probability of being safe $= 0.05 + 0.20 + 0.50 = 0.75$.

And so on.

Column 5: Probability of Being Short if $R = M$**.** Probability of being short is simply 1 minus the probability of being safe. Hence, these values are calculated as 1 minus the corresponding value in column 4.

Column 6: Level of Safety Stock if $R = M$**.** Since leadtime is 2 days, and the average usage rate per day is 10 units, normal R is $10 \times 2 = 20$ units. Hence, if $R = 20$, we have only provided for the normal usage for 2 days of leadtime. That is, if $R = 20$, then safety stock is zero.[8] If $R = 25$, safety stock $= 25 - 20 = 5$. If $R = 30$, safety stock $= 30 - 20 = 10$.

Let us now determine $Q*$ as if we are under conditions of certainty. Then, from (13.4),

$$Q* = \sqrt{\frac{2DS}{h}} = \sqrt{\frac{2(3,000)(450)}{30}} = 300 \text{ units}$$

Since the annual demand, D, is 3,000 units and the value of $Q*$ is 300 the number of orders per year (and hence the number of reorder cycles) is

$$N = \frac{D}{Q} = \frac{3,000}{300} = 10 \text{ reorder cycles/year}$$

It is clear from the above discussion and from column 6 of Table 13.5 that, in this problem, we must consider the consequences of three strategies regarding the size of the safety stock (i.e., safety stock of 0, 5, or 10 units). We want to calculate two types of costs in conjunction with *each* level of safety stock: (1) holding costs of safety stock, and (2) expected stockout costs.

---

[8] Safety stock, SS, is calculated as $R - \overline{M}$, where R is the reordering point and $\overline{M}$ is the average or *expected* units demanded during leadtime. That is, SS $= R - \overline{M}$.

Calculation of Holding Costs of Safety Stock

The holding cost associated with *each* safety stock level is calculated by multiplying the safety stock level, SS, by h (holding cost per unit per year).[9] Thus, since $h = \$30$, we have the results shown in Table 13.6.

Table 13.6

Safety Stock, SS	Holding Costs of Safety Stock, SS × h
0	0 × 30 = 0
5	5 × 30 = $150
10	10 × 30 = $300

Calculation of Expected Stockout Costs

Expected stockout costs per year

$$= \begin{pmatrix} \text{expected units} \\ \text{short per reorder} \\ \text{cycle} \end{pmatrix} \times \begin{pmatrix} \text{penalty cost} \\ \text{per unit} \end{pmatrix} \times \begin{pmatrix} \text{reorder cycles} \\ \text{per year} \end{pmatrix}$$

$$= \frac{\text{expected stockout (units)}}{\text{reorder cycle}} \times \frac{\text{penalty cost}}{\text{unit}} \times \frac{\text{reorder cycle}}{\text{year}} \quad (13.5)$$

It is clear from Table 13.5 that if the safety stock is zero (i.e., $R = 20$), there is either the possibility of being short 5 units (when $M = 25$) with a probability of 0.20, *or* there is the possibility of being short 10 units (when $M = 30$) with a probability of 0.05. Hence, the expected units short *per reorder cycle*, when SS = 0, is

$$5(0.20) + 10(0.05) = 1.5 \text{ units}$$

Similarly, if the safety stock is 5 (i.e., $R = 25$), then the only possibility of being short is when $M = 30$ (the shortage will be 5 units with a probability of 0.05). Hence, the expected stockout per reorder cycle, when SS = 5, is

$$5(0.05) = 0.25 \text{ units}$$

Finally, if the safety stock is 10 (i.e., $R = 30$), the probability of being short is zero. Hence, the expected stockout per reorder cycle, when SS = 10, is zero. That is, expected stockout is zero units. We can now cast Equation (13.5) in a tabular format, as shown in Table 13.7.

Calculation of Optimal Safety Stock, SS, and Reorder Point, R

If we combine column 5 of Table 13.7 with Table 13.6, we get the data shown in Table 13.8. Since the minimum total cost results when safety stock is 5, the optimal level of safety stock is 5 units, and the optimal reorder point, R, is 25 units. The number 25 is derived as follows:

[9] Note that we do *not* divide SS by 2, since the safety stock is present for the entire year and does not normally deplete to zero.

Table 13.7

(1)	(2)	(3)	(4)	(5)
		Expected		
		Stockout		*Expected*
		Cost per		*Stockout*
Safety	*Expected*	*Reorder*	*Reorder*	*Cost per*
Stock	*Units Short*	*Cycle,*	*Cycles*	*Year,*
Level,	*per Reorder*	*Column 2 × K*	*per*	*Column 3*
SS	*Cycle*	*(Here K = 20)*	*Year*	*× Column 4*
0	1.5	30	10	300
5	0.25	5	10	50
10	0	0	10	0

R = average usage (per day) during leadtime × leadtime + optimal safety stock

$$= (10 \times 2) + 5 = 25 \text{ units}$$

Alternatively,

$$R = \bar{M} + SS = 20 + 5 = 25 \text{ units} \leftarrow$$

13.3.2 FIXED-PERIOD SYSTEM

To complete the discussion of this section, we present in Figure 13.4 the behavior of a probabilistic (dynamic) model under the fixed-period system. The most complicated case will assume both a probabilistic demand and a probabilistic leadtime. However, to simplify the explanation (but still preserving the essence of the fixed-period system), we assume in Figure 13.4 a constant demand (that is why the lines representing demand are parallel to each other), but probabilistic leadtime (that is why, in the second review period, we experience delayed delivery and hence stockout).

Let us discuss how the fixed-period system shown in Figure 13.4 can be analyzed and operated. Basically, we need to know two things: (1) level of safety stock,[10] SS, and (2) decision rule (formula) for calculating order quantities, Q_i, at the end of each review period.

Table 13.8

Safety Stock Level SS	Holding Costs of Safety Stock	Expected Stockout Costs	Total Cost
0	0	300	300
5	150	50	200 ← minimum
10	300	0	300

[10] As stated earlier, the fixed-period system requires a larger safety stock (as compared to the fixed-order system with the same service policy).

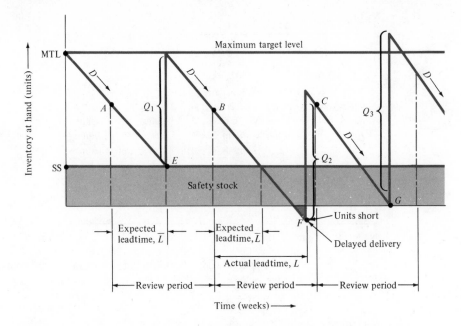

Figure 13.4. Probabilistic Model (fixed-period system with safety stock; constant demand; probabilistic leadtime; instantaneous buildup of inventory)

Calculation of Safety Stock, SS

Since we have assumed a constant demand, we do not need any safety stock to absorb the fluctuations (uncertainty) in the demand rate. However, we do need safety stock to accommodate the fact of probabilistic leadtime.

Now, focus on the concept of a discrete distribution of leadtime, L, from which we can calculate expected leadtime, $\bar{L}$ (i.e., $\bar{L} = L_1 p_1 + L_2 p_2 + L_3 p_3 + \cdots + L_n p_n$). Since "usage rate during leadtime," u, is constant, we can say that

$$\text{expected units demanded during leadtime} = \bar{M} = (u)(\bar{L})$$

In general, for a fixed period system such as shown in Figure 13.4, safety stock can vary from a value of $u \times \bar{L}$ (i.e., we *plan* to experience a stockout 50 percent of the time) to a value obtained by multiplying u by the highest value of L (i.e., we *plan* to experience no stockouts). However, the optimal level of safety stock must be calculated, as before, by minimizing the sum of two opposing costs: (1) holding cost of safety stock, and (2) costs of being out of stock.

Calculation of Order Quantities (Q_i)

The calculation of order quantities requires that we establish a maximum target level, MTL, to which we *expect* the inventory to reach when goods are received. We establish MTL as shown in Equation (13.6).

$$\text{MTL} = \text{SS} + Q^* \tag{13.6}$$

Inventory Control—Probabilistic Models   Chapter 13

where

$$Q^* = \sqrt{\frac{2DS}{CH}}$$

Next, we can calculate order quantity Q_i at the end of any review period by using Equation (13.7):

$$\left.\begin{array}{r}\text{order quantity } Q_i = (\text{MTL} - \text{inventory at hand}) \\ + \text{ expected units demanded} \\ \text{during leadtime} \\ + \text{ back orders (if any)}\end{array}\right\} \tag{13.7}$$

As shown in Figure 13.4, orders are placed at the end of each review period, and that in the fixed-period system order quantity *can* vary. Let us examine Figure 13.4 again and make the following observations.

1. The safety stock, SS, is the *optimal* safety stock.
2. Orders are placed at the end of a review period at points *A*, *B*, and *C*.
3. Goods are received at points *E*, *F*, and *G* (after leadtimes of different lengths).
4. The first order, Q_1, and the first leadtime are such that, upon receiving the goods, inventory at hand reaches MTL. Note that in the second cycle, upon receipt of goods, inventory at hand does not reach MTL—while in the third cycle it exceeds MTL. We emphasize this to point up the probabilistic nature of leadtime and varying order sizes, Q_i.

13.4
The Concept of Service Level

In the preceding section, we illustrated the determination of the safety stock and the reorder point *R* in a probabilistic (dynamic case) inventory problem with the assumption that stockout costs were known. However, there are circumstances when it is extremely difficult to reliably estimate stockout costs. Furthermore, in certain industries there is a "norm" regarding *service level*, and in order to remain competitive, these norms must be observed. Therefore, the inventory policy in such cases is designed by utilizing the concept of *service level*.

Service level is usually defined as the ratio of the number of customers receiving goods to the number of customers demanding goods.[11] For example, if during a given year, 200 customers demanded goods but the inventory situation was such that only 190 customers could be supplied goods on demand, then the service level was $\frac{190}{200} = 0.95$ or 95 percent. This means that, in this situation, the probability of stockout was 0.05 (or 5 percent).

From the above discussion, we can establish the following relationships between "service level" and the "probability of stockout."

service level $= 1 -$ probability of stockout

---

[11] See Section 13.5 for other measures that directly or indirectly reflect service level.

Alternatively,

$$\text{probability of stockout} = 1 - \text{service level}$$

We mentioned in Section 13.3.1 that in a fixed-order system the stockouts can occur only during the leadtime. Hence, while determining the level of safety stock we must know the history and pattern of units demanded during leadtime. The pattern of units demanded during leadtime is represented by a probability distribution (*discrete* such as shown in Table 13.5 or *continuous* such as a normal distribution). Two things are important when "units demanded during leadtime" is represented by a continuous probability distribution. First, we should know $\overline{M}$— the *expected* number of units demanded during leadtime (i.e., how much *on the average* is needed during leadtime). Second, we should know the standard deviation of the distribution of M—that is, σ_M. The σ_M is indicative of the *range* of M and hence affects the determination of safety stock. For example, if $\overline{M}$ is 20 units and the range of M is from 18 to 22, the maximum safety stock should be only 2 units (i.e., reorder point $R = 22$ units). (Remember that safety stock, SS $= R - \overline{M}$.) However, if the range of M is from 5 to 35 units (and $\overline{M}$ is still 20), then the maximum safety stock will be 15 units (i.e., $R = 35$ units). In practice it is often too expensive to provide full safety (i.e., 100 percent service level). The inventory policy is designed by providing a service level that is deemed by management to be in line with the "norm" of the industry, or the service level that is acceptable to the company in view of its own circumstances.

Example 13.6

The Garg manufacturing company has kept full records of the behavior of M, "units demanded during leadtime," of one of the parts purchased from an outside vendor. The records show the pattern of M to be such that it can be represented by a normal distribution shown in Figure 13.5 with a mean of 1,500 and a standard deviation of 150. That is, $\overline{M} = 1,500$ and $\sigma_M = 150$. The management has decided to provide a service level of 95 percent. Determine the level of safety stock, SS, and the reorder point R to meet the service level goal of the company.

Solution. It is clear from Figure 13.5 that area under the curve to the right of $\overline{M}$ is 50 percent of the total area under the curve. This means that if we carry a safety stock of zero (i.e., reorder when stocks fall to 1,500 units), then we will be safe only 50 percent of the time and hence will be short 50 percent of the time. This will correspond to a service level of 50 percent. However, our service goal of 95 percent requires that we be safe 95 percent of the time and hence short only 5 percent of the time. That is, we should find an R (reorder point) in Figure 13.5 so that the area under the normal curve to the right of R is exactly 5 percent. This means that area under the curve between points $\overline{M}$ and R is 45 percent. As can be ascertained from Table I of Appendix E, this corresponds to a distance of 1.64 standard deviations between points R and $\overline{M}$. Therefore,

$$R - \overline{M} = 1.64 \times \text{(standard deviation of } M\text{)}$$
$$R = \overline{M} + 1.64\sigma_M$$
$$= 1,500 + 1.64(150)$$
$$= 1,500 + 246 = 1746$$

Hence, in order to provide a 95 percent service level, the reorder point, $R = 1,746$ units. That is, we are providing a safety stock of 246 units

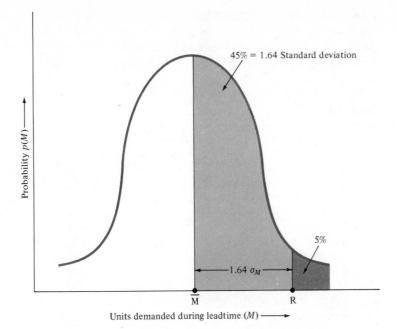

45% = 1.64 Standard deviation

5%

1.64 σ_M

$\overline{M}$ R

Units demanded during leadtime (M) ⟶

Probability $p(M)$ ⟶

Figure 13.5. Probability Distribution of Units Demanded During Leadtime (M).

$$\overline{M} = 1,500 \qquad \sigma_M = 150$$

Note that $M = \mu L$, where
μ = usage rate during leadtime
L = leadtime

($1,746 - 1,500 = 246$). That is,

$$SS = R - \overline{M}$$
$$= 1,746 - 1,500 = 246$$

If we carefully examine the calculations for Example 13.6 in conjunction with Figure 13.5, we can observe that when M is normally distributed, the safety stock can be calculated directly as

$$SS = Z\sigma_M \qquad (13.8)$$

where

Z = the distance between R and $\overline{M}$, stated in "standard deviation" units. [See Table 1 in Appendix E and Section A.6.1 (step 2) on p. 499.]

σ_M = standard deviation of M (units demanded during leadtime).

For our example, from (13.8)

$$SS = (1.64)(150) = 246 \text{ units}$$

Note that if h = holding cost per year, then

$$\text{holding cost of safety stock per year} = (Z\sigma_M)h \qquad (13.9)$$

It is obvious that the higher the desired service level, the higher the safety stock; and hence the higher will be the costs of maintaining the safety stock.

However, the relationship between the service level and the costs of safety stock is *not* linear. It costs much more to go from a service level of 95 to say 99 percent than it will to go from 50 to 54 percent. We show in Table 13.9[12] the cost behavior of providing different service levels with respect to Example 13.6.

Table 13.9

Service Level (%)	Probability of Stockout	Number of Standard Deviations Between R and $\bar{M}$ (Z)	Safety Stock, SS $(Z\sigma_M)$	Holding Costs of Safety Stock per Year $(Z\sigma_M)h$
50	0.50	0	0	0
80	0.20	0.84	126	630
95	0.05	1.64	246	1,230
98	0.02	2.05	308	1,540
99	0.01	2.33	350	1,750
99.9	0.001	3.09	464	2,320

Calculation of Optimal Safety Stock (Continuous Probability Distribution Case)[13]

In Section 13.3.1 we illustrated, with the aid of an example, how to calculate the optimal level of safety stock, SS, in the face of discrete demand distribution. In this section, we set down the procedure for calculating the optimal safety stock level in the face of a continuous (normal) probability distribution of demand.

The framework of the procedure for the continuous case is the same as in the discrete case. That is, for *various levels of safety stock* (these levels correspond to different service levels and are calculated as shown in Table 13.9), we compute: (1) holding costs of safety stock per year (as shown in Table 13.9), and (2) expected stockout costs per year (see Equation 13.5). Then the total cost, T, for *each* safety level, is calculated by adding (1) and (2). The optimal safety level will then correspond to that strategy which yields the minimum total cost, T.

- holding costs of safety stock per year $= (Z\sigma_M)h$ (13.9)
- expected stockout cost per year = (expected units short per reorder cycle)
  × (stockout penalty cost per unit)
  × (reorder cycles per year)

$$= E(M > R) \times K \times \frac{D}{Q} \quad (13.10)$$

[12] The procedure for calculating the safety stock for a specified service level has already been illustrated. The annual cost of holding each safety level is calculated by multiplying the safety stock by h (assume that the holding cost, h, is \$5/unit/year).

[13] This section may be omitted without loss of continuity.

where

$$(Z\sigma_M) = \text{safety stock, SS (see Equation 13.8)}$$
$$h = \text{holding cost per unit per year}$$
$$K = \text{stockout penalty cost per unit}$$
$$E(M > R) = \text{expected value (in physical units) that } M \text{ (units demanded}$$
$$\text{during leadtime) is greater than reorder point } R$$

[*Note*: The meaning of $E(M > R)$ becomes clear if we focus in Figure 13.5 on the area, under the normal curve, to the right of point R. It is the *expected value* of stockout units per order cycle. Mathematically, it is calculated as follows:

$$E(M > R) = \int_{R}^{\infty} (M - R)p(M)\,dM$$

where $p(M)$ is the probability distribution of M. For further discussion, see footnote 13 in Section A.4 on p. 494].

13.5
Selected Measures of Managerial Efficiency in Inventory Control

It is clear that the purpose of inventory management is to minimize total inventory cost (or maximize profits) and yet provide good customer service and avoid stockouts or shortages. The higher the level of average inventory, the better the customer service and the less the danger of stockouts. However, higher inventory levels also mean larger inventory costs. Hence, the job of the manager is to design an inventory policy that carefully balances costs associated with holding inventories against the costs of being out of stock. Mathematical models of inventory control offer a great opportunity to practicing managers in designing optimal inventory policies. These models are built into computerized inventory control systems such as IMPACT and PICS developed by IBM (Section 13.7). The manager can also benefit from some elementary measures of managerial efficiency in inventory control. These measures are *quantitative* and their *acceptable limits* are usually set by the norms of the industry. They can be used as supplementary tools of control, in conjunction with the decision rules (*when* and *how much*) provided by the mathematical models of inventory control. Listed below are six such measures.

1. Inventory turnover ratio $= \dfrac{\text{monthly (or annual) sales}}{\text{average value of monthly (or annual) inventory}}$

2. Percentage of shortages $= \dfrac{\text{number of units short}}{\text{number of units demanded}} \times 100$

3. Service level $= \dfrac{\text{units demanded} - \text{units short}}{\text{units demanded}} \times 100$

4. Service level $= \dfrac{\text{number of customers receiving goods}}{\text{number of customers demanding goods}} \times 100$

5. Percent stockout days $= \dfrac{\text{number of working days with zero inventory}}{\text{total number of working days}} \times 100$

6. Percentage of stockouts $= \dfrac{\text{number of order periods with zero inventory}}{\text{total number of order periods}} \times 100$

13.6
Sensitivity Analysis in Inventory Control

The purpose of sensitivity analysis in inventory control is to examine the impact on the inventory policy (i.e., *when, how much,* and *total cost*) of possible changes and errors in such parameters (input data) as D, C, S, and H. Let us examine the basic EOQ model of Equation (12.7), reproduced as Equation (13.11):

$$Q^* = \sqrt{\frac{2DS}{CH}} \qquad (13.11)$$

We note that because of the presence of the square root in the formula for Q^*, the impact of changes in D, S, C, and H is greatly dampened. That is, optimal order quantity, Q^*, is not very sensitive to changes (or errors) in the four parameters. Let us illustrate this with the aid of an example.

Example 13.7 | Let us consider a deterministic inventory situation such as described in Section 12.11.1. Assume that $D = 6{,}000$, $S = 25$, $C = 20$, and $H = 0.06$. Hence,

$$Q^* = \sqrt{\frac{2DS}{CH}} = \sqrt{\frac{2(6{,}000)(25)}{(20)(0.06)}} = 500 \text{ units/order}$$

Table 13.10 *Illustration of Sensitivity Analysis*

	Q^*	Comments
• The basic EOQ model with given data in Example 13.7	500	Initial economic order quantity
• Let D increase by 100 percent	707	Initial economic order quantity increases by a factor of $\sqrt{2}$. This is to be expected in view of the EOQ formula given by Equation (13.11).
• Let S increase by 100 percent	707	Same comments as above
• Let C increase by 100 percent	354	Initial economic order quantity is decreased by a factor of $1/\sqrt{2}$, again because of the structure of Equation (13.11)
• Let H increase by 100 percent	354	Same comments as above

Let us now examine how sensitive Q^* is to changes in D, S, C, and H. The sensitivity analysis is summarized in Table 13.10.

The sensitivity analysis can now be extended to show the impact of changes in the four parameters on total cost, T. We leave this task to the reader.

13.7
Computerized Inventory Control Systems

Inventory control is but one part of the organizational system that coordinates planning, forecasting, production, scheduling, and related activities. A multitude of computer programs for inventory and production control systems are available in the market. In Table 13.11 we provide a selected list of these programs, along with the name of company or source that can be contacted for full details.

Table 13.11 *Computer Routines or Programs for Inventory Control*

Name of Company or Source	Computer Routine or Program
International Business Machine Corporation	• Disk Order Point of Inventory Management (DOPTIM) • Gross Explosion Technique of Inventory Control for Manufacturers • Inventory Management Program and Control Techniques (IMPACT) • Management Planning and Control System (MPACS) • Material Planning System • Net Explosion Technique of Inventory Control for Manufacturers • Order Point Technique of Inventory Control for Manufacturers (OPTIM) • Production Information and Control System (PICS) • Retail Inventory Stock Control System • System/360 Model 20 Requirements Planning and Inventory Control System (RICS) • Statistical Inventory Management • Wholesale Inventory System
Burroughs Corporation	• Project Audit Report (PAR)
National Aeronautics and Space Administration	• NASA PERT and Companion Cost
Scientific Time Sharing Corporation	• L-707 Materials Management Analysis and Simulation • L-747 Materials Management System

13.8
Summary

The focus of this chapter has been on the basic probabilistic models of inventory control. The inventory model is of the probabilistic variety whenever one or more components of the problem must be described with probability distributions. We utilized the payoff matrix approach and the marginal analysis approach to illustrate a simple probabilistic model (static case). Then we described and illustrated the dynamic case of the basic probabilistic model.

The concept of service level was described and illustrated. We also presented some measures of managerial efficiency that can be used in conjunction with management science models of inventory control.

The basic idea of sensitivity analysis in inventory control was illustrated with the aid of an example. Finally, we provided a selected list of computerized inventory control systems.

References

See the References at the end of Chapter 12.

Review Questions and Problems

13.1. Differentiate between the following inventory control models:

(a) Deterministic versus probabilistic.
(b) Static versus dynamic.

13.2. Describe the rationale of the payoff matrix approach and the marginal analysis approach in solving a probabilistic inventory model (static case).

13.3. What is the role of the safety stock in inventory control? Is the level of safety stock independent of the order quantity?

13.4. Discuss the following statement: "The size of the safety stock in the fixed-period system must be larger than that required for the fixed-order system, assuming the same service policy."

13.5. Explain the concept of service level in inventory control. Why is it necessary that we know both the expected units demanded during leadtime ($\overline{M}$), and the standard deviation σ_M, to determine the appropriate level of the safety stock?

13.6. List and define some of the selected measures of managerial efficiency that can be used as supplementary tools of inventory control.

13.7. Why is the impact of changes in such parameters as D, S, C, and H not very pronounced in the basic EOQ model?

13.8. What is the optimal order quantity for a retailer of *Workman Magazine* if its cost is $1/copy, selling price is $2/copy, and its demand schedule is given by Table 13.12?

Table 13.12

Demand/Week	Probability
0	0.1
10	0.1
20	0.2
30	0.3
40	0.2
50	0.1

(*Note*: If the magazine is unsold, the retailer loses $1/copy.)

13.9. The Boulle Milk Company buys half-gallon cartons for $0.50/carton. The selling price is $0.80 and the company gets $0.05 credit for each unsold carton. What is the optimal order quantity if the demand is as shown in Table 13.13?

Table 13.13

Demand/Day	Probability
100	0.1
150	0.3
200	0.3
250	0.2
300	0.1

13.10. Determine the optimal order quantity, if the cost of stockout is $3/unit, the cost of overstocking is $2/unit, and the demand distribution is as in Table 13.14. Use the marginal analysis approach. (*Hint*: See footnote 3 on p. 368.)

Table 13.14

Demand/Day	Probability
0	0.1
1	0.3
2	0.4
3	0.2

13.11. Dewey, Cheattam & Howe Retail Sales, Inc.'s inventory manager has determined that demand is normally distributed with a mean of 40 units and standard deviation of 10 units. If stockout cost per unit is $3.15 and cost of overstocking is $0.60, determine the reorder point, R.

13.12. What is the minimum cost strategy for a firm given the following information: demand = 20 units/day, cost = $4.50/unit, holding cost = 10 percent per year of average dollar inventory, stockout cost = $2/unit, ordering cost = $20/order, and leadtime is distributed as shown in Table 13.15. Assume 360 working days per year.

Table 13.15

Leadtime (days)	Probability
1	0.1
2	0.2
3	0.4
4	0.2
5	0.1

13.13. What is the production order quantity for a firm if it can produce 200,000 units/year, has a demand of 100,000 units/year, holding cost is $5/unit/year, and cost/setup is $50? Assume that no breakdowns occur and that inventory is built up at a linear rate. How does your answer change if holding cost increases to $10/unit/year? If cost per setup increases by 100 percent, but holding cost is $5/unit/year?

13.14. V. Shaftew Plumbing Supply Co. buys faucets for $2 each and sells them for $5 each. Daily demand for faucets is normally distributed with mean of 75 units and standard deviation of 5 units. Salvage value of unsold faucets is $1. Use the marginal analysis approach to determine how many faucets should be ordered.

13.15. The All Ways Understocking Co. sells ladies' hosiery items. Demand is normally distributed with mean of 850 units and standard deviation of 250 units. What percentage of time will stockouts be experienced if safety stock level is at 292 units? What safety stock level would be necessary to maintain a 99 percent service level?

13.16. Short Electricals Ltd. produces motors and generators. In order to have smooth production runs, management wants to maintain an inventory of motor housings to support a 96 percent service level. Units demanded during leadtime are known to be normally distributed with mean of 350 housings and standard deviation of 50 housings. How much safety stock should be carried? What is the reorder point?

CHAPTER 14
Simulation

MAJOR CONCEPTS AND TOPICS
DISCUSSED IN THIS CHAPTER

Analytical Versus Simulation Procedures

Why Use Simulation Models?

Development and Utilization of Simulation Models

The Idea of Experimentation (Random Sampling) in Monte Carlo Simulation

Devices for Generating Chance (Probabilistic) Outcomes

Simulation and Financial Analysis

Simulation and Inventory Control

Simulation and Network Models

Computer Languages and Programs for Simulation

Classification of Simulation Models

Monte Carlo simulation
Heuristic programming
Operational gaming
Artificial intelligence

14.1
Introduction

In Section 4.6, we presented several possible classifications of models. One classification, developed according to the *type of procedure employed to derive solutions to mathematical models*, divided management science models into two categories: (1) analytical models, and (2) simulation models. Our focus up to this point has been on analytical models. The following analytical models have thus far been presented: various decision-theory models, network models (PERT and CPM), linear programming models, transportation model, assignment model, game-theory models, and inventory control models. We now turn our attention to the concept of simulation and simulation models.

The purpose of this chapter is to describe simulation and illustrate how simulation models can be used in making managerial decisions. We first differentiate between analytical and simulation procedures and provide the rationale for using simulation models. This is followed by a brief discussion of how a simulation model is developed and utilized. Next, we describe the concept of Monte Carlo simulation and explain the idea of *experimentation* in simulation models. A list of devices that can be used in generating probabilistic outcomes required in conducting simulation is provided. We then illustrate how the simulation approach can be used in financial analysis, inventory control, and network models. A selected list of computer languages or programs for simulation is provided. Finally, we briefly describe four categories of simulation models.

14.2
Analytical Versus Simulation Procedures

In general, solutions to mathematical models can be derived by using two types of procedures: (1) analytical, and (2) simulation. In the analytical procedures, two categories can be identified. In the first category, we have a *general solution* in an abstract form (i.e., the solution is specified by symbols). Further, the general solution is obtained by using mathematical techniques, and it can then be used *directly* to solve a specific problem (i.e., we can obtain the optimal strategy in a noniterative manner). This, for example, was the case in the inventory model presented in Section 2.8. In that model we obtained a general solution for the decision variable Q by taking the first derivative of T [see Equation (2.6) on p. 47] and equating it to zero.[1] The general solution for the optimal order quantity was

---

[1] It should be noted that in Equation (2.6), D, S, C, and H are the parameters and that Q is the *only* decision variable. Hence, we needed *only one* equation (generated by equating the first derivative of T to zero) to solve the model. In general, the number of equations needed to derive an analytical solution equals the number of decision variables. That is, when the model consists of two or more decision variables, we take partial derivatives (and equate them to zero) in order to obtain the necessary optimizing equations. For an illustration, see Section B.7.4.

$$Q^* = \sqrt{\frac{2DS}{CH}}$$

Note that the solution derived by the analytical procedure is quite *general* and it does *not* depend on any specific values of the problem parameters.

In the second category, we have a *general methodology*[2] that is applied to solve a specific problem. This category of the analytical procedure is *iterative* (numerical) in nature. The iterative (numerical) procedure consists of examining various values of the decision variable(s) and choosing those that give the best results (in terms of the value of the stated objective or the criterion variable) in view of *specified* values of the problem parameters. In the iterative case, the specific problem is *not* solved directly. Instead, the general methodology (algorithm) is applied to produce a specific numerical solution and then, on successive trials (iterations), better solutions are produced until the optimal solution is identified. This, for example, was the case when we applied the simplex method to solve a linear programming problem (Chapter 8).

In the *simulation* procedure, the solution is *not* derived deductively. Instead, the model is *experimented* upon by inserting into the model specific values of decision variables, under assumed conditions, and then observing their effect on the criterion variable. For example, we can *test* the effect of different numbers of checkout counters (decision variable) under assumed conditions of customer arrivals, on total cost of operation (criterion variable) of a grocery store. As we shall see in Section 14.5, simulation procedures are inductive in nature and they use the concept of *random sampling*. By taking random samples, we can describe "what is happening" to the system for a selected period of time, and under a variety of assumed conditions. The "state of the system" is simulated by advancing the clock either in uniform time increments (known as *time increment* simulation) or in variable time increments (known as *event increment* simulation). We shall further discuss this aspect of simulation in Section 15.11 on p. 451.

The basic idea of simulation is to utilize *some device* to *imitate* a real-life system in order to study and understand its properties, behavior, and operating characteristics.[3] The device can be physical, mathematical, or any convenient means that can effectively *describe* the behavior of a system that a manager wishes to study, understand, analyze, design, improve, or operate. For example, we can learn a lot about the operating characteristics of a new airplane by simulating (imitating) flight conditions in a wind tunnel. Similarly, as we shall explain in Section 14.9, we can simulate (imitate) the behavior of an inventory system by *experimenting* (i.e., taking random samples) on a mathematical model that represents the system.

The experimentation can be performed on a *physical* model such as testing of airplanes in wind tunnels (*iconic simulation*), on electronic or hydraulic *analog* models of production processes or economic systems (*analog simulation*), or on *mathematical* models of such real-life systems as inventory control, investment

---

[2] Also called an *algorithm* (a systematic step-by-step procedure). Note that the general methodology or algorithm is derived deductively (e.g., the simplex method), but is applied inductively.

[3] A dictionary definition of simulation is "to assume or have the appearance or characteristics" of something. In this sense, all models, to some extent, are simulation models. However, we shall define simulation models as those that are built by using simulation (as opposed to analytical) procedures. Thus, depending upon the procedure of solution employed, we can classify models into the categories of *analytical* or *simulation* models.

planning, production scheduling, and so on (*symbolic simulation*). In any simulation model, the idea is to study, analyze, and understand the behavior of the real-life system by *running* or *testing* the model under a variety of operating conditions.

Simulation based on mathematical models can be *deterministic* or *probabilistic*. When managers conduct sensitivity analysis (commonly referred to as *what-if* analysis in the business world) on the financial projections of an investment project, balance sheet, income statement, or cash-flow statement, they are, in effect, engaged in deterministic simulation (sensitivity analysis was discussed in Section 9.6). *What* will be the impact on the income statement, *if* the inflation rate is 10 percent? *What* will be the impact on the monthly cash flow *if* the OPEC countries raise the price of oil by 20 percent next year? Other examples of deterministic simulation include simulation of plant layout, network analysis, and line balancing. The basic assumption in deterministic simulation models is that the distribution of any random variable can be represented by one value.[4]

A probabilistic simulation deals with *random phenomena* and is often referred to as *Monte Carlo simulation*. Monte Carlo simulation is based on the idea of taking *random samples* from the mathematical model that represents the real-life system. These random samples are of *specified* stochastic variables of the system at different points in time, and under different conditions. The random samples result in a probability distribution that *imitates* the real-life system, and from which the value of the specified stochastic variable is to be *estimated*. Furthermore, by varying the values of certain parameters and independent variables, and then repeating the random sampling process, we can attempt to measure their effect on the chosen stochastic variable. The simulated behavior is used as an input to the decision-making process.

Based on the above discussion, we present a classification of models as shown in Figure 14.1.

In this chapter, we shall limit our discussion to simulation models of the probabilistic type.

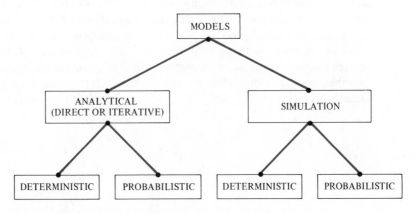

Figure 14.1. Analytical Versus Simulation Models.

---

[4] This *one* value is most often the *expected value* of the random variable.

14.3
Why Use Simulation Models?

Analytical models are very powerful and useful, as is apparent from their application potential described in the previous chapters. However, they have some serious limitations. For one thing, analytical models lack the ability to trace the past or future behavior of a system through finely divided time intervals. They provide the manager with only the *overall* solution—a solution that may be unique and optimum but does not prescribe any operating procedures for time spans shorter than the planning horizon. For example, the linear programming solution to a problem with a planning horizon of 1 year does not prescribe any rules for devising month-to-month, week-to-week, or day-to-day operating procedures. Similarly, when an inventory model assumes a probabilistic daily demand, it gives only an *overall pattern* of daily demand. It does *not* mention as to what specific demand occurred, or will occur, on a particular day. Now, if under these circumstances, the manager wishes to obtain some idea of the *time history* of the behavior of the inventory system, he cannot effectively employ the analytical models.

A second limitation of the analytical approach relates to the fact that large and complex real-life systems cannot adequately be represented by conventional mathematical models. Thus, it would be extremely difficult to build an analytical model to represent an urban system that adequately incorporates the relevant economic, social, and political factors. Furthermore, even if we succeed in building appropriate mathematical models of such complex systems, it may not be possible to solve them by known analytical techniques.

Finally, analytical models are limited in terms of adequately treating uncertainties and dynamic aspects (time factors) of management problems. In the linear programming model, uncertainty regarding *some* of the parameters can be treated with sensitivity analysis (see Section 9.6), and dynamic aspects can sometimes be treated by employing a multiperiod (dynamic) linear programming model. However, if the uncertainty aspects are of major importance, the standard sensitivity analysis is an inefficient device to measure their impact. And, although dynamic programming models can solve some simplified problems, most of the complex dynamic systems cannot realistically be represented by analytical models. How, then, do we overcome these limitations of the analytical models? A possible answer is provided by the concept of simulation and the use of simulation models.[5]

---

[5] Simulation models can also be very difficult to construct and very costly to run. That is why management scientists recommend that, wherever feasible, analytical models should be used in preference to simulation models.

14.4
The Development and Utilization of Simulation Models

The reader will recall the basic structure of a decision model that was illustrated in Section 2.8 and shown graphically in Figure 2.8 on p. 41. It is desirable at this time that we revisit Figure 2.8 and recognize that after step 4 (development of the decision model—i.e., mathematical structure of the decision problem), we used

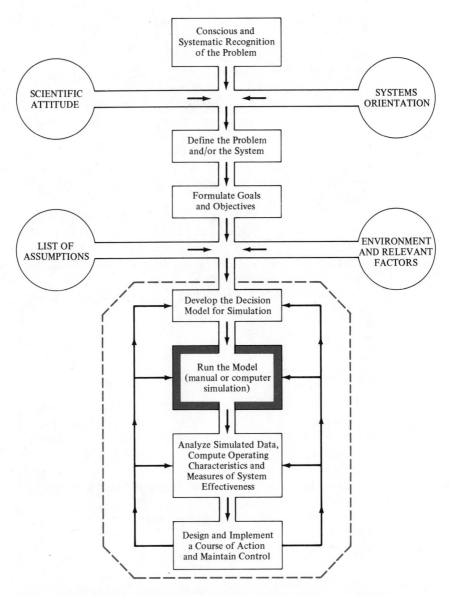

Figure 14.2. Planning, Running, and Implementing a Simulation Model.

the analytical approach to first derive the general solution to the model and then solve the specific problem. In the simulation approach, the modeling steps up to and including the development of the decision model (i.e., mathematical structure) are essentially the same. However, in simulation, after the decision model has been developed, we *run* the model (experiment with it by taking random samples and noting its behavior), as opposed to solving the model analytically. The steps involved in developing and utilizing a simulation model are shown in Figure 14.2.

14.4.1 DEVELOPMENT OF THE MODEL

Development of the *decision model for simulation* involves specification of the *system* that is being studied (e.g., an inventory system); *components of the system* (e.g., the firm, inventory items, customers); *criterion* variable (e.g., total cost); *decision* or *controllable variables* (e.g., order quantity); *uncontrollable variables* (e.g. demand); *parameters* (e.g., cost per unit); *functional* or *system relationships* (e.g., stockout costs = number of units short × stockout penalty per unit). In each simulation experiment, the elements of the decision model just described must be fully specified *before* we *run the model*. Since the focus of this chapter is on the simulation procedure, rather than on the development of the model, we shall not explicitly identify these elements in the illustrative examples. However, the reader is encouraged to think in terms of these elements when considering a simulation model.

A detailed coverage of the various steps shown in Figure 14.2 is beyond the scope of this book.[6] As mentioned earlier, our mission here is to give the reader a general understanding of the simulation approach. Hence, in the sections that follow, we concentrate essentially on the box that is entitled "Run the Model" in Figure 14.2. Furthermore, we present conceptual arguments as to how, in various illustrative examples, the simulated data are to be analyzed and interpreted for making managerial decisions.

14.4.2 RUNNING THE MODEL

Briefly, the task of running the model consists of three parts: (1) state the assumptions and structure of the mathematical model, (2) choose random numbers and translate them into unique values of appropriate stochastic variables, and (3) plug these simulated values into the mathematical model and calculate the numerical value of the criterion variable or other operating characteristics of the system. The results obtained from running the model are then utilized to improve the system.

The concepts described in this section will be illustrated in Sections 14.8 to 14.11 and in Chapter 15.

---

[6] The interested reader is referred to Naylor [1966].

14.5
The Idea of Experimentation (Random Sampling) in Monte Carlo Simulation

The procedure employed to simulate a probabilistic system is known as *Monte Carlo simulation.* The heart of Monte Carlo simulation is experimentation on the probabilistic components of the model. This is done by using some device that enables us to generate probabilistic or chance outcomes. The device is so constructed, or utilized, that the chance outcomes are based upon, and correspond to, the probability distribution(s) assumed by the model. The generation of chance outcomes is the result of random sampling (sampling is conducted by using the chosen device) from the model.

We shall illustrate the idea of random sampling by considering a simple probability distribution that represents the daily demand of fresh bread at a small grocery store. The demand distribution is compiled from the historical records kept by the owner and is shown in the first two columns of Table 14.1.[7] The third column of Table 14.1 contains the device that we shall use to generate chance outcomes.

Table 14.1

Daily Demand, D	Probability of Demand, p(D)	Number and Color of Balls
100	0.20	20 red
110	0.50	50 blue
120	0.30	30 yellow

We shall conduct the simulation experiment by drawing random samples from a bowl that contains 20 red balls, 50 blue balls, and 30 yellow balls. Note that the proportion of balls of a specific color corresponds *exactly* to the probability of a specific level of daily demand. This type of correspondence between the "chance outcome-generating device" and the specified probability distribution is no coincidence. It is, instead, the central requirement of Monte Carlo simulation.

We simulate the daily demand by the following procedure: Draw one ball at a time, note its color, and place the ball back in the bowl.[8] This is obviously an inductive procedure, and it stands to reason that if we repeat this experiment a

---

[7] We repeat what was said earlier regarding the interpretation of a given probability distribution (discrete or continuous) that represents the behavior of a component of a system. It gives us an *overall pattern,* but provides no direct clue regarding the outcome (e.g., daily demand) at a specific point in time. That is, the *time history* or *order* of demand cannot be inferred from the probability distribution. If we need the time history (or order) of the probabilistic phenomenon, we shall have to resort to simulation.

[8] This is *random sampling with replacement,* which is an operational definition of probabilistic simulation.

sufficiently large number of times, we shall reproduce the probability distribution of Table 14.1. That is, by using a device that generates chance or probabilistic outcomes, it is possible to simulate a real-life probabilistic system. This, then, is the general idea and concept of Monte Carlo simulation.

At this time, the reader might wonder and legitimately ask this question: If all that is produced by simulation is a reproduction of the assumed distribution of a specified variable, what is the advantage of simulation? We provide four answers. First, simulation can generate a *time history*. Second, although the probabilistic behavior of *individual* components of a system might be known (e.g., distribution of machine breakdowns and distribution of repair times in a maintenance system), we might not know the behavior of the *entire* system. Through simulation, we can study the behavior of the entire system and the interaction effects of its individual components without having to experiment on the system in real life. Third, simulation permits us to analyze the impact on the entire system of varying inputs through time (this capability is of enormous importance in the design of new systems). Fourth, through simulation (i.e., computer simulation) we can obtain, within seconds, an operational history of the system covering several months or years (*time compression*).

We further explain the idea of experimentation by conducting one simulation run. This corresponds to the second of the three parts involved in "running the model" as listed in Section 14.4.2. That is, we choose random numbers (or employ some other device that can generate chance outcomes) and translate them into corresponding *unique* values of the stochastic variables. Here, we shall experiment with the distribution of only one stochastic variable, "daily demand," D, for fresh bread. Our mission is to project, by simulation, the demand for fresh bread on each of the next five days (Monday through Friday). We accomplish this task by taking random samples from the set of 100 colored balls of Table 14.1 and then translating each sample to a *unique* value of daily demand. We proceed to take just five samples, with the understanding that the first sample corresponds to the customer demand on the first day, the second sample to the second day, and so on. A possible result of *one experimental run* consisting of five random samples is shown in the first two columns of Table 14.2. By noting the color of ball for each sample and referring to Table 14.1, we project (simulate) the customer demand on each of the five days as shown in the fourth column of Table 14.2. Note that in Table 14.2 the *expected value* (average) of the *simulated* demand is 112 units/day. If we calculated the *expected value* by *analytical* means, we find (see Table 14.1) that

$$\text{expected daily demand} = 100(0.2) + 110(0.5) + 120(0.3)$$

$$= 111 \text{ units}$$

It should be noted that the greater the number of experimental runs, the closer will be the simulated value to the value derived by analytical means.[9]

In Table 14.2, we have simulated only one experimental run covering 5 days. The manager might want to make several runs before basing a policy decision (e.g., optimum order quantity) on the results of simulation. How many runs to make? What should be the length of each run (in terms of time periods)? These are two of the most important questions in designing a simulation experiment. However, the discussion of these issues is beyond the scope of this book.[10]

[9] It should be emphasized that Monte Carlo procedure results in extreme *variability* in the *short run*, and yet it assures highly *predictable* behavior in the *long run*.

[10] For a detailed discussion of simulation design, we refer the reader to Naylor [1966].

Table 14.2

Sample Number	Color of Ball	Day of the Week	Simulated Demand
1	Blue	Monday	110
2	Blue	Tuesday	110
3	Yellow	Wednesday	120
4	Yellow	Thursday	120
5	Red	Friday	100

14.6
Devices for Generating Chance or Probabilistic Outcomes

In Section 14.5, we used colored balls to generate chance outcomes that simulated (imitated) daily demand for fresh bread at a specific grocery store. A number of other devices can also be used to generate such chance or probabilistic outcomes. The only requirement is that the device be so constructed, or utilized, that chance outcomes are based upon, and correspond to, the probability distribution(s) assumed by the model. In Table 14.3, we present a number of such devices.

It should be obvious that, instead of using physical devices, it is much more convenient and practical to conduct simulation experiments by the use of random numbers. A set of random numbers is provided in Table 14.5.

The random numbers can be used in manual simulation, as illustrated in several of the illustrative examples that follow. However, in real-life situations, simulation is conducted by digital computers, and chance outcomes are generated by random numbers that are either stored in the computer memory or provided, when needed, by computer subroutines.[11]

14.7
Monte Carlo Simulation—An Illustrative Example

In this section, we shall explain the mechanics and rationale of using random numbers and establish a five-step procedure for performing Monte Carlo simulation.

Step 1. *Obtain a probability distribution for each of the stochastic variables that must be analyzed.*

---

[11] The internally generated random numbers (i.e., produced by computer subroutines) are called *pseudo random numbers*. The term "pseudo" refers to the fact that these numbers are not truly random. They are generated by a deterministic mathematical process that is repeatable. The pseudo random numbers generated in this manner can pass certain statistical tests for randomness, and hence they can be considered as random numbers.

Table 14.3 *Devices for Generating Chance Outcomes*

Device	Comments
• An unbiased roulette wheel with 100 slots.	• Divide the slots in *exactly* the same proportion as the probability distribution of demand. This means that each slot is "associated with" a specific level of daily demand. Spin the wheel and simulate the demand by noting the specific slot where the ball stops.
• A perfectly balanced pointer wheel with a stationary outer ring calibrated from 0 to 1.	• Divide the outer ring in *exactly* the same proportion as the probability distribution of demand. This means that the outer ring has been segmented; and each segment is "associated with" a specific level of daily demand. Spin the wheel and simulate the demand by noting the segment in which the pointer stops.
• An urn containing 10 balls marked 0, 1, 2, 3, 4, 5, 6, 7, 8, and 9.	• Assign the 10 balls to different demand levels in such a way that their percentages correspond *exactly* to the probability distribution of demand. That is, for Table 14.1, let balls marked 0 and 1 correspond to a demand of 100 units; balls marked 2, 3, 4, 5, and 6 correspond to a demand of 110 units; and balls marked 7, 8, and 9 to a demand of 120 units. Choose a ball at random and simulate the demand by noting its number.
• A table of random numbers for manual sampling.	• A random number has the property that, in a sequence of numbers, it has the same probability of occurrence as any other number in the sequence. The random numbers are assigned in such a manner that their proportion *exactly* equals the probability distribution. That is, each random number is "associated with" a unique level of demand. We simulate demand by choosing the random number and noting its corresponding demand level.
• A computer program that is capable of either picking from its memory, or generating, random numbers.	• This device is used when the simulation is conducted with the aid of a digital computer. The rationale is the same: Each random number is "associated with" a unique outcome.

The probability distribution can be discrete or continuous and is obtained from sampling the actual process, historical data, or managerial forecast based on experience. The distributions can be empirical or they can be represented by such known distributions as Poisson, exponential, binomial, or normal.

We shall work with the probability distribution shown in column 2 of Table 14.4, and graphed in Figure 14.3a. That is, we are dealing with only one stochastic variable (daily demand).

Step 2. *Build a cumulative probability distribution corresponding to each probability distribution chosen for analysis in step 1.*

The cumulative probability distribution can be of the "less than or equal to" or "greater than or equal to" type. In this particular case, the cumulative distribution $P(\text{demand} \leq D)$ of the stochastic variable (daily demand) from step 1 is shown in the third column of Table 14.4 and is graphed in Figure 14.3b.

Step 3. *Assign an appropriate set of random numbers to represent each value, or range of values, of the stochastic variable(s) chosen in step 1.*

The task in this step is twofold. First, we have to decide on the entire range of random numbers and, second, we have to divide the range in appropriate intervals. Each interval corresponds to a *unique* outcome, and the length of an interval relates to the proportion of the corresponding unique outcome.

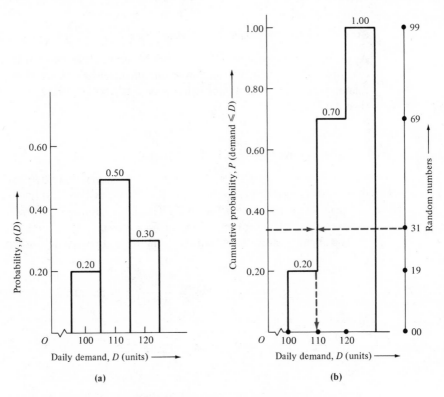

Figure 14.3. (a) Probability Distribution of Daily Demand; (b) Cumulative Probability Distribution of Daily Demand.

Table 14.4 *Probability Distribution of Daily Demand*

Daily Demand, D (in units)	Probability Distribution, p(D)	Cumulative Probability Distribution, P(demand ⩽ D)	Random Numbers
100	0.20	0.20	00–19
110	0.50	0.70	20–69
120	0.30	1.00	70–99

The range of numbers can be from 00 to 99 if probabilities are specified in two significant digits, 000 to 999 if probabilities are specified in three significant digits, and so on. From the chosen range a sequence of random digits is assigned to a specific outcome, corresponding *exactly* to the proportion of that outcome. Hence, since in Table 14.4 a daily demand of 100 units occurs only 20 percent of the time, we assign 20 random numbers to this outcome (00 to 19). Similarly, exactly 50 random numbers are assigned to a daily demand of 110 units (interval of 20 to 69), and exactly 30 numbers are assigned to a daily demand of 120 units (interval of 70 to 99).

In the fourth column of Table 14.4 we show the assignment of random numbers corresponding to each value of the probabilistic process (i.e., daily demand).

Step 4. *Conduct the simulation experiment (Run the Model) by means of random sampling.*

As mentioned in Section 14.4.2, the task of running the model (experimentation) consists of three parts. We shall illustrate the mechanics of experimentation with reference to our grocery store that sells fresh bread 5 days a week (Monday through Friday).

Assumptions and Structures of the Model

First, we make the assumption that daily sales equal daily demand. That is, the grocery store never runs out of bread. Second, we assume that the sale of each loaf of bread yields a *net profit* of $0.25. Third, we assume that our objective is to forecast expected (average) weekly profit by using simulation.

The above assumptions lead to the mathematical model shown in Equation (14.1):

$$\text{average profit per week} = \frac{5 \text{ days}}{\text{week}} \times \text{expected daily demand} \times \$0.25$$

or

$$R = 1.25(\text{EDD}) \tag{14.1}$$

where

$$R = \text{average profit per week}$$
$$\text{EDD} = \text{expected daily demand}$$

Choose Random Numbers and Translate Them into Unique Values of the Stochastic Variable

This part involves choosing a random number, manually or by computer. The random number is then translated into a *unique* value of the variable under study.

Each random number corresponds to a *unique* value of the probabilistic process, as can be seen from the nature of the random-number intervals in the fourth column of Table 14.4, and from Figure 14.3b. As we choose the random number, we are, in effect, entering the cumulative probability distribution from the vertical axis and hitting a *unique* daily demand on the horizontal axis.

We take a sample of 10 random numbers (i.e., we are simulating daily demand for 2 weeks) from a table of random numbers. A set of random numbers is provided in Table 14.5. We shall start sampling from the top of the first column and move down vertically.[12] The results of the 10 random samples are shown in Table 14.6.

The sequence of 10 random numbers in the first column of Table 14.6 represents the sequence of 10 samples. Each random number here is a sample of the daily demand for a specific day. These simulated daily sales are shown in the second column of Table 14.6. Let us now explain the construction of Table 14.6.

Our first random number is 31. This means, as can be ascertained from Table 14.4, that our first sample falls in the interval 20–69 and hence the simulated units sold on the first day is exactly 110. Our second random number is 70, and this implies that the simulated units sold for the second day is 120. Similarly, by utilizing Table 14.4, each chosen random number shown in Table 14.6 can be translated into a *unique* daily demand (units sold) for a specified day.[13]

Plug These Simulated Values into the Mathematical Model and Calculate the Numerical Value of the Criterion Variable or Other Operating Characteristics of the System

We see from Table 14.6 that

$$\text{EDD (for the first week)} = 114 \text{ units}$$
$$\text{EDD (for the second week)} = 110 \text{ units}$$

We can now plug these simulated values into the mathematical model given by (14.1). Hence,

$$R(\text{for the first week}) = 1.25(114) = \$142.50$$
$$R(\text{for the second week}) = 1.25(110) = \$137.50$$

---

[12] While taking random samples from a random-number table, we can start with any number in any column or row, and proceed vertically or horizontally to the next random number. That is, the sampling process should follow a *consistent* pattern and we should not jump from one number to another indiscriminately. Here, we shall start with the first random number in the first row and first column. Then we proceed down the first column and when the first column numbers are exhausted, we can begin to work on the second column, and so on. One more comment is in order at this time. If we are taking random samples for more than one stochastic variable, it is a good idea to use different random numbers for each variable, since using the same random numbers would imply independence among different variables, an assumption that may or may not be valid.

[13] The single "run" here consisted of 10 days. It projected the behavior of the system for 2 weeks. Obviously, we could have increased the sample size (more than 10 days) or conducted more than one run.

Table 14.5 *Random-Number Table**

31	28	18	10	23	22	64	47	64	55	20	08	73	58	23	68	15	05	98	02	65	49	55	01	44
70	57	67	23	50	96	71	90	54	97	38	51	52	68	05	48	65	41	20	68	81	75	60	38	49
53	60	16	61	30	58	35	21	75	64	51	91	16	21	17	39	78	07	66	15	56	23	57	15	57
86	17	71	47	09	08	90	59	06	04	59	87	02	88	80	64	86	75	54	56	96	11	35	80	97
32	64	43	25	99	16	30	54	73	53	63	72	22	97	12	60	77	90	86	69	37	70	82	36	48
78	20	68	39	06	43	90	16	10	28	03	21	60	00	74	78	11	97	74	00	47	91	15	03	63
26	27	47	34	87	97	28	63	20	04	61	84	49	97	37	46	17	67	77	75	83	67	47	03	18
64	58	24	35	52	31	91	22	62	83	19	28	50	22	64	54	42	67	60	74	91	17	36	72	10
45	61	19	70	01	76	72	22	70	82	88	16	72	88	80	97	19	46	73	59	11	01	62	78	16
12	30	97	68	72	81	32	90	52	04	20	69	31	24	92	52	74	26	47	29	85	77	83	06	70
99	23	92	98	47	50	02	85	04	23	62	94	57	89	72	59	54	31	75	89	67	17	77	25	00
52	41	03	37	85	91	76	22	55	62	46	48	17	65	38	70	74	85	71	28	85	23	92	95	04
43	47	35	04	66	95	51	19	36	22	83	09	82	55	73	06	83	59	23	99	09	06	37	90	05
84	48	60	05	72	10	64	58	00	13	90	83	76	20	63	39	20	72	19	71	94	34	49	48	68
38	19	91	38	70	59	54	14	91	26	20	38	99	08	25	46	65	97	16	11	91	75	64	15	76
40	07	27	09	17	69	02	87	98	10	47	34	18	20	58	71	74	17	32	23	93	92	35	55	87
19	90	69	64	65	51	17	63	35	87	46	02	71	28	27	47	20	07	92	00	28	05	16	96	10
87	02	22	38	45	62	81	38	30	86	19	18	37	44	99	02	00	18	38	47	38	47	29	10	77
83	57	82	37	02	47	38	82	02	47	83	37	29	37	19	28	19	92	72	82	62	28	19	03	72
73	28	64	19	37	28	26	28	29	09	00	72	18	36	81	36	46	77	18	23	77	19	01	39	56
84	29	36	44	91	11	39	92	92	63	82	16	37	28	46	28	93	74	92	01	03	95	68	82	99
29	83	80	30	84	82	19	36	63	92	40	92	38	67	72	38	19	12	99	03	00	01	72	89	27
09	58	27	34	33	19	16	68	39	43	13	34	13	82	19	75	50	65	11	15	33	27	43	49	63
02	41	09	60	21	45	62	38	97	42	84	18	42	61	08	83	98	23	09	55	80	51	25	59	46
20	13	59	97	91	68	58	38	18	38	00	03	52	43	93	15	12	18	82	50	06	53	71	15	11
54	55	13	20	70	33	82	28	24	66	04	22	99	66	64	38	05	71	90	08	23	16	33	85	68
57	68	61	37	30	94	81	21	84	81	48	64	45	69	32	98	09	74	59	37	19	06	56	98	02
00	16	45	84	18	33	38	37	39	97	98	76	78	63	98	40	58	73	58	54	21	02	29	62	69
83	28	82	36	91	09	81	24	55	21	57	22	92	50	49	20	35	46	61	97	85	62	08	62	88
95	14	80	68	53	34	79	75	32	54	70	68	46	93	45	04	93	02	84	40	12	33	29	09	14
78	40	29	92	21	20	63	46	16	45	41	44	66	87	26	78	36	57	03	28	77	10	07	89	85
80	62	74	64	26	23	57	99	84	51	29	41	11	66	30	41	40	97	15	72	31	11	42	59	46
23	08	87	23	90	69	65	07	39	85	96	62	74	75	90	70	04	10	86	23	21	88	75	35	97
31	26	65	08	36	08	30	22	68	27	92	06	69	77	16	14	84	34	36	23	43	63	28	36	51
72	70	81	68	17	31	54	16	54	22	09	00	75	02	07	91	93	72	93	16	48	57	27	58	37
90	88	22	92	49	56	85	89	61	84	84	19	32	56	54	85	26	83	79	40	04	30	46	29	24
60	14	25	68	61	37	74	68	79	87	10	67	14	96	92	28	66	44	67	40	79	82	23	53	09
34	56	82	00	93	47	29	47	58	29	02	17	38	46	8	29	93	64	06	99	00	16	12	08	11
82	36	92	10	03	83	63	92	26	27	29	63	91	73	10	10	39	28	84	82	92	62	90	11	88
29	71	83	72	92	01	94	72	39	49	59	92	72	19	00	09	18	38	72	39	03	16	20	69	16

* This table was generated by David Cadden, Department of Management, Baruch College. A Texas Instruments SR-51 calculator was used to generate the numbers.

It is obvious that by following the above procedures for, say 52 weeks, we shall obtain a distribution of weekly profit for the whole year. For that matter, with the aid of a computer, we could "run the model" for several years in order to trace the behavior of *R*.

Table 14.6 *Simulated Daily Demand*
(Sample Size = 10)

Random Number	Daily Demand (units sold)
First Week	
31	110
70	120
53	110
86	120
32	110
Expected daily demand = 114 units	
Second Week	
78	120
26	110
64	110
45	110
12	100
Expected daily demand = 110 units	

Step 5. *Design and implement a course of action and maintain control.*

In this step, we study the simulated probability distribution(s) and use them for estimating parameters and taking managerial actions. For example, the simulated profit distribution can be used to study the pattern of profits, and to obtain an estimate of *mean* and *standard deviation* of profit. Should the pattern of profits be unsatisfactory to the manager, new ways to improve demand or improve profit margin can be investigated. As in other managerial situations, the system is continually monitored for the purpose of maintaining control.

We shall always apply these five steps in the simulation examples that follow. However, for the sake of economy, we might combine them and as such we might not specifically identify each step.

Before leaving this section, we note that in our grocery store example, we simulated only one stochastic variable (i.e., daily demand). However, in most real-life problems we need to simulate the behavior of several stochastic variables and then note their impact on the criterion variable (e.g., total profit). We illustrate such a case next.

14.8
Simulation and Financial Analysis

When simulation is used in financial analysis, the term applied is *risk analysis.* The purpose of risk analysis is to consider the impact of various factors (selling price, market size, market growth rate, etc.) on a financial parameter such as ROI. The simulation model takes samples from the probability distributions of *each* of the relevant factors and then computes the rate of return on investment. For each trial, the output is a specific rate of return, and thus the result of several trials is a *distribution* of ROI. From this distribution we can calculate the *expected value* as well as the *standard deviation* of ROI.[14] A conceptual representation of this type of simulation for financial analysis is shown in Figure 14.4.

We shall illustrate, in a very rudimentary fashion, the idea of risk analysis (i.e., financial simulation) with the aid of an example.

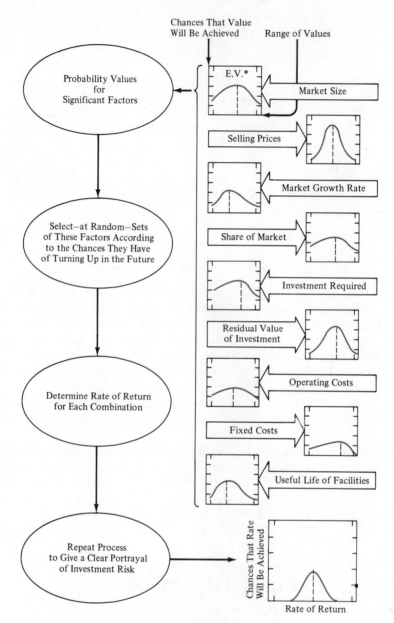

Figure 14.4. Simulation for Investment Planning. * = Expected Value. From David B. Hertz, "Risk Analysis in Capital Investment," *Harvard Business Review*, January–February 1964, Copyright © 1963 by the President and Fellows of Harvard College; all rights reserved. Reprinted by permission.

[14] The availability of standard deviation is helpful in assessing the *quality* of risk. See Appendix A.

Example 14.1

An entrepreneur is considering the purchase of a small business firm that has been operating in the local area for the last 10 years. He knows the local conditions and some of his friends also own similar business outlets in the neighboring communities. Our entrepreneur is familiar with Monte Carlo simulation and he would like to obtain an idea regarding the difference, positive or negative, between sales revenue and costs. Based on marketing research and in consultation with his friends, he projects a probability distribution of monthly costs (Table 14.7) and a probability distribution of monthly revenue (Table 14.8). The *expected* monthly cost is $23,000 and the *expected* monthly revenue is $24,800. Since we have to conduct simulation, we construct cumulative probability distributions of monthly costs and revenues and assign appropriate random numbers, as shown in Tables 14.7 and 14.8.

Table 14.7

Monthly Cost, Y (thousands of dollars)	Probability, $p(Y)$	Cumulative Probability, $P(cost \leqslant Y)$	Random Numbers
21	0.10	0.10	00–09
22	0.15	0.25	10–24
23	0.50	0.75	25–74
24	0.15	0.90	75–89
25	0.10	1.00	90–99
Expected value of monthly cost = $23,000			

Table 14.8

Monthly Revenue, X (thousands of dollars)	Probability, $p(X)$	Cumulative Probability, $P(revenue \leqslant X)$	Random Numbers
22	0.08	0.08	00–07
23	0.12	0.20	08–19
24	0.20	0.40	20–39
25	0.30	0.70	40–69
26	0.17	0.87	70–86
27	0.08	0.95	87–94
28	0.05	1.00	95–99
Expected value of monthly revenue = $24,800			

Our mathematical model here is:

$$Z = X - Y \tag{14.2}$$

where

Z = monthly net = monthly revenue − monthly cost

X = monthly revenue

Y = monthly cost

Next, we simulate the system for 25 months by taking 25 samples from the monthly cost distribution, and 25 samples from the monthly revenue distribution. Then, for each sample, we compute the simulated monthly net, Z, by plugging the simulated values of the two stochastic variables (X and Y) into the model given by (14.2). The results of the simulation are shown in Table 14.9. The simulated monthly net, shown in the last column of Table 14.9, can now be represented as a probability distribution (see Table 14.10). The probability distribution of monthly net, shown in Table 14.10, has an *expected value* of 1.96 ($1,960) and a standard deviation of 1.661 ($1.661). This simulated picture of the potential investment can be compared with other available opportunities before the decision to invest is finalized.

It should be emphasized that one measure of the *quality* of risk of a proposed investment is the *standard deviation*, or *variance* of the distribution of return on investment (see Appendix A). For example, consider the two hypothetical distributions representing returns on investment (ROI) on two different projects

Table 14.9

Sample Number	Random Number for Cost (Use Column 2 of Table 14.5)	Simulated Cost, Y	Random Number for Sales (Use Column 3 of Table 14.5)	Simulated Revenue, X	Simulated Monthly Net, Z = X − Y
1	28	23	18	23	0
2	57	23	67	25	2
3	60	23	16	23	0
4	17	22	71	26	4
5	64	23	43	25	2
6	20	22	68	25	3
7	27	23	47	25	2
8	58	23	24	24	1
9	61	23	19	23	0
10	30	23	97	28	5
11	23	22	92	27	5
12	41	23	03	22	−1
13	47	23	35	24	1
14	48	23	60	25	2
15	19	22	91	27	5
16	07	21	27	24	3
17	90	25	69	25	0
18	02	21	22	24	3
19	57	23	82	26	3
20	28	23	64	25	2
21	29	23	36	24	1
22	83	24	80	26	2
23	58	23	27	24	1
24	41	23	09	23	0
25	13	22	59	25	3

Table 14.10 *Probability Distribution of Simulated Monthly Net*

Monthly Net, Z	Observed Frequency	Probability, p(Z)
−1	1	0.04
0	5	0.20
1	4	0.16
2	6	0.24
3	5	0.20
4	1	0.04
5	3	0.12

(*A* and *B*), as shown in Figure 14.5. Note that the distributions have the same *expected* ROI, but the variance of project *A* is much higher than that of project *B*. Hence, other things being equal, project *B* is less risky and, accordingly, should be the preferred choice for investment.

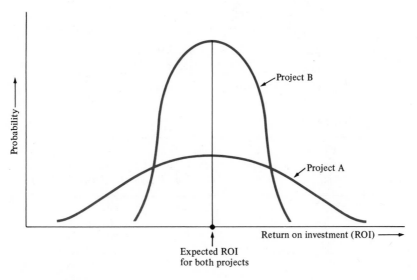

Figure 14.5

14.9
Simulation and Inventory Control

It is quite useful to analyze different inventory policies (in terms of their cost or profit consequences) by using simulation procedures. For example, by using simulation we can investigate the effect of different inventory policies (e.g., different combinations of order quantity, Q, and reorder point, R) on a probabilistic inventory system.

Let us consider an inventory system that is represented by the demand distribution shown in Table 14.11, and by the leadtime distribution shown in Table 14.12.

Assume that we want to simulate and compare these two inventory policies:[15]

first policy: $Q = 50, R = 30$

second policy: $Q = 45, R = 25$

In our inventory system we have two stochastic variables (*demand* and *leadtime*). As before, we build cumulative distributions and assign appropriate random numbers in the case of each stochastic variable, as shown in Tables 14.11 and 14.12.

The next task would be to simulate the behavior of the inventory system for a specified period of time by random sampling from the two distributions and calculating the daily status of such system variables as beginning inventory, demand, ending inventory, inventory on order, leadtime, stockout units, and so on. The procedure for simulating would consist of the same steps as outlined in Section 14.7. Finally, various simulated values would be plugged in a specified inventory model for cost minimization or profit maximization.

It should be noted that the inventory system will have to be simulated for *each* inventory policy. Then, the cost or profit consequence of each policy can be calculated and compared. The reader is encouraged to simulate this system for 25 days and calculate corresponding total cost, T, for each policy, assuming that

holding cost, $h = \$1/\text{unit}/\text{day}$
ordering cost, $S = \$20/\text{order}$
stockout penalty, $K = \$5/\text{unit}$

Table 14.11

Daily Demand, D (units)	Probability, $p(D)$	Cumulative Probability, $P(\text{demand} \leqslant D)$	Random Numbers
10	0.20	0.20	00–19
11	0.50	0.70	20–69
12	0.30	1.00	70–99

Table 14.12

Leadtime, L (days)	Probability, $p(L)$	Cumulative Probability, $P(\text{leadtime} \leqslant L)$	Random Numbers
1	0.10	0.10	00–09
2	0.30	0.40	10–39
3	0.60	1.00	40–99

[15] The Q and R combinations can be calculated by the inventory models discussed in Chapters 12 and 13 under assumed values of holding costs, ordering costs, stockout costs, and so on.

14.10
Simulation and Network Models

In Section 6.8, we analyzed a PERT network by applying analytical procedures. We can analyze the same network by simulation and trace the behavior of the network during a specified number of runs. For *each* activity of the network we need: (1) probability distribution of completion time, (2) cumulative probability of completion time, and (3) associated random numbers. Then we conduct simulation by taking random samples from each completion time distribution and, *for each run*, complete the following tasks by using appropriate models: (1) determine the critical path (and thus identify activities on the critical path), (2) compute the project completion time (this can be converted into a distribution of project completion time), and (3) compute the relative frequency with which each activity falls on the critical path during the simulated runs (*critical path index* of the activity).

Let us illustrate the idea of simulating a PERT network by considering the network in Figure 14.6. Note that we have three stochastic variables: activities 1–2, 2–3, and 1–3. In Table 14.13 we show the necessary date for simulation. The notation $P(\leqslant)$ implies P(completion time $\leqslant T$). That is, it gives the cumulative probability that the completion time of an activity is "less than or equal to" some specified number T.

We simulate the system for 10 runs by taking random samples from each of the three probability distributions (follow the same procedure as applied in previous

Table 14.13

Activity 1–2				Activity 2–3				Activity 1–3			
Completion Time, T	$p(T)$	$P(\leqslant)$	Random Numbers	Completion Time, T	$p(T)$	$P(\leqslant)$	Random Numbers	Completion Time, T	$p(T)$	$P(\leqslant)$	Random Numbers
7	0.20	0.20	00–19	8	0.30	0.30	00–29	16	0.40	0.40	00–39
8	0.50	0.70	20–69	9	0.40	0.70	30–69	17	0.20	0.60	40–59
9	0.30	1.00	70–99	10	0.30	1.00	70–99	18	0.40	1.00	60–99

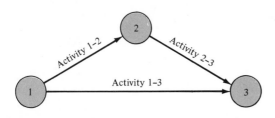

Figure 14.6. PERT Network.

examples). The results are summarized in Table 14.14.[16] The critical path index shows the relative frequency (probability) with which an activity falls on the critical path.

The analysis by simulation is more informative in the sense that it indicates the relative critical path index (and hence importance) of each activity.

The procedure for simulating a PERT network consists of the following steps:

Step 1. *Obtain a probability distribution of each activity, and calculate t_e (expected completion time) and σ (variance) of each activity.*

Step 2. *Build cumulative distributions and assign appropriate random numbers.*

Step 3. *By using random numbers, generate "time consumed" for each activity in the network. Then record the critical path and the project completion time.*

This step completes one simulation run.

Step 4. *Repeat step 3 several times in order to generate simulated behavior of the network.*

The output of the simulation experiment is a distribution of project completion time (as opposed to one project completion time obtained by the analytical method). The distribution will have its own t_e and $\sigma_{project}$, and they can then be used for conducting a more realistic probabilistic analysis.

Table 14.14

Simulation Run	Critical Path	Activities on Critical Path			Completion Time (days)
		1–2	2–3	1–3	
1	1–2–3 and 1–3	×	×	×	16
2	1–2–3 and 1–3	×	×	×	18
3	1–2–3	×	×		17
4	1–3			×	18
5	1–2–3 and 1–3	×	×	×	17
6	1–3			×	18
7	1–3			×	17
8	1–2–3	×	×		17
9	1–2–3	×	×		17
10	1–3			×	18
Frequency of activity on critical path		6	6	7	
Critical path index of activity		0.6	0.6	0.7	

[16] We have used column 3 of Table 14.5 to enter the simulated values of the completion times of activities 1–2, 2–3, and 1–3.

14.11
Computer Languages (Programs) for Simulation Models

As shown in Figure 14.2, after the decision model for simulation has been developed (i.e., specification of the system, system components, functional relationships that relate system components, criterion variable, decision variables, uncontrollable factors, and parameters), we can *run* the model (simulate the system) either manually or by using computers. In all of the illustrative examples presented thus far, we have conducted manual simulation. However, in large-scale and real-life problems, simulation experiments are almost always performed by using computers.

The first step in computer simulation is to develop a flow chart[17] (a step-by-step schematic description of how the system operates). For example, a flow chart of how we generate simulated demand for Table 14.4 is shown in Figure 14.7. The flow chart is then translated (coded) into a computer language. The computer language can be a *general-purpose* (e.g., FORTRAN, ALGOL, COBOL) or a *special-purpose* simulation language (e.g., SIMSCRIPT, GPSS, DYNAMO, GASP). The general-purpose languages have the advantage of being flexible, but they present serious programming difficulties. The special-purpose simulation languages are restricted in scope, but they are very suitable for specific areas (e.g., queuing, scheduling, and production problems). The special-purposes languages have special output formats and they include such subroutines as random-number generators.

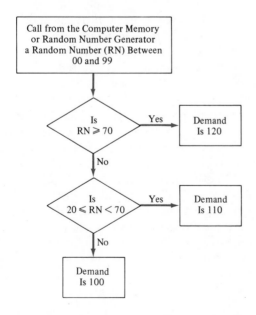

Figure 14.7. Flow Chart for Generating Simulated Demand for Table 14.4.

[17] A flow chart is desirable even in manual simulation.

In Table 14.15, we provide a list of selected special-purpose simulation languages, along with the name of the company that can be contacted for further details.

Table 14.15 *Computer Languages and Programs for Simulation*

Company or Source	*Computer Language or Program*
Elliott Corporation	* Elliott Simulation Package (ESP)
International Business Machine Corporation	* General Activity Simulation Package (GASP II)
	* General Purpose Simulation System (GPSS)
Massachusetts Institute of Technology	* DYNAMO II
Rand Corporation	* Simscript 1.5
Univac Corporation	* Simula 67
	* Simpac

14.12
Classification of Simulation Models[18]

Simulation models can be classified into four main categories: (1) Monte Carlo simulation, (2) heuristic programming, (3) operational gaming, and (4) artificial intelligence. We have already discussed Monte Carlo simulation. In this section we present a very brief description of the remaining three categories.

Heuristic programming refers to a method of problem solving based on the application of "rules of thumb" or "shortcuts." A *heuristic* is an aid to discovery, or a rule of thumb to solve a particular problem; and a *heuristic program* is a computer program consisting of a set of heuristics to be applied at different stages of the solution process. Heuristic programming is useful in solving two specific types of problems. First, it is used in solving large-size, combinatorial problems because by applying heuristics at each decision point, one of several possible paths is chosen, thereby considerably reducing the size of the problem as well as the computational effort.[19] Second, it is applied for simulating decision processes that are applied in solving specific ill-structured problems.[20] The purpose of simulating the decision-making activities of ill-structured decision problems is to delegate to the computer those duties that the heuristic program can effectively imitate. Heuristic programs do not yield optimal solutions (because they simply do not evaluate all the available alternatives). Instead, heuristic programs develop "good-enough" or satisfactory solutions within the cost or budgetary constraints.

[18] This section is adapted from Section 13.4 of Levey and Loomba [1973].

[19] Wiest [1966, p. 132].

[20] Clarkson and Meltzer [1960].

Heuristic programs have been applied with a varying degree of success to such problems as: (1) assembly line balancing, (2) facilities layout, (3) portfolio selection, (4) job shop scheduling, (5) electric motor design, (6) warehouse location, (7) inventory control, (8) resource allocation to large projects, and (9) department store pricing.[21]

Operational gaming is the name given to simulation experiments in which human beings are involved in a role-playing capacity. The two major sub-categories of this branch of simulation are: (1) business games, and (2) military games. Operational gaming can be used for educational, training, experimental, and problem-solving purposes—although in many cases it lacks realism. In operational gaming, we simulate a decision environment within which real decision makers make decisions under competitive conditions. An observation of the decisions and their consequences sheds light on the behavior of the decision maker as well as the decision system. Although used mainly to study and improve decision-making skills under competitive situations, operational gaming has also been applied in many functional areas under a noncompetitive environment.

The history of military games dates back to 1780, when the Prussians used war games for purposes of training their army. Since that time war games have been, and are being employed, by all major powers in order to design and test military strategies under simulated environments. Since World War II, the idea of gaming has been extended to study business systems, organizational behavior, and political problems. A business game may be defined "as a *sequential* decision-making exercise structured around a model of a business operation in which participants assume the role of managing the simulated operation."[22] Business gaming is very much akin to educational and training methods, such as case study, role playing, sensitivity training—except that a business game centers around a model to be manipulated within the boundaries established by a set of rules. The model consists of a set of mathematical statements that simulate the decision system and define the relationships between decisions and operating results. The participants play by a set of rules that provide for *sequential* decision making, to bring dynamic realism to the game.

Artificial intelligence refers to that branch of simulation models that attempts to imitate purposeful behavior. It is essentially an extension of heuristic programming designed to duplicate behavior patterns of individual decision makers. It is simultaneously the boldest and most difficult branch of simulation—since it attempts to simulate human thinking. Herbert Simon cites computer programs that have been developed for proving geometrical theorems, playing checkers, and playing chess.[23] Artificial intelligence is based on the familiar components of problem solving: search, pattern recognition, inductive inference, and learning.[24]

---

[21] Wiest [1966, p. 129].

[22] Greenlaw et al. [1962, p. 5].

[23] Simon [1960, pp. 30–32].

[24] The reader is referred to Meinhart [1966], Minsky [1966], Jackson [1974], Feigenbaum and Feldman [1963], and Newell and Simon [1958] for relevant material on artificial intelligence.

14.13
Additional Remarks

In view of the previous discussion and recognizing that computers are an integral part of simulation experiments, we present the following definition of a simulation model.

> A simulation model is computer-assisted experimentation on a mathematical structure of a real-life system in order to describe and evaluate the system behavior through real time under a variety of assumptions.

This definition implies that there are at least four distinct parts to any computer simulation model. First, there must be a mathematical structure representing the essential properties of the real-life system that it imitates. Second, experiments are conducted on the mathematical structure under a variety of assumed conditions to explore the impact of changes in inputs on a set of output variables. Third, provisions are built into the model for advancing time (fixed or variable time increments). Fourth, the experimental results are evaluated in terms of identifying preferred decision rules, alternative courses of action, and contemplated policies.

The essential differences between analytical and simulation models can be summarized as follows. First, while both possess mathematical structures, simulation models cannot be "solved" by mathematical techniques. Second, the mathematical structure of simulation models is of a different type. It *describes* what *is*, and traces information flow of the problem—what happens, where does it happen, and in what sequence, and so on. These relationships are traced through time by experimentation in order to arrive at a solution. The mathematical structure of the analytical model, on the other hand, reflects relationships that are not instructions or information flows. The third element of distinction is that while analytical models yield *optimum* solutions, the solutions obtained through simulation models are usually only "good-enough" or near-optimal solutions. Fourth, while simulation models are essentially *descriptive*, analytical models are usually *prescriptive*. The simulation models are descriptive in the sense that they trace and describe the behavior of a system through time. From an analysis of this behavior, it is possible to design a system that attempts to minimize costs. Hence, we see that even though simulation models are descriptive, it is possible to identify, in a prescriptive sense, preferred courses of action from the simulated results.

The fifth, and a very important, element of distinction between analytical and simulation models relates to causality. In analytical models, the relationships among various variables are structured on the clear assumption that there is causality between certain system outcomes and a set of input variables. In simulation models, however, it is often not possible to clearly assign causality—we simply *observe* changes in certain output variables as changes in specified input variables are made.

14.14
Summary

The purpose of this chapter was to describe the ideas, concepts, and methodology of simulation. We explained the difference between analytical and simulation procedures for solving mathematical models.

Monte Carlo simulation is one of four categories of simulation models. Monte Carlo simulation deals with probabilistic systems and is based on the idea of random sampling. Several devices for taking random samples were listed. Then we provided a few illustrative examples of Monte Carlo simulation in the areas of financial analysis, inventory control, and network models.

A very brief discussion of computer programs for simulation models was presented. Finally, we evolved a descriptive definition of a simulation model and listed the essential differences between analytical and simulation models.

References

Brigham, E., and J. Pappas. *Managerial Economics*, 2nd ed. New York: Holt, Rinehart and Winston, 1976.

Carlson, J. G., and M. J. Misshauk. *Introduction to Gaming: Management Decisions Simulations*. New York: John Wiley & Sons, Inc., 1972.

Clarkson, G. P., and A. H. Meltzer. "Portfolio Selection: A Heuristic Approach." *Journal of Finance*, Vol. 15, No. 4 (Dec. 1960), 465–480.

Feigenbaum, E., and J. Feldman. *Computers and Thought*. New York: McGraw-Hill Book Company, 1963.

Forrester, J. W. *World Dynamics*. Cambridge, Mass.: Wright-Allen Press, 1971.

Goronzy, F. "A Simulation Model of Corporate Growth." *Management International Review*, Vol. 12, No. 4–5 (1972), 77–94.

Greenlaw, P. S., et al. *Business Simulation*. Englewood Cliffs, N.J.: Prentice-Hall, Inc., 1962.

Hertz, D. B. "Risk Analysis in Capital Investment." *Harvard Business Review* (Jan.–Feb. 1964), 102.

Jackson, P. C. *Introduction to Artificial Intelligence*. New York: Petrocelli/Charter, Inc., 1974.

Levey, S., and N. P. Loomba. *Health Care Administration*. Philadelphia: J. B. Lippincott Company, 1973.

Meinhart, W. A. "Artificial Intelligence: Computer Simulation of Human Cognitive and Social Processes, and Management Thought." *Academy of Management Journal*, Vol. 9 (Dec. 1966), 294–307.

Minsky, M. L. "Artificial Intelligence." *Scientific American*, Vol. 215 (Sept. 1966), 246–260.

Naylor, T. H., et al. *Computer Simulation Techniques*. New York: John Wiley & Sons, Inc., 1966.

Newell, S., and H. Simon. "Chess Playing Programs and the Problem of Complexity." *IBM Journal of Research and Development*, Vol. 2, No. 4 (Oct. 1958), 320–335.

Norton, J. H. "Simulation for Planning and Review." *Management Review*, Vol. 61, No. 2 (Feb. 1972), 18–27.

Simon, H. A. *The New Science of Management Decision*. New York: Harper & Row, Publishers, 1960.

Wagner, J., and L. J. Pryor. "Simulation and the Budget: An Integrated Model." *Sloan Management Review*, Vol. 12, No. 2 (Winter 1971), 45–58.

Wiest, J. R. "Heuristic Programs for Decision Making." *Harvard Business Review*, (Sept.–Oct. 1966), 129–143.

Review Questions and Problems

14.1. Distinguish between analytical and simulation procedures for deriving solutions to mathematical models.

14.2. What are the advantages and limitations of analytical models? Simulation models?

14.3. What is Monte Carlo simulation? Describe the idea of experimentation (random sampling) in simulation.

14.4. List a number of devices for generating chance outcomes. What are random numbers? How are they generated?

14.5. What is a heuristic? Describe the idea of heuristic programming.

14.6. What is operational gaming? Artificial intelligence?

14.7. A man at a skeet shooting range is using a single-barrel shotgun. His time to reload (i.e., time between firings and being in position to aim) has the distribution shown in Table 14.16. His time to track a clay pigeon and fire is given by the distribution shown in Table 14.17. The probability of a hit varies with the tracking time and is shown in Table 14.18. Assume that he begins with a loaded gun and the time is given in seconds. If clay pigeons are launched on his command, what is the total time for completing 15 shots? What is the total number of hits?

Table 14.16

Reload Time	Probability
8	0.15
9	0.25
10	0.40
11	0.20

Table 14.17

Tracking Time	Probability
4	0.05
5	0.15
6	0.30
7	0.40
8	0.10

Table 14.18

Tracking Time	p(hit)	p(miss)
4	0.80	0.20
5	0.75	0.25
6	0.50	0.50
7	0.35	0.65
8	0.25	0.75

14.8. The Federal Aviation Agency (FAA) is evaluating two landing approach systems. Each system is designed to: (1) detect light civilian aircraft, (2) determine its range and heading, and (3) feed information to the pilot for a glide-approach landing. The evaluation is based on cost, detection range, and control range. System 101 has a cost of $1,101,000, while System 707 has a cost of $1,875,000. The distributions for detection and control for each system are given in Table 14.19.

Table 14.19

System 101		System 707	
Detection Range	Probability	Detection Range	Probability
35	0.10	41	0.15
34	0.25	40	0.25
33	0.35	39	0.40
32	0.20	38	0.20
31	0.10		
Control Range	Probability	Control Range	Probability
32	0.15	34	0.05
31	0.25	33	0.20
30	0.35	32	0.23
29	0.25	31	0.27
		30	0.10
		29	0.09
		28	0.06

Simulate both systems for 10 aircraft. If the FAA uses the following utility function, choose the best system.

$$U = \log[\text{detection range} + 1.2(\text{control range}) - (\text{cost}/\$1,000,000)]$$

14.9. The Nevor-Cey-Dye Hospital is seeking to simulate a fleet of ambulances from a cost-effective standpoint. The vehicles must be purchased in lots of threes. Each vehicle has a unit cost of $15,000, which is fully depreciated at the end of the year, and an annual operating cost of $1,750. The number of calls an ambulance can respond to is distributed as shown in Table 14.20. The number of calls the hospital receives every day is distributed as shown in Table 14.21.

Table 14.20

Calls/Day/Ambulance	Probability
5	0.05
6	0.10
7	0.30
8	0.40
9	0.15

Table 14.21

Total Calls/Day	Probability
45	0.10
46	0.15
47	0.20
48	0.25
49	0.20
50	0.10

If the hospital assigns a "paper cost" of $100 for each failure to respond, determine the number of vehicles that will minimize cost over a 10-day period. (Assume that the distribution in Table 14.20 holds for all ambulances. Also assume 365 days in a year.)

14.10. Mr. Manuel Laboor has just been appointed manager of inventory control at Snafu, Inc. Not being familiar with inventory control theory (he did not read Chapters 12 and 13 of this book), he has decided to analyze the inventory system by simulation. He has gathered information on the leadtime and demand distributions, shown in Tables 14.22 and 14.23, for a particular item. Simulate the system for 20 days, to determine the reorder point R. (Hint: Determine average leadtime and average demand.)

Table 14.22

Leadtime (days)	Probability
4	0.20
5	0.50
6	0.20
7	0.10

Table 14.23

Demand/Day	Probability
100	0.10
110	0.20
120	0.40
130	0.15
140	0.10
150	0.05

14.11. Paper Pushers, Inc., wholesalers of stationery items, wants to determine the order size for desk calendars. The demand and leadtime are probabilistic and their distributions are given in Tables 14.24 and 14.25, respectively.

Table 14.24

Demand/week (thousands)	Probability
0	0.2
10	0.4
20	0.3
30	0.1

Table 14.25

Leadtime (weeks)	Probability
2	0.3
3	0.4
4	0.3

The incremental cost of placing an order is $50 and the holding cost for 1,000 units is $1/week. The stockout cost is $10/thousand. The inventory manager is considering two policies: quantity per order is 50,000 units and reorder point is 20,000 units; and quantity per order is 40,000 units and reorder point is 30,000 units. Choose the least-cost policy by simulation. Assume the following: (1) The beginning inventory is 30,000 units; (2) no back orders are permitted; (3) each order is placed at the beginning of the week following the drop in inventory level to (or below) the reorder point, R; and (4) goods are received at the beginning of the week. Simulate to the time when the goods from the 5th order have arrived.

14.12. The Jaws Loan Company has been examining the possibility of using simulation to study their cash flow. A study of past records shows the probability of rejecting an applicant and the size of loans (Table 14.26). The company charges 20 percent interest on all loans, collected at the end of each year. The debtor has the option of repaying any portion of the loan at interest collection time. The collectors have seen that there is a difference between repayment for loans of $500 or less, and those loans greater than $500. The probability of repayment at the end of 1 year is shown in

Tables 14.27 and 14.28. Simulate 1 year's cash flow generated by 10 applicants. Assume *all* loans are made on the same day and that *at least* the interest is repaid at the end of 1 year.

Table 14.26

Loan Size	Probability
Rejection ($0)	0.05
$100	0.10
250	0.40
500	0.20
1,000	0.15
2,000	0.10

Table 14.27

Percent Repayment for Loans of $500 or less	Probability
0	0.05
10	0.10
20	0.50
40	0.15
60	0.12
100	0.08

Table 14.28

Percent Repayment for $1,000 and $2,000 Loans	Probability
0	0.05
20	0.15
40	0.20
50	0.25
60	0.30
100	0.05

14.13. Only one patrol car is assigned to answer calls in a specific precinct sector. The time required to answer and service each call is distributed as shown in Table 14.29. If calls arrive every 30 minutes, simulate the system for 15 calls.

Table 14.29

Service Time (minutes)	Probability
15	0.15
30	0.40
60	0.30
120	0.15

14.14. For Problem 14.13. determine the total waiting time for the callers. The Police Department assigns a cost of $11 for each minute of waiting time. The cost of running one patrol car in the precinct is $500/day. Determine the number of patrol cars that minimize total cost. (Note that this is a queuing-type problem. See Chapter 15.)

14.15. Simulate the network depicted in Figure 14.6 for a total of 20 runs using columns 4, 5, and 6 of Table 14.5. Construct the critical path index of each activity. What is your understanding of the term "critical path index"?

Queuing Models

15.1
Introduction

The concept of providing, and receiving, service is inherent in today's specialized and interdependent world. Indeed, one of the most common phenomena of modern life is that *customers* (human beings or physical entities) requiring service arrive at a set of *service facilities* that provide service. If, upon arrival, the service facilities are free, the customers are provided service without any delay or waiting. However, if the service facilities are not free, the customers either wait in a *queue* (or *waiting line*) to receive their turn for service—or they get discouraged by seeing the length of the line and decide not to join the line. Airports, banks, barbershops, gasoline stations, grocery stores, machine shops, motels, patient clinics, restaurants, and toll booths are but a few examples of real-life situations in which we can identify the nature of customers, the type of service, the number and nature of service facilities, and the problem of *queuing* or waiting in a line.

In queuing situations, three things can happen. First, there may be a *perfect match* between the requirements of the customers and the capacities of the service facilities. In such a case, we do not have a queuing problem. Second, the relationship between the pattern of customer arrivals and the pattern of service rate may be such that the customers have to "wait" for service. Third, the relationship between the patterns of customer arrivals and service rate may be such that the service facilities have to "wait" or remain idle. In the latter two cases a *queuing process* is operative and we face a *queuing problem*.

In general, a queuing, or waiting-line, problem arises whenever the demand for *customer service* cannot perfectly be matched by a set of well-defined *service facilities*. The perfect match cannot be achieved because, in many situations, neither the *arrival times* (or *arrival rate*) of the customers nor the *service times* (or *service rate*) of the service facilities can be accurately predicted (i.e., both customer arrivals and service times are *random*). Consequently, as mentioned earlier, either the customers have to "wait" for service (i.e., the *queue* emerges) or the service facilities have to "wait" (i.e., service facilities remain idle). Obviously, specific costs are associated with: (1) the waiting of customers, and (2) the idle service facilities. Further, these two categories of costs move in opposite directions. For example, by adding more service facilities we decrease the cost of customer waiting but increase the cost of idle facilities. Conversely, by decreasing the number of service facilities, we increase the cost of customer waiting but decrease the cost of idle facilities. The purpose of queuing models is to help design a system that will minimize a stated measure of performance such as the sum of the costs of customer waiting and costs of idle facilities.

In this chapter, we first present the basic structure and components of a queuing system and discuss the characteristics of these components. We then explain the idea of operating characteristics of a queuing system, and provide equations for calculating their numerical values for a very simple queuing model. Finally, we illustrate how queuing problems can be solved by simulation as well as analytical procedures.

15.2
Basic Structure and Components of a Queuing System

The general framework of a queuing system is shown in Figure 15.1. As shown in Figure 15.1, a queuing system essentially consists of the following four components.

1. An *input source* or *calling population* that generates customers. Consider, for example, a machine shop in which the mechanics are required to go to a central tool crib to receive tools. The mechanics represent the input source because it is the population of mechanics that generates customers requiring service ("calls" on the service facilities).

As another example, consider a very busy and long turnpike. The driving motorists very often seek to break their journey and spend a night in one of the motels located on or near the turnpike. Then the pool of driving motorists is the input source.

2. A *service system* that consists of one or more *service facilities*. In the machine shop example, the tool crib is the service system with one or more clerks (service facilities). In the turnpike example, the service system consists of one or more motels (service facilities).

3. A *queue* that indicates the number of customers waiting for service (the queue does *not* include the customers being served). When the customers arrive at the service facilities, they examine the queue conditions and then decide whether or not to join the queue. Some customers are discouraged by the length of the queue and therefore do not join the line (this is known as *balking*). Some customers, after waiting in the queue for some time, become *impatient* and drop out of the queue (this is known as *reneging*).

4. A *queue discipline* or *service discipline* according to which the customers are selected for service. The queue discipline indicates the decision rule for service. For example, in machine shops the mechanics are usually served on a "first-come, first-served" basis. However, in a hospital emergency room, the service may be rendered on the basis of some medical priority.

Next we discuss some additional aspects of each of the four components of a queuing system shown in Figure 15.1.

15.3
Input Source

The *input source* or *input process* generates customers for the service facilities. The characteristics of the input source are given by the *size of the calling population* (finite or infinite), *arrival size* (single or batch), *arrival control* (controllable or noncontrollable), *arrival distribution* (Poisson, exponential, etc.) and the *attitude of the customers* (patient or impatient).

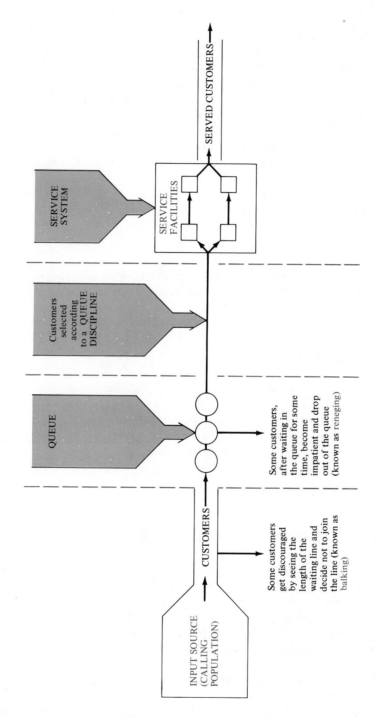

Figure 15.1. Basic Framework of a Queuing System.

15.3.1 SIZE OF THE CALLING POPULATION

The size of the calling population is *finite* if the number currently in the system (customers being served plus those in the queue) is a significant portion of the number of potential arrivals. Consider, for example, an input source of six machines that break down from time to time and require repairs. In this case, it is obvious that the number of actual machine breakdowns varies from 1 to 6, and hence the number in the service system (i.e., the number of machines being repaired) at any time is a significant portion of the number of potential arrivals. Hence, this is a case of *finite* population size.

The population size is *unlimited* or *infinite* when the number currently in the system is an insignificant portion of the number of potential arrivals. This, for example, would be the case on a busy day at the toll-booth entrance to the George Washington Bridge in New York City.

15.3.2 ARRIVAL SIZE

An arrival can be *single* (e.g., a person entering a bus station, a doctor's office, or a barbershop) or *batch* (e.g., a party of two or more entering a restaurant).

15.3.3 ARRIVAL CONTROL

Most of the arrivals are subject to some degree of influence and control. For example, grocery stores can influence, to varying degrees, the arrivals of their customers by advertising special sales and by regulating the days and hours during which they remain open for business. The queuing literature classifies arrival control in the categories of *controllable* (e.g., registration days for college students) and *noncontrollable* (e.g., emergency room of a hospital).

15.3.4 ARRIVAL DISTRIBUTION (PATTERN OF ARRIVALS)

The *pattern of arrivals* is usually given by: (1) the *distribution of times between successive arrivals* (i.e., *interarrival times*), or (2) the *distribution of the number of arrivals per unit of time* (i.e., *arrival rate distribution*). A unit of time refers to a specified time interval, such as 5 minutes, 15 minutes, or 1 hour.

The pattern or distribution of arrivals can be *constant* or *random*. A *constant distribution* means that the time intervals between arrivals (interarrival times) are constant. Constant distributions are common in automated assembly line operations where parts, subassemblies, and finished goods arrive after *predetermined* time intervals.

A *random distribution* means that the interarrival times cannot be predicted with certainty, and hence their pattern is given either by actual empirical data or can be approximated by some theoretical probability distribution, such as the exponential distribution.[1] The interarrival times of many real-life phenomena (arrivals at bank windows, arrivals of machines for repairs, etc.) can be approximated by exponential distributions. In Figure 15.2, we show an exponential distribution. It is obvious from Figure 15.2 that the probability of long interarrival times is rather small and that short interarrival times occur with high probability.

The distribution of *arrival rates* (i.e., the number of arrivals per unit time) of many real-life phenomena can often be approximated by the *Poisson distribution*.[2] In Figure 15.3 we present a Poisson distribution with $\lambda = 5$.

The Poisson distribution corresponds to completely random arrivals, and it assumes that an arrival is completely independent of other arrivals and the probability of arrival during a very small time interval remains constant. If we assume very small time intervals, then the telephone requests for claims at a

---

[1] Since interarrival times are *measured* (as opposed to *counting*), an interarrival time distribution must be of the *continuous* type. The exponential distribution (also referred to as "the negative exponential distribution") is a continuous distribution whose density function is given by

$$f(X) = \mu e^{-\mu X}$$

where

$f(X)$ = density function that is used to calculate the probability of X

X = interarrival time (or service time)

$e = 2.71828$

μ = (Greek letter mu)

Note that X is the continuous random variable. It can be shown that, for the exponential distribution,

$$\text{mean} = \frac{1}{\mu} \quad \text{and} \quad \text{variance} = \frac{1}{\mu^2}$$

Hence,

$\dfrac{1}{\mu}$ = mean interarrival time (or mean service time)

μ = mean arrival rate (or mean service rate)

Note, also, that μ is the only parameter in this distribution. Hence, if we know the value of μ, the exponential distribution is completely described. See Appendix A and the note on p. 501.

[2] Since the number of arrivals per unit time is *counted* (as opposed to *measurement*), the arrival rate distribution must be of the *discrete* type. The Poisson distribution is a discrete distribution and is given by

$$p(X) = \frac{\bar{e}^{\lambda} \lambda^X}{X!}$$

where

$p(X)$ = probability of X arrivals

X = number of arrivals per unit time (arrival rate)

λ = (Greek letter lambda)

$e = 2.71828$

Note that X is the discrete random variable. Also, for the Poisson distribution, mean = λ and variance = λ. Hence,

λ = mean arrival rate (or mean service rate)

$\dfrac{1}{\lambda}$ = mean interarrival time (or mean service time)

Note also that λ is the only parameter in this distribution. Hence, if we know the value of λ, the Poisson distribution is completely described. See Appendix A.

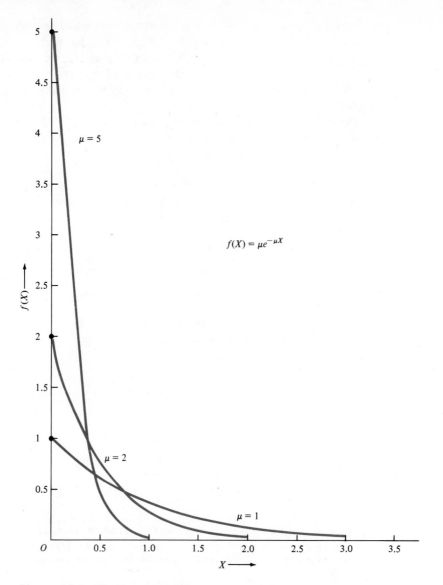

Figure 15.2. The Exponential Probability Density Function.

centralized insurance office, arrival of customers at a large department store, and arrival of cars at a toll booth would produce Poisson distributions.[3] It should be noted that Poisson arrival rate distribution gives rise to exponential interarrival times (and vice versa). The means of the two distributions are inversely related, as follows:

Poisson Arrival Rate

mean arrival rate

$= \lambda = 5$ arrivals per hour

Exponential Interarrival Times

mean interarrival time

$= \dfrac{1}{\lambda} = 12$ minutes $= \dfrac{1}{\mu}$

[3] *Erlang* and *hyperexponential* distributions are also used quite frequently in the queuing literature to approximate arrival and service distributions. See Morse [1958].

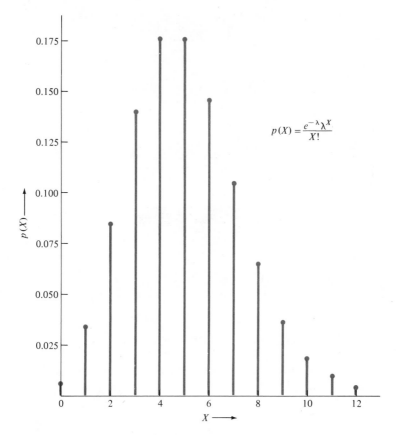

$$p(X) = \frac{e^{-\lambda}\lambda^X}{X!}$$

Figure 15.3. The Poisson Probability Distribution for $\lambda = 5$.

15.3.5 ATTITUDE OF THE CUSTOMERS

The attitude of the customers is important because it affects the length of the queue. The attitude is a reflection of different types of customers: (1) impatient customers (balking or reneging), and (2) patient customers (voluntary or involuntary).

When the customers arrive for service, they can either be immediately served (if the service facility is free), or they have to stand in a queue (if they wish to receive service). The customers who either do not join the queue (balking) or leave the queue before receiving service (reneging) are called *impatient* customers. The *balking* customers are those who, upon arrival, are discouraged by the length of the queue, and, therefore, do not join the waiting line (this often happens when we go to see very popular movies). The *reneging* customers are those that join the line, but after waiting in the queue for some time, become impatient and leave the queue (this can happen when we wait in long lines to buy special bargains on Washington's birthday). The customers who either voluntarily (e.g., patients in a physician's office) or involuntarily (e.g., prisoners or physical entities) remain in the queue until they are served are called *patient customers.*

The purpose of recognizing the attitude of the customers is that if a waiting time of extraordinary length produces a substantial number of impatient customers, then there is the potential of lost sales.

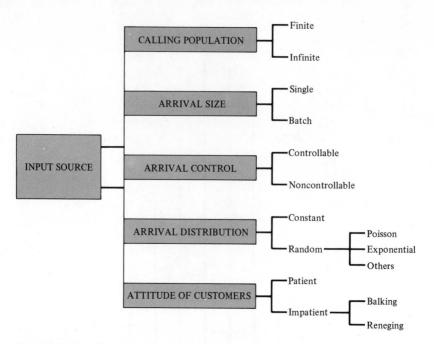

Figure 15.4. Characteristics of the Input Source.

The ideas pertaining to the input source can be summarized as shown in Figure 15.4.

15.4
The Service System

The service system is characterized by the *configuration (structure) of the service facilities* and the *service distribution*.

15.4.1 CONFIGURATION (STRUCTURE) OF THE SERVICE FACILITIES

Depending upon the nature of the service process, we can classify service facilities in terms of their configuration of channels (single or multiple) and phases (single or multiple). The term *channel* refers to the number of points of entry to the service system. A *single channel* means that there is only one point of entry. *Multiple channels* refer to the *parallel* arrangement of service facilities (i.e., two or more points of entry exist so that two or more service stations can simultaneously begin the service process).

The term *phase* refers to the number of service stations through which the customer must pass before the service is considered complete. A *single phase* implies that there exists only one service station. *Multiple phases* refer to the *series* arrangement of service facilities (i.e., customers must go through two or more service stations in *sequence* before the service is considered complete).

An example of the *single-channel, single-phase model* is the purchase of a ticket at a suburban train station with only one ticket window (single channel) and taking the train ride to the city (single phase).

An example of the *single-channel, multiple-phase model* is the production of an item if it is being produced on only *one* assembly line (single channel) but must go through two or more sequential operations (multiple phase).

An example of *multiple-channel, single-phase model* is the purchase of a ticket at a large train station with two or more ticket windows (multiple channel) and taking the train ride to a destination (single phase).

An example of the *multiple-channel, multiple-phase model* is the production of an item if it is being produced on two or more assembly lines (multiple channel) and must go through two or more sequential operations (multiple phase).

Arrangements that cannot be subsumed under any of the four configurations described above are called *mixed arrangements*.

In Figure 15.5, we show the basic configurations of service facilities.

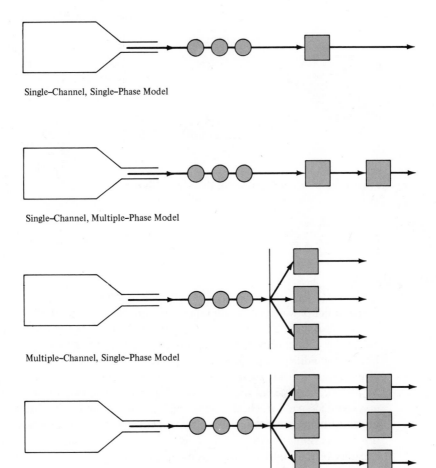

Single–Channel, Single–Phase Model

Single–Channel, Multiple–Phase Model

Multiple–Channel, Single–Phase Model

Multiple–Channel, Multiple–Phase Model

Figure 15.5. Basic Configurations (Structure) of Service Facilities.

15.4.2 SERVICE DISTRIBUTION (PATTERN OF SERVICE)

The pattern of service can be recorded by: (1) the *distribution of service times*, or (2) the distribution of the number of customers served per unit time (i.e., *service rate distribution*).

As in the case of arrivals, the distribution of service time can be *constant* or *random*. The constant service time occurs mostly in mechanized operations. In most real-life situations, service times are random and can often be approximated by the exponential probability distribution.

If the service is random but is specified in terms of service rates, it can often be approximated by the Poisson distribution. We should mention again that exponential service-time distribution gives rise to Poisson service rate (and vice versa). The means of the two distributions are inversely related.

The ideas pertaining to the service system can be summarized as shown in Figure 15.6.

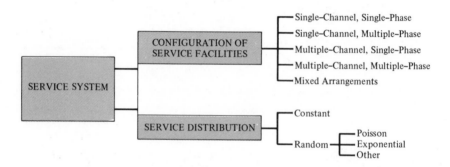

Figure 15.6. Characteristics of the Service System.

15.5
The Queue

The number of waiting lines and their respective lengths are the two basic aspects of the component labeled "Queue" in Figure 15.1. The *number of waiting lines* is essentially a function of the configuration of the service facilities (e.g., one waiting line for each different point of entry into the service system). Thus, we can have a *single* queue or *multiple* queues.

The *length* or *size* of the queue is influenced by such factors as physical space (e.g., limited space at gas stations), legal restrictions (e.g., city ordinance against forming queues on specified city streets), attitude of the customers (e.g., long lines discourage some customers from joining the queue), and relationship of the capacity of the input source to the capacity of the service facilities.

The length of the queue can be finite or infinite. The queue is *finite* (*truncated*) when there is a limit beyond which it cannot increase (e.g., the queue at a gas station). The queue is *infinite* when there is no limit on its size (e.g., the number of mail orders for development of photos).

The nature and analysis of queues is important because the expected length of the queue affects the number of lost customers. For example, if the queue at a service facility is *often* found by the customers to be near or at its maximum possible length, the service organization will lose a large number of customers.

The ideas relating to the queue are summarized in Figure 15.7.

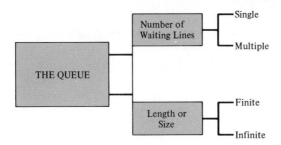

Figure 15.7. Characteristics of the Queue.

15.6
The Queue Discipline

The *queue discipline* indicates the decision rule by which the customers are selected from the queue for service. In most queuing systems, the queue discipline is the *first-come, first-served* (FCFS) rule.[4] However, other types of queue disciplines can be specified. For example, the service can be provided on the basis of *assigned priorities.* Some examples in the category of assigned priorities are given by the following decision rules for selecting the customer: *emergency first* (e.g., in a hospital emergency room), *reservations first* (e.g., in a restaurant), *shortest processing time first* (e.g., in a job shop), and *preemptive priority* (when service to one customer is interrupted to provide service to another).

Another type is the *random* queue discipline that reflects a service system not operated in a well-organized manner (e.g., service in a liquor store with several salesmen).

The specification and analysis of the queue discipline is important because it affects the operating characteristics of the queuing system.

The queue disciplines described in this section are shown in Figure 15.8.

15.7
Operating Characteristics of a Queuing System

The behavior of a queuing system is described by such *variables* as *arrival rate, waiting time in the queue, service time, idle time of service facilities, total time spent by a customer in the queuing system,* and so on. We need to know the distributions of such variables, along with the numerical value of their means, standard deviations, and probability measures that the variable be less than, or more than, certain

---

[4] The first-come, first-served rule can also be called FIFO (first in, first out).

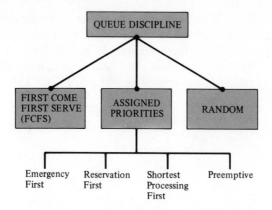

Figure 15.8. Different Types of Queue Discipline.

specified numbers (e.g., what is the probability that the waiting time is 5 minutes or less?) The *operating characteristics* of a queuing system refer to the values (i.e., mean, standard deviation, etc., of different variables) that are needed to either *evaluate* the performance of an existing queuing system or to *design* a new system. For example, while designing a new system, we may impose such specifications as: "The probability of the waiting time being 5 minutes or more should be less than 0.20." Examples of operating characteristics include: *average waiting time in the queue, percent idle time of service system, average arrival rate, average service rate,* etc.

The operating characteristics emerge as a result of interaction among the different components of a queuing system. The numerical values of various operating characteristics of an existing queuing system can be calculated either analytically (i.e., by using mathematical equations relating to specified queuing models) or by simulation. Both approaches shall be illustrated in subsequent sections.

A knowledge of the operating characteristics is useful in improving an existing queuing system. For example, service rate can be accelerated to reduce average waiting time in the queue, provided such a change is viable in terms of economic and other criteria. Operating characteristics can also be used as a guide in designing new queuing systems (e.g., average waiting time for customers must be less than 10 minutes).

15.8
Design of a Queuing System

The design of a queuing system requires that we choose the characteristics of various components of the system (input source, queue discipline, service facilities, etc.) in such a way that specified objectives are met. For example, the system can be designed to minimize costs or maximize profits. Alternatively, the system can be designed so that certain operating characteristics are within specified limits. The analysis and design of a queuing system requires that we assign costs to customer waiting as well as to machine idle time. The cost data can then be used in conjunction with the information generated by the queuing model in order to make managerial decisions on such things as physical facilities, service mechanisms, service levels, and measures of system effectiveness.

15.9
Queuing Models

Depending upon the assumptions made with regard to the size of the calling population, arrival distribution, balking, reneging, service discipline, service channels, service phases, service distribution, and state of the queuing system (*transient* versus *steady state*[5]), we can develop an extremely large number of queuing models. The development and analysis of even the simplest queuing models requires an advanced level of mathematical and statistical knowledge. For this reason, we shall not undertake the task of developing any queuing models in this introductory book. However, we shall present equations that can be used to calculate the *operating characteristics* of one of the basic queuing models (single channel, single phase). The model will then be illustrated (analytical approach) with the aid of a simple queuing problem.

Queuing models can be "solved" by applying either the analytical or the simulation approach. Both approaches are illustrated in this chapter.

15.10
A Single-Channel, Single-Phase Model (Analytical Approach)

In the analytical approach we represent the arrival rates and service rates by appropriate mathematical distributions. Then we develop, or retrieve from the queuing literature, mathematical equations for the operating characteristics of the model under consideration. We then calculate the numerical values of various operating characteristics of the queuing system (assuming that relevant parameters of the distributions are known). With this information in hand, and provided we can estimate relevant costs, the queuing model can be used to identify the optimal alternative that will minimize costs or maximize profits.

In this section, we consider a single-channel, single-phase model. This is one of the simplest and most commonly illustrated models.

15.10.1 ASSUMPTIONS

1. The size of the calling population is *infinite*. This assumption implies that the input source is unlimited (this assumption is also warranted in cases where the

---

[5] A *transient system* indicates that the behavior of the system is dependent upon time. That is, the impact of the starting conditions has not "settled" as yet. A *steady-state system* indicates that the behavior of the system is independent of time (i.e., long-run conditions prevail).

number of customers is finite but, after being serviced, customers rejoin the input source).

2. The arrival-rate distribution is approximated by a Poisson distribution.
3. There is no *balking*. This assumption implies that arriving customers always join the queue.
4. There is no *reneging*. This assumption implies that customers stay in line until served (i.e., patient customers).
5. The queue discipline is *first-come, first-served* (FCFS).
6. The permissible length of the queue is *infinite*.
7. The service-time distribution is approximated by an exponential distribution.
8. The rate of service is greater than the rate of arrivals (i.e., $\mu > \lambda$).
9. The queuing system is in *steady state*.

15.10.2 OPERATING CHARACTERISTICS

Next, we present some of the commonly used operating characteristics of the single-channel, single-phase queuing model. Although the equations or formulas for calculating the numerical values of these operating characteristics differ from model to model, they are useful in describing the behavior of all types of queuing models.

- Mean (average) arrival rate $= \lambda$

- Mean (average) interarrival time $= \dfrac{1}{\lambda}$

- Mean (average) service time $= \dfrac{1}{\mu}$

- Mean (average) service rate $= \mu$
- Utilization factor, ρ (Greek letter rho) = probability of the service facility being busy

$$= \rho = \frac{\lambda}{\mu} \tag{15.1}$$

Since $\mu > \lambda$ (by assumption 8),

$$0 \leqslant \rho < 1$$

- Percent idle time, I = probability of no units in the queuing system

$$= I = 1 - \rho = 1 - \frac{\lambda}{\mu} \tag{15.2}$$

- Mean (average) number of customers in the queue $= L_q$

$$= \frac{\lambda^2}{\mu(\mu - \lambda)} \tag{15.3}$$

- Mean (average) waiting time in the queue $= W_q$

$$= \frac{\lambda}{\mu(\mu - \lambda)} \tag{15.4}$$

- Mean (average) number of customers in the entire system

(waiting plus those being served) $= L_S$

$$= \frac{\lambda}{\mu - \lambda} \qquad (15.5)$$

- Mean (average) time per customer in the entire system

(waiting time plus service time) $= T_S$

$$= \frac{1}{\mu - \lambda} \qquad (15.6)$$

- Probability of n units in the entire system $= P_n = \left(1 - \frac{\lambda}{\mu}\right)\left(\frac{\lambda}{\mu}\right)^n \qquad (15.7)$

From (15.7) we can derive P_0 (the probability of no units in the entire system).

$$P_0 = \left(1 - \frac{\lambda}{\mu}\right)\left(\frac{\lambda}{\mu}\right)^0 = 1 - \frac{\lambda}{\mu} \qquad (15.8)$$

Note that (15.8) equals (15.2). That is,

$$I = P_0$$

- Probability of k or more customers in the entire system

$$P(n \geqslant k) = \left(\frac{\lambda}{\mu}\right)^k \qquad (15.9)$$

- Probability that number of customers in the entire system is greater than k,

$$P(n > k) = \left(\frac{\lambda}{\mu}\right)^{k+1} \qquad (15.10)$$

Example 15.1 | The Chase Hanover Bank is opening a new suburban branch. Based on preliminary research, it is assumed that customer arrival rate can be approximated by a Poisson distribution, with an average arrival rate of 10 customers/hour. The bank is planning to employ only one teller, and it is assumed that the teller can serve, on the average, 12 customers/hour. It is assumed that the service-rate distribution is also Poisson (i.e., service-time distribution is exponential). Our task is to analyze this queuing system by calculating the numerical values of these operating characteristics: $\rho, I, L_q, W_q,$ $L_S, T_S, P_0, P_n,$ and $P(n \geqslant k)$.

Solution. We know from the problem description that:

1. $\lambda =$ average arrival rate $= 10$ per hour. Hence,

$$\frac{1}{\lambda} = \text{average interarrival time} = \frac{1 \text{ hour}}{10} = 6 \text{ minutes}$$

2. $\mu =$ average service rate $= 12$ per hour. Hence,

$$\frac{1}{\mu} = \text{average service time} = \frac{1 \text{ hour}}{12} = 5 \text{ minutes}$$

3. From (15.1),

$$\rho = \text{utilization factor} = \frac{\lambda}{\mu} = \frac{10}{12} = 0.8333$$

That is, the teller is busy 83.33 percent of the time (hence, he is idle 16.67 percent of the time).

4. From (15.2),

$$I = \text{percent idle time} = 1 - \rho = 1 - 0.8333 = 0.1667$$

That is, the teller is idle 16.67 percent of the time (the same answer as in item 3).

5. From (15.3),

$$L_q = \frac{\lambda^2}{\mu(\mu - \lambda)} = \frac{100}{12(12 - 10)} = 4\frac{1}{6}$$

That is, on the average, $4\frac{1}{6}$ customers will be waiting in the queue for service. [*Note:* The average number of customers waiting in the queue might intuitively appear to be rather high—especially because the average service time is 5 minutes and average interarrival time is 6 minutes. It should be remembered, however, that both the interarrival time and the service time are *random* and what our model measures is the result of *interaction* between these random components over the long run (steady state).]

6. From (15.4),

$$W_q = \frac{\lambda}{\mu(\mu - \lambda)} = \frac{10}{12(12 - 10)} = \frac{5}{12} \text{hour} = 25 \text{ minutes}$$

That is, on the average, a customer will wait in the queue for 25 minutes. (*Note:* The average wait of 25 minutes appears to be unbelievably high in view of the fact that average service rate is greater than average arrival rate. Again, the explanation resides in the assumption of randomness.)

7. From (15.5),

$$L_S = \frac{\lambda}{\mu - \lambda} = \frac{10}{12 - 10} = 5 \text{ customers}$$

That is, on the average, 5 persons are in the entire system (waiting plus those being served).

8. From (15.6),

$$T_S = \frac{1}{\mu - \lambda} = \frac{1}{12 - 10} = \frac{1}{2} \text{ hour} = 30 \text{ minutes}$$

That is, on the average, each customer spends 30 minutes in the entire system (waiting time plus service time).

9. From (15.8),

$$P_0 = 1 - \frac{\lambda}{\mu} = 1 - \frac{10}{12} = 0.1667$$

That is, the probability of no unit in the entire system is 16.67 percent. This corresponds to the value of I (percent idle time) calculated in item 4.

10. We can build the probability distributions for P_n and $P(n \geqslant k)$ by using (15.7) and (15.9), respectively. The results for selected values of n and k are summarized in Table 15.1.

Let us examine the operating characteristics of the queuing system described in Example 15.1. It is clear, first of all, that an average customer waiting time of 25 minutes is unacceptable, as it will result in lost customers. Hence, the manager must immediately look for different means to improve service (i.e., reduce customer waiting time). One obvious course of action is to employ two tellers (alternative 1). Another is to investigate the possibility of replacing the teller with an automated device (alternative 2). A third course of action is to make the teller more efficient by providing him with some better equipment (alternative 3). In each case, the cost of service facilities will increase while the cost of customer waiting will decrease. The idea in each of the three alternatives is to compute the total cost of the system and choose the alternative that yields the *minimum total cost* (cost of service facilities + cost of customer waiting time).

Alternative 1

Since this alternative requires two tellers, the analysis of the system will require the utilization of equations that apply to a multiple-channel, single-phase model. Note that we will have two channels in this case.

Alternative 2

The new system remains under the single-channel, single-phase category. Hence, Equations (15.1) to (15.10) can be used to calculate new values of various operating characteristics. In order to make a rational decision, we need to place a value on customer waiting time and assign an hourly cost to the automated system.

Alternative 3

This is also the single-channel, single-phase model. Again, we can use Equations (15.1) to (15.10) to calculate the numerical values of various operating characteristics. Here, too, we need to place a value on customer waiting time and assign an hourly cost to the new service facility (teller plus the new equipment).

In order to choose the most cost-effective alternative, we can use the format shown in Table 15.2. The numerical values in the table are hypothetical and were chosen only for purposes of illustration. We are assuming a customer waiting cost

Table 15.1

n	$P_n = (1 - \frac{10}{12})(\frac{10}{12})^n$	k	$P(n \geqslant k) = (\frac{10}{12})^k$
0	0.167	0	1.000
1	0.139	1	0.833
2	0.116	2	0.694
3	0.096	3	0.579
4	0.080	4	0.482
5	0.067	5	0.402

of \$10/hour and a 40-hour week. As seen in the table, alternative 3 results in minimum total cost and hence is the optimal course of action.

Table 15.2

	Present System	Alternative 1	Alternative 2	Alternative 3
Weekly cost of service system	300	600	1,500	500
Weekly cost of customer waiting*	1,667	1,000	200	800
Total weekly cost	1,967	1,600	1,700	1,300

* For the present system, weekly customer waiting cost is calculated as follows:

$$\frac{25 \text{ minutes}}{\text{customer}} \times \frac{10 \text{ customers}}{\text{hour}} \times \frac{8 \text{ hours}}{\text{day}} \times \frac{5 \text{ days}}{\text{week}} \times \frac{1 \text{ hour}}{60 \text{ minutes}} \times \frac{\$10}{\text{hour}}$$

$$= \$1,666.67/\text{week}$$

15.11
Analysis of Queuing Problems by Simulation

Whenever a queuing problem cannot easily be structured for, or is not amenable to, the analytical approach, the simulation approach provides an effective means to analyze and solve the problem. That is, by simulating the queuing system we can study its various operating characteristics and then take appropriate actions to improve the system.

The basic rationale and mechanics of the simulation approach have already been presented in Chapter 14. In this section, we shall employ Monte Carlo simulation to analyze a queuing system (a simple machine maintenance problem) and, based on the results of simulation, recommend an optimal course of action.

Example 15.2

Let us consider a machine shop in which small quantities of spare parts for airplanes are being produced by a group of similar machines. Currently, there is only one full-time repairman available to repair the machines that break down and require service. The repair service is provided on a first-come, first-served basis, and the machines wait in queue until they are serviced by the full-time repairman (i.e., there is no balking or reneging and we are dealing with patient customers). The time history of machine breakdowns and machine repair times can be retrieved from actual company records.

Assume that the data for machine breakdowns and machine repair times are as shown in Tables 15.3 and 15.4, respectively.[6] Assume, further, that the cost of an idle machine is \$100/*machine hour* and the prevailing wage rate for repairmen is \$10/*manhour*.

---

[6] It should be reemphasized that if the actual data can be approximated by a theoretical probability distribution (e.g., Poisson distribution), an analytical solution might be preferable. However, here we want to illustrate the simulation approach.

Our decision problem is this: Analyze the behavior of this queuing system and then determine the optimal number of repairmen to employ. That is, the number of repairmen should be such that the total system costs (cost of idle machine time + cost of repairmen's wages) are minimized. We assume that it is not possible to employ a repairman on a part-time basis.

It is clear that we are dealing with a queuing system consisting of these components: (1) the *input source* is the set of machines (broken machines are the customers), (2) the repairmen are the *service facilities*, (3) the machines waiting for service form a *queue*, and (4) the queue discipline is first-come, first-served. As in the inventory problem, we face two types of opposing costs (cost of machine idle time and cost of repairmen's wages) in our queuing system. Our purpose is to determine the number of repairmen that will result in minimizing the sum of these two opposing costs.

We shall analyze the queuing system by employing the Monte Carlo simulation procedure described in Section 14.7.

Step 1. *Obtain a probability distribution for each of the stochastic variables that must be analyzed.*

We need probability distributions for two stochastic variables: (1) number of machine breakdowns per hour[7] and (2) repair times (in manhours). The two distributions based on hypothetical data are shown in Table 15.3 (first three columns) and Table 15.4 (first two columns), respectively.

Step 2. *Build a cumulative probability distribution corresponding to each probability distribution.*

Table 15.3

(1)	(2)	(3)	(4)	(5)
Number of Breakdowns per Hour, X	Frequency, f	Probability Distribution, p(X)	Cumulative Probability Distribution, P(breakdowns ≤ X)	Random Numbers
0	850	0.850	0.850	000–849
1	110	0.110	0.960	850–959
2	40	0.040	1.000	960–999

[7] The information can be in terms of breakdowns per hour or per day. We assumed the distribution in Table 15.3 for purposes of illustration only. A theoretical distribution can be generated by using the Poisson density function

$$p(X) = \frac{\bar{e}^{\lambda} \lambda^X}{X!}$$

which often approximates real-life phenomena in breakdown and maintenance problems. It should be noted that the random variable X represents the number of breakdowns per hour, while λ (the expected value) is a parameter. Construct a distribution for $\lambda = 0.08$, and by letting $X = 0, 1$, and 2. The reader can look up the result in Table II of Appendix E.

Table 15.4

(1)	(2)	(3)	(4)
		Cumulative	
	Probability	Probability	
Repair Time, Y	Distribution,	Distribution	Random
(manhours)	p(Y)	P(repair time ⩽ Y)	Numbers
4	0.400	0.400	000–399
5	0.300	0.700	400–699
6	0.175	0.875	700–874
7	0.100	0.975	875–974
8	0.025	1.000	975–999

The cumulative probability distribution of the number of machine breakdowns per hour, $P(\text{breakdown} \leqslant X)$, is shown in column 4 of Table 15.3. The cumulative probability distribution of repair times, P (repair time $\leqslant Y$), is shown in column 3 of Table 15.4.

Step 3. *Assign an appropriate set of random numbers to represent each value, or range of values, of the stochastic variables.*

Column 5 of Table 15.3 and column 4 of Table 15.4 show the assigned random numbers for the two stochastic variables. Three comments, based on the material covered in Chapter 14, are in order at this time. First, although we know the individual probability distributions of "number of breakdowns per hour" and "repair times in manhours," we have no empirical data regarding the characteristics of waiting time for the machines or the idle time for the repairmen (one or more repairmen). This will have to be generated by the simulated interaction of two components (number of breakdowns per hour, and repair times) whose past behavior is known. Second, we can achieve *time compression* by simulation, since by using computers we can easily simulate in a matter of minutes the behavior of the maintenance system for several months or even years. Third, by considering the options of hiring different number of repairmen, we can study the effect on the system (e.g., total cost) of different levels of inputs (repairmen). Similarly, by carefully designing the simulation experiment, we can analyze the effect and importance of different inputs on various characteristics of the system.

Step 4. *Conduct the simulation experiment (RUN THE MODEL) by means of random sampling.*

As described in Section 14.4.2, the task of running the model consists of three parts. Next, we illustrate these parts as they apply to our maintenance problem.

State Assumptions and Structure of the Mathematical Model

We make the following assumptions:

1. The firm cannot employ repairmen on a part-time basis.
2. Each machine must be repaired in-house.

3. Machine breakdown occurs at the end of clock hour.
4. Repair starts at the beginning of the hour that immediately follows the breakdown hour.
5. Repair always terminates at the end of hour.
6. Repairmen's idle time cannot be utilized in performing other tasks.
7. Each repairman has the same level of efficiency.

The above assumptions lead to the mathematical model described below.

For One Repairman

BD = clock time when a machine breakdown occurs (this is an *instant in time*)

RT = repair time required to repair a breakdown (this is a *period of time*)

IT = idle time for a repairman (this is a *period of time*)

TT = clock time when the repair on a breakdown terminates (this is an *instant in time*)

WT = machine waiting time (this is a *period* of time).

Any of the above symbols can be used with a subscript (1, 2, 3, etc.) to signify the data regarding a specific event. For example, TT_1 signifies the clock time when the repair on the *first* breakdown terminates.

It stands to reason that the clock termination time for the first breakdown, TT_1, can be obtained by adding the repair time for the first breakdown, RT_1, to the clock time when the first breakdown occurred. That is, for the first breakdown,

$$\text{TT}_1 = \text{BD}_1 + \text{RT}_1 \tag{15.11}$$

When we come to the second breakdown, one of the circumstances shown in Figure 15.9 can develop. The analysis related to the second breakdown and shown in Figure 15.9 will also hold for the third, fourth, and subsequent breakdowns. That is, the mathematical model for $i = 2, 3, 4, \ldots$, is given by

$$\left. \begin{array}{l} \text{TT}_i = \text{BD}_i + \text{RT}_i \quad \text{if } \text{BD}_i > \text{TT}_{i-1} \text{ (i.e., repairman is idle)} \\ \\ \text{or} \\ \\ \text{TT}_i = \text{TT}_{i-1} + \text{RT}_i \quad \text{if } \text{BD}_i \leqslant \text{TT}_{i-1} \text{ (i.e., repairman is not idle)} \end{array} \right\} \tag{15.12}$$

For Two Repairmen. It stands to reason that when we employ two repairmen, there is no waiting time for the first and the second breakdown. Hence,

$$\text{TT}_1 = \text{BD}_1 + \text{RT}_1 \tag{15.13}$$
$$\text{TT}_2 = \text{BD}_2 + \text{RT}_2 \tag{15.14}$$

The mathematical model for the third, fourth, and subsequent breakdowns, however, becomes more complicated. For example, we shall have to develop models for TT_i to cover cases when third and subsequent breakdowns occur under these circumstances: (1) both repairmen are just completing their repairs, (2) one is busy and the second is just completing his repairs, (3) both are idle, (4) one is idle and the second is busy, (5) one is idle and the second is just completing his repairs, and (6) both are busy. We shall not develop the mathematical models for the two repairmen's case.

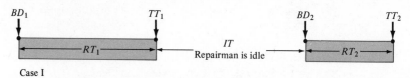

Repairman Is Idle (i.e., $BD_2 > TT_1$)
BD_1
TT_1
BD_2
TT_2
RT_1
IT
Repairman is idle
RT_2
Case I
Repairman Is Not Idle (i.e., $BD_2 \leqslant TT_1$)
BD_1
TT_1
RT_1
BD_2
TT_2
RT_2
(Here $BD_2 = TT_1$)
Case II
BD_1
TT_1
RT_1
BD_2
TT_2
WT_2
RT_2
(Here $BD_2 < TT_1$)

Figure 15.9

Choose Random Numbers and Translate Them into Unique Values of Appropriate Stochastic Variables

Let us first study the behavior of the system with the assumption that the company hires only one repairman. We shall conduct the simulation experiment to cover a period of 25 operational hours. This means that we take 25 samples from the breakdown distribution (Table 15.3). Each such sample will correspond to a specific hour of operation and will indicate one of two things: "machine breakdown" or "no breakdown." Whenever a machine breakdown occurs, we take a sample from the repair-time distribution (Table 15.4), indicating a specific repair time. If two breakdowns occur simultaneously, we take two samples from the repair-time distribution.[8]

The unique values of the two stochastic variables (breakdown numbers and repair times) that correspond to 25 random samples are shown in columns 3 and 6, respectively, of Table 15.5.

Note that since the probability distributions are given in three significant digits, we are using the first three digits (use the first two columns of Table 14.5 on p. 406 and move down, starting from the top) to sample from the breakdown distribution, and the first three digits (use the last two columns of Table 14.5 and move down, starting from the top) to sample from the repair-time distribution. As shown in Table 15.5, there is no breakdown in the first 3 hours of operation. The random number for the fourth sample (hour) is 861, and that indicates 1 breakdown (see Table 15.3 and note that random number 861 corresponds to 1 breakdown). Next, we take one random sample from the repair-time distribution

[8] Note that the number of samples from the repair-time distribution will depend upon the number of simulated machine breakdowns.

Table 15.5 Simulation of the Maintenance System with One Repairman

(1) Hour of Operation	(2) Random Number for Machine Breakdown (First Two Columns of Table 14.5)	(3) Breakdown Number, i (Table 15.3)	(4) Breakdown Occurs at End of Hour, BD	(5) Random Number for Repair Time (Last Two Columns of Table 14.5)	(6) Repair Time, RT (Table 15.4)	(7) Start Repair at Beginning of Hour	(8) Terminate Repair at End of Hour, TT	(9) Machine Waiting Time, WT	(10) Idle Time of Repairman, IT
1	312								⎫
2	705								4 hr
3	536								⎭
4	861	1st (one breakdown)	4	014	4				
5	326					5 ● first breakdown 4 hr			
6	782								
7	262								
8	645						● 8		
9	456								⎫
10	123								3 hr
11	992	2nd and 3rd (two breakdowns)	11	384 and 155	4 and 4				⎭
12	524					12 ● second breakdown 4 hr			
13	434								
14	844								
15	381						● 15		
16	400					16 ● third breakdown 4 hr		Third breakdown waits 4 hr	
17	199								
18	870	4th (one breakdown)	18	809	6				
19	835						● 19		
20	732					20 ● fourth breakdown 6 hr		Fourth waits 1 hr	
21	842								
22	298								
23	095								
24	024								
25	201						● 25		

by using Table 14.5. The first random number is 014, indicating a repair time of 4 hours for the first breakdown (see Table 15.4 and note that random number 014 corresponds to 4 hours of repair time). Since we assumed that the breakdown occurs at the end of the hour and repairs start at the beginning of the hour immediately following the breakdown hour, we start repairs on the *first breakdown* at the *beginning* of hour 5, and after exactly 4 hours, complete the repairs at the *end* of hour 8. This fact is shown in Table 15.5.

As can be seen in Table 15.5, no breakdowns occur from hour 5 to hour 10 (i.e., for these six samples, the random numbers are less than 850). The random number for hour 11 is 992, indicating two breakdowns (see Table 15.3). This means that our second and third breakdowns occur *simultaneously* at the end of hour 11. Hence, we take two random samples from the repair-time distribution (i.e., we choose random numbers 384 and 155 from the last two columns of Table 14.5). This says that repair time for the second and the third breakdowns is 4 hours each (see Table 15.4). Since only one repairman is available, he starts repairing the second breakdown (at the *beginning* of hour 12) and, after 4 hours, completes it at the end of hour 15. That is, the third breakdown must wait for 4 hours (machine waiting time). The remaining simulated data of Table 15.5 is subject to similar explanation and interpretation.

Note that during the 25-hour simulated period we experience 4 machine breakdowns, 18 hours of repair time, 5 hours of machine waiting time, and 7 hours of idle time of the repairman.[9] If we simulate the system (run the model) for more than 25 hours, we can find a more complete *time history* of breakdowns, repair time, idle machine time, and idle time of the repairman.

Let us assume that the manager considers the idle machine time in this system to be excessive. Then the logical question for the manager is: Should another repairman be hired? (Note that the task of testing the effect of hiring the second repairman is part of our original mission in this example.) How does the additional cost of hiring the second repairman compare with the savings due to decreased idle machine time? An analysis of this type can easily be made by simulating the system for longer periods of time, attaching a cost to idle machine time, and knowing the cost of repairman's time.[10]

Plug the Simulated Values of the Stochastic Variables into the Mathematical Model and Calculate the Numerical Values of the Criterion Variable or Other Operating Characteristics of the System

Discussion of Table 15.5 with One Repairman. We can now use Equations (15.11) and (15.12) to fill column 8 of Table 15.5. That is, terminal time (TT) for different breakdowns can be calculated. And, as shown in column 9, we can calculate waiting times of machines (WT) by comparing column 4 (breakdown hour, BD) with column 8 (terminal time, TT). Similarly, we can calculate the idle time of the

---

[9] Actually, in computer simulation, the numerical values of such operating characteristics are calculated by using the mathematical model, as we briefly describe later in this section.

[10] The repairman is indivisible in the sense that he is not available to other parts of the organization. Hence, if he is not repairing a machine, he is assumed to be idle.

repairman. Please remember that all the values are simulated values based on 25 samples.

It is now easy to calculate the total system cost for the simulated time period with *one repairman*.

$$\text{cost of repairman's wages} = \frac{\$10}{\text{hour}} \times 25 \text{ hours} = \$250$$

$$\text{cost of machine waiting time} = \frac{\$100}{\text{hour}} \times 5 \text{ hours} = \$500$$

$$\text{total cost} \qquad\qquad\qquad\qquad = \$750$$

Discussion of Table 15.5 with Two Repairmen. A quick examination of Table 15.5 shows that if the firm were to employ a second full-time repairman, the third breakdown does not have to wait. Further, both the second and the third breakdowns are repaired by the end of the 15th hour. Consequently, the fourth breakdown does not have to wait, because both repairmen are free by the time repairs need to begin on the fourth breakdown (19th hour). Hence, no machine waiting time occurs when we hire two repairmen. That is,

$$\text{cost of repairmen's wages} = \frac{\$10}{\text{hour}} \times 25 \text{ hours} \times 2 = \$500$$

$$\text{cost of machine waiting time} = \qquad\qquad\qquad = \quad 0$$

$$\text{total cost} \qquad\qquad\qquad\qquad\qquad = \overline{\$500}$$

Step 5. *Design and implement a course of action and maintain control.*

Based on the limited sample of 25 hours of operation, the desirable course of action is to employ two repairmen. However, at this stage, before implementation, the manager must question his assumptions and see whether operational procedures can be improved (e.g., can the idle time of repairmen be utilized in other organizational tasks). The model produces a *possible* solution—based on certain assumptions. The manager must not accept this solution blindly. He must weigh its feasibility and viability in terms of realistic environmental and organizational circumstances. The point to emphasize is that management is a dynamic concept and the manager must continually monitor the environment and maintain control.

[*Note:* It should be mentioned here that the queuing problem simulated in Table 15.5 followed what is known as the "time-oriented" mode of simulation (also referred to in the literature as *time increment* simulation or *uniform increment* simulation). This refers to the fact that uniform time increments were used as the guide to simulate the state of the system. After an increment of time had passed, we determined if any events had occurred. Alternatively, we can conduct what is known as the "event-oriented" simulation (also referred to in the literature as *event increment* or *variable increment* simulation). This refers to the fact that the occurrence of the event is used as the guide to simulate the state of the system. Incremental steps are generally uneven and the magnitude of each step is the size of the interval between events. An example of event-oriented simulation is provided in the text entitled *Study Guide and Cases* that accompanies this book.]

15.12
Summary

In this chapter, we defined the queuing problem, discussed the basic structure and components of a queuing system, presented an elementary queuing model (single-channel, single-phase), and illustrated how queuing problems can be analyzed by simulation as well as analytical procedures.

A queuing, or waiting-line, problem arises whenever the demand for customer service cannot perfectly be matched by a set of well-defined service facilities. The queuing system, which provides the general framework for analyzing queuing problems, consists of four components: (1) input source, (2) service system, (3) the queue, and (4) the queue discipline. The characteristics of each of these components were described.

The performance of a queuing system is measured by such operating characteristics as average waiting time in the queue, average length of the queue, and so on. These operating characteristics can be utilized in analyzing, evaluating, and improving a current system or designing a new queuing system. Several operating characteristics of a queuing system were defined and then calculated analytically with reference to a single-channel, single-phase queuing model.

Finally, we illustrated how queuing problems can be analyzed by simulation, and how the results of simulation can be used for making managerial decisions.

References

Bhat, U. N. "Sixty Years of Queuing Theory." *Management Science*, Vol. 15 (1969), B280–B294.

Bhatia, A., and A. Garg. "Basic Structure of Queuing Problems." *Journal of Industrial Engineering*, Vol. 14 (1963), 13–17.

Buffa, E. S. *Operations Management: Problems and Models*, 3rd ed. New York: John Wiley & Sons, Inc., 1972.

Cooper, R. B. *Introduction to Queuing Theory*. New York: Macmillan Publishing Co., Inc., 1972.

Cox, D. R., and W. L. Smith. *Queues*. New York: John Wiley & Sons, Inc., 1961.

De Marco, R. V. "Discussion of the Mathematical and Simulation Approach to Queuing Theory." *Journal of Systems Management*, Vol. 22, No. 1 (Jan. 1971), 26–31.

Howl, J. M. "Queuing Systems." *Automatica*, Vol. 3 (1966), 321–344.

Lee, A. M. *Applied Queuing Theory*. New York: St. Martin's Press, Inc., 1966.

Morse, P. M. *Queues, Inventories, and Maintenance*. New York: John Wiley & Sons, Inc., 1958.

Newell, G. E. *Applications of Queuing Theory*. New York: Barnes & Noble Books, 1971.

Page, E. *Queuing Theory in Operations Research*. New York: Crane, Russak & Company, Inc., 1972.

Panico, J. A. *Queuing Theory*. Englewood Cliffs, N.J.: Prentice-Hall, Inc., 1969.

Ruiz-Pala, E., et al. *Waiting Line Models*. New York: Van Nostrand Reinhold Company, 1967.

Saaty, T. L. *Elements of Queuing Theory with Applications*. New York: McGraw-Hill Book Company, 1961.

White, J. A., J. W. Schmidt, and G. K. Bennett. *Analysis of Queuing Systems.* New York: Academic Press, Inc., 1975.

Review Questions and Problems

15.1. What factors give rise to a queuing problem?

15.2. What are the four basic components of a queuing system? Describe each component.

15.3. Explain the following terms: (a) balking, (b) reneging, (c) patient versus impatient customers, (d) finite versus infinite population size, (e) distribution of interarrival times, and (f) distribution of arrival rate.

15.4. What is the relationship between the mean of the Poisson distribution and the mean of the exponential distribution?

15.5. List various possible configurations of the service facilities in a queuing system.

15.6. What are some of the operating characteristics of a queuing system? How can they be used in the evaluation, or design, of a queuing system?

15.7. A containerized cargo ship, S.S. Kontiki, docks at a small facility. The rate of unloading the containers follows a Poisson distribution, with an average rate of 10 per hour. After unloading, the containers are dispatched by a single truck to their final destination. On the average the dock facility can hold 20 containers. What is minimum rate of dispatching containers from the docks so as to prevent a halt in the unloading process?

15.8. In the Knot-EZ Bakery, an attendant must be present to punch holes in the bagels. The bagels are delivered by a conveyor belt at a Poisson-distributed rate of 2,000 per hour. If the attendant cannot allow on the average more than 50 bagels to back up, what must be his punching rate? If the attendant can punch each bagel on the average in 1.5 seconds (exponentially distributed), what is average waiting time of each bagel?

15.9. At Corro & Zianni's car wash, customers arrive at an average rate of 30 per hour (Poisson distribution). One attendant can clean cars at an average rate of 35 per hour (Poisson distribution). If the attendant is paid $5/hour and the opportunity cost of lost customers is $7.50/car, how many attendants should be present? Assume that a sale is lost if the queue size is 4 or more.

15.10. The Bison Burger Company, a fast food chain, is concerned with the quality of service (they have given up on the quality of food). They have hired consultants to study the queuing problems. The initial study indicates that the following conditions exist: steady-state, single-channel, single-phase system with Poisson arrival rate and exponential service time. Arrivals occur at an average rate of 20 per hour and the mean service time is 2 minutes/customer.

    (a) What percent of the time will the server be idle?
    (b) What is the mean waiting time for a customer?
    (c) What is the average time of a customer in the entire system?
    (d) What is the average number of customers in the system?
    (e) What is the system's utilization factor?

15.11. The Military Air Transport System (MATS) is studying the queuing problems involved with unloading a C-130 aircraft. Cargo is unloaded onto pallets by a special machine, one plane being unloaded at a time. Using only one machine the unloading rate is one plane every 2 hours, varying according to a Poisson distribution. Under peace-time conditions, MATS is concerned solely with the cost effectiveness of the unloading procedure. The cost of using the machine is $50/day and the cost of a waiting aircraft is $120/hour. Is it cost-effective to use only one machine? Assume that the mean interarrival time of aircraft is 3 hours and the arrival times are exponentially distributed.

15.12. The quality-control lab for Ellis-Dee Pharmaceuticals performs tests on samples of a particular drug. Past data, shown in Table 15.6, give the frequency distribution of the time to process one sample.

Table 15.6

Process Time (hours)	Frequency
1	5
2	10
3	20
4	10
5	5

If a sample arrives every 2 hours, simulate the quality-control system for 10 samples. Assume that there is only one chemist in the laboratory. From the simulation, determine:

(a) The average waiting time of the samples
(b) The average processing time
(c) The average time in the system

15.13. Assume a service system with a single service station (one attendant) in which buses arrive for service according to the probability distribution given in Table 15.7. The distribution of service time is also shown in Table 15.7.

Table 15.7

Number of Bus Arrivals per Hour	Probability	Service Time (manhours)	Probability
1	0.10	0.5	0.45
2	0.20	1.0	0.35
3	0.40	1.5	0.15
4	0.30	2.0	0.05

Assume that buses arrive at the beginning of the hour. Simulate the system for an 8-hour period under the conditions that the service to each bus that arrived during the 8-hour interval must be completed. Calculate the following for the simulated time period: (1) average service time for the buses, (2) average waiting time for the buses, and (3) idle time for the service station attendant. Assume that the service station attendant is being paid $15/hour, and the waiting time of a bus costs $20/hour. Will you recommend the hiring of a second attendant? Assume that you want to install a mechanical servicing system that can simultaneously service buses at a rate of 4 buses/hour. The automated system will cost the company $100/hour. Will you recommend installation of the system?

PART V

Implementation

Implementation of Quantitative Models

16.1
Introduction

The previous chapters of this book have been devoted to accomplishing four main objectives: (1) to present a framework for thinking about management theory and practice (with special emphasis on the quantitative approach); (2) to provide conceptual foundations for building, solving, and applying quantitative decision models; (3) to describe and explain a selected set of planning and control models; and (4) to differentiate between and acquaint the reader with the analytical and simulation approaches for deriving solutions to mathematical models. In general, our focus up to this point has been on two aspects of quantitative models. First, we have concentrated on the *logic* and *mechanics* of building quantitative models. Second, we have shown how quantitative models can be used to *derive solutions* to specific managerial problems. However, we have not, as yet, explicitly addressed ourselves to the important topic of "implementation of quantitative models."

The actual implementation of quantitative models is of the utmost importance, both to the manager and the management scientist. This importance derives from the fact that solutions to managerial problems are essentially courses of actions, strategies, or policies that *must be implemented* to produce desired results. Without actual implementation, the building of models and subsequent derivation of solutions to managerial problems (by using these models) will amount to no more than an interesting academic exercise. What, after all, is the value of a quantitative decision model that cannot pass these basic tests of successful implementation: *technical feasibility, economic viability, organizational pragmatism,* and *actual utility*?

The implementation of quantitative models is an extremely complex area, as it involves multifaceted relationships and interactions among the manager, management scientist, top administration, production personnel, and other organizational resources (e.g., computer system). The issues involved in the problem of implementation are rather complex and multidimensional (e.g., they consist of technical, economic, social, political, and psychological components). A thorough discussion of these issues is beyond the scope of this book. However, we do want to alert the reader that, beyond the domain of the scientist, there exists the world of the practicing manager where the organizational action is—and where the problem of implementation must be faced.

The purpose of this chapter is to present some of the important aspects and issues of implementation of quantitative models. We shall address ourselves to these major questions: What is an appropriate framework for discussing the problem of implementation? What are some of the relationships and interactions involved in the process of implementation? What is involved in the three-way interface among the manager, the management scientist, and the computer system? What factors generate the need for developing and utilizing quantitative models? What is needed in terms of *technical requirements* and *behavioral changes* to transform a theoretical model into a practical reality? What technical support and facilities are required to prepare the problem data in the proper format, choose the proper computer program to execute the necessary computations, and arrange the computer output in a format that is meaningful in managerial decision making? What behavioral changes are desirable, and what organizational environment must be created to effectively implement the solution? What is the current state of the art as far as implementation is concerned? These are obviously some of the most important questions and considerations that have real significance to the manager.

16.2
A Framework for Discussing the Problem of Implementation

It is often said that the *process* is as important as the *product*; that the *means* are even more important than the *ends*; and that *effort* is what really counts. These statements, and the philosophy behind them, are important in any field of human endeavor. They are, however, especially relevant to the task of formulating management science models, deriving their solutions, and implementing the programs, procedures, or policies suggested by the model solutions. This is because management science models are invariably quantitative models, and they require the problem to be expressed in quantitative and often mathematical terms. This requirement yields several dividends, not the least of which is an increased understanding of the problem and a more meaningful awareness of the system environment. Hence, whenever a situation arises that calls for the application of management science models, the first task is to define and formulate the problem in quantitative terms. The very attempt to define the problem in a precise and structured manner has several inherent advantages for the manager because he is forced to think about improving technology, developing new contacts and sources for procuring organizational resources, developing new products, eliminating some current products, seeking new markets, and so on. Yet, to derive full benefits from any model, tool, or technique of modern management, the manager must move beyond the stage of problem definition and formulation.[1] That is, the manager must consider the very important aspect of *potential of application* of the specific model and *implementation* of the solution suggested by the model.

16.2.1 THE PROCESS VIEW OF IMPLEMENTATION

The term "implementation" has been examined in the literature from different perspectives. For example, the term has been used to refer to "the manner in which the manager may come to use the results of scientific effort," and accordingly the *problem of implementation* is viewed as the "problem of determining what activities of the scientist and manager are most appropriate to bring about an effective relationship."[2] Another view of implementation adds the element of "control" to the concept of working relationship between the manager

---

[1] See Section 9.7 for a brief discussion of problem formulation.
[2] Churchman and Schainblatt [1965].

and the management scientist. Thus, successful implementation is defined as "the establishment of a viable working relationship between the user and researcher, which continues for a reasonable time period, and during which controls for the continuous review and scrutiny of the researcher's recommended solution are developed and utilized."[3] Other definitions of implementation have concentrated on even more narrow interests of the scientist (e.g., a model is thought to be implemented once the scientist *sells* to the manager the suggestion of using a specific model) or the manager (e.g., implementation takes place *only* if economic dividends flow to the manager and the organization). In our opinion, these and similar definitions lack comprehensiveness and thereby do not render adequate justice to the importance of implementation.

The full impact and potential of implementation can be appreciated only if it is viewed as a *continuous process*—integral to the basic missions of the management scientist, the manager, and the organization. Thus, we shall use the term "implementation" to refer to the entire set of activities, relationships, and interactions involved in the development and utilization of quantitative models—including the technical, economic, political, social, and psychological issues that are inherent in the solutions, strategies, or policies suggested by the model for solving organizational problems.

The topic of implementation of quantitative models, therefore, can best be discussed by viewing implementation as a *continuous process* over time rather than as a fixed event at a particular point in time. For purposes of analysis, we can say that the process of implementation starts with the *perceived need* (on the part of the management scientist and/or the manager) to develop or use a quantitative model and ends when the results of the model are implemented. However, it should be emphasized that the entire process of implementation should more appropriately be seen as a *cycle* in which the model helps produce better results by assisting the manager, and the experience gained from implementation helps improve the model. This interactive and evolutionary mode of model development, and model implementation, is shown in Figure 16.1.

16.2.2 STAGES OF IMPLEMENTATION

One way to examine the process view of implementation is to divide the implementation process into specific stages and then focus on the problems, issues, and aspects that belong to *each stage*. For example, *adoption, systemati-*

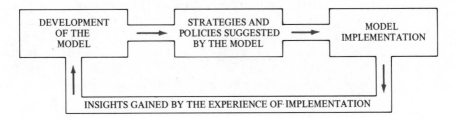

Figure 16.1. Interactive and Evolutionary Mode of Model Development and Implementation.

[3] Markland and Newett [1972, p. 33].

zation, and *institutionalization* can be considered as three stages in the process of implementation.[4] The idea of *adoption* refers to acceptance by management of the philosophy of management science in general, or of the results of a particular study dealing with quantitative models. The *systematization* stage concerns the development of formal procedures for implementing and evaluating the model. Finally, the stage of *institutionalization* focuses on the formal integration of management science into the organization. In this stage, the organizational role of the management scientist is formally defined so that the potential of effective communications is improved, and resistance to change can be minimized.

Another classification divides the process of implementation of a management science project into six "life phases," as described below.[5]

1. *Prebirth Phase.* This phase occurs when either the operating manager or the management science manager perceives a possibly useful management science project. During this phase no formal project exists, but small, informal projects may be in progress within the operating division.
2. *Introductory Phase.* This phase begins with operating management granting a "charter" for a specific management science activity. As a result, specific resources are allocated to the activity.
3. *Transitional Phase.* This phase is characterized by an emphasis on results by operating and top management. During this phase, the management science team is necessarily results-oriented—toward project definition, and model construction and solution.
4. *Maturity Phase.* This phase is signaled by the acceptance of the study by operating management as a decision-making aid. Continued modeling and analytical efforts by the management science team are likely during this phase, but the intensity of commitment of resources is probably diminishing.
5. *Death Phase.* During this phase, all project activities are drawn to a formal completion, by agreement of the user and management science manager. If this study has proven successful, an attempt may be made to "systematize" its results on a recurring basis for the operating manager.
6. *Resurrection Phase.* This phase occurs when a previously "dead" project is resurrected, for any of a number of reasons (e.g., a new manager becomes interested in a "dead" project, or software permitting the solution of a previously unsolvable problem becomes available).

Once the idea of various important stages of the project's life is accepted, the next logical step is to develop an evaluation procedure based on a set of "implementation criteria." In Figure 16.2, we present an implementation evaluation grid based on 10 different criteria.[6] The evaluation scale for the grid shown in Figure 16.2 ranges from 0.0 to 1.0, and a specific scale value is assigned according to the importance, during any particular life phase, of *each* implementation criterion. That is, a value ranging between 0.0 to 1.0 (the closer the value to 1.0, the more important is the criterion) is placed at the intersection of an implementation criterion and a specific life phase. For example, top management interest might have a scale value of 1.00 in the introductory phase, and perhaps a

---

[4] Wolek [1975, p. 38].

[5] From Markland and Newett [1972, pp. 33–34].

[6] The grid, developed by Markland and Newett, was applied to evaluate a simulation model of a distribution system. See Markland and Newett [1972, p. 37].

Implementation Criteria	Prebirth	Introductory	Transitional	Maturity	Death	Resurrection
1. Managerial						
a. Top management interest		1.0		0.0		
b. Operating management involvement						
c. OR management managerial skill						
2. OR/MS Team				0.8		
a. Technical ability						
b. Project management skills						
c. Results orientation						
d. Communicative ability						
3. Project						
a. Technical feasibility						
b. Economic feasibility			0.4			
c. Operational feasibility						
Summation						

Figure 16.2. Implementation Evaluation Grid.

value of 0.0 in the maturity phase. By constructing such a grid, the manager, in conjunction with the management scientist, can focus his resources and efforts in a selective manner, thereby increasing the potential of successful implementation.

16.2.3 RELATIONSHIPS AND INTERACTIONS INVOLVED IN THE PROCESS OF IMPLEMENTATION

As mentioned in the preceding section, one way to examine the problem of implementation is to divide the process of implementation into specific stages and then analyze the issues that belong to each stage. This might be considered a

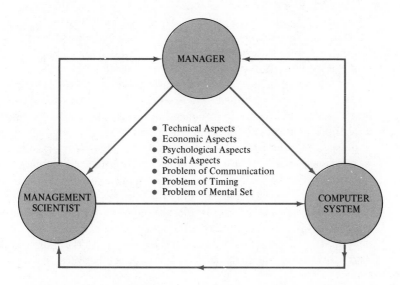

Figure 16.3. Interactions and Relationships Involved in the Process of Implementation.

micro approach to implementation. A second approach, which is *macro* in nature, concentrates on the overall system (and its components) within which the process of implementation takes place. The system consists of several organizational components, but three specific entities are central to the development and implementation of quantitative decision models: (1) the manager, (2) the management scientist, and (3) the computer system. The relationships and interactions that arise among these entities are very complex, indeed.

As mentioned earlier, and as shown in Figure 16.3, these relationships and interactions have *technical* (e.g., is the model technically sound and can it do the job?), *economic* (e.g., will the model save money? Is it cost-effective?), *psychological* (e.g., does the model pose a threat to the manager? What can be done to make him feel secure?), *political* (e.g., what can be done to *sell* the model to the entire organization?), *social* (e.g., how can resistance to change be minimized?), and *organizational* (e.g., how can management science win a formal place in the organization?) aspects. As indicated in Figure 16.3, a three-way interface exists among the manager, the management scientist, and the computer system. The probability of successful implementation can significantly be increased if the nature of this three-way interface is fully grasped by the manager and the management scientist.

Another version of the macro approach to examine the problem of implementation suggests that the degree of successful implementation is determined by two sets of factors.[7] The factors included in one set are related directly to a specific project and hence are called "project particulars." The project particulars include such factors as cost–benefit analysis, technical feasibility, and priority of the project. The factors included in the second set are grouped under the title "implementation climate." The implementation climate takes account of, and is shaped by, the social, political, and psychological environment of the organization—as well as external influences exerted by such sources and entities as government, the economy, the public, competitors, and suppliers. The factors included in the implementation climate determine the *organizational viability* of the project. In Figure 16.4 we show an overview of the implementation process based on the concepts of project particulars and implementation climate. A delineation of the two distinct but intimately related sets of determinants, shown in Figure 16.4, is an important element of any implementation effort. The manager must understand the nature, role, and impact of these and related factors that are crucial in the application and implementation of quantitative models.

We have now examined three approaches for discussing the problem of implementation. These approaches have the same objective: improving the probability of successful implementation by understanding the important issues and aspects of the process of implementation. Let us refer, once again, to the macro view presented in Figure 16.3. The multidimensional issues and problems, depicted in Figure 16.3, are obviously present in *every* interface involved in the process of implementation. The only difference is the *degree of importance* of a specific issue or aspect. For example, although the question of economic viability is relevant in each of the three interfaces shown in Figure 16.3, it is *extremely important* in the interface between the manager and the management scientist. And it is *relatively less important* in the interface between the manager and the computer system.

---

[7] See Turban and Meredith in Turban and Loomba [1976, pp. 369–381].

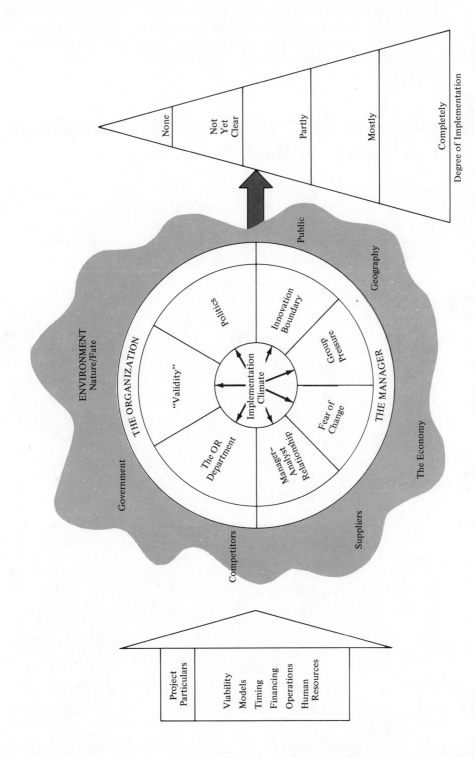

Figure 16.4. Overview of the Process of Implementation. (From Turban and Meredith, in Turban and Loomba [1976, p. 372].)

Similarly, the psychological aspects do not play as important a role in the interface between the management scientist and the computer system as in the interface between the manager and the management scientist. Hence, for the sake of economy, we shall *not* discuss every single issue in every interface. Instead, in any given two-way interface, we shall present only those issues and aspects that we consider to be most important.

16.3
Interface Between the Manager and the Management Scientist in Successful Implementation

We have already mentioned the complexity and multidimensionality (i.e., the existence of technical, economic, psychological, political, social, and organizational aspects) of the issues involved in the process of implementation. In this section, we examine some of the concepts that are most important in the interface between the manager and the management scientist.

16.3.1 PERCEIVED NEED

The interactions between the manager and the management scientist are based on the assumption that there exists a *perceived need*, on the part of the management scientist and/or the manager, to develop and eventually utilize quantitative models. Two separate but interdependent forces are at work along this dimension. First, the management scientist dedicates his energies to model development because, *as a scientist*, he wants to expand the theoretical frontiers of knowledge. Thus, the management scientist continually attempts to improve the quality and scope of existing models (e.g., inventory models that are normally used in production planning and control are refined to solve problems in financial management), and spends his creative efforts to develop new models that can handle new and more complex problems of modern society (e.g., space exploration, ecology, energy).[8]

The second force behind the developmental effort has its origins in the psychology and actions of the manager. What happens in real life is this. The manager comes to know about the availability and success stories of the quantitative models from business publications, professional journals, newspaper articles, papers delivered at professional meetings, and his friends in other organizations. This excites his imagination. Accordingly, as a potential user, and as a potential beneficiary, the manager initiates the necessary search process to acquire the capabilities of using quantitative models (e.g., an outside consulting firm is retained or an in-house management science group is established).

It should be noted that the motivation on the part of the manager is usually rooted in two factors. First, he sincerely believes that the utilization of the new

---

[8] It should be emphasized that for the sole purpose of pushing the frontiers of knowledge, the scientist can legitimately ignore the criterion of cost-effectiveness. For example, it can be argued that our mission to Mars is not really cost-effective today. However, if history is any guide to the future, it will yield significant economic dividends to future generations. (This argument was suggested by my colleague, Lou Stern.)

tools and techniques of management science will produce economic dividends for him and his organization. Second, he does not want to be left behind the times and be labeled as a "backward" manager. Thus, the manager launches a formal organizational effort to utilize science and quantitative models.

16.3.2 CHARACTERISTICS OF THE MODEL

Are there any guidelines that the manager and the management scientist can use in developing or selecting an effective model? Are there certain requirements or characteristics that a model should possess to effectively assist the manager in making decisions and solving problems? The answer is definitely yes.[9] First, the effectiveness of a model is directly related to its *accuracy, reliability*, and *validity*. The accuracy of a model is determined by the quality of information and data fed into the model. The manager can obviously play an important role in improving the quality of data and hence increase the accuracy of the model. The reliability of a model refers to the degree of consistency with which a model produces correct solutions to the problems for which it was developed. The reliability of a model can be improved by checking its internal consistency. The validity of a model concerns the question of whether the model in fact represents the phenomenon it is supposed to represent. The validity of a model is determined by the considerations of appropriateness of assumptions, criteria, and sensitivity to changes in inputs and parameters.

Furthermore, it has been suggested that, to be useful to the manager, a model should be *simple* (easy to understand), *robust* (hard to get absurd answers from), *easy to control* (the manager knows what input data would be required to produce desired output), *adaptive* (the model can be adjusted as new information is acquired), *as complete as possible* (important phenomena will be included even if they require judgmental estimates of their effects), and *easy to communicate with* (the manager can quickly and easily change inputs and obtain and understand outputs).[10]

16.3.3 PROBLEM OF COMMUNICATION

A natural *communication problem* exists between the manager and the management scientist because, by tradition and training, "they are, with rare exceptions, very different types of people along dimensions important for successful implementation."[11] However, this differentiation between the personalities of the manager and the management scientist can be converted to a special advantage if a continuous and conscious effort is made to maintain effective communication and to integrate different viewpoints. The manager must clearly define the problem and communicate his *perception* to the management scientist. On his part, the management scientist must explain *all* the assumptions and weaknesses of the proposed model and earn the full confidence of the manager. The "punch of the model" can be made stronger, and the potential of successful implementation increased, if there is proper diagnosis of the problem, based upon an open, frank, and constructive discussion between the manager and the management scientist.

[9] See, for example, Eilon [1974] and Huysmans [1970].

[10] Little [1970, p. B-466].

[11] Hammond [1974, p. 13].

16.3.4 PROBLEM OF TIMING

An important determinant of successful implementation relates to the question of "proper timing" for developing and utilizing quantitative models. One aspect of proper timing is the existence of a congenial and supportive organizational environment and the degree of top management support. Quite often, the implementation of a model can succeed or fail, depending solely upon who initiates the project. For example, it was demonstrated in a recent study that all but one of the projects initiated by top management were implemented; 75 percent of the projects initiated by the user were implemented; but less than 50 percent of the projects initiated by the operations researcher were implemented.[12] Hence, it is extremely important that the management scientist seek and secure top management support *before* launching a management science project.

Another aspect of proper timing is that economic viability and technical feasibility of the model should be demonstrated at an *early stage* of implementation. In addition, the manager must be fully involved in the difficult decisions affecting the choice of those assumptions and considerations that are likely to mold the very nature and impact of the model. In this manner, the manager can institute proper controls and minimize the possibility of "future surprises."

16.3.5 ORGANIZATIONAL LOCATION

Another important determinant of successful implementation is the organizational location of the in-house management science group. Basically, there are two organizational arrangements and, as in everything else involving human interactions, each has its advantages and disadvantages. One arrangement is to have a centralized management science department located at the corporate headquarters and reporting directly to the president or a vice-president of the company. The main advantage of this arrangement is the appearance, if not the reality, of top management support. The main disadvantage is the fact that the management science group is removed from the actual firing lines that are manned by the manager. And, therefore, the probability of miscommunication and loss of trust between the manager and the management scientist is rather high.

The second arrangement places the management science resource under the direct supervision of line managers. The main advantage of this arrangement is that the manager exhibits a greater willingness to use quantitative models. In this arrangement, the manager has the feeling of security and power because the management scientist is accountable to him—rather than to someone who is organizationally, and perhaps even geographically, far removed from the scene of action. The main disadvantage of this arrangement is that the management scientist tends to adopt the myopic vision that is so common to managers at operational levels.

---

[12] Lonnstedt [1975, p. 25].

16.4
Interface Between the Management Scientist and the Computer System

The most important aspects of the interface between the management scientist and the computer system are economic and technical in nature (although one cannot ignore the psychological and social impact of introducing the role of computers in organizations). Furthermore, the economic and technical aspects are interlinked, as the main problem for the management scientist is to design a new computer system, or utilize the existing system, in such a way that technical demands of the model can be met without incurring excessive costs. Also, questions relating to *speed, precision, file capacity, core memory, turnaround time, cost,* and *specific needs* of the user must be considered.

With the rapid progress in computer technology, the use of computers to implement quantitative models has increased significantly. Only in very rare circumstances is a model excluded these days from potential implementation because of either technical limitations of the computer or the cost of running the model on the computer. Actually, we have a virtual revolution in the economics of computer technology. The scope, power, and economic feasibility of the computer have been expanding at an accelerating rate. For example, with the advent of microprocessor units (MPU), we can now purchase computer power for only $360 that would have cost $18 million twenty years ago.[13] This type of development is having a significant impact on companies in terms of using quantitative models and in terms of designing new organizational strategies.

To increase the probability of successful implementation, the management scientist must work closely with the computer specialist for the purpose of developing computer programs or selecting the proper canned program, designing formal procedures for putting and running the model on the computer, and creating input–output forms that are easy to interpret by the manager.

As the role of computers and such developments as time sharing (see Section 16.6.2) and computer utilities becomes more important, the degree of interaction between the management scientist and computer will increase. Thus, the interface problems shown in Figure 16.3 will demand serious attention of both the manager and the management scientist.

16.5
Interface Between the Manager and the Computer System

The most important aspects of the interface between the manager and the computer system are economic, social, and organizational. Economic viability is obviously a *necessary* condition, and the manager can easily determine the requirements that will make economic sense when computers are used to

[13] See "The Smart Machine Revolution," *Business Week,* July 5, 1976, pp. 38–44.

implement quantitative models. However, the social and organizational issues are not that easily resolved. For they involve people who perceive the power of computers to be a real threat to their positions and security. This is particularly true for middle managers, whose analytical and report-generating functions can easily be transferred to the computer. "Traditional functions, traditional organizational ideas, traditional sources and repositories of information, traditional decision-making prerogatives are bound to be upset when analyses and decisions, once necessarily delegated to various functional managers, become directly accessible to top executives and can be analyzed fast enough to warrant the time of top management."[14] For successful implementation, the manager must understand the basics of a computer system. Furthermore, the manager must develop a sound *management information system* that integrates the efforts, capabilities, and resources of the three entities shown in Figure 16.3 and that provides the manager with timely information for making decisions.

16.6
Management Information Systems and Implementation of Quantitative Models

Modern organizations are inundated with data and information that are either generated by internal transactions (e.g., selling, purchasing, manufacturing, paying wages and salaries) or gathered from outside sources (e.g., forecasts and projections regarding gross national product, employment, inflation, imports, exports, tax laws, government regulations). Such data and information are needed for making managerial decisions. No organization can function without an adequate exchange of relevant information among its various decision centers. However, there is a major problem in arranging such an exchange—the problem of *information overload*. The amount and variety of information have been growing at an exponential rate and society is confronted with an information explosion. The technicians, often ignorant of managerial requirements and in their zeal to "impress the boss," have a tendency to produce computer-processed data that are often unnecessary, unwieldy, expensive, and not very productive. Managers must learn to cope with this phenomenon—they must *manage* information, and not be buried by the avalanche of irrelevant data. That is, a *system* or *structure* must be developed to collect, organize, process, and disseminate right type of information at the right time to the right person. The awareness of this need has resulted in an area called *management information systems* (MIS).

A *management information system* is any system designed to economically collect, carefully organize, properly process, and selectively transmit data and information to designated points in the organization. Management information systems derive their name and meaning from the fact that their focus is on the flow of information and that they represent a *network* rather than an isolated exchange of information required for management decisions. The important considerations in designing a management information system relate to the *type*,

---

[14] Hertz in Turban and Loomba [1976, p. 338].

amount, *form,* and *frequency* of information required in the decision-making processes. In addition, to be effective, information must be timely, relevant, and valid.

Although it is possible to design and operate a *manual* management information system, we assume (and evidence supports this assumption) that the computer is an integral part of any modern management information system. Accordingly, in Figure 16.5, we present the main features of a *computer-based* management information system. It is clear from Figure 16.5 that the implementation and effectiveness of quantitative models depends on a sound management information system. After all, a quantitative decision model is nothing but a device to produce rational decisions. The effectiveness of these decisions is determined by the quality of input data and by the quality of the system that transmits information regarding these decisions to appropriate managers and decision centers. Thus, a management information system provides the "nerve system" and the machinery that permit quantitative decision models to operate effectively.[15]

It is appropriate at this time to present a very brief discussion of a *computer system* and *time sharing.*

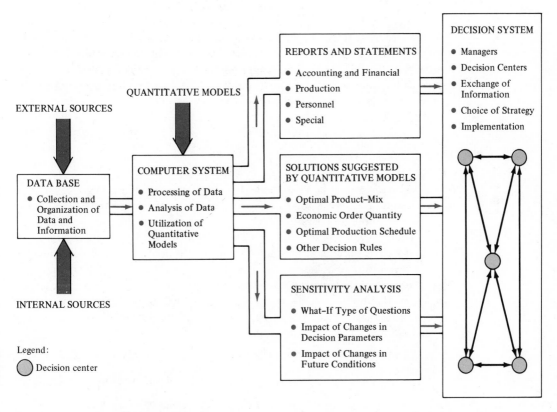

Figure 16.5. Main Features of a Computer-Based Management Information System.

[15] For a discussion of a framework that integrates basic concepts of MIS into the management science function, see Schneyman [1976].

16.6.1 WHAT IS A COMPUTER SYSTEM?

A *computer* is nothing more than a machine that can perform arithmetic operations and make logical choices with high speed and precision.[16] A *computer system* essentially consists of five basic components:[17] (1) hardware, (2) software, (3) programs, (4) procedures, and (5) personnel. The term *hardware* refers to the equipment part of the computer system, the main computer, and its auxiliary parts. The term *software* refers to a program, code, or a set of instructions that must be fed to the computer to execute computing tasks. A *program* is a set of instructions, provided by the computer manufacturer, obtained from an outside vendor of software packages, or designed by the user to perform specialized tasks. A program is written in one of the computer languages, such as FORTRAN, BASIC, and COBOL.[18] For example, it is a simple task to write a FORTRAN program that will systematically execute all the steps of the simplex method. In practice, it is not necessary to write one's own program, because several standard software packages are commercially available.

A computer *procedure* refers to instructions regarding the procurement and preparation of data, operation of the computer, and how to deal with operational contingencies. The *personnel* necessary to a computer system consist of systems analysts, programmers, and computer operators.[19] The total computer system performs the essential functions of preparing the data, inputting the data (along with a program or set of instructions) to the computer in a machine-readable form, processing of the data by the main unit, storing the data in secondary or auxiliary units, obtaining the output from the computer in a specified format, and controlling or monitoring both the input and the output. The basic organization of a computer is shown in Figure 16.6.

16.6.2 TIME SHARING

In this section, we explain two modes of computer processing and give a very brief description of what is known as a *time-sharing system*. There are essentially two modes of computer processing: (1) batch processing, and (2) real-time processing. In *batch processing*, the data are accumulated over a period of time and then processed. The processing of a payroll by using the data contained in keypunched cards is an example of batch processing. In *real-time processing*, the data are not accumulated over a period of time; they are processed as soon as they are received. Examples of real-time processing include airline reservation systems. No waiting is required of a customer who is seeking information regarding the availability of space on a given flight.

---

[16] The discussion here pertains to a *digital* computer, in which the data are represented by discrete sets of digits and are based on the concept of counting. In the *analog* computer, the data are represented in a continuous form by a measurable physical quality (based on the concept of measurement).

[17] See Davis [1971, pp. 13–29].

[18] For a discussion of the computer languages, see Chapter 12 of Davis [1971]. A computer language provides the means to communicate with the computer. In practice, a set of routines, called a *compiler*, translates a program written in, say, FORTRAN, to a machine-readable form.

[19] For job descriptions, see Davis [1971, p. 16].

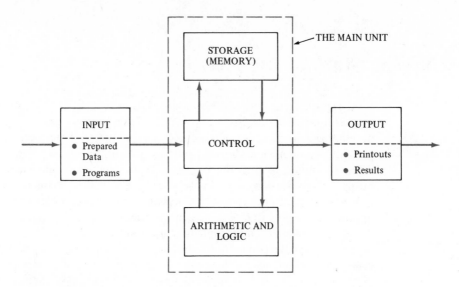

Figure 16.6. Organization of a Computer.

A *time-sharing system* exists when many users can *simultaneously* use a single computer system. The name "time-sharing" is derived from the fact that multiple users can directly and concurrently "share" the "time" of a large computer system. Use of time-sharing systems, which are based on the concept of economy of scale, is growing rapidly. In a typical time-sharing system, the central computer system is located at a central location while the users are at different and often distant places. The central computer system consists essentially of a set of computers that perform the tasks of sequencing incoming requests, performing the necessary calculations according to a set of instructions, and then sequencing the outgoing responses. The users of the time-sharing system communicate with the central computer from remote terminals. The terminals, located at various geographical locations (the terminal can be in an office, a home, a library, or a classroom), are connected with the central computer system through specially designed telephone lines. The user sends his request to the central computer by typing his data and indicating the program on an input device such as a teletype.[20] The incoming request is handled by a communications computer (at the central location) and, in sequence, is fed into the processing computer (also located at the central location). Each user is allocated a unit of time for processing his request. If the job is not completed within the allocated time, the problem is put back in computer storage until the next turn for that particular user. This pattern is repeated until the job is done and the response is sequenced back to the user through the communications center. The response is produced in the form of a printout at the remote terminal. The user can interact with the system by asking specific questions (e.g., questions on sensitivity analysis discussed in Chapter 9). All the activities in a time-sharing system are controlled by a supervisory or executive program stored in the computer memory. And, all this happens at such a fast pace that each user feels as if he had exclusive use of the entire computer system.

[20] A teletype is a device which combines the features of a telephone and a typewriter.

16.7
Current State of the Art

What is the current state of the art as far as the actual impact and implementation of quantitative models is concerned? Available evidence indicates three sets of developments that are extremely encouraging. First, there has been an impressive gain in the *organizational status* of management science, as shown by a recent survey designed to find the organizational trend of management science in business organizations (see Table 16.1).[21] The trend shown in Table 16.1 is indicative of the fact that business organizations are beginning to recognize and appreciate the potential of management science. Hence, we can expect a higher degree of application and implementation in the future.

The second development is the increased frequency with which both the academicians and business managers are beginning to engage in critical appraisal of the actual utility of management science.[22] This is a sign of maturity. Because of the penetrating questions raised in such appraisals we can expect that the *quality* of implementation will show a significant improvement in the future.

The third encouraging development is that the application of quantitative models is being extended from simple and structured operational problems (e.g., inventory control, production scheduling) to complex, ill-structured, problems of top management (e.g., design of a firm's strategy). This trend means that the *scope* of quantitative models is steadily increasing.

The problem of implementation has only recently begun to receive the degree of attention that it deserves.[23] This is only natural, as in the early stages of

Table 16.1 *Organizational Trend of Management Science in Business Organizations (percent)*

Organizational Status of Management Science	Pre–1960	1960–1965	1966–1970	1971–1974
No formal management science function	80	75	37.5	17
Recognizable management science group	20	25	37.5	33
Completely integrated management science resource	0	0	25	50

[21] Shycon [Nov. 1974]. Also, see Turban [1972]. Turban's survey indicated a phenomenal progress in the establishment of formal operations research units at the corporate level.

[22] See, for example, Grayson [1973], Wagner [1971], and Shycon [Feb. 1974].

[23] See, for example, Duncan [1974], Hammond [1974], and Argyris [1971].

development of any tool or technique the major focus of effort is always on perfecting the technical aspects. Once the technical aspects are developed and the application potential of the model is tested in the real world, the problems of implementation begin to assume their due importance. Recent studies on the implementation problems appear to arrive at three major conclusions. The first conclusion is that regardless of several technical and behavioral obstacles, the degree of implementation of quantitative models has steadily been increasing during the last three decades. This is due mainly to increased awareness regarding the actual success of tested models, higher level of technical education of the modern manager, better quality and scope of the model, and reduced cost of computer systems.

The second conclusion is that the degree of successful implementation can be increased by considering *explicitly* the psychological and sociological factors in the design of the model. The possible conflict of goals between management scientists and the user is a case in point. The manager might feel threatened by the potential success of the model. For example, the manager might feel that the model will replace him as a decision maker. This type of fear is, of course, not supported by evidence. The model does *not* replace the manager; it assists him in his decision making. Another source of resistance to implementation is the fear of the operating and production workers that the model might drastically alter their working conditions, and thereby reduce their work satisfaction. This fear is also unfounded. A successful implementation of management science spreads benefits at all levels in the organization and, if managed properly, can increase the quality of life for all organization members, including the production workers.

The third conclusion is that implementation of management science models can be increased only by conducting extensive research into the behavioral areas of interpersonal, group, and intergroup functioning.[24] This assertion recognizes the vital importance of linking behavioral aspects of the process of management with the technical aspects of modern management science models.[25] This emphasis is an inherent part of the definition of management that was developed in Chapter 1.

We conclude this section with a note of caution advanced by Eilon.[26]

> Mathematical modeling has made an immense contribution to management—it has helped to convert muddled thinking and amorphous deliberations into an orderly analysis, allowing crucial issues to be highlighted and purposely debated. It has taken the mystique out of some managerial tasks. It has allowed for many programmable decisions to be programmed and has shown how certain analytical tools cut across conventional boundaries between types of managerial functions, or even industries.
>
> But the present shortcomings of mathematical modeling and the blind belief of some modelers in the infinite power of mathematical analysis have led to a backlash. The criticisms range from accusations that most analysts address themselves to the wrong problems, to suggestions that analytical models are inappropriate for solving managerial problems. It is important for us to recognize the various shortcomings and limitations of the present state of the art in order to appreciate the true contribution that can be made and in order to combat the total rejection advocated by a growing number of skeptics.

[24] Dalton [1968, Chap. 5].

[25] Schultz and Slevin [1975].

[26] Eilon [1974].

16.8
Future: An Overview

Quantitative thinking, based on the foundations of science and scientific method, has enabled man to land instruments on, and receive information from the planet Mars—located at an enormous distance of 220 million miles. The impact of quantitative models on the practice of management may not, at this time, seem to be that spectacular. However, the future is certain to bring a managerial revolution in the use of quantitative models. First, a large majority of future managers will have acquired, by formal education and training, a working knowledge of management and behavioral sciences. Second, advanced computer technology is likely to transform the very mode of management. With the help of innovative and sophisticated management information systems, managers will be able to retrieve information rapidly and make decisions in real time. A reflection of things to come is provided by the following account of a management information system installed at a medium-sized instrument company.[27]

> The company was operating with no formal planning, no budget, no controls, no written job descriptions, no performance reporting, and no accountability measurement. In place of this chaos, the company now has established a management system that precisely defines jobs to be done and has set up a parallel information system that just as precisely provides the data that managers need to perform those jobs. Through 40 newly developed computer programs, information packages that include data in such diverse areas as personnel, order entries, inventories, and even international exchange rates automatically go to managers who need to know.
>
> Engineers who process orders, for example, now sit in front of computer terminals and make instant decisions that cut as much as three weeks from the time it used to take to get an order into production. Each order is first checked against all customer and product information in the data banks to make sure the customer is solid and the production is feasible. Then every component of the order is broken out and estimates of delivery date and component costs are calculated. If approved, a manufacturing order is placed. At the same time, purchase orders for parts may go out, and assembly operations are scheduled.
>
> Each day management gets a report of the dollar volume of orders and the units demand by product and customer, and the finance department is triggered to handle credit checks, purchase orders, or—in the case of a big system—lines of credit needed to finance the job.

Finally, management technology will integrate, in a more formal and effective manner, the behavioral considerations in the actual implementation of quantitative models. Only in this manner can we begin to realize the full potential of management science.

[27] From "Replacing a One-Man Show," *Business Week*, Aug. 16, 1976, pp. 154–156.

16.9
Summary

In this chapter, we presented some of the important aspects and issues involved in the implementation of quantitative models. A framework for examining the problem of implementation was developed. It was emphasized that implementation should be viewed as a continuous process, a cycle, rather than a fixed event.

Two approaches to examine the process of implementation were suggested. One approach, micro in nature, divided implementation into specific stages and focused on the problems, issues, and aspects that belong to each stage. The second approach, macro in nature, concentrated on the overall system (and its components) within which the process of implementation takes place. The macro approach was analyzed by discussing some of the important issues involved in each two-way interface among the manager, the management scientist, and the computer system.

Main features of a computer-based management information system were presented and the role of management information systems in implementing quantitative models was described. The basic organization of a computer system was described, and the concepts of batch processing, real-time processing, and time sharing were discussed.

The current state of the art was established by drawing on recent studies dealing with the "organizational status" of management science and actual utilization of quantitative models. These studies indicated a steadily increasing rate of implementation of quantitative models. Furthermore, they pointed out that the scope of quantitative models will increase and the quality of implementation will improve significantly in the future. We also provided a very brief overview of the future regarding the changes that we can expect in the mode of management.

Finally, and perhaps most important, it should be noted that the quantitative approach to management is not a choice but a requirement for those who wish to become successful managers in the extremely dynamic and technological world of tomorrow. However, the full impact of, and benefits from, the quantitative approach (and quantitative decision models) can be realized only when the manager is able to integrate the scientific and technical elements with the full range of behavioral factors.

References

Argyris, C. "Management Information System: The Challenge to Rationality and Emotionality." *Management Science*, Vol. 17, No. 6 (Feb. 1971), B275–B292.

Boulden, J. B., and E. S. Buffa. "Corporate Models: On-Line, Real-Time Systems." *Harvard Business Review* (July–Aug. 1970), 65–83.

Braunstein, D. N. "Relating the Logic of Management Science to Executive Decision Making." *Interfaces*, Vol. 5, No. 2 (Feb. 1975), 44–46.

Churchman, C. W., and A. H. Schainblatt. "The Researcher and the Manager: A Dialectic of Implementation." *Management Science*, Vol. 11, No. 4 (Feb. 1965), B69–B87.

Dalton, G. W., et al. *The Distribution of Authority in Formal Organizations*. Cambridge, Mass.: Harvard University Press, 1968.

Davis, G. B. *Introduction to Electronic Computers*, 2nd ed. New York: McGraw-Hill Book Company, 1971.

Duncan, J. W. "The Researcher and the Manager: A Comparative View of the Need for Mutual Understanding." *Management Science*, Vol. 20, No. 8 (Apr. 1974), 1157–1163.

Eilon, S. "Mathematical Modeling for Management." *Interfaces*, Vol. 4, No. 2 (Feb. 1974), 32–38.

Grayson, C. J., Jr. "Management Science and Business Practice." *Harvard Business Review* (July–Aug. 1973), 41–48.

Gruber, W. H., and J. S. Niles. "Problems in the Utilization of Management Science/Operations Research: A State of the Art Survey." *Interfaces*, Vol. 2, No. 1 (Nov. 1971), 12–19.

Gruber, W. H., and J. S. Niles. "The Science–Technology–Utilization Relationship in Management." *Management Science*, Vol. 21, No. 8 (Apr. 1975), 956–963.

Hammond, J. S. "The Role of the Manager and Management Scientist in Successful Implementation." *Sloan Management Review* (Winter 1974), 1–24.

Harvey, A. "Factors Making for Implementation Success and Failure." *Management Science*, Vol. 16, No. 6 (Feb. 1970), B312.

Huysmans, J. H. B. M. *The Implementation of Operations Research: An Approach to the Joint Consideration of Social and Technological Aspects*. New York: John Wiley & Sons, Inc. 1970.

Little, J. D. C. "Models and Managers: The Concept of Decision Calculus." *Management Science*, Vol. 16 (Apr. 1970), B466–B485.

Lonnstedt, L. "Factors Related to the Implementation of Operations Research Solutions." *Interfaces*, Vol. 5, No. 2 (Feb. 1975), 23–30.

Markland, R. E., and R. J. Newett. "A Subjective Taxonomy for Evaluating the Stages of Management Science Research." *Interfaces*, Vol. 2, No. 2 (Feb. 1972), 31–39.

Moses, M. "Implementation of Analytical Planning Systems." *Management Science*, Vol. 21, No. 10 (June 1975), 1133–1143.

Schneyman, A. H. "Management Information System for Management Sciences." *Interfaces*, Vol. 6, No. 3 (May 1976), 52–57.

Schultz, R. L., and D. P. Slevin (eds.). *Implementing Operations Research/Management Science: Research Findings and Implications*. New York: American Elsevier Publishing Co. Inc., 1975.

Shycon, H. N. "Perspectives on MS Applications." *Interfaces*, Vol. 4, No. 2 (Feb. 1974), 21–23.

Shycon, H. N. "Perspectives on MS Applications." *Interfaces*, Vol. 5, No. 1 (Nov. 1974), 41–43.

Turban, E. "A Survey Sample of Operations Research Activities at the Corporate Level." *Operations Research*, Vol. 20 (May–June 1972), 708–721.

Turban, E., and N. P. Loomba. *Readings in Management Science*. Dallas, Tex.: Business Publications, Inc., 1976.

Wagner, H. M. "The ABC's of OR." *Operations Research* (Oct. 1971), 1259–1281.

Wolek, F. W. "Implementation and The Process of Adopting Managerial Technology." *Interfaces*, Vol. 5, No. 3 (May 1975), 38–46.

Zeleny, M. "Managers Without Management Science." *Interfaces*, Vol. 5, No. 4 (Aug. 1975), 35–42.

Review Questions and Problems

16.1. What are the basic tests of successful implementation of quantitative models?

16.2. Describe the scope of these *stages* of the process of implementation: (a) adoption, (b) systematization, and (c) institutionalization.

16.3. List and describe the six "life phases" of the process of implementation.

16.4. Explain the rationale of the implementation evaluation grid shown in Figure 16.2. Develop such a grid for a management science project of your own choice.

16.5. Explain, in your own words, the focus of the *micro* approach to implementation. How does the micro approach differ from the *macro* approach to implementation?

16.6. What are the important aspects and issues involved in the interface between the manager and the management scientist in successful implementation? Between the manager and the computer system? Between the management scientist and the computer system?

16.7. What are the important characteristics or requirements that a model should possess to increase its effectiveness?

16.8. What is a management information system? Analyze Figure 16.5 with respect to a managerial environment of your own choice.

16.9. What are the main components of a computer system? Describe the role of these components.

16.10. What is batch processing? Real-time processing? Describe how a time-sharing system works.

16.11. What, in your opinion, are the important determinants of successful implementation?

PART VI

Appendixes

Probability—Basic Concepts and Some Applications

MAJOR CONCEPTS AND TOPICS DISCUSSED IN THIS APPENDIX

The Concept of Probability

Random experiment, random variable
Relative frequency
Objective, subjective, empirical, and a priori probabilities
Sample space and sample points
Frequency and probability distributions
Discrete and continuous probability distributions
Idea of cumulative probability

Classification of Events and Probability Concepts

Mutually exclusive versus joint events
Independent versus dependent events
Marginal, unconditional, conditional, joint, prior, and posterior probabilities

Bayesian Analysis

A Replacement Model

Markov Models

A.1
Introduction

As discussed in Section 4.6, decision models can be classified in terms of *deterministic* versus *probabilistic* models (if "degree of certainty" is employed as the criterion of classification). Also, as explained in Chapter 5, the idea in probabilistic models is that each decision or strategy can lead to a number of *different* possible outcomes (as opposed to a deterministic model in which each decision leads to a unique outcome). A logical question follows: How can we enhance the description of a probabilistic situation so that managers can gain a deeper understanding of the decision problem and base their decisions on rational considerations? The answer resides in the concepts of *probability, probability distribution, expected value, variance,* and related statistical terms which we shall discuss in this appendix. The purpose of this appendix is twofold: (1) to explain, at a very elementary level, some of the basic probability and related concepts, and (2) to illustrate the application of these concepts to decision problems involving Bayesian analysis, Markov analysis, and a replacement model.

A.2
The Concept of Probability

All of us have some idea of the meaning of probability since, in one form or the other, we either use or hear this term every day. For example, the statement "the *odds* are that David will pass this course" is based on the concept of probability. Similarly, when we say "there is a good *chance* that it will rain tomorrow," we are making a probabilistic statement. However, such statements must be *quantified* if they are to be used in formal decision models—and that is done by converting the notion of "chance" or "odds" into specific fractions, decimals, or percentage terms. For example, we can say that odds for the event "sunshine" are "6 in 10" (i.e., $\frac{6}{10}$ or 0.6) or "the chance is 60 percent." When we do this we assign a *probability value* to a *specific event.*

A more formal meaning of the term "probability" is based on the concepts of random experiment and random variable. A *random experiment* (phenomenon) is one in which each object included in the experiment (phenomenon) has an equal chance of becoming an "outcome" of the experiment (phenomenon). A *random variable* is a function of the random experiment, and it assigns a number to each outcome of the experiment. For example, the experiment of flipping a coin is a random experiment. It can result in two possible events (head; tail). However, each *trial* of the experiment can result in only one event (head *or* tail). Now, suppose that we associate a reward of $5 when a head appears, and a penalty of $4 when a tail appears. Then we have defined a random variable (say, X) that assigns a value of $+5$ to one outcome and -4 to the other. It is in this sense that a random variable is a function of the random experiment, and, in this case, it takes only two values. However, depending upon the nature of the random phenomenon, the random variable could assume a large number of values (finite or infinite).

The random variable can be *discrete* (subject to counting—e.g., 1 girlfriend, 2 girlfriends; but not 1.236 girlfriends) or *continuous* (subject to *measurement*—e.g., temperature or height that can be measured with varying degrees of accuracy or significance). Thus, we can associate the notion of probability with either *discrete variables* or *continuous variables*. When the random variable is discrete, we usually have a *finite* (say, *n*) number of outcomes. When the random variable is continuous, we have an *infinite* number of outcomes.

In the context of a random experiment that produces discrete events, the probability of an event is defined in a *relative-frequency* sense. For example, repeat a random experiment *N* times (e.g., flipping a fair coin or throwing a true die). Count the number of times the experiment results in a certain event *E* (e.g., head or tail; a die coming up with one of the values 1, 2, 3, 4, 5, 6). Call this number *f*, which is really the frequency with which the event *E* occurs. The ratio *f*/*N* is then called the *relative frequency* of the event *E*.

Now when we say that the probability of an event *E* is *p*, we mean that the relative frequency of *E* will be close to *p*—provided that *N* is large. This is a definition of what is called *objective probability*. It is based on the idea of relative frequency and is denoted as follows:

$$p(E) = \lim_{N \to \infty} \frac{f}{N} \tag{A.1}$$

In practice, however, we do *not* repeat the experiment an infinite number of times. Instead, managers gather a finite amount of business and economic data subject to the constraints of time and money. For example, data on the number of hours that a repairman takes to repair a machine breakdown are kept over a finite period of time. And, from these data we can calculate the relative frequency (probability) of specified events or outcomes.

Assume that in a machine shop requiring the service of one repairman, records are kept regarding the repair time. Then the repair time (in manhours) is the random variable *X*. Assume that the random variable takes only these values: 4, 5, 6, 7, and 8. Then, based on a total of, say, 1,400 observations, we can arrange the data as shown in columns 1 and 2 of Table A.1 (note that Table A.1 is the same as Table 15.4). We can calculate the probability of each event in Table A.1 by determining its relative frequency (see column 3) and expressing this relative frequency either as a decimal (see column 4) or a percentage (see column 5). Note that in Table A.1 the probability of each event was calculated by utilizing actual empirical data. When calculated on the basis of empirical data, the probabilities can be referred to as *empirical probabilities*. In comparison, we can speak of an *a priori probability* that is based on logic rather than on empirical data. For example, we can say on an a priori basis that the probability of drawing an ace from a deck of 52 cards is $\frac{4}{52}$. In this case, we do not gather actual data or repeat the experiment a large number of times.

A complete description or listing of all the different possible outcomes of a random variable together with their respective frequencies (probabilities) is called a *frequency (probability) distribution*. A frequency or probability distribution can be *discrete* or *continuous*. The distribution shown in Table A.1 is a discrete

Table A.1

(1) Repair Time (manhours) (Values Taken by the Random Variable, X)	(2) Frequency, f	(3) Relative Frequency, f/N	(4) Probability, p (expressed in decimals)	(5) Probability, p (expressed in percentages)
4	560	$\dfrac{560}{1,400}$	0.400	40.00
5	420	$\dfrac{420}{1,400}$	0.300	30.00
6	245	$\dfrac{245}{1,400}$	0.175	17.50
7	140	$\dfrac{140}{1,400}$	0.100	10.00
8	35	$\dfrac{35}{1,400}$	0.025	2.50
Total	1,400	1.000	1.000	100.00

distribution. The well-known normal distribution is a continuous probability distribution.[1]

A frequency distribution can be converted into a probability distribution by expressing frequencies of events as relative frequencies (either as decimals or percentages). In this manner, we *normalize* a frequency distribution, as shown in columns 4 and 5 of Table A.1.

In real life, managers sometimes base their decisions on "intuition" or "hunches." Since these intuitions or hunches are often based on personal experience or personal biases, they are subjective in nature (as opposed to objective observations based on actual data). Hence, if a probabilistic statement is made on the basis of a personal belief, intuition, or hunch, we have a *subjective* probability.

As is shown in Table A.1, the probability measure attached to an event can vary from 0 to 1; however, it can never be negative. Further, the sum of probabilities attached to all possible events of an experiment or phenomenon must be 1 (or 100 percent). These basic axioms of probability are stated as follows (assume a random variable X that can take n discrete values):

$$0 \leqslant p(X_i) \leqslant 1 \tag{A.2}$$

$$\sum_{i=1}^{n} p(X_i) = 1 \tag{A.3}$$

The idea of probability can also be grasped by defining the terms *sample space* and *sample points*. A complete description or enumeration of all the different

---

[1] While we attach a specific probability value to each outcome in a discrete distribution, the idea of probability at a point does not hold in the case of a continuous distribution. In a continuous probability distribution, we measure probability as the area, under the curve, between two different values of the random variable. In Appendix E we provide such measures of probability for the normal distribution.

possible outcomes of a random experiment (i.e., *collectively exhaustive* and *mutually exclusive* values of a random variable)[2] describes a *sample space*. The events are referred to as *points* or *sample points* in the space. For example, the sample space of the experiment of flipping a coin consists of two sample points: head (*H*) and tail (*T*) (these are the only two points and they are collectively exhaustive and mutually exclusive). Then the probability of an event, *E*, is defined as the ratio of the points included in the event divided by the total number of points in the sample space. Hence,

$$p(H) = \tfrac{1}{2} \qquad p(T) = \tfrac{1}{2}$$

The probability of an event considered alone, such as $p(H)$ or $p(T)$, is called the *marginal* probability. More on this in Section A.3.5.

Remember that, in the illustration above, the "ratio" definition hinges upon the fact that the events in the sample space are equiprobable.

A.3
Classification of Events and Probability Concepts

Let us consider a residential coeducational university located in a large city. We can classify the student population of the university in a number of ways, such as males versus females (criterion of sex); black versus white (criterion of race); commuter versus resident (criterion of whether or not the student commutes); and high, middle, or low income (criterion of annual income). Note that, for *each* criterion of classification, we can build a list of collectively exhaustive and mutually exclusive events, and a probability distribution. Let us consider the following data:

total student population = 1,000

male = 500   female = 500

black = 300   white = 700

female *and* black = 100   female *and* white = 400

male *and* black = 200   male *and* white = 300

The data can be represented schematically as shown in Figure A.1. We shall utilize Figure A.1 in illustrating various concepts discussed in this section.

It should be stated here that various definitions and formulas developed in this section are based on the assumption that we are dealing with two events, such as *M* (male) and *F* (female), *M* (male) and *B* (black), and so on. The discussion and the formulas can easily be extended to three or more events. The interested reader is referred to any standard book on probability and statistics.[3]

---

[2] *Collectively exhaustive* implies that no other events than those listed can be the outcomes of the experiment. *Mutually exclusive* implies that no two events can occur together.

[3] See, for example, Tsokos [1972] or Wadsworth and Bryan [1974].

BLACK (300) | WHITE (700)

MALE (500)

$$p(M|B) = \frac{200}{300} = \frac{2}{3} \qquad p(M|W) = \frac{300}{700} = \frac{3}{7}$$

$$p(B|M) = \frac{200}{500} = \frac{2}{5} \qquad p(W|M) = \frac{300}{500} = \frac{3}{5}$$

$$p(MB) = \frac{200}{1,000} = \frac{2}{10} \qquad p(MW) = \frac{300}{1,000} = \frac{3}{10}$$

male *and* black = 200   male *and* white = 300
(M and B)   (M and W)

$$p(M) = \frac{500}{1,000} = 0.5 = \frac{5}{10}$$

FEMALE (500)

$$p(F|B) = \frac{100}{300} = \frac{1}{3} \qquad p(F|W) = \frac{400}{700} = \frac{4}{7}$$

$$p(B|F) = \frac{100}{500} = \frac{1}{5} \qquad p(W|F) = \frac{400}{500} = \frac{4}{5}$$

$$p(FB) = \frac{100}{1,000} = \frac{1}{10} \qquad p(FW) = \frac{400}{1,000} = \frac{4}{10}$$

female *and* black = 100   female *and* white = 400
(F and B)   (F and W)

$$p(F) = \frac{500}{1,000} = 0.5 = \frac{5}{10}$$

$$p(B) = \frac{300}{1,000} = 0.3 = \frac{3}{10} \qquad p(W) = \frac{700}{1,000} = 0.7 = \frac{7}{10}$$

Figure A.1. • Note that the sum of joint probabilities (vertically or horizontally) equals the marginal probabilities; that is,

$$p(B) = p(MB) + p(FB)$$
$$p(W) = p(MW) + p(FW)$$
$$p(M) = p(MB) + p(MW)$$
$$p(F) = p(FB) + p(FW)$$

A.3.1 MUTUALLY EXCLUSIVE VERSUS JOINT EVENTS

We can distinguish between different events of interest in terms of mutually exclusive versus joint events. Events are termed *mutually exclusive* if no two events (from an *exhaustive* list of all the outcomes of an experiment) can occur together. For example, the outcomes head and tail in the experiment of flipping a coin constitute a set of exhaustive and mutually exclusive events. Similarly, the events "male" and "female" are mutually exclusive events, as are the events "black" and "white" shown in Figure A.1.

Events are called *joint events* if they can occur together (i.e., they are not mutually exclusive). Note that in our example the events "male" and "black" are not mutually exclusive and hence are joint events. Note, further, that the joint events require the use of more than one criterion of classification (we can also consider them as the results of two different experiments applied to a specific population of interest).

We can use a *Venn diagram* to depict the occurrence of mutually exclusive events and joint events. For example, in Figure A.2a, the events "male" and "female" are mutually exclusive events. In Figure A.2b, the events "male" and "black" (that are not mutually exclusive) are shown as joint events. Note the existence of overlapping (intersection) in joint events (see shaded area in Figure A.2b).

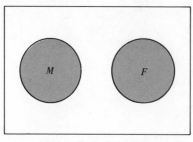
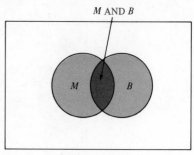

(a) Mutually Exclusive Events   (b) Joint Events

Figure A.2

Assume the existence of two events A and B. Then we are often interested in the following two types of probabilities: (1) $p(A \text{ or } B)$, and (2) $p(A \text{ and } B)$.[4] We shall denote the "probability of A and B" as $p(AB)$ and refer to it as the *joint probability*.

A.3.2 PROBABILITY CONCEPTS FOR MUTUALLY EXCLUSIVE EVENTS

Consider the two mutually exclusive events M and F shown in Figure A.2a. Then we can think of the "probability of M or F"—$p(M \text{ or } F)$ and the "probability of M and F"—$p(MF)$.

In general, we say that while calculating either–or probabilities, the probabilities of mutually exclusive events are added and equal the sum of the relevant marginal probabilities. Thus,

$$p(M \text{ or } F) = p(M) + p(F) \tag{A.4}$$

For our example (see Figure A.1),

$$p(M \text{ or } F) = p(M) + p(F) = 0.5 + 0.5 = 1$$

For mutually exclusive events, the intersection or joint probability is zero. Thus,

$$p(MF) = 0 \tag{A.5}$$

Now refer to Figure A.2a. It is clear that the mutually exclusive events M and F do not overlap. There is no intersection between mutually exclusive events. Hence, we can say that the "intersection" or "joint" probability of mutually exclusive events is zero.[5]

---

[4] If we think in terms of set-theoretic representation of events, then "*either–or*" probability is usually denoted as $p(A \cup B)$—probability of A *union* B. The "*and*" probability is usually denoted as $p(A \cap B)$—probability of A *intersect* B.

[5] Consider two mutually exclusive events A and B. Then we can also think of "the probability of A *given* that B has occurred." This is called *conditional probability* and is denoted as $p(A \mid B)$. For mutually exclusive events, by definition, we have

$$p(A \mid B) = 0 \qquad p(B \mid A) = 0$$

More on conditional probability in Section A.3.5.

A.3.3 PROBABILITY CONCEPTS FOR JOINT EVENTS

Consider the joint events M and B as shown in Figure A.1 and represented in Figure A.2b. Again, we can think of the "probability of M or B" and "the probability of M and B."

For joint events,

$$p(M \text{ or } B) = p(M) + p(B) - p(MB) \tag{A.6}$$

The rationale for (A.6) is that by adding $p(M) + p(B)$ we have double-counted the sample points included in the shaded area MB in Figure A.2b. Hence, the probability of the joint event MB is subtracted to adjust for this double counting.[6] In general, we can say that, while calculating either–or probabilities of joint events, we add the probabilities of relevant marginal probabilities and then adjust for overlapping (or multiple counting of points).

For joint events, the intersection probabilities are expressed in two ways. Assuming *independence*, we have

$$p(MB) = p(M) \cdot p(B) \tag{A.7}$$

Assuming *dependence*, we have

$$p(MB) = p(M) \cdot p(B \mid M) \tag{A.8}$$

or

$$p(MB) = p(B) \cdot p(M \mid B) \tag{A.9}$$

The term $p(B \mid M)$ is an example of *conditional probability*. It is read "conditional probability of B given M." More on the concept of conditional probability in the next section.

It should be noted here that if events B and M were *indeed independent*, then

$$p(B \mid M) = p(B) \tag{A.10}$$

and

$$p(M \mid B) = p(M) \tag{A.11}$$

Consequently, if we put (A.10) in (A.8) and (A.11) in (A.9), we obtain (A.7).[7]

A.3.4 INDEPENDENT VERSUS DEPENDENT EVENTS

Events are called statistically *independent* if the occurrence of one event does not, in any way, affect (correlate with) the probability of occurrence of any other event. For example, the events "head" and "tail" in the experiment of flipping a coin

---

[6] As stated earlier, the existence of joint events requires more than one criterion of classification (e.g., outcomes from two random phenomena). From the nature of the data, the two phenomena might be *independent* of each other (i.e., the probability of an outcome in one is not affected by the occurrence of events in the other) or they might exhibit dependency (i.e., the probability of outcomes from each is *dependent* upon or affected by the occurrence of events from the other). See Section A.3.4.

[7] The data in Figure A.1 are such that we do have dependency between the two phenomena. However, if we let black = 500, white = 500, female *and* black = 250, and female *and* white = 250, we shall find the two phenomena to be independent. That is, (A.10) and (A.11) will be true. The reader is encouraged to verify this assertion.

twice are independent. As stated earlier, for independent events, we can consider the intersection or joint probability (probability of events occurring together or in succession) and calculate it as shown in (A.7).

We illustrate next how joint probability of independent events can be calculated. Consider the experiment of flipping a coin. Then

$$p(HT) = p(H) \cdot p(T) = (\tfrac{1}{2})(\tfrac{1}{2}) = \tfrac{1}{4}$$
$$p(\text{HHT}) = p(H) \cdot p(H) \cdot p(T) = (\tfrac{1}{2})(\tfrac{1}{2})(\tfrac{1}{2}) = \tfrac{1}{8}$$

When the occurrence of one event can be statistically linked to, or is dependent upon, another event, the events are called *dependent* events. For example, statistical evidence has shown that the events "heart attack" and "cigarette smoking" exhibit statistical dependency.[8] For dependent events we need the notion of *conditional probability*. Assume that events A and B are dependent events. Then $p(A \mid B)$ is the "conditional probability of A given B." As stated earlier, for dependent events, we can consider the intersection or joint probability and calculate it as shown in (A.8) and (A.9). We shall illustrate the calculations for joint probabilities of dependent events in Section A.3.6.

Now, with reference to Figure A.1, we have $p(B \mid M)$ and $p(M \mid B)$. It is clear from (A.8) that

$$p(B \mid M) = \frac{p(MB)}{p(M)} \tag{A.12}$$

Also, from (A.9),

$$p(M \mid B) = \frac{p(MB)}{p(B)} \tag{A.13}$$

We shall illustrate the calculations of conditional probabilities in Section A.3.5.

It is obvious that for independent events, $p(A) = p(A \mid B)$, because there is no dependence between events A and B. For example, if there were no dependency between "heart disease" and "cigarette smoking," we could say that

$$p(\text{heart disease}) = p(\text{heart disease} \mid \text{cigarette smoking})$$

Similarly, if there were no dependency between sex and race in the data exhibited in Figure A.1, we would find that

$$p(M) = p(M \mid B) = p(M \mid W) \tag{A.14}$$

A.3.5 UNCONDITIONAL VERSUS CONDITIONAL PROBABILITY

When our focus is on a specified (single) criterion of classification, we speak of *unconditional* probability. For example, the unconditional probabilities in Figure A.1 are:

---

[8] The idea of dependent events requires that we use more than one criterion of classification. However, depending upon the result of certain tests [see (A.10) and (A.11)] statistical data such as shown in Figure A.1 may or may not exhibit statistical dependency. That is, the use of more than one criterion of classification is a necessary but not sufficient condition for statistical dependence.

Sex as the criterion of classification *Race as the criterion of classification*

$$p(M) = 0.5 \qquad\qquad\qquad p(B) = 0.3$$
$$p(F) = 0.5 \qquad\qquad\qquad p(W) = 0.7$$

The unconditional probability is also known as the *marginal* or *prior probability*.[9]

When our focus is on more than one criterion of classification, we think of *conditional* probability. As mentioned earlier, the conditional probability is denoted as follows:

$p(M \mid B)$ is read: "probability of male *given* black"

$p(B \mid M)$ is read: "probability of black *given* male"

It is easy to see that in Figure A.1 we have eight different conditional probabilities (two conditional probabilities exist in each of the four cells of Figure A.1). We can calculate these conditional probabilities by utilizing the concepts of sample points and sample space. For example,

$$p(M \mid B) = \frac{200}{300} = \frac{2}{3} \qquad \text{(note that in the } reduced \text{ sample space of "black" with a total of 300 points, we have 200 points in the subset "male and black")}$$

By applying similar reasoning, we can calculate the remaining conditional probabilities. The specific values are entered in Figure A.1 and are as follows:

$$p(M \mid B) = \frac{200}{300} = \frac{2}{3} \qquad p(M \mid W) = \frac{300}{700} = \frac{3}{7}$$

$$p(B \mid M) = \frac{200}{500} = \frac{2}{5} \qquad p(W \mid M) = \frac{300}{500} = \frac{3}{5}$$

$$p(F \mid B) = \frac{100}{300} = \frac{1}{3} \qquad p(F \mid W) = \frac{400}{700} = \frac{4}{7}$$

$$p(B \mid F) = \frac{100}{500} = \frac{1}{5} \qquad p(W \mid F) = \frac{400}{500} = \frac{4}{5}$$

It is clear that conditional probabilities do not exist for mutually exclusive events. Thus, if two events A and B are mutually exclusive, then

$$p(A \mid B) = p(B \mid A) = 0 \qquad\qquad\qquad (A.15)$$

A.3.6 JOINT PROBABILITY

As mentioned earlier, if two events A and B are joint events, their probability is termed *joint probability* and is denoted as $p(AB)$ or $p(BA)$. The joint probability is read: "probability of A and B" or "probability of A intersect B." It is clear that we can identify and calculate the following four joint probabilities in Figure A.1. (We

[9] The name "marginal" can be thought of in terms of placing the probability on the margin in Figure A.1. The name "prior" reminds us that this probability is prior to any other considerations.

calculate the joint probabilities based on the concepts of sample points and sample space.)

$$p(MB) = \frac{200}{1,000} = \frac{2}{10} \qquad \text{(note that in the entire sample space with a total of 1,000 points we have 200 points in the subset "male and black")}$$

Similarly, from Figure A.1,

$$p(FB) = \frac{100}{1,000} = \frac{1}{10}$$

$$p(MW) = \frac{300}{1,000} = \frac{3}{10}$$

$$p(FW) = \frac{400}{1,000} = \frac{4}{10}$$

A.3.7 RELATIONSHIP AMONG JOINT, CONDITIONAL, AND MARGINAL PROBABILITIES

It is easy to see the relationship among conditional, joint, and marginal probabilities. This relationship becomes obvious when we examine how the conditional probabilities were derived in Section A.3.5. It is also helpful at this time to refer to Figure A.2b. It makes sense to say that

$$p(M \mid B) = \frac{\text{sample points in the shaded area } MB}{\text{total sample points in } B}$$

That is,

$$p(M \mid B) = \frac{p(MB)}{p(B)} = \frac{0.2}{0.3} = \frac{2}{3} \qquad (A.16)$$

$$p(B \mid M) = \frac{p(MB)}{p(M)} = \frac{0.2}{0.5} = \frac{2}{5} \qquad (A.17)$$

Also, we can rearrange (A.16) and (A.17) as (A.18) and (A.19), respectively:

$$p(MB) \quad = \quad p(B) \quad \cdot \quad p(M \mid B) \qquad (A.18)$$

$$p(MB) \quad = \quad p(M) \quad \cdot \quad p(B \mid M) \qquad (A.19)$$
$$\Downarrow \qquad\qquad \Downarrow \qquad\qquad \Downarrow$$
$$\text{joint} \qquad \text{marginal} \qquad \text{conditional}$$
$$\text{probability} \qquad \text{probability} \qquad \text{probability}$$

Now, consider *any* two events A and B. Then the *general formulas for the probability of joint events* (the intersection) are patterned after (A.18) and (A.19) as follows:

$$p(AB) = p(A) \cdot p(B \mid A) \qquad (A.20)$$

$$p(AB) = p(B) \cdot p(A \mid B) \qquad (A.21)$$

Since the left-hand sides of (A.20) and (A.21) are equal, we can equate their right-hand sides. Hence,

$$p(A) \cdot p(B \mid A) = p(B) \cdot p(A \mid B)$$

or

$$p(B \mid A) = \frac{p(B) \cdot p(A \mid B)}{p(A)} \tag{A.22}$$

Note that (A.22) is a simple statement of Bayes' theorem. Briefly, this theorem enables us to calculate $p(B|A)$ provided that we know the value of $p(A|B)$. We shall illustrate the use of Bayes' theorem in Section A.3.8.

Note that if we utilize (A.20) in (A.6)—but assuming A and B to be joint events—the general formula for either–or probability is given by

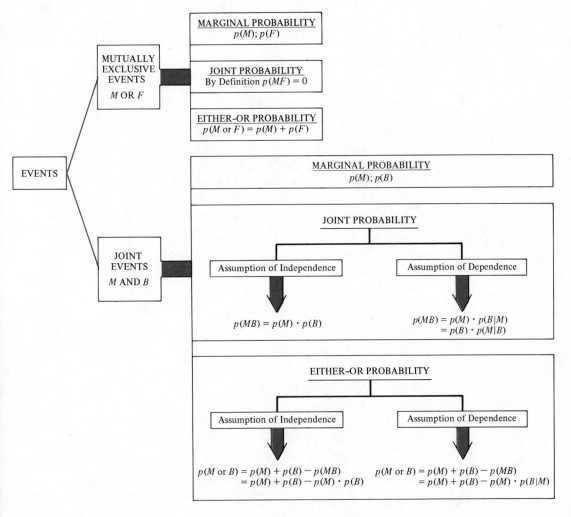

Figure A.3.   *Note*: The events M (male), F (female), and B (black) are the same as shown in Figure A.1.

$$p(A \text{ or } B) = p(A) + p(B) - p(A) \cdot p(B \mid A) \tag{A.23}$$

We have now laid the foundations for understanding the implications of different types of probabilities. Based on the events shown in Figure A.1, we present a summary of these ideas in Figure A.3.

A.3.8 POSTERIOR PROBABILITIES AND BAYESIAN ANALYSIS

The concept of *posterior probability* implies that, after receiving certain additional information, we can revise, and improve upon, the knowledge (degree of certainty or belief) that is available solely from the *prior (marginal) probability* of an event. For example, if we refer to Figure A.1 and examine the prior (marginal) probability of the event M, all we can say is that the probability of a student being "male" is 0.5, or 50 percent. The next question is whether we can improve our knowledge regarding the occurrence of event M by utilizing additional information (e.g., information retrieved by applying the criterion of race). The answer is that quite often we can indeed improve our knowledge of the decision problem by applying more than one criterion of classification, as we shall illustrate with reference to Figure A.1.

Typically, the idea of posterior probability requires the classification of data by more than one criterion of classification (e.g., see Figure A.1). Then we know the prior (marginal) probability of events such as M and F. Assume, further, that we are provided with the information regarding the conditional probability $p(B \mid M)$. Now the question is: Can we calculate the conditional probability $p(M \mid B)$? The answer is yes, and when calculated in this manner [see (A.24)] the conditional probability $p(M \mid B)$ is called the posterior probability.

The posterior probability is calculated by using *Bayes' theorem*:[10]

[10] Here is a simple derivation of Bayes' theorem. From (A.13),

$$p(M \mid B) = \frac{p(MB)}{p(B)} \tag{A.25}$$

From (A.8),

$$p(MB) = p(M) \cdot p(B \mid M) \tag{A.26}$$

Also, $p(FB) = p(F) \cdot p(B \mid F)$

From Figure A.1,

$$p(B) = p(MB) + p(FB)$$

Then,

$$p(B) = p(M) \cdot p(B \mid M) + p(F) \cdot p(B \mid F) \tag{A.27}$$

Now, put (A.26) and (A.27) in (A.25).

Hence,

$$p(M \mid B) = \frac{p(M) \cdot p(B \mid M)}{p(M) \cdot p(B \mid M) + p(F) \cdot p(B \mid F)} \tag{A.28}$$

Now, let us assume a schematic diagram such as Figure A.1 except that we have m horizontal divisions (i.e., $A_1, A_2, A_3, \ldots, A_m$) and n vertical divisions (i.e., $B_1, B_2, B_3, \ldots, B_n$). Then a general statement of Bayes' theorem is patterned after (A.28) and is given as follows:

$$p(A_m \mid B_n) = \frac{p(A_m) \cdot p(B_n \mid A_m)}{\sum p(A_j) \cdot p(B_n \mid A_j)} \qquad j = 1, 2, 3, \ldots, m \tag{A.29}$$

$$p(M|B) = \frac{p(M) \cdot p(B \mid M)}{p(B)} \tag{A.24}$$

$$\begin{array}{l} \text{posterior probability} \\ \text{of } M \text{ given } B \end{array} = \frac{(0.5)(0.4)}{0.3} = \frac{2}{3}$$

Note that without using the information provided by $p(B \mid M)$, all we could say was that $p(M) = \frac{1}{2}$. Now, by using Bayes' theorem, we have calculated the posterior probability and gained a deeper understanding regarding the event M. We can say that probability of being a male is $\frac{2}{3}$ (as compared to just $\frac{1}{2}$), provided we know that the person is black. That is, $p(M \mid B) = \frac{2}{3}$. Incidentally, with reference to Figure A.1, we can now immediately make the statement that $p(F \mid B)$ is $\frac{1}{3}$.

What we have just illustrated, the calculation of a posterior probability, is the cornerstone of what is known as *Bayesian analysis*. The idea of Bayesian analysis is extremely useful in making multistage (dynamic) decisions.[11] Bayesian analysis proceeds along five steps.

Step 1. *The problem is structured in such a manner that the data can be exhibited by using more than one criterion of classification* (e.g., See Figure A.1).

Then, typically, the values for one set of marginal (prior) probabilities are known (the values of the other set of marginal values are to be calculated). Additionally, the values for one set of conditional probabilities are known (the value of the other set of conditional probabilities—the posterior probabilities—are to be calculated). For example, if we know that

$$p(M) = 0.5 \qquad p(F) = 0.5$$

$$p(B \mid M) = 0.4 \qquad p(W \mid M) = 0.6 \qquad p(B \mid F) = 0.2 \qquad p(W \mid F) = 0.8$$

then we need to calculate the marginal probabilities

$$p(B) \, ; \, p(W)$$

and the conditional probabilities

$$p(M \mid B); \, p(M \mid W); \, p(F \mid B); \, p(F \mid W)$$

Step 2. *The purpose of the second step is to calculate the joint probabilities.*

This is possible by using (A.8). For example,

$$p(MB) = p(M) \cdot p(B \mid M) = (0.5)(0.4) = 0.2$$
$$p(FM) = p(F) \cdot p(B \mid F) = (0.5)(0.2) = 0.1$$

Similarly, the remaining two joint probabilities—$p(MW)$ and $p(FW)$—can be calculated.

Step 3. *The purpose of this step is to calculate those marginal probabilities that were not provided in step 1.*

[11] For a simple illustration, see Green and Tull [1975].

This can be accomplished by realizing the axiom that "marginal probability equals the sum of joint probabilities" (this holds true either horizontally or vertically, as shown in Figure A.1). For example,

$$p(B) = p(MB) + p(FB) = (0.2) + (0.1) = 0.3$$

The reader can check that

$$p(W) = p(MW) + p(FW) = (0.3) + (0.4) = 0.7$$

Step 4. *The purpose of this step is to calculate the posterior probabilities.*

This can be done by using Bayes' theorem, as shown in (A.24) or (A.28). For example, we have already calculated the posterior probability, $p(M \mid B)$. There are three other posterior probabilities—$p(M \mid W)$, $p(F \mid B)$, and $p(F \mid W)$—that can be similarly calculated.

Step 5. *This is the managerial step of utilizing the information obtained from Bayesian analysis to choose the optimal strategy.*

For example, realizing that $p(F \mid B)$ is very low, the university might want to offer incentives to encourage additional enrollment of black women.[12]

A.4
The Concept of Expected Value

Since, in any probabilistic situation (e.g., rate of return from a project) each strategy can lead to a number of different possible outcomes, managers want to know at least two things. First, what happens *on the average* (i.e., what is the *average* payoff or *average* value of the random variable)? Second, what is the *risk* involved in the strategy, as measured by *dispersion*, *spread*, *range*, or *variability* of the distribution of different outcomes. Both the *average* value and some measure of *risk* can be calculated by utilizing the concept of *expected value* or *mathematical expectation*.

Let us consider a probabilistic decision problem in which the discrete random variable, X, can assume n different values (e.g., rate of return may be 12 percent, 20 percent, and 30 percent if $n = 3$). Then we define the *expected value* of the discrete random variable X as follows:[13]

$$\text{expected value of } X = E(X) = O_1 p_1 + O_2 p_2 + \cdots + O_n p_n \qquad \text{(A.30)}$$

$$= \sum_{i=1}^{n} O_i p_i$$

---

[12] For an illustration of a business decision problem, see Frank and Green [1967].

[13] The expected value of a continuous random variable is defined as

$$E(X) = \int_{-\infty}^{\infty} X f(X) \, dx$$

For further discussion, we refer the reader to Crowdis et al. [1976].

where

$$O_i = i\text{th outcome}$$

$$p_i = \text{probability of } i\text{th outcome}$$

Note that $E(X)$ is nothing more than a *weighted* average $(\bar{X})$, the weights being the probabilities of different outcomes. Also, it should be stated that in (A.30) the sum of probabilities must add to 1 (i.e., $\sum p_i = 1$), and each probability must be either zero or positive (i.e., $p_i \geqslant 0$).

Now assume that the probabilities of three rates of return (12, 20, and 30 percent) are 0.5, 0.3, and 0.2, respectively. Then, using (A.30), we obtain

$$E(X) = \bar{X} = 12(0.5) + 20(0.3) + 30(0.2) = 18 \text{ percent}$$

Note that the expected value here has been calculated in percentage terms. If the expected value is calculated in terms of dollars, we can call it *expected monetary value* (EMV). In a similar manner, we can calculate expected value or *expected utility*, $E(U)$, of any discrete random variable.

Now consider a discrete random variable, X, with n values $X_1, X_2, \dots, X_n$. We can calculate its expected value, $E(X)$, by using (A.30). Let $E(X) = \bar{X}$, and define a new random variable, $X_i - \bar{X}$. Note that $(X_i - \bar{X})$ can be either positive or negative, as it measures deviations from the arithmetic mean. However, as shown in Table A.2, $(X_i - \bar{X})^2$ must always be positive.

Let $d_i = X_i - \bar{X}$. Then, for our example, $d_i = X_i - 18$. Then, the *variance of X*, denoted by Var(X), is the expected value of the random variable $d_i^2 = (X_i - \bar{X})^2$. Hence,

$$\text{Var}(X) = E(d_i^2) = \sum d_i^2 p_i \qquad (A.31)$$

The positive square root of the variance of X is called the *standard deviation* of X. The standard deviation is denoted by σ (read "sigma"), and it is a measure of the variability of the random variable X.[14]

$$\sigma = \sqrt{\text{Var}(X)} = \sqrt{\sum d_i^2 p_i} \qquad (A.32)$$

As shown in Table A.2, variance of the rate of return is 48.0. That is,

$$\text{Var}(X) = 48.0 \quad \text{and} \quad \sigma = \sqrt{48.0} = 6.93$$

Consider two projects, A and B. Assume that both yield the same expected return (i.e., $\bar{X}_A = \bar{X}_B$). However, the variability of project A is much lower than the variability of project B (i.e., σ_A is very low as compared to σ_B). Then it stands to reason that project B would be more risky (most people are risk averters). Which project a particular manager chooses will depend upon his or her utility function. The reader will recall that we made this point in Section 14.8 (see Figure 14.5 on p. 411).

Two comments are in order at this point. First, if we want to invest in more risky projects, we should expect a relatively higher rate of return. That is why managers think in terms of a *tradeoff* between risk and return. Second, if we use

[14]The reader will recall that in most books dealing with statistics,

$$\sigma = \sqrt{\frac{\sum(X_i - \bar{X})^2}{n}}$$

is the formula for calculating standard deviation.

Table A.2

Percent Rate of Return, X_i	$d_i = X_i - \bar{X}$ $= X_i - 18$	d_i^2	p_i	$d_i^2 p_i$
12	-6	36	0.5	18.0
20	2	4	0.3	1.2
30	12	144	0.2	28.8
Sum→			1.0	48.0

$E(X)$ and σ as means to compare investments that differ significantly in amounts of dollars involved, the σ of the larger project will necessarily be much larger in *absolute* terms. Hence, in comparing projects that involve significantly different amounts of dollars, we use the idea of *relative variation* to measure *relative risk*. One such measure is called the *coefficient of variation*, V, and is defined as

$$V = \frac{\sigma}{\bar{X}} \tag{A.33}$$

In general, the larger the coefficient of variation, the more risky the project is.

Example A.1 | Let us consider two projects, Alpha and Beta. The estimated expected return for Project Alpha is $1 million ($\bar{X}_A$ = \$1,000,000) with a standard deviation of \$20,000 (σ_A = \$20,000). Project Beta has an expected return of \$10,000 ($\bar{X}_B$ = \$10,000), with a standard deviation of \$1,500 (σ_B = \$1,500). It is obvious that, in *absolute* terms, the standard deviation of Project Alpha is significantly greater than that of Beta. Taken by itself, this may indicate that Project Beta is less risky. However, such a conclusion would be erroneous, because the two projects differ significantly in terms of their dollar amounts. Hence, the correct manner of evaluating these projects would be to compare their coefficients of variation, as follows:

Project Alpha	Project Beta
$\bar{X}_A = \$1,000,000$	$\bar{X}_B = \$10,000$
$\sigma_A = \$20,000$	$\sigma_B = \$1,500$
$V_A = \dfrac{\sigma_A}{\bar{X}_A} = \dfrac{\$20,000}{\$1,000,000} = 0.02$	$V_B = \dfrac{\sigma_B}{\bar{X}_B} = \dfrac{\$1,500}{\$10,000} = 0.15$

Based on the values of the coefficient of variation, it is clear that Project Alpha is superior to Project Beta.

A.5
Some Discrete Probability Distributions

As stated in Section A.2, a complete description or listing of all the collectively exhaustive and mutually exclusive values of a random variable, together with their respective probabilities, is called a probability distribution. We can certainly build a probability distribution if we have the empirical data. However, mathematicians have developed some theoretical but very useful probability distributions (discrete and continuous) that can be expressed by mathematical formulas called *probability density functions* (p.d.f.) and often denoted by $f(X)$. In each theoretical distribution, we are given one or more parameters for which specific values are assigned to reflect the specific decision problem.

In a discrete distribution, it is possible to calculate the probability of the random variable X by using the relevant formula (p.d.f.). In this section, we present two widely used discrete probability distributions: (1) the binomial distribution, and (2) the Poisson distribution.[15]

A.5.1 THE BINOMIAL DISTRIBUTION

In several decision problems, we have *only two outcomes* (e.g., in a quality control test we can have a "defective" item or a "good" item; head or tail; pass or fail). Then we can arbitrarily call one outcome "success" and the other "failure."

Further, the probability of "success" or probability of "failure" can remain *constant* from trial to trial, and the *n trials* can be *independent*. This type of behavior is represented by the *binomial distribution.*[16] The probability density function of the binomial distribution is given by

$$f(X) = \binom{n}{X} p^X (1 - p)^{n - X} \tag{A.34}$$

where

$$X = \text{discrete random variable (number of successes)}$$
$$p = \text{probability of "success"}$$
$$1 - p = \text{probability of "failure"}$$
$$n = \text{number of independent trials}$$

Note that n and p are parameters of the binomial distribution. Further, it can be shown that for the binomial distribution,

$$E(X) = np \tag{A.35}$$
$$\text{Var}(X) = np(1 - p) \tag{A.36}$$

A.5.2 THE POISSON DISTRIBUTION

The *Poisson distribution* is useful in describing those situations in which arriving customers (e.g., passengers arriving at an airport, telephone calls arriving at a central exchange, persons arriving at a bank window), during an interval of time, arrive independently and the number of arrivals depends upon the length of the

---

[15] Examples of other well-known discrete probability distributes are the *Pascal distribution* and the *geometric distribution.* See Wadsworth and Bryan [1974].

[16] This type of behavior (i.e., only two outcomes; probability of each outcome remains constant; n independent trials) is also referred to as a *Bernoulli process*

time interval. Further, the probability of two or more arrivals in a small time interval is *considerably* smaller than the probability of one arrival.

The probability density function of the Poisson distribution is given by

$$f(X) = \frac{e^{-\lambda}\lambda^X}{X!} \tag{A.37}$$

where

$$X = \text{random variable (number of arrivals)}$$

$$\lambda = \text{mean arrival rate}$$

Note that λ (read "lambda") is the only parameter of the Poisson distribution, and it can be shown that

$$E(X) = \lambda \tag{A.38}$$

$$\text{Var}(X) = \lambda \tag{A.39}$$

We state, parenthetically, that the Poisson distribution can be used as an approximation for the binomial distribution provided that probability of "success," p, is small (less than 0.05) and the number of independent trials, n, is large (greater than 30).

A.6
Some Continuous Probability Distributions

In the case of a discrete random variable, X, it is possible to attach a probability measure for specific values of X (e.g., see Table A.2). However, we note that the probability of a continuous random variable at a specific value of X is always zero. This follows from the structure of probability density functions of continuous variables (i.e., probability for a continuous variable is defined as the area under the curve generated by $f(X)$—and the area under the curve *at a point* is always zero).

In this section, we present two widely used continuous probability distributions: (1) the normal distribution, and (2) the exponential distribution.[17]

A.6.1 THE NORMAL DISTRIBUTION

The *normal distribution* is a perfectly symmetrical, bell-shaped distribution, as shown in Figure A.4. The normal distribution is one of the most important and widely used distributions. Several natural phenomena (e.g., height of people) and business problems (e.g., demand for commodities) give rise to a normal distribution. Furthermore, if we plot a very large number of the means of samples drawn from *any* distribution, we obtain a normal distribution, regardless of the nature of the original distribution.

[17] Examples of other well-known continuous distributions include the beta distribution, the uniform distribution, and the gamma distribution. See Wadsworth and Bryan [1974].

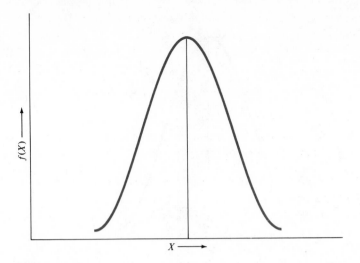

Figure A.4

The probability density function of the normal distribution is given by

$$f(X) = \frac{1}{\sigma\sqrt{2\pi}} e^{-\frac{(X-\mu)^2}{2\sigma^2}} \tag{A.40}$$

where μ and σ are the parameters of the normal distribution. It can be shown that

$$E(X) = \mu \tag{A.41}$$

$$\text{Var}(X) = \sigma^2 \tag{A.42}$$

We illustrate below how the area under the normal curve (between any two points) can be calculated by using the information given in Table 1 of Appendix E. By calculating such areas we compute the probability of the random variable falling between two specified values.

Let us refer to Figure A.5 (recall that Figure A.5 is the same as Figure 6.9 and that it represents a completion-time probability distribution of a PERT network discussed in Chapter 6).

Assume that we want to know the shaded area under the curve between points A and B[i.e., we want to know the probability that the random variable assumes a value between 28 and 30 weeks—$p(28 \leqslant X \leqslant 30)$]. The procedure for finding such probabilities (areas under the curve) consists of the following steps.

Step 1. *Find the absolute difference between the mean of the normal distribution and the relevant specific value of the random variable.*

In our case the absolute difference, $|X - \bar{X}| = |30 - 28| = |2| = 2$.

Step 2. *Divide the absolute difference of step 1 by the standard deviation.*

This yields the deviation in standardized units, and is denoted by Z. In our case,

$$Z = \frac{2}{1.86} = 1.08 \text{ standard deviations}$$

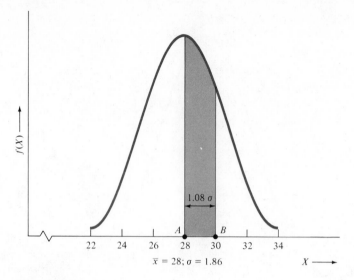

Figure A.5

This means that point *B* is 1.08 standard deviations away from the mean. In other words, the purpose of step 2 is to express distances (from the mean) in units of *σ*.

Step 3. *Look up the area from a table of areas of the normal curve* (see Table I of Appendix E).

In our case, we look under column 2, next to the value of 1.08 in column 1, and find the area to be 0.36. Hence, we can say that

$$p(28 \leqslant X \leqslant 30) = 0.36, \text{ or 36 percent}$$

It is obvious that the area under the curve to the right of point *A* is 0.5. Hence, we can say that

$$p(X \geqslant 30) = 0.50 - 0.36 = 0.14, \text{ or 14 percent}$$

In a similar fashion, by using the three-step procedure outlined above, we can find the probability under the normal curve between any specified values of the random variable.

[*Note*: In executing step 3 we must focus on two things: first, is a point such as *B* located to the right of the mean or to the left of the mean? Second, is the question asking for the area (probability) between two points of which neither is the mean? In each case, Table I of Appendix E yields information *only* with reference to the mean of the distribution. And, we must then answer questions regarding the probability between any two points of the random variable *X* accordingly.]

A.6.2 THE EXPONENTIAL DISTRIBUTION

The *exponential distribution,* also referred to as the *negative exponential distribution,* is useful in describing the behavior of *interarrival times* of arriving

Probability—Basic Concepts and Some Applications   Appendix A customers in queuing problems. The probability density function of the exponential distribution is given by

$$f(X) = \mu e^{-\mu X} \qquad \text{(A.43)}$$

where

X = random variable (interarrival time)

μ = mean arrival rate

Note that μ (read "mu") is the only parameter of the exponential distribution, and it can be shown that

$$E(X) = \frac{1}{\mu} \qquad \text{(A.44)}$$

$$\text{Var}(X) = \frac{1}{\mu^2} \qquad \text{(A.45)}$$

[*Important Note:* To calculate the probability that the random variable X of a *discrete* distribution assumes a specified value [say $X = 5$ in (A.34)], all we have to do is to estimate or assign values to the parameters of the distribution [say $n = 20$, and $p = 0.05$ in (A.34)], and then calculate the probability at $X = 5$ by using the probability density function formula. Thus, if $n = 20$ and $p = 0.05$, then by using (A.34), we calculate $f(X = 5)$ to be 0.0022. That is, the probability of five "successes" is 22 out of 10,000.

Now, when it comes to a *continuous* distribution, we *cannot* calculate the probability *at* a specified value of the random variable. Consider, for example, the exponential distribution whose probability density function (p.d.f.) is given by (A.43). Now, if we calculate the value of $f(X)$ for, say, $X = 0$ and $\mu = 5$, we find that $f(X) = 5$. (See Figure 15.2 on p. 432.) But, we know that probability associated with a specified value of the random variable cannot be greater than 1. Hence, $f(X) = 5$, in this case, gives the numerical value of the p.d.f. at $X = 0$; it *does not* yield the probability that the random variable X assumes a value of zero. Hence, we repeat that, for continuous distributions, we *do not* calculate the probability *at a specified value* of the random variable. Instead, we calculate the probability *between* two specified values of the random variable by calculating the area under the curve, generated by the relevant probability density function formula, *between* the same two specified values of the random variable. This is done by using integral calculus or by simply looking up the relevant tables (e.g., see Table I in Appendix E for the normal probability distribution).]

A.7
Cumulative Probability

It is sometimes necessary to determine the cumulative probability[18] that a random variable (e.g., *demand* for an inventory item) assumes a value of "less than or equal to"—

$P(\text{demand} \leqslant X)$

[18] Note that in the case of cumulative probability, we use the capital letter P.

or "greater than or equal to"—

$$P(\text{demand} \geq X)$$

a specified number, X. Both $P(\text{demand} \leq X)$ and $P(\text{demand} \geq X)$ are examples of cumulative probabilities. However, it is customary to state cumulative probability in "less than or equal to" terms. Then, if we consider "demand" to be a random variable, we denote the cumulative probability as $P(\text{demand} \leq X)$. Since the area under the probability curve is 1, we can say that

$$P(\text{demand} \geq X) = 1 - P(\text{demand} \leq X) \tag{A.46}$$

At this time, we want to note a digression from the normal convention stated above. In Chapter 13, for pedagogical reasons, we directly built cumulative probability of the $P(\text{demand} \geq X)$ type (see Figure 13.2 on p. 371).

Let us now ask this question with reference to the PERT network shown in Figure 6.5 on p. 141. What is the probability that the project will be finished by the 30th week? This question asks for the area under the normal curve to the *left* of point B. This area is obviously 86 percent. Why? We can answer the same question by using a graph of the cumulative probability distribution, as shown in Figure A.6. (Review, at this time, pp. 148–151.)

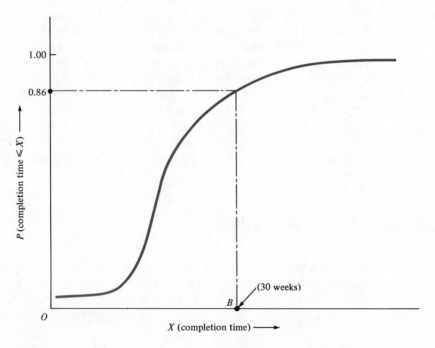

Figure A.6. Point B in this figure is the same B as in Figure A.5.

Probability—Basic Concepts and Some Applications   Appendix A

A.8
A Replacement Model

In Section 4.6.4, we briefly described the nature of replacement models. In this section, we illustrate a replacement model dealing with items (light bulbs) that fail suddenly and completely.

Example A.2 | Let us consider a decision problem in which we wish to compare the cost of two categories of policies dealing with replacing light bulbs in a factory. One policy is the *individual replacement policy*, which calls for replacing a light bulb as soon as it fails. The cost of replacing a bulb on an individual basis is $2.50, owing to the high cost of labor. The other policy is the *group replacement policy*, which is defined as replacing all bulbs at the end of some months *plus* individual replacements. The cost of replacing a bulb in group replacement is $0.50. Assume the mortality distribution for light bulbs shown in Table A.3. Further, assume that the factory has 576 bulbs.

Analysis

Our decision problem can be analyzed in terms of monthly cost. First, we calculate the monthly cost of the individual replacement policy. Then we calculate the monthly cost for the group replacement policy (assuming 1 month, 2 months, or 3 months as possible strategies). Finally, we choose the optimal strategy.

Individual Replacement Policy. By using (A.30),

$$E(X) = \text{expected life of a bulb}$$

$$= X_1p_1 + X_2p_2 + X_3p_3$$

$$= 1(0.15) + 2(0.30) + 3(0.55) = 2.40 \text{ months}$$

Since we have 576 bulbs, we must replace, *on the average* (in the long run),

$$\frac{576}{2.4} = 240 \text{ bulbs/month}$$

Table A.3

Random Variable (Failure During Month After Replacement) X	Probability of Failing (During a Given Month) p(X)	Cumulative Probability P (Failure During Month After Replacement ⩽ X)
1	0.15	0.15
2	0.30	0.45
3	0.55	1.00

Hence, the monthly cost of the individual replacement policy is

$$240\frac{\text{bulbs}}{\text{month}} \times \frac{\$2.50}{\text{bulb}} = \$600/\text{month}$$

Group Replacement Policy. Here we have three possible strategies (S_1, S_2, S_3), which represent group replacement at the end of 1, 2, or 3 months. In each case, the cost of group replacement is the same, $288 (576 bulbs at $0.50/bulb). However, the cost of individual replacements is different, and is determined by the number of bulbs that fail between *successive group replacement times* under each strategy.

Let N_o be the number of original bulbs and let R_1, R_2, and R_3 represent the number of bulbs that failed and have been replaced during the first, second, and third month, respectively. Let p_1, p_2, and p_3 be the probabilities of failure during the first, second, and third month, respectively (see column 2 in Table A.2). Then

$$R_1 = N_o p_1 = 576(0.15) = 86 \text{ bulbs}$$

$$R_2 = N_o p_2 + R_1 p_1 = 576(0.30) + 86(0.15) = 186 \text{ bulbs}$$

$$R_3 = N_o p_3 + R_1 p_2 + R_2 p_1$$

$$= 576(0.55) + 86(0.30) + 186(0.15) = 370 \text{ bulbs}$$

Hence, the number of bulbs that fail and must be replaced individually under the three strategies are:

for S_1: $R_1 = 86$ bulbs; replacement cost $= 86 \times 0.50 = \$43$

for S_2: $R_1 + R_2 = 272$ bulbs; replacement cost $= 272 \times 0.50 = \$136$

for S_3: $R_1 + R_2 + R_3 = 642$ bulbs; replacement cost $= 642 \times 0.50$
$= \$321$

It is now possible to summarize the cost consequences of the three strategies under the group replacement policy covering the 3-month period (see Table A.4).

If we compare the cost consequence of the individual replacement policy with each of the three strategies under the group replacement policy, we note that the best policy is to "group-replace" every 3 months.

Table A.4

Strategy	Cost of Replacing All of 576 Bulbs	Cost of Individually Replacing the Failed Bulbs	Total Cost	Average Cost per Month
S_1: group replacement every month	$288	$ 43	$331	$331
S_2: group replacement every 2 months	288	136	424	212
S_3: group replacement every 3 months	288	321	609	203

A.9
Markov Models

A *Markov model* is a dynamic model and is based on the concepts of Markov processes or Markov chains. A Markov process represents a dynamic system in which we assume that knowledge of the immediate past is helpful in predicting how the system will behave in the future.[19] For example, if the data on market shares of different brands of flour (in a given geographical area) are known, Markov analysis can shed some light on the question of how customers move from one brand to another.

In the Markov model, we assume that the system (e.g., customers), at a given time, can be in one of n *states* (e.g., the customer can be buying one of two brands of flour). As the dynamic system moves from one time period to another, we can expect the customers to change brand loyalty (depending upon the impact of such factors as price, quality, and promotion). The change from one brand to another takes place according to a set of *transition probabilities* (a transition probability, denoted by p_{ij}, is the probability of a customer moving from brand i to brand j).

The transition probabilities can be assumed to stay constant over time (*time-independent* or *stationary* Markov chains), or they can change with time (*time-dependent* or *nonstationary* Markov chains). In this section, we assume that the p_{ij} stay constant over time.

If, for a given system, the probabilities for the various possible starting states and the transition probabilities p_{ij} are known, we can determine the future behavior of the system by Markov analysis. The implication of this assertion is that managers must try to change the transitional probabilities for the benefit of the organization. Let us illustrate a Markov model by using a brand-loyalty problem.

Example A.3 | In a given geographical area, the customers purchase one of two brands of flour: (1) Gold Medal (GM), and (2) Long Life (LL). By using consumer panel data covering a reasonable period, we are in a position to know two things. First, we can determine, in a given month, the number of customers that purchase each brand. From these data, we can calculate q_i, the probabilities of the two *states* of the system ($n = 2$). Note that a customer is in one of two states: he or she either purchases GM or LL. Second, we can calculate the transitional probabilities, p_{ij}.

Assume the following data, at the beginning of a specified month:

number of customers that buy Gold Medal = 10,000

number of customers that buy Long Life = 30,000

Then

q_1 (probability of the event Gold Medal) $= \frac{1}{4} = 0.25$

q_2 (probability of the event Long Life) $= \frac{3}{4} = 0.75$

---

[19] A Markov process can be of the *first order, second order, third order*, and so on, depending upon whether knowledge regarding one, two, or three past periods is utilized for future prediction. In this section, we consider only the first order Markov model.

This probability description of the initial state of the system can be expressed by a row vector,[20]

$$\mathbf{Q}_0 = [q_1 \quad q_2] = [0.25 \quad 0.75]$$

Note that $\mathbf{Q}_0$ describes the probability distribution of the system states in a specified period.

Assume further that, by using the data, we could calculate the relevant transitional probabilities, p_{ij}. For our problem, we would have four transitional probabilities, which can be shown in the form of a matrix, $\mathbf{P}$:

$$\mathbf{P} = \begin{bmatrix} p_{11} & p_{12} \\ p_{21} & p_{22} \end{bmatrix} = \begin{bmatrix} 0.8 & 0.2 \\ 0.6 & 0.4 \end{bmatrix} \tag{A.47}$$

Note that the sum of the transition probabilities in each row is 1. This stands to reason, because the customer starting from one state in one period must end up in one of two possible states in the next period. Let us examine and interpret the transition probabilities as they are displayed in (A.47).

$$\begin{array}{cc} & \text{GM} \quad \text{LL} \\ \begin{array}{c} \text{GM} \\ \text{LL} \end{array} & \begin{bmatrix} 0.8 & 0.2 \\ 0.6 & 0.4 \end{bmatrix} \end{array}$$

$p_{11} =$ probability that a GM customer remains loyal to GM in the next period

$\quad = 0.8$

$p_{12} =$ probability that a GM customer switches to brand LL in the next period

$\quad = 0.2$

$p_{21} =$ probability that a LL customer switches to brand GM in the next period

$\quad = 0.6$

$p_{22} =$ probability that a LL customer remains loyal to LL in the next period

$\quad = 0.4$

We now have the basic ingredients (i.e., a probability vector of the states in the starting period, and a matrix of transition probabilities) for conducting a Markov analysis. With this information we can answer such questions as: (1) what is the probability distribution of the states after 1, 2, or more time periods (i.e., how customers are shifting from one brand to another); (2) what is the probability distribution of the states under equilibrium or steady-state conditions; (3) what is the average staying time (i.e., average time during which the customer sticks to one brand); and (4) what is the average return time? We shall answer only the first two questions.[21]

[20] It is advisable at this time to review Appendix C.

[21] The interested reader is referred to Tsokos [1972].

Probability Distribution of States After Specific Time Periods

After 1 Month

$$Q_1 = Q_0 P = [0.25 \quad 0.75] \begin{bmatrix} 0.8 & 0.2 \\ 0.6 & 0.4 \end{bmatrix} = [0.65 \quad 0.35]$$

Note that, after 1 month, GM increased its customers by 16,000. Why?

After 2 Months

$$Q_2 = Q_1 P = [0.65 \quad 0.35] \begin{bmatrix} 0.8 & 0.2 \\ 0.6 & 0.4 \end{bmatrix} = [0.73 \quad 0.27]$$

Note that, in the second month, GM gained an additional 3,200 customers at the expense of LL. Why? Also, note that

$$Q_2 = Q_1 P = Q_0 (P)^2$$

Similarly, we can calculate the probability distribution of the states after n periods by

$$Q_n = Q_0 (P)^n \tag{A.48}$$

Probability Distribution of the States Under Steady-State or Equilibrium Conditions

Since, under steady-state conditions, the probability distribution of the states is assumed to be constant (i.e., Q does not change), we can calculate the steady-state probabilities by (A.49):

$$[Q][P] = [Q] \tag{A.49}$$

That is,

$$[q_1 \quad q_2] \begin{bmatrix} p_{11} & p_{12} \\ p_{21} & p_{22} \end{bmatrix} = [q_1 \quad q_2]$$

Assume that we have the transition probability matrix, P, of (A.47). Then, for our problem,

$$[q_1 \quad q_2] \begin{bmatrix} 0.8 & 0.2 \\ 0.6 & 0.4 \end{bmatrix} = [q_1 \quad q_2]$$

Hence, by the rules of matrix multiplication, we obtain

$$0.8q_1 + 0.6q_2 = q_1 \tag{A.50}$$
$$0.2q_1 + 0.4q_2 = q_2 \tag{A.51}$$

Solving Equations (A.50) and (A.51) simultaneously, we get

$$q_1 = 0.75 \quad \text{and} \quad q_2 = 0.25$$

That is, the steady-state probability vector

$$Q = [q_1 \quad q_2] = [0.75 \quad 0.25]$$

The managerial implication is that, unless the management of Long Life takes strong measures to change the transition probabilities to their own advantage, they would lose almost two-thirds of their present customers.

References

Boot, J. C. G., and E. B. Cox. *Statistical Analysis for Managerial Decisions*, 2nd ed. New York: McGraw-Hill Book Company, 1974.

Crowdis, D. G., S. M. Shelly, and B. W. Wheeler. *Calculus for Business, Biology and the Social Sciences*, 2nd ed. Beverly Hills, Calif.: Glencoe Press, 1976.

Frank, R. E., and P. E. Green. *Quantitative Methods in Marketing*. Englewood Cliffs, N.J.: Prentice-Hall, Inc., 1967.

Green, P. E., and D. S. Tull. *Research for Marketing Decisions*. Englewood Cliffs, N.J.: Prentice-Hall, Inc., 1975.

Tsokos, C. P. *Probability Distributions: An Introduction to Probability Theory with Applications*. North Scituate, Mass.: Duxbury Press, 1972.

Wadsworth, G. P., and J. P. Bryan. *Applications of Probability and Random Variables*, 2nd ed. New York: McGraw-Hill Book Company, 1974.

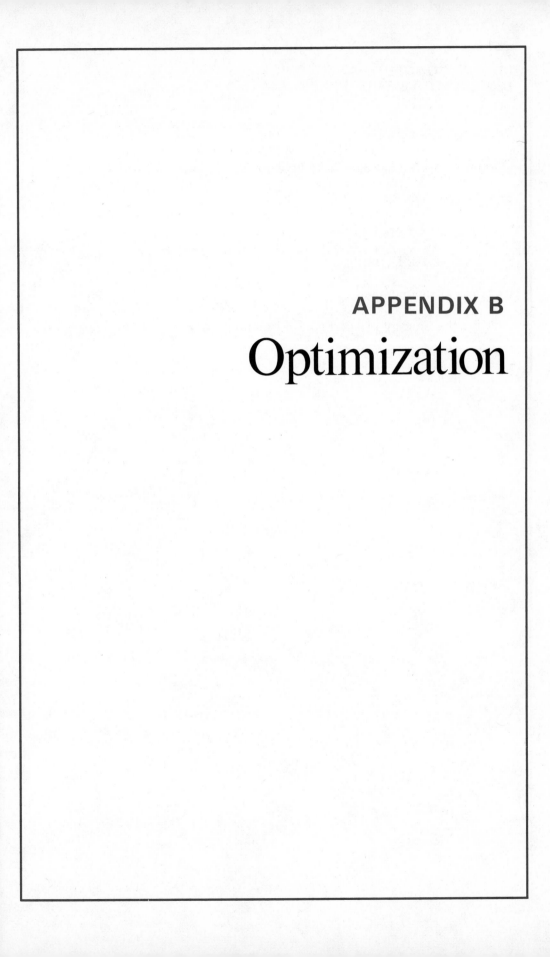

APPENDIX B

Optimization

MAJOR CONCEPTS AND TOPICS
DISCUSSED IN THIS APPENDIX

Process of Optimization

Optimizing Techniques for Different Types of Mathematical Models

The Concept of a Function

The Concept of Slope and Rate of Change

The Concept of a Derivative

Rules of Differentiation

Utilizing the Concept of Derivatives for Optimization

Unconstrained functions
Constrained functions
Lagrange multipliers

B.1
Introduction

The objective in decision problems is to identify or design the best (optimal) strategy (course of action). This is accomplished by either maximizing or minimizing the value of a dependent (criterion) variable or an objective function (by assigning appropriate values to independent or decision variables).[1] The general process of finding the best (optimal) strategies is called *optimization*, and the mathematical techniques employed in finding the optimal strategies are called *optimizing techniques*. The main purpose of this appendix is to illustrate the use of some basic optimizing techniques.

B.2
Optimizing Techniques for Different Types of Mathematical Models

In general, the process of optimization is completed in two steps. First, we develop a mathematical model of the decision problem (the model relates selected variables, parameters, and constants). Second, depending upon the type of the model, we apply an appropriate optimizing technique to identify the optimal strategy.

In Figure B.1, we list some optimizing techniques that can be used in different types of mathematical models. We illustrate them in Section B.7.

B.3
The Concept of a Function

The relationship between the dependent variable and the independent variables can be represented by using the concept of a function. A *function* is a rule that establishes a relationship between different variables. For example, we can state a *general* relationship between *total inventory cost*, T, and *order quantity*, Q, by using the functional notation

$$T = f(Q) \tag{B.1}$$

Equation (B.1) reads "total cost is a function of order quantity." It does *not* mean that T equals f times Q. Furthermore, Equation (B.1) implies that we have decided to make T the dependent variable and Q the independent variable. Note that Q is the sole (single) independent variable in (B.1).

Let us now consider a functional relationship that contains two independent variables. Assume that the quantity demanded, D, of a product is a function of price per unit, C, and the level of advertising expenditure, A. Then the *general*

---

[1] See Figure 2.10 on p. 44 for a classification of variables. Also, review Section 2.8.

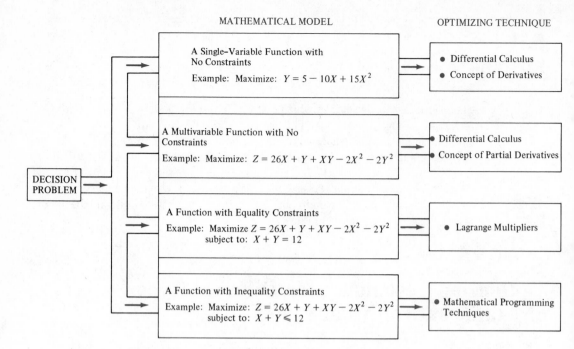

Figure B.1. Optimization Techniques for Different Types of Mathematical Models.

relationship between the dependent variable, D, and the two independent variables, C and A, can be expressed as

$$D = f(C, A) \tag{B.2}$$

The functional notations of the type shown in (B.1) and (B.2) are meant to give a general idea that certain variables are, somehow, related. However, for making managerial decisions, we need a specific and explicit, not a general and implicit, relationship among selected variables. For example, for the purpose of finding optimal Q, we make the general relationship (B.1) more specific by the explicit model shown in Equation (B.3):[2]

$$T = \frac{D}{Q}S + \frac{Q}{2}CH \tag{B.3}$$

Similarly, the general relationship (B.2) must be made specific before it can be used to identify optimal strategies. For example, depending upon the empirical data, Equation (B.2) *could* take a specific form as shown in (B.4):[3]

$$D = 20 + 5C - 2CA + 2A^2 \tag{B.4}$$

Note that both in (B.3) and (B.4) we have established a *rule of correspondence* between the dependent variable and the independent variable(s). That is, as soon as values are assigned to the independent variable(s), the corresponding value for

---

[2] Equation (B.3) is the same as Equation (2.6) on p. 47. It is a mathematical model of the inventory problem presented in Section 2.8. Note that D, S, C, and H are treated as parameters in (B.3).

[3] Note that if we assign numerical values to the parameters in Equation (B.3), we shall obtain a model that is specific to a given problem.

the dependent variable is determined by the specific relationship established by the function. That is why a *function* is sometimes defined as a rule of correspondence between variables.

A function with only one independent variable is called a *single-variable function*. For example, (B.1) contains only one independent variable and therefore represents a single-variable function. Further, a single-variable function can be *linear* or *nonlinear*.

$$Y = 2X \tag{B.5}$$

is *an* example of a linear (single-variable) function.

$$Y = \frac{X^3}{3} - 2X^2 + 3X + 2 \tag{B.6}$$

is *an* example of a nonlinear (single-variable) function.

A single-variable function can always be graphed in a two-dimensional space. The graph of the linear function represented by Equation (B.5) is shown in Figure B.2. The nonlinear function represented by Equation (B.6) is shown in Figure B.3.

A function with more than one independent variable is called a *multivariable function*. For example, (B.2) contains two independent variables and therefore represents a multivariable function. Further, a multivariable function can be *linear* or *nonlinear*.

$$Z = 23X + 32Y \tag{B.7}$$

is *an* example of a linear (multivariable) function.

$$Z = 23X + 10XY + 32Y^2 \tag{B.8}$$

is *an* example of a nonlinear (multivariable) function.

A function (single or multivariable; linear or nonlinear) may or may not be subject to constraints, depending upon the assumptions or realities of the

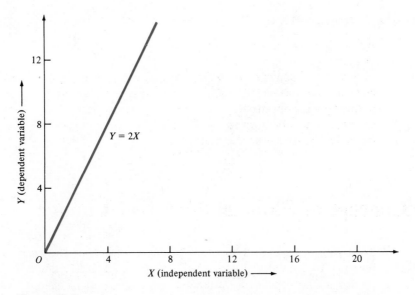

Figure B.2

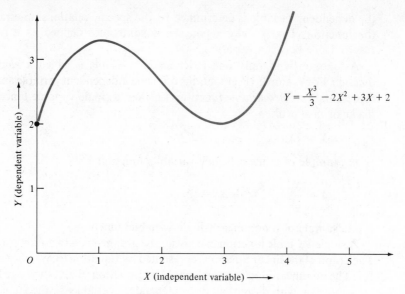

$$Y = \frac{X^3}{3} - 2X^2 + 3X + 2$$

Figure B.3

problem. For example, none of the functions represented in (B.1) to (B.8) have been subjected to any constraints.

As discussed in Section 7.2.3, the maximization (or minimization) of an *unconstrained linear function* does not make any practical sense. (Why?) However, we *can* maximize or minimize *unconstrained nonlinear functions* by using the concepts of *derivatives* and *partial derivatives* (these concepts are presented in Sections B.5 and B.7.3). Recall that we minimized the unconstrained nonlinear function (total inventory cost) shown in Equation (2.6), [on p. 47], by using the concept of derivatives.

Constrained Optimization

A *function subject to equality constraints* can be optimized by using the technique of *Lagrange multipliers* (See Section B.7.4).

A *function subject to inequality constraints* can be optimized by using *mathematical programming* techniques. Recall that a linear programming model is nothing but the optimization of a linear function subject to linear constraints that are often, but not always, stated as inequalities. Linear functions subject to inequality constraints were treated in Chapters 7 to 10.

B.4
The Concept of Slope and Rate of Change

The term *slope* is used to measure the degree of steepness or *rate of change* of a function. In general, the slope or rate of change of a function is defined as the change in the dependent variable caused by 1 unit of change in one of the independent variables.

Optimization   Appendix B

B.4.1 SLOPE OF A LINE

Consider the equation $Y = a + bX$, which is a general mathematical model for a line. Then, the coefficient of the independent variable X (i.e., the value of b) is the *slope* of the line. This is because the value of b measures the change in the dependent variable Y caused by 1 unit of change in the independent variable X.

Consider the equation of a line $Y = 6 + X$. Then, the slope of the line is $+1$. The plus sign indicates that Y and X move in the *same* direction. That is, the line slopes upward, as shown by line A in Figure B.4.

Consider the equation of a line $Y = 6 - X$. Then, the slope of the line is -1. The minus sign indicates that Y and X move in the *opposite* direction. That is, the line slopes downward, as shown by line B in Figure B.4.

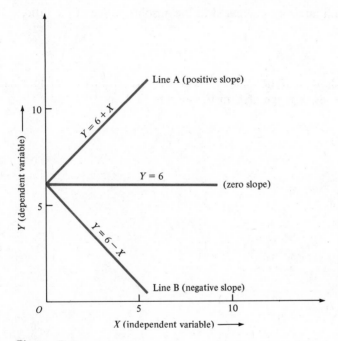

Figure B.4

Consider the equation of a line $Y = 6$ (i.e., $Y = 6 + 0X$). It is obvious that the term involving X has a coefficient of zero, and hence the value of b must be zero. That is, the slope of this line is zero, and hence it is a horizontal line, as shown in Figure B.4. Note that the slope (rate of change) of a line remains constant at all points on the line. However, the slope (rate of change) of a curve (i.e., a nonlinear function) changes from point to point.

B.4.2 SLOPE OF A CURVE (AT A POINT)

The idea that the slope (rate of change) of a curve is different at different points on the curve can best be appreciated if we utilize the symbol Δ (read "delta") to denote very small changes in the variables. For example, let ΔX measure the change in the value of the independent variable X, and let ΔY measure the change in the value of the dependent variable Y. Then the ratio $\dfrac{\Delta Y}{\Delta X}$ measures the change in the dependent variable Y caused by 1 unit of change in the independent variable X. Now, refer to the straight line in Figure B.5 and note that the ratio $\dfrac{\Delta Y}{\Delta X}$ (i.e., slope) remains constant—regardless of the portion of the line selected to build this ratio. But, as shown in Figure B.6, the slope of a curve is different at different points. For example, we note in Figure B.6 that the absolute value of the ratio,

$$\frac{\Delta Y}{\Delta X} = \frac{Y_2 - Y_1}{X_2 - X_1}$$

is much larger as compared to the absolute value of the ratio,

$$\frac{\Delta Y}{\Delta X} = \frac{Y_4 - Y_3}{X_4 - X_3}$$

This shows that the value of Y is much more *sensitive* to changes in the value of X in the lower range of X in Figure B.6.

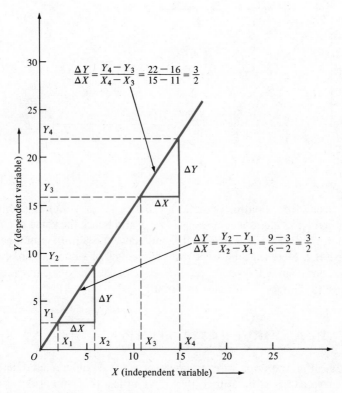

Figure B.5

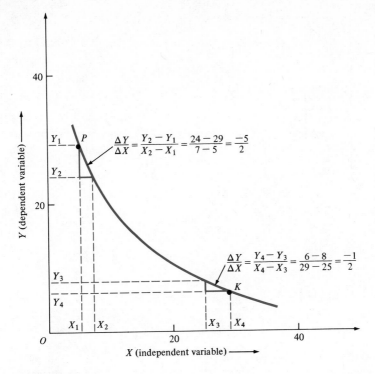

Figure B.6

B.5
The Concept of a Derivative

The term *derivative* is a generalized expression for measuring the rate of change of a function. In mathematical terms, finding the derivative of a function involves the calculation of the ratio $\dfrac{\Delta Y}{\Delta X}$ for an infinitesimal change in the independent variable. The idea of an infinitesimal (close to zero) change is denoted by the symbol $\Delta X \to 0$ (read ΔX approaches zero).

The derivative of Y with respect to X is denoted by such symbols as

$$\frac{dY}{dX}; \; y'; \; f'(X)$$

Mathematically, we define the derivative of Y with respect to X as

$$\frac{dY}{dX} = \lim_{\Delta x \to 0} \frac{\Delta Y}{\Delta X} \tag{B.9}$$

The expression (B.9) is read: "The derivative of Y with respect to X equals the limit of the ratio $\dfrac{\Delta Y}{\Delta X}$ as ΔX approaches zero."

Let us pose this question: What is the slope of the curve in Figure B.7 at a point

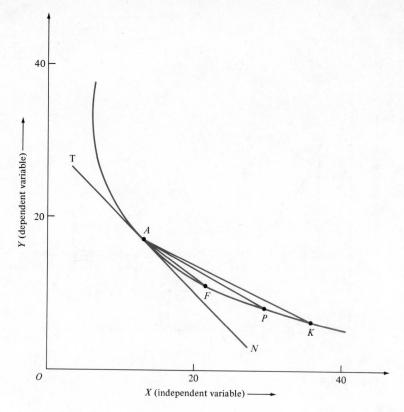

Figure B.7

average slope of the curve between any two points (e.g., between points A and K) is measured by the slope of the line joining those points. Hence, the average slope of the curve between points A and K is

$$\text{slope of the line } AK = \frac{\Delta Y}{\Delta X} = \frac{Y_2 - Y_1}{X_2 - X_1}$$

However, it is always possible to consider *successively smaller* portions of the curve (i.e., smaller intervals of X or, alternatively, smaller values of ΔX). Now, as we keep on making ΔX smaller, we approach a point such as A and we obtain a line that touches the curve only at one point.[4] Thus, at the limit, as $\Delta X \to 0$, the ratio $\frac{\Delta Y}{\Delta X}$ (i.e., the derivative) equals the slope of the tangent (line TAN) at that point of the curve. Hence, we can say that the derivative of a function is a generalized expression for the slope of a function. Further, when we calculate the value of a derivative at a particular point of a function, this value equals the slope of the tangent at that point—and yields *the value of the slope at that point.*

---

[4] This line is the *tangent* to the curve at that point. A tangent at a point is defined as the line that touches the curve *only at that point*—and does not cross the curve at that point.

B.6
Rules of Differentiation

The process of finding the derivative of a function is called *differentiation*. Given below are some of the most commonly used rules of differentiation.

Derivative of a Constant

Let $Y = K$, where K is a constant; then

$$\frac{dY}{dX} = \frac{d}{dX}(K) = 0 \tag{B.10}$$

This can be reinforced by simple reasoning. In Figure B.8, Y always has a value of K, regardless of the value assumed by X. Hence, the rate of change of Y with respect to X is zero, and *the derivative of a constant is always zero.*

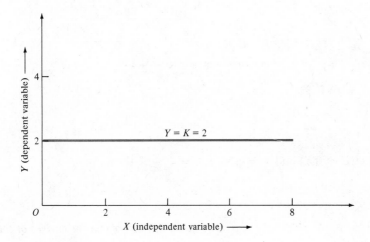

Figure B.8

Derivative of a Power Function

Let $Y = kX^n$, where coefficient k and exponent n are constants; then

$$\frac{dY}{dX} = k \cdot n \cdot X^{n-1} \tag{B.11}$$

That is, *the derivative of a power function equals the coefficient k multiplied by the product of the exponent n and variable X raised to the power $(n-1)$.* Here are some examples:

- Let $Y = X$; then $\dfrac{dY}{dX} = 1$ (see Figure B.9)

- Let $Y = 4X^3$; then $\dfrac{dY}{dX} = 12X^2$

- Let $Y = \dfrac{4}{X}$, so $Y = 4(X)^{-1}$; then $\dfrac{dY}{dX} = 4(-1)(X)^{-2} = -4X^{-2} = \dfrac{-4}{X^2}$

- Let $Y = \dfrac{DS}{Q}$, where D and S are constants, so $Y = DS(Q)^{-1}$; then

$$\frac{dY}{dQ} = DS(-1)(Q)^{-2} = \frac{-DS}{Q^2}$$

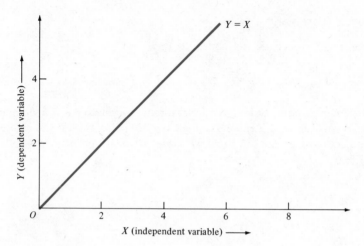

Figure B.9

Derivative of a Sum of Terms

Let $U = f(X)$ and $V = g(X)$. If $Y = U + V$, then

$$\frac{dY}{dX} = \frac{dU}{dX} + \frac{dV}{dX} \tag{B.12}$$

That is, *the derivative of a sum equals the sum of the derivatives of the individual terms.*

Let $U = 4X^2$, $V = -3X^2$, $Y = U + V$. Then $\dfrac{dU}{dX} = 8X$, $\dfrac{dV}{dX} = -6X$. Hence, from (B.12),

$$\frac{dY}{dX} = 8X - 6X = 2X$$

Derivative of a Difference of Terms

If $Y = U - V$, then

$$\frac{dY}{dX} = \frac{dU}{dX} - \frac{dV}{dX} \tag{B.13}$$

That is, *the derivative of a difference equals the difference of the derivatives of the individual terms.*

Let $U = \dfrac{5}{X}$, $V = 2X + 3X^2$, $Y = U - V$. Then $\dfrac{dU}{dX} = \dfrac{-5}{X^2}$, $\dfrac{dV}{dX} = 2 + 6X$.

Hence, from (B.13),

$$\frac{dY}{dX} = \frac{-5}{X^2} - 6X - 2$$

Derivative of a Product

If $Y = U \cdot V$, then

$$\frac{dY}{dX} = U \cdot \frac{dV}{dX} + V \cdot \frac{dU}{dX} \tag{B.14}$$

That is, the derivative of the product of two terms equals this sum: *first term multiplied by the derivative of the second term plus second term multiplied by the derivative of the first term.* Consider, for example, $Y = X(X^2 + 2)$. Let $U = X$ and $V = (X^2 + 2)$. Then, from (B.14),

$$\begin{aligned}
\frac{dY}{dX} &= X \cdot \frac{d}{dX}(X^2 + 2) + (X^2 + 2)\frac{d}{dX}(X) \\
&= X(2X + 0) + (X^2 + 2)(1) \\
&= 2X^2 + X^2 + 2 = 3X^2 + 2
\end{aligned}$$

Derivative of a Quotient

If $Y = \dfrac{U}{V}$, then

$$\frac{dY}{dX} = \frac{V \cdot \dfrac{dU}{dX} - U \cdot \dfrac{dV}{dX}}{V^2} \tag{B.15}$$

That is, the derivative of a quotient equals this: *the denominator multiplied by the derivative of the numerator minus the numerator multiplied by the derivative of the denominator—then this difference divided by the square of the denominator.* Consider, for example, $Y = \dfrac{X}{X + 1}$. Then, from (B.15),

$$\begin{aligned}
\frac{dY}{dX} &= \frac{(X + 1) \cdot \dfrac{d}{dX}(X) - X \cdot \dfrac{d}{dX}(X + 1)}{(X + 1)^2} \\
&= \frac{(X + 1)(1) - X(1 + 0)}{(X + 1)^2} = \frac{1}{(X + 1)^2}
\end{aligned}$$

Derivative of a Function of a Function

Let $Y = f(U)$ and $U = g(X)$; then

$$\frac{dY}{dX} = \frac{dY}{dU} \cdot \frac{dU}{dX} \tag{B.16}$$

Consider, for example, $Y = (4 + 2X)^2$. Let $U = 4 + 2X$; hence, $Y = U^2$. Now

$$\frac{dY}{dU} = 2U = 2(4 + 2X) = 8 + 4X$$

$$\frac{dU}{dX} = 0 + 2 = 2$$

Hence, from (B.16),

$$\frac{dY}{dX} = \frac{dY}{dU} \cdot \frac{dU}{dX} = (8 + 4X)2 = 16 + 8X$$

Other rules for differentiation can be found in any calculus book or in a handbook of differentiation formulas.

B.7
Utilizing the Concept of Derivatives for Optimization

B.7.1 OPTIMIZING SINGLE-VARIABLE FUNCTIONS (UNCONSTRAINED)

We have established that the derivative of a function is a generalized expression for the slope of a function. Now refer to Figures B.10 and B.11. (Note that both figures depict a single-variable function.) Figure B.10 represents a typical total-cost function that is to be minimized (e.g., see Figure 2.9, on p. 42 which shows total inventory cost). Now, it is quite clear that at the point of *minimum* total cost, the slope of the curve must be zero. Hence, we can find the derivative of the dependent variable, T, with respect to the independent variable, Q, and equate the

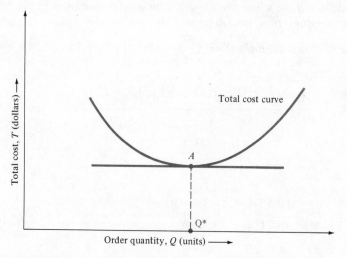

Figure B.10

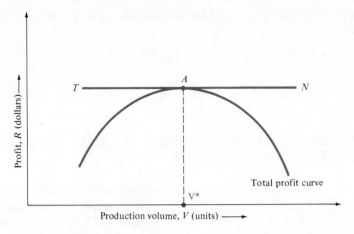

Figure B.11

derivative to zero. Then we can solve for the optimal order quantity Q^* that will result in *minimum* total cost. For example, consider the total-cost function,

$$T = \frac{4,000}{Q}(20) + \frac{Q}{2}(5)(0.20)$$

$$= +\frac{80,000}{Q} + \frac{Q}{2}$$

Differentiating T with respect to Q, we obtain the first derivative,

$$\frac{dT}{dQ} = \frac{-80,000}{Q^2} + \frac{1}{2} \tag{B.17}$$

Since the first derivative must be zero to minimize total cost, we set (B.17) equal to zero:

$$\frac{-80,000}{Q^2} + \frac{1}{2} = 0$$

$$Q = \sqrt{160,000} \qquad \text{or} \qquad Q^* = 400 \text{ units/order}$$

That is, if we order in units of 400, we shall minimize total cost.[5]

Figure B.11 represents a profit function. Again, at the point of *maximum* profit, the slope of the curve must be zero. Hence, we can find the derivative of the dependent variable, R, with respect to the independent variable, V, and equate the derivative to zero. Then we can solve for the optimal production volume, V^*, that will result in maximum total profit. Consider, for example, the total-profit function,

$$R = -5,000 + 600 V - 3V^2$$

Differentiating R with respect to V, we obtain the first derivative,

$$\frac{dR}{dV} = 600 - 6V \tag{B.18}$$

[5] Refer at this time to pp. 345–347.

Since the first derivative must be zero to maximize total profit, we set (B.18) equal to zero:

$$600 - 6V = 0 \qquad \text{or} \qquad V^* = 100 \text{ units}$$

That is, total profit is maximized when production volume is 100 units.

B.7.2 HOW TO DISTINGUISH BETWEEN MAXIMUM AND MINIMUM POINTS OF A FUNCTION

The idea of using derivatives to maximize or minimize the value of a function, as illustrated above, is subject to a hazard that will become evident when we examine a complicated function, such as shown in Figure B.12. When we equate the first derivative of a function to zero, we are saying that the slope of the curve is zero (i.e., the rate of change is zero), and it implies that the curve is neither falling nor rising. However, since this condition holds not only for maxima and minima, but can also hold for points of inflection (e.g., point D in Figure B.12), further tests are necessary.[6] Hence, the equating of the first derivative to zero is a necessary, but not sufficient, condition for optimizing functions. We need an additional test to distinguish between maxima and minima. This test is conducted by utilizing the concept of *second-order derivatives*.

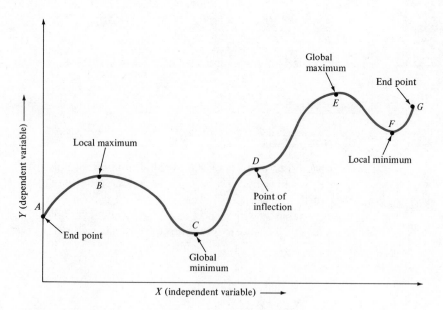

Figure B.12

[6] Maximum or minimum points can be local or global. The term *global* is used to identify the absolute maximum (e.g., point E) as compared to the *local* maximum (e.g., point B). Similarly, we can distinguish between local and global minima.

A second-order derivative is obtained by differentiating the first-order derivative.[7] The procedure for using second-order derivatives to distinguish between a maximum and a minimum point is summarized below (for single-variable functions).

Step 1. *Determine the first derivative,* $\dfrac{dY}{dX}$.

Step 2. *Equate the first derivative,* $\dfrac{dY}{dX}$, *to zero and calculate optimal value(s) of independent variable* X *by solving this equation.*

Denote the optimal value(s) by $X*$

Step 3. *Determine the second derivative,* $\dfrac{d^2Y}{dX^2}$.

Step 4. *Evaluate the second derivative for value(s) of* $X*$ *found in step 2.*

Then, in general, the following will hold.

- If this evaluation yields a *negative* number, we have a *maximum*.
- If this evaluation yields a *positive* number, we have a *minimum*.
- If this evaluation yields a value of *zero*, further investigation is needed to distinguish whether we have a maximum, a minimum, or a *point of inflection*.[8]

The next step is designed to locate the global (as opposed to local) maximum or minimum.

Step 5. *Determine the global maximum or minimum by comparing the values of the function for each optimal* $X*$ *and for the end points* (e.g., points *A* and *G* in Figure B.12).

B.7.3 OPTIMIZING MULTIVARIABLE FUNCTIONS (UNCONSTRAINED)

To optimize a multivariable function, we need to use the concept of partial derivatives. A *partial derivative* of a multivariable function is the derivative of the dependent variable with respect to one of the independent variables, while assuming that all other independent variables are treated as constants. Therefore, a partial derivative measures the change in the dependent variable caused by 1 unit of change in one of the independent variables, while holding constant the

---

[7] The second-order derivative is denoted as $\dfrac{d^2Y}{dX^2}$ or $f''(x)$. Here is a familiar example to illustrate the idea of the second derivative. If the dependent variable d is the distance in miles and the independent variable t is time in hours, then the first derivative, $f'(d) = \text{speed} = \text{miles/hour}$; and the second derivative, $f''(d) = \text{acceleration} = \text{miles/hour/hour}$.

[8] For a more formal and mathematically precise treatment, see Crowdis et al. [1976].

effect of all other independent variables.[9] Consider, for example, the multivariable function

$$R = 26A + B + AB - 2A^2 - 2B^2 \qquad \text{(B.19)}$$

Then the partial derivative of the dependent variable R with respect to the independent variable A is

$$\frac{\partial R}{\partial A} = 26 + 0 + B - 4A + 0 \qquad \text{(B.20)}$$

The partial derivative of R with respect to the independent variable B is

$$\frac{\partial R}{\partial B} = 0 + 1 + A + 0 - 4B \qquad \text{(B.21)}$$

Now, in order to maximize (B.19), we need to equate both partial derivatives to zero and then solve the resulting equations simultaneously. Hence, from (B.20),

$$26 + B - 4A = 0 \qquad \text{(B.22)}$$

And, from (B.21),

$$1 - 4B + A = 0 \qquad \text{(B.23)}$$

Solving (B.22) and (B.23) simultaneously, we get $A = 7$ and $B = 2$. That is, by letting $A = 7$ and $B = 2$, the multivariable function given by (B.19) is maximized.[10]

B.7.4 CONSTRAINED OPTIMIZATION (EQUALITY CONSTRAINTS)

In Sections B.7.1 and B.7.3, we explained the optimization procedure for *unconstrained functions*. In this section, we utilize the concept of *Lagrange multipliers* to optimize a function with one equality constraint.[11] Let us reconsider the function stated in (B.19) except that we impose one equality constraint.

Maximize

$$R = 26A + B + AB - 2A^2 - 2B^2$$

subject to the constraint

$$A + B = 12 \qquad \qquad \text{(B.24)}$$

We now describe the Lagrange multiplier technique by solving the maximization problem stated in (B.24).

---

[9] The symbol ∂ (read "delta") is used to denote a partial derivative. The partial derivative of Y with respect to X is denoted as $\dfrac{\partial Y}{\partial X}$.

[10] Actually, as in the case of single-variable functions, we need additional tests here to determine whether the function is maximized or minimized. However, the additional tests are rather complicated and we do not pursue them here. The interested reader is referred to Loomba and Turban [1974, pp. 455–457].

[11] The Lagrange multiplier procedure is quite general and can be used for any number of equality constraints.

Step 1. *Rearrange each equality constraint so that its right-hand side is zero.*

Here we have only one equality constraint. Hence,

$$A + B - 12 = 0 \tag{B.25}$$

Step 2. *Multiply each rearranged equation (result of step 1) by an unknown factor λ (read "lambda"):*

$$\lambda(A + B - 12) = 0 \tag{B.26}[12]$$

Step 3. *Form the Lagrangian function by subtracting from the original function the left-hand side result(s) of step 2.*

In our problem, the Lagrangian function (denoted by L_R) is

$$L_R = 26A + B + AB - 2A^2 - 2B^2 - \lambda(A + B - 12) \tag{B.27}$$

Step 4. *Optimize the unconstrained Lagrangian function by using partial derivatives* (treat each λ as a variable).

Before we execute step 4, we note that Equation (B.27) has three independent variables, A, B, and λ. Hence, to optimize (B.27) we need to take three partial derivatives, equate them to zero, and simultaneously solve the three resultant equations. This procedure accomplishes two things for us. First, we are assured that the constraint condition is met.[13] Second, the optimization of the Lagrangian function also ensures the optimization of the original function. Next we execute step 4.

$$\frac{\partial L_R}{\partial A} = 26 + B - 4A - \lambda = 0 \tag{B.28}$$

$$\frac{\partial L_R}{\partial B} = 1 - 4B + A - \lambda = 0 \tag{B.29}$$

$$\frac{\partial L_R}{\partial \lambda} = 12 - B - A = 0 \tag{B.30}$$

Solving Equations (B.28) to (B.30) simultaneously, we obtain

$$A = 8.5 \qquad B = 3.5 \qquad \lambda = -4.5$$

We can now make two statements. First, the constrained function of (B.24) is maximized by letting $A = 8.5$ and $B = 3.5$. Second, the value of λ measures the impact on the objective function of changing the constraint by 1 unit. This information is of the utmost importance to the manager, as it indicates the "marginal worth" of the constraint. For example, if the constraint specifies a

---

[12] If we had more than one (say, n) equality constraints, we would have multiplied each rearranged equation by $\lambda_1, \lambda_2, \ldots, \lambda_n$.

[13] This is because the partial derivative with respect to λ, when equated to zero, automatically yields the original constraint. See Equation (B.30) which yields $A + B = 12$.

limited resource (e.g., machine-hours), the value of λ indicates the "marginal worth" of an additional unit of machine-hours. Note that the value of λ is the same thing as the value of the dual variable discussed in Section 9.4.

B.7.5 CONSTRAINED OPTIMIZATION (INEQUALITY CONSTRAINTS)

The product-mix problem described by (7.4) in Chapter 7 is a typical constrained optimization problem. That problem, as the reader will recall, required the maximization of a linear objective function subject to linear constraints that were expressed as inequalities.[14] Insofar as the inequalities can be converted to equalities, we can handle such problems by using Lagrange multipliers, as explained in Section B.7.4. However, mathematical programming techniques are much more efficient in optimizing objective functions subject to inequality constraints. The simplex method, presented in Chapter 8, is one such mathematical programming technique.

References

Crowdis, D. G., S. M. Shelley, and B. W. Wheeler. *Calculus for Business, Biology and the Social Sciences*, 2nd ed. Beverly Hills, Calif.: Glencoe Press, 1976.

Loomba, N. P., and E. Turban. *Applied Programming for Management*. New York: Holt, Rinehart and Winston, 1974.

---

[14] We can also have a nonlinear objective function subject to linear or nonlinear constraints.

Basic Concepts of Matrix Algebra

MAJOR CONCEPTS AND TOPICS
DISCUSSED IN THIS APPENDIX

The Concept of a Matrix

The Concept of a Vector

Operations Concerning Matrices and Vectors

Linear Combination

Linear Independence

Idea of Vector Space

Basis for a Vector Space

Systems of Simultaneous Linear Equations

C.1
Introduction

The simplex method of solving linear programming problems that we presented in Chapter 8 utilizes a branch of mathematics known as *matrix algebra*. *Matrices* and *vectors* are the central concepts of matrix algebra, and they can be used effectively in explaining the mechanics of the simplex method. Furthermore, the concepts of matrices and vectors are used in several other decision models (e.g., Markov models). It is, therefore, desirable that we become familiar with matrices and vectors, their structure and properties, and such operations as addition, subtraction. and multiplication of matrices and vectors. This appendix is devoted to accomplishing this task.

C.2
Matrices

C.2.1 DEFINITION AND NOTATION

A *matrix* is a rectangular array of ordered[1] numbers, consisting of m rows and n columns. The purpose of a matrix is to convey information in a concise fashion and to promote ease of mathematical manipulation. Although a given matrix does not imply any mathematical operation, matrix algebra is a powerful tool for solving a system of linear equations.

Some examples of matrices are

$$A = \begin{bmatrix} 2 & -1 \\ 1 & 3 \end{bmatrix} \quad B = \begin{bmatrix} 2 & 1 & 4 \\ -3 & 2 & 1 \end{bmatrix} \quad C = \begin{bmatrix} 10 & 6 & 2 \\ 5 & 10 & 5 \\ 1 & 2 & 2 \end{bmatrix}$$

Square brackets, [ ], are used in this book to denote a matrix.[2] Any matrix in which the number of rows equals the number of columns is called a *square matrix*. Thus, matrices A and C above are square matrices, whereas B is a rectangular matrix of two rows and three columns.

In this book, we use boldface capital letters, such as A, B, and C, to denote the entire matrix, and lowercase italic letters with proper subscripts, such as a_{11}, $a_{12}, \ldots$, to denote the numbers within the matrix.

Note that the first two columns of matrix C consist of ordered numbers that reflect the technical specification of the linear programming problem described in Chapter 8.

---

[1] The term *ordered* implies that the position of each number is significant and must be determined carefully to represent the information contained in the problem.

[2] Sometimes matrices are denoted by parentheses. ( ). or by pairs of double vertical lines, ‖ ‖.

C.2.2   THE DIMENSION OF A MATRIX

The number of rows and the number of columns in a given matrix determine the *dimension* or *order* of the matrix. For example, consider

$$D = \begin{bmatrix} 2 & 1 \\ -1 & 4 \end{bmatrix} \quad \text{and} \quad E = \begin{bmatrix} -3 & 2 & 1 \\ 2 & 1 & 3 \end{bmatrix}$$

Matrix D is a 2×2 (two by two) matrix, whereas matrix E is a 2×3 matrix. When specifying the order or dimension of a matrix, the first number always refers to the rows of the matrix, the second number to the columns of the matrix. For example, the dimension of a matrix with m rows and n columns is $m \times n$. Rows of a matrix are numbered from top to bottom; columns are numbered from left to right.

C.2.3   COMPONENTS OF A MATRIX

The various numbers within a matrix are referred to as the *components* of the matrix. For example, matrix

$$A = \begin{bmatrix} 2 & -1 \\ 1 & 3 \end{bmatrix}$$

has four components: $2, -1, 1$, and 3. The general form of a 2×2 matrix is

$$A = \begin{bmatrix} a_{11} & a_{12} \\ a_{21} & a_{22} \end{bmatrix}$$

The components of the matrix are denoted by double subscripts. In the component a_{12}, the first subscript refers to the row and the second subscript refers to the column. The double subscripts give us the *address* of the component, indicating the specific row and column in which the component may be found. For example, component a_{ij} is located in the ith row and jth column.[3] A compact notation for a matrix is $A = [a_{ij}]$.

C.2.4   THE REAL MATRIX

If all the components of a given matrix are real numbers, the matrix is called a *real matrix*.

C.2.5   SOME SPECIAL MATRICES

Identity Matrix

The *identity matrix* (sometimes called the *unit matrix*) is a square matrix and is denoted by I. It is characterized by the fact that all components on its main diagonal (the diagonal going from the northwest corner to the southeast corner)

---

[3] Unless otherwise indicated, i's refer to rows and j's to columns throughout this book.

are 1's, whereas all other components are zero. Following are two different identity matrices:

$$I = \begin{bmatrix} 1 & 0 \\ 0 & 1 \end{bmatrix} \qquad I = \begin{bmatrix} 1 & 0 & 0 \\ 0 & 1 & 0 \\ 0 & 0 & 1 \end{bmatrix}$$

The role of the identity matrix in matrix algebra is very similar to that played by the number 1 in ordinary algebra. Provided that they are compatible for multiplication, an identity matrix multiplied by any matrix gives the same matrix.[4] That is, $IA = A$; and $AI = A$.

The Zero Matrix

The *zero matrix* is a matrix in which all components are zero. It is denoted as 0. Given next are three examples of zero matrices.

$$0 = \begin{bmatrix} 0 & 0 & 0 \\ 0 & 0 & 0 \\ 0 & 0 & 0 \end{bmatrix} \qquad 0 = \begin{bmatrix} 0 & 0 \\ 0 & 0 \end{bmatrix} \qquad 0 = \begin{bmatrix} 0 & 0 & 0 \\ 0 & 0 & 0 \end{bmatrix}$$

The role of the zero matrix in matrix algebra is very similar to that of zero in ordinary algebra. Provided that they are compatible for multiplication, the product of any matrix and the zero matrix is a zero matrix.

Transpose of a Matrix

Associated with every $m \times n$ matrix A is an $n \times m$ matrix (denoted by A^T) whose rows are the columns of the given matrix A, in exactly the same order. (See Table 9.2 on p. 240.)

C.3
Vectors

C.3.1   DEFINITION AND NOTATION

A *vector* is an array of ordered numbers, consisting of a *single* row or column. If a vector has n components, it is an *n-dimensional vector* and corresponds to a point in an n-dimensional space. For example, a vector with just two components, 4 and 2, is a two-dimensional vector and corresponds to the point $(4, 2)$. The same vector can also be graphed as line OV_3, which has *magnitude* as well as *direction*[5] (see Figure C.2).

---

[4] As will be explained later, two given matrices are compatible for multiplication only when the number of columns in the *lead matrix* equals the number of rows in the *lag matrix*.

[5] It should be emphasized that a vector is *not* a number. A *scalar*, which is a number, is distinguished from a vector by the fact that a scalar possesses only magnitude.

The concept of a vector as a point in space is important because we can think of the right-hand side of a linear programming constraint set (e.g., the capacity levels of the three departments in Table 8.1) as a vector that corresponds to a point in space; and the solution of the linear programming problem can be thought of as reaching this point in space.

Like matrices, vectors are denoted in this book by square brackets. We shall use boldface capital letters such as U and V to denote the entire vector, and lowercase italic letters with proper subscripts to denote the components of a vector.

In matrix algebra, vectors can be considered as special cases of a matrix. Two types of vectors can be identified: (1) row vectors, and (2) column vectors. A *row vector* is an ordered array of numbers arranged in a row. Following are examples of row vectors:

$$V_1 = [10 \quad 6 \quad 2] \qquad V_2 = [5 \quad 10 \quad 5] \qquad V_3 = [23 \quad 32 \quad 18]$$

Since it is a special case of a matrix, we can say that V_1 is a 1×3 matrix. Thus, in general, a row vector is a $1 \times n$ matrix, when $n = 1, 2, 3, \ldots$. A *column vector* is an ordered array of numbers arranged in a column. Examples of column vectors are

$$U_1 = \begin{bmatrix} 10 \\ 5 \\ 1 \end{bmatrix} \qquad U_2 = \begin{bmatrix} 6 \\ 10 \\ 2 \end{bmatrix} \qquad U_3 = \begin{bmatrix} 2,500 \\ 2,000 \\ 500 \end{bmatrix}$$

Since it is a special case of a matrix, we can say that U_1 is a 3×1 matrix. Thus, in general, a column vector is an $m \times 1$ matrix, where $m = 1, 2, 3, \ldots$. The numbers in a vector are referred to as the *components* of the vector. For example, the column vector U_1 has three components: 10, 5, 1.

Note that the column vector U_3 reflects the capacity levels of the linear programming problem presented in Section 8.3.

C.3.2   SOME SPECIAL VECTORS

Unit Vector

A *unit vector* is a vector in which one component has the value 1 while the rest of the components are zeros. Here are some examples of unit vectors:

$$U_1 = \begin{bmatrix} 1 \\ 0 \\ 0 \end{bmatrix} \qquad U_2 = \begin{bmatrix} 0 \\ 1 \\ 0 \end{bmatrix} \qquad V_1 = [1 \quad 0 \quad 0] \qquad V_2 = [0 \quad 1 \quad 0]$$

Zero Vector

A *zero vector* is a vector in which all the components are zero. Given next are a 1×3 zero row vector and a 3×1 zero column vector:

$$\mathbf{0} = [0 \quad 0 \quad 0] \qquad \mathbf{0} = \begin{bmatrix} 0 \\ 0 \\ 0 \end{bmatrix}$$

C.4
Graphical Representation of Vectors

If we assume that the vectors emanate from the origin of a coordinate system, it is easy to view a vector as a point in space, and vice versa. A given vector can be represented graphically if it has less than four components. Consider, for example, a vector $\mathbf{V}_1 = [5]$, which has a single component. This vector can be represented in a one-dimensional space as in Figure C.1. Similarly, a vector $\mathbf{V}_2 = [-3]$ can be represented in a one-dimensional space as in Figure C.1.

A vector having two components can be represented in a two-dimensional space. For example, the vector $\mathbf{V}_3 = [4 \quad 2]$ can be graphed as shown in Figure C.2. That is, $\mathbf{V}_3 = [4 \quad 2]$ implies that $X = 4$ and $Y = 2$. Similarly, a three-component vector can be represented in a three-dimensional space. For example, the vector

$$\mathbf{V}_4 = [2 \quad 1 \quad 4]$$

is graphed in Figure C.3. That is,

$$\mathbf{V}_4 = [2 \quad 1 \quad 4]$$

implies that $X = 2$, $Y = 1$, and $Z = 4$.

We note that there is no geometric distinction between row and column vectors. Figure C.3, for example, is a graphical representation of

$$\mathbf{V}_4 = [2 \quad 1 \quad 4] \qquad \text{as well as of} \qquad \mathbf{V}_5 = \begin{bmatrix} 2 \\ 1 \\ 4 \end{bmatrix}$$

In general, it takes an m-dimensional space to represent an m-component vector. Evidently, we are limited by our inability to graph a space having more

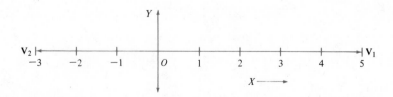

Figure C.1

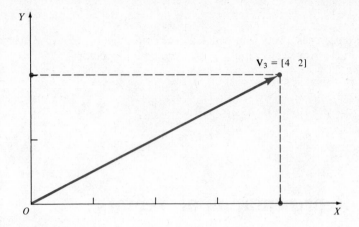

Figure C.2

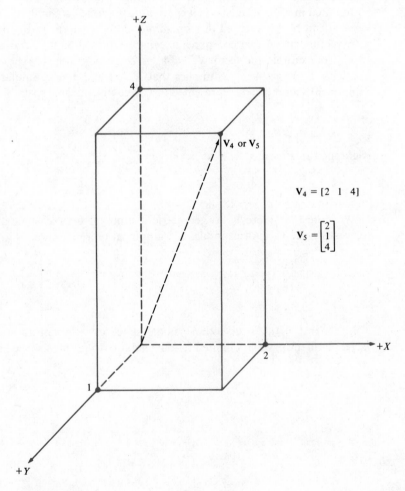

$\mathbf{V}_4 = [2 \quad 1 \quad 4]$

$\mathbf{V}_5 = \begin{bmatrix} 2 \\ 1 \\ 4 \end{bmatrix}$

Figure C.3

Basic Concepts of Matrix Algebra   Appendix C

than three dimensions. However, the concept of correspondence between the number of components in a vector and the number of dimensions required to represent it is very important.

C.5
Vector Notation of a Matrix

If we consider vectors as special cases of a matrix, a given matrix can always be represented as a set of row or column vectors. For example, let $\mathbf{A}$ be a 3×3 matrix:

$$\mathbf{A} = \begin{bmatrix} 10 & 6 & 2 \\ 5 & 10 & 5 \\ 1 & 2 & 2 \end{bmatrix}$$

The matrix $\mathbf{A}$, when represented as a set of three row vectors, $\mathbf{V}_1, \mathbf{V}_2$, and $\mathbf{V}_3$, can be written

$$\mathbf{A} = \begin{bmatrix} \mathbf{V}_1 \\ \mathbf{V}_2 \\ \mathbf{V}_3 \end{bmatrix} \quad \text{where} \quad \begin{aligned} \mathbf{V}_1 &= [10 \quad 6 \quad 2] \\ \mathbf{V}_2 &= [\ 5 \quad 10 \quad 5] \\ \mathbf{V}_3 &= [\ 1 \quad 2 \quad 2] \end{aligned}$$

The same matrix, $\mathbf{A}$, when represented as a set of three column vectors, $\mathbf{U}_1, \mathbf{U}_2$, and $\mathbf{U}_3$, can be written

$$\mathbf{A} = [\mathbf{U}_1 \quad \mathbf{U}_2 \quad \mathbf{U}_3]$$

where

$$\mathbf{U}_1 = \begin{bmatrix} 10 \\ 5 \\ 1 \end{bmatrix} \quad \mathbf{U}_2 = \begin{bmatrix} 6 \\ 10 \\ 2 \end{bmatrix} \quad \mathbf{U}_3 = \begin{bmatrix} 2 \\ 5 \\ 2 \end{bmatrix}$$

C.6
Basic Concepts and Operations Concerning Matrices and Vectors

Since vectors can be considered as special cases of matrices, the rules of operations involving vectors and matrices and their behavior are similar.

C.6.1 EQUALITY OF MATRICES AND VECTORS

Two matrices (vectors) are equal if and only if: (1) their dimension or order is the same, and (2) their corresponding components are equal to each other. Thus, if

$$A = \begin{bmatrix} 2 & 1 \\ -1 & 3 \\ 4 & 2 \end{bmatrix} \quad B = \begin{bmatrix} 2 & -1 & 4 \\ 1 & 3 & 2 \end{bmatrix}$$

$$C = \begin{bmatrix} 2 & -1 & 4 \\ 2 & 3 & 2 \end{bmatrix}$$

then

$A \neq B$ because their dimensions are not the same

$B \neq C$ because their components are not the same

If A and B have the same dimensions, and $a_{ij} = b_{ij}$ for all i and j, then $A = B$. Conversely, if two matrices are equal, their corresponding components are equal. If

$$U = \begin{bmatrix} 2 & 1 & 0 \end{bmatrix} \quad V = \begin{bmatrix} 2 & 1 & 0 \end{bmatrix} \quad X = \begin{bmatrix} 2 \\ 1 \\ 0 \end{bmatrix}$$

$$W = \begin{bmatrix} 2 & -1 & 0 \end{bmatrix} \quad Y = \begin{bmatrix} 2 \\ 1 \\ 1 \end{bmatrix} \quad Z = \begin{bmatrix} 2 \\ 1 \\ 0 \end{bmatrix}$$

then

$U = V$ $U \neq W$

$X = Z$ $X \neq Y$

$U \neq X$ $U \neq Y$

C.6.2 ADDITION AND SUBTRACTION OF MATRICES AND VECTORS

Two matrices (vectors) can be added *only* if they have the same dimensions. Similarly, a matrix (vector) can be subtracted from another matrix (vector) only if both have the same dimensions. Once it is established that the numbers of rows and columns of the two matrices (vectors) are identical, their respective components can be added together (or subtracted from each other).

Example C.1

Let

$$A = \begin{bmatrix} 2 & 3 & 4 \\ 1 & 0 & 6 \end{bmatrix} \quad B = \begin{bmatrix} -1 & 2 & 1 \\ 0 & 3 & 2 \end{bmatrix}$$

Then

$$A + B = \begin{bmatrix} 2 & 3 & 4 \\ 1 & 0 & 6 \end{bmatrix} + \begin{bmatrix} -1 & 2 & 1 \\ 0 & 3 & 2 \end{bmatrix} = \begin{bmatrix} 1 & 5 & 5 \\ 1 & 3 & 8 \end{bmatrix}$$

Two things must be observed in matrix addition. First, the matrix representing the sum of **A** and **B** has the same dimensions as **A** and **B**. Second, the order of addition is not important, for if **A** + **B** equals **C**, then **B** + **A** also equals **C**.

Example C.2

Let

$$V_1 = [2 \quad 3 \quad 4] \quad V_2 = [-1 \quad 2 \quad 1]$$

Then

$$V_1 + V_2 = [1 \quad 5 \quad 5]$$

Let

$$U_1 = \begin{bmatrix} 2 \\ 1 \end{bmatrix} \quad U_2 = \begin{bmatrix} -1 \\ 0 \end{bmatrix}$$

Then

$$U_1 + U_2 = \begin{bmatrix} 1 \\ 1 \end{bmatrix}$$

As in the case of matrices, the order of addition of vectors is not important.

C.6.3 SCALAR MULTIPLICATION AND LINEAR COMBINATION

The simultaneous multiplication of all the components of a given matrix by a real number (scalar) is called *scalar multiplication*. Suppose that an $m \times n$ matrix **A** $= [a_{ij}]$ is to be multiplied by a scalar k. Then

$$Ak = kA = [ka_{ij}]$$

Example C.3

Let

$$A = \begin{bmatrix} -2 & 3 & 1 \\ 0 & 2 & 4 \\ 3 & -5 & 1 \end{bmatrix}$$

Then

$$2A = \begin{bmatrix} -4 & 6 & 2 \\ 0 & 4 & 8 \\ 6 & -10 & 2 \end{bmatrix}$$

Similarly, if we multiply all the elements of a given vector by some scalar (i.e., a real number), we get a *scalar multiple* of the given vector. A *linear combination* is essentially a sum of the scalar multiples of some vectors. What interests us, however, is a linear combination that involves some special type of vectors, namely, linearly independent vectors.[6] The reason for our interest in a set of linearly independent vectors lies in the fact that by forming linear combinations of the vectors in this set, we can reach any point in a space of specified dimensions. For example, by forming a combination of two linearly independent (two-dimensional) vectors, we can reach any point in a two-dimensional space. Similarly, we need three linearly independent (three-dimensional) vectors in order to reach any point in a three-dimensional space. In general, we need m linearly independent (m-dimensional) vectors in order to reach any point in the m-dimensional space. That is, any m-dimensional vector can be expressed as a linear combination of m linearly independent (m-dimensional) vectors. This statement is of extreme significance in solving a linear programming problem. The linear programming problem boils down to expressing an m-dimensional vector as a linear combination of a set of linearly independent vectors.

C.6.4 MULTIPLICATION OF VECTORS

Row Vector × Column Vector

We shall first define the product of a row vector and a column vector, both having the same number of components. Let

$$\mathbf{V}_1 = [2 \quad 3 \quad 4] \qquad \mathbf{U}_1 = \begin{bmatrix} 1 \\ -2 \\ 4 \end{bmatrix}$$

Then

$$\mathbf{V}_1 \times \mathbf{U}_1 = 2(1) + 3(-2) + 4(4) = 12$$

It is to be observed that the number of components in the lead vector is exactly the same as the number of components in the lag vector. If this condition does not

---

[6] The vectors

$$\mathbf{V}_1 = \begin{bmatrix} 1 \\ 0 \end{bmatrix} \quad \text{and} \quad \mathbf{V}_2 = \begin{bmatrix} 0 \\ 1 \end{bmatrix}$$

are linearly independent. A precise definition of linear independence is given in Section C.8. For the time being, the reader can consider that a set of vectors is linearly independent if any one vector in the set cannot be formed by taking a linear combination of the other vectors in the set. For example, if

$$\mathbf{V}_1 = [1 \quad 0 \quad 0], \qquad \mathbf{V}_2 = [0 \quad 1 \quad 0], \qquad \text{and} \qquad \mathbf{V}_3 = [0 \quad 0 \quad 1],$$

then the vectors $\mathbf{V}_1, \mathbf{V}_2$, and $\mathbf{V}_3$ are linearly independent. In the two-dimensional space, two vectors are independent if when graphed they do not lie on the same line. For example, the vectors $\mathbf{V}_1 = \begin{bmatrix} 1 \\ 0 \end{bmatrix}$ and $\mathbf{V}_2 = \begin{bmatrix} 0 \\ 1 \end{bmatrix}$ are linearly independent, but the vectors $\mathbf{V}_3 = \begin{bmatrix} 2 \\ 4 \end{bmatrix}$ and $\mathbf{V}_4 = \begin{bmatrix} 4 \\ 8 \end{bmatrix}$ are not linearly independent.

exist, the vectors are said to be *incompatible* and their multiplication is not defined. Furthermore, in any multiplication involving a row vector and a column vector, the product is treated as a scalar,[7] provided that the row vector is the lead vector. This scalar is the sum of the products of the corresponding components of the two vectors.

Let us illustrate the multiplication operation and then check on dimensionality to ensure compatibility for multiplication. If

$$V_1 = [2 \quad 3 \quad 4] \quad \text{and} \quad U_1 = \begin{bmatrix} 1 \\ -2 \\ 4 \end{bmatrix}$$

then

$$V_1 U_1 = \quad V_1 \quad \times \quad U_1 \quad = \quad 12$$

dimensions: $\quad (1 \times 3) \quad (3 \times 1) \quad (1 \times 1)$

Note that the order 1×1 means that we have a single component.

The following dimensional arrangement must hold for compatibility in vector multiplication:

$$\text{lead vector} \times \text{lag vector} = \text{product}$$

dimensions: $\quad (1 \times n) \quad (n \times 1) \quad (1 \times 1)$

Column Vector × Row Vector

Let

$$U_1 = \begin{bmatrix} 2 \\ 1 \\ -3 \end{bmatrix} \quad V_1 = [1 \quad -2 \quad 3]$$

Then

$$U_1 \times V_1 = \begin{bmatrix} 2 \\ 1 \\ -3 \end{bmatrix} [1 \quad -2 \quad 3] = \begin{bmatrix} 2 & -4 & 6 \\ 1 & -2 & 3 \\ -3 & 6 & -9 \end{bmatrix}$$

It is to be observed again that U_1 and V_1 are dimensionally compatible. However, the product in this case (when the column vector is the lead vector) is a 3×3 matrix.

In general, if the lead vector is an $n \times 1$ column vector and the lag vector is a $1 \times n$ row vector, their product results in an $n \times n$ matrix:

$$\text{lead vector} \times \text{lag vector} = \text{product}$$

dimensions: $\quad (n \times 1) \quad (1 \times n) \quad (n \times n)$

---

[7] Actually, the matrix product of a row and column vector yields a matrix having only one component. However, there is complete equivalence between scalars (real numbers) and matrices with only one component.

C.6.5 MULTIPLICATION OF MATRICES

The definition of multiplication of a row vector by a column vector can easily be extended to cover matrix multiplication. Let us illustrate matrix multiplication by considering a specific example. Let

$$\mathbf{A} = \begin{bmatrix} 2 & 1 & -2 \\ 3 & 2 & 4 \end{bmatrix} \qquad \mathbf{B} = \begin{bmatrix} 1 & 2 \\ 0 & 3 \\ -2 & 1 \end{bmatrix}$$

and let $\mathbf{AB} = \mathbf{C}$. Then

$$\mathbf{A} \times \mathbf{B} = \mathbf{C} = \begin{bmatrix} 2(1) + 1(0) + (-2)(-2) & 2(2) + 1(3) + (-2)(1) \\ 3(1) + 2(0) + 4(-2) & 3(2) + 2(3) + 4(1) \end{bmatrix}$$

or

$$\mathbf{C} = \begin{bmatrix} 6 & 5 \\ -5 & 16 \end{bmatrix}$$

This matrix multiplication consists of the following steps:

1. *Check on compatibility.* Is the number of columns in the lead matrix (**A**) equal to the number of rows in the lag matrix (**B**)? If so, the matrices are compatible for multiplication; otherwise, not. In the above case, the matrices **A** and **B** are compatible.

2. *The operation of multiplication.* The components of the first row of **A**, the lead matrix, are multiplied by the corresponding components of the first column of **B**, the lag matrix. The product is summed and is placed in the first row–first column cell of the resultant matrix **C**. Similarly, the components of the second row of matrix **A** are multiplied by the corresponding components of the first column of matrix **B**; the product is summed and is placed in the second row–first column cell of the resultant matrix; and so on. The resultant matrix, **C**, is a 2×2 matrix. The check on dimensional compatibility is

lead matrix × lag matrix = resultant matrix

$$\mathbf{A} \qquad \times \qquad \mathbf{B} \qquad = \qquad \mathbf{C}$$

dimensions: (2×3) (3×2) (2×2)

In general, if we multiply an $m \times k$ matrix **A** by another $k \times n$ matrix **B**, the dimension of the resultant matrix is $m \times n$:

lead matrix × lag matrix = resultant matrix

dimensions: $(m \times k)$ $(k \times n)$ $(m \times n)$

Example C.4

Obtain the product **BA** when

$$\mathbf{A} = \begin{bmatrix} 2 & 1 & -2 \\ 3 & 2 & 4 \end{bmatrix} \qquad \mathbf{B} = \begin{bmatrix} 1 & 2 \\ 0 & 3 \\ -2 & 1 \end{bmatrix}$$

$$\mathbf{BA} = \begin{bmatrix} 1 & 2 \\ 0 & 3 \\ -2 & 1 \end{bmatrix} \begin{bmatrix} 2 & 1 & -2 \\ 3 & 2 & 4 \end{bmatrix}$$

$$= \begin{bmatrix} 1(2) + 2(3) & 1(1) + 2(2) & 1(-2) + 2(4) \\ 0(2) + 3(3) & 0(1) + 3(2) & 0(-2) + 3(4) \\ -2(2) + 1(3) & -2(1) + 1(2) & -2(-2) + 1(4) \end{bmatrix}$$

$$= \begin{bmatrix} 8 & 5 & 6 \\ 9 & 6 & 12 \\ -1 & 0 & 8 \end{bmatrix}$$

In this example, **AB** and **BA** are both compatible, but note that **AB** ≠ **BA**. This leads to the remark that in matrix multiplication, *order is important*.

The multiplication of a matrix by a vector follows the rules of regular matrix multiplication, as explained previously.

Example C.5

Let

$$\mathbf{A} = \begin{bmatrix} 4 & -1 & 2 \\ 0 & 2 & 3 \end{bmatrix} \qquad \mathbf{U} = \begin{bmatrix} 1 \\ 0 \\ 2 \end{bmatrix}$$

Then

$$\mathbf{AU} = \begin{bmatrix} 4 & -1 & 2 \\ 0 & 2 & 3 \end{bmatrix} \begin{bmatrix} 1 \\ 0 \\ 2 \end{bmatrix} = \begin{bmatrix} 8 \\ 6 \end{bmatrix}$$

C.7
The Inverse Matrix

If, for a given square matrix **A**, there exists another square matrix **B** such that **AB** = **BA** = **I** (the identity matrix), then **B** is said to be the *inverse* of **A**. The inverse of **A** is usually denoted as $\mathbf{A}^{-1}$. When it exists, $\mathbf{A}^{-1}$ plays a role similar to that played by the reciprocal of a given number in ordinary algebra, although it must be noted that not all matrices have inverses. As a matter of fact, only square matrices with nonzero *determinants* have inverses.[8]

---

[8] For a definition of the term determinant, see Loomba [1976, Chap. 5].

Example C.6

Let

$$
\mathbf{A} = \begin{bmatrix} 4 & 0 & 0 \\ 0 & 6 & 2 \\ 2 & 0 & 1 \end{bmatrix} \qquad \mathbf{B} = \begin{bmatrix} \frac{1}{4} & 0 & 0 \\ \frac{1}{6} & \frac{1}{6} & -\frac{1}{3} \\ -\frac{1}{2} & 0 & 1 \end{bmatrix}
$$

Then

$$
\mathbf{AB} = \begin{bmatrix} 4 & 0 & 0 \\ 0 & 6 & 2 \\ 2 & 0 & 1 \end{bmatrix} \begin{bmatrix} \frac{1}{4} & 0 & 0 \\ \frac{1}{6} & \frac{1}{6} & -\frac{1}{3} \\ -\frac{1}{2} & 0 & 1 \end{bmatrix} = \begin{bmatrix} 1 & 0 & 0 \\ 0 & 1 & 0 \\ 0 & 0 & 1 \end{bmatrix}
$$

$$
\mathbf{BA} = \begin{bmatrix} \frac{1}{4} & 0 & 0 \\ \frac{1}{6} & \frac{1}{6} & -\frac{1}{3} \\ -\frac{1}{2} & 0 & 1 \end{bmatrix} \begin{bmatrix} 4 & 0 & 0 \\ 0 & 6 & 2 \\ 2 & 0 & 1 \end{bmatrix} = \begin{bmatrix} 1 & 0 & 0 \\ 0 & 1 & 0 \\ 0 & 0 & 1 \end{bmatrix}
$$

That is,

$$
\mathbf{AB} = \mathbf{BA} = \mathbf{I}
$$

Hence, by definition, $\mathbf{B} = \mathbf{A}^{-1}$. It may be noted that if a given matrix has an inverse, the inverse is unique.[9]

C.8
Linear Independence

A set of vectors $\mathbf{V}_1$, $\mathbf{V}_2,\ldots,$ $\mathbf{V}_m$ of the same dimension is said to be linearly *dependent* if a set of scalars $k_1, k_2,\ldots, k_m$, not all of which are zero, can be found such that

$$
k_1\mathbf{V}_1 + k_2\mathbf{V}_2 + \cdots + k_m\mathbf{V}_m = \mathbf{0} \tag{C.1}
$$

where $\mathbf{0}$ represents a zero vector.

If this relationship holds *only* when the scalars $k_1, k_2,\ldots, k_m$ are zero, the set of vectors $\mathbf{V}_1, \mathbf{V}_2,\ldots, \mathbf{V}_m$ is said to be *linearly independent*.

The above definition implies that a set of vectors of the same dimension is *linearly independent* if none of the vectors in the set can be expressed as a *linear combination* of the remaining vectors in the set.

Example C.7

Test the vectors

$$
\mathbf{V}_1 = \begin{bmatrix} 3 \\ 2 \end{bmatrix} \qquad \text{and} \qquad \mathbf{V}_2 = \begin{bmatrix} 6 \\ 4 \end{bmatrix}
$$

---

[9] See Loomba [1976, Chap. 5] for methods of calculating the value of an inverse.

for linear independence. Let

$$k_1 V_1 + k_2 V_2 = 0$$

or

$$k_1 \begin{bmatrix} 3 \\ 2 \end{bmatrix} + k_2 \begin{bmatrix} 6 \\ 4 \end{bmatrix} = \begin{bmatrix} 0 \\ 0 \end{bmatrix}$$

or

$$3k_1 + 6k_2 = 0 \tag{C.2}$$
$$2k_1 + 4k_2 = 0 \tag{C.3}$$

Clearly, Equations (C.2) and (C.3) are simultaneously satisfied if we let $k_1 = 1$ and $k_2 = -\frac{1}{2}$. Hence, according to the definition given in Equation (C.1), vectors V_1 and V_2 are linearly dependent. That is, V_1 and V_2 do *not* constitute a linearly independent set. Further, if we graph V_1 and V_2, we shall observe that V_1 lies on top of V_2. This type of congruence indicates linear dependency (i.e., the vectors are not linearly independent). Conversely, if plotted, linearly independent vectors, will not lie on top of each other.

Example C.8

Test the vectors

$$V_3 = \begin{bmatrix} 2 \\ 3 \end{bmatrix} \quad \text{and} \quad V_4 = \begin{bmatrix} 4 \\ 2 \end{bmatrix}$$

for linear dependence. Let

$$k_3 V_3 + k_4 V_4 = 0$$

or

$$k_3 \begin{bmatrix} 2 \\ 3 \end{bmatrix} + k_4 \begin{bmatrix} 4 \\ 2 \end{bmatrix} = \begin{bmatrix} 0 \\ 0 \end{bmatrix}$$

or

$$2k_3 + 4k_4 = 0 \tag{C.4}$$
$$3k_3 + 2k_4 = 0 \tag{C.5}$$

Clearly, Equations (C.4) and (C.5) are simultaneously satisfied *only* if $k_3 = 0$ and $k_4 = 0$. Hence, the vectors V_3 and V_4 constitute a linearly independent set.

C.9
Matrix and Vector Representation of Linear Systems, and Vice Versa

Consider a system of two linear equations

$$2x_1 + 4x_2 = b_1 \tag{C.6}$$
$$3x_1 + 2x_2 = b_2 \tag{C.7}$$

If we use matrix notation, this system can be written

$$
\begin{matrix} \mathbf{A} & \times \mathbf{X} & = & \mathbf{b} \\ \Downarrow & \Downarrow & & \Downarrow \end{matrix}
$$

$$
\begin{bmatrix} 2 & 4 \\ 3 & 2 \end{bmatrix} \begin{bmatrix} x_1 \\ x_2 \end{bmatrix} = \begin{bmatrix} b_1 \\ b_2 \end{bmatrix} \tag{C.8}
$$

Equation (C.8) is equivalent to (C.6) and (C.7), as we can verify by matrix multiplication of the left-hand side of Equation (C.8) and equating it to its right-hand side.

A system of the type given in Equation (C.8) reflects the linear constraints of a typical linear programming problem. The matrix $\mathbf{A}$ is called the *input–output coefficient matrix*, $\mathbf{b}$ is the *constant vector* reflecting resource capacities or the requirements, and $\mathbf{X}$ is the *solution vector*.

The two linear equations (C.6) and (C.7) can also be represented with the aid of vectors, as follows:

$$
\begin{bmatrix} 2 \\ 3 \end{bmatrix} x_1 + \begin{bmatrix} 4 \\ 2 \end{bmatrix} x_2 = \begin{bmatrix} b_1 \\ b_2 \end{bmatrix} \tag{C.9}
$$

It is obvious that Equation (C.9), which is a vector representation, can be translated back to the linear equations (C.6) and (C.7).

C.10
Vector Space

Consider the system in Equation (C.9). The problem is usually to find appropriate values of x_1 and x_2 for a given set of values b_1 and b_2. Now, suppose that we generate all possible values of b_1 and b_2 by varying the values of x_1 and x_2. Then the set of vectors $\begin{bmatrix} b_1 \\ b_2 \end{bmatrix}$ generated by all possible choices of x_1 and x_2 is called a *vector space* of two dimensions. Similarly, the set of *all* three-component vectors forms a three-dimensional vector space, and so on. The idea of the vector space is important in linear programming problems because the resource capacity, or the requirement vector, is located in a particular vector space. Our task is to choose a set of vectors that can *span* the particular vector space.

C.11
Basis for a Vector Space

A *basis* for a vector space is a set of linearly independent vectors such that *any* vector in the vector space can be expressed as a linear combination of this set. This set spans the entire vector space. The vectors in such a set are called the *basic vectors*

Let us consider two linearly independent vectors

$$
\mathbf{V}_1 = \begin{bmatrix} 1 \\ 0 \end{bmatrix} \quad \text{and} \quad \mathbf{V}_2 = \begin{bmatrix} 0 \\ 1 \end{bmatrix}
$$

Any two-dimensional vector can be expressed as a linear combination of these two linearly independent vectors. For example,

$$\mathbf{V}_3 = \begin{bmatrix} 200 \\ 100 \end{bmatrix}$$

can be represented as $\mathbf{V}_3 = 200\mathbf{V}_1 + 100\mathbf{V}_2$. We come to the conclusion that vectors

$$\mathbf{V}_1 = \begin{bmatrix} 1 \\ 0 \end{bmatrix} \quad \text{and} \quad \mathbf{V}_2 = \begin{bmatrix} 0 \\ 1 \end{bmatrix}$$

comprise *one* possible set of basic vectors for a two-dimensional vector space. The basis is

$$[\mathbf{V}_1 \quad \mathbf{V}_2] = \begin{bmatrix} 1 & 0 \\ 0 & 1 \end{bmatrix}$$

Similarly, in a three-dimensional vector space, we need a set of three linearly independent vectors to form the basis. The argument can easily be extended to n dimensions.

It should be noted that linear independence is a necessary condition for forming a basis for a vector space in order that any vector in that space may be represented as a linear combination of the basic vectors. To emphasize this point, let us again consider vector

$$\mathbf{V}_3 = \begin{bmatrix} 200 \\ 100 \end{bmatrix}$$

Clearly, $\mathbf{V}_3 = 200\mathbf{V}_1 + 100\mathbf{V}_2$, provided that

$$\mathbf{V}_1 = \begin{bmatrix} 1 \\ 0 \end{bmatrix} \quad \text{and} \quad \mathbf{V}_2 = \begin{bmatrix} 0 \\ 1 \end{bmatrix}$$

where $\mathbf{V}_1$ and $\mathbf{V}_2$ are linearly independent. But if we consider two linearly dependent vectors, say,

$$\mathbf{V}_4 = \begin{bmatrix} 3 \\ 2 \end{bmatrix} \quad \text{and} \quad \mathbf{V}_5 = \begin{bmatrix} 6 \\ 4 \end{bmatrix}$$

then we simply cannot express $\mathbf{V}_3$ as a linear combination of $\mathbf{V}_4$ and $\mathbf{V}_5$. The reader should verify this statement with a graphical representation of these vectors.

The concepts of linear independence and basis are very important in linear programming. The first tableau of the simplex method creates a basis, say, for an m-dimensional space, by using m linearly independent unit vectors. Further, a "degeneracy" occurs in linear programming problems when an m-dimensional vector is represented as a linear combination of less than m independent vectors.[10]

---

[10] Sections 7.5.2 and 8.7.

C.12
Systems of Simultaneous Linear Equations

Since the structural constraints of a linear programming problem can be expressed as a system of simultaneous linear equations, knowledge of such a system is important. Finding a solution to a system of linear equations requires the assignment of values to $x_1, x_2, \ldots$, so that *all* the equations are satisfied. When such a system is expressed in matrix notation as $\mathbf{AX} = \mathbf{b}$, its solution involves the determination of the components of the vector $\mathbf{X}$. A system may have a unique solution, no solution, or an infinite number of solutions.

We classify a system of simultaneous linear equations into three categories.[11]

Category 1. *The system of linear equations contains n equations and n unknowns.*

In this category, we can have one of three cases:

1. The system has a unique solution.
2. The system is inconsistent and has no solution.
3. The system has an infinite number of solutions.

Category 2. *The system of linear equations has more equations than unknowns.*

This type of system of linear equations results whenever there is either redundancy (i.e., one or more equations in the system can be obtained by forming linear combinations of the remaining equations) or inconsistency. When the redundancy exists, the system can be reduced, by eliminating the redundancy, to that of category 1.

Category 3. *The system of linear equations has more unknowns than equations.*

In this case, the system has no solution if the equations are inconsistent. However, if the system can be solved, it has an infinite number of solutions. Various possible solutions are identified by assigning arbitrary value(s) to the excess of unknowns over equations. Of these, one or more are chosen to obtain an optimal value of some objective function.

The reader will realize that linear programming problems fall into category 3.

References

Childress, R. L. *Sets, Matrices, and Linear Programming.* Englewood Cliffs, N.J.: Prentice-Hall, Inc., 1974.

Loomba, N. P. *Linear Programming: A Managerial Perspective*, 2nd ed. New York: Macmillan Publishing Co., Inc., 1976.

Reiner, I. *Introduction to Matrix Theory and Linear Algebra.* New York: Holt, Rinehart and Winston, Inc., 1971.

[11] For further discussion, see Loomba [1976, Chap. 5].

APPENDIX D
Pivoting

MAJOR CONCEPTS AND TOPICS DISCUSSED IN THIS APPENDIX

Elimination Method of Solving a System of Equations

Row Operations

Process and Mechanics of Pivoting

Pivot row
Pivot column
Pivot element

D.1
Introduction

The purpose of this appendix is to illustrate how, through the process of *pivoting*, we can transform a given simplex tableau to produce another tableau. We first present and explain the idea of *row operations*. Next, we describe the mechanics of pivoting in terms of four specific steps. Finally, we illustrate the use of pivoting by solving a maximization linear programming problem.

D.2
Row Operations

All of us are familiar with the *elimination method* of solving a system of linear equations. The elimination method is based on the simple algebraic operations of multiplication, addition, and subtraction. It consists of making the coefficients of all but one variable zero, and then solving for that variable whose coefficient was not zero. The value of this variable is then inserted in the appropriate equation to solve for the remaining variables, either directly or again by the elimination technique. We shall solve the following system of equations by the elimination method:

$$10X + 6Y = 2,500 \tag{D.1}$$
$$5X + 10Y = 2,000 \tag{D.2}$$

Divide Equation (D.1) by 10:

$$X + \tfrac{3}{5}Y = 250 \tag{D.3}$$

Multiply Equation (D.3) by 5:

$$5X + 3Y = 1,250 \tag{D.4}$$

Subtract Equation (D.4) from (D.2):

$$7Y = 750 \tag{D.5}$$

Divide Equation (D.5) by 7:

$$Y = \frac{750}{7} \tag{D.6}$$

Substitute Equation (D.6) in (D.3):

$$X = \frac{1,300}{7}$$

The type of basic algebraic operations that we have just performed can also be performed on the rows of a matrix. When performed on the rows of a matrix, they are called *row operations*. In particular, we define three rules of row operations:

1. Any row can be multiplied by a positive or negative constant.
2. A multiple of one row can be added to another row.
3. Any two rows of a matrix can be interchanged.

Let us apply the first two rules of row operations in order to solve the system of equations given by (D.1) and (D.2). Note that our system of equations represents the first two rows of Table 8.1. It consists of a 2×2 input–output coefficient matrix on the left-hand side of the equalities, and a constant or resource vector on the right-hand side. We shall express the system as a matrix that clearly shows the input–output coefficient matrix $\begin{bmatrix} 10 & 6 \\ 5 & 10 \end{bmatrix}$ and the resource vector $\begin{bmatrix} 2,500 \\ 2,000 \end{bmatrix}$. In addition, the same series of row operations that are performed to solve the given system of equations will be applied, in successive steps, to an identity matrix. This is shown in the third column.

First Column (Algebraic Statement)	*Second Column* (Matrix Notation)	*Third Column*

$$10X + 6Y = 2,500$$
$$5X + 10Y = 2,000$$

$$\begin{bmatrix} 10 & 6 & 2,500 \\ 5 & 10 & 2,000 \end{bmatrix}^1 \quad \begin{bmatrix} 1 & 0 \\ 0 & 1 \end{bmatrix}$$

First row operation: Divide the first row by 10:

$$X + \frac{3}{5}Y = 250$$
$$5X + 10Y = 2,000$$

$$\begin{bmatrix} 1 & \frac{3}{5} & 250 \\ 5 & 10 & 2,000 \end{bmatrix} \quad \begin{bmatrix} \frac{1}{10} & 0 \\ 0 & 1 \end{bmatrix}$$

Second row operation: Multiply the first row above by 5 and subtract this multiple from the second row. Then the system becomes:

$$X + \frac{3}{5}Y = 250$$
$$7Y = 750$$

$$\begin{bmatrix} 1 & \frac{3}{5} & 250 \\ 0 & 7 & 750 \end{bmatrix} \quad \begin{bmatrix} \frac{1}{10} & 0 \\ -\frac{1}{2} & 1 \end{bmatrix}$$

Third row operation: Divide the second row above by 7:

$$X + \frac{3}{5}Y = 250$$
$$Y = \frac{750}{7}$$

$$\begin{bmatrix} 1 & \frac{3}{5} & 250 \\ 0 & 1 & \frac{750}{7} \end{bmatrix} \quad \begin{bmatrix} \frac{1}{10} & 0 \\ -\frac{1}{14} & \frac{1}{7} \end{bmatrix}$$

Fourth row operation: Multiply the second row above by $\frac{3}{5}$ and subtract this multiple from the first row:

---

[1] This is an example of what is known as a *partitioned* matrix. The vertical bar indicates the place of partition.

$$X = \frac{1,300}{7}$$

$$Y = \frac{750}{7}$$

$$\begin{bmatrix} 1 & 0 & \dfrac{1,300}{7} \\[2ex] 0 & 1 & \dfrac{750}{7} \end{bmatrix} \quad \begin{bmatrix} \dfrac{1}{7} & -\dfrac{3}{35} \\[2ex] -\dfrac{1}{14} & \dfrac{1}{7} \end{bmatrix}$$

What the matrix notation (after the fourth row operation) shows is this:

1. We have an identity matrix on the left-hand side of the partition.
2. The identity matrix, associated with the variables X and Y, shows that variables X and Y are the basic variables. Hence, our *basis* in this case is $\begin{bmatrix} 10 & 6 \\ 5 & 10 \end{bmatrix}$.
3. The values on the right-hand side of the partition are the values of the basic variables X and Y.

What we have done is this: By performing a series of row operations on a partitioned matrix (consisting of an input–output coefficient matrix and the constant vector), we produced an identity matrix and simultaneously determined the values of the basic variables. Also, by performing the same row operations, in successive steps, on an identity matrix, we have produced the inverse of the original matrix. Note that

$$\begin{bmatrix} \dfrac{1}{7} & -\dfrac{3}{35} \\[2ex] -\dfrac{1}{14} & \dfrac{1}{7} \end{bmatrix}$$

is the inverse of

$$\begin{bmatrix} 10 & 6 \\ 5 & 10 \end{bmatrix}$$

It should now be clear that the rules of transformation of the simplex method perform exactly the same function. That is, once a basis is identified, the tableau must produce an identity matrix (under the chosen basic variables), generate the values of the basic variables under the "Quantity" column, and create an inverse of the basis under the set of basic variables used to create the identity matrix in the first simplex tableau. This argument is illustrated in Section D.4.

D.3
Pivoting

The preceding discussion was presented to introduce the reader to the process and mechanics of *pivoting*. The use of row operations to produce a simplex tableau that represents a given basis is known as *pivoting*. The purpose of pivoting is to help us proceed from a nonoptimal simplex tableau to the next tableau, which is then tested for optimality by the rules established in Chapter 8. The *process* of pivoting consists of the following four steps.

Step 1. *Identify the pivot column.*

The pivot column is identified by the largest positive $C_j - Z_j$ (in maximization case) or largest negative $C_j - Z_j$ (in minimization case). The *pivot column* is the same as the *key column* described in Chapter 8. The pivot column identifies the incoming variable that will become one of the next set of basic variables.

Step 2. *Identify the pivot row.*

We calculate replacement quantities (for each row) by dividing the numbers under the "Quantity" column by the corresponding positive a_{ij} under the pivot column. The row in which falls the smallest replacement quantity is the *pivot row*. The *pivot row* is the same as the *key row* described in Chapter 8. The pivot row identifies the outgoing variable leaving the current set of basic variables.

Step 3. *Identify the pivot element.*

The element at the intersection of the pivot column and the pivot row is the *pivot element*. The *pivot element* is the same as the *key number* described in Chapter 8.

Step 4. *Transform the current tableau to produce a tableau that represents the new basis.*

It is in this step that the *mechanics* of pivoting are somewhat different from the rules of transformation that were employed in Chapter 8 to proceed from one simplex tableau to the next. It will be recalled that in Chapter 8 we stated two rules of transformation: one for transforming the key row, and the other for the nonkey rows. By applying these two rules of transformation, we can proceed from one tableau to the next. The same results can be produced by pivoting. The idea of pivoting is based on the concept that when we proceed from one tableau to the next, all we do is create a new basis so that there must exist an identity matrix under the new basic variables. *Since the pivot column represents the only new incoming variable, we can produce the new identity matrix (corresponding to the new basis) if, through the use of row operations, we obtain 1 at the pivot element and 0's elsewhere in the pivot column.*

D.4
Illustrative Example

We shall illustrate the mechanics of pivoting by using the same linear programming problem that was solved in Chapter 8. Let us start with Table D.1, which represents the first program to the problem stated in Table 8.1.

Remember that our task is to produce, through the use of row operations, a vector $\begin{bmatrix} 0 \\ 1 \\ 0 \end{bmatrix}$ for the next tableau to replace the pivot column vector $\begin{bmatrix} 6 \\ 10 \\ 2 \end{bmatrix}$ in the current tableau. Thus, we first multiply the pivot row by the reciprocal of the pivot element (or divide the pivot row by the pivot element). In our case, we multiply the pivot row by $\frac{1}{10}$ and obtain

$$200 \quad \frac{1}{2} \quad 1 \quad 0 \quad \frac{1}{10} \quad 0 \tag{D.7}$$

Table D.1 *First Program*

Program (Basic Variables)	Profit per Unit, C_b	Quantity	$C_j \to$ 23 X	32 Y	0 S_1	0 S_2	0 S_3	Replacement Quantity
S_1	0	2,500	10	6	1	0	0	$416\frac{2}{3}$
S_2	0	2,000	5	10	0	1	0	$200 \to$ outgoing variable
S_3	0	500	1	2	0	0	1	250
Z_j			0	0	0	0	0	
$C_j - Z_j$			23	32	0	0	0	

incoming variable

Table D.2 *Second Program*

Program (Basic Variables)	Profit per Unit, C_b	Quantity	$C_j \rightarrow$ 23 X	32 Y	0 S_1	0 S_2	0 S_3	Replacement Quantity
S_2	0	1,300	7	0	1	$-\frac{3}{5}$	0	$\frac{1,300}{7} \rightarrow$ outgoing variable
Y	32	200	$\frac{1}{2}$	1	0	$\frac{1}{10}$	0	400
S_3	0	100	0	0	0	$-\frac{1}{5}$	1	
Z_j			16	32	0	3·2	0	
$C_j - Z_j$			7	0	0	$-3·2$	0	

incoming variable

556   Pivoting   Appendix D

This row of numbers is entered as row 2 (the Y row) in the tableau shown in Table D.2.

Our next task is to create zeros (in rows S_1 and S_3) under the pivot column. The first zero (in row S_1) can be created if we multiply (D.7) by -6 and add the multiple to row S_1 of Table D.1. This will give us the following row for the next tableau (to be placed as first row):

$$1,300 \quad 7 \quad 0 \quad 1 \quad -\frac{3}{5} \quad 0$$

The remaining zero (in row S_3) can be created if we multiply (D.7) by -2 and add the multiple to row S_3 of Table D.1. This will give us the following row for the next tableau (to be placed as third row):

$$100 \quad 0 \quad 0 \quad 0 \quad -\frac{1}{5} \quad 1$$

We have now transformed the simplex tableau of Table D.1 through the process of pivoting (i.e., by using row operations). The new tableau is shown in Table D.2. Note that the second program shown in Table D.2, obtained by pivoting, is the same as the second program of Table 8.4, which was obtained by the two rules of transformation stated in Chapter 8. Since one $C_j - Z_j$ in Table D.2 is positive (maximization case), our second program is not optimal. We identify 7 as the pivot element. Our task now is to produce, through the use of row operations, a

vector $\begin{bmatrix} 1 \\ 0 \\ 0 \end{bmatrix}$ for the next tableau to replace the pivot column vector $\begin{bmatrix} 7 \\ \frac{1}{2} \\ 0 \end{bmatrix}$ in

Table D.2. This can be accomplished easily by just two row operations. First, we multiply the pivot row by $\frac{1}{7}$ to obtain

$$\frac{1,300}{7} \quad 1 \quad 0 \quad \frac{1}{7} \quad -\frac{3}{35} \quad 0 \tag{D.8}$$

This row of numbers is entered as row 1 (the X row) in the tableau shown in Table D.3.

Table D.3 *Third and Optimal Program*

Program (Basic Variables)	Profit per Unit, C_b	Quantity	$C_j \rightarrow$ 23 X	0 32	0 S_1	0 S_2	0 S_3
X	23	$\frac{1,300}{7}$	1	0	$\frac{1}{7}$	$-\frac{3}{35}$	0
Y	32	$\frac{750}{7}$	0	1	$-\frac{1}{14}$	$\frac{1}{7}$	0
S_3	0	100	0	0	0	$-\frac{1}{5}$	1
Z_j			23	32	1	2.6	0
$C_j - Z_j$			0	0	-1	-2.6	0

Second, we multiply (D.8) by $-\frac{1}{2}$ and add the multiple to row Y of Table D.2. This will give us the following row for the next tableau (to be placed as row Y):

$$\frac{750}{7} \qquad 0 \qquad 1 \qquad -\frac{1}{14} \qquad \frac{1}{7} \qquad 0$$

Note that in the pivot column of Table D.2, we already have a zero in the third place. Hence, the third row of the second tableau need not be changed, and will appear "as is" in the third row of the tableau shown in Table D.3. Note that the optimal program shown in Table D.3, and obtained by pivoting, is the same as the optimal program of Table 8.5, which was obtained by the two rules of transformation stated in Chapter 8.

Tables

Table I *Areas and Ordinates of the Normal Curve*

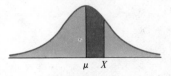

Table of Areas
Column (2) shows

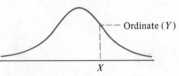

Table of Ordinates
Column (3) shows

$\dfrac{X - \mu}{\sigma}$	Area Under the Curve Between μ and X	Ordinate (Y) of the Curve at X	$\dfrac{X - \mu}{\sigma}$	Area Under the Curve Between μ and X	Ordinate (Y) of the Curve at X
(1)	(2)	(3)	(1)	(2)	(3)
.00	.00000	.39894	.20	.07926	.39104
.01	.00399	.39892	.21	.08317	.39024
.02	.00798	.39886	.22	.08706	.38940
.03	.01197	.39876	.23	.09095	.38853
.04	.01595	.39862	.24	.09483	.38762
.05	.01994	.39844	.25	.09871	.38667
.06	.02392	.39822	.26	.10257	.38568
.07	.02790	.39797	.27	.10642	.38466
.08	.03188	.39767	.28	.11026	.38361
.09	.03586	.39733	.29	.11409	.38251
.10	.03983	.39695	.30	.11791	.38139
.11	.04380	.39654	.31	.12172	.38023
.12	.04776	.39608	.32	.12552	.37903
.13	.05172	.39559	.33	.12930	.37780
.14	.05567	.39505	.34	.13307	.37654
.15	.05962	.39448	.35	.13683	.37524
.16	.06356	.39387	.36	.14058	.37391
.17	.06749	.39322	.37	.14431	.37255
.18	.07142	.39253	.38	.14803	.37115
.19	.07535	.39181	.39	.15173	.36973

SOURCE: J. F. Kenney, and E. S. Keeping, *Mathematics of Statistics*, 3rd ed. (New York: D. Van Nostrand Company, 1954), pp. 565–569.

Table I *Areas and Ordinates of the Normal Curve (continued)*

$\dfrac{X - \mu}{\sigma}$	Area Under the Curve Between μ and X	Ordinate (Y) of the Curve at X	$\dfrac{X - \mu}{\sigma}$	Area Under the Curve Between μ and X	Ordinate (Y) of the Curve at X
(1)	(2)	(3)	(1)	(2)	(3)
.40	.15542	.36827	.90	.31594	.26609
.41	.15910	.36678	.91	.31859	.26369
.42	.16276	.36526	.92	.32121	.26129
.43	.16640	.36371	.93	.32381	.25888
.44	.17003	.36213	.94	.32639	.25647
.45	.17364	.36053	.95	.32894	.25406
.46	.17724	.35889	.96	.33147	.25164
.47	.18082	.35723	.97	.33398	.24923
.48	.18439	.35553	.98	.33646	.24681
.49	.18793	.35381	.99	.33891	.24439
.50	.19146	.35207	1.00	.34134	.24197
.51	.19497	.35029	1.01	.34375	.23955
.52	.19847	.34849	1.02	.34614	.23713
.53	.20194	.34667	1.03	.34850	.23471
.54	.20540	.34482	1.04	.35083	.23230
.55	.20884	.34294	1.05	.35314	.22988
.56	.21226	.34105	1.06	.35543	.22747
.57	.21566	.33912	1.07	.35769	.22506
.58	.21904	.33718	1.08	.35993	.22265
.59	.22240	.33521	1.09	.36214	.22025
.60	.22575	.33322	1.10	.36433	.21785
.61	.22907	.33121	1.11	.36650	.21546
.62	.23237	.32918	1.12	.36864	.21307
.63	.23565	.32713	1.13	.37076	.21069
.64	.23891	.32506	1.14	.37286	.20831
.65	.24215	.32297	1.15	.37493	.20594
.66	.24537	.32086	1.16	.37698	.20357
.67	.24857	.31874	1.17	.37900	.20121
.68	.25175	.31659	1.18	.38100	.19886
.69	.25490	.31443	1.19	.38298	.19652
.70	.25804	.31225	1.20	.38493	.19419
.71	.26115	.31006	1.21	.38686	.19186
.72	.26424	.30785	1.22	.38877	.18954
.73	.26730	.30563	1.23	.39065	.18724
.74	.27035	.30339	1.24	.39251	.18494
.75	.27337	.30114	1.25	.39435	.18265
.76	.27637	.29887	1.26	.39617	.18037
.77	.27935	.29659	1.27	.39796	.17810
.78	.28230	.29431	1.28	.39973	.17585
.79	.28524	.29200	1.29	.40147	.17360
.80	.28814	.28969	1.30	.40320	.17137
.81	.29103	.28737	1.31	.40490	.16915
.82	.29389	.28504	1.32	.40658	.16694
.83	.29673	.28269	1.33	.40824	.16474
.84	.29955	.28034	1.34	.40988	.16256
.85	.30234	.27798	1.35	.41149	.16038
.86	.30511	.27562	1.36	.41309	.15822
.87	.30785	.27324	1.37	.41466	.15608
.88	.31057	.27086	1.38	.41621	.15395
.89	.31327	.26848	1.39	.41774	.15183

Table I   Areas and Ordinates of the Normal Curve

Table I *Areas and Ordinates of the Normal Curve* (continued)

$\dfrac{X - \mu}{\sigma}$	Area Under the Curve Between μ and X	Ordinate (Y) of the Curve at X	$\dfrac{X - \mu}{\sigma}$	Area Under the Curve Between μ and X	Ordinate (Y) of the Curve at X
(1)	(2)	(3)	(1)	(2)	(3)
1.40	.41924	.14973	1.90	.47128	.06562
1.41	.42073	.14764	1.91	.47193	.06438
1.42	.42220	.14556	1.92	.47257	.06316
1.43	.42364	.14350	1.93	.47320	.06195
1.44	.42507	.14146	1.94	.47381	.06077
1.45	.42647	.13943	1.95	.47441	.05959
1.46	.42786	.13742	1.96	.47500	.05844
1.47	.42922	.13542	1.97	.47558	.05730
1.48	.43056	.13344	1.98	.47615	.05618
1.49	.43189	.13147	1.99	.47670	.05508
1.50	.43319	.12952	2.00	.47725	.05399
1.51	.43448	.12758	2.01	.47778	.05292
1.52	.43574	.12566	2.02	.47831	.05186
1.53	.43699	.12376	2.03	.47882	.05082
1.54	.43822	.12188	2.04	.47932	.04980
1.55	.43943	.12001	2.05	.47982	.04879
1.56	.44062	.11816	2.06	.48030	.04780
1.57	.44179	.11632	2.07	.48077	.04682
1.58	.44295	.11450	2.08	.48124	.04586
1.59	.44408	.11270	2.09	.48169	.04491
1.60	.44520	.11092	2.10	.48214	.04398
1.61	.44630	.10915	2.11	.48257	.04307
1.62	.44738	.10741	2.12	.48300	.04217
1.63	.44845	.10567	2.13	.48341	.04128
1.64	.44950	.10396	2.14	.48382	.04041
1.65	.45053	.10226	2.15	.48422	.03955
1.66	.45154	.10059	2.16	.48461	.03871
1.67	.45254	.09893	2.17	.48500	.03788
1.68	.45352	.09728	2.18	.48537	.03706
1.69	.45449	.09566	2.19	.48574	.03626
1.70	.45543	.09405	2.20	.48610	.03547
1.71	.45637	.09246	2.21	.48645	.03470
1.72	.45728	.09089	2.22	.48679	.03394
1.73	.45818	.08933	2.23	.48713	.03319
1.74	.45907	.08780	2.24	.48745	.03246
1.75	.45994	.08628	2.25	.48778	.03174
1.76	.46080	.08478	2.26	.48809	.03103
1.77	.46164	.08329	2.27	.48840	.03034
1.78	.46246	.08183	2.28	.48870	.02965
1.79	.46327	.08038	2.29	.48899	.02898
1.80	.46407	.07895	2.30	.48928	.02833
1.81	.46485	.07754	2.31	.48956	.02768
1.82	.46562	.07614	2.32	.48983	.02705
1.83	.46638	.07477	2.33	.49010	.02643
1.84	.46712	.07341	2.34	.49036	.02582
1.85	.46784	.07206	2.35	.49064	.02522
1.86	.46856	.07074	2.36	.49086	.02463
1.87	.46926	.06943	2.37	.49111	.02406
1.88	.46995	.06814	2.38	.49134	.02349
1.89	.47062	.06687	2.39	.49158	.02294

Table I *Areas and Ordinates of the Normal Curve (continued)*

$\dfrac{X - \mu}{\sigma}$	Area Under the Curve Between μ and X	Ordinate (Y) of the Curve at X	$\dfrac{X - \mu}{\sigma}$	Area Under the Curve Between μ and X	Ordinate (Y) of the Curve at X
(1)	(2)	(3)	(1)	(2)	(3)
2.40	.49180	.02239	2.90	.49813	.00595
2.41	.49202	.02186	2.91	.49819	.00578
2.42	.49224	.02134	2.92	.49825	.00562
2.43	.49245	.02083	2.93	.49831	.00545
2.44	.49266	.02033	2.94	.49836	.00530
2.45	.49286	.01984	2.95	.49841	.00514
2.46	.49305	.01936	2.96	.49846	.00499
2.47	.49324	.01889	2.97	.49851	.00485
2.48	.49343	.01842	2.98	.49856	.00471
2.49	.49361	.01797	2.99	.49861	.00457
2.50	.49379	.01753	3.00	.49865	.00443
2.51	.49396	.01709	3.01	.49869	.00430
2.52	.49413	.01667	3.02	.49874	.00417
2.53	.49430	.01625	3.03	.49878	.00405
2.54	.49446	.01585	3.04	.49882	.00393
2.55	.49461	.01545	3.05	.49886	.00381
2.56	.49477	.01506	3.06	.49889	.00370
2.57	.49492	.01468	3.07	.49893	.00358
2.58	.49506	.01431	3.08	.49897	.00348
2.59	.49520	.01394	3.09	.49900	.00337
2.60	.49534	.01358	3.10	.49903	.00327
2.61	.49547	.01323	3.11	.49906	.00317
2.62	.49560	.01289	3.12	.49910	.00307
2.63	.49573	.01256	3.13	.49913	.00298
2.64	.49585	.01223	3.14	.49916	.00288
2.65	.49598	.01191	3.15	.49918	.00279
2.66	.49609	.01160	3.16	.49921	.00271
2.67	.49621	.01130	3.17	.49924	.00262
2.68	.49632	.01100	3.18	.49926	.00254
2.69	.49643	.01071	3.19	.49929	.00246
2.70	.49653	.01042	3.20	.49931	.00238
2.71	.49664	.01014	3.21	.49934	.00231
2.72	.49674	.00987	3.22	.49936	.00224
2.73	.49683	.00961	3.23	.49938	.00216
2.74	.49693	.00935	3.24	.49940	.00210
2.75	.49702	.00909	3.25	.49942	.00203
2.76	.49711	.00885	3.26	.49944	.00196
2.77	.49720	.00861	3.27	.49946	.00190
2.78	.49728	.00837	3.28	.49948	.00184
2.79	.49736	.00814	3.29	.49950	.00178
2.80	.49744	.00792	3.30	.49952	.00172
2.81	.49752	.00770	3.31	.49953	.00167
2.82	.49760	.00748	3.32	.49955	.00161
2.83	.49767	.00727	3.33	.49957	.00156
2.84	.49774	.00707	3.34	4.9958	.00151
2.85	.49781	.00687	3.35	.49960	.00146
2.86	.49788	.00668	3.36	.49961	.00141
2.87	.49795	.00649	3.37	.49962	.00136
2.88	.49801	.00631	3.38	.49964	.00132
2.89	.49807	.00613	3.39	.49965	.00127

Table I   Areas and Ordinates of the Normal Curve

Table I *Areas and Ordinates of the Normal Curve (continued)*

$\dfrac{X - \mu}{\sigma}$	Area Under the Curve Between μ and X	Ordinate (Y) of the Curve at X	$\dfrac{X - \mu}{\sigma}$	Area Under the Curve Between μ and X	Ordinate (Y) of the Curve at X
(1)	(2)	(3)	(1)	(2)	(3)
3.40	.49966	.00123	3.70	.49989	.00042
3.41	.49968	.00119	3.71	.49990	.00041
3.42	.49969	.00115	3.72	.49990	.00039
3.43	.49970	.00111	3.73	.49990	.00038
3.44	.49971	.00107	3.74	.49991	.00037
3.45	.49972	.00104	3.75	.49991	.00035
3.46	.49973	.00100	3.76	.49992	.00034
3.47	.49974	.00097	3.77	.49992	.00033
3.48	.49975	.00094	3.78	.49992	.00031
3.49	.49976	.00090	3.79	.49992	.00030
3.50	.49977	.00087	3.80	.49993	.00029
3.51	.49978	.00084	3.81	.49993	.00028
3.52	.49978	.00081	3.82	.49993	.00027
3.53	.49979	.00079	3.83	.49994	.00026
3.54	.49980	00076	3.84	.49994	.00025
3.55	.49981	.00073	3.85	.49994	.00024
3.56	.49981	.00071	3.86	.49994	.00023
3.57	.49982	.00068	3.87	.49995	.00022
3.58	.49983	.00066	3.88	.49995	.00021
3.59	.49983	.00063	3.89	.49995	.00021
3.60	.49984	.00061	3.90	.49995	.00020
3.61	.49985	.00059	3.91	.49995	.00019
3.62	.49985	.00057	3.92	.49996	.00018
3.63	.49986	.00055	3.93	.49996	.00018
3.64	.49986	.00053	3.94	.49996	.00017
3.65	.49987	.00051	3.95	.49996	.00016
3.66	.49987	.00049	3.96	.49996	.00016
3.67	.49988	.00047	3.97	.49996	.00015
3.68	.49988	.00046	3.98	.49997	.00014
3.69	.49989	.00044	3.99	.49997	.00014

Table II *Poisson Distribution*

$$p(x) = \frac{\lambda^x e^{-\lambda}}{x!}, \ \lambda > 0, \ x = 0, 1, 2, \ldots.$$

This table contains the individual values of $p(x)$ for specified values of x and λ.

x	0.1	0.2	0.3	0.4	λ 0.5	0.6	0.7	0.8	0.9	1.0
0	.9048	.8187	.7408	.6703	.6065	.5488	.4966	.4493	.4066	.3679
1	.0905	.1637	.2222	.2681	.3033	.3293	.3476	.3595	.3659	.3679
2	.0045	.0164	.0333	.0536	.0758	.0988	.1217	.1438	.1647	.1839
3	.0002	.0011	.0033	.0072	.0126	.0198	.0284	.0383	.0494	.0613
4	.0000	.0001	.0002	.0007	.0016	.0030	.0050	.0077	.0111	.0153
5	.0000	.0000	.0000	.0001	.0002	.0004	.0007	.0012	.0020	.0031
6	.0000	.0000	.0000	.0000	.0000	.0000	.0001	.0002	.0003	.0005
7	.0000	.0000	.0000	.0000	.0000	.0000	.0000	.0000	.0000	.0001

x	1.1	1.2	1.3	1.4	λ 1.5	1.6	1.7	1.8	1.9	2.0
0	.3329	.3012	.2725	.2466	.2231	.2019	.1827	.1653	.1496	.1353
1	.3662	.3614	.3543	.3452	.3347	.3230	.3106	.2975	.2842	.2707
2	.2014	.2169	.2303	.2417	.2510	.2584	.2640	.2678	.2700	.2707
3	.0738	.0867	.0998	.1128	.1255	.1378	.1496	.1607	.1710	.1804
4	.0203	.0260	.0324	.0395	.0471	.0551	.0636	.0723	.0812	.0902
5	.0045	.0062	.0084	.0111	.0141	.0176	.0216	.0260	.0309	.0361
6	.0008	.0012	.0018	.0026	.0035	.0047	.0061	.0078	.0098	.0120
7	.0001	.0002	.0003	.0005	.0008	.0011	.0015	.0020	.0027	.0034
8	.0000	.0000	.0001	.0001	.0001	.0002	.0003	.0005	.0006	.0009
9	.0000	.0000	.0000	.0000	.0000	.0000	.0001	.0001	.0001	.0002

x	2.1	2.2	2.3	2.4	λ 2.5	2.6	2.7	2.8	2.9	3.0
0	.1225	.1108	.1003	.0907	.0821	.0743	.0672	.0608	.0550	.0498
1	.2572	.2438	.2306	.2177	.2052	.1931	.1815	.1703	.1596	.1494
2	.2700	.2681	.2652	.2613	.2565	.2510	.2450	.2384	.2314	.2240
3	.1890	.1966	.2033	.2090	.2138	.2176	.2205	.2225	.2237	.2240
4	.0992	.1082	.1169	.1254	.1336	.1414	.1488	.1557	.1622	.1680
5	.0417	.0476	.0538	.0602	.0668	.0735	.0804	.0872	.0940	.1008
6	.0146	.0174	.0206	.0241	.0278	.0319	.0362	.0407	.0455	.0504
7	.0044	.0055	.0068	.0083	.0099	.0118	.0139	.0163	.0188	.0216
8	.0011	.0015	.0019	.0025	.0031	.0038	.0047	.0057	.0068	.0081
9	.0003	.0004	.0005	.0007	.0009	.0011	.0014	.0018	.0022	.0027
10	.0001	.0001	.0001	.0002	.0002	.0003	.0004	.0005	.0006	.0008
11	.0000	.0000	.0000	.0000	.0000	.0001	.0001	.0001	.0002	.0002
12	.0000	.0000	.0000	.0000	.0000	.0000	.0000	.0000	.0000	.0001

SOURCE: Reprinted with permission from *Standard Mathematical Tables*, 24th ed. (Cleveland, Ohio: The Chemical Rubber Co., 1976). Copyright The Chemical Rubber Co.

Table II   Poisson Distribution   **565**

Table II *Poisson Distribution* (*continued*)

x	3.1	3.2	3.3	3.4	λ 3.5	3.6	3.7	3.8	3.9	4.0
0	.0450	.0408	.0369	.0334	.0302	.0273	.0247	.0224	.0202	.0183
1	.1397	.1304	.1217	.1135	.1057	.0984	.0915	.0850	.0789	.0733
2	.2165	.2087	.2008	.1929	.1850	.1771	.1692	.1615	.1539	.1465
3	.2237	.2226	.2209	.2186	.2158	.2125	.2087	.2046	.2001	.1954
4	.1734	.1781	.1823	.1858	.1888	.1912	.1931	.1944	.1951	.1954
5	.1075	.1140	.1203	.1264	.1322	.1377	.1429	.1477	.1522	.1563
6	.0555	.0608	.0662	.0716	.0771	.0826	.0881	.0936	.0989	.1042
7	.0246	.0278	.0312	.0348	.0385	.0425	.0466	.0508	.0551	.0595
8	.0095	.0111	.0129	.0148	.0169	.0191	.0215	.0241	.0269	.0298
9	.0033	.0040	.0047	.0056	.0066	.0076	.0089	.0102	.0116	.0132
10	.0010	.0013	.0016	.0019	.0023	.0028	.0033	.0039	.0045	.0053
11	.0003	.0004	.0005	.0006	.0007	.0009	.0011	.0013	.0016	.0019
12	.0001	.0001	.0001	.0002	.0002	.0003	.0003	.0004	.0005	.0006
13	.0000	.0000	.0000	.0000	.0001	.0001	.0001	.0001	.0002	.0002
14	.0000	.0000	.0000	.0000	.0000	.0000	.0000	.0000	.0000	.0001

x	4.1	4.2	4.3	4.4	λ 4.5	4.6	4.7	4.8	4.9	5.0
0	.0166	.0150	.0136	.0123	.0111	.0101	.0091	.0082	.0074	.0067
1	.0679	.0630	.0583	.0540	.0500	.0462	.0427	.0395	.0365	.0337
2	.1393	.1323	.1254	.1188	.1125	.1063	.1005	.0948	.0894	.0842
3	.1904	.1852	.1798	.1743	.1687	.1631	.1574	.1517	.1460	.1404
4	.1951	.1944	.1933	.1917	.1898	.1875	.1849	.1820	.1789	.1755
5	.1600	.1633	.1662	.1687	.1708	.1725	.1738	.1747	.1753	.1755
6	.1093	.1143	.1191	.1237	.1281	.1323	.1362	.1398	.1432	.1462
7	.0640	.0686	.0732	.0778	.0824	.0869	.0914	.0959	.1002	.1044
8	.0328	.0360	.0393	.0428	.0463	.0500	.0537	.0575	.0614	.0653
9	.0150	.0168	.0188	.0209	.0232	.0255	.0280	.0307	.0334	.0363
10	.0061	.0071	.0081	.0092	.0104	.0118	.0132	.0147	.0164	.0181
11	.0023	.0027	.0032	.0037	.0043	.0049	.0056	.0064	.0073	.0082
12	.0008	.0009	.0011	.0014	.0016	.0019	.0022	.0026	.0030	.0034
13	.0002	.0003	.0004	.0005	.0006	.0007	.0008	.0009	.0011	.0013
14	.0001	.0001	.0001	.0001	.0002	.0002	.0003	.0003	.0004	.0005
15	.0000	.0000	.0000	.0000	.0001	.0001	.0001	.0001	.0001	.0002

Table II *Poisson Distribution (continued)*

x	5.1	5.2	5.3	5.4	5.5	5.6	5.7	5.8	5.9	6.0
0	.0061	.0055	.0050	.0045	.0041	.0037	.0033	.0030	.0027	.0025
1	.0311	.0287	.0265	.0244	.0225	.0207	.0191	.0176	.0162	.0149
2	.0793	.0746	.0701	.0659	.0618	.0580	.0544	.0509	.0477	.0446
3	.1348	.1293	.1239	.1185	.1133	.1082	.1033	.0985	.0938	.0892
4	.1719	.1681	.1641	.1600	.1558	.1515	.1472	.1428	.1383	.1339
5	.1753	.1748	.1740	.1728	.1714	.1697	.1678	.1656	.1632	.1606
6	.1490	.1515	.1537	.1555	.1571	.1584	.1594	.1601	.1605	.1606
7	.1086	.1125	.1163	.1200	.1234	.1267	.1298	.1326	.1353	.1377
8	.0692	.0731	.0771	.0810	.0849	.0887	.0925	.0962	.0998	.1033
9	.0362	.0423	.0454	.0486	.0519	.0552	.0586	.0620	.0654	.0688
10	.0200	.0220	.0241	.0262	.0285	.0309	.0334	.0359	.0386	.0413
11	.0093	.0104	.0116	.0129	.0143	.0157	.0173	.0190	.0207	.0225
12	.0039	.0045	.0051	.0058	.0065	.0073	.0082	.0092	.0102	.0113
13	.0015	.0104	.0021	.0024	.0028	.0032	.0036	.0041	.0046	.0052
14	.0006	.0007	.0008	.0009	.0011	.0013	.0015	.0017	.0019	.0022
15	.0002	.0002	.0003	.0003	.0004	.0005	.0006	.0007	.0008	.0009
16	.0001	.0001	.0001	.0001	.0001	.0002	.0002	.0002	.0003	.0003
17	.0000	.0000	.0000	.0000	.0000	.0000	.0001	.0001	.0001	.0001

x	6.1	6.2	6.3	6.4	6.5	6.6	6.7	6.8	6.9	7.0
0	.0022	.0020	.0018	.0017	.0015	.0014	.0012	.0011	.0010	.0009
1	.0137	.0126	.0116	.0106	.0098	.0090	.0082	.0076	.0070	.0064
2	.0417	.0390	.0364	.0340	.0318	.0296	.0276	.0258	.0240	.0223
3	.0848	.0806	.0765	.0726	.0688	.0652	.0617	.0584	.0552	.0521
4	.1294	.1249	.1205	.1162	.1118	.1076	.1034	.0992	.0952	.0912
5	.1579	.1549	.1519	.1487	.1454	.1420	.1385	.1349	.1314	.1277
6	.1605	.1601	.1595	.1586	.1575	.1562	.1546	.1529	.1511	.1490
7	.1399	.1418	.1435	.1450	.1462	.1472	.1480	.1486	.1489	.1490
8	.1066	.1099	.1130	.1160	.1188	.1215	.1240	.1263	.1284	.1304
9	.0723	.0757	.0791	.0825	.0858	.0891	.0923	.0954	.0985	.1014
10	.0441	.0469	.0498	.0528	.0558	.0588	.0618	.0649	.0679	.0710
11	.0245	.0265	.0285	.0307	.0330	.0353	.0377	.0401	.0426	.0452
12	.0124	.0137	.0150	.0164	.0179	.0194	.0210	.0227	.0245	.0264
13	.0058	.0065	.0073	.0081	.0089	.0098	.0108	.0119	.0130	.0142
14	.0025	.0029	.0033	.0037	.0041	.0046	.0052	.0058	.0064	.0071
15	.0010	.0012	.0014	.0016	.0018	.0020	.0023	.0026	.0029	.0033
16	.0004	.0005	.0005	.0006	.0007	.0008	.0010	.0011	.0013	.0014
17	.0001	.0002	.0002	.0002	.0003	.0003	.0004	.0004	.0005	.0006
18	.0000	.0001	.0001	.0001	.0001	.0001	.0001	.0002	.0002	.0002
19	.0000	.0000	.0000	.0000	.0000	.0000	.0000	.0001	.0001	.0001

Table II   Poisson Distribution

567

Table II *Poisson Distribution* (*continued*)

					λ					
x	7.1	7.2	7.3	7.4	7.5	7.6	7.7	7.8	7.9	8.0
0	.0008	.0007	.0007	.0006	.0006	.0005	.0005	.0004	.0004	.0003
1	.0059	.0054	.0049	.0045	.0041	.0038	.0035	.0032	.0029	.0027
2	.0208	.0194	.0180	.0167	.0156	.0145	.0134	.0125	.0116	.0107
3	.0492	.0464	.0438	.0413	.0389	.0366	.0345	.0324	.0305	.0286
4	.0874	.0836	.0799	.0764	.0729	.0696	.0663	.0632	.0602	.0573
5	.1241	.1204	.1167	.1130	.1094	.1057	.1021	.0986	.0951	.0916
6	.1468	.1445	.1420	.1394	.1367	.1339	.1311	.1282	.1252	.1221
7	.1489	.1486	.1481	.1474	.1465	.1454	.1442	.1428	.1413	.1396
8	.1321	.1337	.1351	.1363	.1373	.1382	.1388	.1392	.1395	.1396
9	.1042	.1070	.1096	.1121	.1144	.1167	.1187	.1207	.1224	.1241
10	.0740	.0770	.0800	.0829	.0858	.0887	.0914	.0941	.0967	.0993
11	.0478	.0504	.0531	.0558	.0585	.0613	.0640	.0667	.0695	.0722
12	.0283	.0303	.0323	.0344	.0366	.0388	.0411	.0434	.0457	.0481
13	.0154	.0168	.0181	.0196	.0211	.0227	.0243	.0260	.0278	.0296
14	.0078	.0086	.0095	.0104	.0113	.0123	.0134	.0145	.0157	.0169
15	.0037	.0041	.0046	.0051	.0057	.0062	.0069	.0075	.0083	.0090
16	.0016	.0019	.0021	.0024	.0026	.0030	.0033	.0037	.0041	.0045
17	.0007	.0008	.0009	.0010	.0012	.0013	.0015	.0017	.0019	.0021
18	.0003	.0003	.0004	.0004	.0005	.0006	.0006	.0007	.0008	.0009
19	.0001	.0001	.0001	.0002	.0002	.0002	.0003	.0003	.0003	.0004
20	.0000	.0000	.0001	.0001	.0001	.0001	.0001	.0001	.0001	.0002
21	.0000	.0000	.0000	.0000	.0000	.0000	.0000	.0000	.0001	.0001

					λ					
x	8.1	8.2	8.3	8.4	8.5	8.6	8.7	8.8	8.9	9.0
0	.0003	.0003	.0002	.0002	.0002	.0002	.0002	.0002	.0001	.0001
1	.0025	.0023	.0021	.0019	.0017	.0016	.0014	.0013	.0012	.0011
2	.0100	.0092	.0086	.0079	.0074	.0068	.0063	.0058	.0054	.0050
3	.0269	.0252	.0237	.0222	.0208	.0195	.0183	.0171	.0160	.0150
4	.0544	.0517	.0491	.0466	.0443	.0420	.0398	.0377	.0357	.0337
5	.0882	.0849	.0816	.0784	.0752	.0722	.0692	.0663	.0635	.0607
6	.1191	.1160	.1128	.1097	.1066	.1034	.1003	.0972	.0941	.0911
7	.1378	.1358	.1338	.1317	.1294	.1271	.1247	.1222	.1197	.1171
8	.1395	.1392	.1388	.1382	.1375	.1366	.1356	.1344	.1332	.1318
9	.1256	.1269	.1280	.1290	.1299	.1306	.1311	.1315	.1317	.1318
10	.1017	.1040	.1063	.1084	.1104	.1123	.1140	.1157	.1172	.1186
11	.0749	.0776	.0802	.0828	.0853	.0878	.0902	.0925	.0948	.0970
12	.0505	.0530	.0555	.0579	.0604	.0629	.0654	.0679	.0703	.0728
13	.0315	.0334	.0354	.0374	.0395	.0416	.0438	.0459	.0481	.0504
14	.0182	.0196	.0210	.0225	.0240	.0256	.0272	.0289	.0306	.0324

Table II *Poisson Distribution (continued)*

x	8.1	8.2	8.3	8.4	λ 8.5	8.6	8.7	8.8	8.9	9.0
15	.0098	.0107	.0116	.0126	.0136	.0147	.0158	.0169	.0182	.0194
16	.0050	.0055	.0060	.0066	.0072	.0079	.0086	.0093	.0101	.0109
17	.0024	.0026	.0029	.0033	.0036	.0040	.0044	.0048	.0053	.0058
18	.0011	.0012	.0014	.0015	.0017	.0019	.0021	.0024	.0026	.0029
19	.0005	.0005	.0006	.0007	.0008	.0009	.0010	.0011	.0012	.0014
20	.0002	.0002	.0002	.0003	.0003	.0004	.0004	.0005	.0005	.0006
21	.0001	.0001	.0001	.0001	.0001	.0002	.0002	.0002	.0002	.0003
22	.0000	.0000	.0000	.0000	.0001	.0001	.0001	.0001	.0001	.0001

x	9.1	9.2	9.3	9.4	λ 9.5	9.6	9.7	9.8	9.9	10
0	.0001	.0001	.0001	.0001	.0001	.0001	.0001	.0001	.0001	.0000
1	.0010	.0009	.0009	.0008	.0007	.0007	.0006	.0005	.0005	.0005
2	.0046	.0043	.0040	.0037	.0034	.0031	.0029	.0027	.0025	.0023
3	.0140	.0131	.0123	.0115	.0107	.0100	.0093	.0087	.0081	.0076
4	.0319	.0302	.0285	.0269	.0254	.0240	.0226	.0213	.0201	.0189
5	.0581	.0555	.0530	.0506	.0483	.0460	.0439	.0418	.0398	.0378
6	.0881	.0851	.0822	.0793	.0764	.0736	.0709	.0682	.0656	.0631
7	.1145	.1118	.1091	.1064	.1037	.1010	.0982	.0955	.0928	.0901
8	.1302	.1286	.1269	.1251	.1232	.1212	.1191	.1170	.1148	.1126
9	.1317	.1315	.1311	.1306	.1300	.1293	.1284	.1274	.1263	.1251

x	9.1	9.2	9.3	9.4	λ 9.5	9.6	9.7	9.8	9.9	10
10	.1198	.1210	.1219	.1228	.1235	.1241	.1245	.1249	.1250	.1251
11	.0991	.1012	.1031	.1049	.1067	.1083	.1098	.1112	.1125	.1137
12	.0752	.0776	.0799	.0822	.0844	.0866	.0888	.0908	.0928	.0948
13	.0526	.0549	.0572	.0594	.0617	.0640	.0662	.0685	.0707	.0729
14	.0342	.0361	.0380	.0399	.0419	.0439	.0459	.0479	.0500	.0521
15	.0208	.0221	.0235	.0250	.0265	.0281	.0297	.0313	.0330	.0347
16	.0118	.0127	.0137	.0147	.0157	.0168	.0180	.0192	.0204	.0217
17	.0063	.0069	.0075	.0081	.0088	.0095	.0103	.0111	.0119	.0128
18	.0032	.0035	.0039	.0042	.0046	.0051	.0055	.0060	.0065	.0071
19	.0015	.0017	.0019	.0021	.0023	.0026	.0028	.0031	.0034	.0037
20	.0007	.0008	.0009	.0010	.0011	.0012	.0014	.0015	.0017	.0019
21	.0003	.0003	.0004	.0004	.0005	.0006	.0006	.0007	.0008	.0009
22	.0001	.0001	.0002	.0002	.0002	.0002	.0003	.0003	.0004	.0001
23	.0000	.0001	.0001	.0001	.0001	.0001	.0001	.0001	.0002	.0002
24	.0000	.0000	.0000	.0000	.0000	.0000	.0000	.0001	.0001	.0001

Table II   Poisson Distribution

569

Table II *Poisson Distribution (continued)*

x	11	12	13	14	λ 15	16	17	18	19	20
0	.0000	.0000	.0000	.0000	.0000	.0000	.0000	.0000	.0000	.0000
1	.0002	.0001	.0000	.0000	.0000	.0000	.0000	.0000	.0000	.0000
2	.0010	.0004	.0002	.0001	.0000	.0000	.0000	.0000	.0000	.0000
3	.0037	.0018	.0008	.0004	.0002	.0001	.0000	.0000	.0000	.0000
4	.0102	.0053	.0027	.0013	.0006	.0003	.0001	.0001	.0000	.0000
5	.0224	.0127	.0070	.0037	.0019	.0010	.0005	.0002	.0001	.0001
6	.0411	.0255	.0152	.0087	.0048	.0026	.0014	.0007	.0004	.0002
7	.0646	.0437	.0281	.0174	.0104	.0060	.0034	.0018	.0010	.0005
8	.0888	.0655	.0457	.0304	.0194	.0120	.0072	.0042	.0024	.0013
9	.1085	.0874	.0661	.0473	.0324	.0213	.0135	.0083	.0050	.0029
10	.1194	.1048	.0859	.0663	.0486	.0341	.0230	.0150	.0095	.0058
11	.1194	.1144	.1015	.0844	.0663	.0496	.0355	.0245	.0164	.0106
12	.1094	.1144	.1099	.0984	.0829	.0661	.0504	.0368	.0259	.0176
13	.0926	.1056	.1099	.1060	.0956	.0814	.0658	.0509	.0378	.0271
14	.0728	.0905	.1021	.1060	.1024	.0930	.0800	.0655	.0514	.0387
15	.0534	.0724	.0885	.0989	.1024	.0992	.0906	.0786	.0650	.0516
16	.0367	.0543	.0719	.0866	.0960	.0992	.0963	.0884	.0772	.0646
17	.0237	.0383	.0550	.0713	.0847	.0934	.0963	.0936	.0863	.0760
18	.0145	.0256	.0397	.0554	.0706	.0830	.0909	.0936	.0911	.0844
19	.0084	.0161	.0272	.0409	.0557	.0699	.0814	.0887	.0911	.0888
20	.0046	.0097	.0177	.0286	.0418	.0559	.0692	.0798	.0866	.0888
21	.0024	.0055	.0109	.0191	.0299	.0426	.0560	.0684	.0783	.0846
22	.0012	.0030	.0065	.0121	.0204	.0310	.0433	.0560	.0676	.0769
23	.0006	.0016	.0037	.0074	.0133	.0216	.0320	.0438	.0559	.0669
24	.0003	.0008	.0020	.0043	.0083	.0144	.0226	.0328	.0442	.0557
25	.0001	.0004	.0010	.0024	.0050	.0092	.0154	.0237	.0336	.0446
26	.0000	.0002	.0005	.0013	.0029	.0057	.0101	.0164	.0246	.0343
27	.0000	.0001	.0002	.0007	.0016	.0034	.0063	.0109	.0173	.0254
28	.0000	.0000	.0001	.0003	.0009	.0019	.0038	.0070	.0117	.0181
29	.0000	.0000	.0001	.0002	.0004	.0011	.0023	.0044	.0077	.0125
30	.0000	.0000	.0000	.0001	.0002	.0006	.0013	.0026	.0049	.0083
31	.0000	.0000	.0000	.0000	.0001	.0003	.0007	.0015	.0030	.0054
32	.0000	.0000	.0000	.0000	.0001	.0001	.0004	.0009	.0018	.0034
33	.0000	.0000	.0000	.0000	.0000	.0001	.0002	.0005	.0010	.0020
34	.0000	.0000	.0000	.0000	.0000	.0000	.0001	.0002	.0006	.0012
35	.0000	.0000	.0000	.0000	.0000	.0000	.0000	.0001	.0003	.0007
36	.0000	.0000	.0000	.0000	.0000	.0000	.0000	.0001	.0002	.0004
37	.0000	.0000	.0000	.0000	.0000	.0000	.0000	.0000	.0001	.0002
38	.0000	.0000	.0000	.0000	.0000	.0000	.0000	.0000	.0000	.0001
39	.0000	.0000	.0000	.0000	.0000	.0000	.0000	.0000	.0000	.0001

Table III. *Values of e^x and e^{-x}*

$e = 2.71828$

x	e^x	e^{-x}	x	e^x	e^{-x}
0.00	1.000	1.000	3.00	20.086	0.050
0.10	1.105	0.905	3.10	22.198	0.045
0.20	1.221	0.819	3.20	24.533	0.041
0.30	1.350	0.741	3.30	27.113	0.037
0.40	1.492	0.670	3.40	29.964	0.033
0.50	1.649	0.607	3.50	33.115	0.030
0.60	1.822	0.549	3.60	36.598	0.027
0.70	2.014	0.497	3.70	40.447	0.025
0.80	2.226	0.449	3.80	44.701	0.022
0.90	2.460	0.407	3.90	49.402	0.020
1.00	2.718	0.368	4.00	54.598	0.018
1.10	3.004	0.333	4.10	60.340	0.017
1.20	3.320	0.301	4.20	66.686	0.015
1.30	3.669	0.273	4.30	73.700	0.014
1.40	4.055	0.247	4.40	81.451	0.012
1.50	4.482	0.223	4.50	90.017	0.011
1.60	4.953	0.202	4.60	99.484	0.010
1.70	5.474	0.183	4.70	109.95	0.009
1.80	6.050	0.165	4.80	121.51	0.008
1.90	6.686	0.150	4.90	134.29	0.007
2.00	7.389	0.135	5.00	148.41	0.007
2.10	8.166	0.122	5.10	164.02	0.006
2.20	9.025	0.111	5.20	181.27	0.006
2.30	9.974	0.100	5.30	200.34	0.005
2.40	11.023	0.091	5.40	221.41	0.005
2.50	12.182	0.082	5.50	244.69	0.004
2.60	13.464	0.074	5.60	270.43	0.004
2.70	14.880	0.067	5.70	298.87	0.003
2.80	16.445	0.061	5.80	330.30	0.003
2.90	18.174	0.055	5.90	365.04	0.003
3.00	20.086	0.050	6.00	403.43	0.002

SOURCE: Sang M. Lee and Laurence J. Moore, *Introduction to Decision Science*, New York: Petrocelli/Charter, 1975.

Table III   Values of e^x and e^{-x} 571

Table IV *Powers and Roots*

n	n^2	$\sqrt{n}$	$\sqrt{10n}$	n^3	$\sqrt[3]{n}$	$\sqrt[3]{10n}$	$\sqrt[3]{100n}$
1	1	1.000 000	3.162 278	1	1.000 000	2.154 435	4.641 589
2	4	1.414 214	4.472 136	8	1.259 921	2.714 418	5.848 035
3	9	1.732 051	5.477 226	27	1.442 250	3.107 233	6.694 330
4	16	2.000 000	6.324 555	64	1.587 401	3.419 952	7.368 063
5	25	2.236 068	7.071 068	125	1.709 976	3.684 031	7.937 005
6	36	2.449 490	7.745 967	216	1.817 121	3.914 868	8.434 327
7	49	2.645 751	8.366 600	343	1.912 931	4.121 285	8.879 040
8	64	2.828 427	8.944 272	512	2.000 000	4.308 869	9.283 178
9	81	3.000 000	9.486 833	729	2.080 084	4.481 405	9.654 894
10	100	3.162 278	10.00000	1 000	2.154 435	4.641 589	10.00000
11	121	3.316 625	10.48809	1 331	2.223 980	4.791 420	10.32280
12	144	3.464 102	10.95445	1 728	2.289 428	4.932 424	10.62659
13	169	3.605 551	11.40175	2 197	2.351 335	5.065 797	10.91393
14	196	3.741 657	11.83216	2 744	2.410 142	5.192 494	11.18689
15	225	3.872 983	12.24745	3 375	2.466 212	5.313 293	11.44714
16	256	4.000 000	12.64911	4 096	2.519 842	5.428 835	11.69607
17	289	4.123 106	13.03840	4 913	2.571 282	5.539 658	11.93483
18	324	4.242 641	13.41641	5 832	2.620 741	5.646 216	12.16440
19	361	4.358 899	13.78405	6 859	2.688 402	5.748 897	12.38562
20	400	4.472 136	14.14214	8 000	2.714 418	5.848 035	12.59921
21	441	4.582 576	14.49138	9 261	2.758 924	5.943 922	12.80579
22	484	4.690 416	14.83240	10 648	2.802 039	6.036 811	13.00591
23	529	4.795 832	15.16575	12 167	2.843 867	6.126 926	13.20006
24	576	4.898 979	15.49193	13 824	2.884 499	6.214 465	13.38866
25	625	5.000 000	15.81139	15 625	2.924 018	6.299 605	13.57209
26	676	5.099 020	16.12452	17 576	2.962 496	6.382 504	13.75069
27	729	5.196 152	16.43168	19 683	3.000 000	6.463 304	13.92477
28	784	5.291 503	16.73320	21 952	3.036 589	6.542 133	14.09460
29	841	5.385 165	17.02939	24 389	3.072 317	6.619 106	14.26043
30	900	5.477 226	17.32051	27 000	3.107 233	6.694 330	14.42250
31	961	5.567 764	17.60682	29 791	3.141 381	6.767 899	14.58100
32	1 024	5.656 854	17.88854	32 768	3.174 802	6.839 904	14.73613
33	1 089	5.744 563	18.16590	35 937	3.207 534	6.910 423	14.88806
34	1 156	5.830 952	18.43909	39 304	3.239 612	6.979 532	15.03695
35	1 225	5.916 080	18.70829	42 875	3.271 066	7.047 299	15.18294
36	1 296	6.000 000	18.97367	46 656	3.301 927	7.113 787	15.32619
37	1 369	6.082 763	19.23538	50 653	3.332 222	7.179 054	15.46680
38	1 444	6.164 414	19.49359	54 872	3.361 975	7.243 156	15.60491
39	1 521	6.244 998	19.74842	59 319	3.391 211	7.306 144	15.74061
40	1 600	6.324 555	20.00000	64 000	3.419 952	7.368 063	15.87401
41	1 681	6.403 124	20.24846	68 921	3.448 217	7.428 959	16 00521
42	1 764	6.480 741	20.49390	74 088	3.476 027	7.488 872	16.13429
43	1 849	6.557 439	20.73644	79 507	3.503 398	7.547 842	16.26133
44	1 936	6.633 250	20.97618	85 184	3.530 348	7.605 905	16.38643
45	2 025	6.708 204	21.21320	91 125	3.556 893	7.663 094	16.50964
46	2 116	6.782 330	21.44761	97 336	3.583 048	7.719 443	16.63103
47	2 209	6.855 655	21.67948	103 823	3.608 826	7.774 980	16.75069
43	2 304	6.928 203	21.90890	110 592	3.634 241	7.829 735	16.86865
49	2 401	7.000 000	22.13594	117 649	3.659 306	7.883 735	16.98499

SOURCE: Isaac N. Gibra, *Probability and Statistical Inference for Scientists and Engineers*, © 1973, pp. 555–556. Reprinted by permission of Prentice-Hall, Inc., Englewood Cliffs, New Jersey.

Table IV *Powers and Roots* (continued)

n	n^2	$\sqrt{n}$	$\sqrt{10n}$	n^3	$\sqrt[3]{n}$	$\sqrt[3]{10n}$	$\sqrt[3]{100n}$
50	2 500	7.071 068	22.36068	125 000	3.684 031	7.937 005	17.09976
51	2 601	7.141 428	22.58318	132 651	3.708 430	7.989 570	17.21301
52	2 704	7.211 103	22.80351	140 608	3.732 511	8.041 452	17.32478
53	2 809	7.280 110	23.02173	148 877	3.756 286	8.092 672	17.43513
54	2 916	7.348 469	23.23790	157 464	3.779 763	8.143 253	17.54411
55	3 025	7.416 198	23.45208	166 375	3.802 952	8.193 213	17.65174
56	3 136	7.483 315	23.66432	175 616	3.825 862	8.242 571	17.75808
57	3 249	7.459 834	23.87467	185 193	3.848 501	8.291 344	17.86316
58	3 364	7.615 773	24.08319	195 112	3.870 877	8.399 551	17.96702
59	3 481	7.681 146	24.28992	205 379	3.892 996	8.387 207	18.06969
60	3 600	7.745 967	24.49490	216 000	3.914 868	8.434 327	18.17121
61	3 721	7.810 250	24.69818	226 981	3.936 497	8.480 926	18.27160
62	3 844	7.874 008	24.89980	238 328	3.957 892	8.527 019	18.37091
63	3 969	7.937 254	25.09980	250 047	3.979 057	8.572 619	18.46915
64	4 096	8.000 000	25.29822	262 144	4.000 000	8.617 739	18.56636
65	4 225	8.062 258	25.49510	274 625	4.020 726	8.662 391	18.66256
66	4 356	8.124 038	25.69047	287 496	4.041 240	8.706 588	18.75777
67	4 489	8.185 353	25.88436	300 763	4.061 548	8.750 340	18.85204
68	4 624	8.246 211	26.07681	314 432	4.081 655	8.793 659	18.94536
69	4 761	8.306 624	26.26785	328 509	4.101 566	8.836 556	19.03778
70	4 900	8.366 600	26.45751	343 000	4.121 285	8.879 040	19.12931
71	5 041	8.426 150	26.64583	357 911	4.140 818	8.921 121	19.21997
72	5 184	8.485 281	26.83282	373 248	4.160 168	8.962 809	19.30979
73	5 329	8.544 004	27.01851	389 017	4.179 339	9.004 113	19.39877
74	5 476	8.602 325	27.20294	405 224	4.198 336	9.045 042	19.48695
75	5 625	8.660 254	27.38613	421 875	4.217 163	9.085 603	19.57434
76	5 776	8.717 798	27.56810	438 976	4.235 824	9.125 805	19.66095
77	5 929	8.774 964	27.74887	456 533	4.254 321	9.165 656	19.74681
78	6 084	8.831 761	27.92848	474 552	4.272 659	9.205 164	19.83192
79	6 241	8.888 194	28.10694	493 039	4.290 840	9.244 335	19.91632
80	6 400	8.944 272	28.28427	152 000	4.308 869	9.283 178	20.00000
81	6 561	9.000 000	28.46050	531 441	4.326 749	9.321 698	20.08299
82	6 724	9.055 385	28.63564	551 368	4.344 481	9.359 902	20.16530
83	6 889	9.110 434	28.80972	571 787	4.362 071	9.397 796	20.24694
84	7 056	9.165 151	28.98275	592 704	4.379 519	9.435 388	20.32793
85	7 225	9.219 544	29.15476	614 125	4.396 830	9.472 682	20.40828
86	7 396	9.273 618	29.32576	636 056	4.414 005	9.509 685	20.48800
87	7 569	9.327 379	29.49576	658 503	4.431 048	9.546 403	20.56710
88	7 744	9.380 832	29.66479	681 472	4.447 960	9.582 840	20.64560
89	7 921	9.433 981	29.83287	704 969	4.464 745	9.619 002	20.72351
90	8 100	9.486 833	30 00000	729 000	4.481 405	9.654 894	20.80084
91	8 281	9.539 392	30.16621	753 571	4.497 941	9.690 521	20.87759
92	8 464	9.591 663	30.33150	778 688	4.514 357	9.725 888	20.95379
93	8 649	9.643 651	30.49590	804 357	4.530 655	9.761 000	21.02944
94	8 836	9.965 360	30.65942	830 584	4.546 836	9.795 861	21.10454
95	9 025	9.746 794	30.82207	857 375	4.562 903	9.830 476	21.17912
96	9 216	9.797 959	30.98387	884 736	4.578 857	9.864 848	21.25317
97	9 409	9.848 858	31.14482	912 673	4.594 701	9.898 983	21.32671
98	9 604	9.899 495	31.30495	941 192	4.610 436	9.932 884	21.39975
99	9 801	9.949 874	31.46427	970 299	4.626 065	9 966 555	21.47229
100	10 000	10.000 000	31.62278	1 000 000	4.641 589	10.000 000	21.54435

Table IV   Powers and Roots

573

Answers to Selected Problems

Chapter 3

3.8. $N = 25$ orders; $Q = 800$ units

3.9. $Q = 48,990$ units

Chapter 5

5.6. (a) S_1; S_1 (b) S_1

5.7. (a) (i) S_2 (ii) S_1 (iii) S_2 (b) S_2

5.8. S_2

5.9. (a) S_4 (b) 1.5

5.10. S_3

5.11. S_1

5.12. (a) S_1 (b) $0 < p < 0.4375$ (c) 3.6

5.13. Expand inpatient facilities; EV = $44,000

5.14. Do not debate; vote con

5.15. Leave money in bank for 2 years: EV = $1,123,600

Chapter 6

6.4. Critical path 1–2–3–4–5; $T_E = 24.67$

6.5. Normal critical path 1–2–4–6–7, $T_E = 25$; crash critical path 1–3–7, $T_E = 17$; normal cost = $10,200; crash cost = $12,000

6.7. Critical path 1–2–5–7, $T_E = 19$

6.8. Critical path 1–2–3–4–6–8–9–10, $T_E = 14$

6.9. Critical path 1–2–3–5–6–8–10, $T_E = 23$

6.10. Critical path 1–2–3–4–5–6–7, $T_E = 40$

6.11. Critical path 1–2–4–6–8–9, $T_E = 54$

6.12. (b) $T_E = 29$ (c) standard deviation of project completion time = 2.16 (d) 32.54 weeks

6.13. Critical path 1–2–5–7, 13.83 minutes, 18.76 minutes, 73 percent, 33 percent

6.14. Critical path 1–2–4–5–6–7–8–9, $p(30$ weeks$) = 0.022$

6.15. (a) Normal critical path 1–3–4–5–6 (b) crash critical path = 1–3–4–5–6 (c) 64, $3,600

6.16. (a) 1–2–4–5–6 (b) 1–2–4–5–6 (c) First activity 1–2, last activity 4–5 (d) 10 weeks, $11,500. $19,500

Chapter 7

7.10. $X = 15$, $Y = 0$, $Z = 45$. (a) degenerate solution (b) multiple optimal solutions (c) no feasible solution

7.11. $X = 27.9$, $Y = 5$, $Z = 204.9$

7.12. General-use wax = 50 gal, heavy-duty wax = 20 gal, profit = \$190

7.13. TV films = 50, profit = \$25 million
TV films = $33\frac{1}{3}$, profit = \$16.667 million

7.14. (a) 57.3 buses, 21.8 railroad cars   (b) 31.5 buses, 27.9 railroad cars   (c) Remodel the track, 5.75 buses, 33.94 railroad cars

7.15. 10 units of soybean, 5 units of fish meal; minimum cost is \$2.45

7.16. 32 canopies only, profit = \$1600; sanding capacity is not binding and there are 18 hr of unused capacity

Chapter 8

8.10. $A = 450$ mg, $B = 300$ mg, $C = 9{,}250$ mg, cost = \$0.70/pill

8.11. Clay = 140 tons, limestone = 160 tons; cost = \$2,360

8.12. Cream = 130 dozen gals, milk = 120 dozen gals, cost = \$2,520

8.13. Multiple optimal solutions; profit = \$108

8.14. Wooden nails = $\dfrac{26{,}400}{23}$, metal nails = $\dfrac{2{,}400}{23}$; profit = \$68.87

8.15. Long range = $\frac{40}{7}$, medium range = $\frac{15}{14}$, short range = 0, profit = \$32.857 million

Chapter 9

9.7. Capsules = $\frac{90}{19}$, injections = $\frac{200}{19}$; profit = \$41.05
$W_1 = \frac{4}{19}$, $W_2 = \frac{9}{95}$; cost = \$41.05

9.8. (a) $W_1 = 1$, $W_2 = 2$, $W_3 = 3$, cost = \$8,000   (b) No   (c) Basis remains the same

9.9. Burbo's better = $\frac{21}{10}$, Burbo's best = $\frac{9}{5}$, cost = \$96

9.10. Chicken chow mein = $3\frac{1}{2}$ lb, shrimp chow mein = 8 lb, profit = \$19.50

9.11. (a) Iron = $\frac{9}{14}$, nickel = $\frac{5}{14}$, chrome = 0, cost = \$2.429 per kg.   (c) No

9.12. High-quality glove = 4, low-quality glove = 16, profit = \$48

Chapter 10

10.14. $X_{12} = 35$; $X_{21} = 30$; $X_{23} = 25$; $X_{32} = 5$; $X_{34} = 20$; $X_{22} = 5$;   minimum cost = \$310

10.15. J_1 to E_1; J_2 to E_2; J_3 to E_3; minimum cost = \$248

10.16. $X_{11} = 8$; $X_{22} = 11$; $X_{31} = 2$; $X_{32} = 1$; $X_{33} = 9$; minimum cost = \$8,300

10.17. J_A to Jim; J_B to John; J_C to Sally; minimum cost = \$58

10.18. $X_{11} = 600$; $X_{12} = 750$; $X_{13} = 150$; $X_{24} = 1,500$; $X_{25} = 600$; $X_{31} = 1,400$; $X_{43} = 800$; $X_{45} = 1,000$; ..inimum cost = \$51,650

10.19 S_1 to T_1; S_2 to T_2; S_3 to T_5; S_4 to T_4; S_5 to T_3; minimum cost = \$138

Chapter 11

11.10. A_2, B_1, value = 70

11.11. S_1, N_4, yes

11.12. Strategy A_2 50% of the time, A_3 50% of the time
Strategy B_2 62.5% of the time, B_3 37.5% of the time
Value of game = 47.5

11.13. G_1 $\frac{23}{28}$ of the time, G_2 $\frac{5}{28}$ of the time

11.14. A_1 $\frac{5}{14}$ of the time, A_2 $\frac{9}{14}$ of the time

B_1 $\frac{9}{14}$ of the time, B_2 $\frac{5}{14}$ of the time

11.15. D_2 $\frac{7}{15}$ of the the time, D_3 $\frac{8}{15}$ of the time

L_2 $\frac{14}{15}$ of the time, L_4 $\frac{1}{15}$ of the time

11.17. Optimal strategy for Great Dane Ptomaine:
A_2 $\frac{1}{2}$ of the time, A_3 $\frac{1}{2}$ of the time
Optimal strategy for Guts-for-Mutts:
B_1 $\frac{1}{10}$ of the time, B_2 $\frac{9}{10}$ of the time

Chapter 12

12.13. $Q^* = 20$ units/order; total cost = \$150

12.14. $N^* = 40$ orders; $Q^* = 500$ units/order

12.15. I-A; II-B; III-C

12.16. Without discount cost = \$1,005,000; discount cost = \$956,937.50

12.17. $N = 3.16$

12.18. $Q^* = 30,000$ units/order; $R = 4,800$ units

12.19. $Q^* = 1,700$ units/order; cost savings = \$37,676; $R = 800$ units

12.20. Fixed order system yields \$1,000/year savings

Chapter 13

13.8. Optimal order quantity = 30 units/week

13.9. Optimal order quantity = 150 units/day

13.10. Optimal order quantity = 2 units/day

13.11. Re-order point = 50 units

13.12. Minimum cost strategy — Maintain 40 units of safety stock

13.13. $Q^* = 2,000$ units/run; $Q^* = 1,414.2$ units/run; $Q^* = 2,828.4$ units/run

13.14. Optimal order quantity = 78.375 units

13.15. 12.1%; safety stock = 582.5 units

13.16. Safety stock = 88 units; re-order point = 438 units

Chapter 14

14.7. Time = 231 sec; 9 hits

14.8. Choose System 707

14.9. Purchase 9 ambulances

14.10. Average leadtime = 5.35 days; average demand = 115.5 units

14.11. Policy 2 is preferred

14.12. Cash flow = − $3,260

14.14. Minimum cost with 2 cars

14.15. Critical path indices—activity 1–2 = 0.6, activity 2–3 = 0.6, activity 1–3 = 0.75

Chapter 15

15.7. 10.48/hr

15.8 2039.23/hr; 7.5 sec

15.9. Two attendants

15.10. (a) $33\frac{1}{3}\%$ (b) 4 min (c) 6 min (d) 20/hr (e) $66\frac{2}{3}\%$

15.11. Not cost effective

15.12. (a) 6 hr (b) 3.1 hr (c) 9.1 hr

15.13. (1) 0.769 hr/bus (2) 6.06 hr/bus (3) zero; cost with one attendant = $3,450, cost with two attendants = $900, automated system is cost effective.

Author Index

Subject Index

under conflict or competition, 118
operational, 101
phases of, 101
under risk (DMUR), 99
strategic, 101
tabular summary, 113
under uncertainty (DMUU), 99, 112
example of, 106, 113
Decision models, 102
descriptive, 102
normative, 102
prescriptive, 102
rationality in, 102
Decision problem, 50, 102
dynamic, 102
marginal approach to, 51
payoff matrix formulation of, 50
static, 102
Decisions, 102
nonprogrammed, 102
programmed, 6n, 102
Decision sciences, 18
Decision theory, 97
definition of, 99
Decision trees, 119
chance branch, 120
chance nodes, 119
decision branch, 119
decision nodes, 119
deterministic, 121
multistage, 121
single-stage, 121
refinements, 125
stochastic, 122
multistage, 122
single-stage, 122
summary, 125
terminal branch, 120
Deductive approach, 28, 34
Demand, 332
deterministic, 332
probabilistic, 332
Density function, 431n
Dependent events, 487
Derivative, 517
concept of, 517
of a constant, 519
definition of, 517
of a difference of terms, 520
of a function of a function, 521
partial, 525
of a power function, 519
of a product, 521
of a quotient, 521

second-order, 524
of a sum of terms, 520
Deterministic problems, 3n
Diet problem, 256
Differentiation, definition of, 519
Dimensional analysis, 64
Dominance, 321
Dual, 235
concept of, 237
to a maximization problem, 238
symmetrical, 240
Dual simplex method, 205n
Dummy activity, 143
Dynamic programming, 270

Earliest expected even time (T_E), 144
Economic man, 103
EOQ, 40, 341
EOQ model, graphic representation, 42
Events, 142
classification of, 484
dependent, 487
independent, 487
joint, 485
mutually exclusive, 485
Expected monetary value, 495
Expected utility, 495
Expected value, 494
calculation of, 366n
concept of, 494
continuous variable, 494n
criterion of, 106n
discrete variable, 494
Exponential distribution, 431, 500
density function, 431
probability density function, 432t

Financial analysis and simulation, 407
Fixed order system, 335
Fixed period system, 335
Floating slack, 148
Frequency distribution, 482
continuous, 482
discrete, 492
normalizing, 483
Function, 511
concept of, 511
definition of, 511
global maximum, 524, 525
global minimum, 524, 525

Negative exponential distribution, 431n
Network models, 133, 142
  computer programs, 159
  crashing, 155
    graphical representation, 157t
    illustration of, 157
    objective of, 155
  and simulation, 413
  terminology of, 142
    end event, 142
    network beginning event, 142
    network ending event, 142
    predecessor event, 142
    source event, 142
    start event, 142
    successor event, 142
    terminal event, 142
Noncontrollable factor, 44
Nonlinear programming, 172n, 270
Normal curve, areas of, 560t
  ordinates of, 560t
Normal distribution, 498
Northwest corner rule, 274

Objective function, 45
  graphing of, 184
Operations research, 18, 28
Opportunity cost, 40n, 209n, 284
Opportunity loss, 111
Optimal lot size (Q^*), 343
Optimal number of orders (N^*), 346
Optimal review time (Y^*), 347
Optimal safety stock (SS), 380
  calculation of, 380, 384
Optimism, coefficient of, 115
Optimism, criterion of, 115
Optimization, 10n, 31, 38
  constrained, 46
  definition of, 511
  multivariable functions, 525
  single-variable functions, 522
  unconstrained, 46
Optimization techniques, summary of, 512

Parameter, 44n, 54
Parametric programming, 245
Partial derivative, 525, 526n
  meaning of, 525
Payoff matrix, 28

  conditional, 50
PERT, 26n, 133
  analysis versus simulation, 151
  basic concepts of, 141
  evolution of, 137
  five-step working procedure, 135–136
  focus of, 136
  general framework, 135
  mechanics of, 152
  philosophical foundations, 135
  probabilistic analysis, 148
  purpose of, 136
PERT/COST, 153
PERT/TIME, 153
Pessimism, criterion of, 114
Pivot column, 554
Pivot element, 554
Pivot row, 554
Pivoting, 549, 553
  illustrative example, 554
Plane, 179n
Poisson distribution, 431, 497, 565t
  density function, 431
  probability density function, 433t
  values of, 565t
Portfolio-selection problem, 257
Postoptimality analysis, 245
Powers, 572t
PPB, 26
Precedence relationships, 137, 142
Probabilistic distribution, 482
  continuous, 482
  discrete, 482
Probabilistic problems, 3n
Probability, 479
  applications, 479
  a priori, 482
  basic axioms, 483
  concepts, 479, 481
    classification of, 484
    summary of, 491
  conditional, 488
  cumulative, 501
  empirical, 482
  joint, 489
  marginal, 484, 489
  objective, 482
  posterior, 492
  prior, 489
  relative frequency of, 482
  subjective, 505
  unconditional, 488
Probability density function, 432, 433, 497

Product-mix problem, 68, 255
Profit contribution, 68

Quantitative approach, $3n$, 23, 25, 57
  illustrative examples, 57
Quantitative models, implementation of, 455
Queue, 436
Queue discipline, 437
  different types, 438
Queuing models (system), 425, 439
  analytical approach, 439
  arrival distribution, arrival rate, 430
    constant distribution, 430
    interarrival times, 430
    random distribution, 430
  balking, 433
  basic framework, $429t$
  basic structure, 428
  calling population, size of, 430
  component of, 428
  design of, 438
  impatient customer, 433
  input source, 430
    arrival control, 430
    arrival rate, 430
  operating characteristics, 437, 438
    examples of, 438
  patient customers, 433
  pattern of service, 436
  purpose of, 427
  reneging, 433
  service distribution, 436
  service facilities, 434
    configuration of, 434, 435
    multiple-channel, 434
    multiple-phase, 434
    single-channel, 434
    single-phase, 434
    structure of, 435
  service system, characteristics of, 436
  simulation approach, 444
  single-channel, single-phase, 439
    assumptions, 439
    illustrative example, 441
    operating characteristics, 440

Random experiment, 481
Random sampling, 394, 395, 399
Random variable, 481

continuous, 482
discrete, 482
Rationality, 102
Real matrix, 532
Regression analysis, $85n$
Regret, criterion of, 116
Regret matrix, rule for deriving, 116
Revised simplex method, $205n$
Rim requirements, 272
Risk adjustment factor, 107
Risk aversion, 30
Roots, $572t$
Row operations, 551

Saddle point, 313
Satisficing, 38, 103
Scalar multiple, 540
Scalar multiplication, 539
Scientific management, 13
Scientific method, 32
  illustration of, 35
  important aspects of, 32
  stages of, 35
Sensitivity analysis, 66, 235, 244, 245
  changes in a_{ij}, 251
  changes in b_i, 245
  changes in c_j, 245
Service level, 381
Shadow price, 217
Simplex method, 203
  artificial slack variables, 220
  $C_j - Z_j$ numbers, calculation of, 209
    economic interpretation of, 217
  comparison with transportation, 291
  degeneracy, 226
    illustrative problem, 229
  key column, 210
  key number, 212
  key row, 210
    transformation of, 214
  minimization case, 217
  nonkey rows, 210
    transformation of, 214
  physical ratios of substitution, 208, $212n$
  pivot column, $210n$
  pivot row, $210n$
  rationale for, 205
  replacement quantities, 212
  schematic of, 231
  special cases, 226
    multiple optimal solutions, 226